THE

Teatro Solís

150 Years of

Opera, Concert, and Ballet

in Montevideo

Susana Salgado

Wesleyan University Press

MIDDLETOWN, CONNECTICUT

Published by

WESLEYAN UNIVERSITY PRESS

Middletown, CT 06459

© 2003 by Susana Salgado

Printed in the United States of America

5 4 3 2 1

LIBRARY OF CONGRESS CATALOGING-IN-PUBLICATION DATA
Salgado, Susana.
The Teatro Solís : 150 years of opera, concert, and ballet in
Montevideo / Susana Salgado.
p. cm.
Includes bibliographical references.
ISBN 0–8195–6593–8 (alk. paper)—ISBN 0–8195–6594–6 (pbk. : alk.
paper)
1. Teatro Solís (Montevideo, Uruguay)—History. 2.
Music—Uruguay—Montevideo—History and criticism. 3. Montevideo
(Uruguay)—History. I. Title.
ML1717.S35 2003
792.5'09895'13—dc21

2003004624

THE TEATRO SOLÍS:
150 YEARS OF
OPERA, CONCERT, AND BALLET
IN MONTEVIDEO

My heart is steadfast, O God;

I will sing and make music with all my soul.

A PSALM OF DAVID, PSALMS 108:1

CONTENTS

FOREWORD

"ALL LIFE PASSES, ART ALONE ENDURES." So reads the Art Deco lettering that embellishes the stage proscenium of a small theater in rural upstate New York. A mere catchphrase, perhaps. But in the wake of recent world-shattering events, the platitude gains new meaning for theater-going communities hitherto serenely untouched by ideological terrorism. The Uruguayan capital city of Montevideo was not one of those communities during much of the twentieth century: decades of political unrest, followed by years of military dictatorship, inevitably took a toll on the musical well-being of that South American cultural oasis. And yet, amid great turmoil and violence, the city's principal opera house and concert hall, the Teatro Solís, managed to escape destruction.

Now, thanks to the unflagging labor of Susana Salgado, the complete history and chronology of the Teatro Solís, the oldest major theater in the Americas still in operation, can be read, for the first time in English, in one comprehensive volume. This book fills in some important gaps in a widely overlooked chapter in the history of Western opera, ballet, and concertizing.

A list of the famous artists who trod the stage of the Solís from the late nineteenth century until the mid-twentieth amounts to a veritable *Who's Who* of legendary names, among them Enrico Tamberlick, Louis Moreau Gottschalk, Francesco Tamagno, Mattia Battistini, Adelina Patti, Luisa Tetrazzini, Pietro Mascagni, Hariclea Darclée, Enrico Caruso, Mario Ancona, Titta Ruffo, Sarah Bernhardt, Arturo Toscanini, Giuseppe Zenatello, Giacomo Puccini, Riccardo Stracciari, Fernando De Lucia, Richard Strauss, Amelita Galli-Curci, Vaslav Nijinsky, Anna Pavlova, John O'Sullivan, Giovanni Martinelli, Camille Saint-Saëns, Tito Schipa, Rosa Raisa, Ninon Vallin, Artur Rubinstein, Tullio Serafin, Giuseppe de Luca, Beniamino Gigli, Claudia Muzio, Felix Weingartner, Wanda Landowska, Elisabeth Schumann, Feodor Chaliapin, Marian Anderson, Nathan Milstein, Claudio Arrau . . .

No amount of sociopolitical oppression could efface the collective memory of that kind of artistry! So, like the red beacon that has shone atop the Teatro Solís' front cornice ever since the building's inauguration in 1856, Professor Salgado's book serves not only as a reminder of a theater's past glories but also as a symbol of the enduring spirit of a civilized people's musical consciousness.

E. Thomas Glasow
Editor, *The Opera Quarterly*

PREFACE

THE HISTORY OF THE TEATRO SOLÍS of Montevideo epitomizes a relevant event in the spiritual panorama of Uruguay. The reader may realize—as the present work reveals it— that the rise of the republic in 1830 coincided with the time when the nascent society foresaw the urgency to build a theater to fulfill its cultural demands. Sadly enough, that important project was one of the first victims of a bloody civil war that lasted from 1839 to 1851; the aftermath was similar, in many senses, to that of the American Civil War.

As soon as peace was established, the new president Juan Francisco Giró embarked upon a countrywide survey to evaluate the economical and social damage caused by the war. Years before, in 1841, as chair of the Committee for the Building of a New Theater, he had been in charge of the search for a suitable location for a theater in the borough, and also for choosing the best project. Consequently, when the new Giró administration was installed, it was no surprise to anybody that the president put at the same level of urgency the enactment of the judiciary system, the repression of smuggling, the welfare of the rural population, the breeding of the depleted livestock, and the building of a new theater. It took many years for the nineteenth-century Republic of Uruguay to build that magnificent opera house; *The Teatro Solís: Opera,*

Concert, and Ballet in Montevideo is a tribute to architect Carlo Zucchi, the father of the original project.

This scholarly work of Professor Salgado reconstructs the earliest vital spirit of the Uruguayan musical culture. Fortunately, however, she does not stop there. Her meticulous research unfolds and displays in front of our amazed eyes the quality that the Teatro Solís sustained throughout two centuries to maintain its highest cultural mission. Since its opening in 1856, this exceptional house has witnessed both the arrival of the major international lyric figures, and the development of the country into a republic that was integrated culturally, socially, and politically. Susana Salgado gives us the best when she re-creates the Teatro Solís Golden Age—a period between the end of the nineteenth and the first quarter of the twentieth century—and describes the arrival of exceptional musical figures such as singers, instrumentalists, orchestras, chorus, conductors, composers, directors, dancers, choreographers, and vaudeville stars, as well as famous dramatic artists, playwrights, and lecturers.

At the same time, as a scholar, she depicts not only the intellectualism of Uruguay, but also the peculiar social life of that brilliant era. It is extremely important to note that the cultural life of Montevideo, the capital city of

xv

Uruguay, earned for the country a prestige totally out of proportion with its economical
and geographical dimensions. In describing
this paradoxical situation, the author tells us
about the pioneering role of theatrical impresarios who ran great risks in presenting at the
Solís the greatest international artists. In 1856
the national poet Francisco Acuña de Figueroa's stanza welcomed the house's opening
night:

> —"Ora puedes, orgullosa
> por tu digno coliseo
> competir, Montevideo
> con Venecia y con París"
>
> [Now you can, proud
> with your worthy coliseum
> compete, Montevideo
> with Venice and Paris]

Fifty years later, when the Solís Golden Jubilee
was celebrated under Toscanini's baton, that
invocation proved prophetical.

This book, the culmination of thirty years
of research and commitment, represents the
conclusive biography (never was a term so
well applied) of a house with the double significance of being the oldest living theater of
the Americas and an authentic landmark in
the history of our country. A work of love,
this study is the best compendium to explore
the country itself, and an indispensable reference for researchers of the cultural life of
Uruguay and its society.

The Teatro Solís was an eloquent witness
that survived the tragedy that terminated the
SODRE Auditorium in 1971, and more recently the Teatro Carlos Brussa. In spite of the
pain that the end of these houses produced in
the public, the Solís was not fully appreciated
as one of the few survivors in the active pat-

rimony of the culture of the Americas. The
publishing of Professor Salgado's work now
makes it possible for the Solís to recapture its
deserved place in history.

The Uruguay of the twenty-first century
must welcome this remarkable book for many
reasons. First, it represents a high level of maturity in historiographic research. In fact, Susana Salgado is a graduate in musicology from
our School of Humanities and was a pupil of
such relevant figures in our national musicology and music fields as Lauro Ayestarán,
Hugo Balzo, Carlos Estrada, and Héctor Tosar. Absent from our country since her relo-
cation many years ago, Professor Salgado
added to her erudition decades of a growing
experience in another culture through the
daily exposure and interchange with a great
diversity of musicological and scholarly publications.

Second, a work of this magnitude leads to
the challenge that a historical monument like
the Teatro Solís represents for a nation (such
as the actual Uruguayan society is) that con-
fronts the double task of looking toward the
future while preserving the best of its past. In
the same spirit, the second administration
that I had the honor to preside over
launched the building of a new performing
arts complex on the same site where the former burnt SODRE Auditorium had been. I
assume that the raising of this new structure
is surrounded by the same problems, hesi-
tations and perplexities that the founders and
builders of the Teatro Solís had more than a
century ago. With the same awareness and
respect for the culture of the country, this
new venture is my homage to the pioneers
and actual builders.

Susana Salgado's book is thus a timely recollection of what we represent as human be-
ings. At the same time, it raises our spirits
from daily-life commonplaces, reminding us

that the intangible is what elevates a civilized society. That this exhaustive musical history of our Teatro Solís is published in the United States of America realizes the best of the culture of two hemispheres.

H. E. Dr. Julio María Sanguinetti
President of the
Republic of Uruguay
(1985–1990 and 1995–2000)

AUTHOR'S NOTE AND ACKNOWLEDGMENTS

FOR ALMOST THIRTY YEARS many people crossed my path, and in one way or another, have influenced the writing of this book. My mentor, the eminent musicologist Lauro Ayestarán, was responsible for suggesting that I "invade" the chaotic and dusty Solís Archives (practically untouched) and begin my research. Neither my dear late professor nor I could imagine so many years ago the long saga that was being created. Very appropriate, indeed, to the book subject, it is comparable to the best and most entangled opera plot.

This book idea was born in Montevideo, Uruguay, when I initiated research and documentation of materials in the Teatro Solís Archives, organized and prepared the first-ever classification, cataloguing and inventory of scores, musical manuscripts, and other historical-musical items related to performances and artists. My long-term goal was to write, eventually, the musical history of the house. Even if at the moment it seemed a challenging project, I felt comfortable and confident, as I was highly encouraged by the late Luis Gualco, professor of history of the theater at the Escuela Municipal de Arte Dramático, who was planning to write the history of the dramatic performances at the Solís.

Our mutual enthusiasm and conviction of the need to unveil the history of one of the most important cultural centers of the country, gave us the courage to start. Thus, and even unofficially, we launched the venture. Two articles were published in a Montevideo newspaper, outlining the dramatic development one day, and the musical history the next.

Parallel to my daily work of sorting and cataloguing scores, programs, photographs, and the most unimaginable variety of valuable (and chaotically mixed) papers, I was shaping, little by little, the structure of what looked at that time, something too big to be done. However, every score, autographed portrait, and program was telling me, even without knowing it, something: one day, a legend; another, an anecdote; yet another, a standing ovation or a sad happening. I ignored them but continued working, studying the materials and doing the inventory.

Day after day to arrive at my hidden working place of the archives, I needed to go through flights of stairs and endless dark corridors that stopped straight ahead, facing the house and the empty stage. I cannot explain, even now, what happened. I perceived something that was neither calm nor peaceful, and I felt invisibly enveloped. Was I daydreaming? Or was it a ghost? That feeling and being isolated for many hours with "my" old papers, made me ponder and ponder. . . . Then, after finishing my daily work, I would remain there and copy, page by page, one by one, all the *bordereau* (register) books, with the daily performance records. It took a long time, but I was creating without knowing it, the backbone of this book.

At the moment when everything was almost in order, catalogued, organized, and ready to put back on the shelves, I was satisfied that *finally* the archives would be ready soon to offer to readers, scholars, and opera researchers the opportunity, for the first time, to know more than one century of the unknown legacy of the Teatro Solís. At the same time, when I began to write an essay about the Collection of Scores—which contains singers' parts that had been used in the Casa de Comedias in 1830, one with Angela Tani's seal, another with Justina Piacentini's signature—everything changed drastically. The municipal authorities (then Teatro Solís administrators) prevented me from continuing to work in the archives; the Department of Culture of the Municipality adduced that it was a waste of time and money. My job was terminated and with it a dream vanished. That was the beginning of a distressing period of bureaucracy, corruption, and cultural insensibility being experienced by the whole country.

However, what appeared to be the end to all my plans became, miraculously, the beginning of a happy new life. Several months later, my husband and I left Uruguay and came to live in the United States. For the sake of historical preservation, I packed my complete musical files and papers, the original and first incomplete draft of the musical history of the Teatro Solís, and the thousands of notes I took at the archives and at the Biblioteca Nacional of Montevideo. And here, in this country, with the assistance of the valuable collections of newspapers and musical magazines of the Library of Congress, I began—thirty years ago—that long project.

Some years later, I traveled to Montevideo with the final manuscript, ready to discuss its publication. The news, however, was shocking: adducing distressing political, economical, and cultural times, neither my former publisher nor the municipal authorities were willing to publish this type of book.

Just when I was about to give up, I met Professor Andrew Farkas, director of libraries at the University of North Florida, who is also an opera scholar and author. He was the first person with whom I discussed at length what to do with a manuscript written in Spanish on the musical history of the Teatro Solís. After long conversations, he encouraged me to write a book in English, indeed, encouraging so strongly that I would have felt terribly guilty had I not done so. And so I started, again from the very beginning, to write this book, undoubtedly, the most challenging and adventurous enterprise of my professional career.

* * *

BECAUSE THIS WORK circumscribes the musical history of the Teatro Solís, I focused it mainly on opera, which was at that time the most influential genre performed on almost all Latin American houses, followed by operetta, zarzuela, vocal and instrumental recitals, symphonic concerts, and ballet.

However, even if opera and music highlighted the Solís stage during a long period, that stage was also shared with illustrious dramatic artists such as Eleonora Duse, Sarah Bernhardt, María Guerrero, Tina Di Lorenzo, María Tubau, Madeleine Renaud, Margarita Xirgu, Ermete Novelli, Ruggero Ruggieri, Fernando Díaz de Mendoza, Tommaso Salvini, Ermete Zacconi, Louis Jouvet, and Jean-Louis Barrault, as well as playwrights such as Jacinto Benavente, Luigi Pirandello, and Federico García Lorca, to mention only a few.

The book encompasses the musical history of this opera house—inaugurated in 1856—which was for a time, the unique center of cultural life in Montevideo. Yet that life was always framed by the social, cultural, and political background. By the same token, it is not possible to isolate the Teatro Solís from the birth of the theater in Uruguay.

When I cite the highlights of individual seasons, such as the first arrival of any number of singers, many of whom may be unfamiliar to readers, I have added some biographical commentaries, such as high points of their careers. For the better known singers, these commentaries have been reduced to a minimum. The same criteria apply to operas and composers.

Selected reviews from the newspapers and periodicals available in Montevideo have been included. Due to problems of conservation, some newspapers at the Biblioteca Nacional were totally destroyed many years ago. Major gaps were filled by using the fairly complete collection of *El Día* of Montevideo at the Library of Congress, as well as musical magazine collections. The Chronology (Appendix A)—which includes all the musical performances day by day, cast by cast, starting in 1856—serves as a quick reference to the performances given at the theater. Five additional appendixes, arranged in chronological order, are included.

Because the history of the Teatro Solís, and the musical history of Montevideo in particular, is so personal an experience, with the reader's indulgence, I shall allow myself some comments in the first person, when deemed appropriate.

* * *

ONE PERSON WAS ESSENTIAL to the genesis of this project: Professor Andrew Farkas, who without knowing me, believed in me and had confidence in my ability. The second miracle was when Professor Farkas put me in touch with Thomas G. Kaufman, an authority on opera listings from all over the world, who later called me to offer casting information that I was unable to obtain. I feel immense gratitude for their generosity, unconditional and continuous support, advice and friendship, from beginning to end, particularly at disheartening times.

Third is Dr. Allyson F. McGill, not only an English literature scholar but a caring friend who took the heavy task of revising the book. I am especially indebted to her and her husband Michael J. O'Brien for their endless affection and support.

My warmest regards go to the late Professor Luis Gualco, the theatrical scholar and historian, for his generous support, help, and enthusiasm during all the time I worked at the Solís Archives.

Also priceless are the contributions made by pianists Wilhelm Kolischer, Luisa and Esther Giucci, as well as violinist Camillo Giucci, Jr., who through many years of friendship, in long conversations with picturesque anecdotes, shared with me an important part of the concert life during and after World War I, as well as Vaslav Nijinsky's last performance at the Teatro Solís. Also to the late Artur Rubinstein, a dear friend of Kolischer and the Giucci family, with whom I corresponded and who after more than half a century remembered with amazing facility his Montevideo recitals and friends, as well as his memorable performance with Nijinsky. I am truly sorry that even though some of them reached a very old age, none are alive to see this book.

I owe very special thanks to Dr. James W. Pruett and to Jon W. Newsom, former and actual chief respectively, of the Music Division of the Library of Congress and its staff; and to Donald F. Wisdom and to Karen Renninger, late and actual chief respectively, of the Serial and Government Publications Division of the Library of Congress and its staff; and to Ms. Sandra Florence of the Arlington County Public Library, Reference Division.

Equally important are the staff of the Teatro Solís that assisted very generously during my visit to Montevideo and made possible my taking photographs inside the house, especially Rubén Casanova, administration; Rafael Castañón, stage staff; Roberto Jones, services coordinator; Edgar Keuchkerian, stage staff; Cristina Landó, archivist; Alba Marchetti, Escuela Municipal de Arte Dramático staff; Estela Mieres, archivist, and José Luis Pochulo, administration. I also extend my gratitude to the staff of the Biblioteca Nacional of Montevideo: Mabel Batto, assistant chief librarian; Julio Castro, director, Bibliography and Reference Division; Isabel Diana, Special Collections Division librarian; and Graciela Guffanti, Research Division librarian, who made possible the access to documents and programs, and granted permission to photograph them. My appreciation goes to many other people, who in different ways, have contributed to this book, such as the architect Margarita Montañez of the Institute of History at the School of Architecture, University of the Republic, for providing the blueprint of the Teatro Solís; my late friend Professor Olga Papa, for smoothing administrative procedures and establishing contacts at the Biblioteca Nacional on my behalf; and to Professor Elsa Clavero de Mourat and Professor Eneida Sansone de Martínez.

I am very thankful to José Pedro Damiani—grandson of the renowned Uruguayan baritone—for sending me not only Víctor Damiani Teatro alla Scala reviews, but original photographs depicting him as Rigoletto in his performances at the Chicago Civic Opera's 1931 season.

I am also indebted to Professor Bruno Cagnoli, of Terni, Italy; to Dr. Carlo Marinelli Roscioni, of Rome, Italy; to Maestro Jaume Tribó, prompter and historian of the Teatro Liceo in Barcelona, and to Antonio Massísimo, of Mataró, Spain—all provided data and reviews of performances of Uruguayan singers at Italian and Spanish opera houses. Also to the late James B. McPherson, from Ontario; Dr. Alberto Pérez-Amador from Berlin; Charles Mintzer, from Brooklyn; and Juan Dzazópulos, from Santiago.

María Carolina Andrade helped to prepare for the publisher's use many rare and old originals that illustrate this book. In addition, there are many close friends and acquaintances, among them musicians, who were a constant support and help during all those long years. There are pianist Luis Batlle and his wife, Geraldine; Dr. Esperanza Berrocal; Dr. Alejandro Cáceres; Maestro Stephen Crout; Adela Durán Herrera; Louise Garcia-Ziebell; composer Sergio Cervetti; the late Roberto J. G. Ellis; soprano Violeta Erausquin; Dr. Miguel and Ilda Ficher; Dr. John R. Hébert, chief, Geography and Map Division, Library of Congress; music librarian Wilda M. Heiss, Library of Congress; David Hatcher and Lane Goddard; Susana Herrera; oboist Robert Lehrfeld and his wife, Florence; music librarian Kevin M. LaVine, Library of Congress; Carlisle J. Levine; Irma Majó; John Michael Martin, Library of Congress Copyright Office; pianist Alan Mandel and his wife, Nancy; Matías, Mónica, and Marcela Morassi; the late Donald Regier; choreographer Kenneth Rinker; Selwa Roosevelt; Suzanne A. Salgado (no relation); music librarian Charles Sens, Library of Congress; Dr. Richard Traubner; Gustavo A. Win; Margaret Warren Zensinger; my fellow members of the Women's National Book Association; my lawyer, Nina Graybill; and many more. Perhaps there are still some that I forgot to add here. I beg their forgiveness.

My gratitude goes to Dr. Alvaro Diez de Medina, former Uruguayan ambassador to the United States who put time, effort, and personal commitment into this publication. Equally, I feel very honored that the former president of Uruguay, Dr. Julio María San-guinetti, wrote the preface to this book. And it is also extremely rewarding that a highly praised opera scholar such as Dr. E. Thomas Glasow wrote the Foreword.

I am particularly grateful to my friend An-gel Gil-Ordoñez, orchestra conductor and professor, for introducing me to Wesleyan University Press, and to my editor Suzanna Tamminen in whom I found a generous and knowledgeable person who was amenable to all questions and suggestions. And of course, to Thomas R. Radko, director of Wesleyan University Press and all his staff who partici-pated in the making of this book. Also to Mi-chael Burton, who designed this book.

All my best memories and everlasting grat-itude goes to my mother Amelia Gómez-Eirín de Salgado, my brother Dr. Juan Andrés Salgado-Gómez, my aunt Elena Gómez-Eirín, and my cousin Elvira Oliver-Eirín. They gave me, in addition to great encouragement, most valuable personal collections of programs of the Teatro Solís performances, from 1894 to 1986 and some very old newspaper clippings with opera reviews. I also thank other mem-bers of my family who shared with me thousands of captivating stories and anecdotes

about singers, conductors, and actors they saw and heard on the Solís stage during the golden years of the house. My father, Juan Andrés Salgado, was the first to introduce me to opera when he sang "E lucevan le stelle" and "Giunto sul passo estremo"—not exactly lullabies, but they made me fall asleep when I was a toddler. It is a great sorrow that none of them could see the publication of this book.

But even with all that help, never ever could this book have been written without the love and permanent encouragement of my husband Roberto O. Morassi. My deepest ap-preciation goes to him for listening patiently each day during all the years of our marriage to my concerns and frequently depressed comments about the ups and downs of the book. In addition, he took time from an ac-tive life as sculptor, painter, and professor of art, to travel with me to Montevideo, where he took more than two hundred photographs of the Teatro Solís building and of documents, programs, and old newspaper reviews there and at the Biblioteca Nacional collection. In addition, he prepared all the book illustra-tions, including the cover. With all my love and gratitude, I dedicate this book to him.

Susana Salgado
Arlington, Virginia

THE TEATRO SOLÍS:
150 YEARS OF
OPERA, CONCERT, AND BALLET
IN MONTEVIDEO

CHAPTER 1

1516–1829

The Solís Tradition—

A Spanish Colony in the New World—

The Birth of Theatrical Life: The Casa de Comedias—

Tonadilla Escénica, Zarzuela, and Opera

Montevideo's Teatro Solís is the oldest major theater in the Americas still open. For almost a century and a half, it attracted the most important musical figures of the world. Singers of the golden age of opera, great conductors and orchestras, sublime dancers, legendary pianists and violinists—all were fascinated and bewitched by the Solís stage and its renowned acoustic qualities. This fame grew to such an extent that the Teatro Solís, a magnificent theater equal to the opera houses of Europe, could command the attention and respect of countries halfway across the globe, where opera had been born and perfected. To perform on the Solís stage and conquer the knowledgeable and demanding Montevideo audiences became a challenge that European artists strove to meet.

The very name of this theater reaches back in time, evoking the entire history of European presence on the Atlantic coast of South America. Juan Díaz de Solís, a Spanish navigator, was the first European to arrive on the South Atlantic shores, landing in 1516 on the coast of the estuary that later bore his name and became part of the Uruguayan coast: Río de Solís, now called the Río de la Plata. Whatever pride he took in his accomplishment was short-lived, however. Solís did not live to announce the news of his discovery to the king of Spain; he was killed by the natives of the land he had found.

Two centuries later, and on the same spot, the colonial city of Montevideo was established, and in 1856, fully 340 years after the arrival of Solís, an opera house bearing his name, the Teatro Solís, was built in Montevideo.

Thus began the Solís tradition, which included an endless stream of people transplanting their lives, their families, their culture, and their music from Europe to Uruguay. As a consequence, a strong tradition of opera arrived with them from the old European opera houses to the city of Montevideo, an entire world away. From the Solís inaugural season in 1856, there has been a steady migration of singers, musicians, conductors, directors, and designers, whose histories are incomplete if their biographies neglect their South American performances. This is the stage where Arturo Toscanini, with a 285-person opera company (including Enrico Caruso), opened the 1903 Solís season, and where Vaslav Nijinsky made his last stage appearance. This theater has earned a place in the world's musical histories, and yet it has remained shrouded in neglect. The purpose of this study is to remind the musical world of the profound place the Teatro Solís has in opera and to demonstrate that important musical history was made beyond European shores.

* * *

WHILE THE EXPLORER SOLÍS ventured into South America, the world was also opening up in other distant lands. It was an age of vast global exploration. In 1513, near the time of Solís' exploration, the Portuguese reached Canton, China. In the same year, Vasco Nuñez de Balboa discovered the Pacific Ocean from the Isthmus of Panama while Hernán Cortés entered Tenochtitlán (Mexico City) in 1521—an epoch also significant for the coronation, in 1519, of Charles I of Spain as the powerful Charles V, Holy Roman Emperor. England was ruled by the young Henry VIII. While the cultured of Europe were enjoying the music of the Flemish and Venetian madrigalists and the art of Michelangelo and Leonardo, and theologians were being shocked by Copernicus' enunciations, the principal preoccupation of European royalty was the conquest and colonization of the New World.

Many expeditions of Portuguese and English explorers, navigators and pirates—all eager to dispute Spain's power—sailed to America in order to enlarge their overseas empires. It was a rough struggle, a matter of first come,

first served. In the end, with the conquest of Brazil, the Portuguese claimed a huge portion of the continent, leaving much of the Atlantic coast and all the Pacific lands as far as Florida to the Spanish crown. Two centuries later, the English and the French were to fight Spain for the possession of North America.

In the South Atlantic, the caravels of the Portuguese explorer Fernão de Magalhães (Magellan) sailed upstream from the mouth of the Río Solís, in 1520. A watchman on one of the boats, sighting a hill overlooking a natural bay, exclaimed: "Monte Vide Eu!" ("I saw a hill!"); thereafter, this place was known as Montevideo. Such is the folklore at least, and if other hypotheses have been proposed about the name's origins, almost five hundred years have passed, and Montevideo remains the official name of the capital of the Republic of Uruguay on the north bank of the Río de la Plata. The river's original name has been lost since 1526, when crewmen with Sebastián Gaboto (Caboto)[1] began to call it Río de la Plata (River of Silver) instead of Río de Solís. They renamed it thinking, erroneously, that it was the regular route for the shipments of the Peruvian silver mines back to Spain. However inaccurate, after more than five centuries the name Río de la Plata firmly remains.

It was not until 1580 that a Spanish explorer successfully attempted to settle land in this tantalizing new wilderness. After the failures of many explorers, it was Juan de Garay who finally succeeded in founding the first Spanish settlement on the Río de la Plata: the city of the Santísima Trinidad and the port of Santa María de los Buenos Aires on the river's southwestern bank. This first settlement on the Atlantic coast was administratively dependent on the viceroyalty of Perú, founded in 1544 by Charles V. In 1618, also under the same viceroyalty, the Spanish crown established the Gobernación del Río de la Plata with the city of Buenos Aires as its capital.

Bruno Mauricio de Zavala, a prominent governor of Buenos Aires, crossed the Río de la Plata from Buenos Aires to found, by royal command, the city of Montevideo on the north bank of the river by the bay and crowned by the cerro de Montevideo (the hill of Montevideo). The city was formally named San Felipe y Santiago de Montevideo, to honor Philip V, then king of Spain. The exact year of the founding of Montevideo has been the source of endless controversy, the dates varying between 1724 to 1726.[2] These were unstable times for the Spanish crown, rocked by the War of Spanish Succession between the houses of Bourbon and Austria. Trying to strengthen his overseas empire, Philip V, the first Bourbon on the Spanish throne, had a new, fortified city—Montevideo—built at the entrance of the Río de la Plata to protect the gobernación from attacks by other European invaders. In addition to fifty families brought from the Canary Islands, the first population of Montevideo included European families from Buenos Aires. Zavala deployed an army of four hundred soldiers to defend the fortified positions.

In the following decades the population of Montevideo expanded considerably. The new generations were not always pleased by the regulations that Spain imposed and enforced on them. Their sensibilities were further influenced by the transformational ideas of the French Enlightenment and the shocking news of the revolution taking place in the British colonies of North America. The Río de la Plata was not isolated from such startling changes, and its people were beginning to reconsider Spanish rule. The Spanish crown was concerned about losing the Atlantic colonies. Thus in 1776, in order to reinforce his power, Charles III raised the gobernación to the rank of Viceroyalty of the Río de la Plata with Buenos Aires as capital. The new viceroyalty was made up of the present lands of Uruguay, Argentina, Bolivia, Paraguay and Rio Grande do Sul (now a Brazilian state). Nevertheless, the new political arrangement did not work, and the Spanish power began to weaken even as the ideals of freedom began to grow in the minds of the patriots around the Río de la Plata.

Three significant events occurred in succession. On July 4, 1776, thirteen of Britain's North American colonies broke away from English rule and declared independence. Thirteen short years later, on July 14, 1789, the king of France was dethroned by the French Revolution, its supporters spurred on by the cry "Liberty, Equality, and Fraternity." And between 1791 and 1792 Thomas Paine published *The Rights of Man*. It seems a noteworthy coincidence that on August 8, 1776, one month after the Americans became independent in the north part of the continent, Charles III published a Royal Letter proclaiming the new viceroyalty of the Río de la Plata. Although independence for Uruguay and the other countries of the new Viceroyalty arrived fifty years later than that of the United States, the struggle for freedom had its seeds here.

It is when a people are settled that they can transcend the everyday world and begin to think about the world of art—imagination, philosophical inquiry, escape, and self-understanding. A theater, even in the most primitive form, will always be a stage where emotion comes alive and understanding is enhanced through music, drama, and dance. It is always a landmark in time and place when a population feels the need for its own theater, and dedicates a site exclusively to its creation. In 1793, within the walls of the city of Montevideo, the Casa de Comedias was built by order of Governor Antonio Olaguer y Feliú. Ironically, in the case of Montevideo, the reason was far from cultural or artistic. The governor's objective was to divert the population's attention from the political and revolutionary scene and refocus it elsewhere. Portuguese attacks on Spanish lands were still frequent, and tension, bloody events, and lack of the basic necessities were commonplace in Montevideo. But what started as a pastime became a necessity, even a passion and, as political events reached the stage, a new language developed: the use of plays, music, and songs to voice objections against the Spaniards.

Other Latin American cities ruled by Spain constructed their first theaters at about this same period. Some, of course, came from earlier times. The Casa de Comedias of Mexico City, perhaps the first, was erected at the end of 1500; the Corral de Santo Domingo de Lima, at the beginning of the seventeenth century; the Coliseo de Comedias in Potosí, Bolivia, in 1716; and the Teatro de Opera y Comedias in Buenos Aires in 1757. In the very core of Montevideo, on Calle del Fuerte (now called 1°. de Mayo) and a few steps down from today's Plaza Zabala, the Casa de Comedias was built under the governor's orders by Manuel Cipriano de Melo on real estate belonging to prominent Montevideans Francisco Oribe and María Francisca de Alzáibar.[3] According to the last will and testament of de Melo, the house was built with money of the Infantry Regiment and by an express order of the governor. The same document, now kept in the archives of the Escribanía de Hacienda, shows the political reasons the governor gave to de Melo to build the Casa de Comedias: "to deflect the feelings of the inhabitants that could be altered in their fidelity [to the Spanish crown] due to the freedom of the French Republic." It also confirms that de Melo acquired the lot from Oribe, paying him 5,000 pesos six years later, by which time the house had already been built. The cost of the construction was 4,000 pesos, bringing the total cost to 9,000. The site of the Casa de Comedias was located on one side of the block that is now adjacent to the Plaza Zabala and surrounded by the streets of 1°. de Mayo, 25 de Mayo, and Zabala (changed from its original spelling of Zavala).

The Casa de Comedias was a large, warehouselike hut with a South American rancho shape and a sloping, clay Spanish-tile roof (fig. 1). It was a simple, functional structure of a type commonly built by the Spaniards in the eighteenth century in America. Two large front doors gave access to the orchestra; a small entrance led to what we would call the peanut gallery. On the upper floor, three small windows completed the building's façade. According to contemporary stories, the theater's interior was very humble.[4] The floor of the orchestra (or patio, as it was then called) was covered by scraped Portuguese bricks, and there were no seats at all. Servants brought chairs for their masters, and there are many stories of how mulatto servants were totally hidden under the mountain of chairs they carried in for an entire family.

The ceiling was supported by columns and heavy wooden beams and trusses that reduced the visibility of the stage. A row of small boxes located at the upper gallery in the back of the hall showcased the most splendid one, richly decorated and with elaborate velvet armchairs, used to seat the governor and other Spanish authorities. The elaborate stage curtain—made of a heavy fabric and covered with hand-painted allegories of the Muses, cornucopias, Pegasus, angels, and flowers—was practically the only decoration of the Casa de Comedias. Above the house, several lamps hung from the ceiling beams, and the lighting of the stage was provided by candles, the only source of light then available. The ceiling had three large holes, a sort of skylight, to allow some ventilation to the house. These holes were merely covered by crude pieces of lumber and so, many times when it started to rain, it also rained inside. Worst of all, it rained on the stage, one of the drawbacks of this colonial air-conditioning system.

Fig. 1. The Casa de Comedias. Colonial drawing used by Raúl Montero Bustamante to illustrate his article "Montevideo in 1810" in *Caras y Caretas*, May 25, 1910. Reproduced in *La Música en el Uruguay* by Lauro Ayestarán, (Montevideo: SODRE, 1953), 1:406.

Incredible as it may seem, in a city that had so devoted itself to the formation of a theater, as soon as the Casa de Comedias was ready for use, de Melo had a difficult time finding performers to perform in it. Evidently, in these times of continuous struggle it was much easier finding soldiers than someone in the performing professions. With perseverance, however, he finally managed to obtain some actors from Buenos Aires, while others were brought together with the help of the barber and the innkeeper of the city. In colonial days the barbershop was the source for finding everything, and the Figaro character, factotum of the city, was very much alive.

The advertising for this opening performance consisted of handbills posted at the Cabildo, the municipal council building. Until 1807, the date of the appearance of Montevideo's first newspaper, the *Southern Star* (written in English), this building served as the center of news distribution. Nor was the 1807 newspaper long-lived. Curiously, it was published during the short period of the English invasions (1806–7).

*   *   *

JOSÉ SUBIRÁ, THE MOST EMINENT musicologist and scholar to have written on this topic, considers the *tonadilla escénica* the authentic Spanish opera of the eighteenth century.[5] This musical form began to take shape in Spain about 1750, and developed rapidly to reach its peak in the last days of that century with such composers as Pablo Esteve, Blás de Laserna, Pedro Aranaz, Antonio Rosales, Jacinto Valledor, José Castel, and Fernando Ferandiere. From the opening of the Casa de Comedias in 1793 until about 1825, the tonadilla was the most important and most frequently performed type of music on this stage.

From the name tonada (song or tune) came the tonadilla (little song), a simple solo piece sung by an actor, generally a woman, to the accompaniment of the guitar. With the rise of the tonadilla escénica, the form became more elaborate, a sort of lyric-dramatic action for two or more characters with an orchestral accompaniment and an independent musical form. When composed for one, two, or three performers, these pieces were called, respectively, tonadilla a solo, tonadilla a duo, tonadilla a trío. But, when more than five characters or the whole company performed, they were called tonadillas generales, and could resemble a sort of operatic work in miniature, with a prelude, arias, duets, dances, intermezzos, and choral parts, lasting about twenty minutes.

Most of the tonadillas were written with a picaresque or satirical intention, and on a wide variety of subjects. Subirá lists the following categories: costumbristas (based on the local customs), amorous, historical, patriotic, magical, autobiographical, and allegorical.[6] The type of characters remained static, however, drawn from the typical lower-class people of Spain. Barbers, soldiers, bullfighters, seamstresses, washerwomen, priests, lackeys, coachmen and, above all, majas and majos, the most colorful characters of Madrid as immortalized in the pictures of Goya. The majo was a swashbuckler always looking either for a night of amour or a deadly brawl and as sharp with his lively wit as with his clasp knife. The maja, his perfect counterpart, was a spirited woman, all passion and freedom, with few prejudices, a sort of gypsy. The beginning of the nineteenth century saw a change in the tonadillas escénicas of Montevideo; pieces were then interlaced with political intentions and used by the patriots as a protest against Spanish colonialism.

The Casa de Comedias' archives list more than three hundred tonadillas escénicas. Unfortunately, the texts are the only material kept in these archives; the music is lost.[7] We do know that the most frequently performed composers in Montevideo were Laserna, Esteve, and Aranaz, and that it was Aranaz who also introduced the same musical form into Argentina and Chile.

Another form of music now also lost was the melólogo, known originally as melodrama, a monodrama for one actor, with incidental music. With music used as background or interspersed with the action, this form arrived at the Casa de Comedias around 1807 and was generally used there as the classic Fin de Fiesta. Some melólogos were also written in Montevideo in those days, but today only the poetic texts are preserved.

As the popularity of tonadilla escénica and the melólogo declined, a third type of music arose on the Casa de Comedias' stage: the exciting and colorful zarzuela. The original zarzuela, first performed in the early seventeenth-century Spain of Philip IV, derived its name from the Palacio de la Zarzuela, a hunting lodge also used for entertainment, that lay close to Madrid. It was here that comedians presented short pieces in two acts, with music and singing. In about 1657, these performances began to be called Fiestas de la Zarzuela, and then simply zarzuelas.[8]

However, the zarzuela arrived in the Americas much later. Eminent Uruguayan musicologist Lauro Ayestarán gives the year of 1854 as the date of the first zarzuela performed in Uruguay: Jeroma la castañera (Jeroma, the chestnut dealer) by Mariano Soriano Fuertes.[9] From then on the zarzuela gained in popularity and was, in fact, the only Spanish musical form of that time to survive the invasion of the Italian opera. Until the close of the nineteenth century and into the first decades of the twentieth, Spanish companies of zarzuelas arrived every season at Montevideo, bringing a wide repertoire and the best conductors and singers. As an artform that chronologically paralleled opera, the zarzuela maintained its popularity and its listeners, and several zarzuelas were written in Montevideo and performed in the Teatro Solís.

If the composers were important as the creators of this music, it was the singers, dancers, and actors who brought the tonadillas escénicas, the melólogos, and the zarzuelas to life. In the early days of the Casa de Comedias, they were almost itinerant players; as Spain's political struggle grew more dangerous, however, many eminently qualified performers set sail for South America. As the years passed, these expatriates established themselves in Montevideo, married, and produced their own families in their adopted countries. Some of their children also became actors, forming a theatrical dynasty.

Still, from among hundreds of singers, actors, dancers, and all types of musicians, really very few made history. One of the most memorable of these early performers was among the first to arrive to the Casa de Comedias—La Paca. A very young bolero dancer in 1808, she also performed tonadillas escénicas, fin de fiestas, and small plays. During this same period, a boy of thirteen, Juan Aurelio Casacuberta, made his stage debut at the Casa de Comedias as a dancer of bolero with La Paca; he also performed in *sainetes,* a sort of one-act Spanish dramatic farce contemporary to the tonadilla and zarzuela. Twenty years later, Casacuberta became the best dramatic actor of Latin America and an outstanding interpreter of William Shakespeare's *Othello* and plays by Tirso de Molina, Pedro Calderón de la Barca, and Molière. If Casacuberta was the great tragic actor of that time, Felipe David and Joaquín Culebras were *the* comedians. They delighted the Casa de Comedias public

for many years with their amusing characters.

It is the Quijano family that is most remembered as exemplars of an early musical dynasty. From the beginning until the end of the nineteenth century in Montevideo, it was this family that commanded the stage. The founding parents were Juan Quijano, known as El Barba (The Bearded), and Petronila Serrano, a Spanish singer, actress, and dancer who sang tonadillas and performed on the stage for fifty-four years. They were the parents of Luisa and Fernando and, in turn, grandparents of Eloísa and Benjamín Quijano, all of them singers, dancers, and actors. Fernando Quijano was the most multitalented member of the clan, as a singer of opera, zarzuela and tonadilla, a composer, dancer and choreographer, a stage director, pianist, and impresario.

In 1813 Manuel Cipriano de Melo died, and one year later the deteriorating Casa de Comedias had to be restored. From that point on, the theater was simultaneously known as the Coliseo or Casa de Comedias, with the older devotees continuing to call it by its original name. In 1816 the poet Bartolomé Hidalgo became its director. Shortly thereafter, the tonadilla escénica, which had monopolized audiences for more than thirty years, quickly declined, practically forgotten in the enthralling novelty of a newly arrived art form that completely captivated the public: Italian opera. In time the Teatro Solís became renowned for its opera, while on its stage, night after night, life and death, love and hate, passion and hallucination, power and glory were re-created with such authority that Montevideo audiences were forever conquered. Since then operatic life has become a vital part of the Solís stage, with its endless dreams about the joys and sorrows of the human soul: the foundation of opera's immortality.

CHAPTER 2

1830–1856

The Italian Opera in the Americas and the Antecedents of the Teatro Solís

Between 1810 and 1820 the musical scene of the Americas, from New York to Buenos Aires, was totally transformed by the introduction of Italian opera into the New World. This transformation came in two phases, the first marked by the arrival of operatic piano scores of arias and choruses, plus the music of orchestral overtures. It was with the second wave of musical importation that opera in its full form blazed onto the American scene with the first performance of complete operas. This would be the pattern for almost every city in the Americas, with the years 1825 through 1830 witnessing a Gioachino Rossini opera in practically every operatic theater.

During the nineteenth century opera in the Americas was (with the exception of a few cities like New Orleans and Havana that had resident companies) largely a function of touring companies that would go first to one city, then to another. As far the "Southern cone" of South America was concerned, Buenos Ai-

res, Rio de Janeiro, and Santiago were the principal centers, with visiting companies usually staying in these cities for a few months, then continuing to other towns.

It was very unusual for such a company to be engaged only for Montevideo, or even to make its first stop in that city. Most of the time, they would start out in Buenos Aires and, after the conclusion of the season there, would then go on tour. There was no regular pattern for these tours, but the most frequent second stop would be either Rosario (often followed by Córdoba) in Argentina, or Montevideo, just across the Río de la Plata. After Montevideo, they might return to Argentina, or go directly to Brazil, primarily Rio de Janeiro followed by São Paulo. On rare occasions, they might also go to Santiago, but that presented a problem, as it necessitated either crossing the Andes, or rounding South America. More likely, the companies engaged for Santiago would proceed to Valparaíso, possibly Lima, and then return to Italy. On even rarer occasions, companies might travel from either Lima or Santiago and give a season in Montevideo. On other occasions, companies reversed the process, starting in Rio, proceeding to São Paulo, and then Montevideo, followed by Argentina. It is safe to conclude that the only pattern for these tours that was ever established was that there was no pattern.

When the García family arrived in America in 1825 to present the first performance of Rossini's *Il barbiere di Siviglia*, at the Park Theatre of New York, they ushered in a new age in musical history; the history of the legendary family was, to some extent, the history of opera in the nineteenth century. Rossini wrote the character of Almaviva for Manuel del Popolo García, a Spanish singer and composer from Seville, who went on to great acclaim and fame for his creation of this character. Both of his daughters had active musical careers: María Felicitas García (later María Malibran) was one of the most famous sopranos of that century, while Paulina (later Pauline Viardot) was famous throughout Europe as a mezzo-soprano and as the first Fidès in Giacomo Meyerbeer's *Le prophète*. She was also a voice teacher in Paris. His son, Manuel junior, studied medicine, specialized in treating the vocal cords, and invented the laryngoscope. Also a singer, he was a professor at the Paris Conservatoire and taught at London's Royal Academy of Music for forty-seven years (1848–95). This multitalented family gave more than eighty performances in New York and then embarked on a journey by sea and land, finally to reach Mexico City after a year of adventure. In 1827, at Mexico City's Teatro de los Gallos, the Garcías performed the same Rossini opera that Buenos Aires had seen for the first time, at its own Coliseo, two years before.

Four other cities in the Americas were introduced to their first complete operatic work on the new Italian model in 1830: Montevi-

deo, Santiago, Lima, and Rio de Janeiro. The date for Montevideo is somewhat misleading, however; the city had had its first contact with opera six years before, in 1824, when the baritone Miguel Vaccani had sung two arias from operas by Giovanni Paisiello and Rossini. The first performance of the overture of *Barbiere* by the orchestra of the Casa de Comedias was in 1827. A concert performance of *Il barbiere di Siviglia* by soloists, chorus and orchestra opened the 1829 season of the Casa de Comedias.

The year 1830 is a double landmark in the development of Uruguayan society, with significant events in both the historical and musical fields. The 1825 Declaration of Independence from Spain was confirmed by the adoption of the First Constitution on July 18, 1830. At nearly the same time, the music of Montevideo (now a city of nearly fifteen thousand) reached new heights with the performance of Rossini's *L'inganno felice* at the Casa de Comedias on May 14, 1830. *L'inganno felice*, the fourth of Rossini's operas and his first successful work, was premiered in Venice at the San Moisè in 1812, when the composer was twenty years old. As its name suggests, this farce in one act is the typical imbroglio, with the happy ending characteristic of Italian opera buffa. The principal characters in the 1830 Montevideo performance were sung by sister and brothers Angelita, Marcelo, and Pascual Tanni; the orchestra of the Casa de Comedias was conducted by Antonio Sáenz. A few days later another Rossini work, *Aureliano in Palmira*, was premiered on the same stage and by the same cast. Four other operas were performed in the Casa de Comedias before the end of the year, each of them several times, but the season's zenith was reached with the Montevideo premiere of Rossini's *Otello*. Desdemona, Roderigo, and Iago were sung by the Tanni sister and brothers, while Spanish tenor Pablo Rosquellas, celebrated in

Madrid, sang the Moor. *Il barbiere di Siviglia*, having premiered in Montevideo in the 1829 concert version, received its first staged performance by the Tanni family in January 1831.

* * *

THE PERIOD BETWEEN 1830 and 1840 was one of true reaffirmation of the operatic field. As the public learned more about opera, their artistic expectations were heightened and they began to look for better vocal qualifications in the singers. One of the first ensembles to meet these requirements was an Italian company headed by the soprano Justina Piacentini who, together with her father, Fabricio, and her sisters, Elisa and Carolina, gave her first operatic concert on May 8, 1832, at the Casa de Comedias. The public received her enthusiastically and talked about her for weeks on end. The press was equally enthusiastic, congratulating "opera lovers for [the] wonderful and amazing acquisition" of this singer.[1] As one of the regular interpreters of Vincenzo Bellini and Gaetano Donizetti in South America until then, Justina Piacentini sang at the Casa de Comedias for eight consecutive seasons. It was Bellini's *Norma* that became her warhorse, and it was she who introduced *Norma*'s famous "Casta Diva" to Montevideo, even before the entire opera was known.

After this triumph, the house stood dark and silent for more than a decade as the Guerra Grande, a political and civil war begun in 1839, interrupted Uruguayan life. Although no opera was sung in the Casa de Comedias at this time, the hosts and hostesses of Montevideo's homes and colonial mansions began sponsoring concerts and amateur drama to feed the elite's craving for culture. When the siege of Montevideo ended on October 8, 1851, and a new freedom of expression was instituted, these salons expanded, becoming the center of the city's cultural life. There were frequent evening gatherings, with poetry readings and small concerts of chamber music. Even if Justina Piacentini didn't sing at all in the theater during those years, she was still very much in charge of the *bel canto*, establishing herself in Montevideo, and opening a musical conservatory on the outskirts of the city.

The musical activities of the Teatro del Comercio (as the Casa de Comedias was renamed after the first renovation in 1843) returned only four days after the peace treaty of 1851 was signed and Montevideo was newly released from its state of occupation. The soprano Teresa Questa and her company gave the Uruguayan premiere of Bellini's *Beatrice di Tenda* on October 12, 1851. In a short three-month season Questa performed, on November 20, another opera hitherto unknown to Montevidean audiences: Donizetti's *Gemma di Vergy*.

Ida Edelvira made her Montevideo debut in January 1852 and performed there for three seasons. She was enthusiastically received: "Her triumph was complete, with a large attendance and endless applause, both deserved by this eminent artist."[2] In only two years the Montevideo audiences came to know fifteen new operas, all sung by Edelvira and her company: *Norma, La sonnambula, I puritani*, and *Il pirata* by Bellini; *Ernani, Nabucco, Macbeth*, and *I due Foscari* by Giuseppe Verdi; *L'elisir d'amore, Linda di Chamounix, La fille du régiment, Don Pasquale*, and *Belisario* by Donizetti; *Il giuramento* by Saverio Mercadante; and *La fidanzata corsa* by Giovanni Pacini. During the same period, between 1852 and 1854, another Italian opera company, headed by tenor Enrico Rossi-Guerra, gave the local premieres of *I Capuleti e i Montecchi* by Bellini; *Attila, I masnadieri, I lombardi alla prima crociata*, and *Luisa Miller* by Verdi; *Marino Faliero* by Donizetti; and six or seven more works by Pacini and Luigi Ricci. The Rossi-Guerra company spent around eight years in

Fig. 2. The famous rival sopranos. *Left:* Elisa Biscaccianti; *right:* Sofia Vera-Lorini. Reproduced in *La Música en el Uruguay* by Lauro Ayestarán, (Montevideo: SODRE, 1953), 1: 213, 211. Original in *Historia de Nuestros Viejos Teatros* by Taullard, 136 and 146.

America, traveling to Buenos Aires, then Chile, up the coast through Perú and Ecuador to Colombia, then Venezuela, various Caribbean islands, and eventually New York.

* * *

IN ADDITION TO OPERATIC ACTIVITIES, in 1850 Montevideo received its first important performing instrumentalist: Camillo Sivori, an Italian violinist and pupil of Nicolò Paganini at the height of his musical career. Sivori appeared in five recitals with programs that included the best known of Paganini's pieces, as well as some of Sivori's own. Two years later, a French pianist and prize winner from the Paris Conservatoire, Paul Faget, also made his appearance in Montevideo. These two soloists inaugurated the visits by European musicians that have lasted for more than a century, into our own.

* * *

IN MANY RESPECTS, Sofia Vera-Lorini's arrival in Montevideo marked the beginning of new heights for operatic excellence in this city. Married to impresario Achille Lorini, at that time she was the *prima donna assoluta* at the Théâtre des Italiens in Paris, and also at London's Her Majesty's.[3] A pioneer in her field, she was not only the first soprano to be called "diva" by the Montevideo public; she also originated a singing rivalry, provoking—for the first time in the theatrical history of Uruguay—a hot quarrel between the audiences and the press. The myth of the diva relies on such flourishes, but Vera-Lorini's significance in the opera world was hardly limited to extravagant behavior. It was she who definitively established the Verdi repertoire within a two-year period when she sang the great trilogy: *Il trovatore*, *Rigoletto*, and *La traviata*. Tenor Giovanni Comolli and baritone Giuseppe Cima shared the principal roles of the Italian Lyric Company with Vera-Lorini. They performed *Il trovatore* at the Teatro San Felipe (the new name for the Casa de Comedias following in the wake of the Teatro del Comercio) on April 14, 1855, and four months later gave the Uruguayan premiere of *Rigoletto*. It was after seeing her interpretation of Gilda that the public raised Vera-Lorini to a status previously unknown in Montevideo operatic tradition.

It was at precisely this time that soprano

Eliza Biscaccianti (fig. 2) appeared on the same stage to perform Donizetti's *Lucia di Lammermoor*. Born in Boston in 1824, Biscaccianti came from a musical background. Her grandfather was James Hewitt, a composer, conductor, organist, professor, and music publisher in the United States, and a musical leader in his time. Nor did the line of talent end there; nine Hewitt descendants dedicated their lives to music. During Eliza Biscaccianti's first performance, half of the house applauded her with enthusiasm; the other half became incensed, shouting that she had been sent only to steal Vera-Lorini's well-established reputation. The battleground was set, and the quarrel grew more violent, with the public, as well as the press, clearly divided into opposing camps. For the duration of this competition, the newspapers daily carried either compliments for one singer or insidious reviews for the other. The peace of the past musical life was over:

> To appreciate the sacrifice imposed on the public by Signora Biscaccianti it is necessary to have heard Signora Vera-Lorini after Biscaccianti's debut. *Lucia* and *Il trovatore*, those two divine creations, perfectly marked the difference between both artists' interpretations. The one [Vera-Lorini] modest, pleasant . . . became the idol of the public for her merit and talent; the other [Biscaccianti] raced like a terrible meteor through the American theatres, raising tempests and conspiracies, identifying herself with violent passions among local parties, exploiting hatred, curiosity, and people's pockets, manipulating all mediums and influences, all culminating in a doleful performance that we cannot, in respect to her sex, classify as we would like to.[4]

It should be noted that this review, partial to Vera-Lorini, was offset by others, such as a long, grandiloquent poem by poet Luis Domínguez, in which he proclaimed Biscaccianti a "divinity, a mermaid with a voice that mesmerizes, akin to those of the angels."[5]

According to reports of their respective performances before coming to Montevideo, both sopranos were considered to have excellent voices. There were no doubt differences in character, quality, and *tessitura*, as well as in the repertoires they sang. But this does not mean that one was better than the other. The great clash came, simply, because it was the first time that two similar sopranos of a certain prestige sang in almost overlapping performances. The competition, if fiery, burned out quickly when Biscaccianti left Montevideo after a few more performances and Vera-Lorini regained her monopoly on the applause. The reaffirmation of her position came on May 10, 1856, with the first performance of *La traviata* in Montevideo; with her success as Violetta, public and press were again hers. Her biggest success, however, was yet in store for her: the opening of the Teatro Solís.

* * *

IN 1856 URUGUAY had a population of 220,000 inhabitants within an area of 72,172 square miles.[6] The political scene, after all the years of the Guerra Grande, was fairly stable, and on March 1 of that year, Gabriel Antonio Pereira, one of the signers of the Declaration of Independence, became the president of the republic. The Montevideo of 1856 was very much like a European city and was always looking to the lifestyle of Paris for inspiration. Using the French Romantic salon as a pattern, the cultural life of the city had been growing through the medium of intellectual gatherings in private homes. With the opening of the Teatro Solís, there was a shift in what was considered the most fashionable gathering place, as elegant soirées at the theater became the new center of cultural and social life. Although this was still a fledgling society when it came to high fashion, the intellectual circles already enjoyed the nonchalance and *laisser-aller* of the French cultural world. In many of those exclusive gatherings the young generation were raised to know about European poetry and literature, as well as their own national figures. These were the years of Francisco Acuña de Figueroa, Bernardo Prudencio Berro, and Alejandro Magariños Cervantes, three typical poets of Uruguayan Romanticism. A group of brilliant journalists—Juan Carlos Gómez, José Pedro Ramírez, Elbio Fernández, and Carlos María Ramírez—reached not only Buenos Aires and other cities of Latin America with their sharp and controversial articles, but Spain as well.

Such growing fame was not limited to writers. Eduardo Acevedo and Gonzalo Ramírez were internationally known Uruguayan jurists, while Andrés Lamas, was known equally as a diplomat, economist, and historian. Isidoro de María, with his quaint chronicles of old times, was the preeminent historian of his age. In visual art, a young Juan Manuel Blanes began his series of large, historical canvases at the Palacio de San José, General Urquiza's residence in Argentina. No matter what their profession or avocation, every member of the young Uruguayan generation of artists, musicians, writers, and poets had a common dream: a trip to Europe, with a Parisian sojourn. Some of them were fortunate enough to realize it.

By this time Montevideo had already heard works by Handel, Mozart, Beethoven, and Weber. The piano repertoire of Mendelssohn, Liszt, and Sigismond Thalberg were very popular, as was the violin music of Paganini, Louis Spohr, and Charles-Auguste de Bériot. The three classical composers for the guitar—Ferdinando Carulli, Mauro Giuliani, and Dionisio Aguado—frequently had their works played at concerts. José Amat, a Spanish singer and conductor, sang *Der Wanderer* in 1853, the first Franz Schubert lied heard in Montevideo. By 1856 Montevideo knew many Rossini, Bellini, and Donizetti operas; audiences were also acquainted with the French repertoire by Meyerbeer, Daniel-François Auber, Ambroise Thomas, Fromental Halévy, Victor Massé, and Adrien Boieldieu.

From 1852 to the beginning of 1856, the audiences of the Teatro San Felipe were able to see ten Verdi premieres, including *Il trovatore*, *Rigoletto*, and *La traviata*. Indeed, *La traviata* was performed in Montevideo before it was in London or New York. The world premiere of *La traviata* took place in Venice, at La Fenice, on March 6, 1853, and San Felipe's presentation was on May 10, 1856. London audiences saw the opera fourteen days later, on May 24, at Her Majesty's Theatre. Almost seven months later the audiences of the Academy of Music in New York were able to see their first *Traviata* on December 3, 1856.

CHAPTER 3

~ *1839–1856* ~

The Construction of the Teatro Solís—
Project for a New Theater—The Zucchi Project—Eight Years
of Delay—Architect Francisco Xavier de Garmendia
and His New Project—Further Renovations

In 1835 the ramparts encircling Montevideo were being demolished, making way for new development and urbanization. The erection of a new theater in accordance with the growth of the city became an integral element in the project; indeed, the idea had first sprung up as early as May 1834 when the government presented a plan to Congress to build a new house on the same site of the Casa de Comedias. The proposals foundered until July 1837, when the Topographic Committee (created in 1831) encouraged the government to build a new theater. The Theater Committee, created in 1833, and presided over by Francisco Magariños, asked the government for authorization to solicit proposals for building a new theater. This latter issue was discussed by the committee on May 23, 1840, and the petition was presented on May 29. The government responded with a decree dated June 16, 1840: "The Committee is authorized to receive bidding for the building of a new theater, that might be presented to the Government for the final decision. This declaration is signed by Francisco Antonio Vidal, Secretary of Government."[1] With this declaration in hand the committee used the Montevidean press to publish the opening of the bidding on June 25, 1840. Each proposal was required to provide complete design plans, blueprints, an appropriate construction site and completion deadline, the work's total cost, benefits derived from this enterprise, and possible government funding for the realization of this project.[2]

One month later the Committee for the Construction of a New Theater held its first meeting; its board of directors, headed by Juan Francisco Giró, included a group of eminent citizens: Luis Lamas, Juan Miguel Martínez, Juan Benito Blanco, Francisco Solano Antuña, Ramón Artagaveytia, and Vicente Vázquez.[3] By year's end, the considerable number of stockholders made the Sociedad del Nuevo Teatro[4] a strong and sound enterprise. The committee's first concern was to find a site for the theater, and in August 1840 Carlos Zucchi presented a report on the most suitable sites available. Zucchi, a notable Italian design architect and engineer living in Montevideo, was a member of the Topographic Committee and an engineer of Housing and Development. He proposed three different lots, one being the same site that had been suggested back in 1837, in front of the Park of Engineers, on a block now bounded by the streets Juncal, Sarandí, Policía Vieja, and Pasaje Centenario. The second site, owned by Elías Gil, was located south of the marketplace, but it was the third (belonging to Ramón Carreras) on San Sebastián Street (actually Buenos Aires Street) and limited by Bartolomé Mitre, Juncal, and Reconquista streets, that was chosen. It was there that the Solís was built, in the very heart of Montevideo, with its main entrance at 678 on Buenos Aires Street. Today this block is a part of the whole area known as La Ciudad Vieja (the Old Town).

In September 1840 the committee contacted Zucchi with its request for a design; five months later the board of directors acknowledged receipt of his architectural plans. The chosen site had a stunning advantage: a natural spring of water running beneath the theater gave it perfect acoustics, with a large network of subterranean tunnels (probably former underground stream channels, now dry) at foundation level creating a huge, resonant chamber under stage and orchestra.

Zucchi's project was magnificent, but totally unrealistic financially, and on March 24, 1841, the entire project—design, plans, and plates—was returned to the designer. Twice Zucchi claimed payment, but was refused on the grounds that his project followed neither the budget nor the regulations established by the committee.[5] Once more the Solís committee set out to raise more money and develop a viable project, this time demanding

that the theater have a seating capacity of at least fifteen hundred and a building cost not exceeding 125,000 pesos. When this was agreed to, on May 13, 1841, the committee declared a competition among architects a Mr. Bocciardi, Pedro Benoit, Francisco Xavier de Garmendia, Juan Lafine, and José Toribio. Only two, Garmendia and Bocciardi, presented plans, and on August 19 the plans of Garmendia, a thirty-year-old Spanish architect, were approved (fig. 3).[6]

Rafael Hernández was chosen to construct the building's foundation and sewage system, with the committee stipulating that the foundation was to "be constructed of stone and mortar [while] wood from both the red pine of Russia and [the] urunday tree must be used for beams and trusses."[7] The proportion of lime, sand, and water, as well as the way to handle the mortar mixture, were all stipulated by the committee because it was different from the standards previously used in Montevideo. The roof, of slate from Genoa, was under the supervision of Esteban Tiscornia, as were the eight marble columns for the entrance foyer.

But such planning came to nothing with the outbreak of the Guerra Grande in 1839 (see chapter 2). Workers were called to join the army, and panicked stockholders emigrated. Once more, dreams and visions fell victim to reality, and the fate of the Teatro Solís would be postponed for almost ten years.[8] When the peace treaty was signed on October 8, 1851, the society called a meeting of the stockholders, and a survey of the site and materials was ordered. After eight and a half years the place was a disaster, with wood and marble abandoned in the open air, unprotected, and even buried in the mud. Amazingly, much of the original material was usable and, in spite of pessimistic predictions, a meticulous checking of the foundation set nine years before showed it to be in perfect

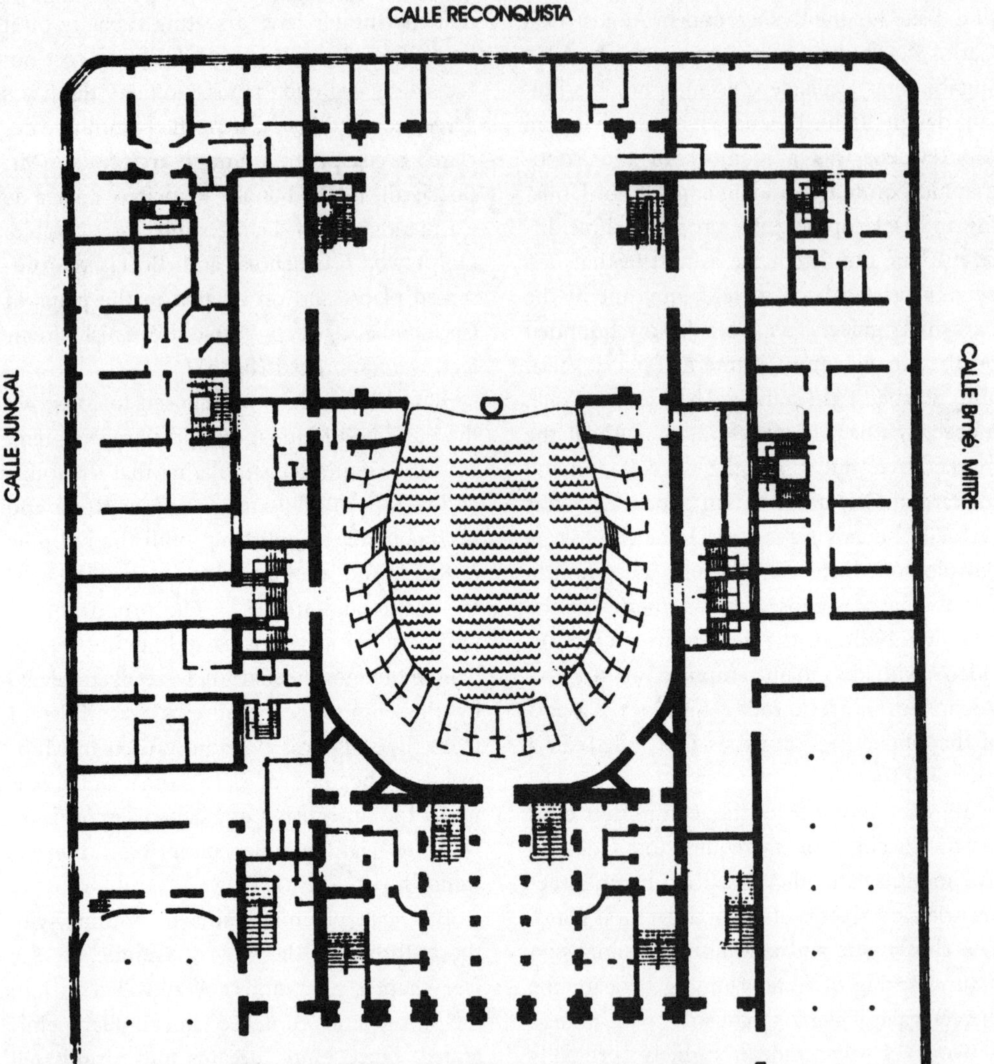

Fig. 3. Floor plan of the Teatro Solís. As the original 1841 plans were never found, this is a blueprint done in 1946 at the time of the existing building's remodeling. Archives School of Architecture, University of the Republic, Montevideo.

condition. Once again the city turned its sights on building its new opera house.

The first task was to remove the obstructions that had been deliberately set up to deter wartime pillage. For almost ten years of war a devoted guard had been living here with his family: part of the foundation had been made into a poultry yard, and another into a pen where he kept the animals to draw his wagons. All this had been done with the knowledge, even approval, of Juan Miguel Martínez and other board members, the only persons among the board and stockholders who had remained in the besieged city. Martínez also thought to rent some of the warehouses surrounded by the foundations so that by war's end it would help defray the cost of clearing the site with a view toward beginning construction once again.

On January 20, 1852, the assembly of Society members appointed a new board of directors consisting of Javier Alvarez, Pablo Duplesis, Joaquín Errazquin, José María Esteves, Jaime Ylla y Viamont, Juan Miguel Martínez, and Antonio Rius, with Martínez as board president. A new meeting was called, and on November 26 Garmendia's plans, with modifications, were approved. The walls of the ellipse, designed originally of bricks and lime, were replaced by iron columns to save space and increase strength. The shape of the ellipse was changed to achieve a more graceful design and to enhance acoustics. However, since the original plans of the house never have been found, there is nothing to be compared with the actual plans of the building to know if that modification reported by the committee is related to the changes done in the auditorium or in the proscenium (see note 10). The orchestra, adjacent corridors, and foyer were all enlarged. José Marino was appointed director of all iron fabrication, while a Mr. Pujole was to see that all marble for columns, walls, stairs, and balustrades was delivered from It-

aly. As exciting as all this was after so many years of inactivity, the committee still prudently called architects Clemente César and A. Penaud to examine the modified plans before giving the final endorsement to the Garmendia project.[9]

The actual capacity of the house was approximately twenty-five hundred seats on the orchestra and five tiers: balcony boxes, dress circle, first tier, and two galleries. The lower gallery (*cazuela,* the peanut gallery) was at the beginning for women only; as the upper called (*paraíso*) was for men only. The name *paradise* came from the French expression *les enfants du paradis* (as the poor students were named in France two centuries ago). And it has been always where usually the cultured but penniless audience sits or stands.

As this history shows, although it was Garmendia who got the assignment to build the Teatro Solís, he cannot truly be considered the theater's sole designer. Furthermore, there is evidence that he based some of his ideas on the designs of Zucchi. In 1841 a complete brochure entitled "Proyecto de Teatro compuesto y dibujado por el ingeniero-arquitecto Carlos Zucchi" (Project of a theater drawn and designed by engineer-architect Carlos Zucchi), was published—the very year of Garmendia's submission. In fact, the Zucchi publication contained the total design with a complete set of drawings and plans, including the specifications. Garmendia must have been familiar with it, because his work was apparently an adaptation and simplification of Zucchi's original ideas. Details, such as the sculpture of the sun emblem at the center of the tympanum, appeared in both projects. While credit should not be taken away from Garmendia, it would more equitable to consider Zucchi as the planning-architect with Garmendia as the adapter and builder of the Teatro Solís. It is important to remember that without Garmendia's ideas for reducing construction costs, the Solís could never have been built. On the other hand, many publications give only Garmendia's name in discussing the background of the Solís. Logically, it would be much better to say that it was a joint project.[10]

Before the bids were published in the press, the committee ordered that a wooden model of what would be one of the theater's boxes, complete with trusses and all details and measures, be constructed to show prospective builders.[11] After a public bid to start the masonry works, builders, foremen, masons, bricklayers, and carpenters resumed work on January 20, 1853. The site must have resembled a giant beehive, but after so many frustrations and setbacks, the noisy hammering would have been celestial music to Martínez!

With construction under way, there was a startling accident on October 16, when the theater's frontispiece (ornamental façade) collapsed, apparently the result of insufficient support. The problem was speedily corrected without further repercussions, but it must have been a shock to the theater's champions. When construction was almost completed, and before the interior decoration was begun, the board appointed a special committee made up by the architects Clemente César, Antonio Paullier, José Toribio, and Aimée Aulbourg to survey the building and report on its soundness and safety. This they did, as noted in their final memorandum dated July 31, 1854.[12]

The committee looked to France for decorating advice for the interior, and sent for proposals and prices relating to crystal chandeliers and other lighting fixtures, and the embellishing of boxes with gilded copper ornaments. They wanted candle chandeliers that could be adapted for gas, similar to those being used in Parisian theaters. In May 1855 the board received a sketch of the principal curtain done by Francesco Gandolfi of Genoa,

chosen because he had taken first prize at the 1854 Genoese painting competition. The curtain had forty-one figures depicting Apollo and Minerva arriving in the Americas, riding in a horse-drawn chariot surrounded by the Muses. Behind the chariot came Fame, laurel crown in hand, flying toward a panoramic landscape of the city of Montevideo. In one corner Liberty, Peace, Commerce, and Abundance, surrounded by nymphs, rejoiced. In another corner appeared War, Envy, and Discord, completely vanquished. A second curtain, painted by Signor Luxiolo (also a Genoese artist), carried a vignette with a scene of nymphs dancing. Vicente Gianello, of Genoa, presented both designs to the theater committee for approval, but they were rejected because of excessive cost.[13] The board agreed on a more modest design: a large red velvet curtain with velvet side cascades, decorated with golden fringes, tassels, and white satin swags in the upper part, all crowned by the national coat of arms. The golden foyer of the second floor was decorated with French chairs and chandeliers, Persian carpets and a Pleyel grand piano of inlay wood (which is still there). And the foyer's doors were upholstered with quilted ivory satin.

At this phase of the construction, the committee decided to rescind Garmendia's technical direction. In a report presented to the general assembly of stockholders on December 21, 1855, the board of directors explained their decision. Garmendia's problems with one of the artists engaged in decorating the theater had led to his denouncing these paintings to the committee, but his lateness in lodging his complaint met with a bad reaction from the board. Already existing conflicts were followed by disputes, and the committee felt further insulted by two statements that Garmendia had made to the press. They also believed that Garmendia lacked the knowledge to handle the interior building and decoration of the house. A feud developed, and Garmendia, offended by his dismissal, claimed 12,000 pesos as indemnification. Garmendia filed two suits against the committee but lost both, and the conflict ended (although the committee paid 741 pesos in legal fees).[14]

As the building's opening date neared, one of the most difficult tasks became the choice of a name. Everyone on the board had a suggestion, and each thought his selection the best. More than a dozen proposals met with endless arguments and confusion: Teatro de la Empresa, Teatro de la Armonía, Teatro de la Libertad, Teatro de Mayo, Teatro de la Paz, Teatro de la Concordia, Teatro del Sol, Teatro Republicano, Teatro de Artigas, Teatro de Montevideo, Teatro Oriental, Teatro de la Opera, and Teatro de la Constancia. All were touted, but, surprisingly, none was selected, and Teatro de Solís was the name sculpted on the frontispiece (fig. 4). The name, chosen in homage to the discoverer of the Río de la Plata, was proposed by Francisco Gómez, one of the society's stockholders. When on September 18, 1871, the society of stockholders made changes to the general contract, the replacement was printed up under the theater's new name: the Empresa del Teatro Solís. Its simplified form, Teatro Solís, was embraced by the public and is still used today.[15]

In December 1855 all the decorations, chandeliers, draperies, grand foyer furniture, and chairs for the boxes were delivered from France. The final pieces of marble for the entrance foyer and stairs were put in place, and the orchestra floor was modified to accommodate stage machinery. All stage materials, stage sets, props, and backstage equipment also arrived. Three complete opera scores and thirty-one other works made up the music library. For safety, the house was furnished with two large fire hydrants, while two lightning rods were installed on the roof. The large

plaza before the building was paved and surrounded by pedestals and gaslight poles, with lateral spaces to park carriages.[16] Total cost, according to existing data, reached 268,239 pesos and 227 reis (approximately $250,000.00 in 1855), with Garmendia's fee set at an additional 10,000 pesos.[17] The original house capacity was 1,584 seats, even if at the opening night 2,500 tickets were sold. (At that time Montevideo had approximately 49,000 inhabitants.)[18]

The idea to enhance the theater façade with three huge marble statues to crown the frontispiece emerged a few years after the opening. One was to depict navigator Juan Díaz de Solís, the man who gave the theater its name, while the smaller statues were to represent comedy and tragedy. Gianello was contracted by the committee to do the work in Europe: but when the three statues arrived in 1860, however, the committee refused to accept them because they were considerably smaller than what had been stipulated. For five years there were endless discussions and arguments among board, committee, and stockholders, and the statues were never put in place; to this day the only decoration on the frontispiece is a bas-relief of the sun.[19]

The exterior of the Teatro Solís has sustained several changes since 1856. A considerable modification was done in 1882, when the original slate roof of the building was replaced by a steel structure, a remodeling that took three months and was planned and supervised by the engineer Juan Alberto Capurro. The addition of two lateral wings to the principal building, both of Zucchi and Garmendia's designs, was thought to be an integral element of the finished theater. As early as 1863 engineer-architect Ignacio Pedralbes y Capua offered the committee his services to design the wings. After several deliberations, the committee was not pleased with his plans, and asked him to make changes. None of his

Fig. 4. Flyer announcing the opening of the Teatro Solís. Reproduced in *La Música en el Uruguay* by Lauro Ayestarán, (Montevideo: SODRE, 1953), 1:227. Original courtesy of Professor Juan Carlos Sábat Pebet.

proposals was accepted, and finally the committee chose French architect Victor Rabu to do the work under the general direction of the Theatre Inspector architect Antonio M. Dupard. The cost of both side buildings was estimated at 210,000 pesos. The two-story wings were constructed between 1869 and 1885, and each semicircular front was decorated with Corinthian columns to match the other eight in the front of the house.[20] Through the years the two lateral wings housed different tenants, from stores to restaurants. The Liceo Musical Franz Liszt—one of the leading Uruguayan musical conservatories, founded by Roman pianist Camillo Giucci—resided in the west wing after the conservatory inauguration on June 28, 1895. Today, the ground level of the west wing is the home of the Natural History Museum. The entire main floor houses the National Committee of Fine Arts and its exhibition galleries. The Escuela Municipal de Arte Dramático (Municipal School of Drama) occupies the main floor of the east wing, with the restaurant El Aguila located on the ground level.

Since the 1532 conflagration in Ferrara, Italy, of the western world's first indoor theater,[21] only good fortune had saved other theaters from the same fate. These Renaissance construction materials of wood, paper, paint, resinous textiles and other fabrics, lighting gelatins, and glue—all highly flammable substances—often resulted in destructive fires. Combine this with the accepted practice of backstage smoking, and it is hardly surprising that so many theaters have been destroyed by fire. The Teatro Solís was lucky, although the upper east wing was not: in the space rented by the Parlante cinema, storm and fire would one day claim the lives of six people and injure many others who had come to see Greta Garbo in *Maria Waleska* [sic].[22]

Because of the Solís' famous acoustics, no one ever dared any major structural interior changes. There have, however, been alterations backstage through the years for the artists' comfort. In 1872 the first bathrooms were installed backstage, and three years later a network of water pipes was installed against the possibilities of fire. Primitive heating was provided by a coal boiler long in use, and the heating system for the occasionally freezing dressing rooms came only years later, in the first years of the twentieth century.

The Teatro Solís' opening was to be illuminated by the new phenomenon of gas lighting; due to problems in Montevideo's gas plant, however, the premiere took place under oil and candle power. The gas system was installed on September 19, almost one month after the inauguration of the house.[23] In 1871 the entire lighting system was considerably improved, and as early as 1879 (the same year that Thomas A. Edison produced and patented the first commercially practical incandescent lamp and developed the complete system of electricity distribution for use with it) the first experiment with electricity to power the theater was launched at a gala performance of August 25. Similar experiments were repeated in subsequent years. In 1892 the grand foyer's large gas chandelier was replaced by an electrical one. The following year, on September 19, 1893, the house's principal chandelier was replaced by electrical power and lighted for the first time (this according to the *bordereau* [register], for a zarzuela performance of the Avelino Aguirre Company). The complete lighting of house, stage, backstage, dressing rooms, cellars, workshops, and machinery was definitively converted to electricity in 1899. The most considerable stage-lighting improvement was done before the opening of the 1903 Solís opera season, with the installation of the most updated system available, requiring an investment of 1,500 pesos by the Solís administration. It was used for the first time at the appearance of the Nardi and Bonetti Company, with Arturo Toscanini conducting and with Enrico Caruso, Hariclea Darclée, Maria Farneti, and Giuseppe De Luca in performance (see chapter 16).

Since October 5, 1856, a red beacon has shone from the apex of the theater roof's front cornice to announce performances at the Teatro Solís. And since its very beginning this beacon has created a problem for navigators entering the port of Montevideo. At night the red light, visible from a long distance, was taken for a lighthouse, creating dangerous false detours: "Instead of a comfortable rest after a long day of navigation more than one ship will leave its ribs in the rocks of Punta Brava."[24] Apparently the problem was solved by putting poles with lights in other parts of the city rather than only on the theater's cornice: by seeing lights around the entire city, ships recognized that this was a city and that the light on the Solís was only one of many. But for Montevideo residents, the Solís light beckoned them to their beloved theater. The tradition is still followed; every time the Solís has a performance the red beacon shines.[25]

CHAPTER 4

August 25, 1856

The Opening of the Teatro Solís

On a chilly winter day, at six o'clock in the evening, the sound of trumpets and bugles filled the air. With pomp and splendor they announced the inauguration of a new theater: the Teatro Solís of Montevideo. It was Monday, August 25, 1856, the thirty-first anniversary of Uruguay's Declaration of Independence. The band's musicians sat in the large square before the Solís, its backdrop the new house with the austere elegance of its eight Corinthian columns (fig. 5).

While a crowd of people pushed and shouted at the box office, others waited, restless and impatient. They had begun arriving in the morning's early hours, wishing to be among the first to enter their splendid new theater. In the midst of this noisy multitude the band played on for two hours—fortissimo! The Solís management grew frightened, fearing the jubilation would give way to a riot. Even though the performance had been announced for eight o'clock, the side doors were opened much earlier to allow access to the galleries and standing-room locations in the hope of averting calamity. Thus was a riot prevented, but the resulting rush swept people upstairs, and many lost their hats and canes in the crush. According to old chronicles, the noise of hundreds of people running up five flights of wooden stairs sounded like a stampede. It is not at all difficult to imagine; night after night many ardent opera lovers still live through the same experience as they dash for a place to see and hear, no matter what heights they must sit in.

Outside the tension built, the box office a battlefield as the management gave the order to stop the sale of tickets. By this time ticket-seller José Soria (a character in himself) had sold 2,500 tickets—and the Solís had only 1,584 seats! Tickets ranged in price from 4 pesos and 640 reis for boxes at the dress circle to 240 reis for standing room. Translated into contemporary U.S. currency, the price of admission ranged between four and a half dol-

Fig. 5. *Upper*: Teatro Solís and Arches of La Pasiva. Drawing by Berthet, lithograph by M. Riviere. Reproduced in *La Música en el Uruguay* by Lauro Ayestarán, (Montevideo: SODRE, 1953), 1: 215. *Lower*: Teatro de Solís at the time of its inauguration in 1856. Drawing by Roesler, printed by Godel. Reproduced in *La Música en el Uruguay*, 1:209. Originals are in the Museo Histórico Nacional, Montevideo.

lars to a few cents. When Soria closed the box office, an even worse struggle erupted between those who had not gotten tickets and the scalpers, who more than doubled the prices.[1]

Only minutes before eight o'clock, the presidential carriage arrived at the Teatro Solís entrance. Juan Miguel Martínez and the members of the board, plus a host of national dignitaries, lined the foyer to welcome the president of the republic, Gabriel Antonio Pereira. As soon as he appeared in the presidential box, an enthusiastic audience greeted him with a standing ovation. The entire house was resplendent with women's velvet, brocades, feathers, and jewels, while the medals and badges of the men glittered majestically. This was more than a gala opening night, more than a patriotic celebration. When the lights dimmed and Sofia Vera-Lorini appeared on the stage with the chorus to sing the Uruguayan national anthem, when Maestro Luigi Preti (fig. 6) raised his baton and the sound of music flooded the house, a new theater— the Teatro Solís—was born.

Count Preti-Bonati, a distinguished European violinist and musician born in Toulouse, France, in 1826, arrived in Uruguay as principal conductor and director with the Italian Lyric Company. Preti launched more than the theater's beginnings that night; he became the Solís conductor and a leading musical influence in Montevideo, where he remained until his death in 1902. Uruguay must acknowledge three important contributions that Preti made to its artistic development. In 1868 he founded the Sociedad Filarmónica, Uruguay's first professional orchestra, and then conducted the Uruguayan premiere of Beethoven's Symphony no. 3 ("Eroica"). His third major contribution was the 1873 creation of the country's first chamber-music ensemble, a string quartet, in which he played first violin.

Three of the musicians who played that

Fig. 6. Maestro Luigi Preti (1826–1902), who conducted *Ernani* at the Solís opening night. Reproduced in *La Música en el Uruguay* by Lauro Ayestarán (Montevideo: SODRE, 1953), 1:261. Museo Francisco Sambucetti at the Escuela Municipal de Música, Montevideo.

night in the Solís orchestra were themselves outstanding personalities in the development of Uruguay's musical life. Francisco José Debali, an Italian born in Hungary who settled in Montevideo in 1838, was not only the author of the music of the Uruguayan national anthem but a prolific and talented composer. Luis Sambucetti Sr.—the orchestra's concert master—was known as conductor, chamber music player, and accomplished pedagogue in his own lifetime; he was also the father of Luis Sambucetti Jr., the best Uruguayan orchestral composer of the nineteenth century. Finally, Pío Giribaldi, an excellent trumpeter himself, had a strong influence on the career development of his brother Tomás Giribaldi, the author of *Parisina*, the first opera to be composed in Uruguay.

The musicians who played under the baton of Maestro Preti, on August 25, 1856, were as follows:

> Violins: Luis Sambucetti (Sr.), Gandolfo, Pérez, Orbera and Demartini.
> Viola: Santiago Dasso.
> Cellos: Debrús and Mari.
> Flutes: Pablo Rossi, Casteletti.
> Bassoon: Francisco José Debali.
> Clarinets: Antonio Garabelli, Dasso, and Ferrari.
> Valves [sic] [Trumpets]: Pío Giribaldi, Tilman, and Keefer.
> French Horns: Molinari and Bastiani.
> Trombone: Silva.
> Other instruments: Scremini, Sincunegui, Subiría, Colombo, Amedé, etc.
> Maestro al cembalo: Amigó de Lara.

With the national anthem over and the excitement for Giuseppe Verdi's *Ernani* mounting, a man rose suddenly from his seat in the middle of the orchestra and began to read aloud something that, according to the newspaper's review, nobody could hear.[2] He then mounted the stage, the lights went on again, and he continued reading—for more than half an hour. What this man, Heraclio Fajardo, was reading were eight-line stanzas written by Francisco Acuña de Figueroa, the national poet who celebrated Uruguay's every important cultural and historical event. Now on his deathbed, Acuña de Figueroa gave Fajardo the long stanzas he had written as an homage to the Solís inauguration. There was no way Fajardo could fail to grant the poet's last wishes, but when he mounted the stage he did it accompanied by another poet, Francisco Xavier de Acha. And when the audience noticed that Acha also had some papers in his hand, many groaned: "We are going to have another speech!" The reading of Acuña de Figueroa's poem was interrupted several times by the audience. (Apparently, loud comments and criticisms were expected!) Written in the emphatic and pompous style of that age—with frequent metaphors and allusions to Greek gods and the Muses—the poem has thirteen eight-line stanzas. The first of them:

> Salve pueblo oriental! con ufanía
> Tu teatro magnífico inauguras;
> Joya monumental de gran valía
> En mármoles, dorados y esculturas;
> Digno templo del canto y poesía,
> Donde fama y aplausos aseguras:
> Bello y sublime el interior contemplo,
> Y grandioso el peristilo del templo.

> [Hail! Uruguayan people, with pride
> You inaugurate your magnificent theater,
> Monumental jewel of great worth
> Of marble, gold and sculpture;
> Worthy temple of song and verse
> Where you assure fame and applause.
> Beautiful and sublime the interior I admire
> Grandiose the temple's peristyle.]

When Fajardo returned to his orchestra seat, Acha embarked on his own recitation, meanwhile circulating printed copies all through the house. His poem begins:

> También tu nombre es inmortal, Solís,
> Y rememora el del audaz piloto
> Que el primero, burlándose del noto,
> en nuestras playas enclavó la cruz.

> [Your name is also immortal, Solís,
> And holds on to that of the brave pilot
> Who first, mocking the South Wind,
> To our beaches nailed the cross.]

In spite of the interruptions, the completed readings of both poems were acknowledged with applause—and shouts. Probably, the first came from the poet's admirers and friends and the latter from an audience frantic for an *Ernani* they must have thought would never begin. However, they still had to put up with three more speeches! Taking advantage of one of the many interruptions, Cándido Joanicó rose in his box to propose that the names of each one of the board members be engraved into the marble columns in the foyer, a notion that although seconded by many of those present was never carried out. During the opera's first intermission, strips of paper printed with these names appeared draped over the columns, but this was the extent of the suggestion's culmination. Once Acha left the stage, Chief of Police Luis de Herrera said a few brief words from his box. He emphasized that one of the Declaration of Independence's signers, Gabriel Antonio Pereira, was present, thirty-one years later— president of the country and now witness to one of the highest landmarks in Uruguayan cultural history. The fourth speech was delivered by Octavio Lapido; this oration, according to the reviewer, had two shortcomings: it was too long and expressed no elation at all. Pity the poor listeners, who only wanted to enjoy opera! The fifth and final of these public addresses was given by journalist Juan José Barboza, editor of the newspaper *El Nacional.*

*   *   *

ERNANI WAS FIRST PERFORMED at La Fenice in Venice on March 9, 1844. In this opera Verdi produced, as he had before in *Nabucco,* what we call a vocal *scontro*: the clashing of vocal archetypes that provide opera with its power and dramatic interest. Those vocal patterns are perfectly drawn in his male characters. First there is the passionate tenor, a lyrical and brave character who usually dies in despair. Next comes the vigorous baritone, very energetic and determined, his forceful

voice pitched about a tone higher than the characteristic Gaetano Donizetti *basso cantante*. Finally, there is the strong bass, severe and independent, who would show his feelings only in the form of a soliloquy. What was more unusual in *Ernani* is that all three males love the same soprano.

As it had already been performed by the Ida Edelvira company in the days of the Teatro San Felipe, why was *Ernani* chosen for the opening of the Teatro Solís? Wouldn't it have been more attractive to give Montevideo a local premiere of another masterpiece? Unfortunately, no written records could be traced about this other than newspaper reviews. Was it just a coincidence that *Ernani* opened two other houses in the Americas? The New York's Astor Place Opera House, inaugurated on November 22, 1847, and the Chilean Teatro Municipal, which opened in 1857, might have had the same reasons as the Solís management. Not only did *Ernani* have novel operatic qualities, but the dramatic development of its political and revolutionary plot attracted the newly independent nations and made this opera one of the biggest draws of its time. Of great importance, too, was the wide popularity gained by the opera's famous chorus, "Si ridesti il Leon di Castiglia," the piano score of which was known to everyone and circulated in Montevideo far in advance of *Ernani*'s first Montevidean performance in 1852.

*   *   *

THE INAUGURAL PERFORMANCE of August 25, 1856, featured the following cast:

Ernani	Giovanni Comolli
Don Carlo	Giuseppe Cima
Elvira	Sofia Vera-Lorini
Don Ruy Gomez de Silva	Federico Tati
Giovanna	Carlotta Cannonero
Don Riccardo	Angelo Chiodini
Jago	Pablo Sardou

Maestro al cembalo	N. Amigó de Lara	
Set designers	Lambert & Pittaluga	
Orchestra conductor, chorus and general		
direction	Maestro Luigi Preti-Bonati	

The middle of the nineteenth century was the time when the prima donna was frequently the star of the company. *Ernani*'s Elvira, Sofia Vera-Lorini, was an outstanding example of the larger-than-life singer—as was her fee. Even if it is difficult to evaluate the currency in which the Italian Lyric Company was paid, a comparison of the figures serves to demonstrate the relationship between salaries. Almost by a miracle, the sheet of the opening two weeks' Bordereau (register) is one of the few things preserved from 1856 (fig. 7). It gives a complete payroll:

CUADRO DE COMPAÑIA/ARTISTAS Y CORISTAS

Primera función del 25 de Agosto al 11 de Setiembre de 1856

Sra. Sofia Vera-Lorini	1a. Dama	500.00
Sra. Preti	2a. Dama	50.00
Sra. Josefina Tati	1a. Contralto	100.00
Sr. Juan Comolli	1er. tenor	300.00
Sr. Arturo Gentili	1er. tenor	300.00
Sr. José Cima	1er. baritono	175.00
Sr. Tati	bajo profundo	45.00
Sr. Angelo Chiodini	2do. tenor	45.00
Sr. Luis Rosea	2do. bajo	22.400 reis
Sr. Bernardo Amigó	Maestro	55.00
Sr. Preti	Dir. Orquesta	75.00
Sr. Sardou	bajo cantante	37.400 reis
Sr. Leon Chanteaufort	corista tenor	15.00
Sr. Monteverde mayor	corista tenor	15.00
Sr. Monteverde junior [*sic*]	corista tenor	15.00
Sr. Bernardini	corista tenor	12.480 reis

Sr. Louis	corista tenor	12.480 reis
Sr. Lacoste	corista tenor	10.00 reis
(illegible)	corista tenor	(illegible)
Sr. Vangool	corista bajo	15.00
Sr. Giuliano	corista bajo	12.480 reis
Sr. Perassi	corista bajo	12.480 reis
Sr. Carrere	corista bajo	12.480 reis
Sr. Quirino	corista bajo	12.480 reis
Sr. Allegre	corista bajo	10.00
Sr. Ferro	cor. 2do. tenor	10.480 reis
Sr. Gari	cor. 2do. tenor	10.480 reis
Sr. Beria	cor. 2do. tenor	5.00
Sr. Doria	cor. 2do. tenor	12.480 reis
Sr. Cusano	cor. 2do. tenor	10.00
Sr. Ricci	cor. 2do. tenor	10.00
Sr. Pompiello	organista y pianista	17.480 reis
Sra. Sardou	corista	12.480 reis
Sra. Sosa	corista	12.480 reis
Sra. Penino	corista	12.480 reis
Sra. Rosita	corista	5.00 reis
Sra. Lanura Beria	corista	3.00 reis
Sra. Pereira	corista	4.00 reis
Sra. Camaure	corista	4.00 reis
Sra. Doria	corista	3.00 199,420
Grand Total patacones		1889.420 reis

There is no doubt about Maestro Preti's professional efficiency in all his work, not only in conducting, but in rehearsing singers, chorus, and orchestra, plus attending to all the hundreds of details that are part of an opera conductor's job. Nevertheless, he received less than one-sixth of what his leading soprano made. Further injury took the form of the next day's review when all credit and homage went, evidently, to Sofia Vera-Lorini: "The performance ended with a rain of flowers at the feet of the fine and exquisite artist, whose name will be forever in the Teatro Solís annals as well as those of its authors."[3]

Because of the many long speeches that may or may not have been part of the original program, this performance of *Ernani* ended

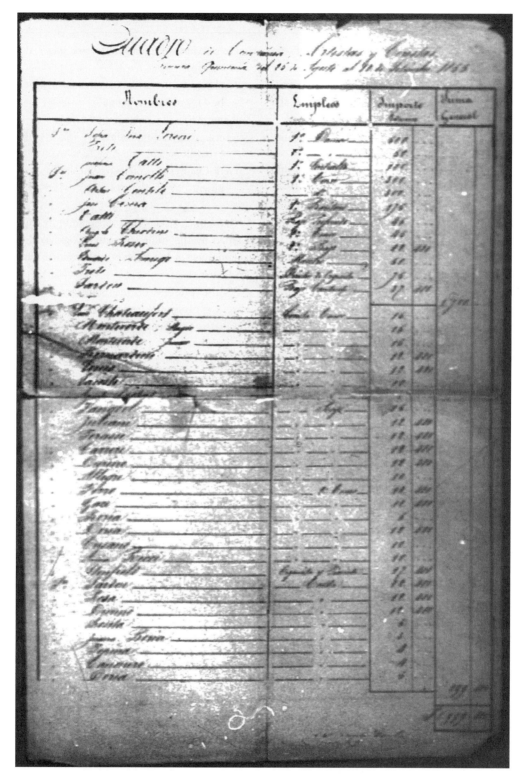

Fig. 7. First page of the original register (*bordereau*) with a list of names and fees of singers, director, conductor, and chorus, in Verdi's *Ernani*, during the week of August 25 to September 11, 1856. Teatro Solís Collection.

close to two in the morning. Yet the end of the celebration was not in sight. Now the audience was joined by large crowds of people who had not been at the opera, as they all stood outside and enjoyed a magnificent display of fireworks in the grand plaza in front of the Solís.

From that special August night to the end of 1856, the same Italian company gave fifty-two performances. In addition to two more *Ernani*s, they gave multiple performances of other Verdi operas: *La traviata, Rigoletto, Il trovatore, Luisa Miller,* and *I due Foscari.* Three Donizetti works—*Lucia di Lammermoor, La favorita,* and *Linda di Chamounix*—were very well received by the public, as were Rossini's *Barbiere di Siviglia* and Vincenzo Bellini's *La sonnambula.* Moreover, *Luisa Strozzi* by Gualtiero Sanelli received its Montevideo premiere.

Even with such a busy schedule, the Solís management was able to book several concerts, some on the stage, others in the more intimate surroundings of the grand foyer, an ideal setting for chamber music. Some theatrical comedies were also produced that year. Among the concerts, the one organized to pay homage to Maestro Preti was especially outstanding. Played by the Solís orchestra on December 20, 1856, it was conducted by the maestro himself. During the concert he also performed some violin pieces with pianist Amigó de Lara. But the highlight of the evening was the world premiere of Preti's First Symphony and two other works of his. The program was made up in part by concert paraphrases of themes from Italian operas, a nineteenth-century form very popular through the piano pieces of Sigismond Thalberg and Franz Liszt, among others. The December 20 program was made up of these works:

Preti: Primera Sinfonía, orchestra under the composer.

Thalberg: Variations on Rossini's *Mosè in Egitto,* by Amigó de Lara, piano.

Bériot: *Aria V,* by Luigi Preti, violin.

Kontsky: Fantasia on Donizetti's *Lucia,* by Luigi Preti, violin and Amigó de Lara.

Preti: Cuadrilla for orchestra, under the composer.

At its conclusion, Preti was soundly applauded by the audience, who recognized his exceptional work as composer, violinist, and conductor.

As the prestige of the Solís grew, there arose a professional and artistic rivalry with the Teatro San Felipe. Sometimes it reached the proportions of disgusting gossip and underground slander. Such competition could not endure. It was childish to compare the two houses, not only in size and category but, above all, in regard to the Solís' stage and backstage facilities, which were simply superior. Eventually the rivalry burned itself out, and the two theaters went back to leading separate lives. Until it was razed in 1879, the San Felipe principally housed zarzuelas—género chico—small operetta and comedy companies. It was the far grander Teatro Solís that hosted the international operatic and dramatic companies as well as the great ballets and symphonic orchestras—as it continues to do, still thriving, still glamorous.

And so ended 1856. The inauguration of the Teatro Solís brought to Montevideo, at this time graced by an already extraordinary cultural life, the opening of a new social era. The golden grand foyer of the second floor was witness to romantic days that may be gone forever. The whispering frou-frou of so many fashionable dresses is silenced. But the house remains.

CHAPTER 5

1857–1858

A Triumphant Enrico Tamberlick Opens the Second Solís Season—
Anna Bishop: A Soprano to Remember—Artur Napoleão
and Oscar Pfeiffer: Two First Piano Virtuosi

"The Covent Garden tenor," they called him—no matter that he had been born in Rome (1820) and debuted in Naples (1841) under the name of Danieli as Tebaldo in Vincenzo Bellini's *I Capuleti e i Montecchi*. Enrico Tamberlick (fig. 8) arrived in London in 1850 and returned there for fourteen consecutive years; as they had done with Handel more than a century before, the British adopted him as one of their own countrymen. At a time when most music criticism was written with extravagant flourishes and what was perceived to be literary merit, London's *The Musical World* carried what were perhaps the first reviews in Europe to analyze technique and true musical content. When the reviewer wrote of Tamberlick's performance, he paid attention to the singer's voice:

Despite many counteracting circumstances, Signor Tamberlick's debut was one of the most triumphant we have witnessed for years on the stage. Signor Tamberlick's voice is a *tenore robusto*, or pure chest voice, of a fine, ringing, sonorous quality, capable of the most varied expression. The upper notes are powerful and clear, the middle round and sweet, possessing a remarkable evenness throughout. He never exaggerates. He adheres conscientiously to his text—at least so far we have heard him—and sacrifices nothing to obtain applause.[1]

When Tamberlick came to Montevideo, the reviewer from *El Comercio del Plata* wrote more typically for his time, a wordy piece saying very little about Tamberlick's artistic qualities. In a very picturesque, but completely uninformative way, it read:

[T]hen he gave off his pure, clear, tender and sorrowful voice, putting will and tears in each word, playing with the most prodigious difficulties of Art. The public, waiting eagerly for the performer, were astonished:

Fig. 8. Tenor Enrico Tamberlick, who sang in 1857. Reproduced in *La Música en el Uruguay* by Lauro Ayestarán (Montevideo: SODRE, 1953), 1:218. Teatro Solís Collection.

as they come for fame and miracles (as do the Neapolitans every year to see St. Gennaro's blood in the Holy Feast), so they came this day to see one artistic and vocal portent. It was as if a divine inspiration had touched everyone's forehead: Each spectator was charmed, frozen and terrified, all at the same time.

. . . [Tamberlick] came as from heaven, an eagle folding his wings.[2]

On and on the review goes, always in the same expansive vein.

It was this tenor that the Teatro Solís welcomed on January 10, 1857, during a brief interlude from one of Tamberlick's English seasons. He was on an extensive tour of South America, opening in Rio de Janeiro in June 1856, and also singing in Buenos Aires. Tamberlick first appeared in Montevideo singing

Il trovatore with members of Lorini's company under the conducting of Maestro Clemente Castagneri. He was accompanied by Sofia Vera-Lorini as Leonora, baritone Giuseppe Cima as Conte di Luna, and contralto Annetta Casaloni as Azucena. The most recent acquisition of the Lyric Company, Annetta Casaloni had been the first Maddalena in the world premiere of Verdi's *Rigoletto* six years earlier in Venice. Tamberlick's second Solís performance was in *Ernani* three days after his *Il trovatore*, then came two more Verdi operas—*Rigoletto* and *Luisa Miller*—after which he repeated his performance in *Il trovatore*. On January 30, 1857, the Lyric Company gave a farewell concert with all of its singers appearing on stage in a gala medley of operatic favorites. Tamberlick performed in a duet from *Rigoletto*, as well as the entire fourth act of Donizetti's *La favorita* with Sofia Vera-Lorini. He completed his showcase performance with Annetta Casaloni and chorus in a scene from *Il trovatore*.

Two more of his characterizations, in addition to Manrico in *Il trovatore*, soon became Tamberlick's warhorses: Arnold in *Guillaume Tell;* and the title role in Gioachino Rossini's *Otello*. It was not only his voice, robust and rich with an easy extension to a powerful C$\sharp''$, that gave Tamberlick his legendary fame. He had the good fortune to be both a very handsome man and a gifted actor—two extremely rare qualities in the opera of the day. Most important, he was blessed with an acute sense of musicianship.

Continuing his tour to other South American cities, Tamberlick was engaged to give a new series of performances at the Solís three months later. Before leaving Montevideo, Tamberlick was received by the president of Uruguay in a special reception at the presidential office. Unfortunately, his arrival back in Montevideo was much less auspicious: when he returned from Buenos Aires in

March 1857, after the opening of the old Teatro Colón, he discovered that all public theater performances, including his own, had been canceled due to a terrible yellow fever epidemic. He left Montevideo forever. Nonetheless, the Solís audience of 1857 was fortunate to hear, at the crown of his career, the best tenor of that time. This was a man renowned for his art, one whose fame included the glory of performing in the world premiere of Verdi's *La forza del destino* at Saint Petersburg's Imperial Theater in 1862. Although his visit to Uruguay was short, even shorter than first planned, it made a lasting impression on Solís devotees.

* * *

IN MARCH 1857 the Solís opened its doors to a Spanish zarzuela company. Under the general direction of José Enamorado and headed by two singers, Matilde Duclós and Rosario Segura, the company performed for most of the month. The remaining portion of that year was shared between a ballet company and the arrival of the first virtuoso pianist to appear at the Solís. This was only the second time that classical ballet had arrived in Uruguay. The first, seven years before, had been the visit of two pupils of the Italian Taglioni school: Henry Finart and Anna Trabattoni. Now the Roussets—Louis, Caroline, Adelaide, Theresine, and Clementine—presented Adolphe Adam's *Giselle* and Paul Taglioni's *Satanella*. As was customary, these performances (running throughout July and August) were interspersed with musical miscellanies by members of Lorini's company.

If the eighteenth century had been characterized by the brilliant display of vocal skills, the nineteenth was to be known as the bravura era of piano. The inventions and improvements, especially the Viennese action in piano building, contributed to the development of the Romantic style of piano music so

well exemplified by Franz Liszt, Sigismond Thalberg, Frédéric Kalkbrenner, and Henri Herz. For audiences Liszt was the personification of that bravura era. The height of this sparkling virtuosity was reached at the Paris salons of 1830s, the world showcase that all pianists dreamed of. But if Liszt had the most charismatic appeal of this century's pianists, it was Frédéric Chopin who even with a short career as a concert pianist, was the great innovator in the use of new harmonic effects in his piano works.

More than twenty years later, Montevideo became acquainted with the first exponent of such piano virtuosity with the arrival of Artur Napoleão. His concerts were the starting point of a concert series of piano virtuosi that would reach its climax with the 1867–69 performances of the legendary Louis Moreau Gottschalk. Born in Oporto, Portugal, in 1843, Napoleão made his Solís debut when only thirteen years old and yet already had six years' experience of public performance. At his first Solís concert on December 4, 1857, the young pianist played a program based on four Thalberg fantasias on operatic themes. The first two were inspired by Donizetti's *La fille du régiment* and *L'elisir d'amore*, the third by Bellini's *La sonnambula*, and the last was a concert paraphrase of Rossini's *Mosè in Egitto*. Napoleão's first appearance was enthusiastically received; the next day's review announced that "after Thalberg, there are very few pianists in the world who can achieve what Artur Napoleão did in his playing."[3]

Knowing the boy's background, it is not difficult to imagine the quality of his performance. After a first recital in Lisbon at age seven, he toured in England, France, and Germany. When in Paris at the age of eleven, he studied for a time under Herz, and Giacomo Meyerbeer presented him at court during Napoleão's 1854 Berlin concerts.[4] The most im portant landmark of his childhood career was his historic visit to Weimar to meet Liszt. So impressed was the musician by young Artur's talent that he gave the boy lessons. Finally, when Napoleão turned twelve he came to the Americas for the first time. In addition to his Montevideo appearance, he gave recitals in many Brazilian cities and in the United States. Napoleão returned to Montevideo in 1863 and afterward settled in Rio de Janeiro. He continued to perform at the Solís and later added his own piano compositions to his repertoire. In 1866 he also attempted—son of a Italian music teacher that he was—to write an opera entitled *Oremorso vivo*.

Less than a year after the young Napoleão's departure, another internationally known concert pianist was heard at the Solís. This was Oscar Pfeiffer, who now returned for the first time to the city where he had been born thirty-four years earlier and that he had left as a small child. His glamorous beginnings had their roots in his parents' international heritage: he was the son of the famous Viennese geographer and explorer, Ida Reyer, and her husband, a lawyer from Lemberg (now Lviv) named Pfeiffer. Reyer was the first woman to reach the source of the Amazon, and her son was born on one of the many trips his parents made around the world. Although also widely traveled, Pfeiffer grew up in Germany. In addition to being a talented composer, Pfeiffer was the best European-trained musician to arrive in Uruguay; he was in all ways, the precursor of virtuoso Gottschalk. At a time when almost no one knew anything about Gottschalk and his music, Pfeiffer was the first to introduce the piano works of the New Orleans composer in his Solís recitals. His concerts included the compositions of Liszt, Thalberg, Gottschalk, and Herz, as well as several of his own concert paraphrases. He was a skilled creator and owner of a deep artistry, competence, and—

especially—compositional technique. These piano paraphrases are of such fine quality that they can be evaluated at the same level as similar works written by Liszt and his followers.

In addition to Pfeiffer's first presentation at the Solís on November 4, 1858, he gave concerts at the San Felipe. In that opening program Pfeiffer played, among other pieces, two of his works: *Fantasía dramática sobre Lucrezia Borgia de Donizetti* and *Introducción y variaciones sobre Carnevale di Venezia*. On the same day, he also performed the first Gottschalk work heard in Montevideo: *El bananero*. His renown extended beyond the concert hall: during this time more than twenty Pfeiffer scores for piano and piano and orchestra were printed, which gives us an idea of his significance not only as a pianist but as a composer. Before Pfeiffer left Montevideo, President Gabriel Antonio Pereira invited him, in homage to his Uruguayan birth, to give a concert at the presidential residence. Pfeiffer later toured extensively, playing in Buenos Aires, Brazil, Mexico, and many European cities. With his return to the Americas in 1882, he settled in Buenos Aires until his death on August 4, 1906. Oscar Pfeiffer was, to be sure, one of the first Uruguayan musical pioneers.

* * *

THE 1858 TEATRO SOLÍS SEASON did not begin on schedule. Any carefully laid plans were ruined by a political revolt against the government, which culminated in the Batalla de Quinteros (Battle of Quinteros).[5] However, when the season's first singer did arrive, she was one of the most picturesque and exceptional sopranos of her century. English by birth, Anna Bishop (fig. 9), endowed as she was with an outstanding voice and the tendency to lead an eccentric and adventurous life, is a memorable representative in the annals of opera lore. After Tamberlick, she was the second celebrated singer to be heard at the Solís. She gave only one concert there, on June 16, 1858. Although she was perhaps not at the peak of her vocal career, this recital was enough to give the audience a sense of one of the century's most famous coloratura sopranos. The program she chose—a display of sparkling virtuosity—did strain her vocal abilities at the time, but it also demonstrated her versatility. She opened the concert with *Norma*'s "Casta Diva," *the* aria of those days, and followed this with an aria from Rossini's *Tancredi;* a *Gratias agamus tibi*, with *flauto obbligato;* an English ballad; and "Si usted lo sabe," an Andalusian song. In the third part of her program she sang the Mad Scene from Donizetti's *Lucia di Lammermoor* and, not stopping there, she added "La catatumba," a popular Mexican song. From Bellini on, she was able to handle all styles of music.

The day after her Solís presentation there appeared the following comments: "Without damaging her reputation, which we don't doubt she holds throughout Europe, we believe that Madame Bishop does not have now all the gift that conquered [*sic*] her fame." The reviewer sought to lessen the sting by acknowledging what years of experience have brought, adding that "Madame Bishop is an outstanding musician."[6]

Contemporary newspaper coverage indicates that Bishop gave only one concert at the Solís. Despite this review's negativity, it is well balanced and demonstrates the knowledge of this Uruguayan music critic. One could cite as support the critique that had appeared in The *New York Daily Tribune* on the occasion of Bishop's premiere performance in Friedrich Flotow's *Martha* at New York's Niblo's Garden on November 1, 1852. Because the newspaper's musical section was under the auspices of the well-known composer William Henry Fry, his evaluation is of real value. According to pre-performance advertising, the opera was sung

Fig. 9. The picturesque and exceptional Anna Bishop. Library of Congress Collection.

in English "translated expressly for Madame Bishop."[7] These are some highlights of a long review:

This is a piece when the greatest perfection is necessary in the artist to render it satisfactory. The music not being remarkable for originality or special beauty nor the plot in itself very interesting, the best singing and acting are required. These we cannot say that it last night received. No doubt Mr. Bochsa the director made the most out of his material, but the material was poor; both vocally and dramatically Madame Bishop, Miss Rosa Jacques, Signor Guidi and Mr. Leach cannot sing well enough for a leading metropolitan opera theatre. However the last evening reaped a liberal harvest of applause from a house more full than critical.[8]

Such an evaluation would indicate that Montevideo's review was not an exaggeration and that even six years earlier Bishop's voice had already lost some of its renowned quality. There is no doubt that at the time of her Solís concert her voice was even further in decline.

The rest of the 1858 season, following Bishop's concert, was made up of the Lyric Company's five-month engagement. Now headed by tenor Luis Lelmi—accompanied by soprano Teresina Bagetti and her husband, baritone and composer Luis Cavedagni—the company gave more than thirty performances of repertoire works under Luigi Preti's baton. Their two Montevidean premieres were Donizetti's *Don Sebastiano* and *Il fornaretto* by Gualtiero Sanelli, a now forgotten but once somewhat successful composer.

The Italian Lyric Company began its Solís season on June 20, 1858, with Verdi's *I lombardi alla prima crociata*. This was followed by several performances of each of the following operas: *I lombardi, Ernani, Belisario, Linda di Chamounix, I due Foscari, Attila, Il trovatore, Il fornaretto, Don Sebastiano*, that were repertory at the time, and some miscellaneous recitals. The company was relatively mediocre in quality, with a roster of internationally unknown singers, Lelmi perhaps the best of them. A very handsome tenor with a good vocal technique, a competent but not extraordinary singer, Lelmi sang at the Solís and other South American theatres for almost twenty years and established a close and warm relationship with its operagoers.

In addition to the opera company's performances, the 1858 season ended with some operatic concerts, but not complete works, given by several different singers: soprano Clarisse Cailly from Brussels; tenor Ugo Devoti; and baritone Giovanni Battista Gianni.

CHAPTER 6

1859–1866

Anna de la Grange and Raffaele Mirate:
Two Stars and Three Companies in the Same Season

When a Montevideo newspaper announced that "De la Grange comes from the same brilliant tradition as Malibran and Sontag," opera fans responded fervently.[1] The comparison of Anna de la Grange to these two extraordinary and legendary singers served only to heighten expectations. From then on, opera fans had one thought: to attend the opening night of the new Solís season (January 18, 1859), when De la Grange was to make her Montevideo debut as Violetta in *La traviata*.

De la Grange arrived with an impressive background, having already conquered Paris and New York. Born in Paris in 1824, she made her professional debut at Varese, singing the title role in Luigi Ricci's *Chiara di Rosemberg* in the autumn of 1842. From 1855 to 1856, in addition to several concerts, she sang eighteen different operas in more than one hundred performances at New York's Academy of Music. It was here that she sang in the world premiere of Luigi Arditi's *La spia*. It is our

misfortune that media coverage was so poor; while the 1856 issues of the *New York Daily Tribune* devote several long columns to the premiere of the new opera and to the composer, only a few lines appear in regard to the opening night performance and cast. Critic William Henry Fry wrote: "The composer enjoyed every advantage [of] a splendid opera house [and] a large and well provided orchestra.... The principal aria of Madame de la Grange was handsomely applauded."[2] This for a soprano of her stature giving a New York world premiere! What makes the omission even more startling is that this singer before coming to New York had a successful career of fifteen years, with performances in the most important opera houses of France, Italy, Vienna, Budapest, Prague, Germany, London, and Saint Petersburg. It was knowledge of this illustrious background that propelled Montevideo opera lovers, especially Solís audiences, to see her opening night as Violetta, even if the New York papers were lacking in acuity.

The singers chosen by the impresario for her Solís performance had appeared earlier with the Vera-Lorini company; his choice thus also included the conductor, Luigi Preti. The following roster details the cast of her company as it appeared on the Solís stage in a varied repertoire:

Prima donna	Anna de la Grange
Second soprano	Rosita Dorina
First mezzo soprano	Angelina Fusoni
First tenor	Giovanni Comolli
First baritone	Giovanni Reina
First basso	Alfred Didot
Second tenor	A. Monteverde
Basso "sui generis"	Pablo Sardou
Basso comprimario	Rosea

Conductor: Luigi Preti

The company sang a total of thirteen performances, from January until the end of February 1859, and each starred De la Grange. In her first season of 1859 (January 18–February 26, and December 1–13) *La traviata* was followed by Bellini's *Norma, La sonnambula*, and *I puritani;* Donizetti's *Lucrezia Borgia* and *Lucia di Lammermoor;* Verdi's *Rigoletto, Il trovatore*, and *Ernani;* and Rossini's *Il barbiere di Siviglia*, with some operas being performed twice. *La Nación*'s music critic again showed his enthusiasm:

> Madame de la Grange's voice has a three-octave range with a brilliant upper register and, at the same time, a strong and sweet vocal quality. In loud or soft passages she handles the dynamic nuances with mastery. Her voice is always fresh, pure, and pleasant. She possesses an extraordinary singing method.[3]

If we bear in mind that in addition to her vocal attributes she was a strikingly attractive singing actress, it becomes easier for us to envision the mesmerizing charm she exercised over her audiences (fig. 10).

Following this, as an interlude before the appearance of a new opera company, the Solís staged a selection of zarzuelas during July 1859, with José Enamorado and the Duclós sisters (Matilde and Carolina) taking the principal roles in a company of Spanish singers and comedians. When the house lights dimmed on August 14, 1859, it signaled the beginning of that year's second opera season. The Lelmi-Cailly company chose Verdi's *Il trovatore* for opening night, although they had performed it in 1858. A new composition of interest was added to the repertoire: the Montevideo premiere of Errico Petrella's first tragic opera, *Marco Visconti*. Hitherto Montevidean audiences had sampled only the comic operas of this composer; now they had a chance to experience a major departure in his work. This opera had received its world premiere five years earlier at the San Carlo in Naples on February 9, 1854, where it enjoyed great success and made Petrella known throughout Italy. In spite of his development as a composer of dramatic works and his notable artistic achievement with *Marco Visconti*, on the basis of his early works Petrella was one of the last composers in the old buffo-style Neapolitan tradition whose works were given in Montevideo.

The 1859 Lelmi-Cailly company roster was enhanced by two singers well known to Solís audiences from previous seasons: baritone Giuseppe Cima, who sang the title role of Marco and Annetta Casaloni as Tremacoldo. Bice and Ottorino, *Marco Visconti*'s other two principal roles, were sung by soprano Clarisse Cailly and tenor Luis Lelmi. Clemente Castagneri, the Italian maestro who had conducted Enrico Tamberlick in his Solís appearance two years earlier, led the orchestra. The opera was well received; nonetheless, *Marco Visconti* was given only twice during the 1859 Solís season.

It is difficult to make the first performance of any work an instant success. Indeed, even the operas of great masters were sometimes scorned at their premieres, and only with the passage of time were some of today's more popular works embraced by the public. *Leonore*, *Il barbiere di Siviglia*, and *La traviata* can be cited as examples of initial failures in opera history. *Carmen, Mefistofele,* and *Madama Butterfly* would all be flops at first. Petrella was competing with the big names in Italian opera. His works would have had to be masterpieces to attain such a level of acceptance and popularity, and this was not the case.

The Lelmi-Cailly Company performed the regular Italian repertoire until the end of November 1859, a four-month period that was followed by De la Grange's return. For this stay she was in Montevideo from the first of December through the thirteenth, performing *Lucia di Lammermoor, Ernani, Lucrezia Borgia, Norma,* and *I puritani,* all of them with the same critical and popular success that they had enjoyed during her initial engagement.

Shortly after the great diva's departure, the house received its third opera company of the year. Retaining some of the Lelmi members (among them Cailly, Casaloni, Giacomo Arnaud, Figari, and Piazzini), this new opera company was headed by leading Italian tenor Raffaele Mirate and his partner, the *prima donna assoluta* Giuseppina Medori. The opera chosen for their December 17, 1859, Solís debut, Verdi's *Il trovatore,* was an immediate success with public and critics alike. *La Nación*'s reviewer enthusiastically embraced the production:

> Mirate has a great voice; his timbre is sweet, and he maintained the same roaring torrent of voice from beginning to end.... [Medori's] voice is powerful, like those of the newest vocal school and singers accustomed to singing in large theaters. Her acting is

Fig. 10. Soprano Anna de la Grange, who debuted at the Solís in 1859, engraving. Reproduced in *La Música en el Uruguay* by Lauro Ayestarán, (Montevideo: SODRE, 1953), 1:223. Teatro Solís Collection.

> very good, and we can say that Madame Medori is a perfect singer.[4]

When Mirate created the Duke of Mantua at the world premiere of *Rigoletto* in 1851, he was thirty-six years old and well suited to the demanding Verdi role. The magnitude of his talent is revealed in librettist Francesco Maria Piave's comparison of Mirate to Napoleone Moriani,[5] one of the most famous Italian voices of the nineteenth century. Born in Naples in 1815, Mirate began his musical career as a violinist at the Academy of San Pietro at Majella. After his voice was discovered and developed, at the age of twenty-two he made his debut at the Teatro Nuovo in Naples. In 1840 he stepped onto La Scala's stage for the first time in Rossini's *Mosè.*

The opera company's appeal, however, lay

not only in its celebrated tenor. Casaloni was the company diva, which increased the pitch of excitement in Montevideo. Everyone dreamed of hearing both singers in *Rigoletto*. But such expectations were to be dashed. Oddly enough, and even though two of the original creators of *Rigoletto* were in the company (Mirate, the first Duke and Casaloni, the first Maddalena), *Rigoletto* was not in the repertory. This caused a great deal of disappointment among the public and a great deal of conjecture in the press. Instead, Mirate was heard in *Ernani*, *Maria di Rohan*, *Lucrezia Borgia*, *Roberto Devereux*, *La traviata*, and *Macbeth*. The final six operas of the season were performed in January 1860. In March of the same year, Mirate was partnered by De la Grange in performances that turned out to be the great French diva's farewell to the Solís and its audience.

* * *

FROM 1860 UNTIL 1870, the year of Carlotta Patti's arrival, the Teatro Solís was home to more than one opera company in the same season. But none of these companies had singers of the caliber of Tamberlick, Anna Bishop, De la Grange, and Mirate. Among the principal female vocalists there were Constanza Manzini, Eloisa de Buil, Carlotta Carozzi-Zucchi, Carolina Briol, Elvira Bruzzone, Teresina Bagetti, and Marietta Mollo. Pozzolini, Ballerini, Duchamont, Emon, Bonetti, Zennari, and Luis Lelmi were the male singers.

The works of Rossini, Bellini, Donizetti, and Verdi made up the Italian repertoire, but several other productions enlarged this repertoire for the Solís audiences: one work by Petrella, another by Giuseppe Apolloni, and three by Giovanni Pacini. One of the most prolific composers in a time of exceptional productivity, Pacini wrote close to eighty operas in addition to several orchestral and sacred

works. He was called *il maestro della cabaletta*, his works graced with an energetic and exuberant melody.

Saffo, Pacini's masterpiece, received its world premiere at the San Carlo in Naples in 1840. Only five years later, excerpts of Pacini's *Saffo* (arias and a chorus) had reached the old Casa de Comedias stage in Montevideo. From 1845 on, this and other Pacini music was frequently heard by Montevideo audiences, even before the first Uruguayan performance of *Saffo* at the San Felipe in 1854. When it was produced at the Solís by the Ballerini Company in March 1861, *Saffo* was reaching almost a second generation of operagoers.

The year 1861 witnessed another Pacini opera, *Bondelmonte*, given by the same company. Produced at the Solís in October, this was the Montevideo premiere of an opera composed five years after *Saffo* and given its world premiere at Florence's Pergola in 1845. Pacini's third opera for Montevideo, *Medea*, was presented on the Solís stage on February 1866 and sung by Carolina Briol and Lelmi. At the same 1866 Solís season that witnessed *Medea*'s premiere, Montevideo audiences heard a Petrella opera for the first time: *Jone* (or, *L'ultimo giorno di Pompei*). Because of its lyricism, and in particular the dramatic consistency of the fourth and final act, *Jone* is considered the best of all Petrella's creations. It was a relatively new opera when Solís audiences saw it, with its world premiere only eight years earlier, at La Scala, on January 26, 1858.

* * *

DURING THIS SAME PERIOD the Solís was enlivened by French grand-opéra and opéracomique as well. The French repertoire consisted largely of the works of Daniel-François-Esprit Auber and Fromental Halévy, with each opera in performance several times. A most unusual treat for the Solís audiences was *Le barbier de Seville*, a French translation of the Italian staple.

Another regular visitor to the Solís stage for many years was also French: the spectacular Les Bouffes Parisiens. With an extraordinary selection of the best light music and the most sensational can-can, each return engagement was eagerly awaited by the public. The troupe was always welcomed by all those mature—and not so mature—gentlemen who, with binoculars in hand, were always seated in the orchestra's first rows.

* * *

THE SOLÍS ALSO HOSTED several good soloists in instrumental concerts during the 1860s. Some of these musicians were already known to the Montevideo audiences. Pianists Artur Napoleão and Oscar Pfeiffer came in consecutive seasons, followed by the famous Louis Moreau Gottschalk in 1867. A new name added to the list of recitalists was the Brazilian pianist Juvenal Sampaio. As was the fashion of the day, he also played all the elaborate concert paraphrases of operas mentioned previously.

Paul Julien, a French violinist, was heard several times, especially during the 1865 season. Another pianist deserving mention is Miguel Hines. Although less talented and of lesser fame than Napoleão or Pfeiffer, Hines had a historical and emotional significance for Solís patrons. Born in 1820 in Colonia del Sacramento, one of the oldest towns in Uruguay, he was able to achieve a musical education sufficient to obtain a professorship. Hines was, in fact, one of the first music teachers in colonial Montevideo. Blind since the age of eighteen, he faced great challenges, thus the October 8, 1861, Solís concert celebrated as a tribute to his artistry must also be considered one to his courage.

Another tribute, completely different, was held at the Solís in June 1862. One must remember that not everyone connected with operas appears onstage. There are hundreds of others, like invisible workers in a beehive, whose nightly contributions bring to life the dreams born on stage. The applause that rewards singers, conductors, directors, dancers, and actors, also belongs to these anonymous laborers. There are stagehands, assistants, machinists, electricians, and finally, box-office attendants who never receive any recognition from the audience, even if a large part of the performance rests on their shoulders. In a time far removed from modern technology, all these functions relied completely on human resources and human efforts. They also carried a very personal touch. Because everybody knows everybody in an opera house, each person was known to everyone by a particular, picturesque nickname. Furthermore, jobs were sometimes inherited, as in a dynasty, and skills were passed through generations from parents to offspring.

People engaged in theatrical activities, even if they are backstage, often have idiosyncrasies. They exist in a histrionic environment, surrounding themselves with theatrical slang and the mannerisms of singers and actors in different roles. Undoubtedly, the magic of the stage is very powerful, and behaviors rub off, especially in a setting that emphasizes and relies on role-playing. Because the Teatro Solís was a traditional house in every respect, this characteristic became almost a rule in the second half of the nineteenth century. When in early 1862 the Montevideo papers carried the news of a public tribute to José Soria, longtime box-office manager of the Solís, they caused a great sensation. Soria was a local legend, an offstage Figaro, and had been since the opening night of the house on August 25, 1856. Through the years he not only sold thousands of tickets from behind the brass bars of the box office, but had managed to handle people in all kinds of moods—from

tears and begging to curses and yelling—
when the house was sold out. At times it was
a human avalanche crushing against those
bars. In addition to controlling sales, Soria
did the bookkeeping, wrote the daily *bordereau* (register), decided how many standing-
room places were to be sold, and helped with
many administrative duties. He knew everything and everyone and was a competent
enough judge of the performances to voice
his criticism about any opera, concert, or
whatever took place on the Solís stage.
Everybody loved him, and because of his position, he was one of the most familiar faces
at the Solís.

The benefit performance chosen to honor
him was an operatic concert given by the Ballerini Company. The box-office receipts of
that night were given to Soria, who, before the
performance, published a note of gratitude in
El Comercio del Plata:

GREAT LYRIC BENEFIT PERFORMANCE
IN HONOR OF BOX OFFICE MANAGER
JOSE SORIA

For the first time in my long career in charge
of the Solís box office. . . . I would like to
dedicate to the esteemed audience a benefit
which the lyric artists Mme. Larrumbe and
Mr. Ballerini offer to me. The gratitude I feel
toward them for their noble gesture prompts
me to await with confidence the public's
support, who by their presence at this
performance will help me thank them and
to show once more my gratitude. JOSE
SORIA.[6]

CHAPTER 7

1867–1869

Louis Moreau Gottschalk, First American Pianist and Composer—

His Monumental Solís Concerts—

The World Premiere of *Symphonie No. 2 "A Montevideo"*

The "pianiste compositeur louisianais"—twenty years old, tall, slender, and possessed of Byronic poise. Such was Louis Moreau Gottschalk when he made his Paris debut in April 1849. His Parisian nickname reflected his native New Orleans, but the young composer was well acquainted with Paris, having arrived there seven years earlier. His musical debut was thus made in the city where the young boy grew into manhood—and the beginning of his sparkling career.

Gottschalk, born May 8, 1829, into a cultured family of colorful background, was the first of seven children. On his mother's side there was a mix of English ancestors and an aristocratic French family of refugees from the Santo Domingo rebellion. His father, Edward Gottschalk, was a successful English businessman, educated in Germany and fluent in seven languages.

As Mikhail Glinka and Frédéric Chopin had once championed their own national medium, so did Gottschalk become a pioneer of American musical nationalism by using folkloric melodies and tunes in his piano works. Before he was twenty his *Bamboula, danse des nègres*, as well as his *La savane, ballade créole*, and *Le bananier, chanson nègre* were popular in Parisian circles. When Gottschalk arrived in New York at the beginning of 1853, he was almost a foreigner in his own country. He spoke English with an accent and remained French in spirit, tastes, and way of life.

Solo piano recitals as they are known today had not yet been adopted in America when Gottschalk began his tour. As with Artur Napoleão and Oscar Pfeiffer in their Teatro Solís presentations in 1857 and 1858, respectively, the concert program was shaped by several artists, instrumentalists, and singers, who played or sang alternately during a two- or three-part concert. Frequently, members of an opera company would perform an entire act from an opera.[1]

From 1853 on, Gottschalk's life was a per-

43

petual adventure, full of extraordinary incidents. Thanks to a diary he began in 1857, we have a wonderful recollection of his life, a life remarkable for its variety and talent. This journal, published as *Notes of a Pianist*, was originally written in French and later translated into English by Dr. Robert E. Peterson, Gottschalk's brother-in-law.

The first two-thirds of Gottschalk's journal covers his cultural and artistic life and his musical opinions, as well as social and political events. The latter certainly supplied him with serious and compelling material; a good part of his writing is dedicated to the sorrows of the American Civil War. Near the end of the journal, and the Latin American period in particular, we find almost nothing about music and a great deal concerning the social and political struggles of the American republics. While historically vital, this political emphasis is most unfortunate for music scholars, all the entries made in Montevideo are devoted not to the people he met there but to the son of the dictator of that time, "who has acquired through his misdeeds the sad celebrity of a bandit!"[2] For those who follow Gottschalk's musical career, it is disappointing that the unpleasant episode fills almost all the journal's Montevideo entries, with only a few lines devoted to musical matters. The journal's final entry, written in Montevideo during Gottschalk's second trip to Uruguay, is dated December 15, 1868: "I am writing at this moment my grand *Tarantelle* for the piano with orchestral accompaniment, which I have dedicated to Her Royal Highness the Princess Marguerite of Italy."[3] There is no mention about his Teatro Solís concerts with the world premiere of his *Symphonie No. 2 "A Montevideo"* performed less than a month before. It is a pity not to have the pianist's own memories of his three Montevideo seasons.

After a long Chilean tour, Gottschalk left Valparaíso on April 30, 1867, sailing toward the south. Passing through the Strait of Magellan, with its desolation, bad weather, and rolling seas, the ship landed for a time in Punta Arenas. Then sailing north, on the Atlantic, the ship reached the entrance of the Río de la Plata, and after a month of antarctic adventure landed at Montevideo. It was May 1867.

The pianist was back to the artistic palestra[4] and ready, once more, to be unreservedly adored. His two-year sojourn at the Río de la Plata was an extraordinary artistic and personal success for Gottschalk, reminiscent of his previous experience in Europe. His charm, artistry, and Don Juanism aroused a kind of worship, especially among Montevideo's audiences. Gottschalk's legendary acclaim in this city began on June 11, 1867, when he gave his first Montevideo recital at the auditorium of the Sociedad Filarmónica on Montevideo's Treinta y Tres Street. A second concert was announced for July 6 in the same hall. As was customary, Gottschalk played to accompaniment and was here joined by Luigi Preti on violin, the organist Mr. Round, and the fifteen-year-old pianist Antonio Maria Celestino, in a program based on pieces for two pianos. Gottschalk and Celestino played two of the pianist-composer's own world premieres: *Fantasía sobre la ópera Martha* and *Glorias italianas*. In addition Gottschalk performed a dance, *Di que sí* (a contradanza) and Chopin's Etude in F Minor. (Unfortunately, these three Gottschalk works are reported lost in the 1970 complete Offergeld catalogue.)

Gottschalk gave two more recitals at Sociedad Filarmónica on July 18 and 20, but the truly important presentations during his Montevideo tour were still to come. The auditorium recitals were now to make way for his four Teatro Solís performances of that 1867 season. The first was programmed for September 11, with Gottschalk's concert set for the third part of the evening (following acts 1 and 2 of Verdi's *Ernani* as performed by the Carolina Briol Lyric Company). Gottschalk played three pieces representative of his style: *Murmures éoliens*, *Ses yeux*, and the already famous *Le banjo*. Four days later Gottschalk gave his second concert, accompanied by second piano player Juan Llovet y Castellet, a talented French performer who had long before established himself in Montevideo, in conjunction with the Briol Lyric Company (see 1867 chronology). The program of Sunday, September 15 was anticipated as "the most interesting and most versatile of all . . . because in addition to playing seven pieces, Gottschalk has chosen the famous *Tarantella* for piano and orchestra and the *Grand fantasía sobre temas de Faust*, just finished in this capital city."[5]

One of Gottschalk's innovative approaches to attracting wide audiences (presaging our era of superstars and massive stage shows) was his "monster" concert festivals. Here ten pianos were played together, an idea that had its inception in the summer of 1865 when Gottschalk was on tour in California. It was a variation on an old idea, harking back to Berlioz's famous monumental 1844 Paris Festivals, where 480 instrumentalists and 500 choristers joined together in a stunning musical display. The idea of the multiple-instrument concert was already in vogue in Europe; Gottschalk attended several of the Berlioz festivals when he was fifteen years old, and he was shrewd enough to include the practice in his Latin American tour. The result was a great public attraction.

For more than a week all Montevideo newspapers carried a daily two-column advertisement announcing the first twelve-piano Gottschalk festival at the Teatro Solís (on October 1), with the *Grand marches sur Tann-*

häuser et Faust on the program. Among the twelve pianists was Paul Faget, a Paris Conservatoire First Piano prizewinner (established in Montevideo since 1850), and future grandfather of Luis Cluzeau-Mortet, one of the first Uruguayan nationalist composers. It is also noteworthy that this performance of the *Tannhäuser* march was the first acquaintance Montevideo audiences had with the music of Richard Wagner.

In 1868 Gottschalk stayed for several months at the Hotel Americano in Montevideo, at the corner of Misiones and Cerrito Streets in the Old Town area. Here he was within walking distance of the Teatro San Felipe, where he gave several concerts during August of that year. Most remarkable were the special benefits Gottschalk offered for the Society of the Friends of Education, founded in 1868 in Montevideo by José Pedro Varela, "the Reformer," a pioneer of new educational systems in Uruguay. One concert alone garnered more than one thousand dollars, a veritable fortune in those days. This generous gesture was widely acclaimed, and Gottschalk was one of the cofounders of this organization.

With the 1868 Teatro Solís season Gottschalk's first concert was programmed in conjunction with Les Bouffes Parisiens. This French vaudeville company performed with great success for more than two months, in part, according to Gottschalk, because (as he commented during its Buenos Aires appearance) "Mademoiselle B. dances pretty well and has also fine legs!"[6] There was also an attempt to be bigger and better than ever, surpassing the previous year's festival, and Gottschalk's showmanship was now heralded by the newspaper announcements for a sixteen-piano festival. This concert became the second segment of a three-part program, bracketed by a vaudeville show (see 1868 chronology).

A few days after the sixteen-piano concerts,

Fig. 11. Advertising for one of Gottschalk's orchestral concerts with the world premiere of his *Symphonie No. 2 "A Montevideo," El Siglo,* November 1868. Biblioteca Nacional Collection, Montevideo.

the following notice appeared in Montevideo newspapers:

> 300—MUSICIANS FESTIVAL—300
>
> All musicians able to play in orchestras that do not belong to any military band or theatrical orchestra can find jobs with Mr. Gottschalk. Also music copyists are needed: 145 Ituzaingó Street, across from the Cathedral. Every day from 12 noon to 2 P.M.[7]

This was the prelude to a concert "à la Berlioz"—a Gottschalk brainstorm, a monumental concert that he himself would conduct at the Teatro Solís on November 10, 1868. The Solís stage would hold two full orchestras, the house orchestra and that of the Teatro San Felipe, plus three military bands, an eighty-voice choir, and, as additional instruments, nineteen clarinets, nineteen trombones, six treble shawms, nine double-basses, four timpani, eighteen tenor drums, six cymbals, one tantan, and four bass drums. Apparently Gottschalk himself was very impressed with the publicity in the press; he reported in a letter to his sisters back home that the entire list of artists covered one whole column of the newspaper.[8] In addition, a cannon plus two kilograms of gunpowder sat outside in the front plaza to be used at the first beat of Meyerbeer's *Le prophète*'s "Triumphal March" (fig. 11).

All this display was clearly a crowd-pleaser; razzle-dazzle aside, however, the truly important part of this memorable evening was the world premiere of Gottschalk's *Symphonie No. 2 "A Montevideo,"* dedicated to Montevideo and performed as the final number on that program. The symphony consists of a single movement divided into seven sections: andante, presto, maestoso (with an arrangement of the Uruguayan national anthem), an untitled section, "Hail Columbia," "Yankee Doodle," and a final section that interweaves the national airs of Uruguay and the United States. It is remarkable how Gottschalk cleverly modulated and linked the passages from one section to another; the work is further notable for its conclusion, where two flutes play "Yankee Doodle." Of course, this piece does not technically follow the symphonic pattern, and the work should really be called a fantasy or overture. When reviews began to appear in Montevideo newspapers two days later, they were incredible for their pomposity of language and style; nonetheless, they also sought to pay homage to the brilliancy of Gottschalk's artistry.

THE GREAT FESTIVAL

It seems as if Gottschalk's creative genius gives us a new surprise every day. Yesterday we were delighted by his incomparable compositions played on sixteen pianos; today we are totally astonished by the lyric harmonies coming from 300 instruments playing together thanks to his magic and marvelous baton! During the unforgettable evening the Solís looked majestic and splendid, and the public was moved and enraptured by Gottschalk's supernatural enthusiasm as the orchestra played—with admirable precision—*Le prophète*, *Prière du Moïse*, *Le jeune Henri*, and the beautiful *Sinfonía Montevideo*. No doubt in all of these pieces there is something both terrifying and sublime, much like the harmonies of the sea!! . . . We are sure that Mr. Gottschalk will remember forever Tuesday evening's concert because a new wreath of glorious triumph has been added to those that encircle his head. Would it be possible, we ask ourselves, for Mr. Gottschalk and all the musicians, to repeat such an outstanding spectacle?[9]

This same concert program (see 1868 chronology) was repeated at the Solís on Decem-

ber 1. Almost one hundred years later, thanks to the Gottschalk Centennial revival and the New Orleans premiere in 1969, the *Symphonie No. 2 "A Montevideo"* enjoyed new-found popularity, and a recording of the work with the Vienna State Opera Orchestra conducted by Igor Buketoff is broadcast fairly often. Curiously, the symphony is celebrated and enjoyed in many places—except for Uruguay!

On April 12, 1869, three days before leaving Montevideo, Gottschalk gave a farewell concert at the auditorium Franco-Oriental (located at Number 252, Treinta y Tres Street) with the collaboration of Preti, violinist and conductor; Carmelo Calvo, organist; and members of the Solís orchestra.

Gottschalk's life was drawing to a tragically early close: after months of rehearsals, concerts, and festivals, working and performing day and night, Gottschalk died on December 18, 1869, in Tijuca, a suburb of Rio de Janeiro. His death was caused by the recurrence of the yellow fever attack he had suffered four months earlier. He was forty years old.

Although now remembered mainly as a composer, Gottschalk was the first American pianistic superstar, with a world-renowned style and talent. He was in the vanguard in bringing American folklore to the concert hall, a wit and raconteur, and the first cultural ambassador to practice the "Good Neighbor Policy" (it would be many years before Franklin D. Roosevelt sent cultural programs to Latin America). He was also the first musician to pay homage to Uruguay by composing an orchestral work bearing the name of its capital, Montevideo.

His sojourn in Montevideo led to other significant ties (fig. 12). It was here that the composer developed a close friendship with Luis Ricardo Fors, an exiled Spaniard who became one of his biographers. Additionally, it was the late Uruguayan musicologist

Fig. 12. *El poeta moribundo*, the only Gottschalk piano work published in Montevideo (Bernareggi y Calvo, 1869). Cover of the score in Lauro Ayestarán Collection at the Library of Congress.

Lauro Ayestarán, who is acknowledged to have had the most important collection of Gottschalk's editions. On the occasion of the eminent scholar's last visit, in 1963, to the New Orleans Library, it was acknowledged that his private collection surpassed by many volumes the Louisianian's. It includes *El poeta moribundo* (The Dying Poet), a Gottschalk piano score published in Montevideo in 1869 by Bernareggi y Calvo.[10]

CHAPTER 8

1870–1876

Carlotta Patti—Pablo de Sarasate—Two Rossini Premieres—A Great Basso
Buffo: Alessandro Bottero—Luisa Gallo—*Il Guarany*

Opera's golden age was often populated by vocal dynasties, and in the 1800s the most prominent artists belonged to families in which three, four, or more members were singers. Parents, children, and other relatives formed their own opera companies, with the Garcías and the Patti-Barilis as the most famous examples.

The Patti-Barilis began their operatic line around 1830, when Salvatore Patti (born in Catania, 1800), a singer with an international career in Italy, France, and Spain, married singer Caterina Barili. At the time of this marriage Caterina Chiesa Barili, a fairly good soprano, was a widow with four children, all of them singers. Her daughter Clotilda was a contralto, while her sons ranged from Ettore, a baritone and excellent voice teacher, to Antonio and Nicòlo, basses. The marriage of Salvatore and Caterina produced three more children, all girls and all singers. Adelina Patti, the youngest, would be the most famous of the three, but Carlotta (a soprano) and

Amalia (a mezzo-soprano) were also talented singers who, for different reasons, left the stage relatively early.

From an early age Carlotta Patti showed a talent for music, with a remarkable ability for the piano. Her oldest half-brother, baritone Ettore Barili (Adelina's first voice teacher) discovered that Carlotta also had excellent vocal material, and he started to train her as a singer. Soon Carlotta found herself on the threshold of a promising career on the concert platform. Though her father would book her in opera, with a debut at the New York's Academy of Music in 1862, Carlotta was not considered suited for the stage, owing to the lameness she suffered since her childhood. Nevertheless, she had an extraordinarily successful debut at London's Covent Garden in a concert on April 16, 1863.

Both Carlotta and Adelina performed at the Solís, in 1870 and 1888, respectively. Carlotta's Montevideo recitals were widely advertised. For almost an entire month, *El*

Siglo published a boldface announcement daily:

At the time of her Solís concerts Carlotta Patti was at the peak of her vocal qualities. Her voice was, according to all the annals, not only of considerable size but also notable for its great flexibility, and she could easily reach G and even G♯ above high C. Carlotta's accompanist was a young violinist who would go on to achieve great renown, although at this time he was still an artistic fledgling. Pablo de Sarasate was only in his early twenties when he played with Carlotta at the Solís, and his spectacular success throughout Europe, especially Vienna and Germany, would come six years later, in 1876. His joint recital with Carlotta Patti was the first time Solís audiences heard him, but in the years to come Sarasate would play several times at the Solís and became a local favorite.

Carlotta Patti gave three concerts in Montevideo, on October 16, 18, and 20, 1870. The great success of all three resulted in the planning of a fourth concert at the Solís for October 22, but it was not to be. First it was postponed to the twenty-seventh, and then canceled when a serious political struggle resulted in the government order to close all public performances in Montevideo, as of October 22, 1870. All the theaters and public performances were to remain closed until the beginning of 1871.

One of the most important musical figures in South America, Amelia Pasi, opened the 1870 Solís operatic season with *La traviata* on April 28. She married the impresario Angelo Ferrari, whose companies toured South America for years (also visiting Montevideo several times, including the Solís). After Ferrari's death, Pasi continued the tradition (for further references see chapter 14). Her Lyric Company performed at the Solís from April 28 until October 2, presenting approximately fifteen works. As part of Pasi's own repertoire, Montevideo operagoers had the chance to see the Solís premiere of two Rossini operas: *Guglielmo Tell* and *Mosè in Egitto*.[2]

On September 2, the last of Rossini's operas, *Guillaume Tell* (sung in Italian under the title of *Guglielmo Tell*) was introduced at the Solís; the French *Moïse*, this time from an Italian libretto translation (as *Mosè in Egitto*), was first performed at the Solís on October 1. The newspaper announcement of the Montevideo premiere was typically bombastic: "First presentation of the 'non plus ultra' four-act opera written by the immortal Rossini !!!Guglielmo Tell!!!"[3] Rossini was only thirty-seven years old at the time of *Guillaume Tell*'s world premiere at the Paris Opéra in 1829. Still, the opera can be considered a work of his maturity, considering that most of his successful operas were produced in his mid- and late twenties, between 1816 and 1822. In *Guillaume Tell* Rossini combined elements of both Italian and French styles; the orchestration is lavish, and the choruses have a central role, both musically and dramatically. Nevertheless, the opera is abundant in solo arias, and the tenor part is composed with an unusually high range. The part of Arnoldo has nineteen high Cs and two D-flats (understandably, the opera seldom appears in modern singers' repertoires).

The era of the 1870s at the Solís was characterized by many ups and downs, due to nonmusical circumstances. The unstable political situation of Uruguay culminated in "The Terrible Year" of 1875, which witnessed a military insurrection and the overthrow of the president, Dr. José E. Ellauri, on January 15, plus continuous revolution from March to December of that year. As if these political troubles were not enough, two yellow fever epidemics followed, one after the other, in 1872 and 1873. Even so, the first half of the decade was not without operatic grace; in 1872 the Solís presented three different opera companies, each of them with a regular subscription series, with a total of 105 performances during the season. Only one Uruguayan premiere was staged that year, the Errico Petrella opera, *La Contessa d'Amalfi*.

The high point of the decade was the 1873 season, with a roster of fourteen internationally known singers plus four Montevideo premieres, giving a high profile to a season that saw 110 performances in the theater. The visiting Italian opera company was headed by the mezzo-soprano Marietta Biancolini and the famous *basso buffo* Alessandro Bottero, and performed under the baton of Maestro Gioachino Salvini. In addition to having a director and chorus master, the company was the first to arrive at the Solís with their own wardrobe master, costume assistant, and chief shifter. The conductor and both principal singers had a close artistic relationship with Antonio Cagnoni, an Italian post-Rossinian composer. Four Cagnoni operas had their Solís premieres in 1873: *Don Bucefalo*, *Michele Perrin*, *Claudia*, and *Papa Martin*.

On May 24, Bottero made his Solís debut singing *Michele Perrin*. First performed nine years earlier in Milan, this *opera comica* had been judged by the well-known Milanese professor Alberto Mazzucato to be the "music of the future." On June 11, 1873, Solís audiences heard the second Cagnoni production, *Papa Martin*. A *semiseria* and the first of Cagnoni's final three operas, it was composed in 1871 as a collaboration with the famous poet Antonio Ghislanzoni, the librettist for *Aida*. While none of his dramatic works brought glory to Cagnoni, *Papa Martin* was probably the best accepted among the Italian audiences.

Eight days after the Solís premiere of *Papa Martin*, Bottero sang a part that had brought him fame all over the world: the title role of *Don Bucefalo*. In spite of its being one of Cagnoni's early works, with its world premiere when he was still at the Milan Conservatory in 1847, this exceptional *opera buffa* remains the singer's most popular. *Don Bucefalo* was not only Bottero's way to success (he sang the Paris premiere in 1865) but also the warhorse of more than one *basso buffo* of that time. As had happened in many opera houses before, Bottero's performance at the Teatro Solís aroused a wave of enthusiasm, preserved in the colorful notice published the same day of the premiere:

DON BUCEFALO GREATEST CAGNONI
THREE ACT OPERA
Composed in 1846[sic], its author gave this opera to Bottero to add even further luster to this singer's glory and fame. It has been sung fifty times in Florence, and also in Naples, Genoa, Madrid, and Lisbon. It is the authentic Bottero warhorse, as was the Bucephalus that accompanied Alexander III [the Great] in his victories. But, there is a difference: while Alexander frightened the people with his horse, Alessandro Bottero enraptured the audiences singing *Don Bucefalo*.[4]

Even if Cagnoni had written many works with Bottero in mind, he also dedicated one opera to mezzo-soprano Biancolini. A Romantic melodrama and perhaps a *verismo* precursor, *Claudia* is a *drama lirico* in four acts, based on a novel by George Sand, and was introduced at Milan's Cannobiana in 1866. As with the world premiere, the August 6, 1873, Solís premiere of *Claudia* was sung with Biancolini in the title role, tenor Piccioli as Silvio, and bass Bottero as Remijio. Although the Italian premiere had been very coolly received, Montevidean critics complimented the music:

> We discovered a well-developed orchestration, better than that of the other two Cagnoni operas performed here by the same Lyric Company. The dominant melancholic melody of *Claudia* broke forth at the end, creating a very pathetic and beautiful effect. Bottero as an actor was as tragic here as he was playful in *Don Bucefalo*. His voice was always powerful, as were those of Biancolini and Piccioli.... All singers were enthusiastically applauded.[5]

Cagnoni's operas were performed frequently during this season, but the only one to be heard in future seasons would be *Papa Martin*. Bottero's triumphs were not enough, in Montevideo as well as elsewhere, to bring lasting popularity to Cagnoni's operas. As has happened with many other operas, these works are now only memories that belong to the past.

* * *

EVEN IF EPIDEMICS and political events prevented regular opera seasons at the Solís, the gap was well filled by remarkable concerts. From the point of view of instrumental music, the years 1874–75 are dates to be remembered in Uruguayan music history. More than once Maurice Dengremont, a seven-year-old violinist, surprised Solís audiences with his musical precocity. His regular concert programs were difficult enough for any adult instrumentalist, and not simplified as sometimes happened with the recitals of a child prodigy. Another rising star was Luisa Gallo (fig. 13),

a unique case in Montevideo's musical circles in the nineteenth century. Her fame rested not only on being a child prodigy (although this was a factor), but also on her being the first Uruguayan concertist given acclaim in the wider world. On September 7, 1874, nine-year-old Luisita Gallo gave her farewell concert at the Teatro Solís, leaving Montevideo a few months later to sail to Italy. Her destination was the Naples Conservatory of Music, but as a foreigner and a child, she was required to pass several examinations before being admitted as a regular pupil. She met these requirements so successfully that she was put under the tutelage of the famous Beniamino Cesi and also in the class of Piccirilli. These men were the best Italian piano teachers of the day, and their pupil responded with flair. Four years later, in 1878, winner of the Conservatory's first prize for piano, Gallo gave a concert in Naples' Teatro Principe Amadeo. When she then returned to Montevideo (and the Solís, on November 12, 1878), she was the first to perform, usually on the Solís stage, all of the current classical and modern repertoire of piano and orchestra concertos. At the age of twenty she married Camillo Giucci (an Italian pianist and a pupil of Liszt), and they founded the Liceo Musical Franz Liszt, now one of the oldest musical institutions in Montevideo.[6] The best-trained Uruguayan musicians and composers of the early twentieth century were formed under their tutelage, among them five of their seven children.

* * *

SINCE 1830 THE PUBLIC's musical preference had been focused in a single direction: Italian opera. The transition to including symphonic music was initially very slow, and it was almost half a century before symphonic works began to interest a select group of Montevidean audiences and to be performed with some regularity. The Teatro Solís remained the opera house par excellence for

Fig. 13. *Left*: Luisa Gallo [de Giucci] was one of the first Uruguayan pianists to premiere the major piano concerti with orchestra. Author Collection, gift from the Giucci family. *Right*: Gallo was also a composer and the first to create a *Fantasía de Concierto* on the Uruguayan national anthem, when she was a thirteen-year-old student at the Naples Conservatory. Cover of the piano score published in Naples, in 1878, in Lauro Ayestarán Collection at the Library of Congress.

more than a century because it was the principal theater of the city, but gradually it became the scene of performances of symphonic music as well. On September 6, 1875, under the baton of Maestro Luigi Preti, the Solís audiences first heard a complete symphonic work: Beethoven's Symphony no. 3 ("Eroica"). Coincidentally, it was on the same evening that a fifteen-year-old violinist, Luis Sambucetti Jr., made his debut. He would later become the best Uruguayan composer of the nineteenth century,[7] an excellent chamber musician, and the founder of a string ensemble and of the Instituto Verdi, then one of the two principal conservatories in Montevideo.

There were two high points at the Solís in the mid- to late 1870s. In 1876 French opera sung in the original language was first introduced; two years later, the first opera written by a Uruguayan composer had its premiere. (For a further discussion of this opera, Tomás Giribaldi's *Parisina*, see chapter 9.)

The French opera company headed by Madame Alhaiza came to the Solís in 1876. Not the first such company to visit Montevideo, it was the first French company in many years that brought brand-new operas—this time, Ambroise Thomas' *Mignon* and *Hamlet*—meeting with acclaim among audiences now influenced by the success of Gounod's *Faust*. Composers eager to build on *Faust*'s popularity turned to Goethe's plays for other subjects. Thomas and Jules Massenet were two such

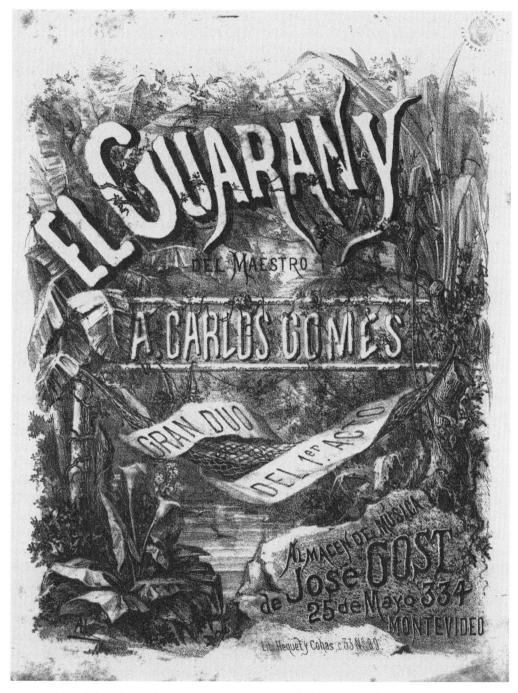

Fig. 14. Cover of the piano reduction score from *Il Guarany*'s first-act duet, in Lauro Ayestarán Collection at the Library of Congress.

composers, with Thomas composing his *Mignon* based on Goethe's *Wilhelm Meister*, and Massenet his *Werther*. The musical qualities of the work, along with the singers chosen for the world premiere (Célestine Galli-Marié in the title role and Marie Cabel as Philine) contributed to *Mignon*'s immediate success. The second Thomas production at the Solís was *Hamlet*, composed soon after *Mignon*. The French composer considered this opera, based on Shakespeare's play, his masterpiece, but the reception in the opera houses of the world varied, and *Hamlet* never reached the popularity of *Mignon*. However, many years later, in 1915, *Hamlet* would return to the Solís stage, as *Amleto*, with extraordinary success, with the title role sung by baritone Titta Ruffo.

The new French productions were not limited to Thomas' operas. On October 23, 1876, Albert Grisar's *Les amours du diable*, written in the style of Giovanni Battista Pergolesi, was first performed at the Teatro Solís. Solís audiences were also introduced to one more French composition, Daniel-François-Esprit Aubert's *Haydée*. Although considered an *opéra-comique*, this 1847 work is more serious and lyrical in style and with richer harmonic qualities than Auber's early operas and *opéra-comiques*. Nevertheless, none of his operas reached the popularity of *La muette de Portici* (which had received its world premiere in Paris on February 29, 1828).

Haydée was first performed at the Teatro Solís on October 17, 1876, with Alhaiza singing the title role. In addition to these four new operas, Solís audiences had the opportunity to hear for the first time the original French-language versions of two very popular operas, Donizetti's *La favorite* and Gounod's *Faust*; they also experienced something most unusual for any opera *habitué* outside of France, Verdi's *La traviata* sung in French.

Although it was not a long season, with only some seventy performances, Solís opera lovers enjoyed not only these French premieres but also two new operas by Brazilian composer Carlos Gomes: *Il Guarany* (fig. 14) and *Salvator Rosa*. As a composition student, the twenty-eight-year-old Gomes arrived in Italy with a scholarship to study at the Milan Conservatory under its director, Lauro Rossi. He remained in Milan for almost his entire life, and it was there that he reached the pinnacle of success, when *Il Guarany* was performed at Milan's La Scala in March 1870. After this premiere, *Il Guarany* entered the repertoire of most major opera companies. The opera owed its success as much to the dramatic lyricism and the high technical competence of the composition as to the libretto, based on a book by Brazilian writer José de Alencar, with its exotic setting that so appealed to nineteenth-century audiences. Of course, *Il Guarany*, as with all of Gomes' works, was composed on the model of the Italian operas, and has nothing to do, melodically or harmonically, with Indian music. (The same pattern and parameters were to be seen almost forty years later, when Uruguayan León Ribeiro's *Liropeya* was performed at the Teatro Solís in 1912.) Gomes' *Salvator Rosa*, premiered at Genoa four years after *Il Guarany*, and at the Solís on September 2, 1876: though composed to Ghislanzoni's libretto, it never reached the success of the earlier opera. No less than Verdi referred to Gomes as a musical genius. He was the first Latin American composer to reach fame with an opera, and it would take almost a century before another Latin American composer—Alberto Ginastera—would get universal recognition for his operas.

CHAPTER 9

1878–1887

The First Uruguayan Opera: Tomás Giribaldi's *Parisina*—Francesco Tamagno's First Season at the Teatro Solís—More Debuts: Gemma Bellincioni and Roberto Stagno, Medea Mei and Nikolay Figner, Eva Tetrazzini

On September 14, 1878, the Teatro Solís occasioned a major landmark in Uruguayan musical history. It was on this evening that the first national opera, Tomás Giribaldi's *Parisina*, has its world premiere. Composed with a Felice Romani libretto (the libretto Donizetti used for his own *Parisina*, with some modifications), this opera is essentially Italian in its style, plot, and text, even more than Carlos Gomes' *Il Guarany*.

Nevertheless, it required a great deal of courage for a thirty-year-old Uruguayan composer without European training to write an opera in the traditional style—the first native-born musician to do so. Giribaldi's choice to compete with the regular Italian repertoire heard at the Solís is particularly striking. *Parisina* was a pioneer work that initiated a musical genre in Uruguay, a country still looking for its own musical language. Though not a masterpiece like *Il Guarany*, there is good me-

lodic material in *Parisina*, with well-written dramatic passages distributed among the principal characters. Of note are the first-act duet between Azzo (baritone) and Ernesto (bass), the second act's soprano aria "V'era un di quando l'alma innocente" and the waltz "Amore e sospiro." This particular waltz became popular overnight, with the piano version of "Amore e sospiro" being heard in every Montevideo home shortly after this opera's premiere (fig. 15).

Sung by soprano Teresa Singer (Parisina), mezzo Lucia Avalli (Imelda), tenor Carlo Bulterini (Ugo), baritone Vincenzo Cottone (Azzo), and bass Achille Augier (Ernesto), under the baton of Leopoldo Montenegro, *Parisina* was warmly received by Solís operagoers, and its creator widely acclaimed. In the pre- and postpremiere excitement, Montevideo's newspapers ran endless previews and reviews about its first national opera. Of greatest importance was music critic Luis Desteffanis'

Fig. 15. "Amore e Sospiro," piano reduction of a waltz from *Parisina* by Tomaso [Tomás] Giribaldi. The opera received its world premiere at the Solís on September 14, 1878. Cover of the score in Lauro Ayestarán Collection at the Library of Congress.

long review after the first performance, partly for his recognition of Giribaldi's use of leit-motif to distinguish his opera's characters:

> If we chose only one phrase to qualify the opera of the young Uruguayan composer, it would be: It is a wonderful promise. Even if some imperfections show the author's inexperience, the opera has enough value to be considered a first-rate work. Evidently, Giribaldi has a deep knowledge of harmony and counterpoint, and the treatment of the melody is great. We also found remarkable the outline of each of the opera's personages. The instrumentation is rich and well done.[1]

As was the custom, when the curtain came down at the end of this first performance the Teatro Solís management, together with the conductor and singers, paid homage to the composer and presented him with gifts. One of the presents that deeply touched him was a gold feather pen given to him by the orchestra musicians. Afterward, as was also the usual practice, Giribaldi gave an ebony and gold baton to Maestro Montenegro, and jewelry to the principal singers. In addition to the laurel wreaths and medals and plaques offered him by musical institutions, a cascade of flowers, most of them coming from the galleries, fell at Giribaldi's feet. The composer, naturally shy, became speechless at such an impressive demonstration. Before the ceremony was over, a representative of the president of Uruguay appeared on the stage announcing that "the Government is conferring a grant to the young composer to allow him to complete his musical studies in Europe." It is unfortunate that so auspicious a moment did not last; as soon as he arrived in Italy, serious family reasons related to his mother's ill health obliged Giribaldi to return to Montevideo, even before he entered the Milan Conservatory. Fortune did not visit him elsewhere either: almost

Fig. 16. Tomás Giribaldi (1847–1930) Author's collection.

until his last days he visited his fiancée's tomb every morning at six o'clock. (The author's mother, a close relative of the Giribaldi family, met the composer when he was in his sixties. She described him as a very quiet, kind, and lonesome man, who carried all his life the sadness of an unaccomplished dream, although he never complained or talked about it.[2]) Giribaldi died on April 11, 1930 at the age of eighty-three (fig. 16).

This is not to say that he did not pursue his music. He composed other operas; sadly, none enjoyed the same resounding success as *Parisina*. After his death, the Municipality of Montevideo placed a plaque in the Teatro Solís foyer. It reads: "To Maestro Tomás E. Giribaldi who in this house premiered *Parisina* on September 14, 1878, and triumphantly gave to his country the first national opera. The Municipality of Montevideo—September 14, 1930."

* * *

THE DECADE OF THE 1880S witnessed a pro-
liferation of singers' debuts on the Teatro Solís stage. The mere list of their names during
these seasons is very impressive.[3] One of the
earliest singers to win renown in this decade
was Romilda Pantaleoni, who made her Solís
debut singing La Regina in Filippo Marchetti's
Ruy Blas. From her debut on June 17, 1882,
through the next five months she performed
ten different heroines; for all her consistently
fine singing, however, the Italian soprano is
most warmly remembered by Uruguayan
opera lovers for creating the role of Yole in
the world premiere—on July 18, 1882—of Giribaldi's *Manfredi di Svevia* under the baton
of Maestro Giuseppe Strigelli. Giribaldi's second opera, the second ever written in Uruguay, is based on an old Italian historic romance written by Francesco Domenico
Guerrazzi. Set in Naples close to the Benevento walls in 1266, Guerrazzi's book had had
an immediate success among readers. Such
was not the case with the opera. Uruguayan
critics found the text, written by poet Giuseppe Emilio Ducatti, "a boring and monot-
onous libretto lacking novel action; its mo-
notony is translated also into the music."[4]
Even if at the end of *Manfredi* Giribaldi received many curtain calls, and all the singers,
"especially Pantaleoni, received many gifts,
flower baskets, and wreaths,"[5] the new five-
act opera was not received with the enthusiasm that had greeted *Parisina* four years earlier.

This time the two principal music critics
had totally opposite points of view. Desteffanis wrote:

It can honestly be said *Manfredi* does not
reach *Parisina*'s splendid triumph. With *Parisina*—his first work—the public could be

generous in encouraging the young composer and his just-born operatic career. But
since *Manfredi* is his second opera, the public now has the right to be more demanding.
In our opinion *Manfredi* lacks lyricism and
variety . . . and musical motifs are too often
repeated.[6]

In the aggrandized style of the less knowledgeable but perhaps more patriotic critic:

With his new *Manfredi di Svevia*, Maestro Giribaldi gives confirmation to our
thoughts: he will be a genius and a glory for
our country. All the beauties of this opera
have surpassed those of *Parisina* and perhaps
we will soon enjoy another new step of our
composer on the way toward success, with
Inés de Castro, a new opera he has just now
finished. Three operas in so short a period
raise hopes about the brilliant imagination
of the young composer. We must congrat-
ulate the musician for *Manfredi*'s accomplished instrumentation. . . . The third act is
perhaps the best of the whole opera, especially the great Final Scene which, beginning
with a tenor vocal line that is then followed
by soprano and mezzo in thirds, and joined
by the baritone, the chorus then comes in to
complete the act in magnificent "stretta"
Meyerbeer-like style.[7]

The lengthy review describes the entire
opera almost bar by bar. The truth is that in
spite of such a chronicle, the audience lost
interest, and after a third performance *Manfredi di Svevia* disappeared from the repertoire. It is hard to judge this opera by today's
standards. The sad consequence is that Giribaldi was so crushed by this failure that neither *Inés de Castro* nor *Magda*, his fourth
opera, has ever been published or performed.
Still, his place in Uruguayan opera is histori-

cally assured. Even if *Parisina* is not a masterpiece, it will always have the merit of being the first opera written by a native son.

* * *

THE CAREER OF SINGER PANTALEONI brought her back to the Solís stage six years later, in 1888, where Montevideo audiences enthusiastically received her. Their warm embrace was not only for the fond memories of the past, but also for knowing that one year earlier, she had created Desdemona (opposite Francesco Tamagno and Victor Maurel as Iago) in the acclaimed La Scala world premiere of Verdi's *Otello*.

Francesco Tamagno, the famous "tenore di forza," was thirty-four when he sang at the Solís for the first time. Four seasons of fame at La Scala preceded Tamagno when he arrived in Montevideo in 1884. Audiences greeted him with good humor when he made his first appearance on the Solís stage to sing *Gli ugonotti*. But it was his fourth appearance, as Fernando in *La favorita*, that conquered Solís opera lovers. In that season, his first in Montevideo, Tamagno sang ten more performances. Nevertheless, for all his success this first year, it was for his second visit during the 1896 Solís season (as we shall see) that he will remain forever in Montevideo musical history.[8]

In 1884 Tamagno shared the applause with two leading sopranos also debuting at the Teatro Solís that year: Elena Teodorini and Medea Mei. The Romanian-born Teodorini (born 1857) was twenty-seven at the time of her Solís debut. Already famous for her La Scala performances, she had an exceptionally wide range, from lyric and dramatic soprano roles to handling mezzo and contralto characters with equal aplomb. Mei, an Italian soprano originally known as Amedea Mei Zovaide, had debuted at a very young age in her native Florence, singing mezzo-soprano roles. She later shifted toward lighter roles until she established herself as a singer of soprano heroines. At the Solís she would sing *Favorita*'s Leonora and *La Gioconda*'s Laura opposite Tamagno.

This season also had the Russian tenor Nikolay Figner alternating such roles with Tamagno as Il Duca in *Rigoletto* and *Martha*'s Lyonel. Only a few years later, Mei and Figner would marry and spend more than twenty years in Russia, but she always remained an Italian soprano—not withstanding Mei and Figner's creating the two leading roles of Lisa and Herman in Tchaikovsky's *Queen of Spades* under the composer's supervision. In 1903 Medea Mei-Figner would return to sing on the Solís stage: her conductor was Arturo Toscanini; her partner, Enrico Caruso.[9]

When these singers continued on their tours, Teatro Solís audiences next welcomed Eva Tetrazzini. Nine years older than her famous sister Luisa, Eva was only twenty-three when she opened the 1885 Solís season on May 23 with *Aida*. Between her debut and November she created more than eight different heroines, during which time she had two leading tenors, Leopoldo Signoretti and Francesco Signorini. The following year Eva Tetrazzini returned to Montevideo for a second opera season, but this time she changed houses, singing at the Teatro Cibils. Here one of her performances was tragically intertwined with Uruguayan political history. In 1886 the president of Uruguay was General Máximo Santos, an opera lover and a great admirer of Eva Tetrazzini. On the night of August 17 he was attending her performance when Lieutenant Gregorio Ortiz shot him in the face. He survived this assassination attempt, but it was the beginning of a political struggle that would result in the president's resignation and eventual banishment.

In 1888 Eva Tetrazzini achieved world recognition for being the first American Desdemona in an *Otello* production at the New York Academy of Music, with Francesco Marconi singing the title role and Maestro Cleofonte Campanini conducting.

The Solís stage was also graced by a tenor whose quality of voice made him one of Tamagno's rivals. Ten years older than the *tenore di forza*, Sicilian tenor Roberto Stagno has a voice that was not so heavy as Tamagno's. What Stagno did have was a rare combination of flexibility and adaptability, which allowed him to sing roles very distant in tessitura, going from *Barbiere*'s Almaviva and *Rigoletto*'s Duke to *L'africana*'s Vasco da Gama and finally Otello, all within the same period in his career. At the time of his first Solís season in 1886, he was forty-six years old and already well known in America for his having sung at the opening season of New York's Metropolitan Opera House three years earlier.

Living as husband and wife in real life,[10] Stagno and Gemma Bellincioni were the creators of Turiddu and Santuzza in the world premiere of *Cavalleria rusticana* in 1890, at the Teatro Costanzi of Rome. In his Montevideo debut, Stagno sang Almaviva opposite Bellincioni's Rosina on the opening night, July 7, of the Solís' 1886 season. This was the first performance in a three-month period in which he sang eight different roles in approximately twenty productions. In addition to *Barbiere*, he performed in *Mefistofele*, *Rigoletto*, *La favorita*, *Faust*, *La Gioconda*, and Meyerbeer's *L'africana* and *Roberto il diavolo*. The last was, at that time, not only Stagno's favorite role but one of the best suited for his voice. Soprano Fanny Copca shared all the female roles with Bellincioni during this Solís season.

Even if we can consider her a very young singer—only twenty-two, thus twenty-four years younger than Stagno—when Bellincioni came to perform at the Solís she already had about five years of operatic experience. And in the same year she sang in Montevideo's Teatro Solís, she also debuted in Milan's La Scala. In 1886, following her *Il barbiere* with Stagno, she was cast in four more operas at the Solís: *Rigoletto*, *Roberto il diavolo*, *Linda di Chamounix*, and *Faust*.

CHAPTER 10

1888–1889

Adelina Patti, Nineteenth-Century Superstar—

Otello's Uruguayan Premiere: Romilda Pantaleoni and Roberto Stagno—

Mattia Battistini, "The King of Baritones"

From the time she was a very little girl, she had dreamed of the enchanted world beyond the footlights; indeed, at the age of seven, she made her first public appearance in a concert. At sixteen she debuted in *Lucia* at the New York Academy of Music, and two years later she conquered London's Covent Garden with her Amina in *La sonnambula*.[1] With an absolute reign of about thirty-five years, Adelina Patti is often considered unique and the most momentous singer of the second half of the nineteenth century. Her career has few parallels in the history of singing.

When in the fall of 1888 Montevideo operagoers read that Patti was coming for an opera season at the Teatro Solís, there was a hum of speculation: what would the famous diva, now forty-five and the highest-paid singer in the world, be like? Would her voice still be fresh, capable of singing with the same grace and mastery as it had twenty years before? Was it true that she spent a fortune on jewelry, with some of it even stitched to her costumes? And what of all the gossip involving her affair with, and subsequent marriage to, Ernest Nicolini? As happened whenever a celebrity was announced, Montevideo opera lovers took up sides. Some were benevolent, influenced by the memories of the Solís' 1858 Louis M. Gottschalk concerts and the composer's anecdotes of the young fifteen-year-old Adelina in his tours. Others, more skeptical, wondered aloud whether the diva's vocal endowment would be worth the ticket price.

The evening of July 8, 1888, arrived. Members of all factions—expectant, euphoric, or critical—waited silently to hear the illustrious Patti. For her long-anticipated performance she sang *Il barbiere*'s Rosina, accompanied by Roberto Stagno as Almaviva and Silla Carobbi as Figaro. Maestro Arnaldo Conti conducted what music critics went on to praise as "a real Patti triumph." The critic for *La Tribuna Popular* continued:

She showed the most extraordinary vocalization skills and brought the house down with the "Echo Song" in the famous Lesson Scene. So grand and endless was the ovation that Patti added the Spanish song "La calesera," capping it with an ardent "Viva Montevideo!" . . . At the beginning of the night the public was divided into two camps: the first were unconditional Patti fans; the second, those who thought they might have paid too much to hear her. But, after "La calesera" the two became a single unity, and as if attracted by some powerful spell they began to applaud with exhilarating excitement. . . . A rain of flowers came down from the galleries at the end of the opera, and then numerous stagehands brought enormous flower baskets to the apron of the stage. Seeing this, Adelina stopped the applause and started to sing the famous Arditi's "Il bacio." When the song finished the gentlemen gave her a standing ovation and the ladies waved their lace handkerchiefs.[2]

If for Solís opera lovers it was a surprise to learn how young and fresh Patti's voice was at forty-five, it was not for the rest of the world. In fact, this was not only one of the years of her prime but, as biographer Herman Klein has written, "[1888 was] her 'banner' year, and the most lucrative in Mme. Patti's whole professional career."[3] According to Klein, writing in 1920, in the first half of 1888 Patti "earned larger sums than have ever been paid, before or since, to any artist in the history of musical enterprise." Certainly, she remains one of the best-paid singers in all opera history. For eight Solís presentations she collected the amount of 20,000 pounds (at that time, approximately $120,000.00).[4]

For her second Solís presentation, on July 11, Patti chose the role of Lucia. Once again the critics raved.

Who designs all those capricious arabesques at the same time poor Lucia is telling her sad story? Who possesses such a perfect singing mechanism, so flexible, so crystal-like, that it allows her to do those incredible trills, ascending and descending scales, roulades, stacatti? Who does all those passages in thirds and fourths or jumps so easily in fifths and sixths with such a mathematical precision dreamed only by the most exigent musician? Adelina Patti, only La Patti! Mme. Patti has, in fact, all those attributes that only have been reached before by Malibran, Cafarelli, or Marchesi.[5]

After her successful *Lucia di Lammermoor*, Patti gave six more performances at the Solís, most of them to a sold-out house with people packed in every cranny. She sang *Barbiere* on July 8 and 24 and also performed *I puritani*, in addition to *Semiramide*, *Linda di Chamounix*, *Lakmé*, and, finally, *La traviata* as her farewell to Montevideo. Such a repertoire demonstrates that Patti was a singer and actress of rare versatility (fig. 17). Able to personify characters that differ drastically in their psychological or physical nature (such as Rosina, Elvira, Lakmé, Semiramide, Lucia, or Violetta), she was never in danger of being typecast.

In her recognition that Leo Delibes' *Lakmé* was a role marvelously suited to her, Patti wisely chose this opera for her Solís *serata d'onore* (a benefit in her honor). Once again the press raved, this time over the well-known Bell Song: "The famous ritornello proved how far she can reach with her vocal flexibility. Hers is a voice that does not lack any of the canorous birds' trills and whose sweetness cannot be imitated either by any instrument or by another human throat." When the Bell Song was over, the ovation was so grand that she granted an encore. Her aria was then capped by an overwhelming display of twenty baskets of flowers and a silver tray filled with jewelry given to Patti by her many admirers.[6]

On July 29 she gave her last Uruguayan performance, singing *La traviata*, with tenor Stagno as her Alfredo. Her first Violetta at Covent Garden, when only eighteen, had made the *Times* critic exclaim, "Mlle. Patti's Violetta, as an artistic display, is more elaborately finished than any previous personification of the character we remember."[7] From that first performance until one of her last *Traviatas* at the age of fifty-two (in the same house in 1895), this particular heroine was one of Patti's greatest achievements. It has been told that when Giuseppe Verdi was asked to name his three favorite singers for interpreting his operas, his answer was: "Number one: Adelina; number two: Adelina, and number three: Adelina!"

In some sense Patti's Solís performance of *La traviata* presaged some of the characteristics of Patti's Covent Garden performance, seven years in the future. Under a bold headline stating "Extraordinary *La traviata* Performance—New and Great Patti Triumph" there appeared an extensive review of that Teatro Solís evening.

> Never ever have we heard anybody sing that sublime Verdi score with such enthusiasm and emotion as yesterday night. The Solís audience can be very proud of having the honor and the glory to be present at a *La traviata* interpretation such as has never been sung in Montevideo before, and only a few times in foreign lands. As soon as Patti stepped on the stage we knew that Violetta's role had a better interpreter than all that we have heard previously. La Patti has a total command of *La traviata*, as [she does] in any other opera, and tenor Stagno was magnificent, greatly contributing to Adelina's colossal triumph.

In order that our readers envision how

Fig. 17. Adelina Patti (1843–1919) in the 1860s. Library of Congress Collection.

> Adelina was dressed last night, I must tell you that she wore five magnificent costumes made of natural silk, brocade, and satin, with golden hand-embroideries and natural flowers stitched all over. And in one act of *La traviata* she displayed gems whose value amounted to a full million francs![8]

When Patti sang *La traviata* at Covent Garden in 1895, the British reviewer's comments were similar:

> In many respects she had never sung the whole opera better. . . . In [one] scene Mme. Patti had conceived the idea of wearing a magnificent white dress, the corsage of which was studded with hundreds of large diamonds, dismounted for the occasion from their settings in some of her finest jew-

els. This mass of coruscating brilliants gave the effect of a veritable blaze of light; and its extraordinary beauty was on a par with the value of the collection, which, according to M. Nicolini, amounted to fully 200,000 pounds.[9]

We can be fairly safe in assuming that some of these jewels were those bought by Patti during her Montevideo sojourn. According to a comment printed in *Montevideo Musical*, a weekly magazine of the last century: "It has been said that the famous artist Adelina Patti had bought from a local Montevideo jeweler diamonds with a value of 12,000 golden pesos. Truly, the trills of *Lucia* and *Barbiere* are worth a great deal!"[10]

From the time I knew what the word "singer" meant, I remember hearing stories about Patti in Montevideo. More than half a century after her performances there, everyone was still impressed by the way she had lived and traveled, always in grand style and surrounded by an almost regal retinue. On her first visit to South America she traveled with her husband, her niece Carlina Patti, her companion Karoline ("Karo") Baumeister, a secretary, three English friends, her faithful maid Patro, a cook, and her favorite and colorful cockatoo, Jumbo. As today some artists travel everywhere with their small lapdogs, fashion then dictated that any prima donna or respectable performer should have a cockatoo or a parakeet as a pet. The quality of her fame was further enhanced by her conjugal state. Unhappily married to the marquis de Caux, a divorce finally enabled her to marry tenor Nicolini. In fact, their love affair was called "the century's greatest stage romance."[11] Although their wedding had taken place in 1886, in the eyes of Montevideo, Patti and Nicolini were almost newlyweds when she sang at the Solís, which only added new luster to her already famous personality.

Patti's possession of incredible gifts, and her shrewd way of managing them, have kept the memory of her Teatro Solís performances clear and vivid, even a century later. It also explains why one of Patti's last Montevideo reviews ends with these words: "Who among us, could ever forget her?"[12] Apparently these feelings were reciprocal. In a long and touching letter of thanks that she sent to *El Siglo* before leaving Montevideo, Patti recounted fond memories of her Montevideo and Buenos Aires appearances: "When I saw the stage covered with flowers thrown by the ladies and saw the [gentlemen's] standing ovation, a genuine happiness made me weep." And after commenting on how sorrowful this farewell would be for her, she expressed her "everlasting gratitude" to Montevideo as she said goodbye.[13]

* * *

THE THUNDEROUS APPLAUSE after Patti's *Traviata* was still resounding when her Alfredo gave Solís audiences an important premiere: on August 4, 1888, Roberto Stagno (in the title role; fig. 18) gave the first Uruguayan performance of Verdi's *Otello*, his Desdemona being Romilda Pantaleoni, the singer chosen by Verdi for the opera's world premiere one year before.

For Montevideo theatergoers, *Otello*'s strong drama always had a fascinating attraction, a magical power to draw audiences into the life of its characters. Rossini's *Otello* had first been performed at the colonial Casa de Comedias in 1830 and was in fact, a production in the very first season of complete staged operas that Montevideo ever knew. The next contact audiences had with the Moor of Venice was neither in Rossini's nor Verdi's operas but in William Shakespeare's drama itself, in Italian translation more than half a century later in performances given at the Solís by three leading Italian dramatic actors: Tom-

Fig. 18. Cover page of *Montevideo Musical*, no. 24, June 24, 1888, issue dedicated to the Uruguayan premiere of Verdi's *Otello* with Roberto Stagno in the title role. Author's collection.

maso Salvini, Ermete Novelli, and Ermete Zacconi. When Verdi's masterpiece arrived in 1888, the public was well versed in the story and able to understand all the subtleties and details of the new opera. Furthermore, since the La Scala world premiere on February 5, 1887, Uruguayan newspapers and musical magazines had provided their readers with extensive information not only about Verdi's score, but of Arrigo Boito's libretto, singers' performances, and all of the opera

world's comments surrounding this spectacular *Otello*. As a consequence, it is not surprising that more than ever there appeared such extensive analysis in Montevideo's newspapers after the first performance of this new operatic work.

Verdi has written a dramatic musical in accordance with the most modern theories, opening in this way his fifth and new style. The venerable Old Master designed a frame of huge proportions, dramatically harmonic and tremendous, deprecating those easy and cheap effects, whose only purpose is "grattare l'orecchio." Six semiquavers in an *Allegro Agitato*, followed by a chord of gigantic sonority that almost shakes the earth, opens the drama. Immediately, Verdi draws a tempest in "quatrinas en quavers" whose fury and uproar stop suddenly in a pianissimo, marked ppp in the score, as a sort of truce to the rage of the elements. But, one second later a flash of lightning, four exclamations of the Cypriot citizens done by the chorus, and terrible thunder prepare Otello's entrance. Esultate! Only twelve bars to sing! And that was enough to show us Otello's character and to know we are already in the presence of a genius![14]

Thus wrote *El Siglo*'s critic Luis Garabelli in a long review that would appear over three consecutive days. He would go on to write of the Credo that "it is built on a very strange harmony, in a base of powerful trills played by the 'epic' instruments of the orchestra, and clearly shows us the diabolical machinery that surrounds the Mephistophelian spirit of the character [Iago]."[15]

Finally, on the third day, Garabelli reviews the three principal characters' performances:

The Opera of the immortal Verdi already has its interpreters in two leading tenors: one the brasslike voice and potent dramatism of Tamagno; the other, Stagno, who adds to a remarkable sound the exquisite mastery of interpretation with a variety of psychological nuances. . . . Romilda Pantaleoni, who learned her role under the composer's supervision, gave all the powerful dramatic talent of her voice in a portrait of passionate feelings. . . . Delfino Menotti was a revelation for all his musical knowledge and dramatic acting. He did not lose for one single moment the IMPASSIVITY, which is Iago's pre-

dominant characteristic. In fact, he showed at the same time, a submission close to servility toward Otello, a kind of politesse with Desdemona, an ironical sarcasm with Rodrigo, and a carefree friendship with Cassio. All the honors go to Maestro Conti who has given us the Montevideo premiere! And our wishes for Verdi's happiness![16]

This review has importance beyond its reflection of the premiere; it is one of the first musical reviews published in Montevideo's newspapers to accomplish something more than a mere collection of superlative adjectives. Here is a critic who is musically trained, able to discover harmonic and melodic treatments that had never been used in such a way before. He is able to highlight—thus teaching his readers at the same time—the outstanding scenes of the opera. In his "Only twelve bars to sing! And that was enough," Garabelli recognized that *Otello*'s opening bars are among the most vocally challenging for a tenor, yet the most impressive. He also analyzed Verdi's use of the "trill effect" to indicate Iago's sinister personality. In other fragments of the same review (not given here) he reemphasized the repetition of trills, appogiature, acciacature, and other musical embellishments, not only on the melodic vocal line but in the accompaniment to accentuate the malevolence of the villainous traitor.

Before this no one had reviewed any musical work from such a point of view, and at first it was an exception. *Montevideo Musical*, Uruguay's leading music magazine, and directed by musicians, said on the same days:

Otello's score is a sublime work because of its inspiration and highest artistic merit. Verdi demonstrates that even in old age he keeps the same young and robust inspiration so popular years before. He is a Master for whom the Divine Art has no secrets. In spite of the taste of certain foolish "wise" critics,

Otello has very inspired moments, some of them as good as those of Verdi's former triumphs. The score is written according to the last word of the science of counterpoint.[17]

Gradually such stylistic contrasts became less noticeable, and by the turn of the century musical reviews not only lost their earlier lyricism and naïveté, but became sharp, exigent, and even captious. The public soon followed the same tendency, becoming more critical in their judgment. In particular, the Solís grew to be the fear of every singer, conductor, actor, or musician to arrive on these shores. Solís operagoers became world-renowned for having to their credit more booing and catcalls than any other opera house. I know from a personal source[18] that even Enrico Caruso could not escape their censure, becoming one of their victims when his voice cracked during a *Manon* performance. There is more to the story, however. After this mishap he went on to complete the opera in marvelous voice. In spite of their demands the audiences were fair, too, and forgave him this bad moment. When the performance was over, he received from the same listeners more curtain calls than he had for the previous acts. But of course, all this happened many years after *Otello*'s Solís premiere.

* * *

IF THE 1888 SOLÍS SEASON had the great appeal of Adelina Patti, the next year's was its equal in the person of Mattia Battistini, proclaimed then as "Il re dei baritoni." He was, in fact, *the* baritone of his time just as years later it would be Titta Ruffo.

Battistini's performance as Alphonse XI in *La favorita* at the Teatro Argentina in Rome in 1878, inaugurated a dazzling career that was to span almost fifty years. Soon he was very much in demand not only in his country, but in all European opera houses, especially in Russia, where he sang each year from 1893 to 1914. He sang very frequently in Spain and Portugal and occasionally in England, Germany, Sweden, and Switzerland. However, he was very much afraid to undertake long sea voyages such as crossing the Atlantic, so he took only two trips to South America. The first (1881–82) took him to Argentina and Brazil,[19] while the second (1889) also took him to Montevideo and Buenos Aires, and in the same company as Angelo Masini.

The Ferrari company arrived in Montevideo that year after a successful season in Buenos Aires. The 1889 Teatro Solís season opened with the annual August 25 gala: this year a performance of Gaetano Donizetti's *Lucrezia Borgia* with two stellar singers, soprano Elena Teodorini and tenor Angelo Masini, under Maestro Marino Mancinelli. Battistini showed his vocal abilities and his famous "velvety" voice during seven performances in the roles of Iago, the *Ernani* Don Carlo, Amleto, Simon Boccanegra, Rigoletto, and Figaro. This showcase was to demonstrate his vocal versatility in roles that differ so much in style, characters portrayed, and vocal demands.

This year also was the only time that Angelo Masini sang at the Solís. The acclaimed tenor performed in five of the operas conducted by Mancinelli, singing Gennaro in the opening night and Almaviva at the close of the season, plus Enzo Grimaldo in *La Gioconda*, Nadir in the Italian translation of Bizet's *Les pêcheurs de perles*, and the Duca di Mantova.

In addition to Teodorini and Masini, Battistini sang some of the other performances with soprano Fanny Torresella and tenor Giambattista De Negri. In Montevideo, however, he did not sing with Tamagno, despite Francesco Palmegiani's statement to that effect.[20] The year was completed with an opera company conducted by Maestro Paolo Balsinelli, with performances in the middle of the summer and a second season in the early fall, with opera and operetta performances.

CHAPTER 11

1890–1894

José Oxilia: The Uruguayan Otello—Young Antonio Scotti's Falstaff—
Edoardo Mascheroni: The First Notable Conductor—
Seven Opera Premieres and a Famous Zarzuela

In the summer of 1887, Maestro Franco Faccio, who had conducted the La Scala premiere of *Otello* six months earlier, brought the new opera to Brescia's Teatro Grande. On this occasion the title role was sung by Giuseppe Oxilia, a twenty-six-year-old Uruguayan tenor. José Oxilia (called Giuseppe in Italy) must have been a first-rate tenor with a well-established reputation for Faccio to have chosen him. Oxilia was joined by Paolo [Paul] Lhérie as Iago and Adalgisa Gabbi as Desdemona in a production at which Giuseppe Verdi was ironically surprised yet pleased by its success: as he wrote to Faccio from Sant'Agata on August 19, 1887: "Well then. . . . *Otello* is making its way even without its *creators*?!! I had got so used to hearing people proclaim the glories of these two [Tamagno and Maurel] that I was almost persuaded they had written this *Otello*. Now you deprive me of my illusions by telling me that the Moor is going well without these stars!! Can it be possible?"[1]

The son of Italian parents, Oxilia had been sent in 1877, at the age of sixteen, from his native Uruguay to Italy in order to pursue the study of medicine. Soon after his arrival he was conquered by the operatic life of the country. Knowing he had a voice, he abandoned his medical career to study singing. Within a few years he had debuted, at twenty-three in the role of Laerzio [Laertes] in the Italian version of Ambroise Thomas' *Hamlet*, on November 21, 1884, at the Teatro Liceo in Barcelona, with Marino Mancinelli conducting and Giuseppe Kaschmann in the title role. In the same 1884–85 Liceo season, he also sang Arturo in *Lucia di Lammermoor*, Rambaldo in *Roberto il diavolo*, Tebaldo in *I Capuleti e i Montecchi*, and Cossé in *Gli ugonotti*, and also a minor role in the premiere of Manuel Giró's *Il renegato Alonso Garcia*. Oxilia sang more performances of Laertes in March and May 1885, when the title role of Hamlet was sung by Victor Maurel (the Iago of Oxilia's Scala debut four years later). Even though young and inexperienced Oxilia had the opportunity to sing the same season the demanding role of Fernando in *La favorita*. It is unusual that a debutante gets a newspaper attention; Oxilia, however, was lucky when *Diario de Barcelona* published a review of *Roberto il diavolo*: "[I]t was not bad at all. Signor Oxilia who sang the role of Rambaldo and who was applauded and called to the proscenium after the fourth-act duet with Signor Vidal [Beltramo] . . . [2]

Oxilia later performed in Madrid, Naples, and Turin, finally reaching Brescia, where he was chosen to sing Otello in the above-mentioned Teatro Grande performance. He then contracted to join the La Scala company for the 1888–89 opera season, making his La Scala debut as Otello on February 19, 1889. The production was performed thirteen times that season and was conducted by Faccio with soprano Aurelia Cataneo as Desdemona and baritone Victor Maurel as Iago. Note that the inclusion of Maurel, the French baritone chosen by Verdi to create Iago two years earlier, was paramount to this cast. To sing Otello for the first time at La Scala with Maurel, an established singer and also an skillful actor, was extremely helpful for the young Oxilia. In the La Scala history of Carlo Gatti, Oxilia is mentioned as follows: "the recent and fine addition to the Theatre, the tenor Oxilia, who will experience a short but acclaimed career."[3]

It has been said that when Verdi later heard Oxilia sing, he thought the Uruguayan tenor quite suitable for the role, admiring his vocal and acting abilities. When Oxilia returned to his homeland in 1890, he was received as a hero. All of Montevideo's newspapers and musical magazines (particularly *Montevideo Musical*, the major music periodical at that time) dedicated long articles to his artistry. The public entertained great expectations when Oxilia debuted at the Solís in Donizetti's *La favorita* on June 3, 1890, along with so-prano Aurelia Kitzu as Leonora under the baton of Cavalliere Giuseppe Pomé-Penna.

Oxilia would be commended for all of his Solís performances, but his debut in *La favorita* met with extraordinary acclaim. When he sang "Spirto gentil" people did not merely applaud; they roared and yelled without cessation until he gave an encore. It happened again when he performed in *Otello* (fig. 19), and the final act was followed by endless curtain calls. His Desdemona, the nineteen-year-old soprano Giuseppina Serra, was also highly applauded, in part because her voice and youthful poise were so suitable for the role of the tragic young wife.

The morning after the Solís *Otello* the newspapers gushed with their typical fervor:

> Oxilia has arrived! The great expectations of the public have been exceeded by the talented Uruguayan tenor. It has already been proved to us that in the matter of Art, first comes truth and second, patriotism. So, nobody can call us conceited if we state that Oxilia was absolutely sublime in *Otello*. He sang the first act's love duet with sweetness in an incomparable "mezza voce." It was amazing how afterward he changed his mood to express with growing passion the doubts, torments, and fury called jealousy. At the final scene he killed himself in a theatrically new and dramatically efficient way. There are times when audiences tremble because they are afraid that dramatic artistry can "kill" the singer's vocal power. In Oxilia this didn't happen because he knows not only how to use his voice but also his histrionic power. The enraptured spectators applauded frantically.[4]

When the Teatro Solís completed its season for 1890, Oxilia sang several performances more at the Nuevo Politeama, also under Maestro Pomé-Penna.[5] He continued to sing

Fig. 19. Uruguayan tenor José Oxilia portraying Otello at the Solís on June 28, 1890, after his Teatro alla Scala debut in February 1889, also as Otello. Teatro Solís Collection.

at the Solís stage for two or three years more. Although it is unclear as to when he again left Uruguay, by 1895 he was back in Italy singing *Lucia*'s Edgardo at the Teatro Alfieri in the Piedmontese city of Asti. Because of his exceptional voice, Oxilia sang more in Europe than in his own country. Even if it was unfortunate for the opera lovers of his native land, it was an honor for Uruguay.

However, it was pathetic that Oxilia began to lose his voice in the middle of his life; as a consequence, he was unable to get a decent contract in Europe. He gave singing lessons in order to survive. Later he sold all his opera mementos, included a golden crown and some jewelry from his past glorious days. At

fifty-eight his life ended in poverty and despair, a few years after a failed suicide attempt, and at the very moment when the Uruguayan parliament was trying to pass a law to grant a pension to him. He died in Montevideo, on May 18, 1919, surrounded by his loving wife and family (the third of his five children was named Otello).[6] The man who was prized by Verdi and once the toast of La Scala was totally forgotten.

* * *

AS SOON AS the Italian Lyric Company left the Solís for the 1890 season, the house received the visit of the Budapest Hungarian National Orchestra, which played twice under Kiss Jancsi.[7] This company was then followed by an English opera and operetta company, which, under the management of Edwin Cleary, brought a repertory based on Gilbert and Sullivan productions. For the first time Solís operagoers experienced operetta in English, and their introduction was the most popular and delicious of Gilbert and Sullivan's oeuvre, *The Mikado*. When Nanki-Poo made his Uruguayan entrance on October 4, 1890, he brought this operetta to South America for the first time. *The Mikado* (in several performances) was followed by *The Pirates of Penzance* and *Trial by Jury*, also new to Solís audiences.

In August 1892, in less than twenty days, Solís operagoers discovered Pietro Mascagni's *L'amico Fritz*, Verdi's *Don Carlo*, and Wagner's *Lohengrin*. This same season presented them with the outstanding Neapolitan baritone Antonio Scotti, who later on held New York Metropolitan Opera House audiences in thrall for more than thirty consecutive years.

L'amico Fritz came to the Solís less than one year after its 1891 world premiere at the Teatro Costanzi in Rome. With *Cavalleria rusticana* had come unprecedented overnight fame, but this, Mascagni's second opera, was not so warmly received in Montevideo. The libretto was a sort of pastoral comedy, very different from *Cavalleria*'s earthy, violent passion. It was easier to move audiences with *Cavalleria*'s verismo and its dramatic Sicilian setting than with the pleasant Alsatian countryside and idyllic and lyric melodies of *L'amico*. Ten months after its disappointing Roman premiere, *L'amico* was performed at the Solís on August 17, 1892. With Arnaldo Conti conducting and twenty-six-year-old Scotti in the cast, the opera was reviewed by composer Antonio Camps as follows:

> *L'amico Fritz* will never enrapture audiences because no great passions exist in the plot. …I am afraid Mascagni has gone beyond the limits that music has been able to reach. Passing beyond these limits is only for the adventurous. There is no doubt that Mascagni was in a state of delirium when he wrote *L'amico Fritz*, for it can be the only explanation for choosing such an antimusical libretto.[8]

Interestingly, Camps recognized the possibility that the experimental music might be better appreciated at a later point in time, adding that he is "curious to know if in the future we might like this opera more than we do today."

It is fairly certain that the emotional impact of *Cavalleria*'s unrivaled success, when Mascagni was only twenty-six damaged his future as an opera composer. He was neither mature enough to live through such an experience, nor had he sufficient time for accruing musical experience and knowledge. To make matters worse, public expectations after *Cavalleria* were far beyond reason.

As mentioned, the season was rounded out by two other novelties for Montevideo, but neither Verdi's *Don Carlo* nor Wagner's *Lohengrin* brought much excitement to Solís au-

diences. Montevideo opera fans already knew these works, composed more than thirty years earlier, through vocal and instrumental concerts and piano scores. Certainly they could not be considered new and different, even in their first stage productions.

A singular and exciting event was found elsewhere, with the theater's first technical modifications since its opening in 1856. The first sign of the approaching twentieth century arrived in brilliant fashion when, on September 19, 1893, the house and stage were lighted by electricity for the first time. Electric bulbs now replaced the old gaslit central chandelier, crystal lamps, and footlights. The first performance to be thus illuminated on the Solís stage was not grand opera but Spanish zarzuela, with the Avelino Aguirre Company in the bizarrely named *El rey que rabió* (The king who got rabies).

* * *

EARLY IN JULY 1894 the Uruguayan newspapers began to publish daily announcements of the approaching debut of an Italian lyric company under the general direction of the Italian conductor and composer Commendatore Edoardo Mascheroni. Chief conductor at La Scala, Mascheroni was one of the first truly notable musicians to conduct opera performances at the Teatro Solís. Only thirty-nine at the time of his La Scala appointment, he had achieved this leading position with the support, among others, of Verdi and Arrigo Boito. There he conducted the world premieres of Verdi's *Falstaff* and Alfredo Catalani's *La Wally*. In addition, *Manon Lescaut*, *La bohème*, *Fidelio*, *Tannhäuser*, and *Der fliegende Holländer* were all introduced to Rome under his baton.

Mascheroni's Lyric Company debuted at the Solís on August 11, 1894, with Wagner's *Lohengrin*. The company also announced a

Fig. 20. Two Uruguayan premieres in 1894. *Left*: Program of Verdi's *Falstaff*. *Right*: Wagner's *Tannhäuser*, program with picture of soprano Teresa Arkel. Author's collection.

season with three new operas for Montevideo: Puccini's *Manon Lescaut*, Verdi's *Falstaff*, and Wagner's *Tannhäuser* (fig. 20). Besides Mascheroni, the company's roster included twenty soloists, a sixty-member chorus, a twenty-dancer ensemble, as well as its own music band, chorus master, and stage director and choreographer. The Solís' own orchestra was enlarged to eighty musicians when augmented by Mascheroni's. Never before had the Solís seen such a stellar company.

The management of the Ferrari Company offered several advance subscription series with a price range between 5 pesos to 0.80 centésimos for a single performance. It was the highest-priced ticket a Montevideo operagoer had yet paid, two and a half times the prices to which the audience was accustomed.

Puccini's *Manon Lescaut* with Elisa Petri in the title role and Giuseppe Cremonini as Des Grieux was first performed under Mascheroni's baton at the Solís on August 14. This was the first acquaintance with Puccini's music that Montevideo audiences had made, and a few days after *Manon*'s Montevideo premiere a multicolumn review appeared in *El Día*. Excerpts from this review indicate high praise:

> We can divide [*Manon Lescaut*] into two different parts: before and after the second act, second scene. In the first part the music is gay, light and coquettish, as in the "first" *Manon* [i.e., Massenet's]; the second part, passionate and moving, becomes very pathetic at the end. Puccini has reached the perfect balance between two dangerous extremes: the exaggeration of pure melody and lack of it. The whole opera looks like one single musical idea divided into four acts, so that the musical fragments are related to each other. This is far from saying that Puccini repeats or copies himself; on the contrary, we like the recurrent motifs for each character, so that the same musical idea

alerts the spectator to the character even before his or her entrance.[9]

Petri is acclaimed as one "born to play this role," while Maestro Mascheroni is also duly applauded.

There were numerous curtain calls for the artists of this *Manon Lescaut*. The review demonstrates a mature understanding of the Puccini opera and its style. *Manon Lescaut* had been a great success since its first production at Turin's Teatro Regio in February 1893. Puccini's third opera, it was the first one for which the composer chose the topic and practically wrote his own libretto. In his *Manon Lescaut* Puccini was able to incorporate all the concepts and characteristics he had developed regarding opera: the importance of the libretto; his new harmonic language (almost Wagnerian in some scenes), plus his use of parallel fifths (even before they were used by the French Impressionists prior to Debussy); the use of leitmotifs; the heroine—sometimes guilty and fragile—who dies for love and is the center of the plot; and finally, the treatment of the chorus as a vital personage of the drama (e.g., *Manon*'s embarkation scene in act 3). On the occasion of Covent Garden's first production, exactly three months before the opera's Solís premiere, then music critic George Bernard Shaw remarked "Puccini looks to me more like the heir of Verdi than any of his rivals."[10]

As the century drew to its close, the period between an opera's world premiere and its first performance in South America diminished considerably. Usually these South American premieres took place in Buenos Aires, which was the first stop on the circuit. After Buenos Aires the company generally, but not always, proceeded to Montevideo and sometimes Brazil. The Teatro Solís now had the prestige of a leading opera house, and more than once the Solís audience had the same conductor or leading singer as had appeared in the opera's world premiere.[11] Verdi's *Falstaff* was conducted at its 1893 Milan premiere and at the Solís, one year later, by Mascheroni. The Milanese conductor gave the Solís' first performance of Verdi's last opera on August 21, 1894, so that Montevideo audiences knew *Falstaff* even before it reached the Metropolitan in New York. This was an outgrowth of Verdi's planning: the composer had not only asked Mascheroni to be *Falstaff's* conductor for its La Scala premiere, but had entrusted him with many opera performances in Italy and overseas. Because of this close composer-conductor relationship, Verdi used to call Mascheroni "*Falstaff's* third author" (the second one being the librettist, Boito).

> *Falstaff* was received in Montevideo with surprise and admiration: We came back from the Solís in a most excited state. Why? The reader asks. Wasn't it a comic opera? Yes, but the funny and the witty could also be cause for enthusiasm for anyone with heart and brains. The opera is admirable, and the stage production was done with such precision, harmonic design, and perfect sense of ensemble that we do not believe it could be better done in Europe, before the pot-bellied rascal decided to sail, exposing himself to the ocean storms, and come to America. . . .
>
> The illustrious Maestro [Verdi] has made much more evident the evolution he barely started with *Aida* and increased in *Otello*. He has become a master of instrumentation without leaving his old melodic sense. So wisely is everything combined here that the result is really a masterpiece.[12]

A different, equally extensive, review provided more detailed musical analysis:

> Verdi broke the old patterns of the *opera buffa*, designing a true comedy with all the

resources of musical science going toward a new style. The Rossinian style, previously fashionable, has disappeared, maybe forever. Verdi does not write either romanzas or cavatinas; his total new music is a continuous musical phrase that closely follows the intention of the words, discovering and supporting the action with a wise and simple orchestration. . . . One of *Falstaff's* high points appears in the first scene with a sort of *duetto* between piccolo and cellos—four octaves apart—that underlines "Se Falstaff s'assottiglia." Also remarkable is the beautiful fugue at the opera's end. It is a pity that it was almost unnoticed by some of the spectators, because it was one of the better moments, if not the best! The public did not quite appreciate this and other masterly musical passages; perhaps a second performance will help them to better understand this marvelous opera. . . . Our warm congratulations to Maestro Mascheroni, for we are sure that the *Falstaff* we heard is the interpretation Verdi asked for. Scotti has been immersed in the spirit of the complex Shakespearian character and translated it with realism and vocal expressiveness.[13]

This second review shows a far more professional musical approach than does the first, and provides us with a perspective by which to see which concepts remain after more than ninety years, and which have changed. The Rossinian style is not only still alive; we are now in the midst of a revival of his more rarely produced operas, with *Maometto II*, *Mosè in Egitto*, and others being given as part of the current vogue of producing lesser known works throughout the opera repertoire. In addition to the Rossini Opera Festival held in his birthplace of Pesaro (instituted in 1980 by the town council of Pesaro) many concerts, in the Americas and Europe, contain a good portion of Rossini's works on their programs.

Two days after *Falstaff*, Mascheroni conducted the third new opera of the season, the Solís premiere of Wagner's *Tannhäuser*, on August 23, 1894. Mascheroni, like Toscanini, had championed Wagner in Italy, when Wagner was being sung exclusively by Italian opera companies throughout the Ibero-American countries and leading Italian opera houses.[14]

Teresa Arkel, the excellent dramatic soprano who had opened the 1894 Solís season with *Lohengrin*, was a *Tannhäuser* heroine as well. The title role was sung by Benedetto Lucignani, with Scotti as Wolfram. Both of Arkel's performances were reviewed, beginning with her portrayal of *Lohengrin*'s Elsa:

> La Arkel is a notable singer, not only for her exceptional voice, but for what she invested in her roles. She reached such an artistic and musical pinnacle on Saturday night [August 11, 1894] that we can without doubt be assured that for many years we will not hear so outstanding an interpretation of the romantic and difficult role of Elsa in this house.[15]

Two weeks later another music critic wrote about *Tannhäuser*'s first performance:

> Maestro Mascheroni! Thank you! Thank you very much! Last night we felt as though possessed! All the mystic, the terrible, the sublime of *Tannhäuser* have been a revelation to us through the magic power of your baton! . . . It will be difficult to find another Wagnerian interpreter like Teresa Arkel. Yesterday Saint Elizabeth was the twin sister of Elsa's a few days ago. She sang again without any effort, with a tender and mystic mood in a vocal and artistic way whose secret only the great artists have.[16]

Three years earlier (in 1891) Arkel had been invited to sing Venus in the La Scala first performance of *Tannhäuser*. Since that time, and in spite of being from German extraction, she sang all the Wagnerian heroine roles in Italian. Arkel was also known for her Desdemona opposite Tamagno's Otello and for her performance in Bellini's *Norma*.

* * *

ON A VERY DIFFERENT LEVEL, we must mention another Solís premiere because of its phenomenal triumph. *La verbena de la paloma* (The Feast of Our Lady of the Dove), a popular Spanish zarzuela by Tomás Bretón, was first performed at Madrid's Teatro Apolo on February 19, 1894, by the Julián Romea Company, and the same artists who brought Bretón's zarzuela to Montevideo only a few months later. This work belongs to the *género chico*, as the one-act zarzuelas are known, and is the most popular of this musical genre, not only in Spanish-speaking countries, but worldwide.

Dealing with popular life in Madrid, *La verbena* has a habanera concertante— "¿Dónde vas con mantón de Manila?" (Where are you going with that shawl from Manila?)— that turned out to be one of the catchiest tunes in musical history. Merely to hum this melody awakens an immediate response in anyone who knows anything about Spain or Spanish music. It has been told in contemporary chronicles that when *La verbena* was first performed at the Solís, all the house people, from the management to the stagehands, hummed the popular tune all day long. The public success was so great than the Romea Company gave fifty consecutive sold-out performances. However many other Bretón works (such as his opera *La Dolores*) were performed at the Solís, none of his nine operas could reach this zarzuela's popularity.[17]

Bretón, a pupil of Emilio Arrieta at the Madrid Conservatory, was a champion of Spanish musical nationalism his entire life, and very active in the pursuit of his ideal. He fought hard against the Spanish composers who used Italian librettos and the monopoly of Italian singers over Madrid's Teatro Real. His active campaign culminated with the presentation to the First Artistic Congress, held in Madrid in 1919, of a motion in favor of the creation of a National Lyric Theatre. By this time Bretón enjoyed immense prestige in Spain and abroad, both as composer and conductor. When he died in Madrid four years later at age seventy-three, he was particularly admired by the young generation of Spanish composers. Conrado del Campo, Jesús Guridi, Manuel de Falla, Oscar Esplá, Manuel Penella, and Federico Moreno Torroba were all committed to furthering Spanish opera.

CHAPTER 12

1895–1897

La bohème Premiere with Hariclea Darclée and Emilio De Marchi—
Francesco Tamagno Singing Otello—An Ideal Werther: Fernando De Lucia—
Edoardo Mascheroni Conducts Seven New Operas—
Florencio Constantino's Debut

As the nineteenth century drew to a close, with every passing year more and more first-rate artists came to the Teatro Solís to sing the leading roles. Emilio De Marchi first arrived in 1895, Hariclea Darclée in 1896, and in the same season, Francesco Tamagno once again, this time at the peak of his fame. The year 1897 welcomed one of the most brilliant tenors, Fernando De Lucia.

It was the 1896 season that introduced Montevideo to La bohème, an opera of such enduring fame and popularity that it is amusing to read the New York Times music critic's comment: "Nevertheless, we cannot believe that there is permanent success for an opera constructed as this one is."[1] When W. J. Henderson wrote this one day after La bohème's first Metropolitan Opera performance he hardly was clairvoyant! Today, almost one century later, La bohème, together with Carmen and Aida, are the three most popular and frequently performed operas in the world. Of

course, Henderson might have known that the 1896 Turin premiere of La bohème was not an immediate success. But he wrote this review four years later, when the opera was already beginning to build its reputation, and his claim was soon proved faulty.

When Edoardo Mascheroni conducted the first Uruguayan performance of La bohème at the Solís on August 1, 1896, exactly six months after the Turin premiere, it was a tremendous success. The critics' reviews were glowing, which raises questions about these greatly different responses. Could it be possible that Montevideo audiences were more capable of judging and accepting La bohème's musical merits than was the "distinguished" New York City critic W. J. Henderson? Why was he so far off the mark? A different perception is shown in the reviews published after the Solís premiere. From one of them:

The first performance of the last Puccini score has been a significant musical event.

Fig. 21. Hariclea Darclée, who debuted at the So-lís in 1896, and sang Mimì in the first Uruguayan performance of Puccini's *La bohème*, on August 1 of that year. Picture from a 1903 Solís program. Author's collection.

Singers, conductor, orchestra, "mise en scène"—everyone contributed to make a masterly interpretation of the new opera that we call a "capolavoro" [a masterpiece]. . . . In fact, *La bohème*, more than being an opera written by a new, young, talented composer in the beginning of his celebrity, looks like the mature fruit of an experienced maestro, and vindicates those who ever since *Manon Lescaut* foresaw that Puccini would be the heir of the Italian lyric art.[2]

In the opening paragraph of his review, another Uruguayan music critic gives us a synthesis of his reactions to the first performance: "*La bohème* is extraordinarily interesting for its originality, for the strange pattern of all its musical parts, and for its surprising and new effects—everything in the midst of a new textured harmony." Commenting on *La bohème*'s cast, he continues: "La Darclée was a sensitive and charming Mimì, with extraordinary dra-

matic skills. Her last scene, particularly, had a heartbreaking melody that touched profoundly the Solís' audience."[3]

If there are some special reasons for the opera's Solís success it could be the exceptional cast—headed by Darclée and De Marchi—who sang this *La bohème*. Four years later, these same artists would be chosen by Giacomo Puccini to give the world premiere of *Tosca* at the Teatro Costanzi in Rome. In addition to having a superior voice—characterized by excellent technique, power, sweetness, and a great versatility—the Romanian soprano was famous for her beauty, elegance, and poise on the stage (fig 21).

It also becomes clear when reading the Montevideo reviews that the Solís audiences accepted *La bohème*'s novelty, and the music critics were not frightened by the famous progression of parallel fifths at the beginning of act 3 or the unresolved dissonances or the augmented triads, so greatly criticized by conservative theoreticians in Italy who did not consider this new opera a masterpiece.

After this successful *La bohème*, Solís audiences were treated to Tamagno's starring roles in two productions, *Aida* and *Otello*. Of his *Aida* (sung with Darclée), a critic said:

It is very difficult to include in only one review the greatness of last night's performance [August 6, 1896]. Everything was perfect: singers, conductor, orchestra, "mise en scène," everything, without one single mistake. La Darclée's singing surpassed even her best admirers' expectations. And Tamagno . . . ! We were especially surprised by the sweetness and pianissimo with which he sang *Aida*'s final scene. Hard to believe! Finally, the enthusiasm reached such a point that women almost began applauding![4]

This last comment reveals the etiquette of theater attendance at the time: if a lady expressed her enthusiasm by applauding, she was in danger of losing her reputation!

Otello's review is also very impressive, with a reminder that the Solís audience was hearing the tenor chosen by Giuseppe Verdi to premiere his opera. Of Tamagno's performance as the Moor one critic wrote that:

> Last night's performance was sensational. In addition to the interest generated by the fact that this great Verdi work had not been heard here for almost three years, there was immense anticipation to hear Tamagno's Otello, *the* Otello of worldwide fame. Last night's performance did not disappoint. Tamagno enunciated each phrase, especially the culminating moments of the opera, in a way we had never heard before, in these moments proving once again that only he can sing Otello as its composer had envisioned it. His is an extraordinary art and vigor that only he is able to master.[5]

In addition to these two performances Tamagno received a grand ovation after singing the "Hymn of Triumph" from the third act of Meyerbeer's *Il profeta*, another of his favorite roles, in a performance of that opera on July 25. Anyone seeing Tamagno's vitality and strength at the age of forty-six, and hearing his famous trumpetlike top notes and ringing voice would never think he had only five more years of singing before him, and that he would pass away in 1905. The greatest *tenore di forza* of his day, he left the arena to an up-and-coming young tenor: Enrico Caruso.[6]

The memorable 1896 Solís season ended with two tributes. First, Darclée was feted on the night of her benefit, the *serata d'onore* as it was called. In a tradition going back to the eighteenth century and still alive in the closing years of the nineteenth, it was customary to give special performances, usually two or three at the end of each company season, in which the proceeds went to the stars and sometimes to the orchestra conductors. In a ceremony that followed the evening's opera, and that assured a sold-out house, operagoers came prepared with various tributes, such as chocolate bouquets or flowers. The pageantry was long remembered by my grandparents, who used to reminisce of those glorious Teatro Solís days.

When Darclée finished singing *La traviata* on the night of her benefit—in a performance that ended with a shower of flowers at her feet—she parted the Solís curtains and walked out onto the apron of the stage. There she graciously received her presents—Tamagno's offering of a golden bracelet with an onyx cameo representing Aida's profile; tenor De Marchi's setting a pearl-and-diamond diadem upon her head; and impresario Ferrari's wife presenting her with a pearl-and-diamond ring. These munificent gifts were further embellished by dozens of other tokens, as well as flowers, plaques, laurel wreathes, and so on, according to the chronicler's quaint and seemingly endless list.[7]

The second tribute took place two days after the season's end, and was a farewell concert in honor of conductor Mascheroni. This took place at the Liceo Musical Franz Liszt, the prestigious musical institution headed by pianists Camilo [Camillo] Giucci and Luisa Gallo de Giucci. After a concert given by all of Montevideo's principal musicians, there was a reception in which Maestro Mascheroni was presented with numerous presents.

*   *   *

THE 1897 SEASON at the Teatro Solís had four remarkable singers and four new operas that received their first Uruguayan performances. For the first time Solís operagoers heard soprano Cesira Ferrani, tenor Fernando De Lucia, and baritone Mario Sammarco.

Four years prior to her arrival in Montevideo, Ferrani had created Manon Lescaut at its 1893 world premiere and *La bohème*'s Mimì in 1896. At the Solís, Ferrani's partner was Neapolitan tenor De Lucia. After a successful debut as Faust[8] when only twenty-five years old, De Lucia had what would be his only New York Metropolitan season in 1893–94. When he came to the Solís three years later, he was preceded by a respectable reputation in the opera world. But Faust was not his only acclaimed role: Met and Solís audiences heard him in his second specialty, as the Conte di Almaviva in Rossini's *Barbiere*, one of the warhorses of his youth. Celebrated as a *tenore di grazia*, particularly in this role, from 1890 onward De Lucia sang the new verismo repertoire, and his fame grew up around the fiery roles of Turiddu and Canio. His choice of roles at the Solís indicates a more eclectic repertory, where he took advantage of his outstanding vocal qualities: a bright enunciation and a wide range of nuances paired with an excellent technique.

Technique alone was not responsible for his popularity. Some years ago I knew two ladies, then in their nineties, who had both seen De Lucia. When I asked about their memories of his performances, both had the same answer: a deep sigh followed by "Oh! you cannot imagine how handsome he was!" They added, "You know, at the Solís he sang Werther, Rodolfo, and Des Grieux." Of course, the most romantic roles of the opera repertoire!

When De Lucia and Ferrani sang *Werther* on August 28, 1897, at the Solís, Jules Massenet's opera was only five years old. Yet some of the novelties of early twentieth-century music were beginning to show: the dissolution of formal melodic structures and *recitativo accompagnato*, for example. The appearance of chromatic modulating phrases, in particular to underline the moments of heightened tension, is another of *Werther*'s characteristics. According to newspaper reviews, De Lucia received a standing ovation after the third act's "Ah! Non mi ridestar" and so he encored it.

A few days before *Werther*'s premiere Solís audiences had heard another Uruguayan premiere of the 1897 season: Umberto Giordano's *Andrea Chénier*. Although not of the caliber of a Verdi or Puccini opera, it was enthusiastically received, perhaps because of its patriotic and emotional fervor. Stylistically, some moments of *Andrea Chénier* came very close to the new verismo style then in fashion. Two arias, totally different in intention and mood, got the attention of the public. In act 3, Sammarco was soundly applauded for "Nemico della patria?" an aria often compared to another emotionally heavy aria for baritone: *Pagliacci*'s prologue. Also well received was the famous act 4 tenor aria, "Come un bel dì di maggio," sung by Michele Mariacher. Sammarco had another success a few days later when he sang a memorable *Manon Lescaut* with Ferrani and De Lucia. Sammarco had debuted at La Scala one year earlier (1896), but it was later that he achieved fame when he created Cascart in Leoncavallo's *Zazà* at Milan's Teatro Lirico in 1900, and Carlo Worms in Alberto Franchetti's *Germania* world premiere in 1902.

The end of the 1897 season introduced Montevideo audiences to another new opera: Amilcare Ponchielli's *Il figliuol prodigo*. First performed at Milan's La Scala in 1880, the Solís production gave theatergoers the opportunity to appreciate mezzo Virginia Guerrini as Nefte. The creator of Afra in Catalani's *La Wally* world premiere (La Scala, 1892), Guerrini was very talented and one of Verdi's favorites (she had sung in *Falstaff*'s 1893 premiere). She debuted at the Solís in 1895 and visited many times, among them the memorable 1903 season with Arturo Toscanini.

* * *

ARTURO BERUTTI WAS THE FIRST Argentinean composer to write opera with South
American settings, although formally his
works are purely classical and technically belong to European harmony. When twenty-
two, he left Argentina and entered the Leipzig
Conservatory to study with Carl Reinecke and
Salomon Jadassohn. Continuing his studies of
Argentinean native subjects, he moved to Berlin, where he wrote symphonic pieces. After
passing through Paris he finally settled in
Milan, having decided to be an opera com-
poser, and all his works from this period re-
ceived their premieres in Italy. Most were a
re-creation of native stories, although *Taras
Bulba*, an opera first performed at the Teatro
Regio in Turin on March 9, 1895, has a plot
based on the 1600 Cossack war against the
Polish. In the same year, following its Buenos
Aires premiere, *Taras Bulba* was given at the
Teatro Solís, on August 22, 1895, by such fine
singers as baritone Edoardo Camera as Taras
Bulba, tenor De Marchi, soprano Emilia
Corsi, mezzo Guerrini, and bass Remo Ercolani. The reviews were lukewarm, but all
agreed on the strength of the performance
and the splendor of the scenery.

Two seasons after *Taras Bulba*, a second
Berutti opera arrived. The first Argentinean
operatic work written essentially with native
roots, *Pampa*'s plot was based on Eduardo
Gutiérrez's play *Juan Moreira*, a story of the
adventures of a gaucho of the Argentinean
pampas. Solís premiered *Pampa* on September 1, 1897, with soprano Carmen Bonaplata,
tenor Mariacher, and baritone Sammarco under Mascheroni's baton, and with scenery
painted by the Argentinean painter Ballerini.
Unfortunately, however enticing the story and
excellent the cast and conductor, the opera
suffered a kind of dislocation. As the critics
perceived; "The music is inspired, but it isn't

appropriate for this drama. . . . This looks like
a native drama written by a foreigner, and its
totally European style disappointed us."[9]

Evidently, neither the public nor the critics
could stomach any longer those operas that
combined a European style with a native plot.
Thirty years earlier the romantic idealization
of indigenous music in *Il Guarany* (1870) had
been a success, but Indians singing in Italian
were no longer acceptable.[10]

* * *

A DIFFERENT KIND OF EXCITEMENT in this
time of plenty was created when the Teatro
Solís presented the first Uruguayan performance of a Spanish regional opera, Tomás
Bretón's *La Dolores*. Its 1895 Madrid world
premiere had been an immediate success,
with 66 consecutive performances in Madrid
and 112 in Barcelona. Its success did not stop
in Spain; it was later given in Milan and even
in Prague. *La Dolores* was soon performed
throughout Latin America, with its peak performance in a Mexico City bullring in 1923,
when the leading role of Lázaro was sung by
the then-celebrated tenor Miguel Fleta.

Unlike the Bretón zarzuela *La verbena de
la paloma* (see chapter 11), *La Dolores* develops
in an atmosphere of drama. Dolores, a young
maid at an inn in Calatayud, has three suitors,
one of whom brags unseemingly about enjoying her favors. Lázaro, a young theological
student, secretly in love with Dolores, kills the
braggart to protect her, and she, in turn, takes
the blame to save him. Nevertheless, Lázaro
confesses to the crime as vengeance for the
villain's having dishonored Dolores.

Even with so dramatic a plot, the opera
demonstrates universal characteristics of
Spanish music and life: there is a continuous
dualism between life and death, joy and sorrow, light and dark. Stereotypically, life for
Spaniards has these sudden cataclysms; no
Spanish play, novel, piece of art, or music

does not contain this contrast. And so, as had already happened with *La verbena*'s "habanera concertante," people began to hum and sing Bretón's opera, particularly the famous lines, "Si vas a Calatayud / pregunta por La Dolores" (If you go to Calatayud / ask for La Dolores . . .).

While *La verbena de la paloma* concludes happily, and *La Dolores* ends in darkness, the songs and dances of both are similar in spirit, with the color of local life in the Spanish villages and cities. Both works lent themselves to being remembered and hummed, and within days after *La Dolores*' Montevideo premiere, it was heard in streets throughout the city.

This production of *La Dolores* was performed by a lyric company of Italian singers brought by the Pastor Opera Company, with Maestro Francisco L. Máiquez as conductor. The Montevideo premiere was on February 6, 1896, with the title role sung by Spanish soprano Amalia Bourman and the character of Lázaro by tenor Leopoldo Signoretti. It was emphasized that "the artists made a great effort to sing the opera in Spanish."[11]

On February 11 Lázaro was sung by tenor Florencio Constantino in his stage debut.[12] This twenty-seven-year-old Spaniard had been a farmer until seven months previously, and had briefly studied with Signoretti in Buenos Aires.[13] He debuted on June 6, 1895, with a concert at "La Colmena Artística," a club in Buenos Aires. While there, he sang also at the Club Español and in several soirées given by prominent families of Buenos Aires society. After one last concert at the Teatro Argentino in La Plata, on December 28, 1895, Constantino proceeded to Montevideo, where four days before his stage debut at the Solís he sang arias from *La favorita* and *La Gioconda*, plus a selection of popular Spanish songs in a concert at the Club Español, on February 7.[14] Within a few years his fame had grown, and when he returned to Montevideo in 1903 it was under Toscanini's baton and singing Massenet's *Griselda* (see chapter 16, and 1903 chronology). In 1896 a Montevideo critic had anticipated his future in this review of *La Dolores*:

> The novelty of last evening at the Solís was the debut of the tenor Florencio Constantino. Few tenors who stride the stage for the first time, and in front of a full house, have received such spontaneous applause as did this artist. While some singing was obscured by moments of stage fright, veiling somewhat the sweetness, beauty, and freshness of his voice, we anticipate that with hard study and dedication, one day our public will applaud him as a great artist.[15]

In addition to the above-mentioned 1903 season Constantino was back twice in Montevideo. He sang in 1909 at the Teatro Urquiza, first on August 24, in a production of *Aida* with Eugenia Burzio, Elisa Petri and Giuseppe de Luca conducted by Luigi Mancinelli; and afterward in 1911 *Rigoletto* with María Barrientos, Titta Ruffo, and Nazzareno de Angelis, under Edoardo Vitale at the same house.[16]

1898–1899

Montevideo and Its New Theaters—Luisa Tetrazzini—
Two *Bohèmes* and a Young Conductor: Giorgio Polacco—
Regina Pacini—Luis Sambucetti's *Suite d'orchestre*

As the nineteenth century came to an end, Montevideo grew in population and culture, becoming the home of several theaters. Big and small houses were built; some endured many years, others had short lives. As happened in those days, many were destroyed by conflagrations, and others, victims of progress, were demolished to make room for new constructions.

Between 1856 and 1914 twenty-two new houses were opened in Montevideo; only a few of them, however, can be considered, in both architectural and cultural senses, as major theaters. The Teatro Cibils, inaugurated in 1871, was destroyed by fire in 1912. The Nuevo Teatro San Felipe—built on the same site of the old Casa de Comedias—opened in 1880, and was demolished in 1909 to erect the Palacio Taranco, actually a branch of the Ministry of Culture and Education. The Teatro Nuevo Politeama, inaugurated in 1889, had only six years of life, and following the Cibils' destiny was destroyed by flames. These three prestigious medium-size houses shared, more than once, artists who came to the Solís.

The Teatro Stella d'Italia, founded by Italians in 1895, was a small, pretty house with a character of its own. Enduring more than eighty years, its stage witnessed every imaginable performance, from opera to comedy, from soap opera and radio programs to movie houses, and even the onstage marriage celebration of an actress.

The Teatro Politeama, which opened at the beginning of the twentieth century (in 1901), burned down the last day of 1919.

In 1905 the second important Montevidean theater was inaugurated: the Teatro Urquiza. With a capacity of around three thousand seats, it attracted first-rate opera and drama companies, and even competed with the Solís for a while. (For further discussion of this theater, see chapters 17, 24, and 26.) Another comfortable house was the Teatro 18 de Julio (opened in 1910), which was for almost fifty years the setting for important music recitals, for Spanish zarzuela and comedy companies. Years afterward, it was transformed into a cinema.

* * *

AS THEY ONCE DID with Carlotta and Adelina Patti (in 1870 and 1888, respectively), Montevideo and the Teatro Solís once again hosted a famous pair of sisters. The first to arrive was Eva Tetrazzini, who sang in 1885 at the Teatro Solís, and then in 1886 and 1889 at the Teatro Cibils. Then in 1894 came her younger sister, Luisa (who would eventually become the more famous of the two) who sang at the Teatro Nuevo Politeama. Luisa returned in 1898 to sing at the Teatro Solís. It is interesting to note the significance of the Italian opera seasons in the Cibils and the Nuevo Politeama. Both acquired top-quality singers, mainly from 1886 to 1894, many times, the same that performed during those years at the Solís stage.

Only twenty-seven at the time, Luisa Tetrazzini had debuted eight years earlier in her native city of Florence, singing Inez in Meyerbeer's *L'africana*. *Lucia di Lammermoor* was the opera she chose for her Solís debut on August 24, 1898, of which reviewers remarked that her technical gifts were already of the highest order. She dazzled the public with the extraordinary agility of her chromatic scales and her warm, clarinetlike tone:

> Tetrazzini . . . has a beautiful tonal emission and a marvelous agility. . . . [Her] art has been improved by her interpretive feeling, where she puts all her warmth and expressiveness into each note. With the rondo she was given a huge ovation, and with prodigious agility she finished the famous cadenza with admirable assurance. In our memory, only Patti was capable of such singing, especially in these clean and clear top notes.[1]

While Luisa was still developing vocally, she already possessed the qualities that allowed her to become a world celebrity by 1907, and to remain in her prime until the early 1920s. People who followed her career after that Solís season have told me how amazingly her voice developed until reaching its peak in the years between 1907 and 1916. During that time she came back to Montevideo, in August 1907, to sing Lucia and Rosina at the Teatro Urquiza (see chapter 19).

After her *Lucia* debut under the baton of Riccardo Bonicioli, Luisa Tetrazzini sang in almost all performances of that 1898 Teatro Solís season, doing Rosina, Gilda, Margherita in *Faust*, the *Fra diavolo* Zerlina, Elvira in *I puritani*, and Violetta.

The last year of the nineteenth century found the Teatro Solís especially busy. In addition to two opera seasons with two different companies, and the arrival of soprano Regina Pacini and conductor Giorgio Polacco, there were important recitals and one Uruguayan symphonic world premiere. On March 4, 1899, Polacco's company debuted with *La Gioconda* and performed throughout the month, bringing Montevideo theatergoers two new and different works: an opera and an oratorio. Two days after a performance of Puccini's *La bohème* on March 9, Polacco conducted the "other" *La bohème*, Leoncavallo's opera. With a world premiere one year after Puccini's blockbuster, the competition between the two versions was to Leoncavallo's disadvantage. The same singers were cast in both performances, but because the characters correspond to different vocal tessitura in each opera, tenor Elvino Ventura sang Rodolfo in Puccini and Marcello in Leoncavallo; such role reversals were consistent throughout the entire cast of characters. When Montevideo newspapers reported on the "new" *Bohème*, the emphasis was on how Leoncavallo's opera more faithfully followed the original Henri Murger novel, *Scènes de la vie de bohème*, than did Puccini's.

The short first season was marked by the first Uruguayan performance of Lorenzo Perosi's oratorio *La risurrezione di Lazzaro*, on March 24, 1899—one year after the composer was appointed music director of the Sistine Chapel in Rome. Parallel to his career as composer of church music, Father Perosi was becoming an internationally known conductor of his own oratorios. The success of *La risurrezione di Lazzaro* was so great that Maestro Polacco decided to repeat the performance. As the Teatro Solís was already booked, the second performance was held (the next day) at the auditorium of the Catholic Club with the same soloists, choir, and orchestra of the Italian opera company. As at the Solís performance, Polacco conducted the Prologue to *Mefistofele* prior to the oratorio. It is remarkable that the weight of this successful short season was on the shoulders of a twenty-six-year-old conductor. Even more amazing is that Polacco had been conducting since he was seventeen and an assistant conductor at London's Covent Garden.

*   *   *

WHEN THE 1899 SOLÍS list of singers was published in early autumn 1898, Montevideo newspapers carried announcements of "the two great surprises of the coming season: Pacini and De Segurola." Maestro Arnaldo Conti, a favorite with Teatro Solís audiences, returned at the beginning of July 1899 as musical director and conductor of the second opera season of that year.

After the opening night of *Aida*, the new artist everybody had been waiting for arrived. Born in Portugal, Regina Pacini had debuted at barely seventeen years of age as Amina in *La sonnambula* in Lisbon's San Carlos. Pacini's 1899 Solís season took place almost eleven years after this event, and audience enthusi-

asm had grown accordingly with her developing talents. Following her Solís success in *Lucia di Lammermoor*, her performance as *Il barbiere di Siviglia*'s Rosina the following week met with even greater acclaim. I have been told that by the time Pacini had finished the delicious cavatina "Una voce poco fa," the audience's ovation was ringing throughout the house. In addition to her excellent singing technique, vocal agility, and easy handling of all the coloratura embellishments, Pacini had an extraordinary combination of beauty, charm, and a sharp and amusing personality, very much like the wily character of Rosina. The daughter of an Andalusian mother, Regina belonged (on her father's side) to an old and noble Roman family with an extensive musical background; her father was Pietro Andrea Giorgi Pacini who, in addition to being an actor and a well-known baritone, was also tied to the history of the Teatro San Carlo in Naples as impresario and director. But what is almost unknown is that the brother of her grandfather Luigi (a basso buffo) was Giovanni Pacini—one of the most prolific opera composers in the first half of the nineteenth century.[2]

The day after Pacini's ravishing performance, Montevideo newspapers competed for the distinction of publishing the best review. The most striking was written by "Suplente," the nom de plume of well-known author and playwright Samuel Blixen:

> For me La Pacini—with all the prodigiousness of her vocalizations, all the magic of her singing, all her pearl-like notes—would be another excellent Rosina, as are many divas around the opera stage. But no one can match "her" Rosina, with all the Andalusian sun in her eyes and all the "salero" of her smiling. . . . [If] as an artist and singer she is portentous, as an Andalusian Rosina from Seville she is at the pinnacle.[3]

Fig. 22. Spanish maestro Manuel Pérez-Badía, who conducted the Solís orchestra, and founded and conducted the Orquesta de la Sociedad Beethoven until his death, in 1901. Author's collection.

Pacini's performance was also complemented by the presence of baritone Guglielmo Caruson, one of the best Figaros of the day. During the rest of that 1899 Solís season, in addition to repeat performances as Lucia and Rosina, Pacini sang Margherita de Valois in *Gli ugonotti*, Elvira in *I puritani*, Gilda, and Amina.

World fame came quickly to Pacini, and after leaving Montevideo she performed in all the leading opera houses. During the 1902 Covent Garden season she again sang Lucia, this time with a young Caruso at the beginning of his career: "On June 4 [1902] [Caruso] sang the role of Edgardo in *Lucia di Lammermoor*. The dramatic role of the heroine, sung by the Portuguese soprano Regina Pacini . . . dominated the evening and Pacini's success was tremendous."[4]

In 1907 Pacini retired from the stage to marry the man who in 1922 would become president of Argentina: Dr. Marcelo T. de Alvear. From that time on she sang only in ben-

efit and social concerts. Nevertheless, as first lady she worked hard for artists' welfare, organizing and founding in 1938 La Casa del Teatro, a house for needy, retired, and sick actors and singers, an institution similar to Verdi's Casa di Riposo per Musicisti in Milan. Until her death in 1965, at ninety-four, Pacini remained greatly attached to Argentinean cultural and musical life, and was always concerned about the career of many musicians in her adopted country.

The other eagerly awaited singer of the season was Spanish bass Andrés Perelló de Segurola (known in Italy as Andrea de Segurola), who was active at the Metropolitan Opera during part of the Giulio Gatti-Casazza years, from his debut on March 3, 1902, as the King in *Aida*,[5] to 1920. He had earlier acquired a strong European reputation, so when he first came to Montevideo for the 1899 Solís season, audience expectations were running high. Unfortunately, he sang only once that season but returned to the Solís many times.

* * *

THE FOUNDING OF THE ORQUESTA de la Sociedad Beethoven in August 1897—conducted by Maestro Manuel Pérez-Badía (fig. 22) a fine Spanish musician—was a landmark in the development of the symphonic repertoire in Montevideo. It also acted as a link between the colonial music ensembles of the Sociedades Filarmónicas and the new Orquesta Nacional of 1908. Symphonic music in Montevideo had long been championed by Maestro Luigi Preti, whose peak achievement had been the first Uruguayan performance, in 1875, of one of Beethoven's symphonies. These efforts were continued and considerably enlarged by the newly created orchestra.

Equally important, Pérez-Badía encouraged the presentation of young, talented Uruguayan musicians as orchestra soloists. Perhaps the most important of these was Luisa Gallo, an outstanding pianist who returned to

Fig. 23. *Left*: Maestro Luis Sambucetti (1860–1926). Author's collection. *Right*: Last page of Sambucetti's *Suite d'orchestre*, with the composer's signature and date. Holograph score in Museo Histórico Nacional, Sección Musicología, Montevideo.

Montevideo after two years of European studies (see chapter 8). Pérez-Badía also proposed to use the new orchestra to play world premieres by Uruguayan composers. By the time the orchestra had been performing for two years, Pérez-Badía had conducted the premiere of what turned out to be the most important symphonic work in the history of nineteenth-century Uruguayan music: Luis Sambucetti's *Suite d'orchestre* (fig. 23). Heard at the Teatro Solís on September 29, 1899, the *Suite* was also the fifth of his orchestral pieces to receive its world premiere at the Solís.

The *Suite* (score dated March 9, 1898) is an orchestral triptych: the movements are "Rêve des bois," "Sérenade à la lune," and "Farandole." The *Suite's* first section, as its name suggests, is a peaceful evocation, a sort of meditative air that ends in a well-orchestrated crescendo. "Sérenade à la lune," with muted string effects and a dreamlike atmosphere, is perhaps closer to an Impressionist style. The last section, "Farandole," has an extraordinary vigor and strong rhythm that build to a final, whirling crescendo, creating in fact a marked contrast to the subdued palette of tones at the beginning movements.

Sambucetti's *Suite* presents a clear and skilled instrumentation with three particular high points: a strongly articulated string section, a remarkable use of woodwinds, and a solid compositional technique. All of these qualities reflect the composer's talent backed by deep knowledge. Not in vain had he spent three years at the national Conservatoire in Paris, studying violin with Hubert Léonard and composition and harmony with such masters as Jules Massenet, Ernest Guiraud,

Ambroise Thomas, Léo Delibes, and Théo-
dore Dubois. He had also been concertmaster
of the Théâtre Châtelet's orchestra under
Edouard Colonne for a year, a position that
he won in competition with forty other Conservatoire contestants.

Even more important than this education
were Sambucetti's friendships with Claude
Debussy, Maurice Ravel, Erik Satie, and Paul
Dukas, which allowed him to witness the
birth of musical Impressionism during his
three years in Paris. When he returned to
Montevideo at age twenty-eight, he had a
complete vision and perspective of Parisian
musical life—when Paris was the music capital of the world. Gifted with energy and vision as well as talent, within a few years Sambucetti founded a musical conservatory (the
Instituto Verdi), a string quartet, and the Orquesta Nacional; as the latter's conductor he
was the first to introduce and perform in
Montevideo the twentieth century's new orchestral and chamber music repertoire.

The Solís performance of Sambucetti's
Suite generated much enthusiasm among the
public and critics; La Razón's critic Adalberto
Soff (the pen name of Alberto Bastos) proclaimed that

> Sambucetti is a "rafiné" who knows how to
> express perfectly the music created by his
> mind and his talent. He does not pursue
> complex forms—he goes directly toward
> that difficult simplicity that discloses the real
> value of good technique and orchestration.
> His wise employment of the orchestra . . .
> reaches a level never before achieved by any
> Río de la Plata composer in the symphonic
> field. Although we detected a French influ-
> ence, the Suite is nevertheless personal, orig-
> inal, and beautiful. For this Sambucetti re-
> ceived thunderous applause. If our country
> did not before now have a symphonist, now
> we not only have one, but we have the best.[6]

A photocopy of the holograph score of the
Suite d'orchestre with Sambucetti's complete
biographical data is now part of The Edwin
A. Fleisher Music Collection of orchestral music in the Free Library of Philadelphia.[7]

* * *

AS THE CENTURY CLOSED, it had been forty
years since Solís audiences thrilled to Louis
M. Gottschalk's pianistic fireworks. Now a
new generation of virtuosos were arriving on
the same stage, and only a few years later,
from the beginning of the First World War,
through the years of tragedy, and afterward,
an impressive array of artists poured into the
Americas. It was an exodus from a shattered
Europe, where opera houses and concert halls
were closed, if not destroyed. José Vianna da
Motta, a young Portuguese musician, was one
of the first to arrive in Montevideo in those
years. From 1897 he would perform many
times at the Solís, with his 1912 performances
regarded as the most memorable. An outstanding pianist and friend and collaborator
of Ferruccio Busoni at the Berlin Academy,
Vianna da Motta gained fame through an extensive world tour in 1927, when he played
Ludwig van Beethoven's thirty-two piano sonatas in honor of the composer's centennial.
When in his teens, Vianna da Motta often visited Weimar, and during these stops he often
took lessons from Franz Liszt. As a result he
became a Liszt scholar, and edited Liszt's
complete piano works with his (that is,
Vianna da Motta's) own fingerings and an-
notations.

The 1890s saw the arrival of another Portuguese musician: violinist Bernardo Valentin
Moreira de Sá. Like Vianna da Motta, Moreira
was not only an excellent performer but also
a scholar. A member of the Société Interna-
tionale de Musique, he published several
works, including a history of music, and es-
says on a variety of topics. Above all he must

be acknowledged for his extensive musicological works on Wagnerian theories. As an instrumentalist Moreira toured extensively as soloist while also performing in a string quartet. When he retired from the recital arena, he became director of the National Music Conservatory of Oporto until his death in 1924, at the age of seventy-one.

Andrés Gaos was another violinist who performed at the Solís as a soloist in the Orquesta de la Sociedad Beethoven. A child prodigy, he began playing the violin in his native city of La Coruña, Spain. He later received lessons at the Madrid Conservatory and was awarded a scholarship to study in Brussels with the celebrated Eugène Ysaÿe. For many years, during his South American tours, Gaos was a familiar figure and a favorite of Montevideo audiences until he went to Buenos Aires and established himself there as professor and composer.

Felice Lebano, a renowned Italian harpist and composer, was also a very colorful musician. A typical fin de siècle specimen, he had all the virtues and weaknesses of this decadent period. At the beginning of his musical career he had counted royalty among his pupils, notably Edward VII, king of England, and Queen Isabella II of Spain. I have been told that when Lebano performed at the Solís, he was famous for spreading many royal anecdotes backstage, to the great delight of the stagehands. Between Solís seasons Lebano performed a series of concerts in Paris, greatly publicized, with pianist Ignaz Paderewski.

With a remarkable balance of first Uruguayan performances (one opera and one oratorio), plus the world premiere of the century's most celebrated Uruguayan symphonic piece, and a display of outstanding instrumentalists, the Solís—after almost fifty years of continuous performances—closed the nineteenth century in triumph. The approaching new century would prove a harbinger of a kind of musical renaissance, its endless succession of prominent artists earning it the name of the Golden Age of the Teatro Solís.

CHAPTER 14

1900

The Turn of the Century: From "La Belle Epoque" to Challenging Times—
Opera as a Fashionable Social Event—Impresarios and Opera Business—
Teatro Solís Carnival Masked Balls—Opera Programs
and a Vanishing Collection

From the stage to drawing-room gatherings, a strong French influence swept away the remains of Romanticism and revolutionized the face of Montevideo literary and artistic circles. A considerable increase in population (at that time 300,000 inhabitants) altered the face of the city, bringing with it increased construction and development. The arrival of well-known French architects such as Joseph P. Carré, and Gardelle meant the building of such new and imposing public structures as the University, the Athenaeum, the Jockey Club, the Railroad Station, the Law and Medical Schools, the Hotel del Prado, and the Club Uruguay. Private mansions, particularly in the then-fashionable El Prado neighborhood, ornamented the surroundings of the city. Graceful curves and volutes, colored marbles, balconies, and balustrades now replaced the former austere Spanish style, and French style and taste have since reigned as the standard style among Montevideo's fashionable inhabitants.

Literary circles were invaded by the poetry and eroticism of Paul Verlaine, Stephane Mallarmé, Théophile Gautier, and Charles Baudelaire, the French Décadentisme. A whole new generation of Uruguayan poets and writers grew up under their shadow and that of the young Symbolists. With Baudelaire's *Les fleurs du mal* as their literary bible, and naming themselves the 1900s Generation of the Modernists, these writers transformed the Uruguayan literary world. The influence is reflected in the French titles of most of these Uruguayans' poems and musical pieces. Pablo Minelli-González and other French-speaking Uruguayan poets went so far as to transform their names (in this case, to Paul Minely). Julio Herrera y Reissig, whose poetry was filled with orientalist exoticism and metaphor, convened a coterie in his *Torre de los Panoramas*, a famous watchtower, for their evening and nocturnal gatherings. Other intimate literary groups formed, among them the *Consistorio del Gay Saber*, hosted by the famous Horacio

Quiroga, whose strong and sharp narrative style also influenced the cultural development of Montevideo.

The theater and these exclusive literary gatherings were the two principal showcases where members of high society enjoyed and displayed themselves. As stated in chapter 13, when the twentieth century opened, Montevideo had several theaters with daily performances, alternating comedy, drama, opera, ballet, zarzuela, and concerts. Those theaters were augmented by the concert halls associated with musical conservatories, which provided an additional regular schedule of chamber music and solo recitals. Roughly eighty percent of the artists, whether musicians, actors, or singers, were of European origin, and were occasionally joined (particularly in concerts) by the young local talent.

*   *   *

THE IMPRESARIO was one of the most respected figures in the show-business world of the 1900s. Most were prosperous men, correctly dressed, fat and bearded, always with their Havana cigars and with golden chains across their stomachs, men whose mere presence was the representation of their status. If this sounds like a caricature, it is also a valid portrait of Camillo Bonetti, partner to Attilio Nardi of the Nardi and Bonetti Italian Company, the most prominent name in opera business management, and the man who brought Arturo Toscanini and Enrico Caruso to South America.

Sometimes the impresario acted as a barrier between artists and audiences, giving press releases and statements on behalf of the artists they represented. Music critics and the press generally respected them, publishing interviews that enticed readers with the news of their business and which artists they were able to engage for upcoming seasons. Some impresarios were not only powerful but capri-

cious, holding artistic lives and destinies in their hands, able to change fame into doom with only one word. At other times prima donnas might marry their impresarios and thus combine career and family life. (Amelia Pasi, for example, who married Angelo Ferrari.) But it did not always work ideally.

Business in the Teatro Solís (until June 1937, when the house was acquired by the Municipality of Montevideo) was a private enterprise; the theater was leased periodically under contract to local ventures that made transactions with foreign impresarios in order to run the house's various seasons of opera, drama, zarzuela, ballet, concerts, and recitals. One of the first impresarios to arrive during the early days of the house was Avelino Aguirre, a Spaniard who brought a zarzuela company from the Teatro Apolo in Madrid. One year later the renowned Maurice Grau came with a French opera company, and a succession of leaders, such as Cesare Ciacchi (1883), and impresario Crodara (1885) presented operetta and opéra-comique seasons. The first important Italian impresario actually to be announced in the Teatro Solís programs was Angelo Ferrari, who first came to Montevideo in 1884, although he was not mentioned in a program until 1894. He had been to Buenos Aires as early as 1868. After he died around 1898, his widow, the former singer Amelia Pasi, ran the company for another two years. Their opera company brought many local premieres to Montevideo, including that of Verdi's *Falstaff*. A notable zarzuela company, the Francisco Pastor Company, arrived in 1896 and offered a month and a half of zarzuela performances led by the bass Rogelio Juarez. Between 1900 until the late 1910s, the five impresarios in charge of the lyric companies that visited Montevideo were (in addition to Ferrari) Rendina, Tornessi (not topnotch, who in 1911 brought Boninsegna), Bernabei (who brought María Barrientos to the Solís for the first time), and the already mentioned Nardi and Bonetti. These impresarios handled the first-rank conductors and singers. Others brought the second-rate companies (that is, companies that were talented enough but lacked divas or stars). Starting in 1912 and into the late 1920s came another: Walter Mocchi, who at first competed with, and then succeeded, Nardi and Bonetti as the leading impresario touring the Río de la Plata and southern Brazil.[1] It must be understood that when these companies traveled to South America, it was not only to visit the Montevideo theaters; that is, the Solís, and once in a while the Cibils (especially during the late 1880s), and the Urquiza. Generally speaking, Ferrari started his opera tour in Buenos Aires, went to Montevideo, then Rio de Janeiro and São Paulo. Ciacchi frequently visited Buenos Aires, and sometimes Santiago de Chile. Nardi and Bonetti followed in Ferrari's footsteps, Mocchi (who visited every year from 1912 to 1925) had no set itinerary—but invariably went also to Buenos Aires, Rio, São Paulo, frequently Rosario, and Córdoba, and occasionally Tucumán, Santa Fé, Santiago, and Santos. In Montevideo these companies alternated between the Teatro Solís and the Teatro Urquiza; in Buenos Aires it was between the Coliseo and the Colón.

These impresarios, magicians conjuring up splendid singers and entertainment, circulated in a world of wealth and high society. As at New York's Met, boxes at the Solís were private property, owned by Montevideo's most prominent and aristocratic families. This was an exclusive group (also including wealthy businessmen and politicians), attending the balls and parties of the winter social season, and strolling in El Prado, the classic fin de siècle fashionable park, in the summer. The boxes at the Solís were a sort of prolongation of club or salon life, with people often more interested in who was in the audience than in the performance. During intermission it was fashionable to receive other society members in one's box; here an aspirant might have an opportunity for an introduction to the girl of his dreams. Tails, white tie, and white gloves were de rigueur attire for gentlemen seated in the boxes or orchestra at any Teatro Solís evening performances. Women and girls wore a glittering display of evening gowns "à la mode de Paris," complemented by the most expensive jewelry. And if they did not have a new dress for each performance, they were sure to stay at home!

In addition to the opening nights of each company, one evening per week was declared "fashionable," the only time at which some box-owners would think it suitable to attend the opera. For many years this special evening at the Teatro Solís was held on Monday nights, to the point that by 1910 nobody who considered himself important would dare to put a foot in the Solís during weekends. This was, after all, the servants' day off, and many seized the chance to attend the opera seated in the gallery. No doubt the theater (and the Solís was no exception) was more than simply a place to present music and drama. Nor did all the drama play out onstage: many among the audience had an extraordinary flair for gossip, handling intrigue with a mastery parallel to the best performers.

The opera was not limited to social butterflies and lively servants. In accordance with rigid social rules, women in mourning were absolutely forbidden to go to any social or public event, even though this was sometimes at variance with their real feelings or wishes. The dictates of formal grieving were also very wearing, with mourning periods ridiculously extended to two, even three years. But not all widows, especially young ones, were ready to close themselves off from all diversion, and many, garbed in heavy veils and crepes, took their carriages and went to the Solís. Once there they enjoyed the performance, comfortably seated in a "grillé" box[2], without being seen by the audience. Discretion was assured and "chacun à son goût"!

From the very opening of the Solís, every year during Carnival season the theater held a series of masked balls that Montevidean chronicles describe as spectacular. All orchestra seats were removed and the house elaborately decorated—each year, and sometimes for each ball—in a different way. For one White Ball, on one single night, wall-to-wall white carpeting was installed over the entire orchestra area. Women were dressed in lavish and original costumes designed by European couturiers, competing for the "best costume" award. The published announcements for these balls required not only tails, white tie, and white gloves, but also the use of black velvet masks for women.[3] Gentlemen distinguished themselves in their satin-lined capes, Montevidean dandies. The flamboyant characters of Montevideo society never missed these famous Solís masked balls.

Orchestras of approximately thirty musicians sat on stage and played cotillions from ten o'clock until the early morning hours. Some guests danced, while others savored the night chatting in their boxes, eating and drinking at the grand foyer buffet, or strolling to admire the sparkling, fairy-tale atmosphere. Nevertheless, these "Veglioni" (their traditional Italian name) had another face: not so glittering or pretty, perhaps, but more authentic. Many love affairs started here, and many marriages dissolved as well—beneath the brilliance of such show and hidden behind each mask was human desire, seeking ways to drink deeply. As with the Paris Opéra's masked balls of the Belle Epoque, society and scandal sometimes held hands.

In the middle 1920s, these Veglioni underwent a change in character. Because society ladies seldom attended, little by little the

events became the province of women of easy virtue; for others it was a chance to taste a forbidden fruit or to have a good time thanks to the anonymity of a mask. However, with the participation of two or three very good modern and popular orchestras, the masked balls retained their tremendous success until about 1950. The Solís' Veglioni ended forever, remaining only in the memories of its former habitués and in colorful posters that have become valued collector's items. (See 1923 Carnival color poster.)

*   *   *

SCENIC DISPLAYS were part of this world even outside the fantastic setting of the ball. In an era when tears, sighing, and fainting were expected of women, back when the covers of musical scores were decorated with cupids, cherubs, lyres, flowers, and cornucopias, opera programs became a forum for unexpected advertisement. In sharp contrast to the nineteenth-century's romantic symbols, the Solís' programs in the new century displayed commercial advertisement that spoke of a more practical world. More than once these programs were startling in their near-oblivious juxtaposition of the ideal and the mundane. In the central pages of one program, next to a highly romanticized portrait of Hariclea Darclée wrapped in laces, there appears an advertisement for laxative water. Elsewhere appears the notice "Saiz de Carlos—Stomalix Elixir—tone the digestive organs and thus cure headache, dysentery, dyspepsia, diarrhea, ulcers, flatulency and all diseases. Be sure the bottle says Stomalix." This, too, appears close to the photograph of a singer. (fig. 24).

Other advertisements touted French champagne, Havana cigars, hair tonic, French perfumes, and "beautiful corsets to keep in marvelous shape your wasp-waist." Here was the elegance missing from the health panaceas.

Fig. 24. *Upper*: A typical central page of a Solís program in the 1900s with cast, singers' photographs, and the most dissimilar collection of advertising. *Lower*: A page with the piano-voice first-page score of the first-act tenor's aria. Program of Wagner's *Die Meistersinger* [I maestri cantori] with Darclée and Zenatello under Toscanini, on August 24, 1903. Author's collection.

Every ad was designed to appeal to (and profit from) people's fantasies and dreams. Perhaps these dreams differed from those that appeared on the stage but they serve to show us the times and tastes of the Solís audiences.

The Solís programs of the 1900s have six or eight pages, with the cast appearing midway, surrounded by a dozen or more advertisements. The rest of the program alternates pages of announcements with oval pictures of leading singers, the plot of the opera being performed, and usually one page of the voice and piano version of that performance's best-known aria.

Considering that there has been almost a century and a half of continuous performance at the Solís, its program collection, housed in the theater, is distressingly incomplete, with many of the most valuable items missing. Among these casualties is a program of Vaslav Nijinsky's final stage performance—together with a Rubinstein piano concert—on October 26, 1917 (see this program picture in chapter 21, fig. 40. The remaining material, exposed to humidity and temperature variations, is in an unfortunate state of decay. During my years of research, I worked on the organization and first inventory ever made of all the materials, including the manuscript and score collections. It was clear that the municipal authorities cared nothing for the conservation of these historical treasures. Not only did my efforts to save the priceless and unique materials meet with minimal attention; they refused to show any material, claiming that the archives do not exist. (This situation endured from 1973—the beginning of the military dictatorship—until March 1985, when democracy was enacted in Uruguay.)

Nowadays the Teatro Solís is closed for a comprehensive restoration, emphasizing fire safety and structural security. The heartbreaking neglect of darker years will pass—and surely a renovated old-splendor will return, not only for the Solís building, but also for its archives.

CHAPTER 15

1901–1902

Two New Stars at the Solís: María Barrientos and Giuseppe Anselmi—
A *Tosca* to Remember with Hariclea Darclée and Edoardo Garbin—
The Death of Maestro Luigi Preti, the Solís' First Conductor

In 1898, six days after her fourteenth birthday, she stepped up on the Barcelona's Teatro Novedades stage for the first time. By age seventeen (in 1901), she was paid 25,000 francs a month. Twelve years later she could command 100,000 francs a season, making her the highest-paid singer in the world.[1] Who was this remarkable singer and what of her rise to stardom? María Barrientos—one of the brightest stars ever to blaze in the Solís firmament.

Since the opening of the 1901 season, Montevideo newspapers had continuously been publishing reviews extolling the "glorious Buenos Aires debut of María Barrientos." When August 1 arrived, the atmosphere crackled with excitement surrounding her debut at the Solís. The opera was Bellini's *La sonnambula*, with tenor Gino Betti as Elvino, under the baton of Arnaldo Conti in his fourth Solís season.

When a fourteen-year-old Barrientos made her debut at the Teatro Novedades in Barce-

lona, it was as Inez in Meyerbeer's *L'africana*. Now she was Amina in Bellini's *La sonnambula* for Buenos Aires (Teatro Politeama) as well as the Solís, and later also Rosario.

Indeed Barrientos' first Solís season covered all of August 1901 (fig. 25). She was cast in eight operas, receiving the best audience response for four roles: Amina, Rosina, Lucia, and in the title role of *Lakmé*. According to an interview published on March 16, she declared that although she sang a wide repertoire, her preference was for precisely these four roles.[2]

The morning after Barrientos' Solís debut this review appeared:

From the first act [Barrientos] conquered the audience, not only because of the beauty of her voice and the purity of her timbre, extending from the most dramatic and powerful moment to *pianissimi* as soft as a sigh, but because she has all the qualities an opera such as *La sonnambula* demands. All her very high pitch trills, her *staccati* and embellishments were done with such an amazing agility and artistry that the audience's applause interrupted her several times.[3]

A review for *Il barbiere*, sung two nights after *La sonnambula*, details an even spectacular performance:

Last evening the Solís was completely packed, more than the opening night, because everyone was extremely eager to hear Miss Barrientos in a role that had been said to be her best. She did an outstanding Rosina, effervescent with the character's youth. It was a girlish interpretation of a witty, coquettish, lovable, and naughty character. To this was added her heavenly voice, doing whatever she liked with astonishing facility, keeping it fresh and crystal-like through all the opera's more difficult passages. Her voice, her smile, and her poise mesmerized the audience in such a way that people sat in amazed silence until they broke into wild applause. After the Lesson Scene the applause was endless. It stopped only when she sang—as a bis—the Waltz from [Charles] Gounod's *Mireille*.[4]

Similar reviews appeared after each one of her Solís performances. Nor is this strange. A child prodigy who had conducted a symphony of her own composition when she graduated from the Barcelona Conservatory at age twelve, Barrientos was a singing phenomenon, especially during the first years of her career. In fact, as Catalan author Antonio Massísimo points out, "She was the youngest debutante singer in all operatic history."[5] Years later and still in her prime, Barrientos was back in Montevideo more than once. (Barrientos will be further discussed in chapter 20 in terms of her memorable 1916 season, when she shared the Solís stage with such

Fig. 25. Program of Italian Lyric Company under conductor Arnaldo Conti with soprano María Barrientos in her debut season at the Solís, August 1901. Biblioteca Nacional Collection, Montevideo.

great artists as Giovanni Martinelli, Tito Schipa, and Titta Ruffo.)

That same August season, the Italian Lyric Company, which had brought Barrientos, presented two new operas to Montevideo audiences, both by Pietro Mascagni. In fact, two days after Barrientos' *Lucia*, Maestro Conti conducted soprano Amadea Santarelli and tenor Elvino Ventura in the first Uruguayan performance of Mascagni's *Iris*. One week later, on August 17 and exactly seven months after its world premiere on January 17, 1901, the same conductor and singers performed Mascagni's *Le maschere*. Since the overnight success, still unmatched, of *Cavalleria rusticana* in 1890, Mascagni had composed six other operas that did not add any measurable fame to his reputation. When *Iris* arrived, with its Japanese flavor (six years before Giacomo Puccini's *Madama Butterfly*), it was the second opera to earn accolades for its composer, partly because in 1898 orientalism was very much in fashion in European cultural circles. *Le maschere*, compared to *Iris*, was received very differently. Its publisher, Sonzogno, planned *Le maschere*'s simultaneous world premieres in six Italian opera houses,[6] thinking it would be a clever way to promote Mascagni. But his plans backfired: the opera failed, and the composer was mocked. The weakness of the opera could not support such grandiosity.

At the Solís performances, neither *Iris* nor *Le maschere* was very much applauded, and only *Iris* was sung more than once. It is probable that the excitement of Barrientos' presentation at the same time overshadowed both Mascagni operas, and it must be admitted that only extremely strong operas could have stood up to Barrientos.

On April 15, 1901, Solís audiences attended a vocal and symphonic concert to honor the memory of Giuseppe Verdi, whose death on January 27 of the same year had worldwide repercussions. That day's program was conducted by Manuel Pérez-Badía, a familiar and much-loved figure in Montevideo. What nobody could foresee was that Pérez-Badía would die suddenly only a few days later. Such unexpected news shocked everyone who knew the extensive career of this Spanish musician as conductor, leader, teacher, mentor, and promoter of symphonic music in Montevideo. Three months later, on July 29, 1901, the young violinist and composer Luis Sambucetti for the first time conducted the Orquesta de la Sociedad Beethoven—the very orchestra Pérez-Badía had so recently conducted—in a concert to honor the memory of the venerated maestro. It was in these somber circumstances that Sambucetti's long and successful conducting career began.

* * *

IN THE SHORT PERIOD of one week, during the 1902 Solís season, operagoers had the opportunity to attend *Tosca* with a cast of Hariclea Darclée, Edoardo Garbin, and Mario Ancona, and to hear *Manon* sung by Darclée and Giuseppe Anselmi. Tenors Garbin and Anselmi were appearing in Montevideo for the first time, as were other stars, all brought by impresarios Nardi and Bonetti for the second opera season of that year. Others to appear were sopranos Adelina Stehle and Matilde de Lerma. In addition to leading baritone Ancona, a young Ruffo was taking the first steps of his career.

Edoardo Garbin, one of the leading tenors prior to Caruso's era, debuted at twenty-six singing Don Alvaro in *La forza del destino* at Vincenza. It was 1891; two years later, after successful presentations in Naples and Genoa, he was chosen to create the first Fenton at La Scala's world premiere of *Falstaff*. This production's Nanetta was Stehle, who eventually became Garbin's wife. Two years before his first Solís season, Garbin created Dufresne in the world premiere of Leoncavallo's *Zazà*, a role he repeated at the end of the 1902 Solís season in its first Uruguayan performance.

An outstanding generation of baritones was produced at the middle of the nineteenth century in Italy, the most famous of whom was the legendary Mattia Battistini, who had sung at the Solís in 1889. Next in the chronological line of superb vocalists was Ancona, one of the finest representatives of his generation. After his La Scala debut in 1890 he soon became a European and American favorite. Four years after his first Solís season, Ancona was cast as Riccardo in Bellini's *I puritani*, along with Regina Pinkert and Alessandro Bonci, to open New York's Manhattan Opera House on December 3, 1906.

Tosca arrived in Montevideo two years after its January 14, 1900, world premiere at Rome's Teatro Costanzi. Solís audiences were wound up to fever pitch. They knew that the Puccini opera was to be sung by Darclée, originator of the title role under the baton of Leopoldo Mugnone, who would be conducting this Solís performance. On August 17, 1902, *Tosca* opened the Solís grand opera season, with the three principal characters sung by Darclée (in her second Teatro Solís visit), Garbin, and Ancona. Surprisingly, the press gave the new Puccini opera a lukewarm reception; it seems incredible that the famous "Recondita armonia" went unnoticed. Today, more than eighty years later, reading these reviews of the Solís' first *Tosca* makes us smile with indulgence:

> We believe that with *Tosca* Puccini has not moved forward, and this opera is neither better nor worse than his others. The "Vissi d'arte" aria is a real jewel, but we thought that it was out of place. La Darclée was hugely applauded, which she answered with an encore. The last tenor aria ["E lucevan le stelle"] is very elegant, and its melody is pure and spontaneous.[7]

New York Tribune music critic Henry Krehbiel had been equally dismissive in his review of *Tosca*'s Metropolitan premiere on February 4, 1901 (with Milka Ternina, Giuseppe Cremonini, and Antonio Scotti):

> And the melodramatic music upon which Sardou's play floats? What is it like? Much of it like shreds and patches of many things with which the operatic stage has long been familiar.... Phrases of real pith and moment are mixed with phrases of indescribable balderdash, yet these phrases recur with painful reiteration and with all the color tints which Puccini is able to scrape from a marvelously varied and garish orchestral palette.[8]

Perhaps critics were surprised with Puccini's first excursion into *verismo*, a sharp turn after the poetic *La bohème*. In any event, Italian critics also attacked the composer for the brutality and cruelty of this opera's action. Now that we can look back with the perspective of a full century, we can see how remarkable it is that Puccini was able to endow the "bloody scenes" with such magnificent lyricism.

In the same singing tradition as Fernando De Lucia, and with the looks of a matinée idol, Anselmi first arrived in Montevideo in 1902. At his Solís debut on August 23 he was a handsome twenty-six-year-old Des Grieux and, according to old chronicles, "the best romantic personification of a young and desperate lover of all the Massenet *Manons* that Solís operagoers have ever seen."[9] His Manon on that occasion was Darclée. One year earlier this gifted tenor had enjoyed success singing Turiddu at the San Carlo in Naples and the Duca di Mantova at Covent Garden. Anselmi came back to the Solís several times during his prime, and the lovely quality of his voice, especially his famous *pianissimi*, had an overwhelming effect on Montevideo audiences.

*   *   *

THE DAY AFTER Darclée and Anselmi's extraordinary *Manon*, Solís opera lovers attended another debut, this time of Stehle as Mimì in Puccini's *La bohème*. It was she who created Nanetta in *Falstaff* opposite Garbin as Fenton. In 1892 she also sang Nedda at the Teatro Dal Verme in Milan opposite Fiorello Giraud's Canio in the world premiere of *Pagliacci* with Victor Maurel as Tonio and Mario Ancona as Silvio (Toscanini conducted). In the Solís *Bohème*, Stehle and Garbin were together again, singing Mimì and Rodolfo in a re-creation of their real-life romance.

A third well-known soprano included in the roster of that Teatro Solís season was Matilde de Lerma. In addition to singing Aida opposite Julian Biel's Radamès, she performed at the Uruguayan premiere of Alberto Franchetti's *Germania*. The performance of the latter met with a very different critical response than had *Tosca*, much as it bemuses us now:

> It is not difficult to highly proclaim that Alberto Franchetti is the most powerful, most strict, most scholastic and most varied of all the contemporary Italian composers. We do not see in him the preoccupation toward cheap musical effects. His melody always flows easily and spontaneously, strongly impassioned. Even if he is influenced by Wagnerian musical processes, he keeps the richness of the Italian melodic form intact.[10]

Today very few remember *Germania*, and even fewer consider Franchetti one of the most important opera composers of his generation. Even though Caruso himself sang the lead role, as he had done at the La Scala premiere, the first U.S. performance of *Germania* under Toscanini at the Met (January 22, 1910) did not keep *Germania* in operatic repertoire. Franchetti's best achievement as a composer was *Cristoforo Colombo*, with its monumental and dramatic display of choruses and masses of people on stage, in the grand style of Mey-

erbeer. In 1992, on the occasion of the five hundredth anniversary of Columbus' discovery of America, Franchetti's neglected opera—commissioned a century ago to commemorate the four hundredth anniversary—was once again performed.

On August 31, the first Uruguayan performance of Leoncavallo's *Zazà* closed an outstanding 1902 Solís season. It has been said that *Zazà*, which sometimes fails dramatically, needs a brilliant cast to survive, in particular a soprano able to reach the necessary dramatic climax and to project it to the audience with a great stage presence. This Solís cast, under the baton of Maestro Mugnone, was superb. To start with, the principal male character of Milio Dufresne was sung by the same singer who had created the role in the Milan world premiere two years before, Garbin. If Toscanini had Rosina Storchio as Zazà and Mario Sammarco as Cascart at the Teatro Lirico, Mugnone's Solís premiere glittered with Darclée and Ruffo. Which was the better cast would be hard to say. Solís opera lovers were delighted, and so was the press:

> *Zazà*'s act three contains wonderful dramatic highlights, especially Milio's aria, which Garbin sang admirably, thus inspiring a grand, ovationed encore. The other [highlight] was the famous encounter between Zazà and Totò—her lover's young daughter—which was played by the little Cabrini girl as though she were a mature actress, seconding Darclée's spectacular singing. . . . Titta Ruffo, a young and new baritone, is also a talented actor, and his performance was excellent. The opera's act four is absolutely beautiful.[11]

Although none of the composer's works could achieve *Pagliacci*'s world acceptance, there is no doubt that after *Pagliacci*, *Zazà* was Leoncavallo's best opera, even if some distance in dates of composition separates them.

In 1902 Ruffo was only twenty-five years

old, and very young for his voice. It would not be until after his La Scala and Covent Garden debuts, the year after this Solís appearance, that he would begin to gain recognition as an important singer. After his American debut at the Chicago-Philadelphia Grand Opera Company in 1912, he became "The Baritone" and possessor of one of the largest and most beautiful voices in the world. Fortunately for Solís audiences, they had the privilege of hearing him often during his prime.

As happens in all the world's best opera houses, besides great successes there are failures, empty houses, and third-class opera companies; the Solís was no exception. What *was* an exception, indeed, was when a less-esteemed company had on its roster a fairly good singer. Such was the case of Maria Galvany. According to the sources available to us, the company that came in June 1902 was "not bad, but horrible, with the exception of Maria Galvany."[12] At that time the Spanish soprano was only twenty-four; perhaps that was why she was booked with a company that got only catcalls. Although Galvany had already sung at Milan's Dal Verme, her triumphs would only really start about 1908 and later, when

she appeared in London at the same time as Luisa Tetrazzini, seven years her senior. There, in spite of the great diva's presence, Galvany enjoyed quite a success. It was the same standard coloratura repertoire as Luisa Tetrazzini and Regina Pacini were singing, and that she performed at the Solís: Amina, Rosina, Lucia. Many years later, there were still people in Montevideo who remembered Galvany's skills in *staccato* passages. She also recorded extensively, often with other great voices, such as De Lucia and Ruffo. In spite of their age, these records display Galvany's lovely vocal qualities: the sweetness of her middle range and the brightness of her upper register.

*   *   *

A YEAR AND A HALF AFTER the sudden death of Pérez-Badía, Montevideo music lovers, and especially Solís audiences, received the news of the death of Luigi Preti on November 20, 1902. At seventy-six the oldest European musician living in Montevideo, and a great part of Solís life, Preti was mourned by his adopted city with profound and fervent sorrow.

CHAPTER 16

❧ *1903* ❧

The Rise of a Golden Age:
The Arrival of Arturo Toscanini and Enrico Caruso

The 1903 Grand Italian Opera season surpassed the former year's excellence and raised the Teatro Solís to its Golden Age. Again the top-flight Nardi and Bonetti company produced the most ambitious event Montevidean opera lovers could ever dream of. The prominent impresario Camillo Bonetti featured Arturo Toscanini and many of the artists who had sung in the preceding season at the Teatro alla Scala. Perhaps even more important than Toscanini was the man whom many now consider the greatest tenor in history: Enrico Caruso. In 1903, Caruso had not yet reached the peak of his fame. His Metropolitan Opera debut was to come only after the Solís season, a short visit to Rio de Janeiro, and a long sea voyage. But he was already famous enough to arouse great anticipation on the part of the audiences of Montevideo.

Another important factor was the proposed ten-title repertoire the company was bringing, with four operas new to Montevideo: Hector Berlioz's *La damnation de Faust* to open the season, plus Jules Massenet's *Grisélidis*, Richard Wagner's *Die Meistersinger*, and Francesco Cilea's *Adriana Lecouvreur*, the tenor role of which had been created by Caruso. It was announced in Montevideo's newspapers as "the arrival of the Teatro alla Scala Company" and "the cultural event of the year." However, one suspects that the impresarios had indulged in a little hyperbole. This was not the La Scala Company, nor had Caruso sung at La Scala during the 1902–03 season: he had been in Rome, Lisbon, and Monte Carlo instead.[1] In fact, when Toscanini asked the La Scala management to be "excused from the last Scala performance, in order to leave for Genoa and South America, the request [was] denied."[2]

The following excerpt from *La Razón* reflects the atmosphere of intense excitement surrounding the projected season:

Today, in the early hours of a cold morning the steamships "Venus" and "Paris" arrived from Buenos Aires, anchoring in the bay. Among their passengers were the 285-member Opera Company from Milan's Teatro alla Scala [sic], including Toscanini and Caruso. As soon as authorities gave the order, dozens of small rowboats began endless trips to carry people from the steamers to the docks. Soon there was pandemonium, with porters unloading hundreds of crates of furniture, scenery, huge boxes of scores, and thousands of pieces of luggage. The confusion was terrible, with people yelling and porters cursing loudly—while from the dock, the Teatro Solís' reception committee looked on helplessly.[3]

From that sort of chaos it is hard to imagine the scene in the opera house that evening. Board members observed Toscanini directing his assistants: according to a contemporary report, this is what they saw:

For such a man he looks amiable. Small of frame, he is slender, with an angular face and well-trimmed black moustache. Toscanini has small eyes—but the sharpest and most vivid I have ever seen. He looks natural, without the pose and mannerisms of many of his colleagues, but his voice sounds rough and husky, like someone in the habit of giving orders all the time.[4]

This preview heralded the resplendent 1903 Solís season in which secondary and even tertiary roles were being cast with exceptional singers. The company was headed by Toscanini as *maestro concertatore e direttore d'orchestra*. In most nineteenth-century Italian opera houses, well into the late 1870s, there were two "heads" of the orchestra: the *maestro concertatore e direttore della musica*, who prepared the score for performance and rehearsed the orchestra, and the *primo violino e direttore dell'orchestra*, who actually "led" the orchestra with the bow of his violin during the performance. Sometimes the *maestro concertatore* was a famous name, perhaps even a well-known composer; at other times it was the *primo violino* who was the more famous of the two. This situation gradually changed, and eventually the positions were combined (as was the case almost universally by the time Toscanini had reached the scene, this interesting and ambiguous matter has been thoroughly discussed elsewhere).[5] Certainly, by 1903 Toscanini's wishes were paramount: to have complete control of the performances, and to prepare and conduct each opera himself. The era of the all-powerful conductor had arrived, and Toscanini was the first among equals.

Nardi and Bonetti's roster from that Solís 1903 season was glorious: sopranos Maria Farneti, Esperanza Clasenti, and Anna Sallaz; mezzo Teresina Ferraris; tenors Enrico Caruso, Giovanni Zenatello, and Gaetano Pini-Corsi; baritones Giuseppe de Luca, Eugenio Giraldoni, and Pietro Giacomello; and bass Constantino Thos—all of them new to Montevideo (fig. 26). Others already well known to Solís audiences completed the exceptional company: Hariclea Darclée, Medea Mei-Figner, Virginia Guerrini, Florencio Constantino, Michele Wigley, Remo Ercolani, and Vittorio Arimondi. Toscanini's two assistants, Maestros Pietro Sormani and Francesco Romei, came accompanied by a band conductor, a band of twenty musicians, numerous secondary-role singers, a seventy-musician orchestra, an eighty-person chorus, a choreographer, and a thirty-dancer corps de ballet. Designers Rovescalli and Ferri's scenery came from Milan, with their own personnel. The costumes, from the famous house of

Fig. 26. The debut of Toscanini and Caruso was the beginning of the Solís Golden Age. Poster advertising the memorable 1903 Nardi and Bonetti season. *Second row from the left:* Caruso, Darclée, Toscanini, Mei-Figner and Constantino. Teatro Solís Collection.

Zamperoni, arrived with the house wardrobe master, while the props from Rancatti's house were also sent from Milan.

The beginning of the 1903 season at both the Teatro Solís and the New York's Metropolitan was marked by the first important remodeling of the buildings since their respective openings. In a remarkable coincidence, Caruso, in his Montevideo and New York debuts, was the artist to perform first under the new lighting of both stages. Only a few months before the arrival of the Nardi and Bonetti company, at the end of summer 1903, the Solís pit was remodeled and enlarged by the rebuilding of the proscenium arc at the level of the "avant-scène" boxes. A new acous-

tical wall was also built all around the pit. According to numerous newspaper articles, a major improvement came with the installation of a state-of-the-art lighting system, for which the Solís administration spent more than 1,500 pesos. *La Razón* reported:

Ricci, Teatro Solís' electrical engineer, thought big! We have been told that the Solís will have some newly invented fixtures called "dimmers," which will avoid the regular and unpleasant flashes of the past and allow for the gradual change of shades. The new system consists of 100 new sixteen-candle-power footlights, ten overhead-lighting poles of fifteen lights each, and seven sidelight poles with 100 lights each. In total, there will be 1,000 lights on the stage.[6]

When Toscanini arrived at the Solís, he had established an impressive career, conducting two hundred opera performances during a period of more than fifteen years. After several world premieres of operas, among them Leoncavallo's *Pagliacci* and Puccini's *La bohème*, he reached La Scala at age thirty-one, making his debut there as artistic director conducting *Die Meistersinger* on December 26, 1898. Toscanini was absolutely inflexible about the importance of the composer's wishes, and he was often ready to do whatever was needed to remain faithful to his principles. To him, laziness, mediocrity, routine, and lack of study or discipline were sins; the result was a fierce and perpetual battle with those he believed governed by such unpardonable traits. Far from the "amiable" Toscanini described in *La Razón,* the real Toscanini was well known for his fits of temper and all that entails: cursing, tearing up scores, breaking batons, and throwing music stands.

At La Scala, besides struggling to overcome artists' bad habits, Toscanini attempted to educate the audience. The terrible resistance he met with when trying to abolish encores within performances led to his resignation as a director of La Scala in April 1903.[7] Exactly four months later Toscanini climbed to the Solís podium to conduct the 1903 season's opening night. On August 15, 1903, the first Uruguayan performance of Berlioz's *La damnation de Faust* took place. A lavish production, costing 50,000 lire, the Berlioz opera and Toscanini's Montevidean debut were fervently praised:

> In a masterful interpretation of the work, Maestro Toscanini appeared as his fame has told: severe, calm, serious, completely self-

assured, confident of his musicians and singers, all without casting a single glance at the score during the entire performance. He was always restrained, never posturing, using clear and sober gestures. From the moment he stepped onto the podium we could feel his authority: immediately all fell under the spell of his influence and strong magnetism.[8]

The critics rightly commented that Montevideo audiences had never seen such an elaborate production; it featured the same conductor, tenor, sets, and costumes that had opened the previous Teatro alla Scala season in December 1902.

When Giovanni Zenatello sang *La damnation de Faust* (in Italian, of course) at the Solís, the young tenor was twenty-seven years old and had already sung in Malta, Trieste (Austrian at the time), Lisbon, Rio, São Paulo, and Buenos Aires. If Toscanini monopolized all the attention at the Solís on opening night, when the tenor sang Radamès a few days later (opposite Darclée's Aida), he was the hero of the evening:

> [Zenatello] has a beautiful, big, round, and powerful voice, with superb, ringing notes. His upper tones are warm, and he has a spontaneous and clear enunciation. His outstanding timbre and color and his management of them place Zenatello among the few who use the entire voice easily and without restraint. . . . Guerrini's Amneris was notable for her art, voice, beauty, dramatic talent, and regal poise. Giraldoni was one of the best Amonasros we have ever heard. Orchestra and chorus were unsurpassed—only Toscanini can reach such perfection.[9]

A few days later the applause rang even more loudly when Zenatello sang the "Preislied" in the first Uruguayan performance of Wagner's *Die Meistersinger*, which was, of course, given

Fig. 27. *Left*: Caruso debuted in Montevideo as Des Grieux in Puccini's *Manon Lescaut*, on August 16, 1903. Biblioteca Nacional Collection, Montevideo. *Upper right*: Soprano Maria Farneti who sang the title role. Author's collection. *Lower right*: Caruso. Library of Congress Collection.

in Italian. The roles of Eva and Maddalena were sung, respectively, by Darclée and Guerrini.

Baritone Giraldoni also triumphed, singing Hans Sachs in this production. In addition to this Wagner role, Giraldoni sang in the Solís performances of *La damnation de Faust*, *Aida*, and *Tosca*. He had created Scarpia three years before this Solís season at *Tosca*'s world premiere.[10] Giraldoni, who would return to sing in other Solís seasons, was characterized by the diversity of characters he interpreted in the best opera houses throughout the world.

Early on the morning of August 16, 1903, an anxious crowd waited for the opening of the Solís box office. With the Toscanini debut still fresh in their minds, these were the people who had not been able to get a ticket to hear Caruso. They waited, hoping only to be standees at a time when even a scalper was hard to find.

Caruso debuted at Montevideo as Des Grieux in Puccini's *Manon Lescaut* (fig. 27). He was accompanied by Farneti singing the title role and baritone Giacomello as Lescaut, both of them new voices for the Solís audiences. The conductor, of course, was Toscanini. While Caruso's first encounter with Toscanini at his La Scala debut had not been at all congenial, compounded by a poor performance due to the tenor's illness, less than two months later (1901), after a successful *L'elisir d'amore*, the conductor confided to Arrigo Boito that the "young tenor sings like an angel."[11] The maestro's enthusiasm eventually receded from such a celestial height; by the time of the Solís performances their relationship had returned to normal (as normal of course, as could be expected between two such diverse and powerful personalities as theirs).

Caruso's first Solís performance was warmly praised, but music critics gave almost the same admiration to the young Farneti, as the following review shows:

> Tenor Caruso is number one among the world's tenors. As an artist he has the largest number of qualifications: a beautiful voice, talent, good taste, admirable singing technique and, above all, his soul and his spirit are exclusively at the service of art. Maria Farneti is twenty-four [*sic*] years old, very pretty, with not only a good and powerful voice but a wide range, a beautiful timbre, and enough talent to handle all these together. She conquered the public with her beauty, her grace, the freshness of her voice, and her elegance without pose.[12]

Caruso sang at the Teatro Solís five more times that season, including another *Manon Lescaut*. Nevertheless, his greatest successes of the 1903 season were *L'elisir d'amore* and, especially, *Tosca*. Thirty years old, the tenor now added Montevideo to his triumphs, along with Bologna, Rome, Milan, Saint Petersburg, and Buenos Aires.

For his second night at the Solís, Caruso sang in the first Uruguayan performance of Cilea's *Adriana Lecouvreur*. The critics raved over Caruso's performance, and the new opera conquered Solís audiences, influenced perhaps by the knowledge that only a few months earlier, on November 6, 1902, the tenor had created the opera's role of Maurizio de Saxonia for the world premiere at Milan's Teatro Lirico. Not counting the famous "Lamento di Federico" from *L'arlesiana*, *Adriana Lecouvreur* soon became the most successful of all of Cilea's operas, and Caruso was associated with four later local premieres of *Adriana Lecouvreur* in Lisbon, Buenos Aires, Montevideo, and the New York Metropolitan in November 1907.

Samuel Blixen ("Suplente"), the leading

Uruguayan critic, with years of experience in Europe's major opera houses, especially those of Italy, said of Caruso's second Solís performance:

> Even in the years ahead it will be impossible to find an interpreter such as Caruso in the role of Maurizio de Saxonia. In him are combined the most fortuitous requirements of a superior tenor. His voice is unique in the sweetness of its timbre, vigor, extension, and flexibility. Caruso never rests on his triumphs, as did [Julián] Gayarre and [Angelo] Masini. On the contrary, he studies hard to be the most complete of tenors, mixing his prodigious voice with a permanent concern for the improvement and development of his interpretive talent.[13]

While still a mezzo at the beginning of her career, Medea Mei had been coached by Toscanini on the maestro's famous 1886 Brazilian tour; now she sang the title role at the Solís opposite Caruso. Toscanini was always very fond of this Italian soprano, casting and conducting her frequently. (As noted in chapter 9, Mei sang at the Solís for the first time in 1884, nineteen years before this illustrious 1903 season.)

The night after Zenatello's triumph as Radamès, Solís opera lovers heard Caruso sing again with the young Farneti in one of his most appreciated creations of these years: Osaka in Pietro Mascagni's *Iris*. Of Caruso in this Solís performance of *Iris* on August 23, critics wrote that "Caruso was again one of the heroes of the evening."[14] When Caruso reached the end of "Una furtiva lagrima" in *L'elisir d'amore* the following evening, it was not only applause that followed but a roar of unending euphoria that demanded—and received—an encore. Even the almighty Toscanini would yield to the demand of the audience on rare occasions!

Caruso's performance was well matched by that of his Adina. According to the reviews, Esperanza Clasenti had "one of the most beautiful soprano voices and a truly outstanding vocal agility."[15] Born in Cuba in 1883, Clasenti, just twenty years old at the time of the 1903 Solís season, was another singer new to Solís music lovers. Her vocal abilities, her talent, and the excellence of her training had won her the privilege of being chosen by Toscanini to sing with Caruso in the 1903 season. Shortly thereafter she debuted at the Teatro alla Scala; eventually she would return to the Solís to sing again under Toscanini's baton.

After a second performance of *Manon Lescaut*, the 1903 Solís opera season closed with Puccini's *Tosca*, featuring a cast of glittering stars: Darclée, Caruso, and Giraldoni, soprano and baritone the creators of their respectives roles only three years earlier. Oddly, Caruso's "Recondita armonia" went relatively unnoticed, the first encore being that of Darclée's "Vissi d'arte," the soprano pièce de résistance for the whole opera. In a surprise turnaround from Toscanini's "encore affair" at La Scala, the conductor not only allowed one encore for Darclée, but multiples for Caruso:

> Caruso was the one and only hero of the night, with the ovation for "E lucevan le stelle" being, without doubt, the grandest we ever heard in this house. . . . The public rose to its feet and in an outburst of spirit, a flight of doves was released, followed by banners bearing the inscription "Caruso—E lucevan le stelle." The tenor sang his famous third-act aria not only superbly but three times. We have never heard such sublime interpretations as these of last night with Caruso, Darclée, and Toscanini.[16]

Three times! There is no doubt that Toscanini forever remembered the end of that season: triple encores, streamers, and doves.

Fig. 28. Announcement of Massenet's *Griselda*, a new opera to Montevideo audiences that was performed at the Solís by Farneti, Constantino and De Luca, under Toscanini. *La Razón*, August 17, 1903. Biblioteca Nacional Collection, Montevideo.

A novelty for Solís audiences was *Griselda* (fig. 28), an Italian translation of Massenet's original *Grisélidis*. *Griselda*, subtitled a "conte lyrique," has a prologue and three acts based on a medieval legend. The work had its world premiere (in French) at the Paris Opéra-Comique two years prior to the Solís performance. The new production was welcomed by Solís audiences and the press:

> The Massenet opera we heard last night [August 18, 1903] at the Solís is a delicious frivolity. Griselda neither suffers like Werther, nor does she cry like Manon, but she has plenty of freshness and mischievousness. In some aspects the opera's knavery, deceit, and sharpness remind us of a Mozart opera. The audience not only liked it but loved it, and we were delighted by the young Farneti singing the title role, as well as by tenor Constantino and baritone De Luca, who is very young and already an excellent singer and actor. Above all we must praise the Lucifer character, how Massenet wrote his scene, and how marvelously it was performed by the bass Ercolani. Toscanini, as always, kept a perfect balance between voices and orchestra. We are really dazzled by the talent of this celebrated young conductor.[17]

While Zenatello and Caruso were perhaps the best known of the three tenors featured in the 1903 season, the third, Florencio Constantino, was almost as famous. This was Constantino's second visit to the Solís, seven years after his 1896 world debut as Lázaro in *La Dolores* at the same theater (see also chapter 12). This Basque tenor had a controversial and sad career. Three years after his 1903 Solís performance he debuted in Boston, and two years later (1908) was acclaimed when he sang *Rigoletto* at New York's Oscar Hammerstein Company with Luisa Tetrazzini and Mario Sammarco. Unfortunately for him, he was involved in a series of lawsuits and counter-suits (both as plaintiff and defendant). These litigations ruined his artistic reputation, and, adding to his own downfall, he began drinking between acts during opera performances. When his then chronic dementia was almost cured, he succumbed to encephalitis, and he died in Mexico City, on November 19, 1919.[18]

It may be instructive to contrast the career of Constantino with that of De Luca, the baritone who had sung with Constantino in the Solís *Grisélidis* premiere. Together with Pasquale Amato, Antonio Scotti and Titta Ruffo—all of them quite familiar to Montevideo audiences—De Luca was one of the finest voices in the world of opera, with a remarkable career of fifty years of singing, among them

twenty consecutive seasons at the Metropolitan. At the beginning of his career De Luca sang bass/baritone and bass roles, as he did twice at that 1903 Solís season with Beckmesser and Dulcamara. Shortly after his South American tour, De Luca created the role of Sharpless for the disastrous world premiere of *Madama Butterfly* at La Scala. He would also return to the Solís, including a special performance under Toscanini's baton to celebrate the Teatro Solís Golden Jubilee Gala in August 1906.

The 1903 season ended with performances by an Italian dramatic company, followed by a series of concerts in November: world-renowned Belgian violinist César Thomson was accompanied by his pupil, Uruguayan Eduardo Fabini, who returned to Montevideo with the Brussels Royal Conservatory's Golden Medal Award. Fabini later became Uruguay's best-known nationalistic composer. Despite such brilliance, Solís' music lovers had memories of only one event: the arrival of Toscanini and Caruso. As the years passed, and as both conductor and tenor returned several times, their first Solís appearance together was relived through anecdotes that are still being recounted, from one generation to the next.

CHAPTER 17

1904–1906

Rosina Storchio and *Madama Butterfly*—The Opening of the Teatro Urquiza—
Puccini Visits Montevideo—Toscanini Conducts the Teatro Solís Golden
Jubilee—Salomea Kruszelnicka

For all his prestige and growing fame, the star of the 1904 Solís season was not Arturo Toscanini, but soprano Rosina Storchio. When she first appeared at the Solís in August 1904, Storchio was at the height of her fame, propelled by her successful creation of the title role in the world premiere of Leoncavallo's *Zazà* at the Teatro Lirico in Milan in 1900. In this, his second Teatro Solís season, the maestro brought almost the same 1903 roster, with the exception of Enrico Caruso. There were, however, four important newcomers: tenor Giuseppe Borgatti, baritone Pasquale Amato, bass Adamo Didur, and soprano Angelica Pandolfini (the Eva when Toscanini made his La Scala debut in the local premiere of Richard Wagner's *Die Meistersinger* in 1898).

From January through July 1904, a political revolution closed all the theaters of Montevideo; as a consequence, the Solís season was the shortest of the era. Nonetheless, Toscanini brought two important new operas to Montevideo: Puccini's *Madama Butterfly*, remembered as one of the greatest evenings in Solís history, and Alfredo Catalani's *La Wally*. The 1904 opera season opened on August 18 with Wagner's *Lohengrin* starring Borgatti, then one of the leading La Scala tenors, in the title role. Maria Farneti, celebrated for her 1903 Solís debut, sang Elsa opposite him. In addition to Borgatti, Amato and Didur, two singers with long and brilliant careers, also made their Montevideo debuts in this *Lohengrin*. The performance was reviewed favorably, one writer noting that:

> Mr. Borgatti, who is now singing Wagner almost exclusively, was an exceptional Lohengrin because of his voice and his dramatic interpretation of the Swan-knight. He has an unusual timbre and—at the same time—a marvelous flexibility. . . . Baritone Amato's voice is one of the most beautiful we have heard at the Solís, with a wide register that he has mastered superbly.[1]

Fig. 29. *Left*: Cover of 1904 Nardi and Bonetti season program. *Right*: first page with Uruguayan premiere of Catalani's *La Wally* with Farneti and Garbin conducted by Toscanini, on August 24, 1904. Author's collection.

Although Storchio had already debuted in Montevideo with Donizetti's *Linda di Chamounix* on August 20, her first big triumph of the 1904 season came in *Manon*. As still happens, the great divas' private lives were often a source of gossip, and Storchio's was no exception, her tempestuous love affair with Toscanini causing widespread commentary.[2] The story piqued interest in her performances, enhancing her reputation as one of the best soprano voices of her time, remarkable for her sensitive and plaintive interpretation of her heroines. The review of her August 21 *Manon* captures much of this excitement:

> Last night La Storchio achieved the greatest triumph a lyric artist can reach. Her voice is

pure, sweet, warm, and very flexible. Her passionate and sensitive personification of Manon made Solís opera lovers weep.... Beside her, with his impeccable training and dramatic talent, Garbin was an ideal Des Grieux. Toscanini's conducting, as usual, reached celestial heights.[3]

Two days after *Manon*, Storchio sang again, this time in Charles Gounod's *Faust* with Piero Schiavazzi, one of Pietro Mascagni's young pupils, in the title role. However, the singer most applauded that evening was the Polish bass Didur, "one of the best interpretations of Méphistophélès we have ever seen and certainly one of the best bass voices that has been heard at the Teatro Solís in many years."[4] Fortunately, Didur returned to sing many times at the Solís and later became the leading bass of New York's Metropolitan Opera Company. Amato enjoyed a similar career, with a long Metropolitan tenure, during which he created important roles.

Toscanini had been not only the closest friend of the composer Alfredo Catalani while he was alive, but also a great admirer and champion of his music. Ever since Catalani's death in 1893 at age thirty-nine, only one year after the La Scala world premiere of *La Wally* (his fifth opera), Toscanini would try to include one or more of his operas in each season under his control. The Uruguayan premiere of *La Wally* took place on August 24, 1904, with Farneti singing the title role (fig. 29). Solís audiences had eagerly anticipated the performance. Before the premiere Montevideo newspapers published long articles about the composer and his works. The reviews afterward were equally keen:

> *La Wally* was composed when modern musical theories had not yet influenced the Latin composers; it is a truly Italian opera, with all the magnificence of the old school. However, in spite of today's snobbery among public and composers, *La Wally* impressed itself upon audiences as a masterpiece and a prodigy of marvelous inspiration, translated into admirable instrumentation. . . . With neither vulgar effects nor exotic harmonic combinations, *La Wally* is sublimely and simply beautiful, with only the purity of musical sounds. . . . We must thank Toscanini, in the name of Lyric Art, for the great contribution he made in reviving this superb Catalani opera.[5]

The review also comments on all the cast members, especially Farneti as Wally, Edoardo Garbin as Hagenbach, and Amato as Gellner. Undoubtedly, *La Wally* demonstrated a great advance over Catalani's earlier operas, and musically it is the best constructed of his works. For Catalani's sake, it must also be said that having died so young he did not reach full maturity as a composer.

Just twenty-four hours after *La Wally*, Toscanini conducted the Solís premiere of *Madama Butterfly*. This was only three months after Cleofonte Campanini had conducted the triumphant second version of Puccini's opera at the Teatro Grande in Brescia, on May 28. The world premiere of *Madama Butterfly* at La Scala on February 17, 1904, had been one of the greatest fiascos ever seen in opera history, but after some cuts and the recasting of the original two acts into three, *Madama Butterfly* conquered the world forever. Solís operagoers were apprehensive about the soprano Storchio, who had been subjected to whistling and shouting at the disastrous La Scala debut. (see this chapter, note 2) At the Solís she met with a much kinder (and well-deserved) reception:

> Yesterday Storchio once more displayed her exceptional singing and acting qualities. She sang the title role deliciously, passionately, and with a touching impulsiveness. We believe that it is impossible to find another soprano who can surpass La Storchio as Cio-Cio-San. . . . The general impression about the new opera, in spite of having only one hearing, is that Puccini's genius is now not only recognized but admired.[6]

With the fragile, sensitive, and melancholic Cio-Cio-San, a character quite distant from the dramatic and realistic verismo school of singing so much in fashion in those days, Toscanini and Storchio brought the 1904 Solís opera season to a happy close (fig. 30).

The excitement over Puccini's visit to Montevideo began to build very early in the summer of 1905. Even the prospect of once

Fig. 30. Rosina Storchio debuted at the Solís at the height of her fame, and overshadowed Toscanini as conductor of that 1904 season, in her plaintive depiction of Cio-Cio-San in *Madama Butterfly*. From a Teatro Solís program. Author's collection.

paid him 50,000 francs in advance to have the composer appear with their opera company.[8] Ultimately Puccini, after his visit to Buenos Aires, came to the Teatro Solís with Bernabei's opera company, and Nardi and Bonetti's more prestigious lyric company lost out. Although Bernabei brought Barrientos and Burzio for this season, his company could seldom compete with Nardi and Bonetti, as year after year they brought stellar casts to the Solís stage. Nevertheless, the knowledge that two companies were fighting for the privilege of presenting Puccini in his first American appearance only heightened the excitement of an already thrilling event.

Bernabei's eight-production season opened on August 5, with Puccini's *Tosca* under the baton of Maestro Ettore Perosio and with soprano Burzio singing the title role. "A woman of great beauty, voice and talent," as she was described at her Solís debut, Burzio was at that time a promising dramatic soprano who would eventually sing at La Scala with Toscanini conducting.[9]

After a four-year absence, Barrientos returned to the Solís. This time she was no longer a teenage soprano at the beginning of her career, but a singer who had swept Milan's La Scala with an impressive performance of Meyerbeer's *Dinorah*. Her new Montevideo appearance in *Lucia di Lammermoor* on August 6 was considered, together with four other coloratura roles she sang, the best of that year's opera repertoire. Newspapers overflowed with articles about "her prodigious voice of velvet, her incredible trills and pianissimi"; in one glorious outburst, a reviewer claimed that "she has a throat like a nest of nightingales on a spring morning."[10]

On August 9 Puccini arrived in Montevideo, surrounded by hundreds of fans as soon as he disembarked from the steamship *Venus*. He and his wife Elvira went directly to the Hotel Lanata, where they would stay during

again having Storchio and María Barrientos, in addition to Eugenia Burzio, Giannina Russ, Rina Giachetti, Giuseppe Anselmi, Giovanni Zenatello, Eugenio Giraldoni, and Didur, could not overshadow the enthusiasm of seeing the famous composer in person.

In the early autumn many Montevideo newspapers began to announce that the winter of 1905 would be an exceptional one for the Teatro Solís: three different opera companies—with a total of sixty-seven first-role singers and six conductors—were planning to come and perform. To the shock of Montevideo's operagoers, along with this good news came the notice of a lawsuit brought against Puccini by Nardi and Bonetti for breach of contract. Apparently, Puccini signed a contract with the competing impresario Bernabei[7] even though Nardi and Bonetti had already

their one-week visit to Montevideo. The day following Barrientos' success in Donizetti's *L'elisir d'amore* was the breathlessly anticipated gala. The Solís was resplendent to receive Puccini, and the audience greeted the composer with a standing ovation. *Tosca* was the opera chosen for this special gala, its stage direction supervised by Puccini. Strangely enough, while the next day's reviews commented widely on Puccini and his wife, their lifestyle, and his operas and future projects, not a single word was written about the performance itself. Evidently, the performance on stage was not the show everyone was interested in.

> A production of *Manon Lescaut* was scheduled at the Solís on August 16 to give Puccini a farewell gala. In spite of the composer's supervision, the performance was not at all successful: Young soprano Ida Gobatto was not yet ready to sing Manon, nor was tenor Armanini ready to be a Des Grieux. This was quite a bad performance, with disastrous moments. The audience, in consideration of Puccini's presence, did not show their disapproval, but wildly applauded the composer.[11]

Before leaving the country, Puccini was received at the Conservatorio Musical Montevideo, where the general director Maestro Virgilio Scarabelli paid homage to Puccini in a moving speech.

With the emotion of Puccini's farewell still in the air, the Lyric Company brought by Nardi and Bonetti arrived to perform the so-called grand opera season. For years this had been the province of these impresarios, and it always included the August 25 Independence Day gala performance. Maestro Leopoldo Mugnone, remembered for his 1902 season, returned, this time bringing three new operas for Montevideo: his own *Vita brettone*, Mas-

cagni's *Amica*, and Catalani's *Loreley*. Two new singers, Russ and Giachetti, shared the leading soprano roles with Storchio. Solís audiences were also able to again hear two star tenors, Anselmi and Zenatello.

Aida, with Russ, Zenatello, and Didur as Ramfis, opened the season on August 19, 1905. The next day a reviewer wrote that Zenatello "is one of the best Radamès of our times, now that Tamagno is retired."[12] Coincidentally, Francesco Tamagno died a few days later, on August 31, 1905, in Varese, Italy, at the age of fifty-four. Giannina Russ, this production's Aida, came to Montevideo in the year of her La Scala debut. She would later become famous for her Verdi dramatic soprano roles and for being the best Norma of her day. When talking about her at the time of her 1905 Aida, one reviewer said, "Very seldom have we heard 'Oh, patria mia!' with such strong feeling as Giannina Russ sang it last night."[13]

Having two performances in a row of both *Manons*, with Puccini's sung on August 20 by Giachetti and Zenatello, and Massenet's two days later by Storchio and Anselmi can only be called an opera luxury. Rarely could two outstanding pairs of singers put on such a display. Solís audiences were truly fortunate in these years. At twenty-five, Giachetti's career was in the ascendant since her successful Covent Garden debut one year earlier[14] when she sang Puccini's heroine opposite Caruso. "A Manon insuperable for her voice, [Giachetti] has a brilliant future in store" commented one reviewer after her Solís performance.[15] About Storchio and Anselmi the same critic raved, "An artistic couple, truly sensational! Rarely could such a complete Des Grieux be found. He reminds us of the famous [Angelo] Masini of old."[16] Another critic said: "Mr. Anselmi's ovation following 'Il sogno' is one of those that he will remember forever in his singing career; of course, he also gave a resounding encore. Rosina Storchio's Manon, so poetic, fragile, and perfidious at the same time, surpassed any ideal characterization of the Massenet heroine we could ask for."[17]

On August 29, Mugnone conducted the Montevideo premiere of his own opera *Vita brettone*. The reviews were disappointing, claiming that "it did not add anything to operatic history, neither new language nor aesthetic discovery. *Vita brettone* is, in the original and primitive meaning of the word, just an opera."[18] The last of Mugnone's works for the stage, this opera had its world premiere at the San Carlo in Naples just before the conductor came to Montevideo. In spite of having written his first opera when he was twelve years old, Mugnone never attained the reputation as a composer that he garnered as a conductor.

Amica, Mascagni's tenth opera, was first performed on the Solís stage only five months after its Monte Carlo world premiere on March 16, 1905. Even the Monte Carlo casting with Geraldine Farrar, Charles Rousselière and Maurice Renaud, and the Solís casting of Russ, Anselmi, and Giraldoni, could not save it from a lukewarm reception, from audiences on both continents.

Finally, for his third new operatic offering, Mugnone chose Catalani's *Loreley*, widely known during this period thanks to Toscanini's promotion of the composer. It was certainly far more successful than *Amica*, being lauded as "beautiful, with plenty of inspiration and interesting and well-done instrumentation, *Loreley* produced, indeed, a deep emotion among Teatro Solís audiences."[19]

With the departure of Mugnone and his artists, impresario Rendina brought to the Solís a third Italian Lyric Company, under the baton of Maestro Rinaldo Giovanelli. He conducted eight productions, including two operettas and a concert, but since this was off-season, none of these productions were of note. The principal singers in that late spring season were sopranos Ida Gobatto (for the second time that year) and Elvira Barbieri, tenors Pietro Gubellini and Atilio Perico, and baritones Emmanuele Bucalo and Mario Roussel.

* * *

A NEW THEATER was also opened in Montevideo during 1905: the Teatro Urquiza (fig. 31), inaugurated on September 5 by Sarah Bernhardt in Victorien Sardou's *La sorcière*. The new house, in Art Nouveau style, was an architectural expression of the Belle Epoque, and a novelty for the Montevideo of that time. Located on the corner of Andes and Mercedes streets, in the heart of the modern city, it was built by Uruguayan engineer Guillermo West by request of Dr. Justo G. Urquiza.[20] Although he spent his youth in Argentina, Dr. Urquiza wished to recognize his natal city by giving it a new theater to be proud of.

As its owner did not spare expense in the building of the new house, all the materials for the decoration were imported from France by the best Buenos Aires stores and brought to Montevideo. The result was a surprise for theatergoers: to begin with, it had avoided the classic red and gold of all other houses, replacing them by subdued shades of Nile green and pale rose.

The Urquiza had a six hundred–seat auditorium and four tiers: lower boxes, second tier or *tertulia*, and two galleries (*cazuela* and *paraíso*) (see chapter 3). The total capacity at that time was approximately twenty-eight hundred seats. The curtain was in Nile green velvet, with embroideries in rose and silver silk, and the orchestra chairs, upholstered in green velvet, were framed in natural oak. It is also interesting to point out the shape of the auditorium. Instead of the horseshoe design (as in the Solís), the Urquiza seating was arranged in an open-fan shape, with the narrow

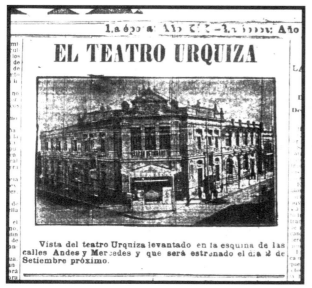

Fig. 31. *Left*: The new Teatro Urquiza, *El Día*, August 22, 1905, front page. Library of Congress Collection. *Right*: Program of the opening of the Teatro Urquiza with Sarah Bernhardt in Victorien Sardou's *La sorcière*, on September 5, 1905. [The program, printed in advance, says September 2]. Biblioteca Nacional Collection, Montevideo.

end near the stage, and the wide, rounded end toward the rear of the house, in order to achieve a better view of the stage.

However, one of the most original things of the new house was the design of the balconies of the four tiers. They were made of convex metal with a bulged lower part, with cuts of voluptuous lines and lotus shapes, and covered with painted chrysanthemums. With the opening of the Urquiza, Montevideo theatergoers had firsthand experience of the Art Nouveau style. The walls of the boxes, as well as those of the anterooms, were covered by hand-painted green silk wallpaper with golden flowers. And the lavish extravagance of the epoch were fans installed in each anteroom, so that the people of the boxes had fresh air during performances. The lights of the house were a chic display of metal sconces with crystal tulips in flowerlike shape. The ceiling was a light frame of curved wooden ribs covered with painted papier-mâché, and with arches that were supported by the capitals of the upper gallery columns.

Even though Dr. Urquiza was the new house owner, he lived in Buenos Aires and also overseas, so the person in charge of everyday business, impresario José Crodara, acted in many ways as a permanent administrative manager. The owner's first idea was to open the theater in August with an Italian opera company. And early in 1905, the Montevidean press reported negotiations in progress with Nardi and Bonetti.[21] However, the delay in the construction of the building changed the plans. As a result, impresario Cesare Ciacchi was contacted, and was able to bring Sarah Bernhardt for the inauguration season.

The opening night was announced for September 2, but it was postponed due to an indisposition of the famous actress, who had surgery on the same day, performed by the well-known Uruguayan physician Dr. Alfredo Navarro. (The programs, which were printed in advance, of course showed the date as September 2.) Finally, the Teatro Urquiza opening took place on September 5, 1905, with the presence of the president of Uruguay Dr. José Batlle y Ordoñez.[22] As was expected, Mme. Bernhardt was the queen of the evening, with several standing ovations at the end of each act of *La sorcière*. The short season continued with six more productions, and the "divine" Sarah, as she was at that time frequently called, triumphed to the point of apotheosis, with extended reviews and interviews in all Montevideo newspapers. Everybody was pointing out that it was a luxury for Montevideo that an actress of such world magnitude came to open a new theater. The rest of the season continued with an Italian operetta company, various concerts, and the Sagi-Barba Spanish Zarzuela Company.

In 1931 the Urquiza building was bought by the government (Uruguayan Broadcasting Service) and became the studio-auditorium of the SODRE (Servicio Oficial de Difusión Radio Eléctrica). Forty years later, in 1971, the house burned down as a consequence of the tragic political turmoil of that epoch. (For further discussion of this theater see chapters 24 and 26.) Even with such sudden bursts of glory as this 1905 opening, and some interesting seasons with first-rank artists, the Urquiza never displaced the Teatro Solís as the country's leading stage.

* * *

THE TEATRO SOLÍS Golden Jubilee Year—1906—saw a dazzlingly array of performances. It was a year of three different Italian lyric companies, a fall opera season brought by impresarios Bonelli and Marranti; the winter short season brought by Bernabei; and the Nardi and Bonetti Grand Opera season in August. The house received a total of seventy-seven leading-role singers, four conductors, sixty opera performances, twelve Spanish opera and zarzuela evenings, and a French operetta company. We know that Toscanini was among the conductors, giving the first Uruguayan performance of Wagner's *Tristan und Isolde*, with Salomea Kruszelnicka, the new opera star of the season, who did sing as Krusceniski in Italy and in Italian seasons abroad.

The singers of the 1906 Solís season were Hariclée Darclée, Storchio again, Ines De Frate, Esperanza Clasenti, Luisa Garibaldi, Anselmi, Garbin, Amato, Giuseppe de Luca, Riccardo Stracciari, Didur, and Gaudio Mansueto, to name only those that sooner or later would be traveling to Milan, London, Saint Petersburg, and New York. It is also worthwhile to remember the great Spanish singers Emilio Sagi-Barba, Luisa Vela, and José Mardones, who gave Puccini's *La bohème* and *Tosca* (both in Spanish versions). While Toscanini's season was clearly the year's highlight, other performances during the 1906 theatrical year are worth mentioning. Immediately before Toscanini's arrival, Maestro Arnaldo Conti conducted a short season that opened with Massenet's *Manon* on August 2, with a remarkable cast headed by Darclée, Carlo Dani, and celebrated bass Mansueto.

Toscanini inaugurated the Grand Opera season on August 18 with Massenet's *Manon*. This meant that for the third consecutive year

Storchio repeated one of her most successful roles, while also appearing in a revival of *Madama Butterfly* as Cio-Cio-San, and displaying her versatile personality as Rosina, Norina, and the *Don Giovanni* Zerlina in the days that followed. On opening night *Manon* also featured the debut of Riccardo Stracciari as Lescaut, together with the well-known Anselmi as Des Grieux. Stracciari came to Uruguay on the way from Milan and Buenos Aires to his New York Metropolitan debut.

Toscanini was known as a Wagner advocate in Italy, and he also was instrumental in introducing many of the composer's operas to South America. On August 19 he conducted *Tristan und Isolde*, translated, of course, into Italian. This performance was hyped by the press even before the conductor's arrival; newspapers published lengthy articles on Wagner, his philosophical and aesthetic theories, and the history of *Tristan und Isolde*. The idea was to immerse everyone in the complexity of Wagner's musical drama. It is thus surprising to read one critic's commentary, calling it a work of "absolute classicism." Even if Wagner is the most controversial composer of the nineteenth century, there is one point on which almost everybody agrees: a musical revolution began with the chromaticism of *Tristan*, the "floating tonality" derived from the famous "*Tristan* chord," considered by many as the starting point of modern music.

This performance marked the Montevideo debut of Salomea Kruszelnicka, a young Ukrainian soprano who would return to the Solís often in her career. Born in Tarnopol, she had made her debut at Lemberg (now Lviv) in 1892, when she was twenty years old, and she inaugurated her Italian career at Cremona in the 1895–96 season. Her first big success came with her Cio-Cio-San in the second version of *Madama Butterfly*, under Cleofonte Campanini. One year after appearing in the 1906 Solís season, Kruszelnicka debuted at La Scala as the leading soprano of the German repertoire.

During her first Solís season Kruszelnicka sang four roles: Tosca, Loreley, Wally, and the Isolde of her debut. In all operas she displayed her singular beauty with what was considered an enigmatic, Eastern softness, a warm voice, and a dramatic and vigorous style occasionally combined with highly stylized gestures. In a long review of this *Tristano e Isotta*, one critic exults in the qualities of Kruszelnicka's voice: "After Toscanini, the high point of the night was Krusceniski [*sic*] as the ideal interpreter of Isotta. . . . She is an artist of great value and talent who sings passionately with a voice of wide register admirably handled."[23]

Riccardo Stracciari, who had sung Kurwenal in the opening-night Wagner, gave one of his best performances of the season in *La traviata* with Storchio and Anselmi two nights later. Considered one of the best baritones of his time and rival to Amato and Titta Ruffo, his Solís debut was praised by the press:

> The hero of the night was the baritone Stracciari. He has a very extended and resonant voice, of a beautiful velvety quality that he manages with mastery. It must be said that he is one of the most famous and talented baritones we have ever heard. In the famous act two aria ["Di Provenza il mar . . ."] the public pressed hard for an encore. Everyone remembers the maestro's policy of no encores at all, but this time Maestro Toscanini was forced to accede to the public request. There followed a prolonged ovation as a tribute to Stracciari.[24]

August 25, 1906, was a day of joy and emotion when the Teatro Solís curtain rose and Toscanini mounted the podium to conduct a

Fig. 32. Solís Golden Jubilee Gala performance on August 25, 1906, featuring *Tosca* with Salomea Kruszelnicka [Krusceniski] in the title role, tenor Edoardo Garbin, and baritone Riccardo Stracciari, with Toscanini conducting. Biblioteca Nacional Collection, Montevideo.

multistellar *Tosca* with Kruszelnicka, Garbin, and Stracciari (fig. 32). Some of those lucky enough to be in the house were reminded of the time fifty years earlier when the Solís curtain was raised for the first time. Since then, hundreds of leading musical and dramatic artists gave life, night after night, to new dreams and fantasies. The entire house was filled with pride that a man of Toscanini's stature was participating in this Jubilee celebration, conducting not only an opera season, but a symphonic-vocal concert as well.

Toscanini's twelve-performance sojourn cannot be discussed without including a colorful (and clever) episode. "The coffee for the Maestro! Let me pass, please, let me pass, the coffee for Maestro Toscanini!" So saying, a waiter from the Tupí-Nambá café—a traditional Montevideo café in fin de siècle style, just across the street from the Solís—hurriedly entered backstage carrying a tray with coffee and a glass of water. Or so it appeared. In a time when autograph hunters had begun to chase Solís celebrities, Toscanini gave stagehands and ushers strict orders not to allow anybody backstage. The rule did not apply to people serving him, and so, one morning an opera lover paid the café's real waiter to exchange clothes with him; picking up the coffee tray, he entered Toscanini's dressing room. Chatting conversationally while the conductor drank his coffee, he dared to ask for Toscanini's autograph, which Toscanini graciously gave him—as well as a tip! Once back in the corridors of the house, this fan again exchanged his clothes with the true waiter and left the Solís enthusiastically waving Toscanini's autograph. Neither the stagehands nor the ushers—who saw and clearly understood the ruse—ever said a single word to the conductor. Such a clever ploy deserved a reward.

In the early fall of 1906 a second-rank Italian opera company gave a two-month series, significant only for the world premiere of an opera written by Uruguayan composer Ramón Rodríguez Socas, then only nineteen years old and at the beginning of what would be a long career. *Alda*, based on an Italian libretto by L. Ambruzzi, was a one-act opera, here sung by Uruguayan soprano Romilda Berti and conducted by her husband, Maestro Antonio Marranti. This opera "had an outstanding success, in spite of having been greatly influenced by Puccini and Mascagni."[25]

The 1906 spring season saw a French opera-and-operetta company giving more than fifteen renowned operettas and five of the most popular French operas. According to the company's advertisements the "étoile" of the season was soprano Vera Courtenay, in her Teatro Solís debut. She sang Micaëla and the title role in Delibes' *Lakmé*, closing the 1906 season with Massenet's *Manon* on November 29. She was the third singer to sing that role in 1906,[26] but the only one to do so in French. Her Uruguayan triumph was apparently based on "her warm voice and scenic poise and her five years in the roster of the Paris Opéra-Comique.

The Teatro Solís Jubilee Year was completed by several concerts, among them two by Florizel von Reuter, a talented boy-violinist, and three by the German pianist and composer Conrad Ansorge, famous for having been one of Liszt's pupils. Although little known today, Ansorge was then considered one of the most successful pianists and pedagogues of all Europe.

CHAPTER 18

~ *1861–1918* ~

Glitter and Gaiety at Solís Operetta Seasons—The First American Musical: *The Black Crook*—An Outstanding English Operetta Season—Lehár Works Close Half a Century of Frivolous and Nonchalant Operettas

*L*ate in the nineteenth century Montevideo fell under the spell of things French: as had happened with the poetry of the French Symbolists, operetta fascinated the circles of Montevideo's high society. Many people, from the youngest to the oldest, dreamed of themselves whirling 'round the dance floor to waltz tunes, or being at Maxim's in Paris drinking champagne in the midst of piquant girls. Contagious melodies, lovely chorus girls, and sometimes risqué couplets all attracted audiences. Operetta seasons at the Teatro Solís always had more eager fans than tickets.

Operetta companies came fairly early to Montevideo, predating Gustav Mahler's introduction of operetta into Hamburg's Stadt-Theater by thirty years. In 1861 the famous Troupe des Bouffes-Parisiens performed such works as Jacques Offenbach's *Le savetier et le financier* and Alfred Dufresne's *Maître Baton* on the Solís stage. Later on, the Operetta

Company Emon and Marti brought such popular works as *Le domino noir* and *Les diamants de la couronne*, both by Daniel-François-Esprit Auber, and Fromental Halévy's *Les mousquetaires de la Reine*—clear exponents, with their captivating dance rhythms, of the early French style, circa 1835–1850.[1]

Croquefer, *Tromb-al-ca-zar*, and *Les deux pêcheurs* were among the early Offenbach works presented in 1866 under the baton of Poppe in a new Solís season of the Bouffes-Parisiens. Two years later the same company offered the charming and amusing one-act Offenbach operetta *La chatte métamorphosée en femme*, sharing the stage with a Louis Moreau Gottschalk concert. With the visiting companies presenting the same operettas that they had premiered in France, Solís audiences were able to enjoy major Offenbach works and witness the development of French operetta. In 1868 the Bouffes-Parisiens presented this composer's *La Grande Duchesse de Gérolstein*, and that year the season culminated with the Uruguayan premiere of *Orphée aux enfers*.

Even if the operetta—with its jokes, double entendres, and puns—often loses something when it is translated into other languages, most operettas heard in Montevideo were heard in the language of the performing company. Thus, Franz Lehár's *Die lustige Witwe* (The Merry Widow) was sung in the original German only once in 1910 by a German operetta company. Thereafter, it was performed in Italian as *La vedova allegra* by an Italian company, in French as *La veuve joyeuse* by a French company, and in Spanish as *La viuda alegre* by a Spanish company. In 1874 Solís audiences were able to see what is considered the first American musical comedy ever created: *The Black Crook*. Based on a book by Charles M. Barras and first performed eight years earlier at New York's Niblo's Garden, the music was a hodgepodge of numbers by various composers. The only Montevideo presentation by this "American Operetta Company from Niblo's Garden"[2] was sung in English and performed from October 21 to November 6, 1874. Although there does not seem to be an extant critical review of *The Black Crook*, the fact that an English-language production lasted for almost three weeks in a city of approximately 90,000 inhabitants reveals the existence of an eager audience. After *The Black Crook*'s stay, sixteen years would pass before Solís audiences could hear another operetta sung in English. More than one hundred years later the significance of *The Black Crook* as a pioneering work in American musical comedy is clearly acknowledged: "Though not an operetta by any means, *The Black Crook* was a significant milestone in American musical theatre history as an early example of showmanship and publicity, and an early confirmation that Americans would

crave spectacle, dancing, and attractive girls in their musical entertainments."[3]

Like a dream of my childhood, I remember hearing my French grandmother hum some very catchy operetta tunes. When I asked where they came from my grandmother answered, "*La fille de Madame Angot*." In fact, since its Belgian premiere, when Paris was still suffering the consequences of the 1870 Franco-Prussian War, Charles Lecocq's masterpiece was one of the more frequently performed operettas around the world. Even before the company from L'Opéra-Comique in Paris presented *La fille de Madame Angot* at the Teatro Solís in 1875, all Montevideo music stores displayed the operetta piano score, and shelves were soon emptied of successive editions. Soon the operetta's catchy melodies had spread among Montevideo aficionados. Among all the operettas performed at the Solís between 1870 and the end of the century, *La fille de Madame Angot* could be matched in popularity only by *Les cloches de Corneville*. One of the most popular of all French operettas ever composed, this latter work, by Robert Planquette was presented at the Solís in 1878, one year after its world premiere at Les Folies-Dramatiques in Paris.

French operetta, which introduced composers such as François Bazin and Adrien Boieldieu, reached its peak in 1881, when a French opera company under the general direction of Maurice Grau, with the conductor Gravenstein at the podium, arrived at the Solís to perform a five-week season. They brought an extensive repertoire of operas and operettas, including the French version of Verdi's *La traviata*, Georges Bizet's *Carmen*, Donizetti's *La fille du régiment*, Ambroise Thomas' *Mignon*, and the South American premiere of Victor Massé's *Paul et Virginie*. Among the fifteen different operetta titles were two new works: Offenbach's *La Périchole* and Lecocq's *Giroflé-Giroflá*. The company of singers included the excellent soprano Hélène Leroux, tenor Paul Mauras, and bass-baritone monsieur F. Maugé. Two other company members must also be pointed out. Mezzo-soprano Paola Marié was the star of Paris with a record of 411 performances as Clairette in *La fille de Madame Angot*. This preceded her Solís season by eight years, when she sang the title roles in *Carmen* and *Mignon* (which, co-incidentally, had been created by her sister, Célestine Galli-Marié). Paola and Célestine were both taught by their father, Félix Mécène Marié de L'Isle, a double-bass player, tenor, and conductor.

The second noted company member was its own director, Maurice Grau. Czech in origin, he was an interesting combination of impresario, entrepreneur, and lawyer. He began his career nine years before his Uruguayan stopover, organizing tours with artists such as Offenbach and Sarah Bernhardt. Grau's career began in the United States, where after graduating from Columbia Law School he served for almost ten years as director of the Metropolitan Opera. Unfortunately, such an interesting character, "suave, multilingual, apparently conciliatory—and tough as nails—who could talk on the phone with his stockbroker while laying out casts," was at the Solís only one season.[4]

Two years after this outstanding French period, Solís operetta fans first became acquainted with one of the finest representatives of the Vienna golden age of operetta, Franz von Suppé, through his three most famous operettas, *Boccaccio*, *Donna Juanita*, and *Fatinitza* (the latter in its first South American performance). As the creator of a style that would become famous for its irresistible rhythms, elegance, and joie de vivre, Suppé's melodies can be compared only to those of his immediate successor, Johann Strauss. (Strangely enough, considering the relish with which Montevideo enjoyed operetta, Strauss' operettas arrived in Montevideo twenty-five years after those of Suppé.)

If *Boccaccio* was the best known of Suppé's operettas in Europe, it was *Donna Juanita* that could claim fame as the operetta most frequently heard in Montevideo. Since its premiere in 1883, for thirty consecutive years Solís spectators enjoyed the adventures of the young French cadet disguised as the coquettish Spanish girl, Juanita. Such popularity was not confined to South America; as early as 1881 the New York public applauded the first English production of *Donna Juanita* at the Fifth Avenue Theatre. This same Suppé operetta, conducted by Artur Bodanzky, appeared on New York's Metropolitan Opera stage as late as January 2, 1932 (sung in German by Maria Jeritza).[5]

In the midst of this Viennese operetta craze, Montevideo received an English operetta company, this time from the very core of the Savoy Theatre tradition. On the opening night of October 4, 1890, Maestro Barter Jones conducted the English Comic Opera Company in the Uruguayan premiere of Gilbert and Sullivan's *The Mikado*. The 1890 Solís season finished off with two more Gilbert and Sullivan comic operas, *The Pirates of Penzance* and *Trial by Jury*.

In spite of *The Mikado*'s being the most famous and most popular of Gilbert and Sullivan productions, *Trial by Jury* remains one of the most successful operettas of all times. Perhaps the only one in the operetta genre without spoken dialogue, its tunes are influenced by the French school, but the plot is absolutely English. The peculiar situation of presenting a bride all dressed in her wedding gown in the middle of an austere English courtroom was very unusual for the Solís audiences of 1890. Nevertheless, with its originality and freshness it was a good choice for closing that brief English operetta season.

Other productions of that season were Alfred Cellier's *Dorothy* and Edward Solomon's *Pepita, or the Girl with Glass Eyes*. Cellier was celebrated for being the almost official conductor of the Sullivan operettas at London's Savoy Theatre, and of his own compositions *Dorothy* was the most successful operetta. Solomon, often thought of as Sullivan's successor, was known to American audiences for more than his music: his favorite star and one of *Pepita*'s singers was the legendary Lillian Russell; known as America's Operetta Queen, she also became the second Mrs. Solomon.

With *The Mikado*'s success, the turn of the century witnessed an Oriental vogue on the European stages. (The zenith of this fashion would of course be Puccini's *Madama Butterfly*, in 1904.) Eleven years after *The Mikado* another English operetta re-created the same flavor. This time it was Sidney Jones' *The Geisha* which, since its opening night on April 25, 1896, was a tremendous success not only in England but also in continental Europe and America. Part of such success came from the ability of George Edwardes, the famous London Daly's Theatre impresario, who engaged a member of the Japanese legation as his adviser to create an authentic look. The first Uruguayan performance took place at the Solís, on July 3, 1902, with an Italian operetta company under the baton of Ciro Sconamiglio. *The Geisha* (*La geisha* in its Italian version) was performed many times until 1918. Interestingly, while all of the previously mentioned English operettas were sung in the original language, *The Geisha* was sung in Italian, German, and Spanish, but never in English. The 1918 Solís performance, sung by soprano Clara Weiss with conductor Riccardo Cendalli, was one of the best of the Solís *La Geisha* productions.

Put together a waltz, champagne, laughter, a touch of passion, some suggestive jokes, and an insinuating smile—all set off by wonderful gowns, tails, and white gloves—and you will have a perfect operetta from la belle époque. Using these ingredients, the fulcrum of the Viennese operetta was the élan and elegance of the waltz, from 1905 immortalized in Lehár's *Die lustige Witwe* (fig. 33).

Operetta thus underwent an evolution, with the substitution of a new romantic and sentimental atmosphere for the old satiric plot. Montevideo swayed to the music and romance of all such operettas until the end of the First World War. Different companies, sometimes two or three in the same year, came to perform the Viennese repertoire. In addition to enjoying works by Strauss and Lehár, Solís audiences were able to hear operettas by Leo Fall, Emmerich Kálmán, Carl Millöcker, Carl Michael Ziehrer, and Carl Zeller, as well as the French and Italian repertoire, including one of Leoncavallo's operettas. Italian companies were the ones to perform most frequently at the Solís, with three leading ensembles coming to Montevideo, sometimes during the same year: the Ettore Vitale Operetta Company, the Città di Milano Operetta Company, and the Sconamiglio Operetta Company. They were responsible for most of the Uruguayan premieres of the most famous operettas. For example, on July 20, 1909, the Ettore Vitale Operetta Company gave Lehár's *La vedova allegra* with soprano Giselda Morosoni singing the title role. Another renowned Hanna Glawari was Clara Weiss, who performed at the Solís in 1913, 1918, and 1926.

Two important German operetta companies arrived in 1910. The first one, under the baton of Maestro Kapeller, opened its season with the first Uruguayan performance of Lehár's *Der Graf von Luxemburg* and ended with Strauss' *Die Fledermaus*. Two conductors, A. Peisker and Carl Dibbern, headed the second company and, in addition to presenting the original Lehár *Die lustige Witwe*, performed a wide repertoire that included works by Oscar

Straus, Millöcker, Rudolf Nelson [Rudolf Lewysohn], and of course Strauss.

Jean Gilbert's *Die keusche Susanne* was the big Solís novelty of the 1911 spring season. It was performed as *La casta Susanna* in its Italian version by the Ettore Vitale Company only one year after its world premiere in Magdeburg. Born in Hamburg in 1879, Max Winterfeld adopted the nom de plume Jean Gilbert when he composed his first operetta in 1901. Gilbert and *La casta Susanna* found great favor among Río de la Plata operetta fans. In fact, when Gilbert was forced to leave Berlin in 1933, after traveling from place to place, he settled in Buenos Aires. Gilbert later returned to Uruguay, this time to conduct a brief but very successful operetta season at the SODRE, which ended with a triumphant performance of *La casta Susana*.

On June 1912 Maestro Marchetti gave the premiere of another popular Lehár operetta, *Eva*. This was followed three months later by the first performance of *La reginetta delle rose* at the Solís. This work, a recent Leoncavallo operetta, received its world premiere in Italy, and its Solís performance gave Montevideo audiences the opportunity to know the last phase of this composer.

In addition to a brilliant season by the Italian operetta company Città di Milano, with Clara Weiss, the Teatro Solís opened its doors

Fig. 33. *Upper Left*: the Ettore Vitale Company introduced the Uruguayan premiere of *La vedova alegra* (The Merry Widow) on July 1909. *Upper Right*: the Ciro Sconamiglio Company presented the popular *Saltimbanchi* in the 1902 season. *Lower*: the French Music Hall from Paris's Théâtre Ba-Ta-Clan, directed by Madame Rasimi brought, for the first time to Montevideo, the famous Mistinguette. Review from *La Razón*, July 18, 1923 [with the wrong spelling of the dancer's name]. Biblioteca Nacional Collection, Montevideo.

in 1913 to a French operetta company from Paris' Opéra-Comique. In an opening night when glitter and glamour were as much in the house as on the stage, Lehár's French version of *La veuve joyeuse* was presented on July 3. Hanna Glawari and Count Danilo were sung by Angèle Van Loo and tenor Henri Dutilloy. Dutilloy debuted as a very young man with the Paris Opéra-Comique, singing in a style called "baryton-Martin"; that is, in a high baritone voice with falsetto singing, a style originated by the famous Opéra-Comique star Jean-Blaise Martin. Dutilloy continued his career singing baritone roles in France and America (although he occasionally sang tenor roles as well, as he did at the Solís as Danilo, and at the Metropolitan Opera as Pomponnet in *La fille de Madame Angot* at about the same time). In 1914 Solís music lovers were once again able to hear a famous Lehár work. This time it was a Spanish operetta company that gave (according to the nostalgic memories of my family) a ravishing version of *La viuda alegre*.

Until the end of the First World War all of these companies continued to offer extended operetta seasons at the Teatro Solís. Later on, the operetta vanished from the stage as la belle époque faded away, banished by the hard and more realistic postwar period. Nevertheless, people refused to give up all fantasy, and more than ever sheet-music sales of operetta highlights soared. Montevideo was not the exception; operetta remained a staple in drawing-room musical gatherings. And as the years passed, two of the most famous operettas, Lehár's *Die lustige Witwe* and Strauss' *Die Fledermaus*, found places at all opera houses. Unbelievable as it now seems, at the time of *Die lustige Witwe*'s premiere, Lehár was offered 5,000 crowns by Wilhelm Karczag (then director of the Theater an der Wien) if he withdrew the operetta before opening night. Thank God Lehár did not accept!

CHAPTER 19

1907–1914

Leopoldo Mugnone Conducts Massenet and Wagner Uruguayan Premieres—
An Overnight Star: Amelita Galli-Curci—Mascagni's Arrival—
Isabeau—Celestina Boninsegna—*Guglielmo Ratcliff*—*Parsifal*—
The Ballets Russes: Vaslav Nijinsky and Tamara Karsavina

uring a four-year period Montevideo opera lovers who frequented the Solís had the opportunity to hear some of the best representatives of the French and German opera repertoire. To start with, Maestro Rodolfo Ferrari, in his first and only season at the Solís, introduced two French operas in 1907: Jules Massenet's *Hérodiade* and Henri Leroux's *Theodora*. One year later Leopoldo Mugnone gave the Uruguayan premiere of *Die Walküre*, as well as Massenet's *Thaïs*. The celebrated maestro, well remembered for conducting the first Uruguayan performances of *Tosca*, *Zazà*, *Don Giovanni*, *Germania*, and his own *Vita brettone*, offered Richard Wagner's *Götterdämmerung* and Gustave Chapentier's *Louise* in 1910.

A stellar group of singers, some of them new to Solís audiences, contributed to the success of those productions. French tenor Charles Rousselière was one of the new artists of the 1907 Solís season. Recipient of the 1900

Singing Award of the Paris Conservatory, he debuted the same year at the Paris Opéra with *Samson et Dalila*. When Rousselière stepped onto the Solís stage on August 18 in the title role of Verdi's *Don Carlo*, he was preceded by his Metropolitan debut and his creation of Andrea in *Theodora*'s world premiere at Monte Carlo's Opera House on March 19, 1907. The day after his *Don Carlo* Solís debut, Rousselière charmed Solís audiences with his Andrea, one of his favorite characters.[1]

Maestro Rodolfo Ferrari was also greatly praised for his remarkable conducting skills. The beginning of the 1907 Solís season saw the publication of the following notice: "Young conductor Ferrari, born in Bologna in 1863, made his conducting debut at Milan's Teatro Lirico. As soon as the present Solís season is over he will head for New York's Metropolitan Opera House, where he has been engaged for the amount of 20,000 francs."[2]

According to music news in the Montevideo newspapers, at the beginning of August

1908 a complete crew from Empresa Nardi and Bonetti, plus the Solís' own machinists and electricians, worked frantically to prepare the scenery for opening night, Charles Gounod's *Romeo e Giulietta*, with Frances Alda and Giuseppe Anselmi in the title roles and Mugnone conducting. But the two events everybody was looking for took place some days later: Massenet's *Thaïs* on August 20 and Wagner's *Die Walküre* on August 22, both in their Uruguayan premieres. While *Die Walküre* had a very enthusiastic reception, Massenet's new opera was not well received by the critics, although the performers were warmly praised:

> We saw and heard a very modern *Thaïs*, almost Parisian in influence. The composer never plumbed the psychology of the characters, as had been achieved in Anatole France's original novel, because Massenet commented only on the surface of people without going deeper. Nevertheless, we recognize the composer's great technical skills and good taste. The musical interpreters of *Thaïs* were outstanding, in particular [Riccardo] Stracciari's Athanaël. The baritone performed his part admirably, both vocally and scenically. La Berlendi performed very well until the last act. Orchestra and chorus were excellent, and the "mise en scène" was magnificent.[3]

Wagner elicited much more favorable press. In an article published five days before *Die Walküre*'s first Uruguayan performance, it was reported that by "7 o'clock there wasn't a single ticket at the Solís box office, not even for general admission or standing room. It was sad to see frustration on the faces of the people. . . . But no one was ready to give up, and the scalpers were practically assaulted by an anxious multitude."[4]

If the success of *Thaïs* was due to soprano

Livia Berlendi and baritone Riccardo Stracciari, Wagner's work had an even more impressive cast: Salomea Kruszelnicka [Krusceniski], Elena Rakowska (the future Mme. Tullio Serafin), Marie Claessens, Charles Rousselière, Adamo Didur, and Andrés Perelló de Segurola, with Mugnone conducting. This is a fragment of one of the extensive reviews that appeared the day after this *Die Walküre* performance:

> There never could be two different opinions about *La walkiria*'s [*sic*] interpretation because it was superb. Nevertheless, the warmest compliments must go to La Krusceniski [*sic*], a Brunhilda without rival, whose interpretation goes from an almost masculine energy in some scenes to a touching tenderness in others. Her voice is outstanding, and her fiery war cry was followed by a huge ovation. La Rakowska was a magnificent Siglinda, of Junoesque beauty, but with a volume of voice smaller than her physique.
>
> Rousselière displayed his excellent school of singing, and his acting was elegant yet convincing. The personification of Wotan done by Didur was, as he always is, notable, and Segurola was excellent as Hunding. Mugnone deserves the highest praise, almost a dithyramb, for his conducting. He interprets Wagner with all the fire of his meridional temperament. The ride of the walkirias, the second-act tempest and the Magic Fire scene were superbly otherworldly.[5]

Mugnone's remarkable opera season ended on August 25 with a *Rigoletto* starring Alda, Anselmi, and Giuseppe de Luca. In addition to her opening-night Giulietta, Alda sang Gilda, Violetta, Philine, and Margherita in *Faust*. This was the only time she sang these roles in Montevideo. The New Zealand–born Alda, twenty-nine at the time of her Solís performances, debuted at New York's Metropol-

Fig. 34. Amelita Galli-Curci, an understudy who, singing Gilda in *Rigoletto*, became an overnight star. Library of Congress Collection.

itan Opera four months later in the same *Rigoletto* opposite Caruso. Alda was trained in Paris by the famous Mathilde Marchesi who, in addition to suggesting the adoption of "Alda" in lieu of the singer's original last name of Davis, prepared her triumphal 1904 debut at the Opéra-Comique in *Manon*. Frances Alda's mother, soprano Leonora Simonsen (1860–1884), was born in Montevideo after her parents, German violinist Martin Simonsen and his French wife, soprano Fanny de Simonsen, gave three presentations on the Solís stage at the end of 1859. The couple performed two operatic recitals on November 10 and 19 with pianist Arthur Loreau, plus an orchestral concert on November 12 with opera excerpts, in which the couple were soloists (see 1859 chronology). In her famous book *Men, Women and Tenors*, Alda writes about her own visit to Montevideo in 1908 to sing on the same stage her grandparents sang on

forty-nine years earlier. "When the company moved across the bay (from Buenos Aires) to Montevideo for an engagement, I experienced the joy of singing in the city where my mother had been born. It seemed to bring me closer to her than I had ever been . . . I drove about Montevideo, through the old Spanish streets, telling myself it was this frowning fronted old house, or there that Grandmother had had her lodgings and where her baby Leonora— my mother—had been born."[6]

The day after Mugnone conducted the first Uruguayan performance of *Götterdämmerung*, the schedule called for a *Rigoletto* under the same baton and starring Esperanza Clasenti, Dmitri Smirnov, and Stracciari. According to an article published the next morning, however, the facts of the August 21, 1910, performance were quite different:

In addition to being a great success for the company, yesterday evening's *Rigoletto* brought a big surprise. Esperanza Clasenti was substituted by La Galli-Cursi [*sic*], who was an astonishing revelation. She sang "Caro nome" with great finesse and a perfect pitch, and her voice was a pure and sweet melodic line. Her agility was prodigious. After receiving a huge ovation she effortlessly sang the "terrible" E-flat offstage.[7]

Such was Amelita Galli-Curci's Solís debut (fig. 34). It is interesting to know that a telegram dated in Montevideo, on August 22, 1910, the day after this successful *Rigoletto*, was sent to the *Rivista Teatrale Melodrammatica* with the following news: "Amelita Galli-Curci who sang in *Rigoletto* gave an stupendous performance as Gilda in Buenos Aires. She is a singer of a rare value."[8] Galli-Curci's Solís performance, just a few days after the one in Buenos Aires, corroborated her success as a new opera star. She would no longer be an understudy for the Gilda role. Some days later she debuted at the Teatro Urquiza with *Il barbiere di Siviglia* in a brief six-performance opera season conducted by Edoardo Vitale. Surprisingly, the review castigated the performance, citing only Titta Ruffo's Figaro as "wonderful."[9] This time the reviewer found Galli-Curci "too weak." Perhaps it was a fluke performance (or review), for Galli-Curci went on to become one of the most beloved singers to appear on the Solís stage, with her 1912 and 1915 seasons standing out with particular force.

Besides all those successful productions, Mugnone conducted a symphonic concert in Montevideo; because of Solís rehearsal schedules, however, the concert was held at the Conservatorio Musical La Lira. The program was made up of Beethoven's Fifth Symphony and preludes for works by Verdi, Wagner, and Mozart.

*   *   *

THE AUGUST 12, 1911, EDITION of the Montevideo newspaper *La Razón* reported the arrival of composer/conductor Pietro Mascagni. In a front page almost completely devoted to photographs of the event, it was reported:

> Last night a large popular reception was held at the port, organized by the Mascagni Committee. As the composer landed at the dock from the steamship *Fusia*, the Municipal Band, under the baton of Maestro Aquiles Gubitosi, broke into a fanfare. After the composer and his wife were seated in a landau, Gubitosi approached to give them a brief welcome speech, ending with a thunderous "Viva Mascagni!" and the applause of a massive multitude that accompanied them, walking all the way up to the hotel.[10]

As part of a South American tour to promote his new operas, the composer came to Montevideo to conduct a grand opera season at the Teatro Solís; of the nine operas he brought, five (plus one overture) were his

own. Two of them, *Isabeau* and *Guglielmo Ratcliff*, were both performed in Uruguay for the first time. *Iris* and *Amica* generated much excitement, but it was nothing compared to the thrill surrounding *Isabeau*. This was the most important opera ever to have its world premiere in South America, an event that had taken place at the Teatro Coliseo in Buenos Aires on June 2. It was subsequently given in Rosario, Rio, and São Paulo, making Montevideo only the fifth city in the world to hear it. From the beginning of that Mascagni tour Montevideo newspapers published almost daily articles and reviews concerning *Isabeau*. Of the other operas Mascagni chose to bring, some (such as *Cavalleria rusticana* and *Iris*) were quite familiar to Solís audiences through many earlier seasons. The company's excellent cast brought new voices to Solís audiences, such as soprano Celestina Boninsegna (who had toured South America in 1910, singing at the Teatro Urquiza in Montevideo), mezzo-soprano Ladislava Hotkowska, tenor Gennaro De Tura, and baritone Carlo Galeffi. There were also the already familiar voices of Maria Farneti, remembered for her Solís debut with Caruso in 1903 (she now shared the principal female roles with Boninsegna), and leading tenor Italo Cristalli.

Aida opened the season on August 12, and two days later a long review appeared:

> Mascagni has an obvious predilection for orchestral nuances and carefully brought out all the details of the *Aida* score. He conducts as a romantic and he is a romantic, but of aristocratic romanticism, without chaos or disorder and always within the framework of a superior aesthetic ideal. His conducting, which displays a contrast of shadows and lights and a care for expressiveness, brought him great applause at the opera's end.... Boninsegna is an uneven artist who has a marvelously deep and dramatic voice, but scenically speaking her acting is very poor.

Hotkowska, in contrast, presents herself very well on the stage and her voice is robust and well-modulated.[11]

Boninsegna's lavish and ringing voice made her perfectly suited for such Verdi heroines as Aida. However, these same qualities put her at a slight disadvantage for the Mascagni parts she sang that season, including the title role in *Amica*, Santuzza, and Maria in *Guglielmo Ratcliff*. Her other heroines included the *Trovatore* Leonora and Arrigo Boito's Margherita. She sang some of these roles more than once.

While *Amica* had first been performed at the Solís six years earlier, under Mugnone's baton (see chapter 17), according to some reviewers Mascagni's version was different: "*Amica* was a real surprise. Maestro Mascagni, with his exuberant temperament, gave us a different interpretation: original, vigorous, stupendous!"[12] The critic from a different newspaper chose to emphasize one of the performers, rather than the conductor: "The hero of last night's *Amica* performance was Mr. Galeffi. Rarely have we heard voices on our stage able to compete with his. Mr. Galeffi is a very young baritone, and the future has in store for him the scepter that Titta Ruffo is holding today."[13]

In fact, Galeffi, who would return to perform at the Teatro Solís during the 1920 and 1923 seasons, was an excellent baritone with a deep, velvet voice and superb acting skills. He had been chosen twice by Mascagni to create the principal baritone roles in *Isabeau*, and *Parisina*. Galeffi's remarkable career stretched from New York's Metropolitan and Chicago's to the main houses of South America and Europe. He is especially remembered as one of the best interpreters of Rigoletto and, even if he never reached Ruffo's worldwide fame, he holds a special place in Solís history.

Isabeau, Mascagni's new opera, performed at the Solís on August 17, had a very strong cast with Farneti in the title role, tenor Antonio Saludas as Folco, and Galeffi as Re Raimundo, Isabeau's father (fig. 35). The next morning's reviews glowed:

> The Solís last night was absolutely extraordinary! The totally packed house was full of the crème-de-la-crème: intellectuals, politicians, high-society, musicians, opera lovers. ... After Maestro Mascagni was greeted by huge applause, an impressive silence dominated the house while the curtain rose and King Raimundo's magnificent quarters appeared. The air was filled with expectation, anxiety, curiosity and above all, respect for the composer.... *Isabeau*'s instrumentation places Mascagni among the first modern composers. The second-act chorus is one of *Isabeau*'s better scenes. ...
>
> Among the performers all glory must go to La Farneti and Galeffi. So young and beautiful, Farneti was the perfect symbol of chastity and purity. Her voice and acting talent paralleled and met all of her role's difficult vocal passages. Galeffi was a brave and athletic King and, as always, he was vocally and scenically perfect. Saludas, in a tenor role that demands all of one's vocal resources, deserved his splendid ovation.[14]

The resounding success of *Isabeau* in South America prompted performances throughout Europe, as was reported in Milan's *Corriere della Sera*. The first was to be at Rome's Costanzi in January 1912, with the composer conducting; this would be followed by performances in London, Brussels, Prague, Paris, Turin, Naples, and Milan's Teatro Lirico.[15] However, all the listed European performances were just plans, many of which did not come about. Rome did not hear it until February 1913, the first Italian cities were actually Venice and Milan, with simultaneous productions (on January 20, 1912) conducted by

Plate 1. Teatro Solís, main entrance. (*Photo © Roberto Morassi.*)

Plate 2. View from the side of the front colonnade; the author stands near the back. *(Photo © Roberto Morassi.)*

Plate 3. Inside the house. *(Photo © Roberto Morassi.)*

Plate 4. The stage with proscenium arch and part of the ceiling. At the right, standing on the stage, are the author and a Teatro Solís staff member. *(Photo © Roberto Morassi.)*

Plate 5. A corner of the Golden Foyer. At the right, between the doors, is a marble bust of Juan Miguel Martínez, first president of the Teatro Solís committee. (*Photo © Roberto Morassi.*)

Plate 6. Poster announcing a performance of Verdi's *Otello* at Brescia's Teatro Grande in 1887, six months after the Teatro alla Scala premiere, with the Uruguyan tenor Giuseppe (José) Oxilia in the title role (see chapter 11).

Claro es que me recuerdo de todo lo
que me escribe Vd. de aquellos tiempos de Montevideo,
y especialmente de Cluzeau Mortet muy simpatico com-
pañero de nuestras reuniones.

Su tan simpatica oferta de mandarme
copias del material de las cosas relacionadas con esta
epoca , me llena de placer, y especialmente el programa del Concierto con Nijinsky, y accepto con caloro-
so agradecimiento.

Como sabe·he tenido que escribir mi
libro basandome su mi memoria, fuera algunas cosas
que mi Señora ha podido reunir aqui y alla por el mundo,
es decir cuanto me podrà enviar me servira mucho para
elproximo libro que tengo la intencion de escribir.

Quedandole muy agradecido ,la saluda
con todo respeto.

Arturo Rubinstein

22 square de l'av. Foch,
   75116 Paris, 14 de Febrero de 1974

Plate 7. The author with Artur Rubinstein backstage at Constitution Hall in Washington, D.C., after his last concert, on March 6, 1976. Below is a fragment of a letter, in Spanish, from Rubinstein to the author in which he mentions Uruguayan friends and musicians and Nijinsky's last performance (see chapter 21).

(Photo © Roberto Morassi.)

Plate 8. Poster announcing the famous "Veglioni" (masked balls) at the Teatro Solís during the 1923 Carnival season (see chapter 14).

Fig. 35. *Upper*: Announcement of the arrival to Montevideo of Pietro Mascagni and interview with the composer. *La Razón*, August 12, 1911. *Lower*: Uruguayan premiere of Mascagni's *Isabeau* at the Solís with the composer conducting, on August 17, 1911. Biblioteca Nacional Collection, Montevideo.

Mascagni and Serafin, respectively. Evidently it was never given in London, Brussels, Prague, or Paris—at least not before the war.

On August 22, 1911, the Solís hosted the most recent premiere of the season, *Guglielmo Ratcliff*. Even though Mascagni began work on this opera in 1882, his first year at the Milan Conservatory (eight years before *Cavalleria rusticana*), it was not performed until 1895, at La Scala. As the composer later often commented, in spite of *Cavalleria*'s phenomenal world success, *Guglielmo Ratcliff* remained his favorite opera. It was never a public favorite, however, and Montevideo's critics and public were no exception:

> Mascagni uses [Heinrich] Heine's poem without allowing a single cut from the librettists; the result is a theatrically heavy and very long opera. Unfortunately, this prevents people from enjoying all the beauties of *Ratcliff*'s score, as the monotony of Heine's poem in the "racconto" style is translated into the music. In addition, *Ratcliff*'s libretto lacks two essential conditions theater must have: life and action. In terms of the performance both Boninsegna and [M.] Pozzi sang and acted well, but the hero of the night was Gennaro De Tura: the real hero of Thermopylae! According to what a well-known singer told me, his role has 227 A's! I do not remember ever witnessing a more demanding tenor role.[16]

The season ended with Mascagni conducting a symphonic concert that, in addition to *L'amico Fritz*'s Intermezzo and *Iris*' "Inno al sole," presented his cherished Tchaikovsky's Sixth Symphony.

*   *   *

A NEW IMPRESARIO, Walter Mocchi and his company "La Teatrale" first appeared on the South American scene in 1912, when they went on an extended tour of that continent, with visits to Argentina, Brazil, Uruguay, Argentina again, and Chile. From that time to 1925 Mocchi visited every year and soon had greater stars than Nardi and Bonetti, whose company had peaked some years before (see chapter 14). The 1912 opera season at the Teatro Solís opened with *Aida*, as had some previous seasons. The Russian soprano Elena Rakowska, in her second visit to Montevideo, sang the title role to good reviews. One critic commented that "if not absolutely perfect, she was still very young, and with the acting abilities that were already present, she would develop into a remarkable singer."[17] But in spite of Rosina Storchio and Galli-Curci's presence as the other two leading sopranos and Gino Marinuzzi as the conductor, the 1912 season was described as "one without brilliance."[18] However, Marinuzzi and Rakowska were Solís stars when they came back the following year to perform Wagner's *Parsifal*, on August 15, 1913, its first performance in Montevideo. (*Parsifal*'s copyright expired on December 31, 1913, thirty years after Wagner's death, so New York and Zurich's 1903 performances of the opera had violated Bayreuth's rights.)

The year 1913 also introduced Marinuzzi's presentation of the Sacred Festival Drama in Buenos Aires and Montevideo. A Sicilian musician who had started his opera conducting career when very young, Marinuzzi had led the first performance of *Tristan* in Palermo in 1909, when he was only twenty-seven. Some time after his South American tour, he would succeed Cleofonte Campanini in Chicago.

It was under Marinuzzi's baton that the 1913 Solís season opened with a performance of Mascagni's *Isabeau* on August 5. Ten days later, after conducting *Die Walküre* and *Lohengrin* (among other operas), Marinuzzi gave the Uruguayan premiere of *Parsifal*, sung in Italian (as were the other Wagner operas), with Guido Vaccani in the title role and bass

Giulio Cirino as Gurnemanz. It was an occasion that had music critics in accord over the performance's glories. The *El Día* review was rapturous, calling Maestro Marinuzzi "the hero of *Parsifal*, the only one to conduct so magisterially this complex and beautiful score."[19] *La Razón*'s critic, Teógenes, was equally enthusiastic:

One of *Parsifal*'s characteristics is the unity of its style. To Marinuzzi and the orchestra must go all our praise, because [they were] able to give us the tonal beauty of the score in a notable way. We must also thank Empresa Mocchi for giving us the opportunity to know so important a work, even before the official Bayreuth date, a huge event for any lover of opera. La Rakowska: superb![20]

During this season Marinuzzi conducted another Uruguayan premiere at the Teatro Solís: *Abul*, a new opera by the Brazilian composer Alberto Nepomuceno. Spanish tenor José Palet—whose performances in Spain and South America had already brought him world recognition—sang the title role in Nepomuceno's opera, with Farneti as his Iskah. The reviews were long and interesting. *La Razón*'s critic wrote:

The libretto, based on an English novel by Herbert Ward, reminded me of Meyerbeer's *Le prophète* and Saint-Saëns' *Samson et Dalila*—with religious love above all the human passions. Abul, chief of a Chaldean tribe, believes he is a prophet who knows the way to redemption. Having had its world premiere only a few weeks ago in Buenos Aires, the opera shows the work of an admirable symphonist with first-rate composition skills. However, we do not yet perceive Nepomuceno's position among modern opera composers.[21]

With four works for the stage, Nepomuceno was afterward better known for his chamber, religious, and symphonic works, and his extensive production. The Brazilian composer frequently incorporated the rhythms and tunes of many Afro-Brazilian dances, as he did in his best-known piece, "Batuque," the last movement of his symphonic work *Serie Brasileira*. Nevertheless his relevance as a creator and his contribution to the Brazilian musical culture goes far beyond. In addition to his career as a major composition teacher and director of the National Institute of Music, he must be remembered as a conductor who not only was the first to lead the symphonic works of his young fellow citizens (for example, Heitor Villa-Lobos), but also the Brazilian premieres of the music of Wagner and all the major French and Russian composers of the first half of the twentieth century.

* * *

DURING THE PERIOD encompassed in this chapter, the Urquiza also had brief attractive opera seasons. Impresario Cesare Ciacchi brought Luisa Tetrazzini in 1907, to sing *Lucia* and *Barbiere*. The audience marveled at the uniformity of her voice, noting that even when she sang high notes, around B or C, her voice remained as full and round as ever. Her remarkable coloratura technique was also demonstrated by the ease with which she handled *staccato* passages, trills, and other ornamentation.

It is interesting that the same company that performed at the Solís from July 16 to 24, 1908, continued the season at the Urquiza from July 25 to 30; that happened more than once during the best years of the new theater. Three good voices that never sang at the Solís came also to the Urquiza, tenor Alessandro Bonci, who was regarded sometimes as Caruso's only serious rival, sang in 1909 and 1911,[22] the other were two Spanish sopranos,

Graziella [Graciela] Pareto and Lucrezia [Lucrecia] Bori. The first sang with Bonci in 1909 and 1910; the second in 1911 shared the soprano roles with Maria Barrientos. And finally, conductor Edoardo Vitale gave the Uruguayan premiere of Giacomo Puccini's *La fanciulla del west* on August 26, 1911, with Adelina Agostinelli as Minnie, Edoardo Ferrari-Fontana as Dick Johnson, and Titta Ruffo as Jack Rance.

* * *

EVEN BEFORE THE SOLÍS 1913 opera season was over, Montevideo newspapers began announcing the arrival of Sergei Diaghilev's Ballets Russes, then the artistic sensation of Paris. Montevideo's intellectual and musical circles were consequently touched by an unusual and growing excitement. When the company arrived in the spring of 1913 (between some recitals and a season of Italian operetta), Solís audiences lived a sort of magic dream via spectacular pirouettes, grand-jetés, fouettés, and entrechats. The complete troupe came from Paris under the general direction of regisseur Serge Grigoriev, who was accompanied by artistic director Léon Bakst and master choreographer Mikhail Fokine. An orchestra of eighty musicians was conducted by Maestro René Baton. Prima ballerina Tamara Karsavina and the legendary Vaslav Nijinsky came on this tour, as did the illustrious Alexandra Vassilievska, Mlle. Maicherska, Lubov Tchernicheva, Adolphe Bolm, and Monsieur Vorontzov, and the company's large corps de ballet. An overwhelming fear of the sea prevented Diaghilev from making the trip to South America. Although the company's tour included only two performances at the Solís, it was enough to see and be swept away by the Ballets Russes' glittering repertoire and spectacular dancers.

Karsavina and Bolm were the soloists in Nikolay Tcherepnine's famous *Le pavillon*

d'Armide on opening night; this was followed by the entire company in Robert Schumann's *Carnaval*. Then came the program's supreme moment: Nijinsky and Karsavina in *Le spectre de la rose*. The Solís audience was conquered by the Ballets Russes' performance and totally electrified by Nijinsky's famous leap as the spirit of the rose comes through the window to dance with a young girl in her dreams. The next day's review expresses some of the evening's emotion:

> I remember very few performances in Montevideo that have aroused so much interest as did the Ballets Russes. . . . I will forever remember the gracefulness and delicacy of Mme. Karsavina, but most memorable was Mr. Nijinsky as he drew figures of supreme harmony in the air, in a perfect agreement between the plastic arts and the music, or when he was suspended in the air as no other human being can be.[23]

On this, his first visit to Montevideo, Nijinsky was accompanied by his recent bride, the Hungarian ballerina Romola de Pulszky. They had been married in Buenos Aires a few days before, on September 10, at the San Miguel church in a wedding ceremony half in Latin, half in Spanish. Some of the very old stagehands I knew at the Teatro Solís remembered, after more than fifty years, how Nijinsky repeatedly and very proudly called her "maia zhena" [my wife]. This marriage was the beginning of the dancer's break with the Ballets Russes and of what Romola called a "state of war which Diaghilev had declared against Nijinsky."[24] After all the tribulations the couple and their little daughter Kyra suffered during World War I, Nijinsky made an extensive tour through the United States, Spain, and South America, and his second visit to Montevideo took place in 1917.

CHAPTER 20

1914—1916

Titta Ruffo: "Not a Voice but a Miracle"—Tito Schipa—Elvira de Hidalgo—Rosa

Raisa—Giovanni Martinelli—A *Pagliacci* to Remember—Riccardo Zandonai's

Francesca da Rimini—Uruguayan Opera World Premiere: César Cortinas' *La*

última gavota—Camille Saint-Saëns' Arrival and Performance—The French

Season: André Messager and Xavier Leroux Conduct Their Operas—Ninon Vallin

August 1914. For Europe, the watershed of war. For the Teatro Solís, a new opera season. *Manon* was the chosen showcase for Rosina Storchio and Tito Schipa as Jules Massenet's lovers. Schipa's Montevideo debut was duly noted: "Des Grieux was sung by Tito Schipa. He is a young, very young, tenor, and a good singer and interpreter. His 'Il sogno' was encored and also received a well-deserved ovation."[1] Schipa was only twenty-six years old and had not yet reached his prime. But it was his La Scala Des Grieux, only a few months after that Solís performance, that placed Schipa at the top of this generation's lyric tenors. He returned to Montevideo many times, and his 1916 appearance at the Solís with Titta Ruffo was one of the most striking triumphs of his career.

The other leading male roles of the 1914 Solís season were sung by two Spanish tenors, Hipólito Lázaro and José Palet. Lázaro had sung in the world premiere of Mascagni's *Par-isina* at La Scala shortly before leaving for South America and his Buenos Aires and Montevideo debuts. Coincidentally, the other new voice of the Solís season was also from Spain, soprano Elvira de Hidalgo. Her debut, the day after Schipa's, was as Gilda. While she was received favorably in this role, it was her performance as Norina in *Don Pasquale* that was the best of all her Solís creations: "With a voice of rare sonority and excellent acting skills, the young Elvira de Hidalgo made her Norina the great success of last evening, surpassing and overshadowing the commendable performances of Schipa, Danise, and Schottler."[2] De Hidalgo—who had debuted in 1908 at Naples singing Rosina and appeared two years later at New York's Metropolitan in the same role—belongs to the generation of Graziella Pareto, Maria Galvany, and María Barrientos. She was one of the last of the Spanish sopranos "d'agilità," but is now chiefly remembered for being one of Maria Callas' voice teachers.

With the exception of the debuts of Schipa and De Hidalgo, 1914 was a very quiet season. While the outbreak of the war paralyzed the planning of operatic schedules, the war years surprisingly held some of the most outstanding seasons in the history of the Teatro Solís. Among the female singers who returned were Amelita Galli-Curci and María Barrientos, while those making their Solís debut included Gilda Dalla Rizza (1914), Rosa Raisa (1915), Geneviève Vix (1915), Mercedes Capsir (1916), Jacqueline Royer (1916), and Ninon Vallin (1916). The male roster was equally impressive, with Enrico Caruso again in 1915, and Hipólito Lázaro, Bernardo De Muro, Ruffo, Schipa, and Mario Sammarco returning, and three respected singers—Giovanni Martinelli, Armand Crabbé, and Marcel Journet (all in 1916)—performing for the first time on the Solís stage.

Considering the competitiveness of the world of the performing arts, when a baritone says of his colleague that "his voice is a miracle," it is more than a compliment; it seems another miracle. Yet this is how Giuseppe de Luca described Ruffo's voice. Ruffo had sung at Montevideo for the first time twelve years before, during the 1902 Solís season. Even if the baritone was then only twenty-five, he had performed such important roles as Amonasro in *Aida*, Conte di Luna in *Il trovatore*, and Cascart in *Zazà*. That season's principal baritone, Mario Ancona, had overshadowed Ruffo at the time, particularly since Ancona was the Scarpia of *Tosca*'s Uruguayan premiere. When Ruffo returned in 1915, he came with the reputation of having given thrilling performances worldwide. Now Ruffo was *the* baritone of his generation.

The 1915 Solís Grand Opera season opened on August 14 with Massenet's *Manon* sung by Vix, Caruso, and Sammarco, with Maestro Giuseppe Sturani conducting. For one music critic it was Vix who triumphed, saying that she was "perfectly suited for the role of Manon."[3] But another reviewer, writing about *Manon*'s "Il sogno," gave all the credit to Caruso, seeing him as "one of the few artists today who combines an exceptional voice with exquisite taste. He sang passionately, with mind and soul, that precious gem ["Il sogno"] embedded by Massenet in *Manon*."[4]

One of the unusual aspects of the 1915 (and, again, the 1917) season is that some of the performances that the Walter Mocchi company would normally have given at the Solís were actually at the Urquiza. On some of the dates, the management of the Solís had arranged, presumably, for other entertainments (even if they were not listed in the actually available newspapers). As a result, what is probably the most significant event of the whole "Solís" season actually occurred at the Teatro Urquiza: on August 16, the day after Ruffo sang a successful Figaro, he sang Tonio opposite Caruso's Canio. This was the only time and place in the history of opera that these two giants appeared together in a complete performance of *Pagliacci* (fig 36). As was almost always the case, Leoncavallo's opera was paired with Mascagni's *Cavalleria Rusticana*. Although tenor Lázaro sang an excellent Turiddu, that performance was not so fortunate for him; it "was but a minor attraction in what became a curtain-raiser to the main event of the evening."[5]

Going back, when the company returned to the Solís, Ruffo's first role was as the lead in Ambroise Thomas' *Hamlet* (*Amleto* in the Italian translation). His performance confirms that, comfortable as he was as Figaro, he was always better suited for dramatic and somber characterizations.

Titta Ruffo astonished the audience last night with his powerful voice, his magnificent style, and the beauties of his art. It was a memorable evening for everyone. We

Fig. 36. *Left*: The only time Caruso and Ruffo ever appeared in an entire work together was in Montevideo's Teatro Urquiza in *Pagliacci*, on August 16, 1915. Biblioteca Nacional Collection, Montevideo. *Right*: Lázaro, (who sang Turiddu in *Cavalleria Rusticana*) on the left, with Caruso and Ruffo in their dressing room. Photograph published in Enrico Caruso Jr. and Andrew Farkas, *Enrico Caruso, My Father and my Family*, (Portland, Ore.: Amadeus, 1990).

found that his performance improves daily, if such perfection can be surpassed! His voice becomes purer every day, and his resonance better; his color and timbre with its strange, somber quality and warmth of tone make him unique in his register. We will always remember his *Amleto* and his vigorous and dramatic *Rigoletto*.[6]

Yet another wonderful surprise was in store for Solís opera lovers, with the debut of Rosa Raisa. A Polish refugee, Raisa went to Naples to study when she was fourteen years old, debuting in a recital at Rome six seasons later. In 1913 she was discovered during the Verdi Centennial celebrations in Parma when she sang Leonora in Verdi's *Oberto* under Cleofonte Campanini's baton. When Raisa sang the title role of *Aida* at the Solís, she was at the height of her abilities and had enjoyed successful debuts at Chicago and London. Accordingly, it is not strange that she garnered a splendid review for her first Solís presentation:

> *Aida* was Rosa Raisa's revelation and [Maestro] Marinuzzi's triumph because we now recognize her as an artist who will soon be one of the best contemporary singers. Raisa, still very young at twenty-two, has a wonderful scenic poise, flexible movements, very expressive eyes, and a passionate spirit. All these combined with an extensive and powerful voice and a talent for the interpretation of her role make her unforgettable.[7]

Her Radamès in this *Aida* was Bernardo de Muro, a young Sardinian tenor[8] remembered for singing the part of Folco in the Italian premiere of Mascagni's *Isabeau* years earlier.

On August 22, the day after Ruffo's *Amleto*, Gino Marinuzzi conducted the first of the two new operas of that season, Massenet's *Le jongleur de Notre Dame*. Based on a story by Anatole France, the opera was first performed in the Monte Carlo opera house in 1902. The leading male role of Jean, sung at the premiere by a tenor (as is customary in France), was a trouser role in New York and at the Solís. While sung by Mary Garden in the United States, Geneviève Vix gave the Uruguayan premiere. This French singer, who had opened the season in *Manon* opposite Caruso, was, according to next morning's review, "The real heroine of the night in Massenet's medieval miracle opera . . . in an exquisite interpretation."[9]

Riccardo Zandonai's *Francesca da Rimini* was the last and most important Uruguayan premiere conducted by Marinuzzi during this Solís season. After the premiere of *Conchita*

in 1911, Zandonai's name became familiar to the young generation of Italian composers, but his first international success was the 1914 world premiere of *Francesca da Rimini* in the Teatro Regio in Turin.[10] From then on Zandonai was considered Puccini's successor. It is interesting to see how the Solís performance of *Francesca da Rimini* impressed the Uruguayan critics. *El Día* published a very long and detailed review the next morning, with a picture of Raisa as Francesca. Some excerpts are reproduced here:

> The roles of Paolo and the Malatestino are treated absolutely differently to point out their complexity and Zandonai's ability to create complex characters. Mr. Zandonai shows here, once more, his extraordinary skills as orchestrator, and *Francesca*'s original sonorities make a perfect frame for D'Annunzio's dramatic environment and the internal struggle of each character. His harmonic palette is very subtle yet very rich. . . .
>
> The best interpreters of the evening were baritone Danise, who magisterially performed the sinister Gianciotto, and Miss Raisa. *Francesca da Rimini*'s particular orchestration enabled her to display better than ever the variety of her vocal talent. In terms of her acting she portrayed a Francesca with so much vigor that perhaps we would like to see a more idealistic and subtle interpretation of Dante's heroine. Never mind. Rosa Raisa is very young and has many years to develop and polish her acting skills.[11]

The day after Zandonai's premiere was the August 25 Gala Performance celebrating Uruguayan Independence Day; the opera chosen to mark the occasion was Bizet's *Carmen* with Vix, Lázaro, and Carlo Galeffi in the principal roles. At the opera's conclusion Marinuzzi conducted the world premiere of the Prelude to the opera *La última gavota*, written by the Uruguayan composer César Cortinas (fig. 37). Cortinas had trained since his early youth at the Berlin Royal Academy of Music with Max Bruch, then with Joseph Jongen at Brussels' Royal Conservatory. (Jongen, brother of the conservatory director, Léon Jongen, was considered the best Belgian composer of the twentieth century.) When the twenty-five-year-old Cortinas had shown his opera manuscript to Marinuzzi in Buenos Aires several months earlier, the conductor was so surprised by the maturity of the work that he chose *La última gavota* as the ideal work to be premiered as part of the August 25, 1915, celebration at the Teatro Solís. But when he consulted with the Uruguayan authorities in preparation for the performance, Marinuzzi was astounded by the response: the government was not at all interested in the world premiere of Cortinas' opera. Marinuzzi was justly upset, seeing this as an insult to himself *and* the composer; without any further discussion he premiered the opera's Prelude after *Carmen*.[12] The work was well regarded by both the public and the press:

> The performance of the Prelude to the opera *La última gavota*, prevented from receiving its world premiere during this opera season, left the listeners strongly impressed. At its conclusion, the house applauded with excitement, and composer and conductor were called repeatedly to the stage. First with Marinuzzi and then alone, César Cortinas was paid the homage that was, after all, an act of strict justice.[13]

In addition to *Aida* and *Francesca da Rimini*, Raisa sang the Marschallin in *Il cavaliere della rosa*, the Italian translation of Strauss' *Der Rosenkavalier* during this Solís season. The Octavian of that performance was Dalla

Fig. 37. César Cortinas (1890–1918) composed, at the age of twenty-six, *La última gavota*. The world premiere of that opera, on August 25, 1916, was one of the most moving performances at the Solís. Author's collection, gift of writer Laura Cortinas.

Rizza, while Sophie was sung by Galli-Curci. A *Rigoletto* sung by Galli-Curci, Lázaro, and Ruffo was the farewell performance of this outstanding 1915 Solís opera season.

*   *   *

THE 1916 SEASON at the Teatro Solís opened under the auspices of French music. Three major composers came to play and conduct: Camille Saint-Saëns, André Messager, and Xavier Leroux. The war years also made possible an impressive succession of French singers, including Ninon Vallin, Jacqueline Royer, Journet, and Léon Lafitte. Two French operas,

Messager's *Béatrice* and Leroux's *Les cadeaux de Noël,* had their Uruguayan premiere, while Saint-Saëns' *Samson et Dalila* was heard for the first time in its original French.

Two other new operas were presented in the same season, both written by Latin American composers. The first, Cortinas' *La última gavota* (whose Prelude had been premiered the year before) received its world premiere on August 26, 1916, under Gennaro Papi, with Dalla Rizza, Schipa, and Giacomo Rimini. *La última gavota* was the first work in the operatic genre composed by then twenty-six-year-old Cortinas; it is a one-act opera based on a text written by the composer, with a plot built on an episode from the French Revolution. The opera follows a group of nobles, among them the Chevalier de Saint Lambert (a poet) and the woman he loves, the Duchess de Bouffers. Knowing that they will soon be led to the guillotine, they all decide to bid farewell to life by dancing one last gavotte, the preferred dance of the queen. The opera's musical style can be placed between Neoclassicism and early Impressionism, with a strong lyricism in the melodic line that resembles the Puccinian vocal style. The new opera was praised, and Solís opera lovers were very proud of their talented composer, forced by the war's outbreak to return from the Royal Conservatory in Brussels.

The audience gave the composer seven curtain calls, and the reaction of the Uruguayan press was positive. *La Razón* wrote that "Cortinas' triumph was one of those that consecrates a musician forever. *La última gavota* is a well-written opera, with a deep lyricism, and it shows a young composer who knows all the secrets of instrumentation and theatrical effects."[14] The musical critic for *El Día* said:

> We cannot ask of a new composer who— having just started an operatic career and still young—the musical personality that can be obtained only by years of study, experience, and wisdom. From this vantage point we recognize that here is a young composer who has the nature of a competent opera composer, and nobody can deny that he understands theatrical effects. We also acknowledge his ability to effectively treat the human voice. . . .
>
> The Prelude also demonstrates a strong knowledge of instrumentation. The unaffected style of *La última gavota* gave Mr. Cortinas' world premiere a striking triumph last night. The Prelude and the gavotte, with its graceful and lyrical strings, and the last duet between soprano and tenor, were the opera's three finest moments, eliciting applause from an enthusiastic house. We must also praise Maestro Papi—who, in spite of few rehearsals, accomplished a genuine success—and Dalla Rizza, Schipa, and Rimini.[15]

Unfortunately, Cortinas' death at age twenty-eight ended a brilliant and promising career that had started with his composing chamber music at fourteen.

The second new opera that season was *Huemac* by the Argentinean Pascual De Rogatis. Unlike *La última gavota* it was not a success, perhaps because of the incongruity between its indigenous plot, set among a population of South American Indians, and its interpretation by Italian singers.

Early in fall 1916 it was announced in the press that Saint-Saëns and Enrique Granados were coming to Montevideo. It was also revealed that Granados would conduct his new opera *Goyescas* at the Solís stage, with Gilda Dalla Rizza and Martinelli singing the principal roles, on August 22.[16] Only a few days after the announcement, Montevideo was shocked with the news that the Spanish composer had died at sea on March 24, 1916, when the steamship "Sussex" was torpedoed in the

Fig. 38. *Left*: Camille Saint-Saëns leaving the Solís during his visit to Montevideo in July 1916, with French ambassador to Uruguay Jules Lefèvre at his right, and Secretary of the Interior Francisco Ghigliani, walking behind them. Author's collection, gift of Eduardo Cluzeau-Mortet in memory of his brother the composer Luis Cluzeau-Mortet. *Right*: Program of Saint-Saëns concert on July 13, 1916, where he performed as conductor and soloist. Biblioteca Nacional Collection, Montevideo.

English Channel. They had been returning to Spain from New York after attending *Goyescas'* world premiere at the Metropolitan Opera House, on January 28, 1916. Granados' death affected the world of music beyond opera; although he composed only one opera and two minor stage works, in large part his opus was made up of vocal and piano pieces, and it is these works that are commonly performed today.

On July 12 all the front pages of Montevideo's newspapers were covered with photo-

graphs showing Saint-Saëns being received upon his arrival by the French ambassador and Mrs. Lefèvre and the conductor Mauricio Geeraert (fig. 38). The venerable composer, who at eighty showed an incredible vigor and strength, raised great expectations among the musicgoing public. A Saint-Saëns Gala Concert was planned for the evening of July 13, with the composer performing as pianist and conductor. The day following the gala, *El Día* published a portrait of Saint-Saëns and a long review, which included the following:

For many years we will retain the memories of this Saint-Saëns concert. In Mozart's "Concerto in A-Major" we could appreciate his brilliant "tocco" and the agility and security he displayed in both energetic and pianissimo passages. We realized once more that we were in the presence of an extraordinary pianist. . . .

At the end of the evening he conducted his own *Marche héroïque* with tremendous vigor—and after thrice being the piano soloist! Maestro Geeraert was an excellent orchestra conductor in all the other works. When the concert ended, many people waited for Saint-Saëns in the outside plaza, where they gave him an impressive ovation and amid applause and shouts of "Vive la France!" accompanied him to his hotel.[17]

With all the excitement of Saint-Saëns' presentation still in the air, the Sconamiglio Operetta Company arrived for a one-month stay. As soon as they had left, Raisa opened the new opera season in *Aida*, with Giulio Crimi as Radamès and Rimini as Amonasro. This same cast opened the Chicago Opera season three months later, on November 13, 1916. Eventually, Raisa and Rimini married and settled in Chicago where, years later, they opened a singing academy.

The 1916 Montevidean opera season had a particular distinction. The podium had been shared among four conductors: Giuseppe Barone, Gennaro Papi, André Messager, and Xavier Leroux (the last two being leading French composers of opera). That the company consisted of both Italian and French singers, used interchangeably in productions, resulted in some unusually splendid performances. Among the famous singers to appear at this time, Vallin and Martinelli were the new voices of the year, while highlights included a *Falstaff* sung by Raisa, Vallin, Elvira Roessigner, Paula Bertolozzi, Ruffo, Schipa, Sinai

Maury, and Gaudio Mansueto, and a notable *Gli ugonotti* sung in Italian by Raisa, Esperanza Clasenti, Martinelli, Crabbé, and Journet.

By the time Martinelli came to South America, he was already an established star at the Metropolitan Opera. When Caruso died some years later, Martinelli was to inherit many of his more heroic roles, such as Radamès, Manrico, and Don Alvaro. Later, as Martinelli matured, Samson, Eléazar and a particularly memorable Otello were to be added. In 1916 he made his Solís debut as Raoul de Nangis opposite Raisa's Valentina in Giacomo Meyerbeer's *Gli ugonotti*. The critics recognized him as

an exceptional Raoul because of his outstanding vocal features and his art in acting. From the very beginning, starting with the racconto ["Bianca al par di neve alpina"], and throughout the entire performance he was intensely applauded. Still, he saved his energy until the end of the opera, culminating in the duet with Valentina "O ciel che fare!" Martinelli astonished the auditorium with his voice and his interpretation.[18]

Maria Barrientos, in her third Solís season, was at the height of her career. On the night following *Aida*, Barrientos sang one of her traditional and beloved signature pieces: Bellini's *La sonnambula*. This time the Elvino was Schipa, back on the Solís stage after a short absence: "In the last two years the beautiful voice of this young and intelligent tenor has become notably better in the growth of his outstanding vocal features, flexibility, and impeccable style. His triumph last evening was one of those Solís events to be remembered."[19] Barrientos' second triumph of that 1916 season occurred when—for the first time in South America—she, Schipa, and Ruffo sang together *Il barbiere di Siviglia* as a part of the centennial celebration of the premiere of Rossini's masterpiece.

If the Italian operas had an impressive roster of singers and an excellent repertoire, their French counterparts was equally grand. Two distinguished composers (Leroux and Messager) conducted their own operas, with singers Vallin, Lafitte, and Crabbé.[20] Messager was widely known as a composer of operetta and as an orchestral conductor; he also wrote operas, but they are seldom performed today. *Béatrice*, subtitled "légende lyrique" and with a libretto based on a medieval story, was premiered at Monte Carlo in 1914. An excellent French cast presented *Béatrice* at the Solís under the composer's baton, meeting with critical success:

> Messager has a deep understanding of all theatrical skills, not needing strange instrumental novelties to bewilder the listener or noisy effects in order to reach and shock the spectator's feelings. Maybe he does not show new forms of expression, but the score is full of rich orchestral nuances. The second act is profoundly reminiscent of Wagner's *Tristan* in both melodic and orchestral treatment. . . . *Béatrice*'s interpretation was admirable from all points of view. It could be no other way since Messager is not only one of the best contemporary French composers but also an excellent orchestral conductor. The principal interpreter of the vocal part was Mademoiselle Vallin, an exquisite singer and actress.[21]

Leroux's *Les cadeaux de Noël* was the season's second Uruguayan premiere of a French opera. A short, one-act opera, it is a Christmas tale, a sort of patriotic peace message composed in response to, and performed in the middle of the war. It was conducted by the composer and appeared in a double-bill program after Bellini's *La sonnambula*.

Without doubt the most prominent singer of the French roster was Vallin. In addition to her operatic career, which started as Micaëla at the Opéra-Comique in 1912, she devoted a good part of her professional life to lieder recitals. Her fame most securely rests on her being one of the best interpreters of Manon, Charlotte, Louise, Juliette, Thaïs, and a dozen more roles that she performed during her prime (between 1915 and 1935). Vallin returned to the Solís three more times after the war. After World War II, she returned to the city once again, this time in her early sixties, as a voice teacher engaged by the Conservatorio Nacional of Montevideo. There many Uruguayan singers received the benefits of her valuable experience.

After seventeen exciting performances, among them a world premiere and three presentations new to Uruguay, the 1916 season closed with Massenet's *Manon* conducted by Leroux and sung in French by Vallin, Schipa, Crabbé, and Journet, a performance that "was a brilliant *Manon*, the best we have heard at the Solís since Hariclea Darclée more than twenty years ago."[22]

1917

A Unique Performance: Artur Rubinstein and Vaslav Nijinsky—Ernest
Ansermet and a New Season of the Ballets Russes—New Voices: Fanny Anitúa
and Marcelo Urízar—Uruguayan World Premiere: César Cortinas' *La sulamita*—
Gino Marinuzzi Conducts Puccini's *La rondine* Premiere

"When we arrived at that early
hour, I spotted at the dock
the familiar face of Wilhelm
Kolischer, a Polish pianist who had studied
with my professor Heinrich Barth and with
whom I used to spend whole days in Cracow
or Berlin or wherever we met. Now he was
accompanied by some friends of his, all young
musicians, among them Eduardo Fabini, a
composer, and Joaquín [*sic*] [Florencio]
Mora, a violinist, who turned out to have
been Paul Kochanski's roommate in Brussels,
where they both had studied. Kolischer and
his friends became my constant companions
and remained so whenever I returned to
Montevideo."[1] These are the memories of Artur Rubinstein sixty-three years after his first
visit to Montevideo in July 1917. What is surprising is that his opinion of Uruguayan musical culture preceding his first concert was
exactly the same in 1980 when he wrote his
second book. Here is part of an interview
published in Montevideo on July 21, 1917:

INTERVIEWER: Are you satisfied with your South
American tour?
RUBINSTEIN: I have no words to express my joy in
view of so many compliments I have been receiving since my arrival to Buenos Aires.
INTERVIEWER: What are your projects for Montevideo?
RUBINSTEIN: I am not sure if I can play more concerts than those already booked, due to the
schedule of my other performances. However,
knowing how severe the Uruguayan people are
in matters of art, I am very impatient to debut
here and receive their approval.[2]

After more than half a century of performances, Rubinstein would go on to say that
"Montevideo had few conservatories, but the
people there were more devoted to good music than those in Buenos Aires."[3] There is no
doubt that the Rubinstein concerts (fig. 39)
created a fervor among Uruguayan music lovers and that his charming personality, plus his

Fig. 39. *Left*: Artur Rubinstein's first concert in Montevideo, on July 21, 1917, was proclaimed "a national event." Author's collection. *Right*: Rubinstein's signature and comments after a concert he played on a national Uruguayan holiday, in 1920. From the album of Haydée Olondriz, Roberto Morassi Collection.

reputation as a womanizer, conquered audiences.

Rubinstein found a musical circle in Montevideo that added to his regard for the city. His friendship with Wilhelm Kolischer and the circle of Uruguayan musicians, and his fluent Spanish, made a sort of perfect chemistry. The connections that he made there remained in his mind throughout his life. Kolischer was a pianist with a very different musical history. Unlike Rubinstein, who toured the world until almost his last years, Kolischer gave few concerts in South America and rarely returned to Poland after the First World War was over. Finally, he and his family settled in Montevideo, where he founded the most prestigious modern conservatory of the country. He and his daughter, Janina (the unforgettable Yanka who taught me piano for several years) dedicated their lives to teaching. Many of today's internationally known Uruguayan pianists were Kolischer pupils.

The day after Rubinstein's first concert—with the house completely sold out—one music critic wrote: "For some moments when Rubinstein played Beethoven's Sonata Op. 53, the music was delivered in such a monumental way that instead of being at the Solís concert we thought we were hearing the hoarse roar of the cannons in the horrible and recent battle of Verdun!"[4] Another critic reported Rubinstein's first two concerts with equal enthusiasm:

> The Spanish press had the most enthusiastic praise and called Rubinstein "the magician of the keyboard." . . . After hearing him twice we are convinced that all these opinions were nothing in comparison with what we heard for two evenings at the Solís. He is colossal and sublime; his interpretation has no equal, and he overcomes even the most recondite fiber of the soul. His playing is beyond comparison.[5]

During the last years of Rubinstein's life I corresponded directly with him in Spanish until he was no longer able to write for himself. I was greatly saddened when I received his first dictated letter in English, for I knew it was a result of the rapid development of his blindness. Because he had lost many documents during both world wars, I sent him information relating to all his Montevideo recitals for a third book he never wrote. He frequently inquired about all the musicians he had met in Montevideo during his thirties to know if they were still alive. Finally, when he played for the last time in Washington, D.C., in a Constitution Hall recital, I met him for the first and only time. It was the Saturday evening of March 6, 1976, and an absolutely unique and astonishing moment. Rubinstein was in his dressing room, accompanied by his youngest daughter, Alina, and talking with us: Patrick Hayes (then manager of the Washington Performing Arts Society) and his wife, pianist Evelyn Swarthout; a Polish couple who were friends of Rubinstein; and my husband and me. To the surprise of all six of us, he conversed animatedly and almost simultaneously in English, Polish, and Spanish. To me he addressed very concrete questions about Montevideo musicians, one by one, and the present musical life there; he remembered, too, his always famous encore with Isaac Albéniz's *Navarra*, a piece he never included in the printed program but saved for his signature piece at the end of his concerts. Before leaving I asked him why he no longer played in Montevideo. His answer was: "None of my friends are living, and even as sad as it is, I cannot live in the past." After a pause he added with a mischievous smile, "I must live in the present . . . and in the future." What a lesson from someone aged eighty-nine!

With the last resounding chords of the *Navarra* and the audience's cheers that followed still reverberating in the house, the Solís curtain rose again during that year of 1917. It was for a new season of the Ballets Russes that, in contrast to the mere two performances of 1913, now brought more than twenty different ballets. The company also had a new prima ballerina, Lydia Lopokova, and an excellent conductor, the renowned Ernest Ansermet. According to the critic of *El Día*: "The audience was stunned with so complex and exotic an exhibition, not easy to analyze; and shocked and moved by the gestures and jumps of the warrior dances in *Prince Igor.* . . . On the other hand, the poetry and delicacy of Lydia Lopokova was the best of all. Ernest Ansermet accomplished a true miracle conducting such difficult orchestral works."[6]

* * *

THE 1917 SOLÍS OPERA SEASON again brought Maestro Gino Marinuzzi, as well as Vincenzo Belleza, as conductors, and a very attractive roster of singers, such as Fanny Anitúa, Gilda Dalla Rizza, Ninon Vallin, Enrico Caruso, Armand Crabbé, Eugenio Giraldoni, Marcel Journet, and Marcelo Urízar. Two of these must be noted as exceptional new voices: Fanny Anitúa and Marcelo Urízar. Mexican mezzo-soprano Anitúa studied in Rome, where she debuted at the Teatro Costanzi singing *Orfeo* in 1909 at age twenty-two. When she debuted at the Solís as Dalila in Saint-Saëns' *Sansone e Dalila* (Italian version), she had already appeared in the world premiere of Ildebrando Pizzetti's *Fedra* at La Scala in 1915. However, the review of *Sansone e Dalila* indicates that her performance was not so excellent as her background promised: "There is no doubt that Miss Anitúa knows her métier perfectly well. But, it is a pity that since her lows are so good, her voice is, sometimes, a little uneven in the high pitch. Nevertheless, we don't like to judge her by her debut."[7] Evidently Anitúa's voice improved; six years later she was chosen by Toscanini to

sing at La Scala, where she performed from 1923 on.

Marcelo Urízar, an Argentinean baritone, debuted at the Teatro Colón in Buenos Aires singing Tonio, with Caruso as Canio. One month later, when Urízar was twenty years old, he was engaged by the same company to debut with the same role at the Solís. *El Día* said that "Tonio was the novel baritone, Urízar, who has a beautiful voice. Scenically, he is still a little immature, but with so good and so big a voice that he has a promising singing career in store."[8] Years later Urízar became not only an excellent actor but one of the Solís' favorite singers. He made too an outstanding international career in Europe's principal opera houses.

The year 1917 was the last time Montevideo audiences heard Caruso. The tenor was then at the peak of his fame, and nobody would willingly miss his performances in either of the principal houses of Montevideo: at the Teatro Urquiza, he sang *Carmen*; at the Teatro Solís, *L'elisir d'amore*, *Pagliacci*, *Tosca*, and, again, *Carmen*. His August 16 presentation at the Solís as Nemorino acquired almost the level of a national event and earned him one of the best reviews of all of his Montevideo seasons:

> We must state that the audience left the Solís with a particular joy, absolutely sure that they will seldom find a singer with so many qualifications as Caruso. The Neapolitan tenor had one of his greatest evenings, in voice and in acting, particularly his performance in the second act. It is not possible today to find a tenor who can so perfectly personify Nemorino. If we add so colossal a voice it is easy to see how everybody was astonished with Caruso in this *L'elisir d'amore*.[9]

Four new operas were performed for the first time that Solís season: Carlos Pedrell's

Ardid de amor, Henri Rabaud's *Mârouf*, Puccini's *La rondine*, and Umberto Giordano's *Siberia*. The world premiere of one of the last works of the Uruguayan César Cortinas was also given: *La sulamita* was conducted by the composer on August 9, the day of his twenty-seventh birthday. Performed by a narrator, soprano, and members of the Asociación Lírica del Uruguay chorus and orchestra, *La sulamita* was the incidental music to the poem of the same name written by the Argentinean poet Arturo Capdevila. Cortinas, then terminally ill, made a superhuman effort to appear in public and conduct for the last time. *La sulamita*'s debut was a success:

> The complete work, poem and music, complemented each other so well that many people thought that composer and poet were working together, which was not the case. . . . The preludes are the best-conceived parts of the entire work, especially that of act two. Hearing them we realized not only the superb qualities of the composer but the feeling reached by Maestro Cortinas in total command of his art.[10]

Seven months later, on March 23, 1918, the composer died in the Sierras de Cordoba of Argentina.

The season's first new opera was Rabaud's *Mârouf, le savetier du Caire*, based on one of the tales of the *Thousand and One Nights*:

> Even if *Mârouf* is not one of the highest representatives of musical art and did not reach the quality that D'Indy, Debussy, Dukas, and Charpentier operas have, neither is it one of those works that torture the minds of the audience. *Mârouf* is a very easy opera to understand, yet is not vulgar. . . . Maestro Marinuzzi and director Romeo Francioli are the real heroes of last evening's performance. . . . Henri Rabaud's music has very delicate and exquisite sonorities, and even its more pow-

erful orchestral effects are not noisy. With its joyful plot and splendid scenery and costumes, *Mârouf* is a good antidote against sadness.[11]

In 1913 Puccini received a profitable offer to write an operetta by then directors of Vienna's Karltheater Erbenschutz and Berté. At first undecided on the text, Puccini eventually chose Giuseppe Adami to write the Italian libretto on a second text offered by A. M. Willner and Heinz Reichert. Two years later the work was still progressing slowly, and in the interim Italy had entered World War I, declaring war on Austria in 1915. The war had put the composer and directors on opposite sides; as a consequence the Viennese management resigned their claim to the opera premiere, while holding a part of the performing rights. And since the Ricordi firm was not interested in the work, Puccini approached the Lorenzo Sonzogno company, the other renowned Milanese music publisher and Ricordi's competitor. This time, however, it would be the composition of a lyrical comedy instead of the originally planned operetta. Thus, almost five years passed between the initial concept and the performance when *La rondine* finally had its world premiere in Monte Carlo (neutral territory) on March 27, 1917. It was conducted by Marinuzzi and starred Dalla Rizza as Magda de Civry, Tito Schipa as Ruggero Lastouc, and Gustave Huberdeau as Rambaldo. Just four months after this production, the same conductor and soprano gave this opera its Solís premiere. The press was excited by the prospect of a new Puccini work, and the reviewer, insisting on calling it an operetta, wrote:

> *La rondine* is an operetta in the sense that operettas are written today, an operetta written with talent by a very skillful composer who knows the taste of contemporary audiences. *La rondine* is a sentimental work

with very affectionate touches, an operetta of great quality. . . . In Marinuzzi this work has also found a conductor . . . who not only loves *La rondine* but protects it, giving it an excellent performance and "mise en scène."[12]

Eleven years later *La rondine* was first performed at the Metropolitan Opera House, on March 10, 1928, with Lucrezia Bori in the Dalla Rizza role. This Spanish soprano, creator of the first American Magda de Civry, also made her operatic farewell with *La rondine*, on the same stage, on March 21, 1936, followed by a farewell concert one week after.[13]

* * *

IT WAS ALSO DURING THIS SEASON that Solís spectators witnessed one of the greatest tragedies that could happen on a stage, even if at the time nobody imagined the consequences. On October 26, 1917, as part of a Gala Benefit Performance for the International Red Cross, Artur Rubinstein and Vaslav Nijinsky appeared together (fig. 40). In his biography seventeen years later Romola Nijinsky looked back: "The public went wild with enthusiasm at this performance, but, as I followed Vaslav's floating movements on the stage in his mazurka in *Sylphides*, little did I think that I had seen him dance for the last time in the theatre."[14] The house was alive with the glitter and frivolity of a common social event, where the diplomatic corps and Montevideo high society made their usual appearance. But backstage wore a different face, where darkness, tension, and the misery of human drama unfolded. The next morning's review carried a long list of the people who had attended, with some remarks about "the important social event," but not a single word about the performance. What had happened? There was no better witness than the other performer of that evening: Rubinstein. Over a number of years I have collected many loose

pieces through verbal sources, correspondence, and my conversation with Rubinstein (later added to recollections he included in the second volume of his autobiography). In this way I was able to confirm the facts.

To begin with, the organization of this performance had been placed in the hands of a women's committee, a group of wonderful goodwill but absolutely no knowledge of how to put together a theatrical event. As a result the first victim of the Gala Benefit was Rubinstein himself, when he realized that his part in the program was to take only twenty minutes of playing from beginning to end. There followed a series of mishaps, beginning on the night before the performance:

> [T]hree ladies appeared. "We are in charge of this gala but we had nothing to do with the program. We sent it to the printer without looking at it." I told them coldly that I refused to take part in this kind of gala. The ladies were panic-stricken. "This is impossible!" they cried. "The President of Uruguay is coming, all the embassies have taken boxes, the house is sold out, and there is tremendous excitement building up in the city. Can't you find a way to help us?" . . .
>
> "Yes dammit, I'll help you. Instead of my three wretched pieces, I shall play the first part of a usual piano recital." . . . And I scribbled wretchedly the pieces I was prepared to play which wouldn't interfere too much with my own subscription programs. The ladies left after trying to kiss my hand. I returned to my room to rest from this new disaster.[15]

Rubinstein has written that a few minutes later he was interrupted again, this time to ask if he would allow the Montevideo's Banda Municipal to play the Allies' national anthems at the beginning of each part of the performance.[16] Rubinstein had hardly finished saying yes when some ladies came back to him

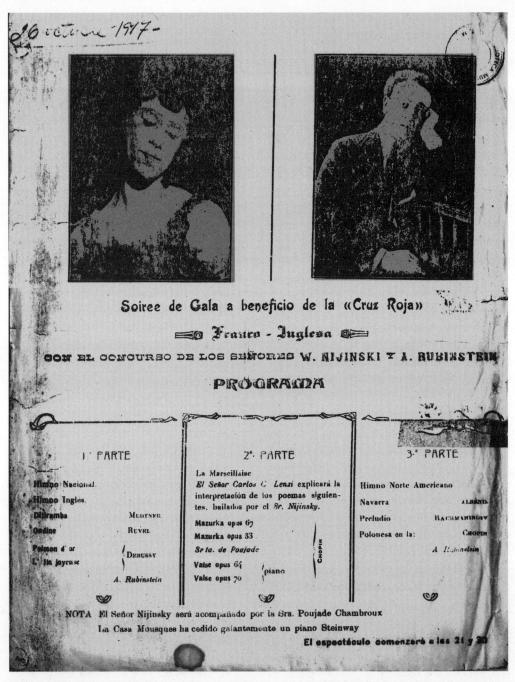

Fig. 40. The Nijinsky-Rubinstein recital to benefit the International Red Cross was the last time that Nijinsky danced on a stage. Center page of the program. Teatro Solís Collection [item lost].

with the news that they had "a brilliant idea." They thought that Nijinsky's part would be very short, so they had invited a poet to read some pages titled "La Danza." The poet (unnamed by Rubinstein) was Carlos César Lenzi, then greatly involved as a collaborator in many lieder written by Uruguayan composers. Again Rubinstein agreed, although he did not like it at all. The pianist's wish at this point was probably only that the performance were over! However, all those inconveniences would have been nothing, even a humorous aside, if it were not for the real tragedy brewing. What Rubinstein had accepted with annoyed but philosophical resignation strongly affected Nijinsky, already in a critical state of stress, and furthered his impending destruction.

When Rubinstein's part in the program was over, with the pianist resting in his dressing room, French ambassador Jules Lefèvre, in a state of agitation, tapped at his door. He explained that Nijinsky was in a terrible state because the dancer was having problems with his feet, and the ambassador feared that the god of dance might decide not to dance at all. He begged Rubinstein to play the program's second part, thus allowing Nijinsky to recuperate and dance afterward. This gala, unique in Teatro Solís history, vacillated from comedy to farce and tragedy. The pianist, relinquishing himself once again, suggested that someone go out on stage to announce the program change. Rubinstein's account describes what followed:

This time I was adamant and the situation became untenable. The French diplomat went to consult with his British colleague, a curious fellow who looked exactly like Don Quixote. Smiling amenably, he said, "No trouble, I can tell them myself." He walked out, obtained the silence of the audience, and laughing uproariously between each

short sentence, spoke more or less the following: "Nijinsky"—he laughed—"con los feet, something, ho, ho"—clapping the sole of his shoe in the air. "Nada, nada"—he waved his hand consolingly—"ballet go on, but ahora"—laughing again and playing an imaginary piano in the air. "Rubinstein, ho, ho!" I don't know if anyone in the audience made sense of this, but the charming man told us triumphantly, "You see, very simple; they understood perfectly." My usual sense of humor got the better of me and I laughed uproariously too.[17]

Still Nijinsky did not make his appearance. After another series of mishaps—or comic interludes, as Rubinstein called them—people from the galleries shouted insults at the "famous poet" as soon as Lenzi began to read his essay. As it was already past midnight, it is easy to see why the audience's patience was over. Worse was to come. According to Rubinstein, the stagehands forgot to sprinkle the stage with water, so that when Nijinsky did dance, it was on a dry and dusty floor, a dancer's nightmare. Rubinstein wrote of the event with anguish:

To me, he looked even sadder than when he danced the death of Petrushka. I must confess unashamedly that I burst into tears. The horrible mixture of a seemingly endless farce with one of the most heartbreaking tragedies was more than one could bear. We gave him an endless ovation. I suddenly knew that everyone in the audience was aware of the drama on the stage. This was the last appearance of Vaslav Nijinsky, the greatest dancer of my time, who still after so many years remains unforgotten.[18]

Wilhelm Kolischer and members of the Giucci family later often told me of that memorable evening, having experienced the same emotions as Rubinstein when they saw this same Nijinsky performance. Fifty years later, perhaps during our last conversation, these witnesses insisted it was impossible to forget Nijinsky's eyes, with their strange expression of sadness and ecstasy, as of someone who no longer belongs to this world. His life ahead was shrouded in despair and madness. And it was the Solís that last bore witness to his glory.

CHAPTER 22

1918–1922

Beniamino Gigli and Claudia Muzio—Lucien Muratore—Four Uruguayan
Premieres: *Madame Sans-Gêne, Monna Vanna, Fedra,* and *Le roi de Lahore*—
Anna Pavlova—Recitals: Yolanda Merö, Frances Nash, Edouard Risler,
Artur Rubinstein, and Ricardo Viñes—Felix Weingartner and
the Vienna Philharmonic Orchestra

Even if the 1918 Solís season was filled with hundreds of operettas and a few second-rate opera performances, the 1919 shone with new operas and talents. Before considering that successful Solís year, we should note that the Teatro Urquiza had one of its longest seasons the same year, with fifteen repertory operas and a new Montevideo premiere. Mocchi and Da Rosa impresarios brought Maestro Gino Marinuzzi who shared the podium with conductor Franco Paolantonio. Both conductors, as well as many of the singers, were the same that had come one year before, in 1917, to the Solís stage. Those singers were sopranos Rosa Raisa, Ninon Vallin, Amelita Galli-Curci, and Hina Spani; mezzosopranos Gabriella Besanzoni, Ida Canasi, and Matilde Blanco-Sadun; tenors Aureliano Pertile; and Charles Hackett; baritones Armand Crabbé, Giacomo Rimini, and Mariano Stabile; and basses Marcel Journet, Gaudio Mansueto, and Teofilo Dentale. In addition, this array of stars was completed with three new

artists (who never sang at the Solís): the Spanish coloratura soprano Angeles Ottein, who sang Rosina and Gilda; the French dramatic tenor Paul Franz, who portrayed Sansone; and baritone Luigi Montesanto, who performed the title role of *Rigoletto*. Marinuzzi also conducted the Montevideo premiere of his own opera *Jacquerie*, a medieval war story, sung by Pertile, Vallin, Dentale, and Montesanto. *Jacquerie* had received its world premiere in Buenos Aires three weeks earlier, at the Teatro Colón, on August 11, 1918.[1]

* * *

THE SOLÍS 1919 OPERATIC YEAR sparkled with new performances, conductors and singers. Two new conductors, Tullio Serafin and Arturo Vigna, and two Uruguayan premieres— Umberto Giordano's *Madame Sans-Gêne* and Henri Février's *Monna Vanna*—were complemented by the Solís debut of two young opera stars, Claudia Muzio and Beniamino Gigli (fig. 41). French tenor Lucien Muratore also

157

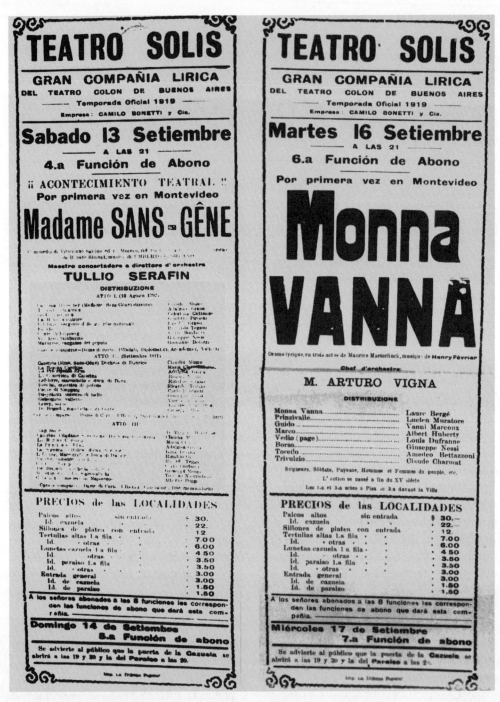

Fig. 41. Impresario Camillo Bonetti brought two new operas to the Solís 1919 season. *Left*: Giordano's *Madame Sans-Gêne* with Claudia Muzio conducted by Tullio Serafin. *Right*: Février's *Monna Vanna* under Arturo Vigna, with Laura Bergé on the title role. Author's collection.

came to create the first Uruguayan Prinzivalle in *Monna Vanna*, ten years after he sang the world premiere at the Paris Opéra.

Muzio arrived in Montevideo between her third and fourth seasons at the New York Metropolitan Opera. From the time she debuted at twenty-one in Jules Massenet's *Manon* at Arezzo, her success was swift and brilliant, marked by her La Scala debut during the 1913–14 season as Desdemona. Muzio was thirty when she opened the 1919 Solís opera season in Alfredo Catalani's *Loreley*, a production in which she sang at the Solís again in 1920 and 1924. On this opening night in 1919, Hina Spani (the stage name of Higinia Tuñón de Serantes), a talented Argentinean soprano, also appeared on the Solís stage as Anna in Catalani's opera; Spani had debuted at La Scala in 1915, when only nineteen years of age, singing Anna.[2]

In spite of Muzio having a great success in *Loreley*, her truly grand night came two weeks later when she sang the title role of *Madame Sans-Gêne* in its Uruguayan premiere under the baton of Serafin. The new Giordano opera had received its world premiere with Arturo Toscanini at the Metropolitan Opera in January 1915; Geraldine Farrar created the role of Caterina.[3] The general comment, however, was that *Madame Sans-Gêne* was more effective theatrically than musically. And indeed, the Montevideo newspaper review, while praising Muzio's performance, shows mixed feelings about *Madame Sans-Gêne*:

> We believe this opera does not add glory to Maestro Giordano, for the subject is too improper and salacious to be treated in a respectable work. Even if the composer has theatrical skills and finds the effects he seeks, the music of *Madame Sans-Gêne* lacks unity. The episodic character of the libretto is translated into the music so that the result is a fragmentary score. . . . To two persons

must go all praise: Serafin and Muzio. The conductor, as usual, did a wonderful job, and the soprano—whom we have already applauded in *Loreley*—was a perfect vocal interpreter and actress last evening. She personified Caterina with charm and energy and deserved the huge applause she received.[4]

In spite of the excitement generated by the Giordano premiere, Solís audiences were eager to hear the season's other star: Beniamino Gigli. Five months after Arrigo Boito's death, Toscanini conducted a memorial performance of *Mefistofele* at La Scala in November 1918; the evening's Faust was the twenty-eight-year-old Gigli. With that performance, only four years after his Rovigo debut, Gigli reached the first summit of an outstanding career. This 1919 South American tour was Gigli's first overseas trip. On the second night of the Solís season, the tenor debuted, singing one of his cherished roles: Enzo Grimaldo in Amilcare Ponchielli's *La Gioconda*.

> The true revelation for the Uruguayan audience was last night's tenor, Beniamino Gigli. Nor are we speaking merely of a promise for lyric art, but a reality. Even though still very young, Gigli is already a great artist who knows how to use his marvelous tenor voice. His voice is, in fact, very fresh, sweet, of a pleasant timbre, considerable volume, and velvety quality. He received a standing ovation after "Cielo e mar." Maestro Serafin gave us an admirable version of *La Gioconda*, with plenty of nuances and color, reaching orchestral effects and sonorities we had never heard before in an opera performance.[5]

Serafin came to Montevideo after being La Scala's principal conductor for several seasons and before his ten-year tenure at the Metropolitan. Maestro Serafin will be remembered always for the balance he achieved between voices and orchestra, as demonstrated during his Solís seasons. He was also highly praised for helping develop the career of many young singers.

Notwithstanding *La Gioconda*'s success, when Gigli sang *La bohème* and *Tosca* with Muzio a few days later, they enthralled the audience. Of *La bohème* the critic raved: "It has been a very long time since I have heard a Puccini opera with singers so splendid as Claudia Muzio and Beniamino Gigli. The audience was fascinated and amazed!"[6] And his *Tosca* was equally embraced: "After 'E lucevan le stelle' the ovation reached such a point of delirium that people whistled and stamped their feet furiously until they got an encore."[7] In 1920, one month before his Metropolitan Opera debut, Gigli returned to Montevideo to sing five different operas at the Teatro Urquiza. That season opened on October 4 with Wagner's *Lohengrin*, featuring Gigli in the title role under the baton of Felix Weingartner, with Lucille Marcel-Weingartner (the conductor's wife) singing Elsa, Elvira Casazza as Ortrud, Giulio Cirino as Heinrich, and José Segura-Tallien as Telramund. Gigli sang also in Pietro Mascagni's *Iris*, Massenet's *Manon*, Giacomo Puccini's *Tosca*, and Ponchielli's *La Gioconda*, the last four operas being conducted by Edoardo Vitale.[8]

While Gigli sang more than sixty principal roles during his entire career, Rodolfo and Cavaradossi will remain as those that brought him most applause. "E lucevan le stelle," sung with his particular sentimental style of breaking the line by sobs, became Gigli's signature aria. It has been said that three leading tenors were Enrico Caruso's heirs: Giacomo Lauri-Volpi, who specialized in the most difficult roles; Giovanni Martinelli, who inherited the less difficult dramatic roles; and Gigli, who took over Caruso's lighter repertoire.

Many years later, when close to retirement,

Gigli returned to Montevideo to sing *Tosca* with Maria Caniglia and Víctor Damiani at the SODRE Auditorium. In the same 1948 SODRE opera season he also sang *La traviata* and *Pagliacci* together with his daughter Rina, as well as a concert. Even if his large ego was still intact, so was the sweetness and fluency of his voice. It is interesting to note that five years earlier Rina Gigli debuted at the Teatro Regio of Parma "singing Violetta in *La traviata*, on May 23, 1943, with [her] father in the part of Alfredo."[9]

Together with Muzio and Gigli, Muratore (in his Solís debut) capped the great success of that 1919 season in Massenet's *Manon*. The review reflects the audience's expectations:

No one went to the Solís last evening to enjoy *Manon*, but to see and hear Muratore's debut. He came to Montevideo preceded by long fame—and for Muratore, as for Caesar: "Veni, vidi, vici." His stage entrance and gallant poise, the way in which he carried himself, his acting abilities, and his talents as a great singer—all indicated that we were in the presence of a superior Des Grieux. His Des Grieux was the man who suffers, loves, and implores—this was not just a tenor playing a role. Muratore's voice is warm and full with a tendency to the baritone range. He is very attentive about his acting, taking care with the least details. His "Le rêve" was a surprise because it was different, sung with passion but with measure, musically and vocally perfect, and without the "fiorituri" used by the Italian divos.[10]

Before his vocal studies at the Conservatoire National in Paris, Muratore had initially embarked on an acting career. He debuted as a tenor at twenty-six, singing Le Roi in Reynaldo Hahn's *La Carmélite* at the Opéra-Comique in 1902. He later performed for several seasons at the Paris Opéra, where he created many roles, in particular those of Massenet's operas.

Monna Vanna, Février's second opera, had its world premiere at the Paris Opéra in January 1909. Based on a play by Maurice Maeterlinck, the opera had enjoyed a fairly good success for several seasons. Muratore, the first Prinzivalle, sang the same role in the Uruguayan premiere of *Monna Vanna* at the Solís. In contrast to *Madame Sans-Gêne*, this second new production of the season was heartily welcomed.

> This opera is a superior spectacle and from the artistic point of view the best of the whole lyric season. Rarely have we been so interested in a new opera. *Monna Vanna*, without being the most representative among those of the French modern composers, has notable values. Tenor Muratore was absolutely admirable as Prinzivalle, and baritone Jean Vanni-Marcoux was an extraordinary Guido. The "mise en scène" was magnificent; nevertheless, we greatly missed Maestro Serafin at the podium.[11]

Baritone Vanni-Marcoux was the son of a French father and an Italian mother born in Turin. His real name was Giovanni Marcoux [Jean Emile Diogène Marcoux in French]. Later his nickname (Vanni) and his last name were combined. He was a talented singer and also a fine actor. Among other characters he was well known for his portrayal of the title character in Massenet's *Don Quichotte*.[12]

Monna Vanna was led that year by assistant conductor Maestro Vigna. Vigna was well known in opera circles, and had gone from La Scala to conduct productions at the Metropolitan, among them the first Caruso season in 1903; nevertheless, in New York he was considered a crude conductor.

The Solís audiences also preferred Serafin, who conducted a Wagnerian concert in the same season. Elena Rakowska, known as a

singer to Solís audiences for many years and then as Serafin's wife, was one of the soloists in this 1919 Wagner program. In the 1920 Solís season, again conducted by her husband, she sang *Tristan und Isolde* in Italian: "This *Tristan* under Serafin was superior to the production Marinuzzi conducted three years ago. Serafin's version has more balance, and the cast was more homogeneous. Rakowska was a splendid Isolda, even if her Italian diction was not clear."[13]

The 1920 Solís opera season opened with Muzio singing Violetta. Serafin also presented Ildebrando Pizzetti's *Fedra* and another new opera for Montevideo audiences: Massenet's *Le roi de Lahore*, translated into Italian. Almost forty years separated the composition of Massenet and Pizzetti's operas. But at the time of these operas' composition, both composers were thirty-five years of age, and each opera helped each composer garner his first public recognition. In fact, in April 1877, many years before his triumphs with *Manon* and *Werther*, Massenet presented *Le roi de Lahore* at the Paris Opéra.

Arriving on the Solís stage long after all other distinguished Massenet works, *Le roi de Lahore* met with a tepid reception: "The opera was interesting only as a historic document that belongs to the 'grand opéra' style, but does not add any higher artistic value. For us Massenet will always be the great creator of *Manon* and *Werther*, but never of *Thaïs*, *Hérodiade*, or *Il re di Lahore*."[14]

When Pizzetti's *Fedra* was produced at La Scala in 1915, he began his collaboration with Gabriele D'Annunzio, and thus began to build a name in the circles of Italian opera. *Fedra*, performed for the first time at the Solís on August 21, 1920, the day preceding Massenet's opera, met with the following reaction:

> Highly interesting, the poet and the composer [D'Annunzio and Pizzetti] have achieved an excellent combination. Notwith-

standing some grandiloquent passages and the lyricism of a new musical language, the music follows the words without destroying the poetic rhythm. Pizzetti's use of Greek tones is colored by the classical concept of Palestrina and Victoria. He has spontaneity and freshness, and the performance was perfect from both the vocal and the dramatic point of view.[15]

In addition to Rakowska and Muzio, several other singers appeared at the Solís that season: Fanny Anitúa was an excellent Ortrud in a *Lohengrin* production, tenor Edoardo Ferrari-Fontana sang Tristan opposite Rakowska, bass Pavel Ludikar was an outstanding Re Marke in the same Wagner, the young Ismaele Voltolini accompanied Muzio as Radamès, and the vigorous baritone Carlo Galeffi sang Amonasro.

In 1920 a correspondent from New York's *Musical Courier* reported on many of the operas of this Solís season. Let us see the Solís through the eyes of a 1920s New Yorker:

GAY FESTIVITIES OPEN GRAND OPERA

SEASON IN MONTEVIDEO

It has been the custom for years gone by to give a fortnight season of grand opera in the Solís Theatre of Montevideo. This fortnight is the social event of the whole year, and it is only right to add that the capital of the Republic of Uruguay assumes quite a gay and animated character during this short period. . . . It is a very old theatre, but despite this its acoustics are among the best I have so far experienced. . . .

With the performance of *Aida* on August 19, it is only fair to say that Impresario Bonetti fully redeemed himself with the public of Montevideo, discontented because of the standard of the preceding three performances [which were] not what one would expect on a basis of twelve dollars gold for a stall. The atmosphere in the auditorium was distinctly jubilant and enthusiastic. Claudia Muzio sang Aida and her success was spontaneous. . . . In the role of Radamès the new tenor Voltolini was fairly good. Galeffi was Amonasro and his success was great. The contralto Fanny Anitúa made her bow to the public in the role of Amneris. She possesses a powerful voice, but her register is uneven. Lazzari as Ramfis proved to have a good voice. The chorus did some excellent work and contributed largely to the great success of the evening. A word of praise is due to Maestro Serafin who conducted the opera in grand style and managed to get wonders out of his orchestra.[16]

* * *

A LONELY DANCER wandering the world from stage to stage, no matter if it was a leading opera house, a small provincial theater, or the smallest music hall—such was Anna Pavlova after her break with the Ballets Russes in 1910. When Vaslav Nijinsky sprang to sudden fame, he was immediately as famous as Pavlova, but Sergei Diaghilev could not have two stars of the same magnitude. In his company only one could shine, and, of course, his choice was Nijinsky. Pavlova was relegated to second place and, refusing this humiliation, she began her lonely pilgrimage. It was never a question of there being two Nijinskys. Pavlova was just as unique, and in the world of dance her presence changed ballet forever. The zenith of all her performances was her interpretation of *La morte du cygne*, choreographed for her by Michael Fokine and set to the music of Camille Saint-Saëns. It is this ballet that is most closely associated with Pavlova; here she transferred her own lonely soul into the solitude of the dying swan, with a mastery never matched.

On her second visit to Montevideo, Pavlova debuted with her company at the Solís in the fall of 1919, on May 15 (fig. 42). During her second performance, two days later, the program ended with *La morte du cygne*. The next day's review shows the impact Pavlova's interpretation produced on the audience:

> When we heard the last notes of Saint-Saëns' moving melody, and the dancer's winged body folded down slowly in a death song full of poetry—after she had sung with her whole body, especially her arms and hands— Solís audiences were open-mouthed. As an echo to the song of the dying bird, an exclamation rose at once, and all spectators broke into great applause that became a standing ovation of several minutes. Very seldom do audiences show spontaneously such unanimous admiration.[17]

Among the six performances Pavlova and her company gave at the Solís, she danced *La morte du cygne* three times. Alexander Volinine, famous for being Katerine Geltzer's partner at Moscow's Bolshoi Theater, came as the first male dancer in Pavlova's company.

Three months after her last Solís presentation, Pavlova came back with Volinine to the Teatro Urquiza to dance with her corps de ballet as part of the Da Rosa–Mocchi opera company. She and Volinine gave also some short shows by themselves at the end of opera performances. It is pathetic that the greatest ballerina of her time was required to do so in order to survive.

* * *

WITH MOST EUROPEAN HALLS and houses still dark and suffering tremendous economic problems, during the war and postwar years the Teatro Solís became the host for hundreds of recitals and concerts performed by the world's finest singers, instrumentalists, and conductors. From 1919 to 1921, the Solís again received Artur Rubinstein, along with nine other outstanding pianists: José Arriola, Ernesto Drangosch, Maurice Dumesnil, Ignaz Friedman, Yolanda Merö, Tina Lerner, Frances Nash, Edouard Risler, and Ricardo Viñes. Among the string instrumentalists that Solís audiences were lucky enough to hear were Agustín Barrios, Gaspar Cassadó, Francisco Costa, Juan Manén, Wasa Prihoda, Andrés Segovia, and Ferenc de Vecsey. The greater number of these performers gave a series of recitals, with a total of eighty concerts. While all were of highest quality, two artists deserve special notice: Risler and Viñes. Two other artists must also be highlighted when we look at this spectacular season: Ninon Vallin (already familiar to Solís audiences) and Felix Weingartner.

Although the French soprano had previously performed at the Solís, Vallin did so as an opera singer; this time she gave two lieder recitals accompanied by Risler and Viñes, something unprecedented in this kind of concert. With Risler she gave the first Uruguayan performance of the complete cycle of Robert Schumann's *Dichterliebe* and Wagner's *Wesendonk Lieder*, plus works by Henri Duparc, Déodat de Séverac, and Gabriel Fauré. In her second recital Vallin (with Viñes) performed works by César Franck, Maurice Ravel, Claude Debussy, Nikolay Rimsky-Korsakov, Alexander Glazunov, and Manuel de Falla, most of them never heard before in Montevideo (see 1920 chronology).

The great expectations that centered on Risler, then considered the best interpreter of Ludwig van Beethoven, became even greater when a joint concert was announced with this Franco-German pianist and Rubinstein. Of special interest is one critic's opinion of how the chemistry of these two celebrities worked together: "Risler and Rubinstein smoothly overcame all the inconveniences of having such different temperaments and styles of playing. Both being geniuses, each one

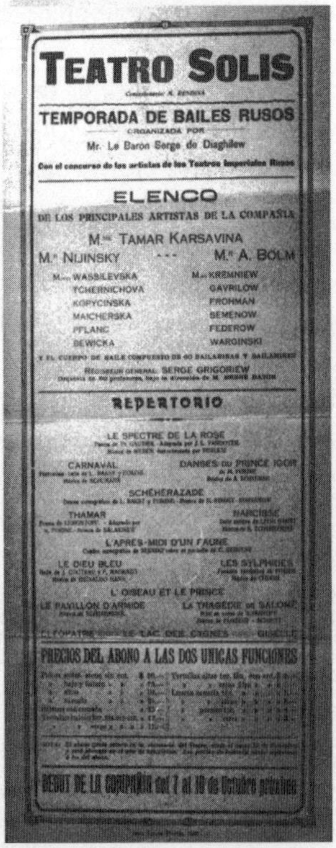

Fig. 42. Famous singers, instrumentalists, and ballet companies performed at the Solís during its Golden Age. *Upper Left*: Titta Ruffo's last recital at the Solís on October 31, 1928. *Upper right*: Pianist Edouard Risler's concert in 1919. Both author's collection. *Lower Left*: The only season Anna Pavlova appeared at the Solís was in May 1919, when she offered six recitals and danced her signature role, Saint-Saëns' *La morte du cygne*. *Lower Right*: The Ballets Russes' first Uruguayan season with the debuts of Vaslav Nijinsky and Tamara Karsavina, October 1913. Lower programs Biblioteca Nacional Collection, Montevideo.

attained an extraordinary balance, also adjusting the style of each interpretation. Concerts like this do not happen every day. It was a master class!"[18]

Another exceptional pianist in the first half of the twentieth century was Viñes. Repeatedly called "the foremost champion of new works," and often to the detriment of his own artistic career, Viñes traveled with a repertoire difficult to promote; people neither knew it nor considered the works of value. As a close friend of Debussy, Ravel, Séverac, Enrique Granados, Isaac Albéniz, and other composers of that period, Viñes fought hard to place their music in the concert repertoire. He also espoused the piano works of the Russian masters Modest Musorgsky, Mily Balakirev, and Sergey Prokofiev. A crusader for modern music, Viñes gave only one concert at the Solís during these years (1919–21); nevertheless, from the musical point of view his presentation must be considered one of the most important performances Solís audiences heard at that time. He did return to Montevideo several times, in 1931 to the SODRE's Estudio Auditorio as soloist in Rimsky-Korsakov's piano concerto with the OSSODRE (Orquesta Sinfónica del SODRE) under the baton of Virgilio Scarabelli, and also in November of the same year when he gave a recital at the same house. He visited again in 1934 and in 1935.

Two young female pianists, Hungarian Yolanda Merö and American Frances Nash, performed at the Solís with very distinct styles. Merö (a fellow student of Rubinstein and Wilhelm Kolischer in Berlin) surprised Solís audiences with her brilliant and vigorous temperament. Reflecting the prejudices of his time, one critic commended her for "her almost manly attack," surprised that such a sound could come from a woman.[19] After many years of touring, Merö established herself in New York City, where she married Herman Irion, one of the associates of Steinway and Sons. Nash, on her first visit to South America, gave the first Uruguayan performance of Edward MacDowell's *Sonata Eroica*. (Born nine years before Louis Moreau Gottschalk's death, MacDowell was considered the best American composer at the beginning of the twentieth century.)

After Toscanini's visit in 1906, Solís audiences did not enjoy a conductor of such magnitude again until 1920, with the arrival of Felix Weingartner (fig. 43). The Dalmatian maestro came to lead the Asociación Coral's orchestra in three concerts. The house was sold out many weeks in advance, and the standing-room line began to form very early in the morning of these performances. Montevideo wanted to see and hear the man who was then thought of as the best classical conductor of the century. Each concert's review, besides applauding Weingartner's genius, had two themes in common: how the conductor communicated his personal style to the orchestra (it being the first time he had conducted those musicians), and his economy and clarity of beat.

> I cannot remember ever attending a symphonic concert in Montevideo such as last evening's, conducted by the celebrated Felix Weingartner. To the lucky people at the Solís he gave the unique opportunity of knowing the authentic essence of Beethoven's symphonic style. I remembered again the last time I had seen Weingartner in Vienna, in 1911—his noble and dignified poise, almost motionless and even sometimes with arms crossed, and how he had the power to extract such unmatched sonorities from an orchestra.[20]

Montevideo music lovers had already had the opportunity to see, three days before his first concert at the Solís, the acclaimed Weingartner as an opera conductor at the Teatro Urquiza.

Fig. 43. The most remarkable event of 1922 was the visit of the Vienna Philharmonic conducted by Felix Weingartner. Announcement of his first concert with the composer's autograph and a few bars of his own *Dame Kobold* overture, and his arrival at Montevideo. *La Razón*, August 5, 1922. Biblioteca Nacional Collection, Montevideo.

If the 1920 Weingartner visit was highly praised, when the conductor returned two years later, this time with the complete Vienna Philharmonic Orchestra, to perform three concerts at the Solís, the city's enthusiasm was unbounded. To understand what qualified as the "Great Musical Event," we must remember that it was the first time in Montevideo musical history that its audience would see and hear the most famous orchestra in the world. Although the words of that time sound a bit exaggerated today, this euphoria is the sincere reaction of someone in the presence of a masterpiece:

We have been extremely lucky to receive the best European ensemble with the most noble tradition in the history of contemporary music, one of the most perfect of the world. For the first time Solís audiences were able to see a conductor like Weingartner with his own orchestra, long having worked together to achieve the magnificent results we witnessed yesterday. The conductor carefully elicited the different styles of the works on the program. If in Beethoven he brought out the best in his musicians, we were happily surprised with the interpretations of Berlioz and Respighi. In the *Symphonie fantastique* Weingartner achieved one of the richest orchestral palettes we can remember. This performance could never be surpassed! Only Weingartner, with such marvelous sobriety and economy of beat, can reach such perfection and, at the same time, lead the orchestra through all the nuances of the Berlioz score.[21]

After each of his concerts the public gave Weingartner standing ovations and then, applauding and shouting, followed him to the plaza in front of the Solís. The Vienna Philharmonic Orchestra would come again in 1923 with Richard Strauss conducting, but the fervor of Weingartner's visits and his first orchestra presentation were never again equaled.

CHAPTER 23

1923–1928

Richard Strauss Conducts *Elektra* and the Vienna Philharmonic—Debut of Nine Celebrated Singers—"A Gentleman of the Stage": The Baritone Víctor Damiani—Two Premieres: *Boris Godunov* and *La cena delle beffe*— Beethoven Centennial Concerts

However brief, the 1923 Teatro Solís season was one of the most significant in the history of the house, comparable only to that of 1903. If the earlier season featured the spectacular arrival of Enrico Caruso and Arturo Toscanini, 1923 had Richard Strauss conducting the Uruguayan premiere of *Elektra*, plus eight of his tone poems with the Vienna Philharmonic Orchestra; two separate rosters of artists from Italy and Germany; and a total of twenty-two singers, with nine especially illustrious performers making their Solís opera debuts: Toti Dal Monte, Elsa Bland, Maria Olczewska, Aureliano Pertile, Miguel Fleta, Walter Kirchhoff, John O'Sullivan, Emil Schipper, and Víctor Damiani (who in 1922 had given a concert at the Solís).

When Strauss arrived in Montevideo in July 1923, he already enjoyed wide fame; all his symphonic works had been performed at least once (even though not very popular in that part of South America) and two of his

operas, *Salome* and *Elektra*, were objects of controversy in many cultural circles. His renown at that time also proceeded from his directorship of the Vienna's Staatsoper.

This was the Vienna Philharmonic's second visit, so the audience expectations focused not on the orchestra but the unknown conductor and, in particular, his tone-poem premieres. For his first concert in Montevideo, Strauss chose a program made up exclusively of his own compositions, while in the remaining four concerts, he included at least two of his works on each program (fig. 44). The critic from *El Día* responded to the first concert:

The artistic interest of the first Vienna Philharmonic concert was greater than that of two years ago because this time we had the opportunity to hear famous Strauss compositions. Surprisingly, *Ein Heldenleben* was not received with the warmth we expected but with some coldness. We suspect that the work is not easy to understand; there was

168

Fig. 44. *Upper*: For the second year in a row the Vienna Philharmonic came again to the Solís, this time led by Richard Strauss. Preview to the first concert with an all-Strauss program, illustrated by a pen drawing by Peña-Plata. Biblioteca Nacional Collection, Montevideo. *Lower*: Program of the fifth and last concert of the Vienna Philharmonic under Richard Strauss, on August 5, 1923. Author's collection.

also the strain of an overlong program. In contrast, *Till Eulenspiegels*, with all its richness of orchestral combinations and superior merriment, got the first ovation of the night. However, enthusiasm reached its peak after Salome's dances, a very familiar piece to the audience's ear.[1]

When the Vienna Philharmonic gave its third concert, *La Razón*'s critic reported:

The second and third part of the program were reserved for two of Strauss' works, *Don Juan* and the *Symphonia domestica*. The productions of such an extraordinary figure of modern art have already conquered all the hostilities of former criticism and are now accepted by all cultivated audiences. The *Symphonia domestica* is a highly original piece with rich instrumentation and a genial addition to the same style as D'Indy and Chausson. Our audience, as always when offered an exceptional example of art, gave Strauss a standing ovation.[2]

A few days after the Vienna Philharmonic concerts ended, violinist Bronislaw Huberman performed a series of recitals, immediately after which the Solís 1923 winter opera season opened with Claudia Muzio singing *Aida* on August 21. This time Radamès was a singer new to Solís audiences: Aureliano Pertile. He was, however, already known in Montevideo, as he had sung at the Urquiza during 1918 (see chapter 22). At the time of his arrival to the Solís this tenor's career was reaching its peak; it had been only a few months before that he achieved fame at La Scala in *Mefistofele* under Toscanini. After this Faust he not only became the conductor's favorite tenor but was engaged by Milan's opera house until 1937. Nevertheless, following his Montevideo production of *Aida*, the review was not at all flattering:

Signor Pertile found difficulties in the role of Radamès that surpassed his vocal means and goodwill. Perhaps he was having a bad night, although he managed very well when delivering "Celeste Aida." The final duet was more successful, enabling him to demonstrate his emotion, voice, and sensitive acting.[3]

Pertile sang again to close that opera season, this time as Edgardo in *Lucia*, and the same critic found him "in better condition than when he made his debut in *Aida*. In fact, in [*Lucia*] his performance was very good."[4] After leaving Montevideo Pertile went to La Scala to create the title role in the posthumous world premiere of Boito's unfinished opera *Nerone*, performed under Toscanini's baton on May 1, 1924.

In 1922, between a successful opera season in Buenos Aires, Rosario, Córdoba, and the Rio de Janeiro presentation, the Mocchi-Da Rosa company proceeded to Montevideo for an extremely brief season at the Teatro Urquiza with three performances only: *Iris*, on August 24, *La Favorita* on the morning of August 25, and *Tosca* in a gala performance in the evening of the same day. *Tosca*, conducted by Maestro Gabriele Santini, was sung by Ofelia Nieto in the title role, with Fleta as Cavaradossi and Luigi Rossi-Morelli as Scarpia.[5]

On the second night of the 1923 Solís season, Montevideo audiences watched a full German cast in *Tristan und Isolde* conducted by Gino Marinuzzi. According to the next day's review, two artists especially merited the applause: "Walter Kirchhoff, who sang Tristan, performed with dexterity, keeping his voice intact throughout the long second-act duet and in the final aria. Maria Olczewska interpreted an excellent Brangäne, with her voice full of passion and dramatic conviction."[6]

A pupil of Lilli Lehmann, Kirchhoff stood

out as a heldentenor, even if he also sang lyric roles. Beginning his singing career in Berlin, he later performed at Covent Garden and, after his South American tour, debuted at the Metropolitan in 1927. At the time of her Solís performances, Olczewska was part of the Vienna Staatsoper, and the role of Brangäne together with other Wagnerian and Straussian characters became her favorites, bringing her worldwide critical acclaim as one of the most gifted and intelligent mezzo-sopranos of her time.

Going from success to success, the day after *Tristan*, the Solís offered a striking *Rigoletto*. Seldom had the three principal characters in Giuseppe Verdi's opera been under thirty years of age, and two of them already possessors of international reputations, as were soprano Dal Monte and tenor Fleta in his second visit to Montevideo. This *Rigoletto* performance was publicized widely, not only because of the fame of Fleta and Dal Monte but because baritone Damiani (fig. 45) was just launching of his international career.

There will be a special gala performance with *Rigoletto* to present our fellow citizen, baritone Damiani, who will sing Verdi's opera with Fleta and Dal Monte under the baton of Maestro Franco Paolantonio. The Uruguayan public will be able to applaud a singer who will hereafter appear on the rosters of opera companies worldwide.[7]

The next day Montevideo's *El Día* carried a lengthy review of Damiani's Rigoletto (a sketch of whom accompanied the article). Under the bold title, "An Exceptional *Rigoletto*," it trumpeted:

Last evening the Solís hosted the extraordinary performance of a *Rigoletto* sung by Dal Monte, Fleta, and Damiani in the title role— the same role in which this Uruguayan bar-

itone had made his debut. This performance was a triumph for our fellow citizen, and this *Rigoletto* demonstrates this singer's progress in both the quality and handling of his voice. Free of the former nervousness, last night his voice had an extremely pleasant timbre, a warm quality with heartrending modulations that reached its peak in the tremendous aria ["Cortigiani, vil razza"] that he sang magnificently to an approving audience.[8]

Damiani had made his debut June 19, 1919 as Amonasro at the Teatro Coliseo in Buenos Aires. Of all the Verdi baritone roles, Rigoletto is one of the most demanding. For a twenty-six-year-old singer, it becomes an even greater challenge, yet this challenge was Damiani's triumph. This Solís performance marked the first time he shared the stage with singers of such caliber as Fleta and Dal Monte. From then on, Damiani enjoyed a brilliant career of forty years, with a repertoire of ninety-seven operatic roles, plus five oratorios. All South American opera houses, in particular Buenos Aires' Teatro Colón, where Damiani sang for eighteen consecutive seasons, had the baritone on their rosters. After his Solís *Rigoletto* he again performed with Fleta on the opening night of Madrid's Teatro Real 1925 opera season, and on March 3, 1925, they sang *Carmen* in a gala performance to celebrate the fiftieth anniversary of Bizet's opera. When Damiani was thirty-one he was engaged for the 1927–28 and 1928–29 seasons by the Teatro alla Scala, debuting there under Ettore Panizza's baton. He sang more than forty performances in eleven different operas at La Scala, including the world premiere of Guido Bianchini's *Thien-Hoa*. Among the standard repertoire were his performances in *Falstaff*, *La traviata*, and *Lucia di Lammermoor* under Toscanini's baton.[9]

When the 1927–28 La Scala season was over,

TEATRO SOLIS

Empresa Walter Mocchi y Cia.   TEMPORADA OFICIAL 1923

Gran Compañía Lírica del Teatro Colón de Buenos Aires

JUEVES 23 DE AGOSTO (A las 21.15)

Gran Función Extraordinaria :: Con asistencia de S. E. el
Presidente de la República y Cuerpo Diplomático

Presentación del Barítono Uruguayo VICTOR DAMIANI

Y DEBUT DE LOS ARTISTAS
TOTI DALMONTE, MIGUEL FLETA y GIULIO CIRINO

Con la ópera en 4 actos, de G. VERDI:

Rigoletto

Maestro Concertador y Director de Orquesta:
FRANCO PAOLANTONIO

Regisseur General:
Comm. MARIO SAMMARCO

REPARTO

Gilda	TOTI DALMONTE
Duca di Mantova	MIGUEL FLETA
Rigoletto	VICTOR DAMIANI
Magdalena	LUISA BERTANA
Sparafucile	GIULIO CIRINO
Monterone	MIGUEL FIORE
Conte di Ceprano	GINO DEVECCHI
Borsa	Nello Palai
Marullo	Ciro Scafa
Contessa di Ceprano	María Lilloni
Un Page de la Duquesa	N. N.
Giavanna servente	Gina Cattaneo

Caballeros, Damas, Pages, Alabarderos, Cortesanos, Etc.

GRAN CUERPO DE BAILE

PRECIOS DE LAS LOCALIDADES

Palcos bajos y balcones, sin entrada	$ 40.00	Lunetas de cazuela, 1.ª fila	$	4.00
Palcos altos, sin entrada	» 20.00	Lunetas de cazuela, otras filas	»	3.00
Palcos de cazuela, sin entrada	» 10.00	Lunetas de paraíso, 1.ª fila	»	4.00
Tertulia alta, primera fila	» 6.00	Lunetas de paraíso, otras filas	»	3.50
Tertulia alta, otras filas	» 5.00	Entrada general	»	5.00
		Entrada a cazuela y paraíso	»	1.20

SILLON DE PLATEA . . . . . $ 8.00

VIERNES 24: 3.ª Función de Abono, con el estreno de ELECTRA,
del maestro Strauss y COMPAGNACCI, del maestro Primo Riccitelli.

Fig. 45. *Left*: The first major performance of Víctor Damiani was Rigoletto, with Miguel Fleta as the Duca di Mantova and Toti Dal Monte as Gilda, conducted by Franco Paolantonio. Author's collection. *Upper Right*: Damiani around 1950s. Author's collection. *Lower Right*: Damiani as Rigoletto, when he sang at the Civic Opera; photograph taken in 1931 by a Chicago photographer. Author's collection, gift of José Pedro Damiani.

Milan's prestigious newspaper, *Il Corriere della Sera*, published a complete article devoted exclusively to Damiani. The article demonstrated the regard in which the Uruguayan baritone was held by Milanese audiences:

> La Scala's season is over. Between November and May, Víctor Damiani has interpreted eight operas in our grand theater. Each one has been a beautiful and incontestable testimony to his value as a singer and interpreter, owner of a beautiful, warm, and mellow voice. He is a very steady artist, unique, with an irreproachable correctness.... Reviews have registered the applause and support of La Scala's audiences during this long season. They also evince his experience, talent, artistry, and marvelous voice: always steady, always different. Thus, the Teatro alla Scala joins the large group of international opera houses that have witnessed the performances of Vittorio [*sic*] Damiani and his well-deserved triumphs. Damiani, who is leaving soon to visit his parents in Montevideo, will return to Italy in a few months.[10]

When in the next season (1928–29) he sang the role of Enrico in Donizetti's *Lucia di Lammermoor*, this same newspaper reported: "We give our unconditional applause to the baritone Víctor Damiani, who sang the role of Enrico with dramatic effectiveness, an authentic sharpness and impetuosity, a correct and noble poise, and all with a warm, robust, and stable voice in both intonation and diction."[11]

In addition to La Scala, Damiani—internationally known as "a gentleman of the stage" because of his extraordinary personality, poise, and professionalism—performed in almost all the cities of Spain and Italy, including such major opera houses as Barcelona's Liceo, Madrid's Real, Naples' San Carlo, Parma's Regio, and Palermo's Massimo. In the

United States he sang at the Boston Opera House and Chicago's Civic Opera.[12] In 1962 an *El Plata* critic wrote, "Without doubt he was until the present the most acclaimed and internationally known Uruguayan opera singer, with a warm and resonant voice of extraordinary power, as well as being an outstanding dramatic actor," especially as Verdi's Rigoletto, Germont, Renato, Amonasro, Di Luna, and Iago—the last in an unforgettable interpretation opposite Ramón Vinay's acclaimed Otello, that they sang in many opera houses, with powerful mastery, during the late 1940s.[13]

His was a career without pause until his death on stage on January 28, 1962, during a concert of his pupils, after delivering *Andrea Chénier*'s "Nemico della Patria." As the famous baritone turned to shake hands with his piano accompanist and then thank his audience, he fell, victim of a heart attack, and died immediately. Sudden and sad as this was, it can still be said that forty-three years after his Buenos Aires debut, Damiani's career ended as it had started, with applause.

Two other new singers shared the Solís stage with Damiani in 1923: Dal Monte and Fleta, both of whom experienced short and brilliant careers. Soprano Dal Monte had appeared as one of the soloists in Beethoven's Ninth Symphony under Toscanini in 1919 and was invited by him to perform Gilda at La Scala in 1922. She gave another example of her prodigious vocal talent when she closed the 1923 Solís opera season with a spectacular *Lucia di Lammermoor*: "Toti Dal Monte is already a rising star of the first magnitude, and her gifted vocal attributes allow her to face the difficult role of Lucia without a single problem. Dal Monte was quite sensational in the Mad Scene, where she sang with a clear and warm voice and, at the same time, with extraordinary agility."[14] Dal Monte continued to sing in the principal opera houses until the beginning of the 1930s, after which she occasionally sang in concerts and performed as an actress until 1949, when she retired. She then appeared in film and taught until her death in 1975, aged eighty-two.

If Dal Monte was extraordinary, her Duca di Mantova in Verdi's opera was not only a handsome twenty-eight-year-old tenor but another rising star. In fall 1923, when Fleta arrived at the Río de la Plata, *El Día*'s music critic interviewed the Spanish tenor. Here we have, in Fleta's own words, some of his future plans:

FLETA: As soon as the three-month South American tour has ended, I will go to New York. I have already signed my contract to sing at the next Metropolitan season a French *Carmen*, *Aida*, *L'amico Fritz*'s New York premiere,[15] *Tosca*, *Rigoletto*, *Andrea Chénier*, *Mefistofele*, and *La bohème*.

INTERVIEWER: What is the reason you have not yet sung at Milan's La Scala?

FLETA: I was asked to go there to perform when I was in Mexico and when all my booking had been done. As a result, it was impossible to arrive in Milan on time for the season.

INTERVIEWER: Will you debut soon at La Scala?

FLETA: Oh yes! I will sing there this year, and Toscanini will conduct.[16]

Three years after Fleta's first Solís performance, the memorable posthumous world premiere of Puccini's *Turandot* was given at the Milan opera house on April 25, 1926, and Fleta was Toscanini's choice to create the first Calaf. Sadly, Fleta's career did not end in distinction. After 1928, when he was only thirty-five, his career was already in decline because he had mistreated his voice; in 1938 he died at the age of forty-five.

Tenor John O'Sullivan was the last new artist to make his local debut during the 1923 Solís opera season. With a brilliant cast that included Hina Spani, Flora Perini, Carlo Gal-

effi, and Giulio Cirino, O'Sullivan sang the role of Arnoldo in a production of Rossini's *Guglielmo Tell*. However, O'Sullivan's greatest Montevideo triumph would take place when he returned to the Solís in 1925.

Besides bringing back the great voices of Gilda Dalla Rizza, Claudia Muzio, Fanny Anitúa, Giulio Crimi, Marcelo Urízar, Giuseppe Borgatti and Italo Cristalli (in addition to Damiani and Fleta), and Maestros Vincenzo Bellezza and Edoardo Vitale, the 1924 and 1925 Solís opera seasons offered other highlights.[17] These included two Uruguayan premieres; an entire Russian opera company; the debut of soprano Maria Zamboni; and, outside of the field of opera, the visit of Spanish composer Amadeo Vives to direct some of his most popular works.

Eleven Russian singers, led by bass Sigismund Zalewsky, gave the first performances of Modest Musorgsky's *Boris Godunov* that Montevideo audiences ever knew (the two exceptions to the otherwise Russian cast were two Italian singers: Anna Gramegna as Xenia's nurse, and tenor Luigi Nardi as the Simpleton). After Zalewsky's two *Boris* performances had met with great success and applause, the renowned bass sang an outstanding Mefistofele in Boito's opera, where the Margherita was Zamboni. This young soprano, not yet noticed, would be Toscanini's choice to create the first Liù in the world premiere of *Turandot* two years later (1926).

The 1925 Solís opera season began with a traditional *Aida*, which was followed by the regular repertoire of Verdi, Puccini, Rossini, Massenet, and some Henry Février, Christoph Gluck, Meyerbeer, and so forth. The excitement of a *Madama Butterfly* sung by Dalla Rizza in a gala performance honoring the Prince of Wales was eclipsed by John O'Sullivan's three presentations, which brought new life to the season. These were Camille Saint-Saëns' *Sansone e Dalila*, Meyerbeer's *Gli ugonotti* and Février's *Monna*

Vanna, as they had not been performed for several seasons, O'Sullivan's performances sparked new interest in the productions. They met with warm approval. "*Gli ugonotti*," wrote the critic for *El Día*, "is the best of the season. Tenor O'Sullivan impressed us greatly; he possesses a magnificent voice, not only for its great volume but for the richness of its timbre, very strong and firm in the high notes. He was the hero of the night, garnering most of the evening's applause."[18]

Three days later, O'Sullivan's Sansone opposite Fanny Anitúa was equally praised:

> Tenor O'Sullivan has, in this particular case, "le physique du rôle," and he delivered his part in French with extraordinary dramatic expression and a powerful voice.... [Unfortunately] Anitúa, who was having one of her best days, sang in Italian. It is a pity, for this bilingualism took away part of the original brightness from the duets.[19]

In addition to O'Sullivan's performances, the hit of the season was Umberto Giordano's *La cena delle beffe* in its first Solís production. The opera, having had its world premiere at La Scala only eight months earlier, elicited an interesting review from the Montevideo press:

> Even if Giordano's new opera follows the verismo school, it has an eclecticism too close to the old Italian operatic style. At the same time, the composer uses the schemes of the new school of composition.... Act one has a preponderance of declamatory passages that efficiently outline the sense of the words without missing the melodic element. The climax of the opera can be found in the third scene of the second act, with a prelude followed by a comic dialogue that reminds me of the Puccini of *Gianni Schicchi*. Musically, it is an admirably well-composed octet.... *La cena delle beffe* was very well interpreted, and Maestro Vitale

and the orchestra should be singled out for special praise. Baritone Apollo Granforte, having one of his best nights, was by far the outstanding member of the cast. Soprano Revalles was adequate, but she had some problems with the high "tessitura" of her part.[20]

* * *

ALTHOUGH THE BEETHOVEN CENTENNIAL year (commemorating the composer's death) was not until 1927, concerts and recitals of his music started much earlier at the Teatro Solís. The zenith of the 1926 season, among the instrumentalists who played that year, was reached with the six recitals offered by the celebrated London String Quartet, which included Beethoven in each of their programs. Local musical ensembles joined in the celebrations in the early fall of 1927. The two leading groups, the Orquesta Nacional and the Asociación Coral, opened the season on April 18, 1927, in the first of six concerts that presented the complete cycle of Beethoven's nine symphonies, plus all of the concertos and some overtures. The orchestra was conducted by Vicente Pablo, a pupil of Ferruccio Busoni and José Vianna da Motta at the Berlin Academy of Music, and the best Uruguayan instrumentalists and singers of that time appeared as soloists. Another local ensemble, the Asociación de Música de Cámara, performed the piano, violin, and chamber music in a series of five concerts with all-Beethoven programs. However, regarding soloist performances, the high point of the year was the recital of Wilhelm Backhaus. Considered one of the finest Beethoven interpreters of his age, the German pianist dedicated a whole recital to the keyboard sonatas, which (according to the *El Día* critic) were masterly played.

Two singers were also welcomed by Solís opera lovers that year: Tito Schipa and Titta Ruffo returned to the stage of their past successes, in 1927 and 1928 respectively.[21] On these occasions both gave vocal recitals, but Ruffo did not fare well; at fifty-one the baritone was past his prime:

> Unfortunately, Titta Ruffo is no longer the wonder of voice and energy we heard at the Solís years ago. After the Brindisi from *Amleto* [*Hamlet*], his famous warhorse, he was extensively applauded by the audience. But it was very sad and painful to see the evident signs of fatigue he showed after that effort. At the end he sang several encores and the audience responded with a standing ovation, accompanying him afterward outside the house.[22]

That year two singers at the height of their careers, Sofía del Campo and Damiani, both gave recitals to say farewell to Solís audiences. The fine Chilean soprano was leaving South America for Philadelphia, where she was expected to open the opera season singing Gilda, while the Uruguayan baritone left Montevideo for Italy.

The 1928 Solís season also contained a group of outstanding instrumentalists. Among them were two twenty-five-year-old newcomers to the Solís: pianists Claudio Arrau and Carlo Zecchi. Arrau reached Montevideo after many European tours and had recently won the Grand Prix International des Pianistes in Geneva. Arrau chose Chopin, Brahms, Debussy, Liszt, and Mily Balakirev for his second program:

> Yesterday we recognized the appearance of a piano virtuoso of exceptional technique.... His Chopin interpretations communicated a

transparency and richness of sound rarely heard.... The overwhelming Brahms *Variations on a Theme by Paganini* were played with dazzling technique, with extraordinary strength, and an assurance that shows his superior control of the keyboard. The recital ended with a performance of Balakirev's *Islamey* that met with bravos.[23]

On April 28 Arrau played works by J. S. Bach, Beethoven, Liszt, Ravel, Debussy, and Stravinsky. Again the review glowed: "His interpretation of Stravinsky's *Three Movements from Petroushka* showed that Arrau is one of the best and most reliable interpreters of modern music. Very few surpass him in the domain of technique, and perhaps none in purity and quality of sound."[24]

Zecchi was considered one of the finest interpreters of Domenico Scarlatti's piano works. His September appearance, in which he performed Scarlatti, J. S. Bach, Ferruccio Busoni, César Franck, Mario Castelnuovo-Tedesco, Nicolò Paganini, and Liszt, was highly regarded:

> Zecchi's interpretations are very moving, steadily and broadly phrased, and simultaneously sober, with an efficient use of chiaroscuro.... He was extremely competent as an interpreter of modern music in Castelnuovo-Tedesco's *Le danze del re David*, with a special color for each one of the movements.... The program, culminating with the Paganini-Liszt's *Three Studies*, demonstrated his exceptional agility and absolute command of piano technique and confirms his fame as great virtuoso.[25]

CHAPTER 24

1929–1930

A Russian Opera Season—Bidú Sayão and Jan Kiepura—Rosette Anday's Carmen—Ottorino Respighi Conducts and Plays His Works—Guiomar Novaës—Wanda Landowska—Elisabeth Schumann—Jacques Thibaud— Feodor Chaliapin—The Creation of the SODRE

Ancient folk tales and legends were the source from which Russian composers found the plots for their operas, operettas, and ballets. In 1929, for the first time in Teatro Solís history, a whole season of Russian opera was given at the theater. Five new productions, in a total of fourteen performances, composed the season, opening with Alexander Borodin's *Prince Igor*. The company that brought these operas was known as the Compagnie Russe de l'Opéra Privée (fig. 46). Created in Paris by soprano Maria Kusnezoff, it comprised singers and personnel who had once belonged to Moscow theaters, all under the musical direction and conducting of Gregoire Fitelberg. After a century's reign of Italian opera and a few French and German performances, this unprecedented Russian season brought a new and refreshing style into the old house. With the exception of the Polovtsian Dances of *Prince Igor*, made familiar by the Ballets

Russes, all the repertoire was absolutely new to the Solís audience.

With the exception of a few works by Mikhail Glinka and Alexander Dargomizhsky, operatic tradition in Russia had begun in the same way as it had in western Europe and America, when the native culture was introduced to Italian opera. In fact, an Italian comedy was the first opera heard in Russia, in 1731. From Glinka's disciples—the outstanding group, The Five—and their use of historical and epic events, popular legends, and plots from prominent writers led by Pushkin, Tolstoy, and Gogol, emerged the Russian opera that captivated the West. It was these works that the Russian opera company presented at the Solís in spring 1929. The operas of Borodin, Musorgsky, and Rimsky-Korsakov were performed, as was one of Tchaikovsky's ballets.

With the large headline of "Magnificent Artistic Event" appearing on two consecutive

Fig. 46. In 1929, for the first time in Teatro Solís history, a season of Russian opera was given by the Compagnie Russe de l'Opéra Privée, from Paris, directed by soprano Maria Kusnezoff. *Snegurochka* was one of the five new operas presented. Biblioteca Nacional Collection, Montevideo.

days, this review of the Russian opera season's first performance appeared in *El Día*:

> Borodin's *Prince Igor* showed not only a well-organized opera company but also excellent singers, scenery, costumes, and orchestra. It was the perfect musical and visual setting to introduce the ethnic character of the Russian opera. *Prince Igor*, more than a lyric drama, uses tableaux to illustrate the historical epic on which *Prince Igor* is based. The score presents an opulent melodic richness in the vocal line, with the people as the real protagonists of the opera. . . . The singers were perfectly cast, but soprano Maria Kusnezoff stood out with her incomparable interpretation of Jaroslavna. With a plastic expression to her vocal line, she handled her voice masterfully, showing an extraordinary sweetness and, at the same time, pure and clear top notes of singular beauty.[1]

Rimsky-Korsakov's *Tsar Saltan*, the second production of the Russian company, was also greatly praised:

> Nicolai Evreinoff's exceptional direction and sets, with all the candor and ingenuity of old and primitive engravings, evoke the spectacular and fairy-tale characteristics of an ancient story. The combination of color and music so admirably displayed is a joy for the eyes in *Tsar Saltan*. . . . Among the interpreters, the two principal basses, Sdanovsky as the Tsar and Jukovich as Tailor excelled; however, tenor Piotrovsky did a funny, well-acted, well-sung characterization in his comic role as Prince Guidon.[2]

The very peak of the Russian season was reached with the performance of Musorgsky's *The Fair at Sorochintsï*. At any rate, it was this production that merited the best review:

Although unfinished by Musorgsky, *The Fair at Sorochintsï* must be considered "the masterpiece" of the Russian opera-buffa style. Composed by the greatest of all the Russian masters, this opera reveals extraordinary originality, singular power of expression and a sense of popular emotion. For us, Musorgsky is the highest and noblest embodiment of the Russian soul. The version we heard last evening was Cui's, one of the famous "Five." The opera has an unmatched display of popular flavor and freshness, and the choral parts, as with those of *Boris Godunov*, have a sense of grandiosity. In this case Musorgsky also achieved a special and rare combination of grandeur and fine humor.[3]

The last two premieres, *The Invisible City of Kitezh* and *Snegurochka*, both by Rimsky-Korsakov, were directed by Michel Benois and received enthusiastic reviews.

* * *

IN THE SOLÍS TRADITION of presenting the beginning of the opera season to coincide with the anniversary of the Solís' grand opening, in the middle of August, Bidú Sayão and Jan Kiepura, a young duo, made up of a petite, silver-toned soprano from Brazil and a strikingly handsome tenor from Poland, arrived to open the 1929 season. Sayão, who had debuted three years earlier in her native Rio de Janeiro as Rosina, sang the same role at Rome's Costanzi in 1926; from then on she toured all the principal opera houses of the world. Kiepura had become famous in the United States and Europe after his tremendous 1926 triumph at the Vienna Staatsoper as Cavaradossi. The tenor debuted at the Teatro Solís as the Duca di Mantova opposite Sayão's Gilda in a *Rigoletto* with baritone Apollo Granforte in the title role. According

to the memories of the professor Dr. Marcel Prawy, present director of education of the Vienna Staatsoper and then secretary to Kiepura, "[A]fter each performance in the State Opera in the '30s, [Jan Kiepura] used to jump on the roof of a taxicab and sing encores for his fans outside the stage door."[4] According to the following review, however, Uruguayan opera lovers were not so enthusiastic as the Viennese:

> Tenor Jan Kiepura comes to the Solís preceded by his Colón triumphs, where he was considered the season's revelation; no doubt he is a singer with a wonderful timbre voice, even if not so big, with easy enunciation and secure high notes, but he is still extremely young to sing the Duca di Mantova role in the way we remember the great singers doing. As proof that he did not impress last night's audience, Kiepura was not applauded enough to encore "La donna è mobile," a rare occurrence on our stage.[5]

The great success of the 1929 Italian season was a *Carmen* sung by Rosette Anday, a Hungarian mezzo-soprano now nearly forgotten. But on this occasion she was

> one of the best Carmens we have seen or heard on the Solís stage, with a very different point of view from Besanzoni's characterization. . . . Not too dramatic or excessively warm, not too elegant like many French Carmens we remember, Anday is an artist of exceptional quality, with a beautiful and well-colored voice employed to register all imaginable nuances of character. She was simultaneously graceful and vulgar, nervous and passionate, sweet and insinuating. With much Gypsy blood in her acting, her role grew dramatically in expression as the opera neared its end.[6]

* * *

WHEN THE OPERA SEASON ENDED Montevideo was visited by Ottorino Respighi and his wife, soprano Elsa Olivieri-Sangiacomo, who, in two interesting concerts, gave the first Uruguayan performances of works by the Italian composer. Then fifty years of age, Respighi had recently resigned from the directorship of Rome's Accademia di Santa Cecilia to devote himself to composition, conducting, and accompanying singers in his own works. Almost all of his well-known symphonic poems were premiered at this time, as Respighi and Olivieri-Sangiacomo toured Europe and America. The first Respighi concert at the Solís was all vocal music, performed by Olivieri-Sangiacomo and the composer. In the second concert, two days later, Respighi and Uruguayan Maestro Vicente Pablo shared the orchestral podium in a program of Respighi's symphonic works. At this concert Respighi was also the soloist in the Uruguayan premiere of his *Toccata* for piano and orchestra. Both concerts were highly regarded:

> Madame Olivieri-Respighi is a notable lieder interpreter who sings with a rare expressiveness and has an acute musical sense. She also puts a warm soprano voice at the service of music. A master in her field, Elsa Olivieri shows a strong musical personality. The Respighi compositions, almost all of them known, had a very good reception, in particular "Stornellatrice" and "La Najade."[7]

. . .

Tomorrow night's concert will have the characteristics of an apotheosis: a composer at the peak of a glorious career whom we will also celebrate as a pianist and a conductor. In rehearsal we appreciated the brilliant interpretation of his magnificent *Toccata* for piano and orchestra. Among the other pieces, *Il tramonto* with string accompaniment is an enjoyable composition in modern style and for us one of the most beautiful and inspired of Respighi's works. The end of the concert, with the cycle of *Antiche dance e aire per liuto*, [sic] closed one of the musical events of the season. We have indeed been fortunate to have the visit of such an important composer.[8]

In addition to the Respighi concerts, Solís audiences enjoyed a considerable number of high-quality recitals during both the 1929 and 1930 seasons. Among more than twenty well-known artists, a few must be cited for their particular qualities and for presenting their first performances before Solís audiences.

On June 13, 1929, Wanda Landowska's first Uruguayan recital became a national musical event. At the peak of an international career, the Polish keyboard artist was the leading musician dedicated not only to the revival of the extensive but unknown harpsichord repertoire but also to the pursuit of the development of a modern playing technique for the instrument. She offered four recitals, two in which she played both piano and harpsichord and two in collaboration with the Russian violinist Nathan Milstein, in the year of his American debut. Landowska's playing was utterly perfect, and these performances became a touchstone for repertoire and technique. Moreover, her dedication to music was accompanied by an authentic modesty.

This season also saw Milstein's second visit to the Teatro Solís. One reviewer wrote of a performance devoted to J. S. Bach and César Franck:

> Last evening we heard one of the best recitals of this season. . . . Nathan Milstein is a complete artist, with an exuberant technique and temperament, as well as a polished and steady artistry. He did not allow, at any time, his virtuosity to overshadow his maturity as

an interpreter, and he rejects the popular and empty acrobatics favored by other violinists.[9]

On December 6, 1987, at age eighty-three, Milstein was one of the five recipients of the tenth Kennedy Center Honors in celebration of excellence in the performing arts.

Brazilian pianist Guiomar Novaës was the next keyboard artist to appear at the Solís. A phenomenal prodigy, in 1909 Novaës won first place at the Paris Conservatory besting 389 other entrants before a jury made up of Debussy, Fauré, and Moritz Moszkowski. Nor did her ascent stop when she reached maturity as a performer. At the time of Novaës' 1930 Solís recitals she was thirty-four and had more than fifteen years' experience touring the leading halls of Europe and the Americas. Considered a great interpreter of Schumann and Chopin, she dedicated one of her Solís concerts to the music of the Polish composer.

Violin virtuoso Jacques Thibaud made history during the 1930 Montevideo concert season. The French violinist debuted at the Solís with a gala concert on May 5, giving a four-recital cycle with pianist Tasso Janopoulo. Thibaud was acclaimed for his exquisite purity of tone and for the perfection of his execution. (The time of his Solís appearances coincided with his widely publicized partnership with Alfred Cortot and Pablo Casals, although his Solís recitals were as soloist.)

Two famous string ensembles, the Guarnieri String Quartet and the Aguilar Brothers Lute Quartet, completed the chamber music recitals series offered at the Solís, with each ensemble giving several recitals. The Spanish lute quartet aroused unusual interest because Montevideo music lovers were seldom able to see and hear an ensemble of this nature. Among lute literature, the repertoire brought by the Aguilar brothers—Elisa, Ezequiel, Pepe, and Paco—ranged from ancient pieces

through modern works composed specifically for the lute, and was absolutely fascinating.

From among the Spanish dynasty of international guitarists—Miguel Llobet, Emilio Pujol, and Andrés Segovia—a young Regino Sáinz de la Maza next arrived to play at the Solís. Performer, composer, teacher, music critic in Madrid, and collaborator with Manuel de Falla, Sáinz de la Maza will be remembered as the artist who, in 1939, performed Joaquín Rodrigo's *Concierto de Aranjuez* for the first time. Indeed, the composer dedicated this popular guitar and orchestra concerto to Sáinz de la Maza.

The centennial of the introduction of Italian opera into Uruguay was 1930; it was also the centennial celebration of the Uruguayan constitution. Around the historical date of July 18, a series of gala performances was organized at the Teatro Solís. Six concerts were planned with the participation of local and international figures as soloists. The programs also included works by Uruguayan composers. In addition to Uruguayan baritone Víctor Damiani, "who interrupted one of his 'tournées' to sing in two of the concerts,"[10] the great public attraction of the July celebrations was Elisabeth Schumann. The German soprano, who at the request of Richard Strauss had joined Vienna's Staatsoper in 1919, was an international performer in both opera and lieder. Karl Alwin, her husband and a pianist and conductor at the Staatsoper, accompanied her on records and in concert. Alwin was also chosen to be the principal conductor at the Gala Symphonic Concerts for the centennial celebrations, concerts in which Schumann was the star: "The big attraction of the first two Gala concerts was Elisabeth Schumann. She is an exquisite singer. . . . with one of the purest voices we have heard."[11]

One year after the Russian opera season, Solís audiences welcomed other Russian visitors: an operetta company and Feodor

Fig. 47. Four famous recitalists that played at the Solís. *Upper Left*: Hungarian pianist Yolanda Merö in her first Solís presentation in August 15, 1919. *Upper Right*: French cellist and composer Gaspar Cassadó participated in an homage to France on July 14, 1920. *Lower Left*: Spanish guitarist Miguel Llobet gave a series of concerts in 1925. *Lower Right*: French violinist Ginette Neveu in her only Solís presentation, accompanied by her brother, pianist Jean Neveu, in August 1947. Author's collection.

Chaliapin. The company, which originated in Moscow's Theater Kamerny and was led by Alexandre Tairoff, showed a variety of theatrical art in seven performances. From an Oscar Wilde drama to two of Charles Lecocq's French operettas, as well as Russian popular and folkloric songs and dances, they displayed both the vivid color of their culture and a different way of interpreting the French works.

The legendary Chaliapin visited Montevideo only twice, and his visit in 1930 would be the last time he traveled to the Río de la Plata area. He covered an extraordinary and protean repertoire, from the deep dramatic depiction of Boris to the rascally sarcasm of Don Basilio, the genial madness of a French Don Quixote, and then reaching on to both Boito's and Gounod's Méphistophélès. All this catapulted him into the international arena and earned him one of the greatest places in opera history.

As a result of such genius, he became one of the best-paid singers and was very jealous of how his singing was compensated—so much so that when the Buenos Aires' Teatro Colón performances were broadcast abroad on radio, he did not allow his voice to be heard. Quite likely, no financial arrangement could be reached between His Master's Voice and the SODRE. Incredibly, whenever Chaliapin sang, the broadcast was interrupted and there was only silence. In some operas this meant long stretches of dead air, an unbearable torment for those opera-loving listeners at home. My family, in Montevideo, suffered this inconvenience many times.

The two Chaliapin performances in Montevideo were in 1930, one at the Teatro Urquiza, and one at the Teatro Solís. During the month of August he sang at the Urquiza with Lina Romelli, Carlo Galeffi, Tito Schipa, and Salvatore Baccaloni in Rossini's *Il barbiere di Siviglia* under Ferruccio Calusio. As always,

his Don Basilio was "the high point of the spectacle":

> The presence of the eminent Russian artist was the focus of the performance. Chaliapin acted the part of the old rascal with authentic art, innermost comprehension, and careful attention to detail. His concept of the role and his expression carry this opera into the realm of reality. Chaliapin sang the famous "La Calunnia" aria in a totally different way from the traditional interpretation we have always heard, departing from the abuse of fermatas, so misused by the best of singers. He used his voice to underline the text and even sometimes at "bocca chiusa" achieved a new and extraordinary effect.[12]

One month later Chaliapin's Solís recital, with a program made up of more than twenty songs, from Beethoven and Mozart to the Russian composers, was also enthusiastically received. He was accompanied by pianist Herman Kumok:

> Last night was an unforgettable evening at the Teatro Solís, where the packed house was present for Chaliapin's recital. Never before has such a singer been heard, and it may be many years until we can again see on Montevideo stages such a vocal phenomenon and exquisite artist as Chaliapin. . . . The chosen program demonstrated the thousands of things he is able to do with his voice in both style and intention. During his twenty or more songs, Chaliapin kept the Solís audience in suspense through his unmatched vocal prowess, far removed from the classical divo who seeks the audience's applause. His art, ranging from drama to comedy, has all the qualities and resources necessary to accomplish each style. For us the best—what a difficult choice!—were Glinka's "Midnight Review," Musorgsky's "Song of the Flea,"

Schumann's "The Two Grenadiers," and the incomparable Russian folk songs he added as encores.[13]

The recitals of foreign artists were complemented by presentations given by Uruguayan performers. In the 1930 Solís season the already internationally known Damiani was joined by such distinguished young singers as sopranos Alma Reyles, María Delia Corchs, Marina Rodríguez-Dutra; mezzo-soprano Lily Morton; and tenors Germán Denis and Augusto De Giuli. As the years passed, some of these became active in both opera and recitals and were also engaged for performances abroad.

* * *

SINCE 1890 LOCAL CHAMBER MUSIC and symphonic ensembles had been performing at the Solís, with a considerable increase since the beginning of World War I and lasting through the 1930s (with some activity continuing today). Two symphonic concerts conducted by Maestro Pablo were vital to the history of Uruguayan music. These were the two first concerts organized in 1931 by the Servicio Oficial de Difusión Radio Eléctrica (SODRE), an official institution created (by a national law in 1930) for the development, presentation, and broadcasting of music and other performing arts.

In 1931 the SODRE also bought the Teatro Urquiza building, known from that time on as the SODRE Auditorium. A broadcasting service—the Radio Oficial (CX6)—and a symphony orchestra were the two first SODRE annexations. A string quartet, opera and ballet companies, an opera and dance school, and a film institute were later added to the official institution. The Orquesta Sinfónica del SODRE (OSSODRE), formed by members of the Orquesta Nacional and other local symphonic groups, gave its inaugural concert under Maestro Pablo on June 20, 1931, with a program composed of J. S. Bach's Concerto in F for orchestra, Ferruccio Busoni's *Turandot* march, Eduardo Fabini's *La isla de los ceibos*, Liszt's *Les préludes*, and Beethoven's Third Symphony. For forty consecutive years the OSSODRE made its home in the building acquired in 1931.

This strong, new enterprise was able to engage the best vocal and instrumental artists. As a consequence, this theater (as had happened in 1905 with the opening of the Teatro Urquiza) became for a time a serious competitor to the Teatro Solís.

CHAPTER 25

1931–1955

Solís Versus SODRE: The Struggle for Survival—Lily Pons—The "Soler Miracle"—The Centro Cultural de Música—An Impressive *Porgy and Bess*

For more than half a century the Teatro Solís had eight to ten months per year of opera performances, concerts and recitals, and dramatic companies. Even the opening of other theaters, such as the Politeama, San Felipe, Cibils, and Stella d'Italia, could not outshine the prestige and the glory of the Solís as the leading opera house of the country. But as the years passed, several major changes occurred. The opening of the Teatro Urquiza in 1905 had been a turning point in the musical history of the Solís. With almost the same capacity as the Solís, the Urquiza, with its Art Nouveau decor and comfortable gallery seats was—since its glamorous opening with Sarah Bernhardt—the first serious competitor for the Teatro Solís as champion among Montevideo's theaters. After 1905, foreign opera companies began to perform in both houses. Evidently, the Solís was under a succession of weak managements, and the theater was not able to compete effectively with the wealthy and well-organized Urquiza.

The operatic life of the Solís was slowly fading out; more and more the house held long seasons of performances by dramatic companies interspersed by recitals, mostly by pianists. The best evidence of this shift in the Uruguayan operatic scene could be the 1932 SODRE opera season, which opened on August 20 with *Lucia di Lammermoor* under Maestro Ferruccio Calusio, with Montevideo's first presentation by Lily Pons.[1] Fresh from her Metropolitan Opera debut in January 3, 1931,[2] she conquered the audience immediately with her unique voice, charm, and beauty. In that performance she was accompanied by Antonio Carrión as Edgardo, Víctor Damiani as Lord Ashton, and Umberto de Lelio as Raimondo. Four days after she gave a lieder recital at the same stage. Two years afterward the SODRE 1934 operatic year was opened by Claudia Muzio as Violetta in Verdi's *La traviata*, with Hungarian tenor Koloman von Pataky as her Alfredo and Carlo Tagliabue as Signor Germont, all of them under the baton of Franco Paolantonio. The following evening Ettore Panizza conducted Lily Pons, Tito Schipa, Víctor Damiani, and Salvatore Baccaloni in Rossini's *Il barbiere di Siviglia*. And two days later Pons and Schipa were *Lucia di Lammermoor*'s unfortunate lovers. Since her appearance two years earlier, Lily Pons was the new glowing star adored by the Montevideo public. In another coup Ottorino Respighi conducted the first Uruguayan performance of his new opera, *La fiamma*, on July 17, 1934,[3] with Muzio as Silvana, six months after its world premiere at Rome's Teatro Reale. After its promising beginning as an operatic house, however, the SODRE evolved into more of a concert hall over the next decades.

*   *   *

THE NEXT CRITICAL STEP in Solís history, and perhaps one of the reasons for its demise as an opera house, began when on June 24, 1937, the Municipality of Montevideo bought the Teatro Solís building. Ten years later and after some major structural rebuilding (see chapter 3), on April 17, 1947, a municipal decree established the Comisión de Teatros Municipales, a board of directors in charge of administering and directing the Teatro Solís. One of the first resolutions of the board was the creation of the Comedia Nacional—a professional, municipal dramatic company— which gave its inaugural performance with Ernesto Herrera's *El león ciego*, on October 2, 1947. The Solís became the official home of the national theatrical company, and a new era in the old house had begun. From 1947 to 1949 the Teatro Solís seasons followed the same pattern: five or six months of daily performances of the Comedia Nacional, which alternated with several short periods of presentations by foreign dramatic companies. Today, more than fifty years later, the Comedia Nacional is still performing there.

From a musical point of view, after the end of World War II very few international ensembles and instrumentalists came to Montevideo. On the other hand, numerous Uruguayan musicians and singers, some of them with solid training, began to give recitals. On two occasions—1948 and 1951—Montevideo once again had the opportunity to enjoy very good opera seasons. In addition to Beniamino Gigli and Maria Caniglia, both in the sunset of their careers, there arrived such strong and beautiful voices as Rina Gigli, Fedora Barbieri, Damiani again, Tito Gobbi, Giulio Neri, and Nicola Rossi-Lemeni. But with the exception of the classical August gala performance at the Solís, this impressive cast appeared both seasons at the SODRE.

*   *   *

THE 1937 SOLÍS PERFORMANCES began with a two-month Italian operetta season, followed by a wide selection of concerts of distinguished singers and instrumentalists, such as Marian Anderson, Wilhelm Kempff, and Nathan Milstein, among others. The year ended with dramatic performances, vocal concerts, and dance recitals. After a period of such dignity and refinement, in the spring of 1937 the impresario Raoul Moretti presented a French operetta company headed by soprano Jacqueline Francell.

This lighthearted season ended with a "succès de scandale" on September 27 with the first Uruguayan presentation of Arthur Honegger's *Les aventures du roi Pausole*. How was it that a work written by the same composer of the oratorios, *Le roi David* and *Judith*, could so perturb Solís audiences? This lesser-known Honegger work is an erotic operetta with a libretto by Albert Willemetz and based on a novel by Pierre Louÿs. To avoid the possibility of a moral uproar, *Les aventures du roi Pausole* was performed under the "franja verde," a green stripe diagonally crossing the posters at the theater's entrance. (Such a mark is equivalent to an X-rating on a movie today.) In addition, newspaper announcements carried the warning that this presentation was "unsuitable for ladies and banned to minors." Of course, this was the best advertising the operetta could have to sell out the house.[4]

* * *

ON AUGUST 25, 1948, Solís opera lovers attended an exceptional *Il trovatore* conducted by Maestro Ettore Panizza. The same evening also saw the presentation of tenor José Soler, fresh from his La Scala debut, as Manrico. Born in Barcelona, Soler had come to Uruguay as a child and grew up in Montevideo; all his life he considered himself a Uruguayan. How an obscure switchboard operator at the SODRE and a member of the house choir came to sing at the Teatro alla Scala and to be cast as Maria Callas' and Renata Tebaldi's leading tenor can be called the "Soler miracle." Soler was forty when Maestro Lamberto Baldi, then music director and conductor of the SODRE symphony orchestra (OSSODRE), discovered him and invited him to sing in Verdi's *Requiem* on April 29, 1944. Two months later Fritz Busch, in Montevideo to conduct the OSSODRE, chose him to be the tenor soloist in Beethoven's Ninth Symphony.

José Soler made his operatic debut as Radamès in *Aida* on May 6, 1945, at the SODRE, with Pablo Komlos in the pit. Another Uruguayan singer, Jorge Algorta, who later became quite noted, was heard as the King in the same production. Months after his Uruguayan operatic debut, Soler appeared again as Radamès, but this time in the Brazilian city of Porto Alegre, the starting point of Soler's international career.

A letter from Maestro Baldi to Ettore Panizza, who was conducting opera at the Teatro Colón in Buenos Aires during the 1946 opera season, was the key to an audition. The Italian maestro, impressed by Soler's voice, hired him to sing Des Grieux at the Teatro Colón Gala

Performance of *Manon Lescaut*, on May 25, 1946. Argentinean soprano Delia Rigal and Uruguayan baritone Víctor Damiani partnered Soler in the Puccini opera, and the Buenos Aires press reacted positively: "Tenor José Soler, a novel artist, approached the role of Des Grieux with gallantry, and in spite of a certain nervousness at the beginning, performed . . . with a warm and generous voice that he handled effortlessly, plus a quite convincing stage composure, notwithstanding his lack of experience as an actor."[5]

As a result of Soler's success at this performance, Maestro Panizza advised him to go to Italy in search of wider operatic horizons. Soler's first Italian appearance was as *La traviata*'s Alfredo at San Remo's Teatro Municipale, where he stole the show. Panizza's advice turned out to be prophetic, and even Soler was surprised when in May 1947, only a few months later, he made his debut in Milan at the Teatro alla Scala singing the same role. The venerable Maestro Tullio Serafin conducted with a cast that included Margherita Carosio and Carlo Tagliabue as Violetta and Giorgio Germont, respectively.

Soler's voice had a profound impact on the Italian opera scene, and his mercurial climb to the stages of Europe's leading opera houses was astonishing. In a very short time he appeared not only in Italy, but in Germany, Portugal, Belgium, Switzerland, and Spain. In fact, when his native Barcelona held a Teatro Liceo Centennial Celebration, he portrayed Lord Richard Percy in a re-creation of the inaugural opera performance of Donizetti's *Anna Bolena* on April 17, 1847. Alfredo Romea, from Barcelona's *El Noticiero Universal*, wrote:

> Tenor José Soler did not disappoint our hopes for his singing. In fact, he surpassed our expectations in such a difficult role. The quality of his voice, especially in the brilliance of the high notes, fits perfectly the role

of Lord Percy, whose melodic line continually moves in this register. . . . A great ovation and many curtains calls acclaimed his performance after each act.[6]

A stellar cast was formed by soprano Sara Scuderi in the role of Anna Bolena, Cesare Siepi as Enrico VIII, Giulietta Simionato as Giovanna Seymour, and Manuel Ausensi as Lord Rochefort. All these, under the baton of Maestro Napoleone Annovazzi, accompanied Soler in this Barcelona production of *Anna Bolena.*

Because of his late start, Soler's career was relatively brief in comparison with that of most opera stars. However, his voice was good enough to sing opposite Maria Callas, Renata Tebaldi, and other leading divas of the late 1940s. Impressively, with Tebaldi and Ugo Savarese he recorded a complete *Andrea Chénier* by Umberto Giordano for Italian Cetra, as well as releases of a variety of operatic arias.

During his retirement years in Montevideo, Soler enjoyed the recognition of the people of his country, and was occasionally visited and interviewed by the press. Remembrances of past glories, colorful anecdotes of an itinerant life on the stage, and a bittersweet nostalgia appeared in his words. It is interesting to bring up some fragments of an interview he gave in his Montevideo home when, still very strong at seventy-seven, he talked animatedly with a reporter. When asked about Maria Callas, he answered:

I have the most beautiful memories about Maria because we met at the time we both were learning the ropes. Maria was very young when we sang *Turandot* in La Fenice. All the time we spent in Venice it was pouring and, you know, we were surrounded by water all around! So the only thing we could do between rehearsals was go to the movies. Even in her early twenties, she already had a powerful personal magnetism and was an

extraordinary woman. But what I appreciated overall was her friendliness on all occasions. Later on, everybody said that she changed and became a different person. Well, I met Maria several times when she was famous and in her prime, and with me she was still the young woman I enjoyed going to the movies with in Venice.

Talking about Maria and Renata [Tebaldi], both were very tall women! And you know, I am and I was very short! It became a real problem on the stage, so the directors found two solutions: first, when we were singing duets or love scenes I might be standing in a higher level or on a step on the scenery, and second, they made me use a pair of shoes five inches high!! Can you imagine me walking on those shoes?! Well, as a memento I brought them to Montevideo and they are still there, in the SODRE costume department.[7]

It is a charming look at a very special singer.

On the occasion of Soler's ninth decade, the press went again to his home to interview the famous tenor. On the actual date of his ninetieth birthday (February 22, 1994), there appeared an article with several photographs. Among the pictures of his many roles in European opera houses and a wealth of souvenirs from his singing glories, there is a picture of the 1956 Solís Centennial performance in which Soler sang Ernani with Argentinean soprano Sofía Bandín as Elvira (see chapter 26). The newspaper photographs of Soler taken in his ninetieth year are of an admirably strong man with a vivid face and piercing eyes. In one photo he stands before a photograph of himself taken as a young and handsome Manrico in Verdi's *Il trovatore*: replicating the same stance and with great pride, Soler holds the embellished sword that he had used more than forty years before in *Aida*'s Radamès (fig. 48). The article relates that while Soler retired at age sixty-five, he returned to the stage at seventy to sing *Pagliacci*'s Canio in a very special and moving farewell performance in his honor and in the company of the best Uruguayan singers of the time.[8] He died on September 1, 1999, at ninety-five.

Soler was one of four memorable Uruguayan voices of this time, along with tenor José Oxilia, who was praised by Verdi for his legendary performance in *Otello*; bass Jorge Algorta, who not only sang in Europe but conquered Buenos Aires' Teatro Colón audiences and became a regular there; and baritone Víctor Damiani, the most famous of them all, who had the longest and most successful career at the Colón and in all the leading European opera houses.

*   *   *

IN 1949 THE CENTRO CULTURAL de música—a private, nonprofit institution founded in 1942 to offer performances by Uruguayan artists—began to present regular concerts on the Solís stage. Its initial reduced budget was improved by productive membership campaigning, which later made it possible to engage international musicians in addition to well-known Uruguayan artists. Pianists Wilhelm Kempff, Rudolf Firkusny, Walter Gieseking, Eliane Richepin, Antonio de Raco, Guillermo Cases, Wilhelm Backhaus, Jorg Demus, Artur Rubinstein, Karl Ulrich Schnabel, Sigi Weissenberg, Alfred Cortot, Maria Tipo, Witold Malcuzinski, Pierre Sancan, Eugene Istomin, Jean Casadesus; string instrumentalists Ginette Neveu, Henryk Szeryng, Enrique Iniesta, Bernard Michelin, Eva Heinitz; guitarist Andrés Segovia; singers Gérard Souzay, Victoria de los Angeles, Erna Berger, Ferruccio Tagliavini; the Végh String Quartet, the Loewenguth String Quartet, the Chorus of the Don Cossacks, the Coral de Pamplona, the Orchestra of Stuttgart under Karl Munchinger, the Ancient Instruments Ensemble of Adolfo Morpurgo—all came to the Solís stage between 1949 and 1955, some of them for several

Fig. 48. *Upper*: Tenor José Soler in his prime when he partnered Maria Callas and Renata Tebaldi. *Lower*: In an interview in occasion of Soler's ninetieth birthday in 1994, the tenor is pictured with his Radamès' sword in hand in front of his portrait depicting himself as a young and handsome Manrico in *Il trovatore*. *El País*, February 22, 1994. Author's collection.

seasons. But even such an effort as done by the Centro Cultural de Música was not enough to match the quantity of musical events of the past. In a chart published at the end of the 1950 Teatro Solís season, the figures speak for themselves.

TOTAL PERFORMANCES DURING 1950
SOLIS SEASON

Comedia Nacional	301
Orchestras and soloists	43
Recitals	14
Pilar López Spanish Ballet	27
French Drama Renaud-Barrault	8
Banda Municipal Concerts	24

The Centro Cultural de Música was never able to support an opera season: top-notch singers came at a cost at least one hundred times that which usually paid for a single instrumentalist. However, the Centro Cultural de Música still managed to offer several operas with excellent national singers, some of them in their first Uruguayan performance. Solís opera lovers heard Domenico Cimarosa's *Il matrimonio segreto* in 1952, Mozart's *Così fan tutte* one year later, and Bedřich Smetana's *The Bartered Bride* (in a Spanish translation, *La novia vendida*) in 1954. Celia Golino, Raquel Satre, Carlota Bernhardt, Lorenzo Rosito, and Eduardo García de Zúñiga, with Juan Protasi in the pit, conducted an excellent *Il matrimonio*. A delightful *Così fan tutte* was given by Raquel Satre as Fiordiligi, Olga Linne as Dorabella, Celia Golino as Despina, de Zúñiga as Guglielmo, Adhemar Otonello as Fernando, and Lorenzo Rosito as Don Alfonso, again conducted by Protasi, as he had at the first Uruguayan Smetana performance. *The Bartered Bride* was sung by Virginia Castro, Carlota Bernhardt, Noemí Gil-Janeiro, Luis Giammarchi, Panchito Pons, Juan Vernazza, and Jorge Botto. Raquel Adonaylo, Socorrito Villegas, Sarah Iglesias, Ercilia Quiroga, and

Walter Mendeguía can complete the list of Uruguayan vocalists who appeared at the Solís stage during the same period.

In addition to these singers, the following instrumentalists performed at the Teatro Solís between 1949 and 1955: pianists Ema Ayala-Vidal, Hugo Balzo, Luis Batlle, Sarah Bourdillon, Norma Giacosa, Lyda Indart, Fanny Ingold, Nibya Mariño, Mercedes Olivera, Nahyr Pantano de Giucci, Mirtha Pérez-Barranguet, Erna Quincke, Paloma de los Reyes, María Luisa Santamarina, Victoria Schenini, Adhemar Schenone, Héctor Tosar, Dinorah Varsi; violinist María Vischnia; cellist Oscar Nicastro; guitarists Oscar Cáceres, Abel Carlevaro, and Olga Pierri. Some of these performers are currently active and have international careers.

In 1950 Solís audiences were amazed when they saw and heard the young Pierino Gamba conducting a symphonic orchestra. The twelve-year-old Italian prodigy, on his second South American tour, led four concerts during this Solís season. He interpreted works by Beethoven, Mozart, Wagner, and Dvořák, as well as Italian operatic overtures. Each performance provoked a thunderous standing ovation.

Although newer than the Teatro Solís by fifty years, the SODRE Auditorium was compelled to close at the end of 1951 and cancel all performances due to serious structural damage in the building. As a result, the 1952 SODRE six-month symphonic series was held at the Solís, with French conductor Paul Paray as music director of the OSSODRE. Carlos Estrada and Nino Stinco alternated as guest conductors with Paray. On October 25, in the closing concert of the season, the OSSODRE was under the baton of Héctor Tosar, who ended the evening program with the world premiere of his *Oda a Artigas*, a work for speaker and orchestra and first-prize winner of the 1952 SODRE Composition Competi-

Fig. 49. The Uruguayan premiere, on July 1955, of Gershwin's *Porgy and Bess*, brought to the Solís a reminiscence of the grandeur of the past opera seasons. Cover and interior page with the cast photographs. Author's collection.

tion. A pupil of Arthur Honegger and Darius Milhaud, as well as Aaron Copland and Serge Koussevitzky at Tanglewood, at age thirty-one Tosar had already a high reputation as the best young Uruguayan composer. Today, Tosar is without doubt remembered as one the leading composers of his country, with many international premieres and awards to his credit. He died on January 17, 2002.

In addition to the OSSODRE cycle, another orchestra, the AUDEM (Asociación Uruguaya de Música) Symphony, also gave several concerts in 1952 at the Solís, most of them under the baton of Maestro Guido Santórsola, a fine composer and violist. One program in this series was sponsored by the Italian Cultural Institute of Montevideo and conducted by the Countess Carmen De Campori, who thus became the first woman to conduct a symphonic concert on the Solís stage.

*   *   *

IN A FLASHBACK OF FADED GLORY, the Teatro Solís presented daily performances of an international opera company when (like the golden times fifty years earlier with Arturo Toscanini and Enrico Caruso) an entire American company with conductor, director, singers, costumes, scenery, machinery, and stagehands arrived at the Solís. An impressive production of George Gershwin's *Porgy and Bess* (fig. 49) was unveiled on July 26, 1955. The Everyman Opera Company came under

the patronage of the American National Theater and Academy (ANTA) in a Robert Breen
production; Breen also directed the opera.
With lavish scenery by Wolfgang Roth, the
principal female roles were sung by Martha
Flowers, Ethel Ayler, Gloria Davy, and Helen
Colbert, while Leslie Scott, Irving Barnes,
John McCurry, Jerry Laws, and Joseph Attler
appeared in the male roles. Montevideo was
fortunate to have Alexander Smallens, the
conductor who had given *Porgy and Bess*' New
York premiere at the Alvin Theatre on October 10, 1935, leading the Solís performances.

Expectation and curiosity were equally
present at the prospect of seeing the Gershwin
opera for the first time. Despite winter wind
and bitter cold, long lines began to form at
the box office very early on the morning that
tickets went on sale. The production was expensive, and prices had been set accordingly,
so the demand for the cheapest tickets and
standing room was high. By noon the house
was nearly sold out for all performances.

But for those of us who were then students
of musicology in the School of Humanities at
the University of Uruguay in Montevideo, the
real saga had just begun. After three hours of
standing in the cold and successfully obtain-
ing tickets, we went to eat a light lunch and
drink something warm, returning immediately to the Solís. This time we waited at the
side entrance of the peanut gallery, hoping to
get the first place in line and then waiting until the doors opened at five o'clock. By now
the sun had gone down and the weather had
turned bitterly cold. As we shivered and
stamped our feet, trying to warm ourselves by
imagining the inside of the theater and the
magic awaiting us, the doors opened suddenly. As though unleashed by a war cry,
more than two hundred people charged up
five flights of wooden steps. In comparison
the "Ride of the Valkyries" was low-key.

I was with a group of friends, and the eight
of us managed to get wonderful locations, in
the middle of the gallery, behind the third row
of seats. By this time we had already been on
our feet a total of six hours, and still needed
to wait another hour and a half until curtain
time. Finally, Maestro Smallens stepped on to
the podium, and the glory of the music and
splendid stage sets made us forget all the cold,
the fatigue, and the wait. We even forgot how
much our feet hurt! The gallery was so
crowded that it was impossible to take off our
coats, woolen scarves, and hats because we
did not have even enough space to move our
arms. There was practically no breathing
space. With the excitement of the opera, no
one cared, but at some point of the performance, I whispered to a friend: "Oh! How
marvelous. It's a revolving stage! It's moving
around!" And as soon as I said these words,
I fainted. In fact, nothing had been moving,
only my head was spinning. But I did not fall
down—there was no room on the floor. After
a few minutes and some air provided by people fanning programs at me, I revived and
stood to see the remainder of the performance. When the curtain fell we gave conductor, directors, and singers a *true* standing
ovation. Keeping in mind that our international operatic knowledge at that time was
based on the few operas we occasionally enjoyed at the Teatro Colón in Buenos Aires, for
all of us that performance was the best of our
lives. After more than thirty-five years and
seeing other productions of *Porgy and Bess*
comfortably seated, that first one—even with
the cold and the sweating, the suffocating
atmosphere, the sore and swollen feet, and
eleven hours' standing—still has for me the
mystery, the excitement, and the impact produced by the first encounter with a masterpiece.

CHAPTER 26

1956–1984

The Teatro Solís Centennial—Political Turmoil and the Fall
of the Cultural Life—The Burning of the SODRE—
From a Military Dictatorship to Democracy

By a happy coincidence, 1956 was both the centennial year of the Teatro Solís and the bicentennial celebration of Mozart's birth. Consequently, the Solís season opened in the early fall with a performance of *Die Zauberflöte*, followed the next day with *Don Giovanni* by the Salzburg Marionetten, under the sponsorship of the Centro Cultural de Música. This outstanding puppet company also performed Mozart's *Bastien und Bastienne*, small works based on other Mozart music, and Johann Strauss' *Die Fledermaus*, with a synchronization and musical quality worthy of the best Viennese opera house. Coincidentally, it was also the centennial of Robert Schumann's death, and several concerts were performed in his memory.

As a musical interlude between this opening and the beginning of the centennial celebrations, the Centro Cultural de Música brought to the Solís stage a considerable number of excellent, internationally known musicians, such as pianists Friedrich Gulda,

Jean Casadesus, Detlef Kraus, Gary Graffman, and Lilian Steuber; violinists Jan Tomasow and Alexander Scholz; the Janacek String Quartet; the Budapest String Quartet; the Berlin Chamber Orchestra under Hans von Benda; the Czech Folkloric Ballet Ludnica; Renate Schottelius and her Contemporary Dance Ensemble; and ballet dancers Tamara Toumanova and Wladimir Oukhtomsky. Of course, the best Uruguayan performers also appeared at the Solís, among them pianists Hugo Balzo, Luis Batlle, Fanny Ingold, Nibya Mariño, Mercedes Olivera, Erna Quincke, Victoria Schenini, and Adhemar Schenone; violinists Mario Bresciani, Juan Fabbri, and Fanny Schwatz; violist Francisco Heltai; flutist Germán Cuevas; trumpeter Walter Pinto; and guitarist Oscar Cáceres. The new Anfión Chamber Orchestra also performed at the Solís, conducted by a woman, the violinist Beatriz Tuset.

After one month of daily performances with the renowned María Guerrero–Pepe Romeu Spanish Company, three other dramatic companies (two from Spain and one from Germany) alternated their performances in the four-month season of the Comedia Nacional, which was celebrating its tenth year.

* * *

THE FIRST EVENT of the Teatro Solís Centennial Celebration was the opening, on August 21, of a theatrical exhibition in the magnificent gold-and-cream grand foyer. There were a variety of documents and memorabilia on display, including the first page of the *bordereau* belonging to the inaugural-night performance on August 25, 1856; a large collection of old sepia pictures of singers, dramatic artists, directors, dancers, conductors, playwrights, lecturers, and impresarios; letters and artists' contracts; orchestral scores and parts; manuscripts; programs; and recent costumes. There were photographs of Enrico Caruso, Vaslav Nijinsky, Artur Rubinstein, María Guerrero, Jacinto Benavente, Louis Jouvet, José Oxilia, Ermete Zacconi, Amelita Galli-Curci, Giuseppe de Luca, María Barrientos, Arturo Toscanini, Adelina Patti, Feodor Chaliapin, Giovanni Martinelli, Anna Pavlova— and hundreds more, most of them with signatures and dedications.

A truly valuable museum item was the program of a benefit held on behalf of the Anglo-French Red Cross at the Teatro Solís on October 26, 1917. It was the event that marked Nijinsky's last performance in a theater in front of an audience and the tragic end of his legendary dancing career (see chapter 21). Another rare piece was a set of soloist and chorus vocal parts from Rossini's *L'inganno felice*, the first complete opera performed in Uruguay, at the Casa de Comedias, on May 14, 1830. The yellowed, handwritten, horizontal parchment pages have the seal of Angelita Tanni; it was the Tanni Brothers Company that performed at the Casa de Comedias between 1829 and 1831, with Angelita, Marcelo, and Pasqual

Tanni all singing in this early Rossini opera. Also of interest, if not of such valuable vintage, were several color posters giving notice of the Solís Carnival Masked Balls, richly designed in the style of Art Nouveau and dated from the 1920s and 1930s.

As opening ceremony for both the Centennial Celebration and the exhibition, Professor Juan Carlos Sabat-Pebet, a scholar of theatrical history, gave a lecture entitled "The Artistic Development of the Teatro Solís." In a lecture series five more lectures were given each day by scholars in their fields; held in the grand foyer, each lecture was designed to show a different aspect of the Solís during its first century. Professor Lauro Ayestarán, the internationally known musicologist, delivered the lecture "The Musical History of the Teatro Solís." Architect and professor Carlos Pérez-Montero chose the topic "The Architectural History of the Teatro Solís," while on the following day Angel Irisarri gave a lecture entitled "The Development of the Comedia Nacional." On August 31, Professor Juan Pivel-Devoto, director of the National Museum of History of Uruguay, gave the talk "Portrayal of an Epoch: Uruguay at the Middle of the XIX Century." And finally, Professor Sabat-Pebet closed the series with "The History of the Teatro Solís," this time speaking from the stage to an audience consisting of a full house of almost two thousand high-school students (fig. 50). Concurrent to all these events were open houses and organized noontime guided tours to visit the backstage area, dressing rooms, scenery shop, costume department, and all those places usually closed to the public.

On August 25, 1956, all that took place at the Teatro Solís replicated exactly the theater's opening day of August 25, 1856. Early in the morning the house was both a human beehive and a madhouse. On stage, while stagehands hammered on the last props, conductor, director, orchestra, and singers pretended to

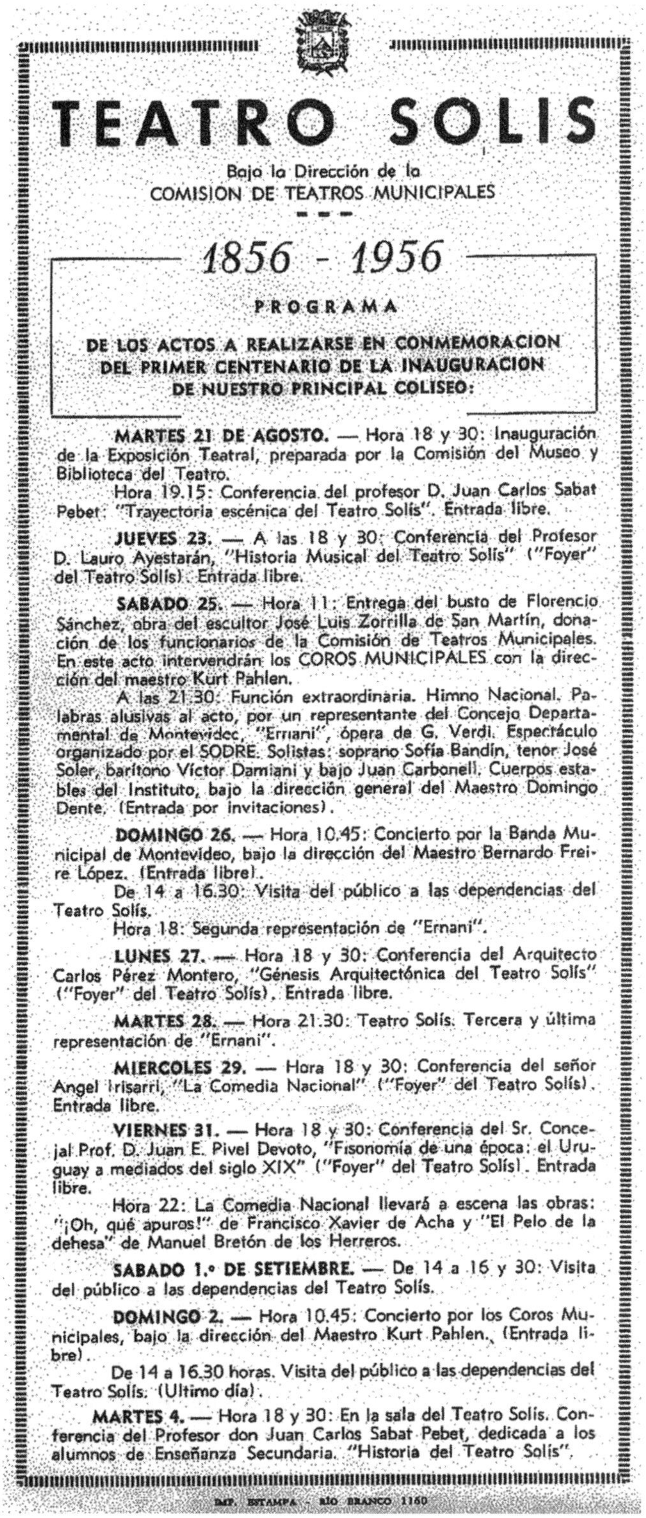

TEATRO SOLIS

Bajo la Dirección de la
COMISION DE TEATROS MUNICIPALES

— — —

1856 - 1956

PROGRAMA

DE LOS ACTOS A REALIZARSE EN CONMEMORACION
DEL PRIMER CENTENARIO DE LA INAUGURACION
DE NUESTRO PRINCIPAL COLISEO:

MARTES 21 DE AGOSTO. — Hora 18 y 30: Inauguración de la Exposición Teatral, preparada por la Comisión del Museo y Biblioteca del Teatro.
Hora 19.15: Conferencia del profesor D. Juan Carlos Sabat Pebet: "Trayectoria escénica del Teatro Solís". Entrada libre.

JUEVES 23. — A las 18 y 30: Conferencia del Profesor D. Lauro Ayestarán, "Historia Musical del Teatro Solís" ("Foyer" del Teatro Solís). Entrada libre.

SABADO 25. — Hora 11: Entrega del busto de Florencio Sánchez, obra del escultor José Luis Zorrilla de San Martín, donación de los funcionarios de la Comisión de Teatros Municipales. En este acto intervendrán los COROS MUNICIPALES con la dirección del maestro Kurt Pahlen.
A las 21.30: Función extraordinaria. Himno Nacional. Palabras alusivas al acto, por un representante del Concejo Departamental de Montevideo, "Ernani", ópera de G. Verdi. Espectáculo organizado por el SODRE. Solistas: soprano Sofía Bandín, tenor José Soler, barítono Víctor Damiani y bajo Juan Carbonell. Cuerpos estables del Instituto, bajo la dirección general del Maestro Domingo Dente. (Entrada por invitaciones).

DOMINGO 26. — Hora 10.45: Concierto por la Banda Municipal de Montevideo, bajo la dirección del Maestro Bernardo Freire López. (Entrada libre).
De 14 a 16.30: Visita del público a las dependencias del Teatro Solís.
Hora 18: Segunda representación de "Ernani".

LUNES 27. — Hora 18 y 30: Conferencia del Arquitecto Carlos Pérez Montero, "Génesis Arquitectónica del Teatro Solís" ("Foyer" del Teatro Solís). Entrada libre.

MARTES 28. — Hora 21.30: Teatro Solís. Tercera y última representación de "Ernani".

MIERCOLES 29. — Hora 18 y 30: Conferencia del señor Angel Irisarri, "La Comedia Nacional" ("Foyer" del Teatro Solís). Entrada libre.

VIERNES 31. — Hora 18 y 30: Conferencia del Sr. Concejal Prof. D. Juan E. Pivel Devoto, "Fisonomía de una época: el Uruguay a mediados del siglo XIX" ("Foyer" del Teatro Solís). Entrada libre.
Hora 22: La Comedia Nacional llevará a escena las obras: "¡Oh, qué apuros!" de Francisco Xavier de Acha y "El Pelo de la dehesa" de Manuel Bretón de los Herreros.

SABADO 1.º DE SETIEMBRE. — De 14 a 16 y 30: Visita del público a las dependencias del Teatro Solís.

DOMINGO 2. — Hora 10.45: Concierto por los Coros Municipales, bajo la dirección del Maestro Kurt Pahlen. (Entrada libre).
De 14 a 16.30 horas. Visita del público a las dependencias del Teatro Solís. (Ultimo día).

MARTES 4. — Hora 18 y 30: En la sala del Teatro Solís. Conferencia del Profesor don Juan Carlos Sabat Pebet, dedicada a los alumnos de Enseñanza Secundaria. "Historia del Teatro Solís".

IMP. ESTAMPA. RIO BRANCO 1160

Fig. 50. Centennial Teatro Solís Celebration, in August and September 1956. Program of events with opera and drama performances, exhibitions, lectures, backstage tours, and choral concerts. Author's collection.

have a dress rehearsal. At the same time, and only yards away, in the entrance foyer house personnel feverishly prepared for the 11:00 A.M. inauguration of a marble bust of dramaturge Florencio Sánchez and for the municipal authorities who were to preside over the first ceremony of the day. In a corner of the same foyer the Municipal Choir tried to get organized and ready to sing the Uruguayan national anthem. Modern technology and one century of experience do very little when openings and celebrations are in the hands of too many special committees.

The evening of August 25, 1956, found the Teatro Solís full of splendor. Hundreds of spots and extra lights were placed behind the colonnade decorated with flags. The wide esplanade in front of the house was transformed into a garden, while a red carpet ran from the street and across the plaza to the principal entrance in honor of the national authorities, diplomatic corps, and special guests who would arrive for the gala. At about nine o'clock Dr. Alberto F. Zubiría, chairman of the Executive National Council, and his wife made their entrance. A few moments later they reached the Presidential Box and were welcomed by the applause of the full house.[1] As in the old days the Solís sparkled: women glittering in gorgeous gowns and men in white tie and tails evoked the golden opera seasons of the Solís at its best.

As expected, Verdi's *Ernani* was the opera chosen in a revival of the opening performance of 1856. The best Uruguayan male voices of that time were cast in the two principal roles: tenor José Soler in the title role and baritone Víctor Damiani as Don Carlo. Argentinean soprano Sofía Bandín, from the Teatro Colón, was invited to sing Elvira. Soprano Marita Perdomo, tenor Jorge Paolillo, basses Juan Carbonell and Miguel Terrasa— all Uruguayan singers—completed *Ernani*'s cast. The baton was given to another national conductor, Maestro Domingo Dente. The

chorus, corps de ballet and orchestra, costume design, and staging were from SODRE. At the end of the performance, artists and special guests were invited to a dinner party in the grand foyer.

Unlike the endless oratory of 1856, this celebration had only one short speech after the Uruguayan national anthem and before the performance, with a member of Montevideo's municipality saying just a few words to underline the cultural importance of the event. If we remember the exhilaration of the opening festivities of 1856, with fights in front of the box office, a band in the plaza, fanfares, and a 2:00 A.M. fireworks display after the performance, we can rate the centennial day as a very low-key event. *Ernani* was repeated twice, on August 26 and 27, and it was, unfortunately, the only opera performances the Teatro Solís held during its centennial year.

During the remainder of the 1956 season, the Municipal Symphony Orchestra and the Banda Municipal gave weekly concerts. Maestro Carlos Estrada, music director and conductor of the orchestra, led several Mozart works, most of them with Uruguayan soloists. Continuing the homage they had started at the beginning of the year, the Centro Cultural de Música also organized a Mozart Festival that included the *Coronation Mass*.

* * *

STARTING IN THE 1940S, and for approximately twenty years, cultural and musical events in Uruguay slowly waned: so slowly that no one then realized it. As Teatro Solís performances deteriorated in quality and quantity, the newly created SODRE expanded, bringing in outstanding conductors for the OSSODRE concerts and excellent international rosters for its first opera seasons.

From at least the 1930s, the insensitivity of official bureaucracy retarded the development of Uruguayan culture. Nevertheless, when the Teatro Urquiza (renamed the SODRE Auditorium) was acquired by the government, it became the new toy of the Department of Culture. After all, the first SODRE winter opera season, opening on August 20, 1932, had featured Lily Pons in her Montevideo debut, singing Donizetti's *Lucia di Lammermoor* (see chapter 25).

After so promising a beginning, it was announced that the next year at the SODRE would bring an outstanding opera cycle under the general direction of conductor Gino Marinuzzi, with such great names as Gilda Dalla Rizza, Claudia Muzio, Beniamino Gigli, and Carlo Galeffi. But it was canceled because not even one-third of the SODRE seats were sold in advance. What was the cause? On March 31, 1933, the president of Uruguay, Dr. Gabriel Terra, staged a coup d'état with the dissolution of the parliament followed by the banishment, arrest, and persecution of several politicians, as well as the temporary censorship of the press. From March 1933 to February 1934, when the president called an election, there was almost a complete year of political turmoil, with all musical and other cultural events numbering among the casualties.

With the absence of international opera companies during World War II, the SODRE, even with continuous setbacks, was able to engage top-flight conductors for its symphony concerts. The opera season, by contrast, reflected the period's absence of first-quality opera singers. The Solís maintained a consistency in its musical programs during this time (see chapter 25) thanks to the efforts of the Centro Cultural de Música; also it periodically featured internationally known Uruguayan singers, such as Soler, Damiani, and Jorge Algorta, then performing at the Teatro Colón in Buenos Aires and in Europe.

A turning point in the musical life in Uruguay came in 1956, which marked not only the centennial of the Solís, but the silver anniversary of the SODRE Symphony Orchestra (OS-

SODRE). Set against these highlights however, would be more than twenty-five years of turmoil as Uruguay passed through one of the worst periods of its history.

*   *   *

URUGUAY WAS ONCE KNOWN as the paradise of democracy, an island of peace in the middle of Latin America. Political stability, with the maintenance of a constitutional tradition, a strong currency, and a high level of education and culture, all contributed to its strength. But two opposed political tendencies, first of the extreme left and afterward of the extreme right, destroyed the social fabric, the economy, and, as a logical consequence, the culture. Almost thirteen years of urban guerrilla infiltration were followed by eleven of military dictatorship, from 1973 to 1984.

Beginning subtly in the late 1950s, a Marxist-Leninist movement supported by Cuba promoted a series of strikes. When the government had evidence that the Cuban embassy was instigating these strikes, Cuban ambassador Mario García-Incháustegui was expelled from the country on January 12, 1961. For a period of about two years (in the early 1960s) the still-unnamed subversive movement slowly infiltrated Uruguayan education, its primary concern being the indoctrination of high-school teachers. The guerrilla force was recruited from high-school and college students belonging to Montevideo's upper-middle-class families, and its leaders were engineers, professors, doctors, architects, and other professionals. Because factories and large corporations were the principal target for destruction, workers and employees were the major enemies, and victims, of the subversion.

By the early 1960s, this group (now known as the Tupamaros and transformed openly into an urban guerrilla movement) began to set incendiary and explosive devices in corporate buildings; they also burned the

cars of two United States diplomats. It was the starting point of a fully developed war of terror.

A massive wave of bank robberies, with death and injuries on both sides, began in 1963–64 and continued for eight years. In 1965 a series of general strikes (sometimes lasting forty-eight hours) interrupted all public utility services, including transportation. For the first time the government enacted emergency security measures (Medidas prontas de seguridad) to protect national security and the rule of law.

Assassinations, the burning of buses and cars, and bombings in factories, clubs, and other public places spread the terror. Hundreds of innocent people were killed or injured as a consequence of that war without truce. Many school laboratories and classrooms were transformed into bomb factories and storage places for ammunition, machine guns, and all type of explosives; more than once an error triggered explosions and fires that killed many students, who became victims of their own thirst for violence. To make things worse, in 1970 there began a series of kidnappings of diplomats and public figures, including the United Kingdom ambassador Sir Geoffrey Jackson; the Brazilian consul, Aloysio Dias-Gomide; the American agricultural expert, Dr. Claude Fry; the ex–secretary of agriculture of Uruguay, Carlos Frick-Davies, and six or seven CEO's of important Uruguayan corporations. After many months of being underground in the so-called People's Jail all were released except the American AID (Agency for International Development) adviser to Uruguay, Dan Anthony Mitrione, who, after being kidnapped, was killed on August 10, 1970.

*　*　*

FOR URUGUAYAN CULTURAL LIFE, one of the most devastating events of this period was the destruction of the SODRE Auditorium: the entire house and stage area were burned on the afternoon of September 18, 1971. A few minutes after 5:00 P.M., the house security discovered a fire in one of the electrical panels; even before there was time to use the extinguishers, huge columns of fire caught one of the side curtains of the stage, reaching the ceiling in seconds. The sound of the crackling of the flames grew louder and louder until a terrible and thundering noise, "like a gigantic stampede" (as described by the people who were there) signaled the collapse of the roof. Columns of flame and smoke from inside the structure reached the sky in a Dantesque and terrifying vision. Firemen worked for more than seven hours before the fire was extinguished, but the destruction was total. With damage estimated in the millions, everything related to the house—scenery, costumes, and all heavy instruments, such as pianos and the timpani—were either trapped and smashed under the ceiling or destroyed by the fire and the water. (Fortunately, firemen and the SODRE Orchestra musicians managed to save the string instruments and small woodwinds.) Hundreds of people outside in the street were speechless or in tears, remembering their own moments in the history of the house that had opened as the Teatro Urquiza on September 5, 1905, sixty-six years and thirteen days before; the younger spectators knew the building only after its 1930 conversion to being the SODRE Auditorium, but their grief ran just as deep.

For all of us at the SODRE site, rumors flew that the fire was the consequence of sabotage by the Tupamaros. All the SODRE telephone lines were dead when security staff tried to call the fire department, forcing them to leave the building and walk half a block, thus losing valuable time. Because of the total destruction, it was impossible to verify those rumors. And if the SODRE burning was an example of the Tupamaros' destruction, the military that succeeded them in February 1973 made no effort to rebuild the house. However, a few years ago and after the enactment of democracy, the construction of a modern performing-arts complex on the same site began. It will house a new auditorium, smaller halls for chamber music, experimental drama, art movies, rehearsal studios, costume and set storage, offices, cafeteria, and other facilities, with state-of-the-art lighting and machinery systems. The building is still under construction.

* * *

BY THE END OF 1972 the political and economic situation of Uruguay was absolutely unbearable, with all education centers in the Tupamaros' hands. President Juan María Bordaberry (elected November 1971 and inaugurated March 1, 1972) and the executive and legislative branches were unable to take drastic steps. The armed forces watched events closely, waiting for the best opportunity to intervene, until Brigadier José Pérez-Caldas and General Hugo Chiappe-Posse turned insubordinate and confronted the president. To avoid bloodshed, Bordaberry yielded his power to the armed forces on February 9, 1973. It was the first military coup in twentieth-century Uruguay.

The first concern of the military was domination of the urban guerrillas, and after some deceptively peaceful days, on June 27 the armed forces forced the president to dissolve the parliament, thus shattering the strongly established Uruguayan tradition of democracy. The military increased in power, becoming a bloody dictatorship that violated all civil and human rights. The use of torture became routine, and Uruguay maintained the highest percentage of political prisoners in the world.

Academic programs of the cultural institutions, from elementary schools to the uni-

versities, were severely trimmed. Philosophy, history, literature, and music were the most damaged. The history of the French Revolution; most of the philosophers; writers and poets such as Fyodor Dostoyevsky, Leo Tolstoy, Jean-Jacques Rousseau, Montesquieu, and Pablo Neruda; Beethoven, Chopin, and Prokofiev (among others); all the musical works and books related to struggle or revolution, including the American wars for independence—all were banned, much to the astonishment of the students who were puzzled at a history with big gaps where apparently "nothing" had happened. Teachers and pupils were equally punished if they did not obey these new programs and regulations. All the performing arts, cultural events, press and publications, television and radio programs were censored, and hundreds of books banned. Half a million people—16 percent of the total population of Uruguay—left the country in thirty years, and with a battered economy the culture was practically decimated. The loss of 75 percent of teachers and professors produced a generation whose education was very poor and incomplete. Youth lost both a sense of responsibility and a methodology of study, with a resulting passivity and laziness. The high level of education and culture of Uruguay, once the pride of Latin America from the beginning of the century until the late 1950s, was gone.

The consequences of this military dictatorship were devastating for the cultural life of the country, particularly for Montevideo. Musical life shrank considerably: all composers, musicians, and singers who opposed the military regime were either banned from performance or fled the country. Foreign performers were too frightened to appear in a country ruled by terror. The former audience for opera, concerts, and ballet lived in fear, concerned with the daily problems of an unstable and dangerous political situation, with neither money to spend nor the mood to enjoy any type of performance.

Finally, pressure from an outside world enraged by human-rights violations, the enormous power struggle, and a terrible economy wore out the military dictatorship. Unfit for leadership, with an unknown and dark future, the military gave way to the existence of political parties as a preparation for a return to democracy. On November 25, 1984, after thirteen years without democracy, the first elections since 1971 were held, and Doctor Julio María Sanguinetti was chosen by the people to be president of Uruguay. A dark age lasting almost twenty-five years was over. This November date was a landmark in the civic history of Uruguay, and the people demonstrated it with indescribable popular celebrations of joy. Hope of a new Uruguay was awakened, and as the inauguration day of March 1, 1985, came closer, the dream of a better future became more real as well.

Epilogue

Opera, Concert, and Ballet on the Teatro Solís Stage—
The Beginning of a New Era—Facing the Future

Even though Montevideo had ten theaters at the dawning of the twentieth century, one hundred years later almost all had been destroyed by fire, demolished, or rebuilt and converted to cinemas. Only the Teatro Solís remains intact. Today the strong structure of the Solís stands as solidly as ever, with daily performances almost a century and a half after it first opened in 1856; it reigns as the oldest of the great opera houses in the Americas. One year younger than the Solís, the Academy of Music in Philadelphia, which opened in 1857,[1] is the oldest in the United States. Curiously both houses, one in the Southern Hemisphere, the other in the Northern, even if totally different in their outside appearance, are very similar in the decorations of their lavish interiors.

With the burning of the SODRE in 1971, the Solís was the only stage able to accommodate symphonic concerts, ballets, chamber-music recitals, and other programs that had been scheduled in advance. Because these productions were given in such distressing times, however, the quality of most of the presentations was very poor. With the SODRE orchestra (OSSODRE) practically depopulated, the only performers to keep the artistic life alive were the few excellent Uruguayan soloists who dared to stay; no outside artist would risk visiting Montevideo at such a dangerous time.[2]

For several years the Centro Cultural de Música was likewise unable to engage any musician. As the atmosphere became more peaceful during the last military days, Argentinean and Brazilian conductors, and some soloists, began to arrive at the Solís to perform with the OSSODRE. With few plays approved by the government, and its roster very much reduced, the Comedia Nacional nonetheless, continued its annual season at the Teatro Solís.

During the early 1980s, before democracy was again reinstated, a transitional period, less rigid and more conciliatory, favored the performing arts. But it was hard to produce performances without money. In an extremely generous act the Argentinean embassy collaborated with the Fabini Foundation (formed by strong foreign corporations once again established in Uruguay) to rescue the operatic life of the city. To the joy of music lovers, two opera productions lent by the Teatro Colón were brought to Montevideo, and the Solís stage came to life again when, on August 10, 1984, the curtain rose on Puccini's *Tosca*. Adelaida Negri, immediately following her New York presentation as *Ernani*'s Elvira,[3] arrived in Montevideo to portray Tosca at the Solís. Her Mario Cavaradossi was the Italian tenor Gianfranco Pastine, and Scarpia was sung by baritone Juan Carlos Gebelin, all of them under the baton of Vicente La Ferla with the SODRE orchestra and chorus. Excellent scenery and costumes were provided by the Buenos Aires opera house.

Following several Toscas, Negri appeared again at the Solís, this time to sing *Aida* in a magnificent staging. Giuseppina Dalle Molle, the Roman mezzo-soprano who at that time sang the same role at the Arena di Verona, opposed Negri as the Egyptian princess Amneris. Piero Visconti had great impact as an unusually handsome Radamès.

With the return of democracy the cultural institutions began to regain their autonomy, but the task remained difficult because of the critical situation of the Uruguayan economy.

After twenty-five years of continuous political struggle, the priority of the new government was the immediate needs of its citizens. Although cultural life was not intentionally displaced, that is what happened.

Eventually, isolated performances, such as the opera productions from the Teatro Colón, and some excellent recitals sponsored by a revitalized Centro Cultural de Música (in a joint effort with the cultural departments of foreign embassies), gave audiences a feeling that a positive change was coming. But in spite of slow improvement, Uruguay has not yet been able to overcome its cultural lag and again enjoy the high intellectual status that had prevailed from the 1900s to the end of World War II.

Musical life in Montevideo continues, but as of now audiences are not being educated in the cultural arts through stellar performances and performers. Sadly, the generations who remember the glories of the Solís are passing away, and younger audiences lack the opportunity to appreciate great works and artists. Nevertheless—regardless of political struggles, civil wars and dictatorships, epidemics from yellow fever to AIDS, a shaken economy, and the new threats posed by the twenty-first century—the Teatro Solís remains, a noble survivor ready to regain its illustrious place in history. As long as the house endures, any miracle could happen on its stage.

Appendixes

A: *Chronology (1856–1956)*

Introduction to the Chronology

Compiling the musical chronology of the Teatro Solís, an opera house that opened in 1856 and that possesses no organized musical archive, was even more difficult than I anticipated when I began research for this project.

The Teatro Solís was leased to many different impresarios before it was purchased by the Municipality of Montevideo on June 24, 1937 (see chapter 3, note 25). Until that date, it was run strictly as a business: there was no concern about the importance of keeping records of the performances given at a venue that, from its beginnings, was at the center of the cultural life of Uruguay. The documentation relating to the construction of the Teatro Solís have been conserved at the theater itself and in other museums and archives in Montevideo. The twenty-volume collection of the box-office register books (*bordereaux*) describing daily accounts and ticket sales (without further information about performances) covers only a short period, from August 1893 to September 8, 1920. The only document retained from the theater's first performance in 1856 is the first page of the register for the period between August 25 and September 11 of that year, with the names of singers, the conductor, and chorus members and the fee they were paid for four opera performances.

Although I spent several years conducting research in the archives of the Teatro Solís I found that many records were incomplete. Therefore, it was necessary to undertake a laborious search of all of Montevideo's newspapers and musical magazines from that time in order to reconstruct the musical history of the Teatro Solís. The chronology is based on several sources of information, including programs, newspapers, musical magazines, and clippings.

1. Teatro Solís Program Collection. Even though this collection is the most reliable historical source, it is incomplete and, from 1856 until the early 1910s, nonexistent. The collection has never been inventoried and was kept in boxes by year of performance only, and in no further chronological order. A part of the collection has been nearly destroyed due to climatic conditions, humidity, mold, dust, and insects. To make things worse, some programs of priceless historical and musical value have been removed (stolen?)—and presumably sold to collectors—since 1971.[1]

2. Newspapers, Musical Magazines, and Clippings. Because the most reliable source of information, programs, was practically useless for the purposes of this chronology, I had to rely on Montevideo's newspapers and musical magazines to provide historical data. Occasionally Italian periodicals printed in Buenos Aires were consulted. With the exception of short periods of time—due to civil wars and political revolutions, in which newspapers were not published—I was able to find almost all the needed information.

This chronology comprises records of opera and operetta, symphonic concerts, recitals, ballets, and some zarzuela performances,[2] each of them listed

205

individually by date. All the nonmusical presentations—dramas, comedies, lectures, and any other sort of entertainment performed on the Teatro Solís stage—are listed by name of the company and/or individual artist. In addition to singers, instrumentalists, dancers, and conductors, the names of directors, chorus masters, designers, and choreographers, when available, have been also included. Newspapers, however, very seldom listed complete opera casts, preferring to publish only the names of the principal characters. The names of conductors were also rarely published during the nineteenth century. Likewise, musical critics hardly ever reviewed singers of secondary roles. The last performances of a season and both matinées and specific shows with reduced prices, were briefly advertised and never reviewed. Listings usually vary from few roles to the complete cast of characters and are listed accordingly to the available information.

Another difficulty is related to singers' first and last names, as their spellings appear in different ways. In such cases secondary spellings are mentioned in parentheses following artists' names. Also, according to the custom of that epoch, singers' first names were sometimes omitted (very common with French artists), and substituted by the titles Soprano, Tenor, Mademoiselle, Signora, or Signor preceding last names. When those names belong to singers who sang secondary roles and were not well known, problems resulted.

Vocal ranges, particularly in the early years of this period, were not so specific as today. I found many discrepancies between voice range and roles in the cast of characters. For example, a singer singing a tenor role could appear in baritone or even bass roles in any given season. The same thing also happened with female voices. Consequently, in the artists list placed at the beginning of each year, their register is indicated concurrently, for example: <s/mez> or <b/bar>.

Opera titles are listed according to the language in which the work was sung. This is often the original language, or the Italian translation of the original title; although exceptions are made when an opera actually exists in two versions, in different languages and both sanctioned by the composer. In these cases it would be misleading to state that a performance in Italian of *La fille du régiment* is

the same work in an Italian translation. *La figlia del reggimento* is actually a slightly different opera, with some music added and other music deleted, from the original French version. The same applied to *Dinorah* and *Le pardon de Ploërmel*.

When the work was not presented in the original, the language of the performance is shown in parentheses (see Abbreviations). It should be noted that until the first decades of the twentieth century most operas performed in Latin America were sung in Italian, because most of the touring activity was by Italian companies. Thus, although *Faust* was actually presented and advertised as *Fausto*, it is listed as *Faust* because of the great fame of the work. However, other operas such as *Les Huguenots* and *Tristan und Isolde* will be listed in Italian as *Gli ugonotti* and *Tristano e Isotta*. Because the operetta companies touring Latin America at the same epoch belong to many different countries, this issue of titles becomes more variable. As a consequence, Léhar's *Die lustige Witwe* can be found listed in its original German and also as *La vedova allegra* (Italian), *La veuve joyeuse* (French), and *La viuda alegre* (Spanish). Curiously, it has never been staged in Montevideo in its English version, *The Merry Widow*.

During the 1870s and 1880s, some operas were performed several times throughout the same year under the same conductor. However, principal roles were sung alternatively by more than one singer. In that case the number that appeared beside the name of the artist means how many times each singer sang the role. For example, Verdi's *Ernani* was sung seven times from April to December 1872. While tenor Setragni sang the title role the seven performances beginning April 12 of that year, three different sopranos shared the role of Elvira. And two baritones sang Don Carlo. So, the listing (see 1872 chronology) appears as follows:

ERNANI (Verdi)
April 12, 16, 23, June 13, Sept 8, Nov 29, Dec 1
Elvira: Mollo (3)/Casanova(1)/Pozzoli(3)
Ernani: Setragni
Don Carlo: Bonetti(5)/Marziali(2)

This means Mollo sang on April 12, 16 and 23; Casanova on June 13, and Pozzoli on Sept 8, Nov 29 and Dec 1. Accordingly, Bonetti sang Don Carlo five times, on April 12, 16, 23, June 13 and Sept 8; while Marziali sang only in two shows, on Nov 29 and Dec 1. The rest of the cast sang in all the performances.

*   *   *

SINCE ITS INAUGURATION in August 25, 1856, the Teatro Solís has been very active, with almost daily performances until today. Nonetheless, and in spite of more than 140 years of continuous existence, the musical chronology covers one century, from 1856 to 1956. That closing date was not chosen at random; the reasons have been extensively explained in chapter 26 and in the epilogue. Finally, in order to correlate and summarize this information, five appendixes have been added to complement the chronology: (B) artists, (C) musical works, (D) instrumental ensembles, (E) vocal ensembles, and (F) ballet companies.

Sources and Acknowledgments

1 Author files, personal and family collections of programs, libretti, and clippings of old unidentified newspapers.
2 Collections of musical magazines, opera libretti, and opera scores from the Library of Congress Music Division, Washington, D.C.
3 Collection of periodicals and magazines from the Library of Congress' Serial and Government Publications Division, Washington, D.C.
4 Collections of periodicals and musical magazines from the Biblioteca Nacional of Montevideo, Uruguay.
5 Teatro Solís Chronology from 1856 to 1860 published in *La Música en el Uruguay* by Lauro Ayestarán, 1:408–35 (Montevideo: SODRE, 1953).
6 Additional casts and singers' names provided by Thomas G. Kaufman.

I extend special gratitude to Dr. James W. Pruett and to Jon W. Newsom, former and current chiefs respectively, of the Music Division of the Library of Congress and its staff; and to Donald F. Wisdom and to Karen Renninger, late and current chiefs respectively, of the Serial and Government Publica-

tions Division of the Library of Congress and its staff. I appreciate the gracious assistance provided by Mabel Batto, Liliane Burwood de Betancor, Julio Castro, Graciela Guffanti and Isabel Diana from the Biblioteca Nacional of Montevideo, Uruguay. Finally I would like to express my deepest thanks to Thomas G. Kaufman, for providing several artists' names and casts, to allow me to share his fabulous lists, and for giving constant encouragement. Without the aid of all of those named, it would not have been possible to complete this chronology.

Abbreviations

a	alto, contralto
ACM	Asociación Coral de Montevideo
AUMC	Asociación Uruguaya de Música de Cámara
b	bass
bar	baritone
bn	bassoon
c	conductor
CCM	Centro Cultural de Música
chor	chorus master
cl	clarinet
d	dancer
db	double bass
dir	opera director
enghn	English horn
fl	flute
gui	guitar
hn	French horn
hpd	harpsichord
mez	mezzo-soprano
ob	oboe
ON	Orquesta Nacional
orch	orchestra
org	organ
OSM	Orquesta Sinfónica Municipal
OSSODRE	Orquesta Sinfónica del SODRE
pf	piano[forte]
s	soprano
sax	saxophone
SODRE	Servicio Oficial de Difusión Radio Eléctrica
SW	Sociedad Wagneriana
t	tenor

tpt	trumpet		***	South American premiere
vn	violin		****	World premiere
vla	viola		(It)	sung in Italian
vc	violoncello		(Fr)	sung in French
*	Teatro Solís premiere		(Sp)	sung in Spanish
**	Uruguayan premiere		(Gr)	sung in German

1856 OPENING SEASON

Female artists
Borra, Rosa <vn>
Cannonero, Carlotta <mez>
Frery, Señora <vn>
Jacobson, Amalia <s>
Merea, Carolina <s>
Tati, Giuseppina <mez>
Vera-Lorini, Sofia <s>

Male artists
Amat, José <t>
Amigó de Lara, Señor <pf>
Aulés, Antonio <pf>
Cariano, Vicente <bar>
Chateauford, León <bar>
Chiodini, Angelo <b>
Cima, Giuseppe <bar>
Comolli, Giovanni <t>
Ferranti, Pedro
Figari, Pietro <b>
Figari, Roberto <t>
Francisco, Julián <t>
Lambra, Carlos <pf>
Rosea, Luis <b>
Sardou, Paul <t>
Stanfield, Silvestre <t>
Tati, Federico <b>
Tati, Felicio <t>

INAUGURAL ITALIAN OPERA SEASON
Aquiles Lorini, Impresario
Aug 25 to Dec 23
Conductor: Luigi Preti
Designer: Lambert & Pittaluga

Aug 25, Oct 30, Nov 8
INAUGURATION GALA
Uruguayan National Anthem
ERNANI (Verdi)
Elvira: Vera-Lorini
Ernani: Comolli
Don Carlo: Cima
D. Ruy Gomez de Silva: Tati
Don Riccardo: Chiodini
Giovanna: G. Tati
Iago: Sardou

Aug 30
Spanish Dramatic Company
Torres–Fragoso–Enamorado

Sept 2, 14, Oct 9, Nov 11, Dec 7, 20
LA TRAVIATA (Verdi)
Violetta: Vera-Lorini
Flora: Tati
Annina: Cannonero
Alfredo Germont: Comolli
Giorgio Germont: Cima
Gastone: Sardou
Barone Douphol: Tati
Marchese D'Obigny: Rosea
Dottore Grenvil: Figari
Giuseppe: Chateauford
Un domestico: Francisco

Sept 7, 11, Nov 6
RIGOLETTO (Verdi)
Il Duca di Mantova: Comolli
Rigoletto: Cima
Gilda: Vera-Lorini
Sparafucile: F. Tati

Maddalena: G. Tati
Monterone: Sardou
Marullo: Chateauford
Ceprano: Rosea
Contessa di Ceprano: Cannonero
Mateo Borsa: Chateauford

Sept 15
Spanish Dance Company

Sept 18, Nov 13
I DUE FOSCARI (Verdi)
Francesco Foscari: Cima
Jacopo Foscari: Comolli
Lucrezia Contarini: Merea
Jacopo Loredano: Tati

Sept 28, 30, Oct 14
LA FAVORITA (Donizetti) (It)
Leonora: Vera-Lorini
Fernando: Comolli
Alfonso XI: Cima
Baldassare: Figari

Oct 1
Concert at the Foyer
The artists: Amat, Figari, Aulés, Borra, Lambra

Oct 4
Operatic Concert

Oct 7, 12
LINDA DI CHAMOUNIX (Donizetti)
Linda: Vera-Lorini
Marquis de Boisfleuris: Sardou

Visconte Sirval: Comolli
Antonio: Cariano
Pierotto: G. Tati
Prefetto: Figari
Intendente: Chateauford

Oct 18, 19, Nov 18
IL TROVATORE (Verdi)
Leonora: Vera-Lorini
Azucena: G. Tati
Manrico: Comolli
Conte di Luna: Cima
Ferrando: Tati
Inez: Cannonero
Ruiz: Chateauford
Zingaro: Stanfield

Oct 25, Nov 4, Dec 11
LUCIA DI LAMMERMOOR
(Donizetti)
Lucia: Merea(2)/Jacobson (1)
Edgardo: Comolli
Enrico: Cima

Oct 31, Nov 1, 16
IL BARBIERE DI SIVIGLIA
(Rossini)
Rosina: Merea
Conte di Almaviva: Comolli
Figaro: Cima
Don Bartolo: Sardou
Don Basilio: Figari
Fiorello: Stanfield

Nov 18
IL TROVATORE (Verdi)
and Concert homage to
Giuseppina Tati

Nov 22, 23, 25, 29, 30, Dec 8
LUISA STROZZI (Sanelli)**
Luisa Strozzi: Merea
Luigi Capponi: Comolli
Alessandro dei Medici: Cima

Nov 29
LUISA STROZZI (Sanelli)
and Concert homage to José
Cima

Nov 30
LUISA STROZZI (Sanelli)
and Concert homage to Carolina
Merea

Dec 13, 17, 25
LUISA MILLER (Verdi)
Luisa: Merea
Federica: G. Tati
Miller: Cima
Il Conte di Walter: F. Tati

Dec 14
Operatic Concert

Dec 18, 21
Concerts
F. Tati and Lyric Company
artists

Dec 20
LA TRAVIATA (Verdi)
Symphonic Concert
Preti: Primera sinfonía****
Thalberg: Variations after Mosè
in Egitto, Amigó de Lara
Beriot: Fifth Aria: Preti <vn>
Kontsky: Fantasia after Lucia di
Lammermoor, Preti <vn>,
Amigó <pf>
Preti: Cuadrilla para orquesta

Dec 23
LA SONNAMBULA (Bellini)
Amina: Merea
Elvino: Comolli
Rodolfo: Chiodini
Teresa: Cannonero
Lisa: G. Tati
Alessio: Rosea
Notario: F. Tati
and Norma, act 1
with Carolina Merea

Dec 31
Concert
Guglielmo Tell Overture
(Rossini)
Spanish Dance Festival

Female artists
Bedey, María (Marietta)<s>
Cannonero, Carlotta <mez>
Casaloni, Annetta <mez>
Duclós, Matilde <s>
Jacobson, Amalia <s>
Tati, Giuseppina <mez>
Vera-Lorini, Sofia <s>

Male artists
Amigó de Lara, Señor <pf>
Chateauford, León <bar>
Cima, Giuseppe <bar>
Enamorado, José <t>
Figari, Pietro <b>
Gianni, Francesco <bar>
Napoleão, Artur <pf>
Sardou, Paul <t>
Susini, Signor <bar / b>
Tamberlick, Enrico <t>
Tronconi, Giovanni <harp>
Van Marke, Gustave <vn / pf>

SUMMER ITALIAN OPERA SEASON

Aquiles Lorini, Impresario
Jan 10 to Feb 7
Conductor: Clemente Castagneri

Jan 10, 24
IL TROVATORE (Verdi)
Manrico: Tamberlick
Conte di Luna: Cima
Leonora: Vera-Lorini
Azucena: Casaloni
Ferrando: Figari
Inez: Cannonero

Jan 13
ERNANI (Verdi)
Ernani: Tamberlick
Don Carlo: Susini
Elvira: Vera-Lorini
D. Ruy Gomez de Silva: Figari
Giovanna: Cannonero
Don Riccardo: Cima

Jan 20
RIGOLETTO (Verdi)
Il Duca di Mantova: Tamberlick
Rigoletto: Cima
Gilda: Vera-Lorini
Sparafucile: Figari
Maddalena: Casaloni

Jan 27
LUISA MILLER (Verdi)
Luisa: Vera-Lorini
Rodolfo: Tamberlick
Miller: Cima
Federica: Casaloni
Il Conte di Walter: Figari
Wurm: Susini

Jan 30
Operatic Concert

Feb 7
STABAT MATER (Rossini)

Feb 12 to 17
Spanish Dance Festival

Feb 22, 23, 24
Carnival Masked Balls
Orchestra conducted by Preti

SPANISH ZARZUELA SEASON
Matilde Duclós Company
March 3 to 28

March 24
LES NOCES DE JEANETTE (Massé)
(It)
Conductor: Luigi Preti
Juan: Sardou
Juanita: Jacobson
Tomás: Chateauford

April
[Theaters closed due to a yellow
fever epidemic.]

**ROUSSET BALLET COMPANY
SEASON**
July 26 to Aug 15
Ballet / concert conductor: Luigi
Preti
Dancers: Adelaide, Carolina,
Clementine, Louis and Theresina
Rousset, Mr. Szollozy

July 26
GISELLE (Adam)

Aug 1, 2
Divertisements

Aug 9, 15
Operatic Concerts and Ballet

SPANISH ZARZUELA SEASON
Sept 3, 12, 13, Nov 14
Duclós—Enamorado Company

Sept 10
Recital: G. Tronconi <harp>
Souvenir de Naples (Fantasy)
Fantasy after La traviata
Fantasy after Lucrezia Borgia

Dec 1
Operatic Concert

Dec 4
Orchestral Concert
Soloist: Napoleão <pf>
Thalberg: Fantasia after La
sonnambula
Kuhe: Fantasia after Il trovatore
Thalberg: Fantasia after L'elisir
d'amore
Thalberg: Fantasia after La fille
du régiment for pf and orch

Dec 12
Orchestral Concert
Soloist: Napoleão <pf>
Prudent: Fantasia after Lucia di
Lammermoor
Ascher: Fantasia after La traviata

Thalberg: Fantasia after Mosè in
Egitto
Hertz: Fantasia after La fille du
régiment for pf and orch

1858

Female artists
Bajetti, Teresa <s>
Bastoggi, Signora <mez>
Bishop, Anna <s>
Cailly, Clarisse <s>
Duclós, Matilde <s>
Duclós, Carolina <s>
Fusoni, Angelina <mez>
Liard, Vittorina <s>

Male artists
Bastoggi, Gaetano <bar>
Bergamaschi, Giovanni <bar>
Casanova, Carlo <b>
Cavedagni, Luigi <bar>
Costa, Pablo <b>
Cusano, Antonio <bar>
Devotti, Ugo <t>
Enamorado, José <t>
Ferrari, Angelo <pf>
Gianni, Giovanni B. <bar>
Gianni, Francesco <bar>
Hipolito, Señor <t>
Lelmi, Luis <t>
Loreau, Arthur <pf>
Loredano, Signor <bar>
Monteverde, A. <t>
Oliveira, Claudino J. de
<ophicleide>
Pfeiffer, Oscar <pf>
Tronconi, Giovanni <harp>

May 15, 20, 29
Recitals: Tronconi <harp>

June 16
Operatic Concert
Soloist: Bishop <s>
Norma: Casta diva
Tancredi: Scene and aria

Gratia agamus tibi (with flute
obbligato)
English Ballad
Si usted lo sabe (Andalusian
song)
Lucia di Lammermoor: Mad
scene
La catatumba (Mexican song)

ITALIAN OPERA AND
CONCERT SEASON
June 20 to Dec 12
Lelmi-Bajetti-Cavedagni
Company
Conductors: Luigi Preti and
Celestino Griffon (assistant)

June 20, 26
I LOMBARDI ALLA PRIMA
CROCIATA (Verdi)
Giselda: Bajetti
Oronte: Lelmi
Arvino: Cavedagni
Pagano: Casanova
Viclinda: Bastoggi
Pirro: Costa

June 24, 29, July 17
ERNANI (Verdi)
Elvira: Bajetti
Ernani: Lelmi
D. Carlo: Bastoggi
D. Ruy Gomez de Silva:
Casanova

June 29 [same as June 24]
ERNANI (Verdi)
and *Concert*: Bajetti/Cavegdani

July 3, 18, 29
BELISARIO (Donizetti)*
Justiniano: Costa
Belisario: Bastoggi
Antonina: Bajetti
Irene: Fusoni
Almiro: Lelmi
Eutropio: Monteverde

July 10
LINDA DI CHAMOUNIX
(Donizetti)
Linda: Bajetti
Marquis Boisfleuris: Cavedagni
Visconte Sirval: Lelmi
Prefetto: Casanova
Pierotto: Fusoni
Intendente: Monteverde
Maddalena: Bastoggi

July 14, Aug 20
I DUE FOSCARI (Verdi)
Francesco Foscari: Bastoggi
Jacopo Foscari: Lelmi
Lucrezia Contarini: Bajetti
Jacopo Loredano: Cavedagni
Barbarigo: Monteverde
Servo: Costa

July 19, 31, Aug 18
ATTILA (Verdi)
Odabella: Bajetti
Foresto: Lelmi
Ezio: Bastoggi
Attila: Cavedagni

July 20
Operatic Concert

July 31
ATTILA (Verdi) [same as July 19]
and *Concert*

Aug 3, 8, 14, 28, 30
IL TROVATORE (Verdi)
Leonora: Bajetti
Manrico: Lelmi
Conte di Luna: Cavedagni
Azucena: Bastoggi

Aug 7, 12, 22
IL FORNARETTO (Sanelli)**
Clemenza: Bajetti
Nella: Bastoggi
Pietro: Lelmi
Marco Tasca: Cavedagni

Aug 14
IL TROVATORE (Verdi) [same as
Aug 3]
and *Concert*
Soloist: Ferrari <pf>
Fantasia after Lucia di
Lammermoor
Quindant: Concert Galop

Aug 17, Sept 18 to 30, Oct 12,
Nov 7
Zarzuela Company Duclós-
Enamorado

Aug 25
Uruguayan National Anthem
ERNANI (Verdi) [same as June
24]
and *Concert*

Aug 28
IL TROVATORE (Verdi) [same as
Aug 3]
and *Concert*

Sept 3
DON SEBASTIANO (Donizetti)
(It)**
Don Sebastiano: Lelmi
Zaida: Fusoni
Antonio, regente: Monteverde
Don Giovanni: Cavedagni
Camoens: Casanova
Ben-Selim: Costa
Abujaldo: Bastoggi

Sept 11
DON SEBASTIANO (Donizetti)
[same as Sept 3]
and *Concert*

Oct 21, 31
Operatic Concerts
Conductor: Luigi Preti
Artists: Duclós, Cavedagni,
Bergamaschi

Nov 4
Recital: Pfeiffer <pf>
Pfeiffer: Fantasia Lucrezia Borgia
Gottschalk: Le bananier**
Dohler: Souvenir de Naples
Pfeiffer: Introduction and
Variations after Carnaval de
Venezia

Nov 20
Recital: Loreau <pf>
Hertz: Variations after La fille
du régiment
Thalberg: Fantasia after La
muette de Portici

Nov 23, Dec 8, 12
Operatic Concerts
Conductor: Luigi Preti

1859

Female artists
Bajetti, Teresa <s>
Bedey, Marietta <s>
Cailly, Clarisse <s>
Casaloni, Annetta <mez>
De Camilli, Matilde <s>
De la Grange, Anna <s>
Dodero, Rosa <mez/s>
Dorina, Rosita <mez>
Duclós, Carolina <s>
Duclós, Matilde <s>
Fusoni, Angelina <mez>
Medori, Giuseppina <s>
Simonsen, Fanny de <s>

Male artists
Arnaud, Giacomo <bar>
Astengo, Carlos <pf>
Bengochea, Pedro D. <vn>
Cambroni, Vicente <bar>
Cavedagni, Luigi <bar>
Cima, Giuseppe <bar>
Comolli, Giovanni <t>
Contini, Luis <t>
De Camilli, Antonio <bar>

Devotti, Ugo <t>
Didot, Alfred <b/bar>
Enamorado, José <t>
Figari, Pietro <b>
Galli, Balestra <t>
Gazzo, Luis <b>
Ghinon, Signor <t>
Gianni, Giovanni B. <bar>
Laserre Brisson, Louis <fl>
Lelmi, Luis <t>
Loreau, Arthur <pf>
Mirate, Raffaele <t>
Monteverde, A. <t>
Reina, Giovanni B. <bar>
Rosea, Luis <b>
Sardou, Paul <t>
Scarabelli, L. <b>
Simonsen, Martin <vn>

**SUMMER ITALIAN OPERA
SEASON**
Jan 18 to Feb 26
Conductor: Luigi Preti

Jan 18
LA TRAVIATA (Verdi)
Violetta: De la Grange
Flora: Dorina
Annina: Fusoni
Alfredo Germont: Comolli
Giorgio Germont: Reina
Gastone: Monteverde
Barone Douphol: Didot
Dottore Grenvil: Sardou
Giuseppe: Rosea

Jan 21, Feb 23
LUCIA DI LAMMERMOOR
(Donizetti)
Lucia: De la Grange
Edgardo: Comolli
Enrico: Reina
Raimondo: Didot

Jan 30
IL TROVATORE (Verdi)
Leonora: De la Grange
Manrico: Comolli

Conte di Luna: Reina
Azucena: Fusoni
Ferrando: Didot
Ruiz: Figari

Feb 2, 6
IL BARBIERE DI SIVIGLIA
(Rossini)
Rosina: De la Grange
Conte di Almaviva: Comolli
Figaro: Reina
Don Basilio: Didot
Don Bartolo: Sardou
Fiorello: Monteverde
Berta: Dorina and Polka sang by
De la Grange

Feb 4, 18, 25
NORMA (Bellini)
Norma: De la Grange
Adalgisa: Fusoni
Clotilde: Dorina
Pollione: Comolli
Oroveso: Didot
Flavio: Monteverde

Feb 8
RIGOLETTO (Verdi)
Il Duca di Mantova: Comolli
Rigoletto: Reina
Gilda: De la Grange
Sparafucile: Didot
Maddalena: Fusoni
Monterone: Sardou
Marullo: Rosea
Mateo Borsa: Monteverde
Ceprano: Gazzo
Contessa di Ceprano: Dorina

Feb 11, 26
LUCREZIA BORGIA (Donizetti)
Lucrezia: De la Grange
Gennaro: Comolli
Duca Alfonso: Didot
Maffio Orsini: Fusoni
Gubetta: Reina
Rustighello: Sardou

Feb 16
LA SONNAMBULA (Bellini)
Amina: De la Grange
Elvino: Comolli
Rodolfo: Didot
Teresa: Dorina
Lisa: Fusoni
Alessio: Rosea
Notario: Monteverde

Feb 20
Operatic Concert
I puritani: Act 2: De la Grange,
Didot, Reina
Ernani: Act 3
Lucia di Lammermoor: Act 3
Duet Gli ugonotti: De la Grange
/ Didot

**SPANISH ZARZUELA
COMPANY SEASON**
Carolina and Matilde Duclós–
José Enamorado Company
July 18 to Aug 4

**WINTER ITALIAN OPERA
SEASON**
Aug 14 to Nov 13
Conductor: Clemente Castagneri

Aug 14, 15
IL TROVATORE (Verdi)
Leonora: Cailly
Manrico: Lelmi
Conte di Luna: Cima
Azucena: Casaloni

Aug 21
LA FAVORITA (Donizetti) (It)
Leonora: Casaloni
Alfonso XI: Cima
Fernando: Lelmi
Inez: Dodero
Baldassare: Figari
Gaspare: Monteverde

Aug 25
Uruguayan National Anthem
ERNANI (Verdi)
Elvira: Cailly
Ernani: Lelmi
Don Carlo: Cima
D. Ruy Gomez de Silva: Figari
Giovanna: Casaloni

Sept 3, 25, Nov 20
MARCO VISCONTI (Petrella)**
Bice: Cailly
Tremacoldo: Casaloni
Ottorino: Lelmi
Marco Visconti: Cima
Lodrisio Visconti: Monteverde
Conte Oldrado: Scarabelli
Laura: Dodero
and La Cenerentola: Act 2 (Nov
20)

Sept 10
Operatic Concert
Uruguayan National Anthem
French National Anthem

Sept 18
LUCREZIA BORGIA (Donizetti)
Lucrezia: Cailly
Gennaro: Lelmi
Duca Alfonso: Cima
Maffio Orsini: Casaloni
Gubetta: Figari
Rustighello: Scarabelli

Oct 2
LA TRAVIATA (Verdi)
Violetta: Bedey
Flora: Dodero
Annina: Dorina
Alfredo Germont: Lelmi
Giorgio Germont: Cima
Gastone: Ghinon
Dottore Grenvil: Scarabelli

Oct 4
I MASNADIERI (Verdi)
Amalia: Cailly
Carlo: Lelmi

Francesco: Cima
Massimiliano: Figari

Oct 16
LA CENERENTOLA (Rossini)
Cenerentola (Angelina): Cailly
Clorinda: Bedey
Tisbe: Casaloni

Oct 23
LUISA MILLER (Verdi)
Luisa: Bedey
Rodolfo: Lelmi
Federica: Casaloni
Miller: Cima
Il Conte di Walter: Figari
Wurm: Scarabelli
Laura: Dodero

Oct 30
NABUCCO (Verdi)
Abigaille: Bajetti
Ismaele: Lelmi
Nabucco: Cima
and *Concert*
Cavedagni: La bendición de las
banderas
orientales, for orchestra

Nov 9, 13
MARIA DI ROHAN (Donizetti)
Maria: Bajetti
Riccardo: Devotti
Armando: Cavedagni

Nov 10
Recital: F. de Simonsen <s>,
Loreau <pf>, M. Simonsen <vn>
Cavatina: Il trovatore <s / pf>
Fantasia: La muette de Portici
<pf>
Fantasia: Ricordo de Bellini <vn
/ pf>
Ballad: Kathleen Mavourneen
<s / pf>
Introduction and Variations
after La fille du régiment <vn /
pf>

Variations Les diamants de la
couronne <s / pf>
Gottschalk: Le bananier <pf>
Liszt: Hungarian Melody <pf>
Ernst: Andante spianato <vn / pf>
Paganini: Carnival of Venice
<vn / pf>

Nov 12
Orchestral Concert
Soloists: F.de Simonsen <s>, M.
Simonsen <vn>
Variations Ocean Life <vn / orch>
Schubert: Serenade <s / vn / orch>
Fantasia after Ernani <vn / orch>
Rode: Al dolce canto <s / orch>
Ernst: Andante spianato <vn /
orch>
Paganini: Carnival of Venice
<vn / orch>

Nov 13
MARIA DI ROHAN
(Donizetti)[same as Nov 9]
and PEPA LA CIGARRERA
(zarzuela)
Pepa: Bajetti
Curro: Contini
Estudiante: Cavedagni
Sacristán: Jover

Nov 19
Recital: F. de Simonsen <s>, M.
Simonsen <vn>, Loreau <pf>
Cavatina: La gazza ladra <s / pf>
Souvenir from Germany <vn / pf>
Romanza Guglielmo Tell <s / pf>
Introduction and capriccio after
Belisario <vn / pf>
Bolero Chanteuse voilée <s / pf>
El pájaro en el árbol(Rondo
Burlesque) <vn / pf>

**FIRST SUMMER ITALIAN
OPERA SEASON**
Dec 1 to 13
Conductor: Luigi Preti

Dec 1
LUCIA DI LAMMERMOOR
(Donizetti)
Lucia: De la Grange
Edgardo: Lelmi
Enrico: Cima

Dec 4
ERNANI (Verdi)
Elvira: De la Grange
Ernani: Lelmi
Don Carlo: Cima
Iago: Galli
D. Ruy Gomez de Silva: Figari

Dec 8, 31
LUCREZIA BORGIA (Donizetti)
Lucrezia: De la Grange / Medori
Gennaro: Lelmi / Mirate
Duca Alfonso: Cima / Arnaud

Dec 11
NORMA (Bellini)
Norma: De la Grange
Pollione: Lelmi
Oroveso: Cima

Dec 13
I PURITANI (Bellini)
Elvira: De la Grange
Lord Arturo: Lelmi
Riccardo Forth: Cima
Lord Gualterio: Scarabelli
Sir Giorgio: Didot
Enriqueta: Dodero
Sir Bruno: Monteverde
and *Concert* by Anna De la
Grange

**SECOND SUMMER ITALIAN
OPERA SEASON**
Dec 17 to Jan 22, 1860
Conductor: Luigi Preti

Dec 17
IL TROVATORE (Verdi)
Leonora: Medori
Manrico: Mirate
Conte di Luna: Arnaud

Azucena: Casaloni
Ruiz: Figari

Dec 18, 28
ERNANI (Verdi)
Elvira: Medori
Ernani: Lelmi (1) / Mirate(1)
Don Carlo: Cima (1) / Arnaud(1)
Iago: Galli
D. Ruy Gomez de Silva: Figari

Dec 23
MARIA DI ROHAN (Donizetti)
Maria: Medori
Riccardo: Mirate
Armando: Arnaud

Dec 31
LUCREZIA BORGIA (Donizetti)
Lucrezia: Medori
Gennaro: Mirate
Duca Alfonso: Arnaud
Maffio Orsini: Casaloni

1860

Female artists
Antoni, Giulietta (Giuditta)
<mez>
Bedey, Maria (Marietta) <s>
Cailly, Clarisse <s>
Casaloni, Annetta <mez>
De la Grange, Anna <s>
Manzini, Constanza <s>
Medori, Giuseppina <s>

Male artists
Antoni, Pietro de <b>
Arnaud, Giacomo <bar>
Ballerini, Emidio [Emilio] <t>
Bassori, Pietro <t>
Bertolini, Giuseppe <bar>
Bezzoni, Pietro <bar>
Chizzoni, Antonio <t>
Cima, Giuseppe <bar>
Didot, Alfred <b / bar>
Figari, Pietro <b>
Franchi, Paolo <b-buffo>

Hericourt, Luis <t>
Lelmi, Luis <t>
Mirate, Raffaele <t>
Sardou, Paul <t>
Scarabelli, Vincenzo <b>

**SUMMER ITALIAN OPERA
SEASON**
[continuation of the 1859
season]
Jan 4 to 22
Conductor: Luigi Preti

Jan 4, 8, 10
I MARTIRI (Donizetti)
Paolina: Medori
Poliuto: Mirate
Severus: Arnaud
Callisthenes: Figari
Felice: Sardou

Jan 6
IL TROVATORE (Verdi)
[same cast as Dec 17, 1859]

Jan 12
ROBERTO DEVEREUX (Donizetti)
Elizabetta: Medori
Roberto Conte di Essex: Mirate
Sara: Cailly
Nottingham: Arnaud

Jan 15
NORMA (Bellini)
Norma: Medori
Adalgisa: Cailly
Pollione: Mirate
Oroveso: Figari
and *Don Pasquale: Act 1*
Norina: Medori
Don Pasquale: Arnaud

Jan 19, 24
LUCIA DI LAMMERMOOR
(Donizetti)
Lucia: Medori
Edgardo: Mirate
Enrico: Arnaud
Arturo: Sardou

Raimondo: Figari
Alisa: Antoni
Normanno: Bassori
and *I lombardi: Trio*

Jan 22
LUCREZIA BORGIA (Donizetti)
[same cast as Dec 31, 1859]

Feb 11 to March 4
Carnival Masked Balls

**FALL ITALIAN OPERA
SEASON**
March 18 to April 22
Conductor: Clemente Castagneri

March 18
IL BARBIERE DI SIVIGLIA
(Rossini)
Rosina: De la Grange
Conte di Almaviva: Lelmi
Figaro: Cima
Don Bartolo: Sardou
Don Basilio: Didot

March 21, April 13
LA TRAVIATA (Verdi)
Violeta: De la Grange
Alfredo Germont: Lelmi
Giorgio Germont: Cima
Flora: Antoni
Gastone: Chizzoni
Barone Douphol: Bezzoni
Marchese D'Obigny: Didot
Dottore Grenvil: Scarabelli

March 24, April 8
I PURITANI (Bellini)
Elvira: De la Grange
Lord Arturo: Lelmi
Riccardo Forth: Cima
Sir Giorgio: Didot

March 27, April 25
NORMA (Bellini)
Norma: De la Grange
Adalgisa: Cailly

Pollione: Lelmi
Oroveso: Didot

April 10, 20
LUCREZIA BORGIA (Donizetti)
Lucrezia: De la Grange
Gennaro: Lelmi
Duca Alfonso: Cima
Maffio Orsini: Casaloni

April 15
DON PASQUALE (Donizetti)
Norina: De la Grange
Ernesto: Lelmi
Don Pasquale: Franchi
Dottore Malatesta: Cima

April 18
MACBETH (Verdi)
Lady Macbeth: De la Grange
Macbeth: Arnaud
Banquo: Figari

April 22
IL TROVATORE (Verdi)
Leonora: De la Grange
Manrico: Lelmi
Conte di Luna: Cima
Ferrando: Figari
Ruiz: Sardou

June 23, July 21, 31, Aug 1
Concerts Sociedad de
aficionados españoles
Conductor: Luigi Preti
and drama: GUZMAN EL BUENO
(Gil y Zárate)

July 18
Masked Ball in celebration of
the Thirtieth Anniversary of the
Uruguayan Constitution

Aug 19
Concert and Spanish Dramatic
Company
Conductor: Luigi Preti

Aug 20 to Oct 13, Nov 21
Spanish Dramatic Company
Fernando Quijano

Sept 22, 28, Oct 4
Concerts by Lyric Italian
Amateur Company
Conductor: Luigi Preti

**SUMMER / FALL ITALIAN
OPERA SEASON**
Manzini-Ballerini Company
Dec 8, 1860 to May 14, 1861
Conductor: Luigi Preti

Dec 8
LA TRAVIATA (Verdi)
Violetta: Manzini
Alfredo Germont: Ballerini
Giorgio Germont: Bertolini
Flora: Antoni
Gastone: Chizzoni
Barone Douphol: Bezzoni
Marchese D'Obigny: Hericourt
Dottore Grenvil: Scarabelli

Dec 13, 23
ERNANI (Verdi)
Elvira: Manzini
Ernani: Ballerini
Don Carlo: Bertolini
D. Ruy Gomez de Silva: de
Antoni

Dec 16, 25
LUCIA DI LAMMERMOOR
(Donizetti)
Lucia: Manzini
Edgardo: Ballerini
Enrico: Bertolini
Arturo: Chizzoni
Raimondo: de Antoni
Alisa: Antoni
Normanno: Bassori

Dec 22
I DUE FOSCARI (Verdi)
Francesco Foscari: Bertolini
Jacopo Foscari: Ballerini
Lucrezia Contarini: Manzini

Dec 27
LUISA MILLER (Verdi)
Luisa: Manzini
Rodolfo: Ballerini
Miller: Bertolini

Dec 30
NORMA (Bellini)
Norma: Manzini
Adalgisa: Bedey
Pollione: Ballerini
Oroveso: Didot

1861

Female artists
Antoni, Giulietta (Giuditta)
<mez>
Arditi, Giulietta <s>
Bedey, Maria (Marietta) <s>
Buil, Eloisa <s>
Dodero, Rosa <mez>
Manzini, Constanza <s>
Perini-Verdini, Margherita de <a>

Male artists
Antoni, Pietro de <b>
Ballerini, Emidio (Emilio) <t>
Bassori, Pietro <t>
Bertolini, Giuseppe <bar>
Bussoni, Pietro <b>
Chiodini, Angelo <b>
Chizzoni, Antonio <t>
Hines, Miguel <pf>
Lelmi, Luis <t>
Sachetti, Pietro <pf>
Scarabelli, Vincenzo <b>
Vignoli, Giuseppe <vn>

**SUMMER / FALL ITALIAN
OPERA SEASON**
[continuation of the 1860 season
to May 14]
Manzini-Ballerini Company
Conductors: Alessandro Marotta
and Luigi Preti

Jan 5
NORMA (Bellini)
Norma: Manzini
Adalgisa: Bedey
Pollione: Ballerini

Jan 6
LUISA MILLER (Verdi)
Luisa: Manzini
Rodolfo: Ballerini
Miller: Bertolini
Laura: Antoni
Il Conte di Walter: de Antoni
Wurm: Scarabelli

Jan 10
ATTILA (Verdi)
Odabella: Manzini
Foresto: Ballerini
Ezio: Bertolini
Attila: de Antoni

Jan 12
RIGOLETTO (Verdi)
Gilda: Manzini
Il Duca di Mantova: Ballerini
Rigoletto: Bertolini
Maddalena: Dodero
Sparafucile: de Antoni
Monterone: Scarabelli
Ceprano: Bussoni

Jan 17, 22
ERNANI (Verdi)
Elvira: Manzini
Ernani: Ballerini
Don Carlo: Bertolini
D. Ruy Gomez de Silva: de
Antoni

Jan 19
LA TRAVIATA (Verdi)
Violetta: Manzini
Alfredo Germont: Ballerini
Giorgio Germont: Bertolini

Jan 24, Feb 27
AROLDO (Verdi)**
Mina: Manzini
Aroldo: Ballerini
Egberto: Bertolini

Jan 27
GEMMA DI VERGY (Donizetti)
Gemma: Manzini
Tomasso: Ballerini
Conte di Vergy: Bertolini

Jan 31, Feb 7
IL TROVATORE (Verdi)
Leonora: Manzini
Manrico: Lelmi
Conte di Luna: Bertolini
Azucena: Buil
Inez: Arditi
Ferrando: de Antoni
Ruiz: Chiodini

Feb 9 to 23
Carnival Masked Balls

March 9
SAFFO (Pacini)
Saffo: Manzini
Faone: Ballerini
Alcandro: Bertolini
Climene: de Perini-Verdini
Olimone: Buil
Dirce: Antoni
Ippia: Chiodini
Sirimaco: Scarabelli

March 31, April 4
NORMA (Bellini)
Norma: Manzini
Adalgisa: Buil
Pollione: Ballerini

April 1
Acrobatic Company
Manzini-Ballerini Company
April 6 to May 9
Conductor: Luigi Preti

April 6
LA BATTAGLIA DI LEGNANO
(Verdi)**
Lida: Manzini
Arrigo: Ballerini
Rolando: Bertolini

April 8
LA TRAVIATA (Verdi)
[same cast as Jan 19]

April 9
I DUE FOSCARI (Verdi)
Francesco Foscari: Bertolini
Jacopo Foscari: Ballerini
Lucrezia Contarini: Manzini

April 11
AROLDO (Verdi)
[same cast as Jan 24]

April 17
RIGOLETTO (Verdi)
[same cast as Jan 12]

April 21, 25, May 14
LUCIA DI LAMMERMOOR
(Donizetti)
Lucia: Manzini
Edgardo: Ballerini
Enrico: Bertolini
Raimondo: de Antoni
Alisa: Dodero
Arturo: Chizzoni
Normanno: Bassori

April 28
LUISA MILLER (Verdi)
[same cast as Jan 6]

May 1, 5, 12
L'EBREO (Apolloni)

Leila: Manzini
Adel-Musa: Ballerini
Issachar: Bertolini
Ferdinando Re di Aragona: de
Antoni

May 7
GEMMA DI VERGY (Donizetti)
[same cast as Jan 27]
Conductor: Luigi Pret:

May 9
IL TROVATORE (Verdi)
Leonora: Manzini
Manrico: Ballerini
Conte di Luna: Bertolini
Azucena: Buil
Inez: Arditi
Ferrando: de Antoni

May 11
ERNANI (Verdi)
[same cast as Jan 17]

**THIERRY COMPANY BALLET
SEASON**
May 26 to July 28
Conductor: Victor Guerin
First ballerina: Virginia Ferrari

June 13
Operatic Concert
Italian Amateur Opera
Company

Aug 1 to Sept 1
Spanish Dramatic Company
Francisco Torres

TROUPE DES BOUFFES PARISIENS
Sept 2
Conductor: Mr. Poppe
LE SAVETIER ET LE FINANCIER
(Offenbach)

Sept 10
MAITRE BATON (Dufresne)

SPRING ITALIAN OPERA SEASON
Second Manzini-Ballerini season
Sept 21 to Nov 3
Conductor: Luigi Preti

Sept 21
LUISA MILLER (Verdi)
[same cast as Jan 6]

Sept 25
LA TRAVIATA (Verdi)
[same cast as Jan 19]

Sept 29, Oct 20
NORMA (Bellini)
Norma: Manzini
Adalgisa: Buil
Pollione: Ballerini

Oct 4, 6, 12, 27
BONDELMONTE (Pacini)**
Beatrice: Manzini
Isaura: Bedey
Bondelmonte: Ballerini
Bianca Donati: Buil
Amedei: Bertolini
Uberti: de Antoni
Gangalandi: Scarabelli
Mosca: Bussoni

Oct 8, 9
Recitals: Hines <pf>

Oct 18
LUCREZIA BORGIA (Donizetti)
Lucrezia: Manzini
Gennaro: Ballerini
and *Concert*
Soloists: Vignoli <vn> / Sachetti <pf>

Oct 24
SAFFO (Pacini)
Saffo: Manzini
Faone: Ballerini
Alcandro: Bertolini

Olimone: Buil
Dirce: Antoni
Ippia: Chiodini
Sirimaco: Scarabelli

Oct 30
ERNANI (Verdi)
Elvira: Buil
Ernani: Ballerini
Don Carlo: Bertolini
D. Ruy Gomez de Silva: de Antoni

Nov 3
IL TROVATORE (Verdi)
[same cast as May 9]
and *Concert*
Soloists: Vignoli <vn> / Sachetti <pf>

Dec 1
Ballet and Comedy Amateur Society

Dec 5 to 20
Spanish Dramatic Company
Francisco Torres

Dec 22
Julio dos Santos Pereira
<Brazilian prestidigitator>

1862

Female artists
Altieri, Giuditta <s>
Bedey, Maria (Marietta) <s>
Bruzzone, Rosita <s>
Dodero, Rosa <mez / s>
Duchamont, Mlle. <s>
Giovanelli, Matilda <mez>
Guille, Mlle. <s>
Larrumbe, Adelaida <s>
Laura, Mlle.
Lecoutex, Mlle.
Lyon, Pauline <s>
Manzini, Constanza <s>

Marti, Anita <s>
Mazzini, Signora <s>
Parodi, Catalina <mez>
Parodi, Teresa <s>
Piazzini, Signora <s>
Rigotti, Signora <mez>

Male artists
Belli, Signor
Ballerini, Emidio (Emilio) <t>
Bouchet, Monsieur
Chiodini, Angelo <b>
Chizzoni, Antonio <t>
Costa, Pablo <b>
Cusano, Antonio <bar>
Duchamont, Monsieur <t>
Ebendinger, Monsieur <b>
Emon, Monsieur <bar>
Enamorado, José <t>
Fernando, Señor
Figari, Pietro <b>
Gaddi, Luigi <b>
Lelmi, Luis <t>
Malbleid, Monsieur
Marchapp, Monsieur
Mazzi, Giuseppe <t>
Monteverde, A. <t>
Noury, Monsieur <t>
Rossi-Ghelli, Achille <b>
Scarabelli, Vincenzo <b>
Walter, Luigi <bar>

GRAND OPERA AND OPERA-COMIQUE SEASON
Emon and Marti, Impresarios
Jan 6 to Feb 8
Conductor: Monsieur Guille
Director: Monsieur Lecoutex

Jan 6
LE BARBIER DE SEVILLE (Rossini)
(Fr)
Cast: Marti, Duchamont,
Lecoutex, Guille, Laura,
Duchamont, Fernando, Bouchet,
Malbleid, Marchapp

Jan 9, 12
LE DOMINO NOIR (Auber)

Jan 16, 19
LES MOUSQUETAIRES DE LA
REINE (Halévy)

Jan 20, 28, Feb 27 to March 15,
March 25, 26
Thierry Choreographic
Company
Dramatic pantomime and dance

Jan 23
LES DIAMANTS DE LA COURONNE
(Auber)

Feb 2
LA FILLE DU REGIMENT
(Donizetti)
LE MAITRE DE CHAPELLE (Paer)

Feb 8
LA FAVORITE (Donizetti)
LES RENDEVOUZ BOURGEOIS
("Nicolo" Isouard)

March 16 to 24
Carnival Masked Balls

**LARRUMBE-BALLERINI
ITALIAN OPERA SEASON**
April 27 to June 1
Conductor: Luigi Preti

April 27
Operatic Concert
Larrumbe <s>, Ballerini <t>,
Cusano <bar>
Ernani: Act 1
Attila: Arias
Il trovatore: Act 1
Nabucco: Arias
Lucia di Lammermoor: Arias

May 1, 4, 11, 18, 20, 25 and June
1
Operatic Concerts

**TROUPE DES BOUFFES
PARISIENS SEASON**
June 15 to July 18

June 15, 24, July 6, 13 to 18
LA CROIX D'OR(?) and LA
CHANTEUSE D'ANESSE(?)
with soprano Pauline Lyon

Special Performances
Conductor: Luigi Preti

July 2, 3
LUCIA DI LAMMERMOOR
(Donizetti)
Lucia: Manzini
Edgardo: Lelmi
Enrico: Walter
Raimondo: Figari
Arturo: Chizzoni
Alisa: Rigotti

July 9
Federic Decremps
<prestidigitator>

**WINTER ITALIAN OPERA
SEASON**
July 19 to Sept 23
Conductor: Luigi Preti

July 19, Aug 28
LA FAVORITA (Donizetti) (It)
Leonora: Parodi
Fernando: Mazzi
Alfonso XI: Walter
Baldassare: Rossi
Gaspare: Chiodini
Inez: Bruzzone (1) / Dodero(1)

July 22
SAFFO (Pacini)
Saffo: Parodi
Faone: Mazzi
Alcandro: Walter
Olimone: Giovanelli

Ippia: Chiodini
Sirimaco: Scarabelli

July 25, Aug 30
LA TRAVIATA (Verdi)
Violetta: Altieri
Alfredo Germont: Mazzi
Giorgio Germont: Walter
Annina: Dodero
Barone Douphol: Cusano
Marchese D'Obigny: Chiodini
Dottore Grenvil: Costa

July 27, Aug 10
I CAPULETI E I MONTECCHI
(Bellini)
Giulietta: Parodi
Romeo: Giovanelli
Tebaldo: Mazzi
Lorenzo: Chiodini
Capellio: Scarabelli

July 30, Aug 3, 21, 25
IL TROVATORE (Verdi)
Leonora: Altieri
Azucena: C. Parodi
Manrico: Mazzi
Conte di Luna: Walter
Ferrando: Rossi

Aug 1
LA SONNAMBULA (Bellini)
Amina: T. Parodi
Elvino: Mazzi
Rodolfo: Chiodini
Lisa: C. Parodi
Teresa: Dodero
Alessio: Rossi

Aug 6, Sept 14
SIMON BOCCANEGRA (Verdi)**
Simon: Walter
Amelia: Altieri
Gabriele Adorno: Mazzi
Jacopo Fiesco: Rossi
Pietro: Chiodini
Paolo: Scarabelli
Capitan: Chiodini

Aug 8
ERNANI (Verdi)
Elvira: T. Parodi
Ernani: Mazzi
Don Carlo: Walter
D. Ruy Gomez de Silva: Rossi
Giovanna: Dodero
Don Riccardo: Chiodini
Iago: Scarabelli

Sept 3, 8
I VESPRI SICILIANI (Verdi)(It)**
Duchessa Elena: Parodi
Ninetta: Dodero
Arrigo: Mazzi
Simon de Monfort: Walter
Signor de Bethune: Costa
Giovanni de Procida: Rossi
Conte de Vaudemont: Scarabelli

Sept 7
STABAT MATER (Rossini)

Sept 12
LUCREZIA BORGIA (Donizetti)
Lucrezia: T. Parodi
Gennaro: Mazzi
Maffio Orsini: Giovanelli
Duca Alfonso: Rossi
Gubetta: Scarabelli
Rustichella: Chiodini
and Benefit Concert to M.
Giovanelli

Sept 17
IL BARBIERE DI SIVIGLIA
(Rossini)
Rosina: Parodi
Conte di Almaviva: Mazzi
Figaro: Walter
Don Basilio: Rossi
and Concert with same artists

Sept 19, 21, 23
UN BALLO IN MASCHERA
(Verdi)**
Amelia: T. Parodi
Riccardo: Mazzi

Renato: Walter
Ulrica: Giovanelli
Oscar: Altieri
Samuel: Scarabelli
Silvano: Chiodini
Tom: Rossi

SPRING ITALIAN OPERA SEASON

Manzini-Ballerini Company
Oct 3 to Nov 30

Oct 3, 8
NORMA (Bellini)
Norma: Manzini
Adalgisa: Bedey
Pollione: Ballerini
Oroveso: Figari

Oct 12, 19, Nov 23, 30
LUCIA DI LAMMERMOOR
(Donizetti)
Lucia: Manzini
Edgardo: Ballerini
Enrico: Walter
Raimondo: Ebendinger
Arturo: Chizzoni
Alisa: Rigotti

Oct 26, Nov 16
BONDELMONTE (Pacini)
Bondelmonte: Ballerini
Beatrice: Manzini
Isaura: Piazzini
Amedei: Figari
Bianca Donati: Rigotti
Uberti: Ebendinger
Gangalandi: Gaddi
Mosca: Chizzoni
Fifanti: Belli

Nov 9
I LOMBARDI ALLA PRIMA
CROCIATA (Verdi)
Giselda: Manzini
Oronte: Ballerini
Arvino: Figari

Pagano: Scarabelli
Viclinda: Giovanelli

SUMMER OPERA PERFORMANCES

Dec 21, 1862, to Jan 11, 1863
Conductor: Luigi Preti

Dec 21, 28
LA INDIGENA (Wenceslao
Fumi)(Sp)***
Atala: Altieri
Chactas: Lelmi
Padre Aubey: Walter
Simaghan: Enamorado

1863

Female artists
Buil, Eloisa <s>
Dagle, Mariana <s>
Giovanelli, Matilda <mez>
Larrumbe, Adelaida <s>
Mollo, Marietta <s>
Manzini, Constanza <s>
Vitali, Ida <a>

Male artists
Antoni, Pietro de <b>
Ballerini, Emidio [Emilio] <t>
Bertolini, Giuseppe <bar>
Chiodini, Angelo <b>
Julien, Paul <vn>
Lelmi, Luis <t>
Liguori, Ermenegildo <pf>
Monteverde, A. <t>
Napoleão, Artur <pf>
Scarabelli, Vincenzo <b>
Walter, Carlo <b>

Jan 1
TROUPE DES BOUFFES PARISIENS

[continuation of the 1862 opera
season]

Jan 4
IL TROVATORE (Verdi)
Leonora: Larrumbe
Manrico: Lelmi
Azucena: Giovanelli
Conte di Luna: Walter
Ferrando: Scarabelli

Jan 11
Operatic Concert

Feb 1 to March 1
Carnival Masked Balls

March 2 to 16
Italian Dramatic Company

March 17 to April 9, 12 to 30,
Aug 16 to 23
Spanish Dramatic Company of
Toral-Cubas

April 9
Recital: Napoleão <pf>
Prudent: Grande Fantasia after
Lucia di Lammermoor
Napoleão: Fantasia after Un
ballo in maschera
Napoleão: Grand Polka de
Concierto
Herz: Paraphrase after La fille
du régiment

April 10, 11
Concerts: Napoleão <pf> and
orchestra

May 1 to July 26
[No theatrical performances in
Montevideo.]

**SPRING ITALIAN OPERA
SEASON**
Aug 25 to Oct 25
Conductor: Serafino De Ferrari

Aug 25, Sept 17, Oct 11, 13
Uruguayan National Anthem
LA TRAVIATA (Verdi)
Violetta: Mollo
Alfredo Germont: Lelmi
Giorgio Germont: Bertolini
Flora: Vitali
Marchese D'Obigny: Chiodini
Dottore Grenvil: de Antoni

Aug 30, Sept 6, 8, 13
ERNANI (Verdi)
Elvira: Mollo
Ernani: Lelmi
Don Carlo: Bertolini
D. Ruy Gomez de Silva: de
Antoni

Sept 3, 12
IL TROVATORE (Verdi)
Leonora: Mollo
Manrico: Lelmi
Azucena: Vitali
Conte di Luna: Bertolini
Ferrando: de Antoni

Sept 20, Oct 8, 25
NORMA (Bellini)
Norma: Mollo
Adalgisa: Vitali
Pollione: Lelmi
Oroveso: de Antoni

Sept 23, Oct 1
LUISA MILLER (Verdi)
Luisa: Mollo
Rodolfo: Lelmi
Federica: Vitali
Miller: Bertolini
Wurm: de Antoni

Sept 24, 27, Oct 4, 15, 20
UN BALLO IN MASCHERA (Verdi)
Amelia: Mollo
Riccardo: Lelmi
Renato: Bertolini
Ulrica: Vitali
Oscar: Buil

Silvano: Chiodini
Samuel: Scarabelli

Sept 29
LUCIA DI LAMMERMOOR
(Donizetti)
Lucia: Mollo
Edgardo: Lelmi
Enrico: Bertolini
Raimondo: de Antoni
Arturo: Monteverde

Oct 18, Nov 5
IL BARBIERE DI SIVIGLIA
(Rossini)
Rosina: Mollo
Conte di Almaviva: Lelmi
Figaro: Bertolini
Don Basilio: de Antoni
Don Bartolo: Chiodini

Oct 22
RIGOLETTO (Verdi)
Gilda: Mollo
Il Duca di Mantova: Lelmi
Rigoletto: Bertolini
Maddalena: Vitali
Sparafucile: de Antoni
Monterone: Scarabelli
Ceprano: Walter

Oct 25
NORMA (Bellini)
[same cast as Sept 20]
and *Concert* Opera Company
artists

Nov 3
Spanish Zarzuela and Comedy
Company

Nov 8
Lyric Company Concert with
child Liguori <pf>

**SUMMER ITALIAN OPERA
SEASON**
Manzini-Ballerini Company
Nov 12 to Dec 6

Nov 12
BONDELMONTE (Pacini)
Beatrice: Manzini
Bondelmonte: Ballerini
Bianca Donati: Buil
Amedei: Bertolini
Isaura: Dagle
Uberti: de Antoni
Gangalandi: Scarabelli

Nov 14
Concert Benefit to M. Mollo

Nov 22
Operatic Concert

Nov 24
Operatic Concert and Julien <vn>

Nov 29, Dec 3
L'EBREO (Apolloni)
Leila: Manzini
Adel-Musa: Ballerini
Issachar: Bertolini
Ferdinando Re di Aragona: de
Antoni
and *Concert* with E. Liguori <pf>

Dec 6
LUCIA DI LAMMERMOOR
(Donizetti)
Lucia: Manzini
Edgardo: Ballerini
Enrico: Bertolini
Raimondo: de Antoni
Arturo: Monteverde

1864

Female artists
Amey, Giuseppina <s>
Manaresi, Clarise <s>
Morini, Luigia <mez>
Serrano (Sereno), Teresa <s>

Male artists
Arnaldi, Francesco <b>

Cesari, Inocente <bar>
Dondi, Enrico <b>
Giuffra, Señor <pf>
Hericourt, Luis <t>
Manaresi, Giobbe <t>

TROUPE DES BOUFFES
PARISIENS SEASON
Jan 1 to Feb 2
Conductor: Leon D'Hôte

Jan 30
Brak [*sic*] Neck Acts American
Acrobatic Company from
Niagara

Feb 7 to 14, 26 to 28
Carnival Masked Balls

April 11
STILL WATERS RUN DEEP
(Ryssens)
and *Concert* Choir of H.R.H.
Forte

May 28
Spanish Dramatic Company

June 1
Operatic Concert
Conductor: Luigi Preti

WINTER ITALIAN OPERA
SEASON
Aug 7 to Nov
Conductor: Luigi Preti

Aug 7, 18, 21, Sept 25
IL TROVATORE (Verdi)
Leonora: Amey (3) / Serrano(1)
Manrico: G. Manaresi
Conte di Luna: Cesari
Azucena: Morini
Ferrando: Arnaldi
Ruiz: Hericourt
Inez: C. Manaresi

Aug 14
ERNANI (Verdi)
Elvira: Amey
Ernani: G. Manaresi
Don Carlo: Cesari
D. Ruy Gomez de Silva: Arnaldi
Clotilde: C. Manaresi
Don Riccardo: Hericourt

Aug 25, Sept 18, 22
Uruguayan National Anthem
NORMA (Bellini)
Norma: Amey
Adalgisa: Sereno
Pollione: G. Manaresi
Clotilde: C. Manaresi
Oroveso: Cesari
Flavio: Hericourt

Oct 11
LA TRAVIATA (Verdi)
Violetta: Amey
Flora: Morini
Annina: C. Manaresi
Alfredo Germont: G. Manaresi
Giorgio Germont: Cesari
Gastone: Hericourt
Dottore Grenvil: Arnaldi

Oct 16
ERNANI (Verdi)
Elvira: Serrano
Ernani: G. Manaresi
Don Carlo: Cesari
D. Ruy Gomez de Silva: Arnaldi
Clotilde: C. Manaresi
Don Riccardo: Hericourt

Oct 20
Operatic *Concert* and Giuffra
<pf>
[The 1864 Opera Season
continued until the end of
November, but there are no
newspapers or programs
available.]
Performances announced for
Nov:

UN BALLO IN MASCHERA (Verdi)
I DUE FOSCARI (Verdi)

Dec 8
Italian Dramatic Company
Homage to Garibaldi

1865

Female artists
Briol, Carolina <s>
Buil, Eloisa <mez>
Julien, Elodie <pf>
Mariotti, Rosina <mez>
Mollo, Marietta <s>
Morini, Luigia <mez>
Serrano, Teresa <s>

Male artists
Arnaldi, Francesco <b>
Celestino, Antonio Ma. <bar>
Hericourt, Luis <t>
Innocenti, Cesare <bar>
Julien, Paul <vn>
Lelmi, Luis <t>
Manaresi, Giobbe <t>
Nerini, Gian-Carlo <b>
Pozzolini, Atanasio <t>
Schramm, Carlos <pf>
Uguccioni, Alejandro <vn>
Werner, Carlos <vn>

March 15 to April 15
Carnival Masked Balls

April 23, 30, May 11
Concerts
Scottish Campanologists (150 bells)

April 25
Concert
German Vocal Societies of
Montevideo and Buenos Aires
and orchestra

May 17, 21, June 11, 15
Symphonic Concerts

Conductor: Luigi Preti
Soloist: P. Julien <vn>

June 1, 4
Symphonic Concerts
Conductor/soloist: Alejandro
Uguccioni <vn>

June 10, 13
Operatic Concerts
Conductor: Luigi Preti
Cast: Serrano, Innocenti,
Manaresi, orchestra and chorus

July 3, 6
Recitals: Werner <vn> and
Schramm <pf>
Works by Bach, Rossini,
Thalberg, Prudent, Servais,
Tedesco, etc.

ITALIAN OPERA SEASON
Mollo-Pozzolini Company
July 8 to Nov 25
Conductor: Luigi Preti

July 8
ERNANI (Verdi)
Elvira: Serrano
Ernani: Manaresi
Don Carlo: Innocenti
D. Ruy Gomez de Silva: Nerini

July 30, Aug 6, 11
Recitals: P. and E. Julien <vn/pf>

Aug 25, Sept 8, Nov 23
Uruguayan National Anthem
ERNANI (Verdi)
Elvira: Mollo
Ernani: Pozzolini
Don Carlo: Innocenti
D. Ruy Gomez de Silva: Nerini

Aug 31, Oct 8, Nov 16
LA TRAVIATA (Verdi)
Violetta: Mollo

Alfredo Germont: Pozzolini
Giorgio Germont: Innocenti
Flora: Buil
Gastone: Hericourt
Barone Douphol: Nerini
Dottore Grenvil: Arnaldi

Oct 11
IL TROVATORE (Verdi)
Leonora: Mollo
Manrico: Pozzolini
Conte di Luna: Innocenti
Azucena: Mariotti
Ruiz: Hericourt
Ferrando: Nerini

Oct 19
UN BALLO IN MASCHERA (Verdi)
Amelia: Mollo
Riccardo: Pozzolini
Renato: Innocenti
Oscar: Briol
Ulrica: Mariotti
Samuel: Nerini

Oct 21
EL DESTINO DE MATOSO
(Preti)****
(First Uruguayan zarzuela)
Cast: Mollo, Mariotti; Pozzolini,
Innocenti

Nov 12
LUCIA DI LAMMERMOOR
(Donizetti)
Lucia: Mollo
Edgardo: Pozzolini
Enrico: Innocenti
Arturo: Hericourt
Raimondo: Nerini

Nov 18
GEMMA DI VERGY (Donizetti)
Gemma: Mollo
Tomasso: Pozzolini
Conte di Vergy: Innocenti
Guido: Nerini

Nov 25
NABUCCO (Verdi)
Abigaille: Mollo
Nabucco: Innocenti
Ismaele: Pozzolini
Zaccaria: Nerini

**SUMMER / FALL ITALIAN
OPERA SEASON**
Antonio Pestalardo, Impresario
Dec 31, 1865, to May 23, 1866
Conductor: Luigi Preti

Dec 31
RIGOLETTO (Verdi)
Gilda: Briol
Il Duca di Mantova: Lelmi
Rigoletto: Celestino
Sparafucile: Nerini
Maddalena: Mariotti

1866

Female artists
Bajetti, Teresa <s>
Briol, Carolina <s>
Buil, Eloisa <mez>
Julien, Elodie <pf>
Lyon, Pauline <s>
Mariotti, Rosina <mez>
Morini, Luigia <mez>
Sánchez, Ramona <s>

Male artists
Cavedagni, Luigi <bar>
Celestino, Antonio Ma. <bar>
Hericourt, Luis <t>
Innocenti, Cesare <bar>
Julien, Paul <vn>
Lelmi, Luis <t>
Nerini, Gian-Carlo <b>
Noury, Mr. <t>
Pozzolini, Atanasio <t>
Sampaio, Juvenal <pf>
Taffurelli, Dario <cl>

Jan 2, 6
RIGOLETTO (Verdi)
Gilda: Briol
Il Duca di Mantova: Lelmi
Rigoletto: Celestino
Sparafucile: Nerini
Maddalena: Mariotti

Jan 5, 7
LA TRAVIATA (Verdi)
Violetta: Briol
Alfredo Germont: Lelmi
Giorgio Germont: Celestino
Flora: Buil
Barone Douphol: Nerini

Jan 9, 10, 14
JONE (Petrella)**
Jone: Briol
Nidia: Mariotti
Glauco: Lelmi
Arbace: Celestino
Burbo: Nerini

Jan 17, 21
UN BALLO IN MASCHERA (Verdi)
Amelia: Briol
Riccardo: Lelmi
Renato: Celestino
Ulrica: Buil
Oscar: Mariotti
and *Concert* with soloist: P.
Julien <vn> (Jan 17)

Jan 19, 20, 25, 30, Feb 7, 9, 16, 18
MARTHA (Flotow)
Lady Harriet: Briol
Lionel: Lelmi
Lord Tristan: Nerini
Nancy: Mariotti
Plunkett: Celestino

Jan 22, Feb 6
ERNANI (Verdi)
Elvira: Briol
Ernani: Lelmi

Don Carlo: Celestino
D. Ruy Gomez de Silva: Nerini

Jan 24, Feb 20
IL TROVATORE (Verdi)
Leonora: Briol
Manrico: Lelmi
Conte di Luna: Celestino
Azucena: Buil

Jan 28
LA FAVORITA (Donizetti) (It)
Leonora: Mariotti
Fernando: Lelmi
Alfonso XI: Celestino

Feb 1
STABAT MATER (Rossini)

Feb 11 to 24
Carnival Masked Balls

Feb 23, 25
NORMA (Bellini)
Norma: Briol
Adalgisa: Mariotti
Pollione: Lelmi
Oroveso: Nerini
and *Concert* by C. Briol

Feb 28
MEDEA (Pacini)**
Medea: Briol
Giasone: Lelmi
Creonte: Celestino
Calcante: Nerini

March 1, 7
Operatic Concerts
Soloist: P. Julien <vn>

March 11
Operatic Concert
Soloist: Taffurelli <cl>

March 24, April 11
Symphonic Concerts
Conductor: Alejandro Uguccioni
Soloist: Sampaio <pf>

April 15, 18
LUCIA DI LAMMERMOOR
(Donizetti)
Lucia: Bajetti
Edgardo: Pozzolini
Enrico: Innocenti
Alisa: Morini

April 22, May 6, 18
UN BALLO IN MASCHERA (Verdi)
Amelia: Bajetti
Riccardo: Pozzolini
Renato: Innocenti
Ulrica: Buil
Oscar: Mariotti

April 28, 29, May 1
I MASNADIERI (Verdi)
Amalia: Bajetti
Carlo: Pozzolini
Francesco: Innocenti
Massimiliano: Nerini

May 10
IL TROVATORE (Verdi)
Leonora: Bajetti
Manrico: Pozzolini
Conte di Luna: Innocenti
Azucena: Buil

May 23
IL BARBIERE DI SIVIGLIA
(Rossini)
Rosina: Bajetti
Conte di Almaviva: Pozzolini
Figaro: Innocenti
Don Basilio: Nerini

June 2, 16
Symphonic Concerts
Conductor: Alejandro Uguccioni
Soloist: Sampaio <pf>

TROUPE DES BOUFFES
PARISIENS OPERETTA
SEASON
June 7 to July 30
Conductor: Mr. Poppe

June 7, 9, 15
LES SALTIMBANQUES (Ganne)

June 10
L'HOMME N'EST PAS PARFAIT
(Thiboush)

June 21
MARIE JEANNE (Mallian)

June 24
CE QUE FEMME VEUT!!!
(Lauzanne)

June 29
LA MARIEE DU MARDI GRAS
(Thiboush)

July 1
ATAR-GULL (Mason)

July 5
CROQUEFER (Offenbach)

July 8
TROMB-AL-CA-ZAR (Offenbach)

July 12, 18
SCHAHABAHAM II (Pope)

July 15
LA PETITE POLOGNE(?)

July 20
LES MISTERES DE L'ETE (Pope?)

July 22
LES FEMMES QUI PLEURENT
(Thiboush)

July 27, 28, 30
LES DEUX PECHEURS (Offenbach)

Aug 4 to 23, 26 to Sept 23
Keller Company Tableaux
Vivant

Aug 25
Uruguayan National Anthem
Concert and Drama
Conductor: Luigi Preti
Soloist: Buil <s>

SPRING / SUMMER CONCERT
SEASON
Sept 21 to Dec 30
Conductor: Luigi Preti

Sept 21, 25
Concerts
Pozzolini <t>, P. Julien <vn>,
E. Julien <pf> Nabucco: Violin
fantasia
Lucia: Tenor aria
Semiramide: Piano paraphrase
Julien: Polka
La favorite: Tenor aria
Marthe: Grand fantasia pour
violon

October 4 to 16
Peyres de la Journade <mime
and prestidigitator>

October 6
Symphonic Concert
Orquesta de la Sociedad
Filarmónica
Soloists: Preti <vn> P. Julien
<vn>, E. Julien <pf>
Stradella: Trio
Il barbiere: La Calunnia
Beriot: Duet for Two Violins
Gottschalk: La dernière
espérance (Meditation)
Schulhoff: Waltz de Concert
Alard: Souvenir de Donizetti
Auber: La muette de Portici
Julien: Bolero venezolano
Gottschalk: Ojos criollos
Carnaval de Venecia: Duet for
two violins

October 19 and 20
Spanish Dramatic Company of
Enrique Revilla

October 21 to November 18
Françoise Peyres <six-year-old
mime>

December 21, 23, 30
Summer Operatic Concerts

1867

Female artists
Barry, Emily <s/pf>
Briol, Carolina <s>
Mollo, Marietta <s>
Sánchez, Ramona <s>
Serrano (Sereno), Teresa <s>
Vassoni (Vassori), Signora <mez>

Male artists
Bengoechea, Pedro <pf>
Bonetti, Edoardo <bar>
Celestino, Antonio María <bar>
Celestino, A., Jr. <pf>
Croner, Rafael <cl / sax>
Costa, Dalmiro <pf>
Faget, Paul <pf>
Faget, Eduardo <pf>
Gottschalk, Louis Moreau <pf>
Jouffre, Monsieur <pf>
Lelmi, Luis <t>
Llovet y Castellet, Juan <pf>
Nerini, Gian-Carlo <b>
Round, Señor <org / pf>
Walter, Luigi <b>

**SUMMER OPERATIC
CONCERTS**
Conductor: Luigi Preti
Jan 6, 13, 20 and 25
Artists: Briol, Sánchez; Lelmi,
Celestino, chorus and orchestra

Feb 3, 9
Recitals: Costa <pf>, A. M.
Celestino <bar>

March 2 to 25
Carnival Masked Balls

ITALIAN OPERA SEASON
Federico Nicolao, Impresario
April 21 to Dec 29
Conductor: Luigi Preti

April 21, 26, Aug 9, 11, 15, Oct 13
ERNANI (Verdi)
Donna Elvira: Briol
Ernani: Lelmi
Don Carlo: Celestino

April 24, 28, Aug 4, 28, 30
LA TRAVIATA (Verdi)
Violetta: Briol
Alfredo Germont: Lelmi
Giorgio Germont: Celestino

May 1
LUCIA DI LAMMERMOOR
(Donizetti)
Lucia: Briol
Edgardo: Lelmi
Enrico: Celestino
Raimondo: Nerini

May 5, 26, Dec 18
NORMA (Bellini)
Norma: Briol
Adalgisa: Sereno
Pollione: Lelmi
Oroveso: Nerini

May 8, 10, 12, Aug 18, Sept 20,
Oct 20
VITTORE PISANI (A. Peri)**
Maria Pisani: Briol
Pietro, pescatore: Lelmi
Vittore Pisani: Celestino
Antonio Barbo: Walter

May 17, 19, June 30, Dec 11, 15
JONE (Petrella)
Jone: Briol
Nidia: Vassoni
Glauco: Lelmi
Arbace: Bonetti
Burbo: Nerini

May 23, 30, June 2, 9, July 19, 24
to 26
LA FORZA DEL DESTINO (Verdi)**
Leonora: Briol
Preziosilla: Mollo
Don Alvaro: Lelmi
Don Carlo: Bonetti
Padre guardiano: Walter
Marchese di Calatrava: Celestino

June 5, 7, 16, 20, 24, 29, Dec 1
MARTHA (Flotow)
Lady Harriet: Briol
Lionel: Lelmi
Lord Tristan: Celestino

June 12, 13
CRISPINO E LA COMARE (Rossi)**
Annetta: Briol
La Comare: Mollo
Contino del Fiore: Lelmi
Fabrizio: Celestino

July 5, 11, 28, Dec 25, 27
FAUST (Gounod)** (It)
Margherita: Briol
Faust: Lelmi
Mefistofele: Nerini
Valentin: Celestino
Siebel: Vassoni

July 7
LUCREZIA BORGIA (Donizetti)
Lucrezia: Briol
Gennaro: Lelmi
Duca Alfonso: Celestino

July 15, 29
UN BALLO IN MASCHERA (Verdi)
Amelia: Briol
Riccardo: Lelmi
Renato: Celestino

Aug 19
Briol Lyric Company Concert
and Gottschalk <pf> playing his
own works, with Celestino Jr.
<2d pf>
La traviata: Acts 1, 2, and 3
Fantasia for two pf on Martha:
Gottschalk and Celestino
I lombardi's aria: Nerini
Fantasia La figlia del reggimento:
Gottschalk
Fantasía sobre el Himno
Uruguayo: Gottschalk
Ernani's aria: Nerini
Recuerdos del Teatro Italiano,
Gran fantasia de bravura:
Gottschalk

Sept 6, 8, Oct 5
LA FIGLIA DEL REGGIMENTO
(Donizetti)
Maria: Briol
Tonio: Lelmi
Contessa: Vassori
Sulpizio: Nerini

Sept 11
Briol Lyric Company Concert
and Gottschalk <pf> playing his
own works, with Bengoechea
<2nd pf>
Ernani: Acts 1 and 2
Gran duo de bravura after Il
trovatore (two pf): Gottschalk /
Bengoechea
Un ballo in maschera's aria:
Celestino
Murmures éoliens: Gottschalk
Il trovatore's aria: Celestino
Le banjo: Gottschalk

Ses yeux, polka for two pf:
Gottschalk / Bengoechea

Sept 15
Briol Lyric Company Concert
and Gottschalk <pf> playing his
own works, with Llovet <2d pf>
La figlia del reggimento:
excerpts
In program:
    1. Tarantelle***
    2. Grand fantasía sobre temas
        de Faust

Sept 18
Briol Lyric Company Concert
and Gottschalk <pf> playing his
own works, with Celestino Jr.
<2d pf>
La traviata: excerpts

Sept 20
VITTORE PISANI (A. Peri)
and Recital: Croner <cl/sax>
Croner: Fantasia after Martha
<sax>
Cavallini: Souvenir de Norma
<cl>
Croner: Variations after La
sonnambula <sax>
Cavallini: Canto greco, fantasia
for clarinet

Sept 22
Briol Lyric Company Concert
and Gottschalk <pf> playing his
own works, with Celestino Jr.
<2d pf>
La figlia del reggimento: excerpts
1. Tarantelle
2. Le carnaval de Venise
3. Lucia de Lammermoor
    Fantasia
4. Souvenirs d'Andalousie,
    caprice de concert
5. Brind al Eré after Sanderson

6. Le poète mourant-Meditation
7. Home Sweet Home, Caprice

Sept 27, 28, 30
American Dramatic Company of
German Mackay

Sept 29
Recital: Croner <cl>

Oct 1
Briol Lyric Company Concert
La traviata: Act 3
and Concert for twelve pianos:
Gottschalk plays his own works
with Bengoechea, Celestino Jr.,
Faget Sr., Jouffre, Round, Faget
Jr., and others <pf>
    1. La dernière espérance
    2. Fantasia sur La favorita
    3. Marche de nuit
    4. The Last Rose of Summer
    5. Bridal Eve
    6. Grande marche sur Tann-
        häuser
    7. Grande marche sur Faust

Oct 5
LA FIGLIA DEL REGGIMENTO
(Donizetti) (It)
and American Dramatic
Company German Mackay

Nov 27, Dec 8
RIGOLETTO (Verdi)
Gilda: Briol
Il Duca di Mantova: Lelmi
Rigoletto: Celestino
Sparafucile: Nerini
Maddalena: Vassoni

Dec 4, 5, 6
IL TROVATORE (Verdi)
Leonora: Briol
Manrico: Lelmi
Conte di Luna: Celestino

Azucena: Vassori
Ferrando: Nerini

Dec 20, 22, 29
BONDELMONTE (Pacini)
Beatrice: Briol
Isaura: Mollo
Bondelmonte: Lelmi
Amedei: Celestino
Uberti: Nerini

1868

Female artists
Buil, Eloisa <s / mez>
Briol, Carolina <s>
Bruzzone, Elvira <s>
Bruzzone, Rosita <mez>
Carozzi-Zucchi, Carlotta <s>
Forlivesi, Felicita <mez>
Petrini, Clotilde <s>
Zacconi Musella, Letizia <s / mez>

Male artists
Basetti, Signor <bar>
Bergamaschi, Adolfo <b / bar>
Bonetti, Edoardo <bar>
Bruzzone, Signor <t>
Celestino, Antonio María <bar>
Chiodini, Angelo <b>
Faget, Eduardo <pf>
Faget, Paul <pf>
Gaddi, Luigi <b>
Gottschalk, Louis Moreau <pf>
Irfré, Héctor <t>
Jouffre, Monsieur <pf>
Lelmi, Luis <t>
Messager, Monsieur <pf>
Nerini, Gian-Carlo <b>
Ordinas, Juan <b>
Pons, Rafael <pf>
Pozzolini, Atanasio <t>
Round, Señor <pf>
Scarabelli, Vincenzo <b>
Zennari, Angelo <t>

ITALIAN OPERA SEASON
[continuation of the 1867 season]
Conductor: Luigi Preti

Jan 1
IL TROVATORE (Verdi)
Leonora: Briol
Manrico: Lelmi
Conte di Luna: Celestino
Azucena: Forlivesi
Ruiz: Gaddi
Ferrando: Bergamaschi

July 5 to 31
Spanish Dramatic Company
Germán Mackay–José
Enamorado

**TROUPE DES BOUFFES
PARISIENS OPERETTA
SEASON**
Aug 8 to Oct 23
Conductor: Leon D'Hote

Aug 8, 11
LES CANOTIERS DE LA SEINE
(A. M.Orey)

Aug 23
LE MARI A LA PORTE
(Offenbach)

Aug 25
Uruguayan National Anthem
Operatic Concert and Spanish
zarzuela and Italian opera
excerpts
Conductor: Luigi Preti

Sept 3
LA GRANDE DUCHESSE DE
GEROLSTEIN (Offenbach)

Sept 4, 11, 17, 27, 28, Oct 18
Spanish Dramatic Company

Sept 6
Three vaudevilles

Sept 19, 20
ORPHEE AUX ENFERS
(Offenbach)

Sept 24, Oct 23
LA CHATTE METAMORPHOSEE EN
FEMME (Offenbach)
and two vaudevilles

Oct 3 to 16
Imperial Japanese Company
Music and Drama

Oct 23
LA CHATTE METAMORPHOSEE EN
FEMME (Offenbach)
and LES CONTRIBUTIONS
INDIRECTES (?) and *Concert* for
sixteen pf: Gottschalk playing
his own works with Faget Sr.,
Faget Jr., Jouffre, Messager,
Pons, Round, and others
  1. Grande fantasie sur Martha
  2. Murmures éoliens
  3. Le banjo
  4. Grande marche Tannhäu-
     ser for sixteen pianos
  5. Grande Fantasie sur
     l'Hymne Oriental
  6. The Last Rose of Summer
  7. Grandetarantelle<pf / orch>
  8. Grand marche sur Faust
     for sixteen pianos

**SPRING / SUMMER ITALIAN
OPERA SEASON**
Oct 25 to September 29, 1869
Conductor: Luigi Preti

Oct 25
LA TRAVIATA (Verdi)
Violetta: Bruzzone
Alfredo Germont: Zennari
Giorgio Germont: Bergamaschi

Oct 27, 28, 29
IL TROVATORE (Verdi)
Leonora: Petrini
Manrico: Pozzolini
Conte di Luna: Bonetti
Azucena: Forlivesi
Ruiz: Gaddi
Ferrando: Bergamaschi

Oct 31
Operatic Concert
and Spanish Zarzuela Company

Nov 6, 8
UN BALLO IN MASCHERA (Verdi)
Amelia: Petrini
Riccardo: Pozzolini
Renato: Bonetti
Ulrica: Forlivesi
Oscar: Briol

Nov 10, Dec 1
Concerts (orchestra of three
hundred)
Gottschalk conducts his works
  1. Marche solennelle sur Le
     prophète
  2. La chase du jeune Henri
  3. Prière du Moïse
  4. Symphonie no. 2 ("A
     Montevideo")****

Nov 13, 14, 15
RIGOLETTO (Verdi)
Gilda: E. Bruzzone
Il Duca di Mantova: Zennari
Rigoletto: Bonetti
Maddalena: R. Bruzzone
Sparafucile: Scarabelli

Nov 20, 25
LUCREZIA BORGIA (Donizetti)
Lucrezia: Petrini / Zacconi
Gennaro: Pozzolini / Zennari
Duca Alfonso: Bonetti / Ordinas
Maffio Orsini: Forlivesi
Gubetta: Bergamaschi

Rustighello: Chiodini
Gazella: Scarabelli
Liverotto: Bruzzone

Nov 21, Dec 3, 6, 8, 20
NORMA (Bellini)
Norma: Zacconi(1) / Carozzi-
Zucchi(4)
Adalgisa: Carozzi-Zucchi(1) /
Zacconi(4)
Pollione: Pozzolini
Oroveso: Nerini

Dec 11, 12, 13
LA FAVORITA (Donizetti) (It)
Leonora: Carozzi-Zucchi
Fernando: Zennari
Alfonso XI: Bonetti
Baldassare: Ordinas
Gaspare: Chiodini
Inez: E. Bruzzone

Dec 15
Spanish Zarzuela Company

Dec 16, 18
ERNANI (Verdi)
Elvira: Carozzi-Zucchi
Ernani: Zennari
Don Carlo: Bonetti
D. Ruy Gomez de Silva: Ordinas

Dec 23
IL TROVATORE (Verdi)
Leonora: Carozzi-Zucchi
Manrico: Pozzolini
Conte di Luna: Bonetti
Azucena: Zacconi
Ruiz: Gaddi
Ferrando: Bergamaschi

Dec 30
POLIUTO (Donizetti)**
Paolina: Carozzi-Zucchi
Poliuto: Irfré
Severus: Bonetti
Callisthenes: Ordinas

Felice: Chiodini
Nearco: Bruzzone

1869

Female artists
Bruzzone, Rosita <mez>
Carozzi-Zucchi, Carlotta <s>
Escalante, Isabella M. <s>
Zacconi Musella, Letizia <s / mez>

Male artists
Bonetti, Edoardo <bar>
Conti Marroni, Luigi <b>
Gaddi, Luigi <b>
Irfré, Héctor <t>
Franco, Señor <harp>
Franco, Señor <vn>
Lelmi, Luis <t>
Nerini, Gian-Carlo <b>
Ordinas, Juan <b>
Sampaio, Juvenal <pf>
Zennari, Angelo <t>

**ITALIAN OPERA AND
BALLET SEASON**
[continuation of the 1868 season
to Sept 30]
Conductor: Angelo Agostini
Principal Dancers: Ernestina
Ardizzoni, Virginia Balsamo,
Enriquetta Bay, Ettore
Poggiolesi, Celestina Ratti

Jan 5, Feb 5, 12, April 7, 9, 21,
29, May 18, June 3, 6, July 28,
Sept 22, 29
IL TROVATORE (Verdi)
Leonora: Carozzi-Zucchi
Manrico: Zennari(5) / Irfré(8)
Conte di Luna: Bonetti(8) /
Conti(5)
Azucena: Zacconi
Ferrando: Nerini
Ruiz: Gaddi

Jan 6, May 15
LUCREZIA BORGIA (Donizetti)
Lucrezia: Carozzi-Zucchi
Gennaro: Zennari
Duca Alfonso: Bonetti

Jan 8, April 16, 19, May 4, 6,
Aug 4, Oct 6
ERNANI (Verdi)
Elvira: Carozzi-Zucchi
Ernani: Zennari(3) / Irfré(4)
Don Carlo: Bonetti
D. Ruy Gomez de Silva: Nerini

Jan 17, 23, 30
Masked Balls

Jan 19, Feb 26, April 24, May 16,
July 7, Sept 5, Oct 3
POLIUTO (Donizetti)
Paolina: Carozzi-Zucchi
Poliuto: Irfré(6) / Zennari(1)
Severus: Bonetti
Callisthenes: Ordinas

Jan 20, July 16
LA TRAVIATA (Verdi)
Violetta: Carozzi-Zucchi
Alfredo Germont: Zennari
Giorgio Germont: Bonetti

Jan 24
Recital: Franco brothers <vn /
harp>

Jan 29, March 12, April 22
LUCIA DI LAMMERMOOR
(Donizetti)
Lucia: Zacconi
Edgardo: Zennari
Enrico: Bonetti
Raimondo: Nerini

Feb 6 to 14
Carnival Masked Balls

Feb 17, 21, March 31, May 12,
June 11
SAFFO (Pacini)
Saffo: Carozzi-Zucchi
Faone: Zacconi
Alcandro: Bonetti
Climene: Bruzzone

Feb 24, March 14, April 18, May
9, July 30,
Aug 22, Dec 8, 15
NORMA (Bellini)
Norma: Carozzi-Zucchi
Adalgisa: Zacconi(6) /
Escalante(2)
Pollione: Zennari(6) / Lelmi(2)
Oroveso: Ordinas

March 3, 6, 10, May 2
FAUST (Gounod) (It)
Margherita: Zacconi
Faust: Zennari
Mefistofele: Nerini
Valentin: Bonetti

March 27
STABAT MATER (Rossini)
and Operatic Concert
Artists: Carozzi-Zucchi,
Bruzzone Zennari, Bonetti,
Ordinas

April 2, 4, 11, May 1, Aug 11
UN BALLO IN MASCHERA (Verdi)
Amelia: Carozzi-Zucchi
Riccardo: Zennari
Renato: Conti
Ulrica: Bruzzone
Oscar: Zacconi
Samuel: Ordinas

April 27, July 19
LA FAVORITA (Donizetti) (It)
Leonora: Carozzi-Zucchi
Fernando: Zennari
Alfonso XI: Bonetti

May 22, 23, 25, 30, June 9, 13,
24, 27, July 4, 18, 23, Aug 1, 13
L'AFRICANA (Meyerbeer)** (It)
Selika: Carozzi-Zucchi
Vasco da Gama: Zennari
Nelusko: Bonetti
Anna: Zacconi

June 19, 21, July 25, Aug 15, Sept
15
LA FORZA DEL DESTINO (Verdi)
Leonora: Carozzi-Zucchi
Don Alvaro: Irfré
Don Carlo: Bonetti
Preziosilla: Zacconi
Marchese di Calatrava: Nerini
Padre Guardiano: Conti

June 26, July 14
Operatic Concerts and Ballet
GISELLE (Adam)

July 9, 11, 21, Sept 8
RIGOLETTO (Verdi)
Gilda: Carozzi-Zucchi
Il Duca di Mantova: Irfré
Rigoletto: Conti
Maddalena: Zacconi
Sparafucile: Nerini
Giovanna: Bruzzone
Ceprano: Gaddi
Monterone: Scarabelli

July 25
LA FORZA DEL DESTINO (Verdi)
[same cast as July 19]
and DORINA (ballet)

Aug 5, 8, 18, 25, 29, Sept 3
UNA VENDETTA (Agostini)**
Don Alvaro de Tellez: Ordinas
Don Rodrigo de Tellez: Irfré
Julia Pacheco: Carozzi-Zucchi
Francisco Pacheco: Bonetti
Floridas de Silva: Zacconi
Sancho Sandoval: Gaddi
and GISELLE (Adam)

Sept 11, 12, 17, 19, 24, 26, 30
ROBERTO IL DIAVOLO
(Meyerbeer) (It)
Alice: Carozzi-Zucchi
Roberto Duca di Normandia:
Irfré
Isabella di Sicilia: Escalante
Rambaldo: Lelmi
Alberti: Bonetti
Bertramo: Conti

Sept 15
LA FORZA DEL DESTINO (Verdi)
[same cast as July 19]
and Ballet with Ettore Poggiolesi

Sept 22, 29
IL TROVATORE (Verdi)
and Ballet performance

Oct 23
Operatic Concert
and J. Sampaio <pf> playing his
own works

Oct 24
Operatic Concert

Oct 27 to Nov 19
Italian Dramatic Company
Adelaida Ristori

Dec 2 to 6
Señor Blach <Catalan
prestidigitator>

Dec 24 to 26
Holiday Masked Balls

————————————

1870

————————————

Female artists
Buil, Eloisa <s / mez>
Escalante, Isabella M. <mez / s>
Estagel, Signora <mez>
Gery, Agzema <s>
Heine, Ada <pf>

Martínez, L. <mez>
Pasi, Amelia <s>
Patti, Carlotta <s>
Sartori, Elvira <d>

Male artists
Antinori, Vicente <t>
Ballerini, Emidio [Emilio] <t>
Bonetti, Edoardo <bar>
Calvo, Carmelo <pf / c>
Camps, Antonio <armonium>
Chiodini, Angelo <b>
Ferrari, P. <b>
Forest, Monsieur <t>
Gaddi, Luigi <b>
Heine, José <vn>
Marchetti, A. <t>
Nerini, Gian-Carlo <b>
Ritter, Teodoro <pf>
Rossi-Ghelli, Achille <bar>
Sarasate, Pablo de <vn>

Feb (all month)
Carnival Masked Balls

March 8, 12, 16
Recitals: A. Heine <pf>, J.
Heine <vn>, Buil <s> and
Sartori <d>

March 25, April 10
French Operetta Company
Estagel-Forest

April 12 to 20
The Passion, Dramatic Religious
Play

ITALIAN OPERA SEASON
April 28 to Oct 2
Conductor: Serafino De Ferrari
Principal dancer: Sartori

April 28, 29
LA TRAVIATA (Verdi)
Violetta: Pasi
Alfredo Germont: Ballerini
Giorgio Germont: Rossi-Ghelli

May 6, 7, 11, 12, 25
NABUCCO (Verdi)
Abigaille: Pasi
Nabucco: Rossi-Ghelli
Ismaele: Ballerini
Zaccaria: Nerini
and Ballet

May 15, June 7, July 17, Aug 25
UN BALLO IN MASCHERA (Verdi)
Amelia: Pasi
Riccardo: Ballerini
Renato: Rossi-Ghelli
Ulrica: Escalante
Oscar: Gery
Tom: Ferrari
Samuel: Gaddi

May 24, Aug 27
ERNANI (Verdi)
Elvira: Pasi
Ernani: Ballerini
Don Carlo: Rossi-Ghelli
D. Ruy Gomez de Silva: Nerini

June 2
LUCIA DI LAMMERMOOR
(Donizetti)
Lucia: Pasi
Edgardo: Ballerini
Enrico: Rossi-Ghelli

June 4, July 18
IL TROVATORE (Verdi)
Leonora: Pasi
Manrico: Ballerini
Conte di Luna: Rossi-Ghelli
Azucena: Escalante
Ferrando: Gaddi
Ruiz: Chiodini

June 11, Aug 9
NORMA (Bellini)
Norma: Pasi
Adalgisa: Escalante
Pollione: Ballerini
Oroveso: Nerini

June 24, Aug 23, 26
MARIA DE ROHAN (Donizetti)
Maria: Pasi(2) / Escalante (Aug
23)
Riccardo: Ballerini
Armando: Rossi-Ghelli
Il Visconte de Suse: Ferrari
De Fiesque: Gaddi
Un famigliare: Chiodini

July 16, Aug 18
LUISA MILLER (Verdi)
Luisa: Pasi
Rodolfo: Ballerini
Federica: Escalante
Miller: Rossi-Ghelli

July 22, 24, Aug 3
IL BARBIERE DI SIVIGLIA
(Rossini)
Rosina: Escalante
Conte di Almaviva: Ballerini
Figaro: Rossi-Ghelli
Don Basilio: Nerini
Don Bartolo: Ferrari

July 25
Concert
Conductor: Carmelo Calvo
Soloists: Camps <armonium>,
Calvo <pf> and Lyric Company
artists

July 27, 29, 31, Aug 14
JONE (Petrella)
Jone: Pasi
Nidia: Escalante
Glauco: Ballerini
Arbace: Bonetti
Burbo: Nerini

Aug 7
MARTHA (Flotow)
Lady Harriet: Pasi
Lionel: Ballerini
Lord Tristan: Nerini

Aug 9
NORMA (Bellini)
and Operatic *Concert*

Aug 11, 30
RIGOLETTO (Verdi)
Gilda: Pasi
Il Duca di Mantova: Ballerini
Rigoletto: Rossi-Ghelli
Sparafucile: Nerini
Maddalena: Escalante

Sept 2, 4, 8
GUGLIELMO TELL (Rossini) (It)**
Arnoldo: Ballerini
Guglielmo Tell: Rossi-Ghelli
Matilde: Pasi
Hedwige: Gery
Jenny: Escalante
Leuthold: Chiodini
Gualterio: Nerini

Sept 14, 16, 18, 25
PIPELET (De Ferrari)**
Rigoletto, seamstress: Pasi
Carlos Duresnel: Ballerini
Jacobo: Bonetti
Cabrión: Rossi-Ghelli
Pipelet, porter: P. Ferrari
Madeleine, his wife: Escalante
Alguacil: Gaddi

Oct 1, 2
MOSE IN EGITTO (Rossini)**
Amenophis: Ballerini
Mosè: Nerini
Anaide: Pasi
Maria: Martinez
Eliezer: Marchetti
Faraone: Rossi-Ghelli
Osidide: Chiodini
Sinaide: Escalante

CARLOTTA PATTI CONCERTS
with Sarasate <vn>, Ritter <pf>
and Antinori <t>
Oct 16, 18 and 20

Oct 16
First Concert
Mozart: Don Giovanni, duet
<vn / pf>

Rossini's Il barbiere cavatina <t/
pf>
Donizetti's Linda di Chamounix:
recitative and aria <s / pf>
Sarasate's Fantasia Faust <vn / pf>
Prudent: Danse des fées <pf>
Donizetti: Spirto gentil (t / pf>
Ritter: La fête, waltz <s / pf>
Ritter: Marche nocturne from Le
postillon <pf>
Sarasate: Jota aragonesa <vn / pf>
Donizetti: Romanza dei bravo
<t / pf>
Donizetti: L'elisir d'amore duet
<s / t / pf>

Oct 18
Second Concert
Osborne-Beriot: Guglielmo Tell
duet <vn / pf>
Donizetti: Una furtiva lagrima
<t / pf>
La traviata: Aria <s / pf>
Alard: La muette de Portici,
Fantasia <vn / pf>
Mendelssohn: Rondo
Capriccioso <pf>
Luisa Miller: Aria <t / pf>
Gounod: Ave Maria for <s / vn /
pf>
Litolff-Ritter: La fileuse and Le
chant du braconnier <pf>
Rigoletto: La donna è mobile <t
/ pf>
Vieuxtemps: Saint Patrick Day
<vn / pf>
Paganini: Le carnaval de Venise
variations <s / pf>

Oct 20
Third Concert
Alard: Duet on Neapolitan
Themes <vn / pf>
Guercia: Non m'amava <t / pf>
Lucia: Mad scene <s / pf>
Beriot: Tremolo <vn / pf>
Liszt: Tourbillon, Etude <pf>
Iradier: Jota de los toreros
<s / t / pf>

I lombardi: Cavatina <t/pf>
Paganini: Le carnaval de Venise,
variations <s/pf>
Sarasate: Habanera and muñeira
<vn/pf>
Bach: Gavotta and presto <pf>
Donizetti: Spirto gentil <t/pf>
I vespri siciliani: Bolero <s/pf>

Oct 22 to end of year
[All theatres closed due to
political revolution]

1871

Male artists
Bignami, César <vc>
Bignami, Pompeo (Pompeyo)
<vn>
Bonetti, Edoardo, <bar>
Celsetti, Signor <harmonium>
Cerioli, F. <bar>
Costa, Dalmiro <pf>
Dionesi, Romeo <t>
Hernández, Félix <sax>
Tappa, P. <tpt>

Jan 8, 14, 15, 22
Masked Balls

Jan 27, July 18
Gala Balls

Feb 2 to March 25
Carnival Masked Balls

April 8, 15, 19, 29, 30
Easter Masked Balls

May 5 to June 29
Italian Dramatic Company
Tommaso Salvini

May 9
Concert
Conductor: Carmelo Calvo

July 23 to 27
American-British Acrobatic
Orrin Company

Aug 1 to 4
Italian Dramatic Company
Ernesto Rossi

Oct 8
Concert
Conductor: Carmelo Calvo
Soloists: Dionesi <t>, Bonetti
<bar>, C. Bignami <vc>, P.
Bignami <vn>, Costa <pf>,
Cerioli <bar>, Celsetti
<harmonium>, Tappa <tpt>
and orchestra

Oct 25
Recital: Hernández <sax>

Nov 17
Choral Concert
Christy's Minstrels
Chorus master: Hart Steel

Nov 18, 19
Italian Dramatic Company
Ernesto Rossi

Nov 24
Benefit Concert
Conductor: Carmelo Calvo
Soloist: Bonetti <bar>

Dec 14
Benefit Gala Ball

Dec 16 to 31
Holidays Masked Balls

1872

Female artists
Bendazzi-Ruiz, Gertrude <s>
Calisto-Piccioli, María <s>
Casanova de Cepeda, Carolina
<s>

Crocci, Clotilde <mez>
D'Hervil, Eloisa <pf>
Estagel, Signora <mez>
Luzzetti, Emilia <mez>
Marziali-Passerini, Julia <s>
Mazzuco, Antonieta <mez/a>
Mollo, Marietta <s>
Pozzoli, Emilia <s>

Male artists
Bonetti, Edoardo <bar>
Buzzi, Attilio <b>
Chiodini, Angelo <b>
Derezzi, Giacomo <t>
Hericourt, Luis <t>
Hernández, Félix <sax>
Limberti, Giuseppe <t>
Marziali, Cristiano <bar>
Mazzoni-Osti, Ludovico <bar>
Menici, Signor <b>
Perotti, Julio <t>
Piccioli, Gerónimo <t>
Ruiz, Luigi <b>
Setragni, Pietro <t>
Tagliapietra, Giovanni <bar>

Jan 5 to March 10
Carnival Masked Balls

March 30 to April 7
Gala Balls

ITALIAN OPERA SEASON
April 10 to Jan 5, 1873
Conductor: Luigi Preti

April 10, June 5, 12, 23, July 5,
Sept 20, Nov 10
LA TRAVIATA (Verdi)
Violetta: Mollo(1) / Casanova(6)
Alfredo Germont: Setragni
G. Germont: Bonetti(1) /
Marziali(6)
Flora: Mazzuco(1) / Estagel(6)
Gastone: Hericourt
Barone Douphol: Chiodini
Dottore Grenvil: Buzzi

April 12, 16, 23, June 13, Sept 8,
Nov 29, Dec 1
ERNANI (Verdi)
Elvira: Mollo(3) / Casanova(1) /
Pozzoli(3)
Ernani: Setragni
Don Carlo: Bonetti(5) /
Marziali(2)
D. Ruy Gomez de Silva: Buzzi

April 14, 19, May 29, Dec 2, 4, 8,
15
IL TROVATORE (Verdi)
Leonora: Mollo(2) / Casanova(5)
Manrico: Setragni(2) /
Limberti(5)
Conte di Luna: Bonetti(2) /
Marziali(5)
Azucena: Mazzuco
Ferrando: Buzzi

April 18, Sept 13, 14, 15, 22, Oct
11, Nov 8, Dec 20, 27
LUCIA DI LAMMERMOOR
(Donizetti)
Lucia: Mollo(1) / Casanova(8)
Edgardo: Setragni(1) /
Limberti(8)
Enrico: Bonetti(1) / Marziali(8)
Arturo: Hericourt
Raimondo: Buzzi

April 21, July 10, 14, 21, Aug 11
IL BARBIERE DI SIVIGLIA
(Rossini)
Rosina: Mollo(1) / Casanova(4)
Conte di Almaviva: Setragni
Figaro: Bonetti(1) / Mazzoni(4)
Don Basilio: Buzzi
Don Bartolo: Menici
Berta: Estagel
Fiorello: Hericourt

April 28, Nov 22, Dec 13
LUCREZIA BORGIA (Donizetti)
Lucrezia: Mollo(1) / Casanova(2)
Gennaro: Setragni(1) /
Limberti(2)

Duca Alfonso: Bonetti(1) /
Setragni(2)
Maffio Orsini: Mazzuco
Principessa Negroni: Luzzetti
Gubetta: Buzzi

April 29 to May 24
[Theaters closed due to a yellow
fever epidemic.]

May 25, June 19, July 18, Aug 28
NORMA (Bellini)
Norma: Casanova
Adalgisa: Mollo
Pollione: Limberti(1) / Setragni(3)
Oroveso: Buzzi
Clotilde: Crocci
Flavio: Hericourt

May 30, June 1, 2, Aug 2, Dec 6,
11
RIGOLETTO (Verdi)
Gilda: Casanova
Il Duca: Limberti(3) / Setragni(3)
Rigoletto: Marziali(3) /
Mazzoni(3)
Maddalena: Mazzuco
Sparafucile: Buzzi
Monterone: Menici
Giovanna: Crocci

June 7, 9, 30, Aug 25, Nov 13, 15,
16, Dec 18, 22
UN BALLO IN MASCHERA (Verdi)
Amelia: Casanova
Riccardo: Setragni
Renato: Marziali
Ulrica: Mazzuco
Oscar: Mollo
Samuel: Buzzi
Tom: Chiodini

June 15, 16, 21, 26, July 26, Aug
15, Oct 2, 9, 24, 25
FAUST (Gounod) (It)
Margherita: Casanova(8) / Calisto-
Piccioli(2)
Faust: Setragni(8) / Piccioli(2)

Mefistofele: Bonetti(4) / Buzzi(6)
Valentin: Marziali(4) /
Mazzoni(6)
Marta: Estagel
Siebel: Mazzuco

June 29, July 16, Aug 13, 21
CRISPINO E LA COMARE (Ricci)
Crispino: Mazzoni
La Comare: Mazzuco
Annetta: Mollo
Contino del Fiore: Setragni
Don Asdrubale: Buzzi

July 3, 7, 12, 13, 28, Sept 4, 18
MARTHA (Flotow)
Lady Harriet: Casanova
Lionel: Setragni
Lord Tristan: Buzzi
Nancy: Mazzuco

July 20, 24, Aug 7
POLIUTO (Donizetti)
Poliuto: Limberti
Paolina: Casanova
Severus: Mazzoni
Callisthenes: Buzzi
Felice: Menici
Nearco: Hericourt

July 31, Aug 4, 9, Nov 3
LINDA DI CHAMOUNIX
(Donizetti)
Linda: Casanova
Maddalena: Estagel
Marquis Boisfleuris: Buzzi
Visconte Sirval: Setragni
Prefetto: Menici
Pierotto: Mazzuco

Aug 17, 18, Sept 11, Nov 17
DON PASQUALE (Donizetti)
Norina: Casanova
Ernesto: Setragni
Don Pasquale: Mazzoni
Malatesta: Buzzi
Notaro: Hericourt

Aug 24, 30, Sept 1, 7
LA CONTESSA D'AMALFI
(Petrella)**
Contessa Leonora: Mollo
Tilde: Estagel
Egidio: Setragni
Duca Carnioli: Mazzoni
Sertorio: Buzzi
Berta: Crocci
Il Conte di Lara: Menici

Sept 4
MARTHA (Flotow)
and Operatic *Concert*

Sept 6
Operatic Concert
Italian Lyric Company artists
and E. d'Hervil <pf>

Sept 13, 14, 15, 22
LUCIA DI LAMMERMOOR
(Donizetti)
and *Concerts* with E. d'Hervil
<pf>

Sept 27, 29, Oct 13, Nov 6, 20,
26
LA SONNAMBULA (Bellini)
Amina: Casanova
Elvino: Piccioli
Rodolfo: Buzzi
Lisa: Estagel
Teresa: Mazzuco

Oct 4, 6, 23, 27, Nov 24, Dec 25,
29
RUY BLAS (Marchetti)
La Regina: Calisto-Piccioli
Ruy Blas: Piccioli

Oct 13
LA SONNAMBULA (Bellini)
and *Concert* with E. d'Hervil <pf>

Oct 18, 20
Concerts
Soloists: Casanova <s>, E.
d'Hervil <pf>, Hernández <sax>

1873

Female artists
Baldi, Carolina <s>
Biancolini, Marietta <s>
Bossi, Carlotta <s>
Calisto-Piccioli, María <s>
Core, Lucia <mez>
Core, Maria <a>
Croce, Luisa <mez>
Escalante, Isabella M. <s>
Fiorio, L. <mez>
Marziali-Passerini, Julia <s>
Vercolini-Tay, <mez / a>

Male artists
Agostinelli, Signor <b>
Bottero, Alessandro <b>
Bulterini, Carlo <t>
Buzzi, Attilio <b>
Cavedagni, Luigi <b / bar>
Ciapini, Signor <bar>
De Bezzi, Signor <t>
Hericourt, Luis <t>
Maffei, Giovanni <b>
Mantinenghi, Antonio <t>
Marucco, Pedro <bar>
Marziali, Cristiano <bar>
Mazzoni-Osti, Ludovico <bar>
Molla, Signor <b>
Perotti, Julio <t>
Piccioli, Gerónimo <t>
Rossi-Ghelli, Achille <bar>
Tagliapietra, Giovanni <bar>
Zucchi, Francisco <t>

Jan 4
Masked Ball

ITALIAN OPERA SEASON
[continuation of the 1872
season]

Jan 5
LUCIA DI LAMMERMOOR
(Donizetti)
Lucia: Marziali-Passerini
Edgardo: Perotti

Enrico: Tagliapietra
Arturo: De Bezzi
Alisa: Fiorio
Normanno: Hericourt
Raimondo: Buzzi

Jan 29 to Feb 6
Royal Japanese Satsuma
Acrobatic Company

Feb 7 to March 29
Carnival Masked Balls

WINTER ITALIAN OPERA SEASON
May 22 to Oct 18
Conductor: Gioachino Salvini
Chorus Master: Francisco Seguí
Director: Luigi Cavedagni

May 22, July 24, 27
LA SONNAMBULA (Bellini)
Amina: Calisto-Piccioli(1) /
Bossi(2)
Elvino: Piccioli
Conte Rodolfo: Buzzi
Lisa: Baldi
Teresa: Core

May 24, 25, 31, Sept 10, Oct 18
MICHELE PERRIN (Cagnoni)**
Michele Perrin: Bottero
Teresa: Calisto-Piccioli
Henri Bernard: Piccioli
Fouché: Marucco
Grussé: Buzzi
Desonné: Cavedagni

May 29, June 1, Aug 28
CRISPINO E LA COMARE (Ricci)
Crispino: Bottero
La Comare: Core
Annetta: Calisto-Piccioli
Contino del Fiore: Piccioli
Don Asdrubale: Marziali
Lisetta: Fiorio

June 7, 8, 14, 15, 24, Aug 21, Sept
17
I CAPULETI E I MONTECCHI
(Bellini)
Giulietta: Calisto-Piccioli
Romeo: Biancolini
Tebaldo: Piccioli
Fray Lorenzo: Cavedagni
Cappelio: Buzzi

June 11, July 5, 15, Aug 15, 19, 31,
Sept 28
PAPA MARTIN (Cagnoni)**
Papa Martin: Bottero
Amelia: Calisto-Piccioli
Olimpia: Core
Genoveva: Baldi
Armando: Piccioli
Charonzon: Buzzi
Feliciano: Marucco
Douvourg: Hericourt

June 12, 21, July 6, Sept 7, 26
LA FAVORITA (Donizetti) (It)
Leonora: Calisto-Piccioli
Fernando: Piccioli
Alfonso XI: Mazzoni
Inez: Fiorio
Baldassare: Buzzi

June 19, 22, 26, 29
DON BUCEFALO (Cagnoni)**
Don Bucefalo: Bottero
Rosina: Calisto-Piccioli
Agata: Baldi
Don Marcos: Buzzi
Giovanna: Fiorio
Conte Belpatro: Mantinenghi
Carlino: Hericourt

June 28, July 3, 9, 19, Sept 5, Oct
10
IL BARBIERE DI SIVIGLIA
(Rossini)
Rosina: Biancolini
Figaro: Mazzoni
Conte di Almaviva: Piccioli

Don Basilio: Bottero
Don Bartolo: Buzzi
Berta: Baldi
Fiorello: Hericourt

July 11, 12, 14, 18, Aug 25
FAUST (Gounod) (It)
Margherita: Biancolini
Faust: Piccioli
Mefistofele: Bottero
Siebel: Core
Valentin: Mazzoni
Marta: Fiorio
Wagner: Chiodini

July 16, 17, 23, 26
UN BALLO IN MASCHERA (Verdi)
Amelia: Bossi
Riccardo: Zucchi
Renato: Mazzoni
Ulrica: Core
Oscar: Baldi
Silvano: Hericourt
Tom: Cavedagni
Samuel: Buzzi

July 30
LA TRAVIATA (Verdi)
Violetta: Bossi
Alfredo Germont: Piccioli
Giorgio Germont: Marziali
Flora: Fiorio
Gastone: Hericourt
Dottore Grevil: Cavedagni

Aug 2, 3
DON PASQUALE (Donizetti)
Norina: Bossi
Ernesto: Piccioli
Don Pasquale: Bottero
Malatesta: Marziali
Notaro: Hericourt

Aug 6, 9, 10, 17, Oct 3
CLAUDIA (Cagnoni)**
Claudia: Biancolini
Silvio: Piccioli

Remigio: Bottero
Tomas: Marziali
Dionisio: Buzzi
Rosa: Fiorio
Teresa: Baldi
Martino: Hericourt

Aug 12, Oct 23, 26, Dec 14
ERNANI (Verdi)
Elvira: Marziali-Passerini
Ernani: Bulterini
Don Carlo: Rossi-Ghelli
D. Ruy Gomez de Silva: Maffei
Anna: Fiorio
Don Riccardo: De Bezzi

Aug 23
I DUE FOSCARI (Verdi)
Francesco Foscari: Marziali
Jacopo Foscari: Zucchi
Lucrezia Contarini: Bossi
Jacopo Loredano: Cavedagni
Pisana: Fiorio
Barbarigo: Hericourt

Aug 30, Sept 3, Oct 25, 31
NORMA (Bellini)
Norma: Bossi(2) / Marziali-
Passerini(2)
Adalgisa: Escalante
Pollione: Zucchi(2) / Bulterini
Oroveso: Buzzi(2) / Maffei(2)
Clotilde: Fiorio
Flavio: Hericourt(2) / De Bezzi(2)

Sept 10
MICHELE PERRIN (Cagnoni) and
Concert
Lucia de Lammermoor: Mad
Scene by Calisto-Piccioli

Sept 11, 13, 14
LA FORZA DEL DESTINO (Verdi)
Leonora: Escalante
Don Alvaro: Piccioli
Preziosilla: Biancolini
Don Carlo: Marziali

Marchese di Calatrava:
Cavedagni
Padre Guardiano: Buzzi
Fra Melitone: Bottero
Curra: Fiorio

Sept 17
I CAPULETI E I MONTECCHI
(Bellini)
and *Concert*

Sept 20, 21
IL TROVATORE (Verdi)
Leonora: Escalante
Manrico: Zucchi
Conte di Luna: Rossi-Ghelli
Azucena: Biancolini
Ferrando: Buzzi
Ruiz: Agostinelli
Inez: Fiorio

Sept 24, Oct 1, 4, 8, 12
RUY BLAS (Marchetti)
La Regina: Calisto-Piccioli
Ruy Blas: Piccioli
Casilda: Escalante
Don Salustio de Bazan: Rossi-
Ghelli
Don Guritano: Buzzi
Don Pedro de Guevara:
Hericourt
Don Fernando de Cordova:
Cavedagni

Oct 15, 16, Dec 24, 25
L'AFRICANA (Meyerbeer) (It)
Selika: Bossi
Vasco da Gama: Zucchi
Nelusko: Rossi-Ghelli
Anna: Baldi

Oct 18
MICHELE PERRIN (Cagnoni)
[same cast as May 24]
and *Concert* Italian Lyric
Company artists

**SPRING-SUMMER ITALIAN
OPERA SEASON**
Oct 31 to Dec 31

Oct 21, Nov 26
LUCIA DI LAMMERMOOR
(Donizetti)
Lucia: Marziali-Passerini
Edgardo: Bulterini
Enrico: Rossi-Ghelli
Arturo: De Bezzi(1) /
Hericourt(1)
Alisa: Fiorio
Normanno: Hericourt(1) / De
Bezzi(1)
Raimondo: Agostinelli(1) /
Molla(1)

Oct 29, Nov 7, 19, Dec 19
IL TROVATORE (Verdi)
Leonora: Marziali-Passerini
Manrico: Bulterini
Conte di Luna: Rossi-Ghelli
Azucena: Vercolini
Ferrando: Molla
Ruiz: Agostinelli
Inez: Fiorio

Nov 5, 11, 28, 29, Dec 3, 10
UN BALLO IN MASCHERA (Verdi)
Amelia: Marziali-Passerini
Riccardo: Bulterini
Renato: Ciapini
Ulrica: Vercolini
Oscar: Escalante
Silvano: Hericourt
Tom: Cavedagni
Samuel: Molla

Nov 9, 14, 16, 30, Dec 27
RIGOLETTO (Verdi)
Gilda: Marziali-Passerini
Il Duca di Mantova: Bulterini
Rigoletto: Rossi-Ghelli
Maddalena: Vercolini
Sparafucile: Maffei
Monterone: Molla

Nov 21, 23
POLIUTO (Donizetti)
Poliuto: Bulterini
Paulina: Marziali-Passerini
Severus: Ciapini
Felice: Agostinelli

Dec 5, 7, 13, 21, 31
IL PROFETA (Meyerbeer) (It)
Giovanni de Leyden: Bulterini
Bertha: Escalante
Fides: Vercolini
Matthisen: Molla
Conte Oberthal: Ciapini
Zaccaria: Maffei

Dec 17, 30
LUCREZIA BORGIA (Donizetti)
Lucrezia: Marziali-Passerini
Gennaro: Bulterini
Duca Alfonso: Marziali
Maffio Orsini: Croce
Gubetta: Buzzi

Dec 31
IL PROFETA (Meyerbeer) (It)
[same cast as Dec 5] and
and Farewell *Concert* by Italian
Lyric Company

1874

Female artists
Brambilla, Elvira V. <s>
D'Amico, Giuseppina <s>
Gallo, Luisa <pf>
García, Josefa <tiple>
Giannini, Clotilde <mez>
Guerrici, Signora <mez>
Guinei, Augusta <mez>
Quesada, Dolores <tiple>
Rosa, Elvira <tiple>
Sanz, Elena <mez / a>
Stoika, Ernestina <mez>
Urban, Alice <s>

Male artists
Ambrosi, Fernando <t>
Buti, Ludovico <bar>
Caneschi, Alceo <vn>
Carmona, Eduardo <t-comico>
Castelmary, Armand <b>
Celada, Augusto <t>
De la Costa, Joaquín <t>
Dengremont, Maurice <vn>
Ferroni, Miguel <vla>
Ferroni, Vicente <fl>
Formentini, Camilo <bn>
Forti, Gaetano <bar>
Galván, Tomás <t-comico>
Gurtubay, Saturnino de <vn>
Hericourt, Luis <t>
Jurkowsky, José <pf>
Larraya, Camilo <b>
Marconi, Raffaele <b>
Pasini, Tomás <b>
Ranzati, Ernesto <t>
Solano, Atilano <bar>

Jan (entire month)
Gala Balls

Feb to March 10
Carnival Masked Balls

March 11 to May 26
Italian Dramatic Company
Jacinta Pezzana

April 28
Recital: Gallo <eight-year-old
pianist>, V. Ferroni <fl>,
Caneschi <vn>, M. Ferroni
<vla>, Formentini <bn>

May 27
Recital: Gallo <pf>, Dengremont
<seven-year-old vn>, Gurtubay
<vn>
Bériot: Violin concerto
Lucia di Lammermoor: Violin
duetto
Capriccio after Martha

June 3
Recital: Jurkowsky <pf>
Opera paraphrases by Thalberg,
Liszt, Gottschalk and Pfeiffer

**WINTER ITALIAN OPERA
SEASON**
Edoardo Bonetti, Impresario
June 16 to Oct 13
Conductor: Timoteo Passini
Chorus Master: Francisco Seguí
Director: Jaime de Bezzi

June 16, 26, 28, July 2, 5, 11, Aug
13
LA FAVORITA (Donizetti) (It)
Leonora: Sanz
Fernando: Celada
Alfonso XI: Buti
Baldassare: Castelmary
Gaspare: Ambrosi

June 17
LA TRAVIATA (Verdi)
Violetta: Brambilla
Alfredo Germont: Celada
Giorgio Germont: Buti

June 18, 20, 21, 29
NORMA (Bellini)
Norma: Urban
Adalgisa: Brambilla
Pollione: Celada
Oroveso: Marconi

June 24, July 4
ERNANI (Verdi)
Elvira: Urban
Ernani: Celada
Don Carlo: Buti
D. Ruy Gomez de Silva:
Castelmary

July 7, 12, 28
LUCREZIA BORGIA (Donizetti)
Lucrezia: Urban
Gennaro: Ambrosi
Duca Alfonso: Buti

Maffio Orsini: Stoika(2) / Sanz(1)
Gubetta: Castelmary
Rustighello: Marconi

July 9, 30
RIGOLETTO (Verdi)
Gilda: Brambilla
Il Duca di Mantova: Celada
Rigoletto: Forti
Maddalena: Sanz
Sparafucile: Castelmary

July 14, 18, Aug 4, Sept 17
UN BALLO IN MASCHERA (Verdi)
Amelia: Urban
Riccardo: Celada
Renato: Buti(3) / Forti(1)
Ulrica: Stoika
Oscar: Brambilla
Tom: Marconi

July 17
LA SONNAMBULA (Bellini)
Amina: D'Amico
Elvino: Ambrosi
Conte Rodolfo: Castelmary
Lisa: Stoika
Alessio: Marconi

July 22, 24, 26, Aug 2, 23, Oct 2
FAUST (Gounod) (It)
Margherita: Urban
Faust: Celada
Mefistofele: Castelmary
Valentin: Buti
Siebel: Stoika(3) / Sanz(2) /
Stoika(1)
Marta: Guerrici(5) / Sanz(1)
Wagner: Forti

Aug 1, 9
RIGOLETTO (Verdi)
Gilda: D'Amico
Il Duca di Mantova: Celada
Rigoletto: Forti
Maddalena: Sanz
Sparafucile: Castelmary

Aug 6, 8, 16, 25, Sept 3, 18
IL TROVATORE (Verdi)
Leonora: Urban
Manrico: Celada
Conte di Luna: Forti
Azucena: Sanz
Ferrando: Castelmary

Aug 11, 15, Oct 1
LINDA DI CHAMOUNIX
(Donizetti)
Linda: Urban
Maddalena: Sanz
Visconte Sirval: Ambrosi
Marquis Boisfleuris: Forti
Prefetto: Marconi

Aug 28, 29, 30, Sept 10, 13, 24
SAFFO (Pacini)
Saffo: Urban
Faone: Ambrosi
Alcandro: Buti
Climene: Sanz
Ippia: Marconi

Sept 2, 5, 8
IL BARBIERE DI SIVIGLIA
(Rossini)
Rosina: Sanz
Conte di Almaviva: Ambrosi
Figaro: Buti
Don Basilio: Castelmary

Sept 6, Oct 13
LUCIA DI LAMMERMOOR
(Donizetti)
Lucia: Brambilla
Edgardo: Celada
Enrico: Ambrosi
Normanno: Buti
Raimondo: Castelmary

Sept 7
Concert
Conductor: Luigi Preti
Soloists: L. Gallo <pf>, M.
Dengremont <vn>, and Italian
Lyric Company, chorus, and
orchestra

Sept 11, 19, Oct 14 to 20
Italian Dramatic Company
Tomasso Salvini

Sept 12, 15, 20, Oct 6
ROBERTO IL DIAVOLO
(Meyerbeer) (It)
Alice: Brambilla
Roberto, Duca di Normandia:
Ambrosi
Isabella di Sicilia: Urban
Rambaldo: Celada
Bertramo: Castelmary
Alberti: Forti

Sept 27, Oct 4, 11
L'EBREA (Halévy)** (It)
Rachel: Urban
Eleazar: Ambrosi
Principessa Eudoxia: Brambilla
Cardinal Brogni: Castelmary
Alberto: Forti

**AMERICAN OPERETTA
SEASON FROM NIBLO'S
GARDEN**
Oct 21 to Nov 6
THE BLACK CROOK (various
composers)

SPANISH ZARZUELA SEASON
Nov 14 to Dec 22
Conductor: Ricardo S. Allú
Repertory:
MARINA (Arrieta)**
EN LAS ASTAS DEL TORO
(Gaztambide)**
EL RELAMPAGO (Barbieri)**
EL MOLINERO DE SUBIZA
(Oudrid)**
CAMPANONE (Mazza)**
LOS MAGYARES (Gaztambide)**
LAS HIJAS DE EVA
(Gaztambide)**
Artists: García, Quesada, Rosa;
De la Costa, Solano, Galván,
Carmona, Pasini and Larraya

Dec 24 to 31
Holidays Balls

1875

Female artists
Belia, Signora <s>
Biancolini, Marietta <s>
Calisto-Piccioli, María <s>
Carozzi-Zucchi, Carlotta <s>
Clotilde, Signora <s / mez>
Corsi-Toressi, Linda <s>
Escalante, Isabella M. <s>
Ollandini, Signora <s>
Oneto de Bruzzone, Signora <s>
Warner, Ermelinda <mez / a>

Male artists
Aubriot, Enrique <t>
Berti, Ernesto <t>
Bonetti, Edoardo <bar>
De Bezzi, Signor <t>
Faget, Paul <pf>
Ferdinando, Signor <t>
Ghizzoni, N. <b>
Jurkowsky, José <pf>
Lelmi, Luis <t>
Manfredi, Eugenio <b>
Marconi, Raffaele <b>
Marziali, Cristiano <bar>
Piccioli, Gerónimo <t>
Pozzi, Natale <b>
Preti, Luigi <vn>
Sambucetti, Luis, Jr. <vn>
Signoretti, Leopoldo <t>
Toressi, Giuseppe <t>
Wagner, Giuseppe <b>

ITALIAN OPERA SEASON
First company: Jan 1 to 23
Conductor: Luigi Preti
Chorus Master: Francisco Seguí
Designer (Scenography): Orestes
Coliva

Jan 1, 3, Feb 18
LA FAVORITA (Donizetti) (It)
Leonora: Biancolini
Fernando: Piccioli
Alfonso XI: Bonetti
Inez: Clotilde
Baldassare: Marconi
Gaspare: Ghizzoni

Jan 6
I CAPULETI E I MONTECCHI
(Bellini)
Giulietta: Calisto-Piccioli
Romeo: Biancolini
Tebaldo: Piccioli
Fray Lorenzo: Ghizzoni

Jan 10, 17
GIULIETTA E ROMEO (Vaccai)
Giulietta: Calisto-Piccioli
Capellio: Marconi

Jan 15, 23
RUY BLAS (Marchetti)
La Regina: Calisto-Piccioli
Ruy Blas: Piccioli
Casilda: E. Warner
Donna Giovanna: Clotilde
Don Salustio de Bazan: Marziali
Don Guritano: Marconi

Feb 6 to 17
Carnival Masked Balls

Feb 20 to 28, March 28
Professors Fay and Keller
<prestidigitators>

March 6 to 27, April 4
Gala Balls

April 6 to 18
Great Silphorama Show from
London
Light and Music with orchestra

**OPERETTA FROM PARIS'
OPERA COMIQUE**
April 24 to 28
LA FILLE DE MADAME ANGOT
(Lecocq)
Clairette: Belia
and Grand Fricassé Comique

ITALIAN OPERA SEASON
Second company: May 1 to 18
Conductor: Luigi Preti
Chorus Master: Francisco Seguí
Designer (Scenography): Orestes
Coliva

May 1
LA FAVORITA (Donizetti) (It)
Leonora: Carozzi-Zucchi
Fernando: Lelmi
Alfonso XI: Bonetti
Inez: Clotilde
Baldassare: Pozzi
Gaspare: Ghizzoni

May 2, 9
IL TROVATORE (Verdi)
Leonora: Carozzi-Zucchi
Manrico: Lelmi
Conte di Luna: Bonetti
Azucena: Biancolini
Ferrando: Marconi

May 4, 6, 11, 13
NORMA (Bellini)
Norma: Carozzi-Zucchi
Adalgisa: Biancolini
Pollione: Lelmi
Oroveso: Pozzi

May 8
I CAPULETI E I MONTECCHI
(Bellini)
Giulietta: Carozzi-Zucchi
Romeo: Biancolini
Tebaldo: Piccioli
Fray Lorenzo: Marconi

May 15
I MARTIRI (Donizetti)
Paolina: Carozzi-Zucchi
Poliuto: Lelmi
Severus: Bonetti
Callisthenes: Marconi
Felice: Berti

May 16
UN BALLO IN MASCHERA (Verdi)
Amelia: Carozzi-Zucchi
Riccardo: Lelmi
Renato: Bonetti
Ulrica: Biancolini
Oscar: Ollandini
Tom: Pozzi
Samuel: Marconi

May 18
IL BARBIERE DI SIVIGLIA
(Rossini)
Rosina: Biancolini
Conte di Almaviva: Signoretti
Figaro: Bonetti
Don Basilio: Pozzi
Don Bartolo: Marconi

May 25 to 31, Aug 25
Spanish Dramatic Company L.
Burón

Aug 3 to 5
Ling Look <magician>

Sept 6
Symphonic Concert
Conductor: Preti
Orquesta de la Sociedad
Filarmónica
Soloists: L. Sambucetti <vn>, P.
Faget <pf>, J. Jurkowsky <pf>,
L. Preti <vn>, E. Aubriot <t>
Beethoven: Third Symphony,
first movement
Donizetti: Fantasia after Linda
<vn/pf>
Beethoven: Third Symphony,
second movement

Chopin: Grand Polonaise <pf>
Donizetti: Aria from La Favorita
Beethoven: Third Symphony,
third movement
Beethoven: Third Symphony,
fourth movement
[First Uruguayan performance
of a complete Beethoven
symphony]
Grand duetto after Guglielmo
Tell<vn/pf>
Gretry: Fantasia for oboe
Gounod: Aria from Faust
Hérold: Overture from Zampa

ITALIAN OPERA SEASON
Third company: Nov 14 to Dec
25
Conductor: Luigi Preti
Chorus Master: Francisco Seguí
Designer (Scenography): Orestes
Coliva

Nov 14, Dec 8
IL TROVATORE (Verdi)
Leonora: Corsi-Toressi
Manrico: Toressi
Conte di Luna: Marziali
Azucena: E. Wagner
Ferrando: G. Wagner

Nov 17, 21
UN BALLO IN MASCHERA (Verdi)
Amelia: Corsi-Toressi
Riccardo: Toressi
Renato: Marziali
Ulrica: E. Wagner
Oscar: Escalante
Tom: Pozzi
Samuel: Marconi

Nov 19
ERNANI (Verdi)
Elvira: Corsi-Toressi
Ernani: Toressi
Don Carlo: Marziali
D. Ruy Gomez de Silva:
Manfredi

Giovanna: Clotilde
Iago: Berti

Nov 24, Dec 10
NORMA (Bellini)
Norma: Corsi-Toressi
Adalgisa: Escalante
Pollione: Toressi
Oroveso: G. Wagner

Nov 28, Dec 15
RUY BLAS (Marchetti)
La Regina: Corsi-Toressi
Ruy Blas: Toressi
Casilda: E. Warner
Donna Giovanna: Escalante
Don Salustio de Bazan: Marziali
Don Guritano: G. Wagner

Dec 1, 5, 19, 26
JONE (Petrella)
Jone: Corzi-Toressi
Glauco: Toressi
Arbace: Marziali
Nidia: Escalante

Dec 12, 25
LUCREZIA BORGIA (Donizetti)
Lucrezia: Corsi-Toressi
Gennaro: Toressi
Duca Alfonso: Marziali
Maffio Orsini: Escalante

———————————————
1876
———————————————

Female artists
Alhaiza, Aline <s>
Andreff, Maria Solowieff <s>
Augier, Signora <mez>
Bálsamo, Virginia <d>
Consolani-Piazza, Signora <a>
Corsi-Toressi, Linda <s>
Dimier, Mlle. <s>
Falconet, Mlle. <mez>
Gerome, Emma <s>
Matray, Mlle. <a>
Missorta, Palmira <s>

Motelli, Signora <mez>
Pascal-Damiani, Signora <s>
Rocca, Clorinda <d>
Tancioni, Annetta <a>
Ubaldi, M. <mez>
Val, Signora <s/vn>

Male artists
Aubriot, Enrique <t>
Augier, Achille <b>
Bazin, Monsieur <b>
Berti, Ernesto <t>
Clergeaud, Monsieur <bar>
De Bezzi, Signor <t>
De Cré, Pomponet <t>
Dondi, Enrico <b>
Formilli, Signor <bar>
Gadilhe, M. <t>
Giordani, Signor <b>
Lafont, Monsieur <b>
Leon, Monsieur <bar>
Marconi, Raffaele <b>
Marino (Marini), C. <bar/b>
Matray, Monsieur <b>
Mazzoli, Agustin <bar>
Moroni, Signor <b>
Parasini, Signor <t>
Pedotti, T. <b>
Pother, Monsieur <b>
Sambucetti, Luis, Jr. <vn>
Subirana, José <bar>
Tansini, Giovanni <b>
Toressi, Giuseppe <t>
Val, Maurice <t>
Vidal, M. <t>
Wagner, Giuseppe <b>
Zabo, Enrique <d>

Jan 5 to 18
Gala Balls

Jan 20
Conte Fabrizio di Castiglioni
<magician>

Jan 21 to Feb 14
French Magic Company
Schumann

Feb 15 to March 20
Carnival Masked Balls

March 25 to 31
Children Dramatic Company
Berenguer Brothers

**FRENCH OPERETTA
COMPANY**
April 16 to 18
LES BRIGANDS (Offenbach)

May 17
Symphonic Concert
Conductor: Luigi Preti
Soloists: Gerome <s>,
Sambucetti Jr. <vn>

**WINTER ITALIAN OPERA
SEASON**
May 24 to Sept 17
Conductor: Luigi Preti
Chorus master: Francisco Seguí
Director: R. Marconi
Designer (Scenography): Orestes
Coliva
Principal Dancers: Bálsamo,
Rocca; Zabo

May 24, 25
RUY BLAS (Marchetti)
La Regina: Missorta
Ruy Blas: Toressi
Casilda: Tancioni
Don Salustio de Bazan: Mazzoli
Don Guritano: Wagner

May 27, 28, July 23
LA TRAVIATA (Verdi)
Violetta: Andreff
Alfredo Germont: Parasini
G. Germont: Mazzoli(2) /
Formilli(1)
Flora: Ubaldi
Annina: Motelli
Gastone: Berti
Barone Douphol: Marini

Marchese D'Obigny: Pedotti
Dottore Grenvil: Marconi

June 1, 7, 11, Aug 13
FAUST (Gounod) (It)
Margherita: Andreff
Faust: Vidal(3) / Parasini(1)
Mefistofele: Dondi
Siebel: Tancioni
Valentin: Mazzoli
Marta: Consolani
Wagner: Pedotti

June 3, 24
IL BARBIERE DI SIVIGLIA
(Rossini)
Rosina: Tancioni
Conte di Almaviva: Vidal
Figaro: Mazzoli
Don Basilio: Dondi
Don Bartolo: Giordani
Berta: Consolani
Fiorello: Berti

June 10, 14, 15, July 21, 22, Aug
30
LA FORZA DEL DESTINO (Verdi)
Leonora: Missorta
Don Alvaro: Toressi
Don Carlo: Mazzoli
Preziosilla: Tancioni
Marchese di Calatrava: Marconi
Padre Guardiano: Dondi
Curra: Ubaldi

June 18
LA SONNAMBULA (Bellini)
Amina: Andreff
Elvino: Vidal
Conte Rodolfo: Tansini
Teresa: Ubaldi
Lisa: Consolani
Alessio: Pedotti

June 22, July 2
L'EBREA (Halévy) (It)
Rachel: Missorta
Eleazar: Toressi

Principessa Eudoxia: Tancioni
Cardinal Brogni: Dondi
Alberto: Marconi
Principe Leopoldo: Parasini
Ruggero: Berti

June 28, 29, July 1, 5, 9, 12
NORMA (Bellini)
Norma: Pascal
Adalgisa: Tancioni
Pollione: Toressi
Oroveso: Dondi
Flavio: Berti

July 7, 8, 11, 14, 16, 18, Aug 4, 17,
19, 25
IL GUARANY (Gomes)**
Scenography: Coliva
Cecilia: Missorta
Pery: Toressi
Gonzalez: Mazzoli
Il Cacico: Dondi
Don Antonio de Mariz: Tansini
Don Alvaro: Berti
Ruy Bento: Marino
Alonso: Giordani
Pedro: Pedotti

July 27, 28, 30, Aug 1, 6
GLI UGONOTTI (Meyerbeer) (It)
Margherita de Valois: Andreff
Raul de Nangis: Toressi
Valentina: Missorta
Urbano: Consolani
Conte di Nevers: Mazzoli
Conte di Saint-Bris: Tansini
Marcello: Dondi

Aug 9, 11, 12, Sept 5
UN BALLO IN MASCHERA (Verdi)
Amelia: Missorta
Riccardo: Aubriot
Renato: Mazzoli
Ulrica: Consolani
Oscar: Andreff
Samuel: Tansini
Tom: Giordani

Aug 15, Sept 1
RIGOLETTO (Verdi)
Gilda: Andreff
Il Duca di Mantova: Vidal
Rigoletto: Mazzoli
Maddalena: Consolani
Sparafucile: Tansini
Giovanna: Ubaldi
Mateo Borsa: Berti
Monterone: Giordani
Ceprano: Pedotti

Aug 23, 24, 27
ERNANI (Verdi)
Elvira: Missorta
Ernani: Toressi
Don Carlo: Mazzoli
D. Ruy Gomez de Silva: Dondi
Giovanna: Ubaldi
Don Riccardo: Berti
Iago: Pedotti

Aug 25
Uruguayan National Anthem
Soloist: Aubriot <t>
IL GUARANY (Gomes)
[same cast as July 7]

Sept 2, 7, 10
SALVATOR ROSA (Gomes)**
Isabella: Missorta
Genariello: Andreff
Salvator Rosa: Toressi
Masaniello: Mazzoli
Il Duca d'Arcos: Dondi
Il Conte di Badajoz: Berti
Fernandez: Marino
Corcelli: Giordani
Bianca: Ubaldi
Sor Inez: Ubaldi
Fra Lorenzo: Pedotti

Sept 6
LA FAVORITA (Donizetti) (It)
Leonora: Tancioni
Fernando: Vidal
Alfonso XI: Mazzoli

Inez: Ubaldi
Baldassare: Dondi
Gaspare: Berti

Sept 8, 9
LUCREZIA BORGIA (Donizetti)
Lucrezia: Missorta
Gennaro: Parasini
Duca Alfonso: Dondi
Maffio Orsini: Tancioni
Gubetta: Giordani
Liverotto: De Bezzi
Gazella: Pedotti
Petrucci: Moroni
Vitelozzo: Marino
Rustighello: Berti

Sept 12
LUCIA DI LAMMERMOOR
(Donizetti)
Lucia: Andreff
Edgardo: Vidal
Enrico: Mazzoli
Normanno: De Bezzi
Raimondo: Tansini
and Concert Signora Val <vn>

Sept 17
IL TROVATORE (Verdi)
Leonora: Signora Val
Manrico: Val
Conte di Luna: Subirana
Azucena: Bruzzone
Ferrando: Marconi

**SPANISH ZARZUELA
COMPANY**
Sept 21, 30

FRENCH OPERA SEASON
Oct 1 to 31

Oct 1, 22, 31
LA TRAVIATA (Verdi) (Fr)
Violette: Alhaiza
Claire: Falconet
Annette: Augier

Rodolphe D'Orbel: Gadilhe
Georges D'Orbel: Clergeaud
Le docteur: Pother
Le Vicomte: De Cré
Le Baron: Bazin
Valet: Matray

Oct 3, 10
LUCIE DE LAMMERMOOR
(Donizetti) (Fr)
Lucie: Alhaiza
Edgard: Gadilhe
Ashton: Clergeaud
Raymond: Pother
Arthur: De Cré
Gilbert: Matray

Oct 5, 8
MIGNON (Thomas)**
Mignon: Falconet
Philine: Alhaiza
Wilhem Meister: Gadilhe
Laertes: De Cré
Lothario: Pother
Giarno: Bazin
Frédéric: Matray
Antoine: Lafont

Oct 12, 15, 19
HAMLET (Thomas)**
Hamlet: Clergeaud
Ophelia: Alhaiza
Claude: Pother
Laertes: Gadilhe
Gertrude: Falconet
Polonio: Lafont
L'Ombre du Roi: A. Augier
Marcellus: De Cré
Polonius: Leon
Horatio: Lafont
1r. Fossoyeur: Bazin

Oct 17
HAYDEE (Auber)**
Haydée: Alhaiza
Loredan: Gadilhe
Malipieri: Pother

Oct 23, 29
LES AMOURS DU DIABLE
(Grisar)**
Urielle: Alhaiza

Oct 26
FAUST (Gounod)
Marguerite: Alhaiza
Faust: Gadilhe
Méphistofélès: Augier
Siebel: Falconet
Valentin: Clergeaud
Marthe: Dimier
Wagner: Bazin

Oct 31
LA TRAVIATA (Verdi) (Fr)
and Concert by French Lyric
Company artists
Soloist: Alhaiza <s>

Nov 19
Symphonic Concert
Montevideo Musical Societies
Conductor: Eduardo Torrens
<composer/pf>

1877

Female artists
Alhaiza, Aline <s>
Carlany, Eva <mez>
D'Adini, Ada <s>
Dimier, Mlle. <s>
Falconet, Mlle. <mez>
Felice, Carlotta <mez>
Henri, Mlle. <s>
Motelli, Signora <mez>
Pagliero, Maria <mez>
Potentini, Vittoria <s>
Pratto-Lalloni, Emma <mez>

Male artists
Aramburo, Antonio <t>
Augier, Achille <b>
Bazin, Monsieur <b>
Boschini, Leonida <bar/b>

Clergeaud, Monsieur <bar>
De Bezzi, Signor <t>
De Cré, Pomponet <t>
Gadilhe, M. <t>
Lafont, Monsieur <b>
Lalloni, Lorenzo <bar>
Lestellier, Signor <t>
Marconi, Raffaele <b>
Matray, Monsieur <b>
Monti, Gaetano <b>
Ortisi, Gaetano <t>
Parmesini, Giovanni <t>
Pother, Monsieur <b>

FRENCH OPERA SEASON
Jan 6 to March 19

Jan 6
LUCIE DE LAMMERMOOR
(Donizetti) (Fr)
Lucie: Alhaiza
Edgard: Gadilhe
Ashton: Clergeaud
Raymond: Pother
Arthur: De Cré
Gilbert: Matray

Jan 7, March 19
LA FILLE DU REGIMENT
(Donizetti)
Marie: Carlany
and LES NOCES DE JEANETTE
(Massé)
Jeanette: Alhaiza

Jan 9
LES MOUSQUETAIRES DE LA
REINE (Halévy)

Jan 11
LA DAME BLANCHE (Boieldieu)
Anne: Alhaiza

Jan 14
MARTHE (Flotow) (Fr)
Lady Harriet: Alhaiza
Lionel: Gadilhe
Lord Tristan: Clergeaud

Jan 17, 28
LA FAVORITE (Donizetti)
Léonor: Carlany
Fernand: Gadilhe
Alphonse XI: Clergeaud
Inès: Dimier
Gaspard: Matray
Balthazar: Pother

Jan 19, 21, 25, 26, Feb 9
LA FILLE DE MADAME ANGOT
(Lecocq)
Clairette: Henri

Jan 24
LA TRAVIATA (Verdi) (Fr)
Violette: Alhaiza
Claire: Falconet
Annette: Augier
Rodolphe D'Orbel: Gadilhe
Georges D'Orbel: Clergeaud
Le docteur: Pother
Le Vicomte: De Cré
Le Baron: Bazin
Valet: Matray

Jan 31
HAYDEE (Auber)
Haydée: Alhaiza
Loredan: Gadilhe
Malipieri: Pother

Feb 2, 28, March 9
RIGOLETTO (Verdi) (Fr)
Gilda: Alhaiza
Le Duc: Gadilhe
Rigoletto: Clergeaud
Sparafucile: Augier
Madeleine: Carlany

Feb 4
LES AMOURS DU DIABLE (Grisar)
Urielle: Alhaiza

Feb 7
FAUST (Gounod)
Marguerite: Carlany
Faust: Gadilhe

Méphistofélès: Augier
Siebel: Alhaiza
Valentin: Clergeaud
Marthe: Dimier
Wagner: Bazin

Feb 9
LA FILLE DE MADAME ANGOT
(Lecocq)
and Hamlet: Act 4 "Le Lac"

Feb 10 to 21
Carnival Masked Balls

Feb 22, 25, March 7
LES HUGUENOTS (Meyerbeer)
Raoul de Nangis: Gadilhe
Marguerite de Valois: Alhaiza
Valentine: Carlany
Comte de Nevers: Clergeaud
Comte de Saint-Bris: Augier
Maurevert: Pother

March 2, 4, 14, 18
LES BRIGANDS (Offenbach)

March 11, 16
LE VOYAGE EN CHINE (Bazin)**

March 19
LA FILLE DU REGIMENT
(Donizetti)
and Farewell *Concert*

March 22 to April 10
Acrobatic Company Maria
Speltrini
"The Niagara's Queen"

May 1
Symphonic Concert
Orquesta Sociedad Musical "La
Lira"

ITALIAN OPERA SEASON
May 17 to Sept 11
Conductor: Oreste Bimboni

May 17, 18, 20, Aug 4, 5
MACBETH (Verdi)
Lady Macbeth: Potentini
Macbeth: Lalloni
Banquo: Monti
Malcolm: De Bezzi
Macduff: Parmesini

May 22, 25, June 3, 16, July 26,
31, Aug 26
IL TROVATORE (Verdi)
Leonora: Potentini
Manrico: Aramburo(6) / Ortisi(1)
Conte di Luna: Lalloni
Azucena: Pratto(3) / Felice(3) /
Pratto(1)
Ferrando: Monti

May 26, June 26, July 3, Aug 21
RIGOLETTO (Verdi)
Gilda: D'Adini
Il Duca: Lestellier(3) /
Aramburo(1)
Rigoletto: Lalloni(3) / Boschini(1)
Sparafucile: Monti
Maddalena: Pratto

May 27, June 2, 10
LUCIA DI LAMMERMOOR
(Donizetti)
Lucia: D'Adini
Edgardo: Aramburo
Enrico: Boschini
Raimondo: Monti

May 28, 30, June 17, Aug 7
POLIUTO (Donizetti)
Poliuto: Aramburo
Paolina: Potentini
Severus: Lalloni
Callisthenes: Monti(2) /
Boschini(1) / Monti(1)
Nearco: Parmesini
Felice: De Bezzi
Cristiano: Lafont

June 6, 8, Aug 2
FAUST (Gounod) (It)
Margherita: D'Adini
Faust: Lestellier
Mefistofele: Monti
Siebel: Pratto
Valentin: Boschini(2) / Lalloni(1)

June 12
NORMA (Bellini)
Norma: Potentini
Adalgisa: D'Adini
Pollione: Aramburo
Oroveso: Monti
Clotilde: Pagliero
Flavio: De Bezzi

June 21, 23, 24, 29, July 1, Aug
18, 19, 23
IL GUARANY (Gomes)
Cecilia: Potentini
Pery: Aramburo(5) / Ortisi(3)
Gonzalez: Lalloni
Il Cacico: Monti(5) / Boschini(3)
Don Antonio de Mariz:
Boschini(5) / Monti(3)
Don Alvaro: Parmesini
Ruy Bento: De Bezzi
Alonso: Marconi
Pedro: Lafont

June 28
ERNANI (Verdi)
Elvira: Potentini
Ernani: Lestellier
Don Carlo: Lalloni
D. Ruy Gomez de Silva: Monti
Giovanna: Pagliero
Don Riccardo: De Bezzi
Iago: Marconi

July 5, 7, 8, 21, Aug 9, 12, 25
LA FAVORITA (Donizetti) (It)
Leonora: Potentini
Fernando: Aramburo
Alfonso XI: Lalloni
Baldassare: Monti
Inez: D'Adini

July 14, 15, 17, 24, 29, Sept 8, 11
AIDA (Verdi)**
Aida: Potentini
Amneris: Felice
Radamès: Lestellier(3) /
Aramburo(2) / Lestellier(2)
Amonasro: Lalloni
Ramfis: Boschini
Il Re: Monti

July 28, Aug 14, 28
I VESPRI SICILIANI (Verdi)
Duchessa Elena: Potentini
Arrigo: Lestellier
Simon de Monfort: Lalloni
Giovanni de Procida: Monti

Aug 14
I VESPRI SICILIANI (Verdi)
[same cast as July 28]
and Operatic *Concert*

Aug 25
Uruguayan National Anthem
LA FAVORITA (Donizetti)
[same cast as July 7]
and Operatic *Concert*

Sept 7
UN BALLO IN MASCHERA (Verdi)
Amelia: Potentini
Riccardo: Lestellieri
Renato: Lalloni
Ulrica: Felice

**ITALIAN OPERA SECOND
SEASON**
Nov 3 to 15
Conductor: Oreste Bimboni

Nov 3
FAUST (Gounod) (It)
Margherita: D'Adini
Faust: Lestellier
Mefistofele: Monti
Siebel: Pratto
Valentin: Lalloni

Nov 4, 11
IL TROVATORE (Verdi)
Leonora: Potentini
Manrico: Ortisi
Conte di Luna: Lalloni
Azucena: Pratto
Ferrando: Monti

Nov 6, 15
AIDA (Verdi)
Aida: Potentini
Amneris: Felice
Radamès: Lestellier
Amonasro: Lalloni
Ramfis: Boschini
Il Re: Monti
and Farewell Company *Concert*
[Nov 15 only]

----- 1878 -----

Female artists
Angioletti, Signora <mez>
Avalli, Lucia <mez>
Blechschmidt, Julia <vn>
Caracciolo-Strozzi, Laura <mez>
Cortesi, Ersilia <s>
D'Orcanti, Signora <s>
Gallo, Luisa <pf>
Henri, Mlle. <s>
Lespagne, Mlle. <mez>
Repetto, Signora <s>
Singer, Teresa <s>
Stampanoni, A. <s>

Male artists
Aubriot, Enrique <t>
Augier, Achille <b>
Blechschmidt, J. <vn>
Bulterini, Carlo <t>
Cottone, Vincenzo <bar>
De Bezzi, Signor <t>
Desiré, Monsieur <t>
Feratoni, Signor <bar>
Forsten (Foster), Signor <bar>
Gottardi, Signor <t>
Maffei, Giovanni <bar>

Milani, Signor <t>
Narberti, Antonio <b>
Sortini, R. <b>
Villanova, Francesco <b>

SUMMER OPERA SEASON
Jan 19 to Feb 3

Jan 19
LUCIA DI LAMMERMOOR
(Donizetti)
Lucia: Repetto
Edgardo: Milani
Enrico: Maffei

Jan 20
LA TRAVIATA (Verdi)
Violetta: Repetto
Alfredo Germont: Milani
Giorgio Germont: Maffei

Jan 23
IL BARBIERE DI SIVIGLIA
(Rossini)
Rosina: Repetto
Conte di Almaviva: Aubriot
Figaro: Maffei

Jan 27, Feb 1 and 3
Operatic Concerts

May 4
Romea Dramatic Company

WINTER OPERA SEASON
First Part, May 24 to July 27
Conductor: Leopoldo
Montenegro
Director: Jaime de Bezzi
Designer (Scenography): Orestes
Coliva

May 24
IL TROVATORE (Verdi)
Leonora: Singer
Manrico: Bulterini
Conte di Luna: Cottone
Azucena: Caracciolo / Avalli

Ferrando: Augier
Ruiz: Villanova

May 25, 29
FAUST (Gounod) (It)
Margherita: Cortesi
Faust: Bulterini
Mefistofele: Narberti
Siebel: Caracciolo
Marta: Avalli
Valentin: Forsten
Wagner: Sortini

May 30, June 16, 20, 23, July 14
LA FAVORITA (Donizetti) (It)
Leonora: Caracciolo
Fernando: Bulterini
Alfonso XI: Forsten
Baldassare: Narberti
Gaspare: Villanova
Inez: Avalli

June 4, 6, July 11, 16, 18
LUCREZIA BORGIA (Donizetti)
Lucrezia: Singer
Gennaro: Gottardi
Duca Alfonso: Cottone
Maffio Orsini: Caracciolo

June 9
LA SONNAMBULA (Bellini)
Amina: Cortesi
Elvino: Bulterini
Conte Rodolfo: Feratoni
Lisa: Angioletti
Teresa: Stampanoni
Alessio: De Bezzi

June 11, 13, 27
UN BALLO IN MASCHERA (Verdi)
Amelia: Singer
Riccardo: Bulterini
Renato: Cottone
Ulrica: Caracciolo
Oscar: Cortesi
Tom: Narberti
Samuel: Villanova
Silvano: De Bezzi

June 18, 24
RUY BLAS (Marchetti)
La Regina: Singer
Ruy Blas: Bulterini
Casilda: Caracciolo
Don Salustio de Bazan: Cottone
Don Guritano: Sortini
Donna Giovanna: Avalli

June 29, July 6, 9
NORMA (Bellini)
Norma: Singer
Adalgisa: Angioletti(1) /
D'Orcanti(2)
Pollione: Bulterini
Oroveso: Augier

July 4, 7
LA EDUCANDE DI SORRENTO
(Usiglio)**
Luisa: Cortesi
Augusto: Giottardi
Placida: Caracciolo
Don Democrito: Sortini
Rodolfo: Foster

July 13
LINDA DI CHAMOUNIX
(Donizetti)
Linda: Cortesi
Visconte di Sirval: Giottardi
Marquis Boisfleuris: Cottone
Prefetto: Sortini
and Concert Italian Lyric
Company artists with
Blechschmidt <vn>

July 14
LA FAVORITA (Donizetti)
and Concert Italian Lyric
Company artists with
Blechschmidt <vn>

July 23, 24, 26, 27
AIDA (Verdi)
Aida: Singer
Amneris: Caracciolo
Radamès: Bulterini

Amonasro: Cottone
Ramfis: Villanova
Il Re: Narberti

WINTER OPERA SEASON
Second Part, Aug 25 to Sept 26
Conductor: Leopoldo
Montenegro
Director: Jaime de Bezzi
Designer (Scenography): Orestes
Coliva

Aug 25
Uruguayan National Anthem
UN BALLO IN MASCHERA (Verdi)
and *Concert* with Giribaldi's Aria
from Parisina**** Singer <s>

Aug 28
RUY BLAS (Marchetti)
[same cast as June 18]

Aug 30
NORMA (Bellini)
Norma: Singer
Adalgisa: Cortesi
Pollione: Bulterini
Oroveso: Augier

Sept 3, 8
FAUST (Gounod) (It)
Margherita: Singer
Faust: Bulterini
Mefistofele: Augier
Siebel: Caracciolo
Marta: Avalli
Valentin: Cottone
Wagner: Sortini

Sept 5, 7, 22
AIDA (Verdi)
[same cast as July 23]

Sept 14, 15, 17, 25
PARISINA (Giribaldi)****
[First Uruguayan opera]
Parisina: Singer
Ugo: Bulterini

Azzo: Cottone
Imelda: Avalli
Ernesto: Augier

Sept 19
IL TROVATORE (Verdi)
Leonora: Singer
Manrico: Bulterini
Conte di Luna: Cottone
Azucena: Avalli
Ferrando: Augier
Ruiz: Villanova

Sept 22
AIDA (Verdi)
and Parisina: Sinfonía

Sept 26
Operatic Concert
Il Guarany: Act 1
Aida: Acts 3 and 4

FRENCH OPERETTA SEASON
Oct 17 to Nov 10
Conductor: L. Cochelin

Oct 17, 20
LA PETITE MARIEE (Lecocq)**

Oct 19, 27
LA FILLE DE MADAME ANGOT
(Lecocq)
Clairette: Henri
Mademoiselle Lange: Lespagne
Ange Pitou: Desiré

Oct 22, 31, Nov 7
LE PETIT FAUST (Hervé)**
Faust: Desiré

Oct 24, 26, 29, Nov 1, 9
LAS CLOCHES DE CORNEVILLE
(Planquette)**

Nov 3
MARCEAU (?)

Nov 5
LES BRIGANDS (Offenbach)

Nov 10
LE PETIT DUC (Lecocq)
and Las Cloches de Corneville:
Act 3

Nov 12
Symphonic Concert
Soloist: Gallo <pf>

1879

Female artists
Antonietti, Ida <mez>
Avalli, Lucia <mez>
Belloni, Signora <mez>
Conti-Foroni, Amalia <s>
Felicio, Mlle. <mez>
Garbini, Adela <s>
Giutti, Emilia <s>
Leuters, Mlle. <s>
Ponte, Carmen del <pf>
Springer-Dominici, Sidonia <s>
Vercolini-Tay, Signora <mez/a>

Male artists
Bazelli, Lorenzo <b>
Belluci, H. <vn>
Bomon, E. <vc>
Bottesini, Giovanni <db>
Charnod, Monsieur <b-buffo>
Cottone, Vincenzo <bar>
Desiré, Monsieur <t>
Dominici, Giuseppe <bar>
Etienne, Monsieur <b>
Felicio, Monsieur
Fradelloni, Achille <b>
Franco, Antonio <t>
Gaito, G. <vn>
Ghignatti, G. <vla>
Giannini, Francesco <t>
Gonzalez, Señor <b>
Mazzoli, Agustín <bar>
Mirabella, Giovanni <b>
Ponte, Signor <pf>
Richard, Monsieur <t>
Villanova, Francesco <b>
White, Mr. <vn>

March 1
Spanish Comedy Company

WINTER OPERA SEASON
May 17 to Sept 7
Conductor: Oreste Bimboni

May 17, 18, 25, June 12, 16
IL TROVATORE (Verdi)
Leonora: Conti-Foroni(3) /
Garbini(2)
Manrico: Giannini(3) / Franco(2)
Conte di Luna: Mazzoli
Azucena: Vercolini
Inez: Avalli
Ferrando: Fradelloni
Ruiz: Villanova

May 19
RIGOLETTO (Verdi)
Gilda: Garbini
Il Duca di Mantova: Franco
Rigoletto: Dominici
Maddalena: Antonietti
Sparafucile: Mirabella

May 22, 27, June 3, 15
LA TRAVIATA (Verdi)
Violetta: Garbini
Alfredo Germont: Giannini
Giorgio Germont: Dominici
Flora: Springer
Annina: Avalli
Barone Douphol: Fradelloni
Marchese D'Obigny: Villanova
Dottore Grenvil: Gonzalez

May 29, June 1, 5, Sept 7
FAUST (Gounod) (It)
Margherita: Conti-Foroni
Faust: Giannini
Mefistofele: Mirabella
Valentin: Dominici

June 7, 8, July 1
L'EBREA (Halévy)
Rachel: Conti-Foroni
Eleazar: Giannini

Principessa Eudoxia: Springer
Cardinal Brogni: Mirabella

June 14, 18, July 4
JONE (Petrella)
Jone: Garbini
Glauco: Franco
Nidia: Vercolini
Arbace: Cottone
Burbo: Mirabella

June 21, 24, 26
LA FAVORITA (Donizetti) (It)
Leonora: Vercolini
Fernando: Giannini
Alfonso XI: Dominici
Inez: Avalli
Baldassare: Mirabella
Gaspare: Villanova

June 28, Aug 6
UN BALLO IN MASCHERA (Verdi)
Amelia: Conti-Foroni
Riccardo: Giannini
Renato: Mazzoli
Ulrica: Vercolini
Oscar: Springer
Samuel: Fradelloni
Tom: Mirabella

July 6, 8, 13, 30
RUY BLAS (Marchetti)
La Regina: Conti-Foroni
Ruy Blas: Giannini
Don Cesar de Bazan: Cottone
Casilda: Vercolini
Don Guritano: Mirabella

July 11, 18, 20, Aug 17
LA FORZA DEL DESTINO (Verdi)
Leonora: Conti-Foroni
Don Alvaro: Giannini
Don Carlo: Dominici
Preziosilla: Vercolini
Padre Guardiano: Mirabella

July 16, 23, 27
IL GUARANY (Gomes)
Cecilia: Garbini
Pery: Franco

Gonzalez: Cottone
Il Cacico: Villanova
Don Antonio de Mariz:
Mirabella
Ruy-Bento: Bazelli
Alonso: Fradelloni
Pedro: Gonzalez

Aug 1, 3, 13, 15, 25, Sept 3
AIDA (Verdi)
Aida: Garbini
Radamès: Giannini
Amneris: Vercolini
Amonasro: Dominici
Ramfis: Cottone
Il Re: Mirabella
Sommo Sacerdote: Fradelloni
Sacerdote: Villanova

Aug 6
UN BALLO IN MASCHERA (Verdi)
[same cast as June 28]
and Instrumental Concert: White
<vn>

Aug 8, 10
LUCIA DI LAMMERMOOR
(Donizetti)
Lucia: Garbini
Edgardo: Giannini
Enrico: Cottone
Raimondo: Fradelloni
Alissa: Avalli
and Concert with soloist White
<vn>

Aug 20, 24
POLIUTO (Donizetti)
Poliuto: Giannini
Paolina: Conti-Foroni
Severus: Cottone
Callisthenes: Mirabella
Felice: Villanova

Aug 22
GEMMA DI VERGY (Donizetti)
Gemma: Conti-Foroni
Tomasso: Giannini

Conte di Vergy: Dominici
Guido: Fradelloni

Aug 30
SAFFO (Pacini)
Saffo: Garbini
Faone: Giannini
Alcandro: Cottone

Sept 5
Operatic Concert

Sept 7
FAUST (Gounod) (It)
[same cast as May 29]
and Farewell Concert by Italian
Lyric Company artists

**FRENCH OPERA AND
OPERETTA SEASON**
Sept 11 to Oct 10
Conductor: L. Cochelin

Sept 11
LA REINE INDIGO (J. Strauss)
Fantasca: Leuters

Sept 13, 28
LA FILLE DU REGIMENT
(Donizetti)
Marie: Leuters
Sulpice: Charnod
Tonio: Desiré
Hortensius: Etienne
La Marquise de Berkenfeld:
Belloni
La Duchesse: Felicio
Un valet: Richard

Sept 14
LE PETIT DUC (Lecocq)

Sept 18, 23, Oct 2, 12
LAS CLOCHES DE CORNEVILLE
(Planquette)

Sept 20, Oct 9
LA FILLE DE MADAME ANGOT
(Lecocq)
Clairette: Leuters

Sept 25
LE DOMINO ROSE (Hennequin)**

Sept 27, Oct 5
ORPHEE AUX ENFERS
(Offenbach)
Eurydice: Leuters

Sept 30
BEBE (Hennequin)

Oct 4
LA GRAND DUCHESSE DE
GEROLSTEIN (Offenbach)

Oct 7
LE GRAND CASIMIR (Lecocq)

Oct 10
LE DROIT DU SEIGNEUR
(Vasseur)

Oct 11 and 13
Vocal-Instrumental Recitals:
Giutti <s>, Bottesini <db>,
Ponte <pf>, Gaito <vn>, Belluci
<vn>, Ghignatti <vla>, and
Bomon <vc>

Oct 19 to Nov 18
Italian Dramatic Company
Ernesto Rossi

**SPANISH ZARZUELA
COMPANY**
from Madrid's Teatro Apolo
Avelino Aguirre, Impresario
Dec 6 to 31
Repertory:
CAMPANONE (Mazza)
LA GALLINA CIEGA (Fernández-
Caballero)
LOS COMEDIANTES DE ANTAÑO
(Barbieri)
MARINA (Arrieta)
EL BARBERILLO DE LAVAPIES
(Barbieri)

LOS DIAMANTES DE LA CORONA
(Auber)
EL POSTILLON DE LA RIOJA
(Oudrid)
JUAN DE URBINA (Barbieri)
EL ANILLO DE HIERRO (Marqués)
LOS MAGYARES (Gaztambide)

1880

Female artists
Avalli, Lucia <mez>
Blume, Bianca <s>
Franco, Matilde <s>
Hellstrom, Luisa <s>
Roca, Gabriela <s>
Stampanoni, A. <s>

Male artists
Bazelli, Lorenzo <b>
Beracoechea, Sebastián <t>
Blanc, Hubert de <pf/
armonium>
Dengremont, Maurice <vn>
Dominini, Giuseppe <t>
Fradelloni, Achille <b>
Galván, Cristóbal <t>
Marasini, Mario <t>
Monti, Francisco de Paula <bar>
Pfeiffer, Oscar <pf>
Subirá, José <b>
Terzi, Titto <bar>

**SPANISH ZARZUELA
COMPANY**
[continuing from 1879]
Jan 1 to 30, May 16 to Sept 29,
Oct 5 to Nov 22, Dec 8 to 31
Avelino Aguirre, Impresario
Repertory: same as 1879 [plus
new zarzuelas listed here]

Jan 31 to March 10
Carnival Masked Balls

ITALIAN OPERA COMPANY
Conductor: Giuseppe Pomè-
Penna
March 31, April 2, 3, 4
LA FORZA DEL DESTINO (Verdi)
Leonora: Blume
Don Alvaro: Marasini
Don Carlo: Terzi
Preziosilla: Avalli
Marchese di Calatrava: Bazelli
Padre Guardiano: Fradelloni

April 14 to 23
Conte Ernesto Patrizio Magic
Company

April 30 to May 11
Hermann Company <Viennese
prestidigitator>

July 18
Uruguayan National Anthem
EL DIABLO EN EL PODER
(Barbieri)
and UN PLEITO (Gaztambide)

Aug 25
Uruguayan National Anthem
LAS HIJAS DE EVA (Gaztambide)

Sept 23
LA GUERRA SANTA (Arrieta)

Sept 30
Symphonic Concert
Conductor: Gioachino Salvini
Soloists: Dengremont <vn> and
Blanc <pf>
Beriot: Violin concerto no.7
Seivri: Grande fantasie from Il
trovatore
Leonard: Variations et fantasie
brillant

Oct 4
Symphonic Concert
In Memoriam Alceo Caneschi
Conductor: Gioachino Salvini
Meyerbeer: Sinfonia Dinorah

Mozart: Turkish march
Gounod: Ave Maria for strings
Wagner: March and chorus
from Tannhäuser
Liszt: Hungarian Rhapsody no.2
Caneschi: Gran batalla (Militar
Fantasy)

Oct 28
OFELIA (Calvo)****
Ofelia: Franco
La Reina: Roca
Hamlet: Beracoechea
El Rey: Monti
Horacio: Subirá

Nov 24
Recital "Concert d'adieu":
Hellstrom <s>, Dengremont
<vn>, Blanc <pf / armonium>
and Pfeiffer <pf>
Leonard: Souvenir de Baden
<vn / pf>
Masnardi: Estasi d'amore <s / pf>
Liszt: Fantasie après Le prophète
pour piano <Pfeiffer>
Corelli: La Folia <vn / pf>
Gounod: Ave Maria <s / vn / pf /
armonium>
Pfeiffer: Piano duet après Robert
le diable: Pfeiffer / de Blanc
Sarasate-Chopin: Nocturne <vn /
pf>
Montenegro: Le rossignol <s / pf>
Wagner: Marche Tannhäuser
Paganini-Ernest: Carnival de
Venice <vn / pf>

Dec 5
"Grand Concert" (two hundred
musicians)
Orchestras: Solís, San Felipe,
and Cibils Theaters
Chorus: Sociedad Musical "La
Lira" and Sociedad Lega
Lombarda
Conductor: Gioachino Salvini

Mercadante: Grande sinfonia
Garibaldi
Rossini: Guglielmo Tell Hunters'
Chorus
Ponchielli: Sinfonia original
Rossini: Sinfonia from Le siège
de Corinthe
Weber: Invitation to the Dance
(Salvini's instrumentation)
Giribaldi: Sinfonia from La
Parisina
Liszt: Hungarian Rhapsody no. 2
Caneschi: Gran batalla (Militar
Fantasy)

1881

Female artists
Blanche, Mlle. <s>
Delorme, Mlle. <mez>
Ferri, Margherita Alda <mez>
Gregoire, Mlle. <mez>
Lentz, Julie <a>
Leroux, Hélène <s>
Malvina, Mlle. <mez>
Marié, Paola <mez>
Maugé, Mlle. <mez>
Merle, Mlle. <mez>
Pirola, Maddalena <s>
Privat, Anais <mez>
Roza, Petronila <mez>
Teresina, Mlle. <s>
Waldteufel, Mlle. <s>
Zanardi, Clotilde <s>

Male artists
Arrigoni, Cesare <t>
Barbé, Henri <bar>
Bazelli, Lorenzo <b>
Bonora, Pietro <b>
Ceresa, Luigi <t>
Dangón, Monsieur <b>
Etienne, Monsieur <b>
Forti, Gaetano <bar>
Ghizone, N. <t>
Giovanini, Signor <t>
Maugé, F. <b / bar>

Mauras, Paul M. <t>
Merle, Monsieur <t>
Mussy, Monsieur <b>
Nigri, Monsieur <b>
Perret, Monsieur <t>
Piroia, Horace <t>
Poyard, Monsieur <bar>
Rebelly, Monsieur <bar>

**MARIMON SPANISH
ZARZUELA COMPANY**
Feb 6, 7, 8
CAMPANONE (Mazza)

March to April 26
Italian Dramatic Company

June and July
Dramatic Company Cuniberti
Brothers

**FRENCH OPERA AND
OPERETTA SEASON**
Maurice Grau, Impresario
July 25 to Aug 28
Conductor: Mr. Gravenstein

July 25
MIGNON (Thomas)
Mignon: Marié
Guillaume: Merle
Philine: Leroux
Lothario: Maugé
Frédéric: Merle

July 26, Aug 14
MADAME FAVART (Offenbach)

July 28
CARMEN (Bizet)
Carmen: Marié
Don José: Mauras
Escamillo: Maugé
Micaela: Leroux
Frasquita: Gregoire
Mercedes: Merle
Zúñiga: Nigri
Le Dancaire: Poyard

Le Remendado: Perret
Morales: Mussy
Lilas Pastia: Merle

July 30
LA FILLE DU TAMBOUR MAJOR
(Offenbach)

July 31
LA FILLE DE MADAME ANGOT
(Lecocq)

Aug 2
LA MASCOTTE (Audran)

Aug 3, 7
SI J'ETAIS ROI (Adams)

Aug 4
LA PERICHOLE (Offenbach)**

Aug 6
LES NOCES D'OLIVETTE (Audran)

Aug 9
LAS CLOCHES DE CORNEVILLE
(Planquette)

Aug 10, 20
LE PRE AUX CLERS (Hérold)

Aug 11
LE PETIT DUC (Lecocq)

Aug 13
LA FILLE DU REGIMENT
(Donizetti)
Marie: Leroux
Tonio: Mauras
Sulpice: Maugé
La Marquise de Berkenfeld:
Delorme
La Duchesse: Malvina

Aug 17
LA TRAVIATA (Verdi) (Fr)
Violette: Leroux
Rodolphe D'Orbel: Mauras
Georges D'Orbel: Maugé

Aug 18
LA MARJOLAINE (Lecocq)

Aug 21, 26
LA GRAND DUCHESSE DE
GEROLSTEIN (Offenbach)

Aug 24
GIROFLE—GIROFLA (Lecocq)**

Aug 27
BARBE-BLEUE (Offenbach)

Aug 28
PAUL ET VIRGINIE (Massé)***
Virginie: Leroux
Paul: Mauras
Meala: Lentz
Madame de Latour: Gregoire
Marguerite: Merle
Dominique: Maugé

ITALIAN OPERA SEASON
Sept 1 to 30
Conductor: G. Ferri

Sept 1, 4, 20
NABUCCO (Verdi)
Abigaille: Pirola
Ismaele: Ceresa
Nabucco: Forti
Fenena: Ferri
Zaccaria: Bonora
Abdallo: Giovanini

Sept 3, 11
IL TROVATORE (Verdi)
Leonora: Pirola
Manrico: Arrigoni
Conte di Luna: Forti
Azucena: Ferri
Ferrando: Bonora

Sept 6
LUCREZIA BORGIA (Donizetti)
Lucrezia: Pirola
Gennaro: Arrigoni
Duca Alfonso: Forti
Maffio Orsini: Ferri

Sept 8, 10, 22
LA TRAVIATA (Verdi)
Violetta: Pirola
Alfredo Germont: Arrigoni
Giorgio Germont: Forti
Flora: Ferri

Sept 13, 16
NORMA (Bellini)
Norma: Pirola
Adalgisa: Ferri
Pollione: Arrigoni
Oroveso: Bonora
Clotilde: Roza
Flavio: Ghizone

Sept 17, 18, 24
RIGOLETTO (Verdi)
Gilda: Zanardi
Il Duca di Mantova: Arrigoni
Rigoletto: Forti
Maddalena: Ferri
Sparafucile: Bonora

Sept 25, 28
ATTILA (Verdi)
Odabella: Pirola
Foresto: Ceresa
Ezio: Forti
Attila: Bonora
Papa Leone: Bazelli
Uldino: Ghizone

Sept 30
LUCIA DI LAMMERMOOR
(Donizetti)
Lucia: Zanardi
Edgardo: Arrigoni
Enrico: Forti
Raimondo: Bonora

FRENCH OPERA AND
OPERETTA SEASON
Oct 1 to 21
Conductor: Victor Dangón

Oct 1, 11
CHARLES VI (Halévy)**
Isabelle de Bavière: Waldteufel
Odette: Privat

Page: Blanche
Charles VI: Barbé
Le Dauphin: Piroia
Raymond: Dangón
Le Duc de Bedford: Rebelly

Oct 2
LE VOYAGE EN CHINE (Bazin)

Oct 4, 5, 9, 15
LA FAVORITE (Donizetti)
Léonor: Waldteufel
Fernand: Piroia
Alphonse XI: Barbé
Inès: Teresina
Balthazar: Dangón
Gaspard: Etienne

Oct 8, 13
LE TROUVERE (Verdi) (Fr)
Manrique: Piroia
Leonore: Waldteufel
Comte de Luna: Barbé
Azucena: Privat
Ferrand: Dangón
Ruiz: Etienne

Oct 16
LAS CLOCHES DE CORNEVILLE
(Planquette)

Oct 21
Farewell Concert French Lyric
Company

1882

Female artists
Casaglia, Giuditta <mez>
Lari-Valero, Raya <s>
Novelli, Giulia <mez>
Pagliero, Maria <mez>
Palacios, Signora <s>
Pantaleoni, Romilda <s>
Pollieri, Signora <s>
Rambelli, Signora <mez>
Ricci, Matilde <s>

Trebbi, Olimpia <s>
Widmar, E. <s>

Male artists
Bazelli, Lorenzo <b>
Bertini, Tobias <t>
Buzzi, Attilio <b>
Capri, Signor <b>
Caroselli, Signor <t>
Cesari, Pietro <b>
Dal Negro, Domenico <b>
De Santis, Angelo <t>
Dondi, Enrico <b>
Forti, Gaetano <bar>
Menotti, Delfino <bar>
Moriami, Gustavo <bar>
Mozzi, Eugenio <t>
Rossi-Ghelli, Achille <bar>
Salvati, Francesco <bar>
Sartori, G. <b>
Valero, Fernando <t>
Vecchioni, Francesco <b>

Jan 2 to 28
Italian Dramatic Company
Adelaide Tessero

SUMMER ITALIAN OPERA SEASON
Angelo Ferrari, Impresario
Jan 29 to Feb 20, March 1 to 10
Conductor: G. Ferri

Jan 29, Feb 20, March 4
LA FAVORITA (Donizetti) (It)
Leonora: Rambelli
Fernando: Bertini
Alfonso XI: Forti
Inez: Pollieri
Baldassare: Buzzi

Feb 2, 4, March 12
LUCIA DI LAMMERMOOR
(Donizetti)
Lucia: Palacios
Edgardo: Bertini
Enrico: Forti
Raimondo: Buzzi

Feb 5
LA TRAVIATA (Verdi)
Violetta: Palacios
Alfredo Germont: Bertini
Giorgio Germont: Forti

Feb 8
RIGOLETTO (Verdi)
Gilda: Palacios
Il Duca di Mantova: Bertini
Rigoletto: Forti
Maddalena: Rambelli
Sparafucile: Buzzi
Monterone: Capri
Giovanna: Pagliero

Feb 11, 15, March 2
IL TROVATORE (Verdi)
Leonora: Ricci
Manrico: Bertini
Conte di Luna: Forti
Azucena: Rambelli
Ferrando: Sartori

Feb 12, 17
ERNANI (Verdi)
Elvira: Ricci
Ernani: Bertini
Don Carlo: Forti
D. Ruy Gomez de Silva: Buzzi

March 1, 5
UN BALLO IN MASCHERA (Verdi)
Amelia: Ricci
Riccardo: Bertini
Renato: Forti
Oscar: Palacios
Ulrica: Rambelli
Tom: Buzzi

March 8, 10
RUY BLAS (Marchetti)
La Regina: Ricci
Ruy Blas: Bertini
Don Cesar de Bazan: Forti
Casilda: Rambelli
Don Guritano: Buzzi
Donna Giovanna: Pagliero

March 22 to April 2
Italian Dramatic Company
Cuniberti Brothers

**WINTER ITALIAN OPERA
SEASON**
Strigelli and Company,
Impresarios
From June 17 to Sept 2
Conductors: Gioachino Salvini
and Giuseppe Strigelli

June 17
RUY BLAS (Marchetti)
La Regina: Pantaleoni
Ruy Blas: Mozzi
Don Cesar de Bazan: Moriami
Casilda: Casaglia
Don Guritano: Vecchioni
Donna Giovanna: Pagliero

June 18, July 2
FAUST (Gounod) (It)
Margherita: Pantaleoni
Faust: De Santis
Mefistofele: Vecchioni
Valentin: Moriami

June 22, 24
IL GUARANY (Gomes)
Cecilia: Pantaleoni
Pery: Mozzi
Gonzalez: Forti
Don Antonio de Mariz:
Vecchioni

June 25, 27, July 9
IL BARBIERE DI SIVIGLIA
(Rossini)
Rosina: Novelli
Conte di Almaviva: Caroselli
Figaro: Moriami
Don Basilio: Rossi
Don Bartolo: Cesari

June 29, July 11
RIGOLETTO (Verdi)
Gilda: Widmar
Il Duca di Mantova: De Santis

Rigoletto: Moriami
Maddalena: Casaglia
Sparafucile: Vecchioni
Monterone: Capri
Giovanna: Pagliero

July 1
UN BALLO IN MASCHERA (Verdi)
Amelia: Pantaleoni
Riccardo: De Santis
Renato: Moriami
Oscar: Palacios
Ulrica: Casaglia
Tom: Buzzi

July 4, 6, 8, 13, 23, 27, Aug 5, 27
L'AFRICANA (Meyerbeer) (It)
Conductor: Strigelli
Selika: Pantaleoni
Vasco da Gama: De Santis
Nelusko: Moriami
Don Pietro: Vecchioni

July 16
LA FAVORITA (Donizetti) (It)
Conductor: Strigelli
Leonora: Novelli
Fernando: De Santis
Alfonso XI: Moriami
Inez: Pollieri
Baldassare: Vecchioni

July 18, 19, 22
Uruguayan National Anthem
MANFREDI DI SVEVIA
(Giribaldi)****
Conductor: Strigelli
Yole: Pantaleoni
Imelda: Casaglia
Manfredi: Moriami
Ruggero: Mozzi
Roberto: Bazelli
Ghino de Jacco: Vecchioni

July 25, Aug 30
LA FORZA DEL DESTINO (Verdi)
Conductor: Strigelli
Leonora: Pantaleoni

Don Alvaro: Mozzi
Don Carlo: Moriami
Preziosilla: Novelli
Marchese di Calatrava:
Vecchioni
Curra: Casaglia
Fra Melitone: Bazelli
Padre Guardiano: Vecchioni

July 29, 30, Aug 3
L'EBREA (Halévy) (It)
Conductor: Strigelli
Rachel: Novelli
Eleazar: De Santis
Principessa Eudoxia: Widmar
Cardinal Brogni: Vecchioni
Alberto: Moriami

Aug 8, 10, 12, 15, 22, 25, 29
AIDA (Verdi)
Aida: Pantaleoni
Radamès: De Santis
Amneris: Novelli
Amonasro: Menotti
Ramfis: Moriami
Il Re: Vecchioni
Sommo Sacerdote: Bazelli

Aug 17, 20
LA TRAVIATA (Verdi)
Violetta: Pantaleoni
Alfredo Germont: Mozzi
Giorgio Germont: Moriami

Aug 26
LUCIA DI LAMMERMOOR
(Donizetti)
Lucia: Pantaleoni
Edgardo: Mozzi
Enrico: Moriami
Raimondo: Vecchioni

Sept 2
IL TROVATORE (Verdi)
Leonora: Pantaleoni
Manrico: De Santis
Conte di Luna: Forti

Azucena: Casaglia
Ferrando: Sartori

Aug 24
French Operetta Company
Cochelin
LE PETIT DUC (Lecocq)
and LA FILLE DU TAMBOUR
MAJOR (Offenbach)

Sept 3, 4, 7 to 15
Italian Dramatic Company
Tomasso Salvini

Sept 5
Spanish Dramatic Company
Victoriano Tamayo

**SPRING ITALIAN OPERA
SEASON**
Cesare Ciacchi, Impresario
Oct 25 to Nov 7
Conductor: Emilio Rajneri

Oct 25, 29
RIGOLETTO (Verdi)
Gilda: Lari-Valero
Il Duca di Mantova: Valero
Rigoletto: Menotti
Maddalena: Casaglia
Sparafucile: Dondi
Monterone: Capri
Giovanna: Pagliero

Oct 26, Nov 1
IL TROVATORE (Verdi)
Leonora: Trebbi
Manrico: Valero
Conte di Luna: Salvati
Azucena: Casaglia
Ferrando: Sartori

Oct 28
AIDA (Verdi)
Aida: Pantaleoni
Radamès: Mozzi
Amneris: Casaglia
Amonasro: Salvati

Ramfis: Vecchioni
Il Re: Dal Negro
Sommo Sacerdote: Bazelli

Oct 31
LA FORZA DEL DESTINO (Verdi)
Leonora: Pantaleoni
Don Alvaro: Mozzi
Don Carlo: Salvati
Preziosilla: Casaglia
Marchese di Calatrava: Sartori
Curra: Casaglia
Fra Melitone: Menotti
Padre Guardiano: Vecchioni

Nov 3, 5, 7
GLI UGONOTTI (Meyerbeer) (It)
Margherita de Valois: Lari-Valero
Raul de Nangis: Valero
Valentina: Pantaleoni
Urbano: Trebbi
Conte di Nevers: Salvati
Conte di Saint-Bris: Vecchioni
Marcello: Dondi

Nov 15, 17
Operatic Concerts to Benefit
Italian Floods
Orquesta del Teatro Solís
Conductor: Alejandro Uguccioni
Soloists: Pantaleoni <s>,
Mozzi<t>, Salvati <bar>,
Vecchioni <b>

1883

Female artists
Belmondo, Signora <s>
Bernardi, Signora <s>
Bianchi Mancini, Carolina <mez>
Brogini, Amalia <s>
Bruni, Signora <s>
Buonaguida, Concetta <s>
Cesari, Giulia <s / mez>
Cobianchi, Angelina <mez>
Copetti, Juanita <musical glasses>
Frigerio, Maria <s>

Giglioni, Ida <s>
Leone, Eugenia <s>
Menghini, Signora
Moller, Martha <mez>
Preziosi, Margherita <mez>
Signori, Signora <mez>
Stolzmann, Maria <s>
Wiziack, Emma <s>
Zani, Diomira <mez>

Male artists
Angellini, Mario <bar>
Aramburo, Antonio <t>
Bignami, César <vc>
Bignami, Pompeo (Pompeyo)
<vn>
Bruni, Rinaldi <t>
Cantieri, Luigi <b>
Cellai, Giuseppe <t>
Cesari, Pietro <b>
Cioci, Amos <t>
Cremonesi, Luis <vn>
Dal Negro, Domenico <b>
Dal Negro, Giulio <b>
De Armas, Signor <t>
Deliliers, Vittorio <t>
Ferreti, Signor <b>
Ferroni, Miguel <vla>
Foresti, Oreste <bar>
Formentini, Camilo <bn>
Frank, Antonio <fl>
Galli, Ferdinando <t>
Gallori, Sebastiano <t>
Giamari, Signor
Giannini, Filippo <b>
Gori, Ferruccio <b>
Grassi, Signor <fl>
Lippi, Signor
Mancini, Roberto <b>
Martini, Gaetano <bar>
Masi, Romeo <vn>
Mazzolo, Signor <b>
Milani, Signor <t>
Paolicchi, Domenico <b>
Pogliami, Enrico <bar>
Polonini, Alessandro <bar>
Reggiani, Samuel <b>
Ruotolo, Signor <b>

Santinelli, Giuseppe <t>
Scolari, Giovanni <b>
Soffleti, Serafino <bar>
Zucchi, Signor <b>

Jan 6 to Feb 1
Italian Dramatic Company
Giacinta Pezzana

Feb 3 to April 8
Carnival Masked Balls

May 8, 11
Concerts
Conductor: Gioachino Salvini
Soloists: Scolari <b-profondo>,
Frank <fl>, Grassi <fl>,
Formentini <bn>, Copetti
<musical glasses>, Masi <vn>,
Bignami <vn>, Cremonesi
<vn>, Ferroni <vla>, and
Bignami <vc>

May 31 to June 13
Italian Dramatic Company
Lambertini Brothers

**ITALIAN OPERA BUFFA /
OPERETTA SEASON**
Cesare Ciacchi, Impresario
First season: June 14 to 26
Conductor: Vincenzo Volir
Chorus Masters: Luigi
Franciscolo and Francisco Seguí

June 14, 17, 19, 24, Aug 31, Sept
1, 2
BOCCACCIO (Suppé)

June 16, 28
LES PRES DE SAINT GERVAIS
(Lecocq)

June 22, 29, Sept 25
LA FIGLIA DI MADAMA ANGOT
(Lecocq)
Clairette: Frigerio
Mademoiselle Lange: Cesari
Ange Pitou: Deliliers

June 26
SERAFIN EL GRUMETE (Arrieta)
and I BRIGANTI (Offenbach)

ITALIAN OPERA SEASON
Tartini, Impresarios
July 7 to Aug 8
Conductor: Vincenzo Volir

July 7, 8, 11, 12
IL GIURAMENTO (Mercadante)
Manfredo: Soffleti
Bianca: Zani
Elisa: Leone
Viscardo di Benevento: Gallori
Brunoro: Bruni
Isaura: Brogini

July 14, 15, 18
MOSE IN EGITTO (Rossini)
Mosè: Paolicchi
Amenophis: Gallori
Anaide: Giglioni
Maria: Zani
Eliezer: Cellai
Faraone: Martini
Aufide: Galli
Sinaide: Buonaguida

July 21, 22, 25, 26
I FALSI MONETARI (Rossi)
Raimondo Lopez: Cellai
Don Isidoro: Martini
Annetta: Zani
Don Euticchio: Cantieri
Sinforosa, sua moglie: Giglioni
Alberto: Lippi
Ines: Buonaguida

July 28, 29, Aug 1
LA FAVORITA (Donizetti) (It)
Leonora: Zani
Fernando: Gallori
Alfonso XI: Soffleti
Inez: Buonaguida
Baldassare: Paolicchi
Gaspare: Ferreti

Aug 4, 5, 8
IL TROVATORE (Verdi)
Leonora: Giglioni
Manrico: Gallori
Conte di Luna: Soffleti
Azucena: Zani
Inez: Belmondo
Ferrando: Dal Negro
Ruiz: Bruni

**ITALIAN OPERA BUFFA /
OPERETTA SEASON**
Cesare Ciacchi, Impresario
Second season: Aug 11 to Oct 28
Conductor: Emilio Rajneri
Chorus Masters: Luigi
Franciscolo and Francisco Seguí

Aug 11, 12, 14, 15, 21, 26, Sept 4,
5, 9, 11, 16, 27, 29, 30, Oct 6, 8,
13, 25, 27, 28
DONNA JUANITA (Suppé) **
Donna Juanita: Preziosi
Donna Olimpia: Cesari
Gaston de Fauré: Deliliers
Sir Douglas: Polonini
Don Pomponio: P. Cesari

Aug 18, 19, 25, Sept 8
IL BARBIERE DI SIVIGLIA
(Rossini)
Rosina: Cesari
Conte di Almaviva: Deliliers
Figaro: Polonini
Don Basilio: P. Cesari
Don Bartolo: Ruotolo

Aug 23
LA EDUCANDE DI SORRENTO
(Usiglio)
Luisa: Bernardi
Augusto: Milani
Placida: G. Cesari
Don Democrito: Ruotolo
Rodolfo: P. Cesari

Sept 14
Concert to benefit the victims of
Ischia's earthquake

Sept 19, 20, 22, 23, Oct 14
FATINITZA (Suppé) ***

Sept 28, Oct 2, 4
PAPA MARTIN (Cagnoni)
Papa Martin: P. Cesari

Oct 11, 16
GLI CAMPANI DI CORNEVILLE
(Planquette) (It)

Oct 13
DONNA JUANITA (Suppé)
and Il Barbiere di Siviglia: Act 1

Oct 18, 20, 23
CARMEN (Bizet) (It)
Carmen: Cesari
Don José: Deliliers
Escamillo: Polonini
Micaela: Preziosi

Oct 27
DONNA JUANITA (Suppé) and
Rigoletto: Act 4

Oct 28
DONNA JUANITA (Suppé)
and Farewell *Concert* Italian
Opera and Operetta Company

**SUMMER ITALIAN OPERA
SEASON**
Nov 17 to Dec 24
Conductor: Camilo Formentini
Director: Luis Lelmi

Nov 17, 20, 22, Dec 1
POLIUTO (Donizetti)
Poliuto: Aramburo
Paolina: Wiziack
Severus: Pogliami

Nov 25, 29
ERNANI (Verdi)
Elvira: Wiziack
Ernani: Santinelli
Don Carlo: Angiollini
D. Ruy Gomez de Silva:
Mancini

Nov 27, Dec 2, 4, 19
LA FORZA DEL DESTINO (Verdi)
Leonora: Stolzmann
Don Alvaro: Santinelli
Don Carlo: Angiollini
Marchese di Calatrava: Mancini

Dec 6
RUY BLAS (Marchetti)
La Regina: Stolzmann
Ruy Blas: Santinelli
Don Cesar de Bazan: Angiollini
Casilda: Signori
Don Guritano: Mancini

Dec 8, 11, 13, 15, 16
L'AFRICANA (Meyerbeer) (It)
Selika: Wiziack
Vasco da Gama: Santinelli
Nelusko: Pogliami
Inez: Stolzmann
Don Pietro: Mancini

Dec 21
AIDA (Verdi)
Aida: Stolzmann
Radamès: Aramburo
Amneris: Signori
Ramfis: Angellini
Il Re: Giannini
Sommo Sacerdote: Gori

Dec 24
Farewell Concert by Italian Lyric
Company artists

Dec 25 to 31
A. Hermann <Viennese
prestidigitator>

1884

Female artists
Beloff, Erminia <mez>
Capelli, Clelia <mez>
Cristino, Ida <s>
De Vere, Clementina <s>
Mei, Medea <s>
Pavan-Moretti, Annetta <s>
Preziosi, Margherita <s / mez>
Ravogli, Julia <mez>
Teodorini, Elena <s>

Male artists
Annovazzi, Antonio <t>
Baldelli, Antonio <t>
Borelli, Ettore <t>
Deliliers, Vittorio <t>
Figner, Nikolay <t>
Lambiase, Gaetano <bar>
Limonta, Napoleone <b>
Polonini, Alessandro <bar>
Sillich, Aristodemo <b>
Tamagno, Francesco <t>
Tamburlini, Angelo <b>
Verdini, Albino <bar>

**SUMMER ITALIAN OPERA /
OPERETTA SEASON**
Cesare Ciacchi, Impresario
Jan 3 to 12
Conductor: P. A. de Cesari
Director: Achille Luppi

Jan 3, 6
DONNA JUANITA (Suppé)
Donna Juanita: Preziosi
Donna Olimpia: Cristino
Gaston de Fauré: Deliliers
Sir Douglas: Polonini
Don Pomponio: Sillich

Jan 5, 12
CARMEN (Bizet) (It)
Carmen: Preziosi
Don Jose: Deliliers
Escamillo: Polonini

Jan 8
LA FIGLIA DI MADAMA ANGOT
(Lecocq) (It)

Jan 10
PAPA MARTIN (Cagnoni)

Jan 16 to Feb 28
Spanish Dramatic Company
Rafael Calvo

March 29 to April 5
Italian Dramatic Company
Lambertini Brothers

**ITALIAN OPERA-BUFFA /
OPERETTA SEASON**
Lambiase and Crodara,
Impresarios
May 15 to July 4
Conductor: Paolo Balsinelli
Director: Filippo Bergonzoni

May 15, 17, 18
IL DUCHINO (Lecocq) (It)

May 20, 22, 24, 25, June 3
IL CUORE E LA MANO (Lecocq)
(It)**

May 27, 29, 31, June 1, 5, 15, 17,
22
LE DONNE CURIOSE (Usiglio)

June 7, 8, 14, Nov 1
LA FIGLIA DI MADAMA ANGOT
(Lecocq) (It)
Clairette: Preziosi
Mademoiselle Lange: Cristino
Ange Pitou: Deliliers

June 11, 12, 29, Oct 30
CRISPINO E LA COMARE (Ricci)
Crispino: Lambiase(3) /
Polonini(1)
La Comare: Preziosi
Annetta: Cristino

Contino del Fiore: Deliliers
Lisetta: Pavan

June 18, 19, 21
LE DONNE GUERRIERE (Suppé)
(It)

June 26, 28
L'AMICO DI CASA (Cortesi)

July 4
TUTTI IN MASCHERA (Pedrotti)

July 18 to Aug 15
French Dramatic Company
Massenet

**WINTER ITALIAN OPERA
SEASON**
Angelo Ferrari, Impresario
Aug 22 to Sept 14
Conductor: Niccola Bassi

Aug 22, Sept 3
GLI UGONOTTI (Meyerbeer) (It)
Margherita de Valois: De Vere
Raul de Nangis: Tamagno
Valentina: Teodorini
Urbano: Ravogli
Conte di Nevers: Verdini
Conte di Saint-Bris: Sillich
Marcello: Tamburlini

Aug 23
LA TRAVIATA (Verdi)
Violetta: Teodorini
Alfredo Germont: Tamagno
Giorgio Germont: Verdini

Aug 24, 25, 28
Uruguayan National Anthem
LA GIOCONDA (Ponchielli)**
Gioconda: Teodorini
Laura: Mei
La Cieca: Ravogli
Enzo Grimaldo: Tamagno
Barnaba: Verdini

Alvise Badoero: Tamburlini
Zuane: Limonta

Aug 26
LA FAVORITA (Donizetti) (It)
Leonora: Mei
Fernando: Tamagno
Alfonso XI: Verdini

Aug 29
IL TROVATORE (Verdi)
Leonora: Teodorini
Manrico: Tamagno
Conte di Luna: Verdini
Azucena: Ravogli

Aug 30
MEFISTOFELE (Boito) **
Margherita / Elena: Teodorini
Faust: Tamagno
Mefistofele: Tamburlini
Marta: Ravogli

Sept 2
LUCREZIA BORGIA (Donizetti)
Lucrezia: Teodorini
Gennaro: Tamagno
Duca Alfonso: Verdini
Maffio Orsini: Ravogli

Sept 5, 7, 9
RIGOLETTO (Verdi)
Gilda: De Vere
Il Duca di Mantova: Figner
Rigoletto: Verdini
Maddalena: Ravogli
Sparafucile: Tamburlini

Sept 11
Operatic Concert

Sept 13, 14
MARTHA (Flotow)
Lady Harriet: De Vere
Lionel: Figner
Lord Tristan: Tamburlini

and *Concert*
Giribaldi: Sinfonia from
Manfredi di Svevia

**ITALIAN OPERA-BUFFA /
OPERETTA SEASON**
Cesare Ciacchi, Impresario
Oct 18 to Nov 15
Conductor: Emilio Rajneri

Oct 18, 19, Nov 15
BOCCACCIO (Suppé) (It)**
Boccaccio: Preziosi
Fiametta: Cristino
Pietro: Deliliers
Lambertuccio: Polonini

Oct 21, 25, 26, Nov 11
DONNA JUANITA (Suppé) (It)
Donna Juanita: Preziosi
Donna Olimpia: Cristino
Gaston de Fauré: Deliliers
Sir Douglas: Polonini
Don Pomponio: Sillich

Oct 23, 28
NAPOLI IN CARNEVALE (De
Giosa)**
Artists: Preziosi, Deliliers,
Polonini

Nov 4, 6
IL BARBIERE DI SIVIGLIA
(Rossini)
Rosina: Preziosi
Conte di Almaviva: Deliliers
Figaro: Polonini

Nov 7, 8, 9
LA SONNAMBULA (Bellini)
Amina: Preziosi
Elvino: Deliliers

Nov 13
RIGOLETTO (Act 4)
Gilda: Preziosi
Il Duca di Mantova: Deliliers

Rigoletto: Polonini
and DONNA JUANITA (Act 3)

Nov 15
BOCCACCIO (Suppé)
and Farewell *Concert*

1885

Female artists
Beloff, Erminia <mez>
Falconis, Vittoria <mez>
Ferreti, Adelina (Adele) <s>
Franco, Matilde <s>
Gori-Pasquali, Cesira <mez>
Morbini, Luigia <mez>
Pattini, Raffaela <s>
Pavan-Moretti, Annetta <s>
Tetrazzini, Eva <s>

Male artists
Benucci, Signor
Donati, Vittorio <b>
Menotti, Delfino <bar>
Ottonello, Felix <t>
Pessina, Arturo <bar>
Pizzoloti, Signor <b>
Sampieri, Signor <b>
Signoretti, Leopoldo <t>
Signorini, Francesco <t>
Stagi, Carlo <t>
Tabellini, Gaetano <t>
Tamburlini, Angelo <b>
Vecchioni, Francesco <b>
Voyer, Capitan <pf>

**SUMMER ITALIAN OPERA /
OPERETTA SEASON**
Crodara and Company,
Impresarios
Jan 1 to Feb 5, April 30
Conductor: Paolo Balsinelli

Jan 1, 6, 8
ORFEO ALL'INFERNO (Offenbach)

Jan 3, 4
ARMI ED AMORE (Varney)

Jan 10, 11, 15, 24, 29, Feb 1, 3
LOS SOBRINOS DEL CAPITAN
GRANT (Fernández-Caballero)**

Jan 18
LES BRIGANDS (Offenbach) (It)

Jan 20, 22, 25, 31
DONNA JUANITA (Suppé) (It)
Donna Juanita: Pavan-Moretti

Jan 29
LOS SOBRINOS DEL CAPITAN
GRANT
and *Concert*
Giribaldi: Sinfonia from La
Parisina

Feb 5
BOCCACCIO (Suppé) (It)

Feb 10
Operatic Concert
Soloists: Franco, Gori; Stagi,
Ottonello, chorus, and orchestra

Feb 20
Operatic Concert
Soloists: Pavan and Ottonello

April 4 to 28
Spanish Dramatic Company
Rafael Calvo

April 30
CRISPINO E LA COMARE (Ricci)
and Farewell Concert

ITALIAN OPERA SEASON
Cesare Ciacchi, Impresario
May 23 to Aug 30, Oct 10 to 22
Conductor: Emilio Rajneri

May 23, 24, June 13, 28, July 12,
28, Aug 16, Oct 15
AIDA (Verdi)
Aida: Tetrazzini
Radamès: Signoretti
Amneris: Falconis
Ramfis: Menotti
Il Re: Vecchioni

May 28, June 25, Aug 2
IL TROVATORE (Verdi)
Leonora: Tetrazzini
Manrico: Signorini
Conte di Luna: Pessina
Azucena: Falconis
Ferrando: Vecchioni

May 30, June 14, Oct 22
FAUST (Gounod) (It)
Margherita: Pattini(1) /
Tetrazzini(2)
Faust: Signorini(2) / Signoretti(1)
Mefistofele: Vecchioni
Valentin: Pessina
Marta: Falconis

June 2, 4, 6, 7, 16, 17
LA FORZA DEL DESTINO (Verdi)
Leonora: Tetrazzini
Don Alvaro: Signoretti
Don Carlo: Menotti
Preziosilla: Beloff
Padre Guardiano: Vecchioni

June 10, 11, 21, July 26, Aug 23
UN BALLO IN MASCHERA (Verdi)
Amelia: Tetrazzini
Riccardo: Signoretti
Renato: Menotti
Ulrica: Falconis
Oscar: Pattini

June 18, 20, 23, Aug 14
LA FAVORITA (Donizetti) (It)
Leonora: Falconis
Fernando: Signoretti
Alfonso XI: Menotti

June 24, July 16, 23, Aug 22, Oct
13, 20
RIGOLETTO (Verdi)
Gilda: Pattini (4) / Ferreti(2)
Il Duca di Mantova: Signorini
Rigoletto: Menotti
Maddalena: Falconis
Sparafucile: Donati(4) /
Vecchioni(2)
Monterone: Sampieri

July 2, 5, 11, 25, Aug 4, 19, 20,
Oct 10, 18
L'AFRICANA (Meyerbeer) (It)
Selika: Tetrazzini
Vasco da Gama: Signoretti
Nelusko: Menotti
Inez: Pattini(7) / Ferreti(2)
Anna: Morbini
Don Pietro: Pizzoloti(7) /
Vecchioni(2)

July 8, 9, 21
POLIUTO (Donizetti)
Poliuto: Tabellini
Paolina: Tetrazzini
Severus: Tamburlini

July 18, Aug 11
Uruguayan National Anthem
[July 18 only]
RUY BLAS (Marchetti)
La Regina: Tetrazzini
Ruy Blas: Signoretti
Casilda: Falconis
Donna Giovanna: Morbini
Don Cesar de Bazan: Menotti
Don Guritano: Donati

July 20
SEMIRAMIDE (Rossini)
Semiramide: Tetrazzini
Arsace: Falconis
Idreno: Signoretti
Assur: Menotti
Oroe: Vecchioni

July 30, Aug 1, 6, 9, 18, 25, Oct
11, 17
GLI UGONOTTI (Meyerbeer) (It)
Margherita de Valois: Pattini
Raul de Nangis: Signoretti
Valentina: Tetrazzini
Urbano: Falconis
Conte di Nevers: Menotti
Marcello: Vecchioni

Aug 7, 8, 13, 15
LA TRAVIATA (Verdi)
Violetta: Pattini
Alfredo Germont: Signoretti
Giorgio Germont: Pessina
Flora: Morbini
Marchese D'Obigny: Pizzoloti
Gastone: Tabellini

Aug 11
RUY BLAS (Marchetti)
and Concert
Logheder: Cuor di Donna, waltz
by Eva Tetrazzini

Aug 29, 30
NORMA (Bellini)
Norma: Tetrazzini
Adalgisa: Falconis
Pollione: Signoretti
Oroveso: Vecchioni
and Farewell Concert

SPANISH ZARZUELA SEASON
from Madrid's Teatro Apolo
Avelino Aguirre, Impresario
Sept 1 to Oct 8
Conductor: Manuel Fernández-
Caballero

Sept 9
"Grand Concert"
Conductors: Manuel Fernández-
Caballero, Francisco Spinelli,
and Gerardo Grasso
Orquesta Teatro Solís, Bandas
Militares, Banda Escuela de

Artes y Oficios
Soloist: Voyer <pf>

**ITALIAN OPERA AND
OPERETTA SEASON**
Nov 8 to 22
Conductors: Giuseppe Strigelli
and Giulio Casali

Nov 8, 19
DONNA JUANITA (Suppé) (It)
Conductor: Strigelli

Nov 14, 15
BOCCACCIO (Suppé) (It)
Conductor: Casali

Nov 21, 22
THREE SHORT OPERETTAS
Conductors: Strigelli and Casali

Nov 29
Dr. Fauré Nicolay <French
psychic and illusionist>

1886

Female artists
Bellincioni, Gemma <s>
Camboggi, Signora <mez>
Capelli, Clelia <mez>
Cataneo, Aurelia <s>
Copca, Fanny <s>
Cortini, Zaira <mez>
Ferreti, Adelina (Adele) <s>
Luttichau, Julia de <mez>
Mancini, Signora <s>
Morelli, Adela <s>
Negrini, Signora <s>
Sartori, Ma. Clotilde <mez>
Tescher, Signora <s>

Male artists
Aramburo, Antonio <t>
Capelli, F. <bar>
Carbonetti, Federico <b-buffo>
Chinelli, Angelo <t>

Contini, Achille <b>
Corsini, Baldassare <b-buffo>
Dorini, Signor <t>
Emiliani, Orestes <t>
Engelbrecht, Enrique <pf>
Masi, Romeo <vn>
Parodi, Luigi <t>
Paroli, Paride <t-leggiero>
Pozzi, Francesco <bar>
Pozzi, Natale <bar>
Prevost, Francesco <t>
Reggiani, Samuel <b>
Reinaldi, José <bar>
Remondini, Amilcare <b>
Salvati, Francesco <bar>
Scolara, Francesco <b-buffo>
Seguí, Francisco <pf>
Stagno, Roberto <t>
Tamburlini, Angelo <b>
Ughetti, Pietro <bar>
Uguccioni, Alejandro <vn>

May 6
Concert
Conductors: Francisco Seguí and
Camilo Formentini
Soloists: Aramburo <t>,
Uguccioni <vn>, Engelbrecht
<pf>

May 27 and 30
Concerts
Conductor: Gerardo Grasso
Soloists: Aramburo <t>, Ferreti
<s>, Salvati <bar>, Masi <vn>,
and Seguí <pf>

**OPERETTA AND BALLET
SEASON**
June 6 to June 28
Conductor: Napoleone Maserole
Chorus Master: Enrico Costa

June 6
CRISPINO E LA COMARE (Ricci)
Annetta: Ferreti
La Comare: Luttichau
Contino del Fiore: Parodi

Fabrizio: Reinaldi
Crispino Tachetto: Carbonetti
Don Asdrubale: Reggiani

June 8
FRA DIAVOLO (Auber)
Zerlina: Tescher
Lorenzo: Parodi
Fra Diavolo: Chinelli
Lady Pamela Allcash: Luttichau
Mateo: Carbonetti
Lord Allcash: Reinaldi

BALLET SEASON
June 29 to July 17
Conductor: Enrico Bovi

June 29, July 3, 4, 10, 17
EXCELSIOR (Manzotti)

July 14, 15
BRAHMA (Dall'Argine)

**WINTER ITALIAN OPERA
SEASON**
Cesare Ciacchi, Impresario
July 24 to Aug 29
Conductors: Niccola Bassi and
Mr. Furlotti (assistant)
Director: Mr. Rossi

July 24, Aug 1
ROBERTO IL DIAVOLO
(Meyerbeer) (It)
Alice: Bellincioni
Roberto, Duca di Normandia:
Stagno
Rambaldo: Paroli
Isabella di Sicilia: Morelli
Bertramo: Tamburlini
Alberti: Scolara

July 25, Aug 21
LA FORZA DEL DESTINO (Verdi)
Leonora: Cataneo
Don Alvaro: Dorini
Don Carlo: Pozzi
Preziosilla: Cortini
Padre Guardiano: Tamburlini

July 27, Aug 15, 22, 25
LA GIOCONDA (Ponchielli)
Gioconda: Copca
Laura: Sartori
La Cieca: Cortini
Enzo Grimaldo: Stagno
Barnaba: Pozzi
Alvise Badoero: Tamburlini
Zuane: Scolara
Un cantore: Capelli

July 29, Aug 11
MEFISTOFELE (Boito)
Margherita: Copca
Faust: Stagno
Mefistofele: Tamburlini
Marta: C. Capelli
Valentin: F. Capelli

Aug 4
RIGOLETTO (Verdi)
Gilda: Bellincioni
Il Duca di Mantova: Stagno
Rigoletto: Ughetti
Sparafucile: Tamburlini

Aug 5, 13, 18, 19
L'AFRICANA (Meyerbeer) (It)
Selika: Copca
Vasco da Gama: Stagno
Inez: Morelli
Nelusko: Ughetti
Don Pietro: Tamburlini

Aug 8
IL BARBIERE DI SIVIGLIA
(Rossini)
Rosina: Bellincioni
Conte di Almaviva: Stagno
Figaro: Reinaldi
Don Basilio: Tamburlini
Don Bartolo: Scolara
Berta: Capelli

Aug 12
LA FAVORITA (Donizetti)
Leonora: Copca
Fernando: Stagno

Alfonso XI: Ughetti
Inez: Morelli
Gaspare: Tamburlini
Baldassare: Contini

Aug 14
LINDA DI CHAMOUNIX
(Donizetti)
Linda: Bellincioni
Maddalena: Cortini
Visconde Sirval: Dorini
Marquis de Boisfleuris: Ughetti
Intendente: Tamburlini

Aug 29
FAUST (Gounod) (It)
Margherita: Bellincioni
Faust: Stagno
Mefistofele: Tamburlini
Valentin: Capelli
Marta: Sartori

Sept 3 to 20
French Dramatic Company
Sarah Bernhardt

Sept 26, Oct 3, 7, 13, 17
Operatic Concerts
Aramburo <t> and orchestra

Sept 30
Operatic Concert
Soloists: Aramburo <t>, Negrini
<s>, Camboggi <mez>, Ughetti
<bar>, and orchestra

SPANISH ZARZUELA SEASON
Avelino Aguirre, Impresario
Oct 23 to Dec 26

1887

Female artists
Arpisella-Romano, C. <mez>
Baldassari, Signora <mez>
Bevilacqua, Concetta <s>

Borlinetto-Conti, Erina <mez>
Brambilla, Elvira V. <s/mez>
Busi, Adriana <s>
Caire, T. <s>
Caracciolo-Strozzi, Laura <a>
Cesari, Giulia <s/mez>
Copetti, Juanita <pf>
Dalceo, Clementina <s>
Gori-Pasquali, Cesira <mez>
Lambiase, Elvira <mez>
Leoni, Eugenia <s>
Malvezzi, Stella <s>
Preziosi, Margherita <mez>
Singer, Teresa <s>
Zani, Diomira <mez>

Male artists
Ageno, Enrico <t>
Andreoli, C. <b>
Baldassari, Luigi <bar>
Baracchi, Cesare <bar>
Beccario, Giuseppe <bar>
Benedetti, Oreste <bar>
Bonfanti, Enrico <bar>
Carobbi, Silla <bar>
Cesari, Pietro <bar/b>
Del Re, Enrico <b>
Deliliers, Vittorio <t>
Facci, Pio <t>
Ferrari, Signor
Galassi, Egisto <b>
Giucci, Camillo <pf>
Grondone, M. <bar>
Lambiase, Gaetano <t>
Lebano, Felice <harp>
Lucignani, Benedetto <t>
Marconi, Raffaele <b>
Massimi, Massimo <t>
Menotti, Delfino <bar>
Monchero, Amilcare <b>
Moretti, Giuseppe <t>
Notargiacomo, Gaetano <b>
Reggiani, Samuel <b>
Sartori, R. <t>
Toninelli, Signor <t>
Vecchioni, Francesco <b>
Zucchi, A. <bar>

Jan 13
A. de la Rosa <magician>

FALL OPERA SEASON
March 10 to 25
Conductor: Luigi Franciscolo and
Severino Noli (assistant)
Director: R. Marconi

March 10, 13, 29
LA TRAVIATA (Verdi)
Violetta: Bevilacqua
Alfredo Germont: Facci
Giorgio Germont: Baracchi
Gastone: Toninelli
Barone Douphol: Grondone
Dottore: Marconi

March 12
RUY BLAS (Marchetti)
La Regina: Bevilacqua
Ruy Blas: Facci
Don Cesar de Bazan: Baracchi
Don Guritano: Galassi
Casilda: Zani

March 17, 20
LUISA MILLER (Verdi)
Luisa: Bevilacqua
Rodolfo: Facci
Miller: Baracchi
Il Conte di Walter: Galassi
Federica: Zani
Wurm: Marconi
Laura: Baldassari

March 19
ERNANI (Verdi)
Elvira: Bevilacqua
Ernani: Facci
Don Carlos: Baracchi
D. Ruy Gomez de Silva: Galassi

March 23, 27
I DUE FOSCARI (Verdi)
Francesco Foscari: Baracchi
Jacopo Foscari: Facci
Lucrezia Contarini: Bevilacqua

March 25
IL TROVATORE (Verdi)
Leonora: Bevilacqua
Manrico: Facci
Conte di Luna: Baracchi
Azucena: Zani

April 14
Symphonic Concert
Conductor: Camilo Formentini
Soloist: Copetti <pf>

April 17
Symphonic Concert
Conductor: Camilo Formentini
Soloists: Lebano <harp>, Giucci
<pf>

May 17 to June 20
Italian Dramatic Company
Giovanni Emanuel

WINTER OPERA SEASON
Cesare Ciacchi, Impresario
July 14 to Aug 25
Conductor: Emilio Rajneri

July 14, 17, Aug 9
L'AFRICANA (Meyerbeer) (It)
Selika: Singer
Vasco da Gama: Lucignani
Nelusko: Menotti
Inez: Brambilla
Don Pietro: Vecchioni
Don Diego: Del Re
Anna: Caracciolo

July 16, Aug 2
FAUST (Gounod) (It)
Margherita: Busi
Faust: Moretti
Mefistofele: Vecchioni
Valentin: Carobbi
Siebel: Borlinetto
Marta: Caracciolo
Wagner: Del Re

July 21, 24, Aug 11
RIGOLETTO (Verdi)
Gilda: Brambilla
Il Duca di Mantova: Moretti
Rigoletto: Menotti
Maddalena: Borlinetto
Sparafucile: Monchero
Giovanna: Caracciolo
Monterone: Del Re
Marullo: Benedetti

July 23, 26, Aug 23
GLI UGONOTTI (Meyerbeer) (It)
Margherita de Valois: Brambilla
Raul de Nangis: Lucignani
Valentina: Singer
Conte di Nevers: Menotti
Marcello: Vecchioni

July 28
LA FORZA DEL DESTINO (Verdi)
Leonora: Busi
Don Alvaro: Lucignani
Preziosilla: Borlinetto
Don Carlo: Carobbi
Padre Guardiano: Vecchioni

July 30, Aug 4
LUCREZIA BORGIA (Donizetti)
Lucrezia: Singer
Gennaro: Moretti
Duca Alfonso: Carobbi
Maffio Orsini: Borlinetto
Gubetta: Vecchioni

Aug 7, 14, 20, 25
L'EBREA (Halévy) (It)
Rachel: Busi
Eleazar: Lucignani
Alberto: Carobbi
Principessa Eudoxia: Brambilla
Cardinal Brogni: Vecchioni
Ruggero: Monchero

Aug 13, 18, 21, 26
LA GIOCONDA (Ponchielli)
Gioconda: Singer
Laura: Borlinetto

La cieca: Caracciolo
Enzo Grimaldo: Moretti
Barnaba: Menotti
Alvise Badoero: Monchero

Aug 15, 24
LA FAVORITA (Donizetti) (It)
Leonora: Singer
Fernando: Moretti
Alfonso XI: Menotti

**ITALIAN OPERA AND
OPERETTA SEASON**
Aug 28 to Sept 20
Conductor: Frank Rosensteel

Aug 28
LA MASCOTTE (Audran)

Aug 30
BABOLIN (Varney)

Sept 1
FRA DIAVOLO (Auber)
Fra Diavolo: Deliliers
Zerlina: Malvezzi
Lorenzo: Sartori
Lady Pamela Allcash: Arpisella
Mateo: Reggiani

Sept 3, 4
PAPA MARTIN (Cagnoni)
Papa Martin: P. Cesari
Amelia: G. Cesari
Olimpia: Gori
Armando: Deliliers

Sept 6, 11, 21
DONNA JUANITA (Suppé)

Sept 8
LE DONNE CURIOSE (Usiglio)

Sept 10, 13, 18
CARMEN (Bizet) (It)
Carmen: Preziosi
Micaela: Malvezzi
Don José: Deliliers

Escamillo: P. Cesari
Mercedes: Gori
Frasquita: E. Lambiase
El Remendado: G. Lambiase
Zúñiga: Andreoli
Morales: Zucchi

Sept 15
BOCCACCIO (Suppé)

Sept 16, 17
LA PRECAUZIONE (Petrella)**

Sept 20
L'ELISIR D'AMORE (Donizetti)
Adina: Malvezzi
Nemorino: Deliliers
Belcore: Andreoli
Dulcamara: P. Cesari
Gianetta: Caire

Nov 21 to 27
Imperial Japanese Company
Chas Comelli

1888

Female artists
Borlinetto-Conti, Erina <mez>
Brambilla, Elvira V. <s>
Busi, Adriana <s>
Caracciolo-Strozzi, Laura <a>
Drog, Livia <s>
Fabbri, Guerrina <mez>
Pantaleoni, Romilda <s>
Patti, Adelina <s>
Singer, Teresa (Teresina) <s>

Male Artists
Benedetti, Oreste <bar>
Cardinali, Franco <t>
Carobbi, Silla <bar>
Cesari, Pietro <b>
Fiorini, Signor <b>
Menotti, Delfino <bar>
Monchero, Amilcare <b>
Moretti, Giuseppe <t>

Ribeiro, León <pf>
Ruis, Señor <b>
Sambucetti, Luis <vn>
Stagno, Roberto <t>
Trabucchi, Ceferino <vn>
Vecchioni, Francesco <b>

Jan 21 to Feb 20
Carnival Masked Balls

**FALL ITALIAN OPERA
SEASON**
Cesare Ciacchi, Impresario
Feb 25 to March 27
Conductor: Emilio Rajneri

Feb 25, March 10, 13, 22
LA GIOCONDA (Ponchielli)
Gioconda: Singer
Laura: Borlinetto
La cieca: Caracciolo
Enzo Grimaldo: Moretti
Barnaba: Menotti
Alvise Badoero: Vecchioni

Feb 26
LA TRAVIATA (Verdi)
Violetta: Drog
Alfredo Germont: Moretti
Giorgio Germont: Carobbi
Flora: Caracciolo

March 1, 15
AIDA (Verdi)
Aida: Singer
Amneris: Borlinetto
Radamès: Cardinali
Ramfis: Carobbi
Il Re: Vecchioni

March 3, 25
IL TROVATORE (Verdi)
Leonora: Drog
Manrico: Cardinali
Conte di Luna: Carobbi
Azucena: Borlinetto

March 6
FAUST (Gounod) (It)
Margherita: Busi
Faust: Moretti
Mefistofele: Vecchioni
Valentin: Carobbi
Siebel: Borlinetto

March 8
LA FORZA DEL DESTINO (Verdi)
Leonora: Drog
Don Alvaro: Cardinali
Don Carlo: Carobbi
Preziosilla: Borlinetto
Marchese di Calatrava:
Vecchioni

March 18
GLI UGONOTTI (Meyerbeer) (It)
Margherita de Valois: Brambilla
Raul de Nangis: Cardinali
Valentina: Singer
Conte di Nevers: Carobbi
Marcello: Vecchioni

March 20
RUY BLAS (Marchetti)
La Regina: Drog
Ruy Blas: Moretti
Don Cesar de Bazan: Menotti
Don Guritano: Vecchioni
Casilda: Borlinetto

March 24, 27
MESSA DA REQUIEM (Verdi)**
Soloists: Singer <s>, Borlinetto
<mez>, Moretti <t>, and
Vecchioni <b>

March 31 to April 29
Italian Dramatic Company G.
Modena

May 6 to 20
Magic Company Julio F. Bosco

June 6
Concert
Soloists: Singer <s>, Ruis <b>,
Trabucchi <child-vn>

**GRAND ITALIAN OPERA
SEASON**
Cesare Ciacchi, Impresario
July 8 to Aug 25
Conductor: Arnaldo Conti

July 8, 24
IL BARBIERE DI SIVIGLIA
(Rossini)
Rosina: Patti
Conte di Almaviva: Stagno
Figaro: Carobbi
Don Basilio: Cesari
Don Bartolo: Fiorini

July 10, Aug 14
LA GIOCONDA (Ponchielli)
Gioconda: Pantaleoni
Laura: Borlinetto
La cieca: Fabbri
Enzo Grimaldo: Cardinali
Barnaba: Menotti
Alvise Badoero: Vecchioni

July 11
LUCIA DI LAMMERMOOR
(Donizetti)
Lucia: Patti
Edgardo: Stagno
Enrico: Carobbi

July 12, 28
AIDA (Verdi)
Aida: Pantaleoni
Amneris: Borlinetto
Radamès: Cardinali
Ramfis: Menotti
Il Re: Vecchioni

July 14
I PURITANI (Bellini)
Elvira: Patti
Lord Arturo: Stagno
Riccardo Forth: Menotti
Sir Giorgio: Vecchioni

July 17
SEMIRAMIDE (Rossini)
Semiramide: Patti
Arsace: Fabbri
Idreno: Moretti
Assur: Menotti
Oroe: Vecchioni

July 18
Uruguayan National Anthem
LA FORZA DEL DESTINO (Verdi)
Leonora: Pantaleoni
Don Alvaro: Cardinali
Don Carlo: Menotti
Preziosilla: Fabbri
Padre Guardiano: Vecchioni

July 19
LINDA DI CHAMOUNIX
(Donizetti)
Linda: Patti
Pierotto: Fabbri
Visconte Sirval [Carlo]: Moretti
Marquis Boisfleuris: Cesari
Prefetto: Vecchioni

July 21
LAKME (Delibes) (It)**
Lakmé: Patti
Gerald: Cardinali
Nilakantha: Vecchioni
Frederick: Cesari
Hagi: Benedetti
Malika: Fabbri

July 22, Aug 5
RIGOLETTO (Verdi)
Gilda: Brambilla
Il Duca di Mantova: Stagno
Rigoletto: Menotti
Maddalena: Fabbri
Sparafucile: Vecchioni

July 26, Aug 24
FAUST (Gounod) (It)
Margherita: Pantaleoni
Faust: Stagno
Mefistofele: Vecchioni

Valentin: Carobbi
Siebel: Borlinetto

July 29
LA TRAVIATA (Verdi)
Violetta: Patti
Alfredo Germont: Stagno
Giorgio Germont: Carobbi
Flora: Caracciolo

July 31, Aug 15
L'EBREA (Halévy) (It)
Rachel: Pantaleoni
Eleazar: Stagno
Principessa Eudoxia: Brambilla
Ruggiero: Menotti
Cardinal Brogni: Vecchioni

Aug 4, 6, 11, 26
OTELLO (Verdi)**
Desdemona: Pantaleoni
Otello: Stagno
Iago: Menotti
Emilia: Borlinetto
Cassio: Moretti
Ludovico: Vecchioni
Montano: Monchero

Aug 7, 9, 12
L'AFRICANA (Meyerbeer) (It)
Selika: Pantaleoni
Vasco da Gama: Cardinali
Nelusko: Menotti
Inez: Brambilla
Don Pietro: Vecchioni

Aug 18, 22, 25
I LITUANI (Ponchielli)**
Aldona: Pantaleoni
Walter: Cardinali
Arnoldo: Menotti
Albano: Vecchioni

Aug 21
LUCREZIA BORGIA (Donizetti)
Lucrezia: Pantaleoni
Gennaro: Stagno
Duca Alfonso: Menotti

Maffio Orsini: Fabbri
Gubetta: Vecchioni

Aug 29 to Sept 5
French Dramatic Company
Coquelin

Sept 7
Symphonic Concert
Conductor: Francisco Seguí
Soloist: Ribeiro <pf>
Including León Ribeiro's Piano
Concerto****

Sept 28
Symphonic Concert
Conductor: Francisco Seguí
Soloist: Sambucetti <vn>

Oct 27 to 30
Balabrega Company
<prestidigitator>

SPANISH ZARZUELA SEASON
Cristóbal Galván Company
Nov 10 to Dec 8

Dec 22 to 26
Holiday Balls

─────────────────
1889
─────────────────

Female artists
D'Astragna, Eduvige <mez>
Garagnani, Signora <mez>
Giglioni, Ida <s>
Lambiase, Elvira <s/mez>
Mantelli, Eugenia <mez>
Orejón, Isabel <pf>
Preziosi, Margherita <mez>
Ricetti, Ida <s>
Rossi-Trauner, Carolina <s>
Sommelius, Giorgina <mez>
Teodorini, Elena <s>
Torresella, Fanny <s>

Male artists
Battistini, Mattia <bar>
Bignami, Pompeo <vn>
Bottero, Alessandro <b>
Bouzzoni, Isauro <vla>
Capelli, F. <b>
Cesari, Pietro <b>
De Negri, Giambattista <t>
Formentini, Camilo <db>
Girardi, Vittorio <b>
Ibarguren, Clemente <vn>
Lanfredi, Carlo <t>
Limonta, Napoleone <b>
Masini, Angelo <t>
Massi, R. <bar>
Moreschi, Enrique <vc>
Passett, Alessandro <t>
Polonini, Alessandro <bar>
Quiroli, Giovanni <t>
Salassa, Signor <bar>
Wulmann, Paolo <b>

**ITALIAN OPERA AND
OPERETTA SEASON**
Cesare Ciacchi, Impresario
Jan 19 to Feb 3, March 18 to 31
Conductors: Paolo Balsinelli and
Vincenzo Volir

Jan 19
DON BUCEFALO (Cagnoni)
Don Bucefalo: Bottero
Rosina: Rossi
Conte Belpatro: Quiroli
Don Marcos: Capelli

Jan 20
MIGNON (Thomas) (It)
Mignon: Preziosi
Filea: Rossi
Guglielmo: Lanfredi
Laerte: Polonini
Lotario: Cesari
Giarno: Girardi

Jan 22, 27, Feb 3, March 24, 30
DONNA JUANITA (Suppé)
Donna Juanita: Preziosi
Gaston de Fauré: Passett

Jan 24, 31
PAPA MARTIN (Cagnoni)
Papa Martin: Bottero
Amelia: Lambiase
Armando: Quiroli
Daniel: Cesari
Feliciano: Polonini

Jan 26
CARMEN (Bizet) (It)
Carmen: Preziosi
Don José: Lanfredi
Escamillo: Cesari
Micaela: Rossi
Frasquita: Lambiase
Mercedes: D'Astragna
Morales: Massi
Zúñiga: Girardi

Jan 29
FATINITZA (Suppé)
Wladimiro Dimitrowich:
Preziosi

Jan 31
PAPA MARTIN (Cagnoni)
[same cast as Jan 24]
and Don Bucefalo: Act 2

Feb 2, March 16
LA MASCOTTA (Audran)

Feb 21, 23, 24
Symphonic Concerts
Conductor: Luis Sambucetti
Uruguayan National Anthem
Argentinean National Anthem
Wagner: Tannhäuser Overture
Sambucetti: Two preludes:
  a. Invocación****
  b. Leyenda Patria****
Wagner: Prelude to Lohengrin
Massenet: Sous le tilleul
Paganini: Moto perpetuo
Saint-Saëns: Danse macabre

March 2 to 15
Carnival Masked Balls

March 18, 21
I PESCATORI DI NAPOLI
(Sarria)**

March 19
BOCCACCIO (Suppé)
Boccaccio: Giglioni

March 23
LOS MOSQUETEROS GRISES (?)

March 27
FRA DIAVOLO (Auber) (It)
Fra Diavolo: Lanfredi
Zerlina: Rossi
Lorenzo: Quiroli
Lady Pamela Allcash: Preziosi
Mateo: Cesari

March 31
TUTTI IN MASCHERA (Pedrotti)

April 3 to 11
Spanish Dramatic Company
Juan Reig

April 27 to 30
Italian Dramatic Company
Francesco Pasta

July 4 to 31
Spanish Dramatic Company
María Tubau

**WINTER ITALIAN OPERA
SEASON**
Angelo Ferrari, Impresario
Aug 25 to Sept 10
Conductor: Marino Mancinelli

Aug 25
Uruguayan National Anthem
LUCREZIA BORGIA (Donizetti)
Lucrezia: Teodorini
Gennaro: Masini
Duca Alfonso: Wulmann
Maffio Orsini: Mantelli
Gubetta: Limonta

Aug 27, Sept 5
OTELLO (Verdi)
Desdemona: Teodorini
Otello: De Negri
Iago: Battistini

Aug 29
ERNANI (Verdi)
Elvira: Ricetti
Ernani: De Negri
Don Carlo: Battistini
D. Ruy Gomez de Silva:
Wulmann

Aug 31
L'EBREA (Halévy) (It)
Rachel: Ricetti
Eleazar: De Negri
Principessa Eudoxia: Garagnani
Cardinal Brogni: Wulmann

Sept 1
AMLETO (Thomas) (It)
Amleto: Battistini
Ofelia: Torresella
Gertrudis: Mantelli
Polonio: Wulmann

Sept 3
SIMON BOCCANEGRA (Verdi)
Amelia: Ricetti
Gabriele Adorno: De Negri
Simon: Battistini
Jacopo Fiesco: Wulmann

Sept 4, 12
LA GIOCONDA (Ponchielli)
Gioconda: Teodorini
Laura: Mantelli
Enzo Grimaldo: Masini
Barnaba: Salassa
Alvise Badoero: Wulmann

Sept 7
I PESCATORI DI PERLE (Bizet) (It)
Leila: Torresella
Nadir: Masini

Zurga: Salassa
Nourabad: Wulmann

Sept 8
RIGOLETTO (Verdi)
Gilda: Torresella
Il Duca di Mantova: Masini
Rigoletto: Battistini
Maddalena: Sommelius

Sept 10
IL BARBIERE DI SIVIGLIA
(Rossini)
Rosina: Teodorini
Conte di Almaviva: Masini
Figaro: Battistini
Don Basilio: Wulmann

Sept 21
Concert: Italian Band

Sept 28 to 30
Spanish Dramatic Company José
González

Nov 1 to 5
Italian Dramatic Company
Giuseppe Rizzotto

Dec 6, 8, 18
Recitals: Orejón <pf>, Ibarguren
<vn>, Bignami <vn>, Bouzzoni
<vla>, Moreschi <vc>, and
Formentini <db>

Dec 12 to 17
Portuguese Dramatic Company
J. Abreu

1890

Female artists
Braham, Leonora <s>
Bruce, May <mez>
Ganthong, Nellis <a>
Gear, Pauline <mez>

Gil (Gilboni), Lucia Boni de <s>
Kitzú, Aurelia <s>
Livian, Miss <d>
Lupino, Miss <d>
Manfredini, Signora <s>
Routin, Teresa <s>
Serra, Giuseppina <s>
Sismondi, Miss <d>
Steinbach, Emma <mez>
Turconi-Bruni, Angelina <s>

Male artists
Arimondi, Vittorio <b>
Barbieri, Emilio <bar>
Brombara, Vittorio <bar>
Browne, Walter <bar>
Cadwalar, L. <bar>
Cockburn, George <b / bar>
Ferroni, Miguel <vla>
Gabrielesco, Gabriel <t>
Ghezzi, Signor <cl>
Irigoyen, J. <pf>
Logheder, Luis <pf>
Marneck, G. Walter <bar>
Meroles, Pablo <b / bar>
Moreschi, Enrique <vc>
Oxilia, José <t>
Rimini, A. <t>
Ruis, Señor <b>
Sambucetti, Juan José <vn>
Sambucetti, Luis <vn>
Wilkinson, John <t>

April 24 to May 28, July 1 to 16
Italian Dramatic Company
Ermete Novelli

**WINTER ITALIAN OPERA
SEASON**
Angelo Ferrari, Impresario
May 31 to June 30
Conductor: Giuseppe Pomè-
Penna

May 31, June 4, 19
AIDA (Verdi)
Aida: Gilboni
Amneris: Steinbach

Radamès: Gabrielesco(2) /
Oxilia(1)
Il Re: Arimondi
Ramfis: Meroles
Amonasro: Barbieri

June 3
LA FAVORITA (Donizetti)
Leonora: Kitzú
Fernando: Oxilia
Alfonso XI: Barbieri
Baldassare: Meroles
Gaspare: Rimini
Inez: Manfredini

June 7
RIGOLETTO (Verdi)
Gilda: Turconi-Bruni
Il Duca di Mantova: Gabrielesco
Rigoletto: Barbieri
Sparafucile: Meroles
Maddalena: Steinbach

June 10, 12
MEFISTOFELE (Boito)
Margherita: Serra
Faust: Oxilia
Mefistofele: Meroles
Wagner: Rimini

June 14
LA GIOCONDA (Ponchielli)
Gioconda: Serra
Laura: Manfredini
La cieca: Steinbach
Enzo Grimaldo: Gabrielesco
Barnaba: Barbieri
Alvise Badoero: Meroles

June 17, 18, 21
LUCREZIA BORGIA (Donizetti)
Lucrezia: Gilboni
Gennaro: Oxilia
Duca Alfonso: Meroles
Maffio Orsini: Steinbach

June 21
LUCREZIA BORGIA (Donizetti)
and *Concert*: Oxilia <t>
Donizetti: excerpts from Il Duca
D'Alba

June 24, 26
GLI UGONOTTI (Meyerbeer) (It)
Margherita de Valois: Turconi-
Bruni
Raul de Nangis: Gabrielesco
Valentina: Gilboni
Conte di Nevers: Brombara
Conte di Saint Bris: Arimondi
Marcello: Meroles
Maurevert: Arimondi

June 28
OTELLO (Verdi)
Otello: Oxilia
Desdemona: Serra
Iago: Barbieri
Cassio: Rimini
Emilia: Manfredini
Ludovico: Arimondi

June 30
Operatic Concert
Soloist: Oxilia <t>

July 17 to Aug 20
French Dramatic Company
Coquelin

Aug 27, Sept 2
Symphonic Concerts
Hungarian National Orchestra
Conductor: Kiss Jancsi

SPANISH ZARZUELA SEASON
Garrido and Pastor, Impresarios
Sept 6 to 12
Conductor: Antonio del Valle

Sept 21
Recital: Oxilia <t>, Routin <s>,
Ruis <b>, Logheder <pf>,

Irigoyen <pf>, Ghezzi <cl>, L.
and J. L. Sambucetti <vns>,
Ferroni <vla>, Moreschi <vc>

**ENGLISH COMIC OPERA
COMPANY SEASON**
Edwin Cleary, Impresario
Oct 4 to 10
Conductor: Barter Jones
Dancers: Livian, Lupino, and
Sismondi

Oct 4
THE MIKADO (Sullivan)***
Yum-Yum: Braham
Katisha: Ganthong
Pitti-Sing: Bruce
Peep-Bo: Gear
Nanki-Poo: Wilkinson
Ko-Ko: Marneck
The Mikado of Japan: Cockburn
Pish-Tush: Cadwalar
Poo-Bah: Browne

Oct 5
THE PIRATES OF PENZANCE
(Sullivan)**
Mabel: Braham
Ruth: Ganthong
Frederic: Wilkinson
Major-General Stanley: Marneck
Pirate King: Cadwalar
Sergeant of Police: Cockburn

Oct 6
DOROTHY (Cellier)

Oct 8
PEPITA (Solomon)

Oct 10
TRIAL BY JURY (Sullivan)
and The Mikado: Act 2
and Grand Ballet Performance

1891

Female artists
Braham, Leonora <s>
Cook, Aynsley <a>
Livian, Miss <d>
Lupino, Miss <d>
Monteano (Monteoni), Signora
<s>
Sismondi, Miss <d>
Sormani, Signora <mez>
Trebbi, Olimpia <s>

Male artists
Bettini, Signor <t>
Coop, Colin <bar>
Fisher, Mr. <bar>
Irigoyen, J. <pf>
Jiske, N. <bar>
Oxilia, José <t>
Rossi, Giulio <bar>
Sambucetti, Luis <vn>
Vanni, Roberto <t>
Wilkinson, John <t>

March 12 to May 31
Italian Dramatic Company

**WINTER ITALIAN OPERA
SEASON**
Aug 1 to 11
Conductor: Camilo Formentini
Director: Giulio Dalnegro

Aug 1
ERNANI (Verdi)
Elvira: Monteano
Ernani: Bettini
Don Carlo: Rossi

Aug 4
RIGOLETTO (Verdi)
Gilda: Trebbi
Il Duca de Mantova: Vanni
Rigoletto: Rossi
Maddalena: Sormani

Aug 6
LUCIA DI LAMMERMOOR
(Donizetti)
Lucia: Trebbi
Edgardo: Bettini
Enrico: Rossi

Aug 8
LA FAVORITA (Donizetti) (It)
Leonora: Monteano
Fernando: Bettini
Alfonso XI: Rossi

Aug 9
IL TROVATORE (Verdi)
Leonora: Monteoni
Azucena: Sormani
Manrico: Bettini
Conte di Luna: Rossi

Aug 11
LA TRAVIATA (Verdi)
Violetta: Trebbi
Alfredo Germont: Vanni
Giorgio Germont: Rossi

**ENGLISH COMIC OPERA
COMPANY SEASON**
Edwin Cleary, Impresario
Sept 5 to 15
Conductor: Barter Jones
Dancers: Livian, Lupino, and
Sismondi

Sept 5
PATIENCE (Sullivan)**
Patience: Braham
Lady Jane: Cook
Colonel Calverley: Jiske
Grosvenor: Coop
Bunthorne: Fisher

Sept 8, 13
THE MIKADO (Sullivan)
Yum-Yum: Braham
Katisha: Cook
Nanki-Poo: Wilkinson

Ko-Ko: Jiske
The Mikado of Japan: Coop
Poo-Bah: Fisher

Sept 9
ERMINE (Jakobowski)

Sept 12
DOROTHY (Cellier)

Sept 15
THE PIRATES OF PENZANCE
(Sullivan)
Grand Ballet Performance and
"Good Night" (chorus from
Ermine)

Nov 15
Recital
Oxilia <t>, Sambucetti <vn>,
Irigoyen <pf>

Dec 27
Operatic Concert
Conductors: Camilo Formentini
and Luis Logheder
Teatro Solís Orchestra and
Chorus
Soloist: Oxilia <t>

1892

Female artists
Arreglia, Signora <a>
Bordalba, Concetta <s>
Borlinetto-Conti, Erina <mez>
Cassandro, Lina <s>
Crippa, Emma <a>
Firpo, Signora
Gini-Pizzorni, Adele <s>
Luttichau, Julia de <s/mez>
Manzini (Mancini), Signora <s>
Matarelli, Signora
Pettigiani, Anna <s>
Peydró, Lola <s>

Rappini, Ida <a>
Zani, Diomira <mez>

Male artists
Annovazzi, Antonio <t>
Balbiani, Felice <t>
Bayo, Gioachino <t>
Bello, Luigi <t>
Borrucchia, Ettore <b>
Ercolani, Remo <b>
Falleti, Ernesto
Lauria, J.
Limonta, Napoleone <b>
Mariacher, Michele <t>
Oxilia, José <t>
Passeto, Luigi <b>
Pollero, Emilio <bar>
Raggi, Carlo
Scotti, Antonio <bar>
Serini, Ermenegildo de <b>
Terzi, Titto <bar>
Valenziani, Signor <b>
Vallo, A.

Feb 27 to March 6
Carnival Masked Balls

March 8 to April 15
[Theaters closed due to political
struggle.]

**FALL ITALIAN OPERA
SEASON**
April 16 to May 15
Conductors: Camilo Formentini
and Luis Logheder (assistant)

April 16
FRA DIAVOLO (Auber)
Fra Diavolo: Annovazzi
Zerlina: Manzini

April 21
LUCIA DI LAMMERMOOR
(Donizetti)
Lucia: Manzini
Edgardo: Annovazzi
Enrico: Pollero

April 23, 30, May 5
Lucia di Lammermoor: Acts 2
and 3
CAVALLERIA RUSTICANA
(Mascagni)**
Santuzza: Peydró
Lola: Zani
Turiddu: Annovazzi(1) / Oxilia(2)
Alfio: Pollero
Mamma Lucia: Arreglia

April 26, May 3
ERNANI (Verdi)
Elvira: Peydró
Ernani: Annovazzi
Don Carlo: Pollero

April 27
LA TRAVIATA (Verdi)
Violetta: Manzini
Alfredo Germont: Annovazzi
Giorgio Germont: Pollero

April 30
La traviata: Acts 3 and 4
CAVALLERIA RUSTICANA
(Mascagni)

May 5
Lucia de Lammermoor: Acts 2
and 3
CAVALLERIA RUSTICANA
(Mascagni)

May 10, 14
LA FAVORITA (Donizetti) (It)
Leonora: Luttichau
Fernando: Oxilia
Alfonso XI: Pollero
and Concert by Oxilia <t>
Donizetti: excerpts from Il Duca
d'Alba

May 15
RUY BLAS (Marchetti)
La Regina: Luttichau
Ruy Blas: Annovazzi
Casilda: Borlinetto

July 2 to 31
Italian Dramatic Company G.
Modena

**GRAND ITALIAN OPERA
SEASON**
Angelo Ferrari, Impresario
Aug 4 to 30
Conductors: Arnaldo Conti and
Gaetano Cimini
Band Conductor: Gugliemo
Bellucci
Chorus Master: Oreste Clivio
Choreographer: Cesare Rossi

Aug 4, 25
GLI UGONOTTI (Meyerbeer) (It)
Margherita de Valois: Pettigiani
Raul de Nangis: Mariacher
Valentina: Gini-Pizzorni
Conte di Nevers: Scotti
Conte di Saint-Bris: Borrucchia
Marcello: Ercolani

Aug 6, 14, 27
LA GIOCONDA (Ponchielli)
Gioconda: Gini-Pizzorni
La cieca: Rappini
Laura: Borlinetto
Enzo Grimaldo: Bayo
Barnaba: Terzi
Alvise Badoero: Borrucchia

Aug 7, 18
I VESPRI SICILIANI (Verdi)
Duchessa Elena: Bordalba
Arrigo: Mariacher
Simon de Monfort: Scotti

Aug 9, 24
MEFISTOFELE (Boito)
Faust: Bayo
Margherita / Elena: Gini-Pizzorni
Mefistofele: Ercolani

Aug 11
Operatic Concert
Conductor: Cimini

CAVALLERIA RUSTICANA
(Mascagni)
Santuzza: Gini-Pizzorni
Turiddu: Mariacher
Lola: Borlinetto
Alfio: Terzi
Mamma Lucia: Crippa

Aug 13
L'AFRICANA (Meyerbeer) (It)
Selika: Bordalba
Vasco da Gama: Mariacher
Inez: Cassandro
Nelusko: Terzi

Aug 15
Operatic Concert
Conductor: Conti
Lucia: Act 3
I puritani: Act 3

Aug 17
L'AMICO FRITZ (Mascagni)**
Suzel: Pettigiani
Fritz: Bayo
David: Scotti
Beppe: Rappini

Aug 19
LA FAVORITA (Donizetti) (It)
Leonora: Borlinetto
Fernando: Bayo
Alfonso XI: Scotti
Inez: Gini-Pizzorni

Aug 20
OTELLO (Verdi)
Desdemona: Gini-Pizzorni
Otello: Mariacher
Iago: Terzi

Aug 23
AIDA (Verdi)
Aida: Bordalba
Amneris: Borlinetto
Radamès: Mariacher

Amonasro: Scotti
Ramfis: Ercolani

Aug 25
Uruguayan National Anthem
Soloist: Mariacher
GLI UGONOTTI (Meyerbeer) (It)
[same cast as Aug 4]

Aug 28
DON CARLO (Verdi)**
Elisabetta di Valois: Gini-Pizzorni
La Principessa Eboli: Borlinetto
Don Carlo: Mariacher
Rodrigo, Marchese di Posa: Scotti
Filippo II: Ercolani
Tebaldo, paggio: Cassandro
Il grande inquisitore: Limonta
Un frate: Serini
Un araldo reale: Balbiani

Aug 30
LOHENGRIN (Wagner) (It)**
Elsa di Brabante: Bordalba
Ortruda: Borlinetto
Lohengrin: Mariacher
Federico di Tetramondo: Terzi
Enrico, Re Germano: Ercolani
L'araldo del Re: Limonta

Oct 31
Symphonic Concert, including
Leon Ribeiro's symphonic poem
Colón****

1893

Female artists
Gautier, Georgine <mez>
Millanes, Carlota <s>
Roger, Marie <s>

Male artists
Florit, Jaime <bar>
Godefroy, Monsieur <bar>
Manén, Juanito <vn>

Feb 11 to 26
Carnival Masked Balls

April 1 to May 7
Italian Dramatic Company

OPERETTA AND VAUDEVILLE SEASON
from Paris' Théâtre Châtelet
Angelo Ferrari, Impresario
May 13 to 27

May 13
LES VING-HUIT JOURS DE CLAIRETTE (Roger)
Artists: Roger, Gautier; Godefroy

May 16
LE MAITRE DES FORGES (Ohnet)
(French drama)

May 18
MAM'ZELLE NITOUCHE (Hervé)

May 20, 25
French Comedy performances

May 23, 27
LA RONSETTE (Millaud)

June 3 to 28
Italian Dramatic Company

June 23 to Aug 10
Spanish Dramatic Company

Aug 24 to Sept 4
French Dramatic Company
Sarah Bernhardt

Aug 25
Uruguayan National Anthem
JEANNE D'ARC (Barbier) with
incidental music by Charles
Gounod
Sarah Bernhardt and her
Dramatic Company

SPANISH ZARZUELA COMPANY SEASON
Avelino Aguirre, Impresario
Sept 5 to 30

Sept 19
EL REY QUE RABIO (Chapí)
[Inauguration of the electrical
system in the house.]

Oct 1, 2
Recitals: Manén <vn>

Oct 19
Concert
Benefit to Carlota Millanes

Oct 24
Concert
Soloists: Millanes <s>, Manén
<vn>

Nov 11 to 25
Spanish Dramatic Company
Antonio Vico

1894

Female artists
Arkel, Teresa <s>
Bensberg, Kate <s>
Fons, Luisa <s>
Gazull, Adele <mez>
Giudice, Maria <mez>
López, Isabel <tiple>
Othon, Salud <s>
Perales, Clotilde <s>
Petri, Elisa <s>
Zawner, Carolina <a>

Male artists
Aramburo, Antonio <t>
Barbieri, A. <t>
Bellazi, Vittorio <bar>
Broglio, Luigi <b>
Calvera, S. <fl>
Caruson, Guglielmo <bar>

Cremonini, Giuseppe <t>
Ercolani, Remo <b>
Estevenet, Señor <fl>
Frank, Antonio <fl>
Franzini, Rocco <b>
Gebelin, Juan <fl>
Juárez, Rogelio <b / bar>
Julien, Jorge <fl>
Limonta, Napoleone <b>
Logheder, Luis <pf>
Lucignani, Benedetto <t>
Mario, Señor <fl>
Ramini, Roberto <b>
Sanjuán, Eliseo <t>
Scotti, Antonio <bar>
Zaccaria, Achille <b>

Feb 3 to 10
Carnival Masked Balls

April 1 to 30
[Theaters closed due to a yellow fever epidemic.]

SPANISH ZARZUELA AND SAINETE SEASON
May 1 to 31

SPANISH ZARZUELA SEASON
June 1 to July 7

FRENCH OPERETTA COMPANY
July 8
LES BRACONNIERS (Offenbach)
L'AMOUR AU MOULIN (Lanciani)
LE RETOUR DU SALTIMBANQUE (?)

July 10, 12
ALI-POT-D-RHUM (Bernicat)
UNE NUIT BLANCHE (Offenbach)
LA BELLE MEUNIERE (?)

SPANISH ZARZUELA SEASON
Rogelio Juárez Company
Francisco Pastor, Impresario
July 18 to 30

July 18
Uruguayan National Anthem
LA VERBENA DE LA PALOMA
(Bretón)**
Susana: Perales
Casta: López
Julián: Juárez
Don Hilarión: Sanjuán

GRAND ITALIAN OPERA SEASON
Angelo Ferrari, Impresario
Aug 11 to Sept 1
Conductor: Edoardo Mascheroni
Band Conductor: Gugliemo Bellucci
Chorus Master: Achille Clivio
Director and Choreographer: Rinaldo Rossi

Aug 11
LOHENGRIN (Wagner) (It)
Elsa di Brabante: Arkel
Lohengrin: Lucignani
Ortruda: Giudice
Enrico, Re Germano: Ercolani
Federico di Telramondo: Caruson
L'araldo del Re: Broglio

Aug 12
MEFISTOFELE (Boito)
Margherita / Elena: Petri
Faust: Cremonini
Mefistofele: Ercolani

Aug 14, 19, 30
MANON LESCAUT (Puccini)**
Manon: Petri
Lescaut: Caruson
Des Grieux: Cremonini
Geronte de Revoir: Ercolani
Edmondo: Ramini
Musicante: Zawner

Aug 15, 26, Sept 2
LA GIOCONDA (Ponchielli)
Gioconda: Petri
Laura: Giudice

La cieca: Zawner
Enzo Grimaldo: Cremonini
Barnaba: Scotti
Alvise Badoero: Ramini

Aug 16
L'AFRICANA (Meyerbeer) (It)
Selika: Arkel
Inez: Bensberg
Vasco da Gama: Lucignani
Nelusko: Scotti

Aug 18
AIDA (Verdi)
Aida: Othon
Amneris: Giudice
Radamès: Lucignani
Amonasro: Caruson
Ramfis: Broglio

Aug 21
FALSTAFF (Verdi)**
Sir John Falstaff: Scotti
Ford: Caruson
Fenton: Cremonini
Dr. Cajus: Ramini
Bardolfo: Barbieri
Pistola: Broglio
Alice Ford: Petri
Nannetta: Othon
Dame Quickly: Giudice
Meg Page: Zawner

Aug 23
TANNHÄUSER (Wagner) (It)**
Germano: Ercolani
Tannhäuser: Lucignani
Volframo di Escimbac: Scotti
Walter di Vogelveide: Barbieri
Biterolf: Limonta
Enrico: Ramini
Reimare di Zweter: Franzini
Elisabetta: Arkel
Venere: Arkel

Aug 24
LA FAVORITA (Donizetti) (It)
Leonora: Giudice
Fernando: Cremonini
Alfonso XI: Scotti

Aug 25
Uruguayan National Anthem
GLI UGONOTTI (Meyerbeer) (It)
Margherita de Valois: Bensberg
Raul de Nangis: Lucignani
Valentina: Arkel
Conte di Nevers: Scotti
Conte di Saint-Bris: Ercolani
Maurevert: Ramini

Aug 28
CARMEN (Bizet) (It)
Carmen: Giudice
Micaela: Bensberg
Don José: Lucignani
Escamillo: Scotti
Zúñiga: Broglio
Mercedes: Zawner
Frasquita: Gazull

Sept 1
Concert
Giribaldi: Gran fantasía
orquestal sobre el Himno
Nacional
Mefistofele: Prologue
Tannhäuser: Sinfonía
CAVALLERIA RUSTICANA
(Mascagni)
Santuzza: Petri
Lola: Giudice
Turiddu: Cremonini
Alfio: Caruson
Mamma Lucia: Zawner

Sept 15 to Oct 9
Italian Dramatic Company
Ermete Novelli

Oct 10
Recital
Soloists: Frank <fl>, Estevenet
<fl>, Julien <fl>, Gebelin <fl>,
Mario <fl>, Logheder <pf>

In program:
Sambucetti: Dance bohèmienne,
for four flutes, piccolo, and
piano****

**SPANISH COMIC ZARZUELA
SEASON**
Oct 15 to Nov 30

Dec 2, 6
Operatic Concerts
Conductor: Camilo Formentini
Soloists: Fons <s>, Aramburo
<t>, Bellazi <bar>, Zaccaria
<b>, and Calvera <fl>

1895

Female artists
Angelini, Emma <s>
Ankermann, Carolina <s>
Bonaplata-Bau, Carmen <s>
Carotini, Tilde <a>
Conde, Lola <mez>
Corsi, Emilia <s>
Feroldi, Ippolita <s>
Gazull, Adele <mez>
Guerrini, Virginia <mez>
Luzzardi (Lusiardo), Clementina
<s>
Piccoletti, Giuseppina
Pinkert, Regina <s>
Tancioni, Annetta <s / mez>
Widmar, E. <mez>

Male artists
Appiani, Antonio <b>
Caldi, Angelo <t>
Camera, Edoardo <bar>
Cesarotto, Vittorio <bar>
Cioni, Cesare <bar>
Colli, Ernesto <t>
De Grazia, Giuseppe <b>
De Marchi (Demarchi), Emilio
<t>
Ercolani, Remo <b>
Franzini, Rocco <b>

Grondona, Emilio <b>
Limonta, Napoleone <b>
Marini, Pio <bar>
Michelotti, Signor <t>
Porzi, Luigi <t>
Ragni, Carlo
Rossi, Arcangelo <b>
Signoretti, Leopoldo <t>
Signorini, Francesco <t>
Sivori, Ernesto <bar>
Travi, Francesco <b>
Vecchioni, Francesco <b>
Zucchi, Dante <t>

Jan 1 to Feb 8
Children Theatre Ensemble

March 2 to 10
Carnival Masked Balls

March 13 to April 30
[Theaters closed due to a
cholera epidemic.]

SPANISH ZARZUELA SEASON
Rogelio Juárez Company
Francisco Pastor, Impresario
May 1 to 31

June 1 to 5
Italian Dramatic Company

June 5 to 15
Leopoldo Fregoli <Italian
impersonator>

June 16 to July 10
Italian Dramatic Company

**GRAND ITALIAN OPERA
SEASON**
Angelo Ferrari, Impresario
Aug 11 to 26
Conductors: Edoardo Mascheroni
and Gioachino Vells (assistant)
Chorus Master: Achille Clivio
Band Conductor: Guglielmo
Belluci

Director: Rinaldo Rossi
Choreographer: Cesare Conti

Aug 11
AIDA (Verdi)
Aida: Bonaplata-Bau
Amneris: Guerrini
Radamès: Signorini
Amonasro: Camera
Ramfis: Vecchioni
Il Re: Appiani

Aug 13
MANON LESCAUT (Puccini)
Manon: Corsi
Des Grieux: De Marchi
Lescaut: Cioni
Geronte de Revoir: Ercolani

Aug 15
LUCIA DI LAMMERMOOR
(Donizetti)
Lucia: Pinkert
Edgardo: Signorini
Enrico: Camera
Raimondo: De Grazia

Aug 17
GLI UGONOTTI (Meyerbeer) (It)
Margherita de Valois: Pinkert
Raul de Nangis: De Marchi
Valentina: Bonaplata-Bau
Urbano: Carotini
Conte di Nevers: Cioni
Conte di Saint-Bris: De Grazia
Marcello: Ercolani

Aug 18
LA FORZA DEL DESTINO (Verdi)
Leonora: Bonaplata-Bau
Don Alvaro: De Marchi
Marchese Calatrava: Ercolani
Preziosilla: Guerrini
Don Carlo: De Grazia

Aug 19, 25
LA GIOCONDA (Ponchielli)
Gioconda: Bonaplata-Bau
Enzo Grimaldo: De Marchi

Laura: Guerrini
La cieca: Conde
Barnaba: Camera
Alivise Badoero: De Grazia

Aug 20
LOHENGRIN (Wagner) (It)
Elsa di Brabante: Corsi
Lohengrin: De Marchi
Federico di Telramondo: Cioni
Ortruda: Guerrini
Enrico, Re Germano: Ercolani
L'araldo del Re: De Grazia

Aug 22
TARAS BULBA (Berutti)**
Olga: Corsi
Taras Bulba: Camera
Simska: Guerrini
Andrés: De Marchi
Jankel: Ercolani
Varvoda de Dubno: Marini

Aug 24
IL BARBIERE DI SIVIGLIA
(Rossini)
Rosina: Pinkert
Berta: Gazull
Conte di Almaviva: Colli
Figaro: Camera
Don Bartolo: Ercolani
Don Basilio: Rossi

Aug 26
TANNHÄUSER (Wagner) (It)
Elisabetta: Bonaplata-Bau
Venere: Guerrini
Tannhäuser: De Marchi
Volframo di Escimbac: Camera
Germano: Ercolani

SPRING ITALIAN OPERA SEASON

Beccario and Co., Impresarios
Sept 28 to Oct 12
Conductor: Edoardo Boccalari
Chorus Master: F. Cerioli
Director: A. Ziglioli

Sept 28, Oct 13
AIDA (Verdi)
Aida: Angelini
Amneris: Tancioni
Radamès: Signoretti
Amonasro: Sivori
Ramfis: Vecchioni
Il Re: Appiani

Sept 29
LA FORZA DEL DESTINO (Verdi)
Leonora: Angelini
Don Alvaro: Signoretti
Padre Guardiano: Vecchioni
Preziosilla: Tancioni
Don Carlo: Sivori

Oct 1, 6
LA GIOCONDA (Ponchielli)
Gioconda: Angelini
Enzo Grimaldo: Signoretti
Laura: Guerrini
La cieca: Conde
Barnaba: Sivori
Alvise Badoero: Vecchioni

Oct 3
RIGOLETTO (Verdi)
Gilda: Lusiardo
Il Duca di Mantova: Signoretti
Rigoletto: Cesarotto
Maddalena: Conde
Sparafucile: Ercolani

Oct 5
UN BALLO IN MASCHERA (Verdi)
Amelia: Angelini
Riccardo: Signoretti
Renato: Sivori

Oct 8
GLI UGONOTTI (Meyerbeer) (It)
Margherita de Valois: Conde
Raul de Nangis: Signoretti
Valentina: Angelini
Urbano: Widmar
Conte di Nevers: Sivori
Marcello: Vecchioni

Oct 10
FAUST (Gounod) (It)
Margherita: Angelini
Faust: Michelotti
Mefistofele: Vecchioni
Siebel: Conde
Valentin: Sivori

Oct 12
LA FAVORITA (Donizetti) (It)
Leonora: Conde
Fernando: Signoretti
Alfonso XI: Sivori

Nov 14 to Dec 3
Italian Dramatic Company Tina
di Lorenzo

Dec 14
Symphonic Concert
Conductor: Manuel Pérez-Badía
Assistant Conductors: Carmelo
Calvo, Cruz Cerezo, and Mr.
López
Cleopatra: Overture
Liszt: Hungarian Rhapsody
Gounod: Philémon et Baucis'
excerpts
Massenet: Sevillanas from Don
Cesar de Bazan
Chapí: Fantasía morisca

1896

Female artists
Bourman, Amalia <s>
Bruno, Elisa <a>
Casals, Signora <s>
Crippa, Emma <a>
Darclée, Hariclea <s>
Gibboni, Elisa <s>
Gini-Pizzorni, Adele <s>
Gori-Pascuali, Cesira <mez>
Guerrini, Virginia <mez>
Lafon, Signora
Marchesi, Adela <s>
Molinari, Signora

Orlandi, Sofía
Padovani, Adelina <s>
Paoli, Signora <s>
Torresella, Fanny <s>

Male artists
Andreoli, C. <b>
Aramburo, Antonio <t>
Bensaude, Mauricio <bar>
Betz, Signor
Bolesio, Signor <vc>
Busacchi, Signor
Camera, Edoardo <bar>
Cesarotto, Vittorio <bar>
Constantino, Florencio <t>
Contarini, Signor
De Grazia, Giuseppe <b>
De Marchi (Demarchi), Emilio
<t>
Derubeis, Signor <t>
Ercolani, Remo <b>
Faff, Enrico <b>
Irigoyen, Juan <pf>
Limonta, Napoleone <b>
Maleroni, Signor
Marangoni, Signor
Maristany, Signor <t>
Migliazzi, Signor
Pellegrini, Signor <t>
Poggi, Signor <b>
Pozzi, Natale <bar>
Riera, Miguel <b>
Rossi, Arcangelo <b>
Signoretti, Leopoldo <t>
Tamagno, Francesco <t>

SPANISH ZARZUELA SEASON
Carlota Millanes Company
Jan 1 to 18, July 1 to 15

Jan 19 to Feb 5
JAUJA (Errante)
Atheneum Operetta Festival

SPANISH OPERA SEASON
Francisco Pastor, Impresario
Feb 6 to 15
Conductor: Francisco L. Máiquez

Feb 6 to 12
LA DOLORES (Bretón)**
La Dolores: Bourman
Lázaro: Signoretti
Melchor: Cesarotto
Rojas: Faff

Feb 11
LA DOLORES (Bretón) [same cast
as Feb 6 except for Constantino
(his stage debut) as Lázaro]

Feb 13
La Dolores: Act 1
Cavalleria rusticana:
  a. Siciliana
  b. Raconto
  c. Aria
I puritani: Duet
La Dolores: Act 3

Feb 15 to 23, Feb 29 to March 1
Carnival Masked Balls

Feb 26
Italian Lyric Children Company
Conductor: Luis Logheder

SPANISH ZARZUELA SEASON
Rogelio Juárez Company
Francisco Pastor, Impresario
March 3 to April 15

**OPERA AND OPERETTA
SEASON**
Raffaelo Tomba Company from
Rome
Cesare Ciacchi, Impresario
April 23 to May 28
Conductor: Oreste Lambiase

April 23, May 1, 14
IL RE COSCRITTO (Chapí) (It)
[El Rey que Rabió]
Cast: Padovani, Gori-Pasquali,
Paoli; Poggi, Maleroni, Busacchi

April 24, 26, May 7, 22, 25
Crispino e la Comare: Act 1
PAGLIACCI (Leoncavallo)
Canio: Derubeis
Nedda: Paoli
Tonio: Pozzi

April 25
RIGOLETTO (Verdi)
Gilda: Padovani
Il Duca di Mantova: Pellegrini
Rigoletto: Pozzi

April 26
Rigoletto: Acts 2 and 4
PAGLIACCI (Leoncavallo)

April 28
IL VENDITORE DI UCCELI (Zeller)
(It)
[Der Vogelhändler]
Artists: Marchesi, Gori, Paoli;
Poggi, Betz, Marangoni,
Contarini.

April 29
LUCIA DI LAMMERMOOR
(Donizetti)
Lucia: Padovani
Edgardo: Pellegrini
Enrico: Pozzi

April 30
RAFFAELO E LA FORNARINA
(Maggi)

May 5
LE CAMPANNE DI CORNEVILLE
(Planquette) (It)

May 6, 8, 24
I GRANADERI (Valenti)
Cast: Gori-Pasquali; Marangoni,
Poggi, Contarini

May 7
Lucia di Lammermoor: Acts 2
and 3
PAGLIACCI (Leoncavallo)

May 9
LA MASCOTTA (Audran) (It)
Bettina: Marchesi

May 12, 21
EL VIEJO DE LA MONTAÑA
(Conti)
Artists: Lafon, Molinari, Orlandi

May 13
LA SONNAMBULA (Bellini)
Amina: Padovani
Elvino: Maristany
Conte Rodolfo: Poggi

May 16, 18
BOCCACCIO (Suppé)
Boccaccio: Gori-Pasquali

May 20
IL DUCHINO [Le petit Duc]
(Lecocq) (It)

May 21
EL VIEJO DE LA MONTAÑA
(Conti)
CAVALLERIA RUSTICANA
(Mascagni)
Turiddu: Pellegrini

May 22
DONNA JUANITA (Suppé)
PAGLIACCI (Leoncavallo)

May 23, 26
ORFEO ALL'INFERNO (Offenbach)
(It)
Cast: Marchesi; Poggi

May 25
Uruguayan National Anthem
Rigoletto: Acts 3 and 4
PAGLIACCI (Leoncavallo)

May 27
CARMEN (Bizet) (It)
Carmen: Gori-Pasquali
Don José: Derubeis

Escamillo: Pozzi
Micaela: Marchesi

May 28
LA TRAVIATA (Verdi)
Violetta: Padovani
Alfredo Germont: Pellegrini
Giorgio Germont: Pozzi

**WINTER SPANISH ZARZUELA
SEASON**
Rogelio Juárez Company
Francisco Pastor, Impresario
June 3 to 30

**GRAND ITALIAN OPERA
SEASON**
Angelo Ferrari, Impresario
July 18 to Aug 25
Conductors: Edoardo Mascheroni
and Pietro Nepoti (assistant)

July 18, 21
Uruguayan National Anthem
GUGLIELMO TELL (Rossini) (It)
Arnoldo: Tamagno
Guglielmo Tell: Camera
Matilde: Torresella

July 20, 26
GLI UGONOTTI (Meyerbeer) (It)
Margherita de Valois: Darclée
Raul de Nangis: De Marchi
Valentina: Torresella
Conte di Saint-Bris: De Grazia
Conte di Nevers: Ercolani
Marcello: Bensaude

July 23, Aug 22
MANON LESCAUT (Puccini)
Manon: Darclée
Des Grieux: De Marchi
Geronte de Revoir: Ercolani
Lescaut: Bensaude

July 25, 28, Aug 8
IL PROFETA (Meyerbeer) (It)
Giovanni di Leyden: Tamagno

Fides: Guerrini
Bertha: Torresella
Zaccaria: Ercolani
Conte Oberthal: Bensaude

July 30, Aug 24
LA GIOCONDA (Ponchielli)
Gioconda: Gini-Pizzorni
Laura: Guerrini
La cieca: Bruno
Enzo Grimaldo: De Marchi
Barnaba: Bensaude
Alvise Badoero: De Grazia

Aug 1, 4, 20
LA BOHEME (Puccini)**
Mimì: Darclée
Rodolfo: De Marchi
Musetta: Torresella
Marcello: Bensaude
Schaunard: De Grazia
Colline: Ercolani

Aug 2
OTELLO (Verdi)
Otello: Tamagno
Desdemona: Gini-Pizzorni
Iago: Camera
Emilia: Bruno

Aug 6, 11, 25
AIDA (Verdi)
Aida: Darclée
Radamès: Tamagno
Amneris: Guerrini
Amonasro: Camera
Ramfis: De Grazia

Aug 9
MEFISTOFELE (Boito)
Margherita: Darclée
Faust: De Marchi
Mefistofele: Ercolani

Aug 13, 16
SANSONE E DALILA (Saint-Saëns)
(It)**
Sansone: Tamagno

Dalila: Guerrini
Un vecchio ebreo: Ercolani
Il sommo sacerdote: Camera
Abimelecco: De Grazia

Aug 15
LOHENGRIN (Wagner) (It)
Elsa di Brabante: Darclée
Lohengrin: De Marchi
Ortruda: Guerrini
Federico di Telramondo:
Camera
Enrico, Re Germano: Ercolani
L'araldo del Re: De Grazia

Aug 18
LA FORZA DEL DESTINO (Verdi)
Leonora: Gini-Pizzorni
Don Alvaro: Tamagno
Preziosilla: Bruno
Don Carlo: Camera
Melitone: Rossi
Padre guardiano: De Grazia

Aug 19
LA TRAVIATA (Verdi)
Violetta: Darclée
Alfredo Germont: De Marchi
Giorgio Germont: Camera

Aug 23
POLIUTO (Donizetti)
Poliuto: Tamagno
Paolina: Gini-Pizzorni
Severus: Camera

Sept 12 to Oct 7
Italian Dramatic Company Italia
Vitalini

**SYMPHONIC CONCERTS
SEASON**
Orquesta del Teatro Solís
Conductor: Manuel Pérez-Badía
Oct 9 to 18, Nov 4 to 29

Oct 9
Symphonic Concert [all León
Ribeiro works]
Symphony no. 4
Andante obligatto for
violoncello
Scherzo
En el Olimpo: Suite pantomime
after Samuel Blixen's words
Symphony no. 2
Gondoliera (Andante cantabile-
Minuetto)
Marcha triunfal

Oct 10, 18
Symphonic Concerts
Soloists: Casals <s>, Crippa
<a>, Aramburo <t>, Riera <b>,
Bolesio <vc>

Oct 27 to Nov 2
Neapolitan Comedy Company

Nov 4
Symphonic Concert
Gomes: Sinfonia Il Guarany
Mendelssohn: First Symphony
(andante)
Saint-Saëns: Danse macabre
Gounod: Marche triumphal
Grieg: Peer Gynt (Suite)
Giribaldi: Orchestral suite
Liszt: Hungarian Rhapsody no.
1**
Gounod: Danses de bacchantes
from Philémon et Baucis
Wagner: Forest Murmurs from
Siegfried
Delibes: Suite from Sylvia
Meyerbeer: Marche des torches

Nov 12
Symphonic Concert
Soloist: Riera <b>

Nov 18
Symphonic Concert

Sociedad Orquestal
Conductor: Camilo Formentini
Soloist: Irigoyen <pf>

Nov 29
Symphonic Concert
Including
Giribaldi: Scènes militaires
(symphonic poem)****

1897

Female artists
Berlendi, Livia <mez>
Bonaplata-Bau, Carmen <s>
Cazmill, Adela
Ferrani, Cesira <s>
Gallo de Giucci, Luisa <pf>
Giudice, Maria <a>
Gori-Pasquali, Cesira <mez>
Guerrini, Virginia <mez>
Laurent, Mlle.
Miró, María <s>
Montenegro de Gaos, America
<pf>
Pavan-Bernini (Pavan-Moretti),
Annetta <s>
Roger, Marie <s>
Torresella, Fanny <s>

Male artists
Baños, Avelino <vc>
Beaucaurt, Henri de <t>
Brando, A. <pf>
De Lucia, Fernando <t>
Franzini, Rocco <b>
Gaos, Andrés <vn>
Mariacher, Michele <t>
Michelotti, Signor <t>
Monchero, Amilcare <b>
Moreira de Sá, Bernardo <vn>
Poggi, Titto <bar>
Rossi, Arcangelo <b>
Rossi, Giulio <b>
Sammarco, Mario (Mariano)
<bar>
Scotti, Antonio <bar>

Stampanoni, Americo <t>
Tanci, Camilo
Tisci-Rubino, Giuseppe <bar>
Vianna da Motta, José <pf>
Zucchi, Dante <t>

Feb to March 6
Carnival Masked Balls

March 7 to June 30
[Theaters closed due to political
revolution.]

July 11
Recital: Vianna da Motta <pf>
and Moreira de Sá <vn>

July 14 to Aug 2
Spanish Dramatic Company
María Guerrero—F. Díaz de
Mendoza

Aug 7 to Dec 14
**ORQUESTA SOCIEDAD
BEETHOVEN CONCERTS**
Inaugural Concert
Conductor: Manuel Pérez-Badía
Nicolai: Overture The Merry
Wives of Windsor
Grieg: Peer Gynt Suite
  a. Le matin
  b. Morte d'Ase
  c. Danse d'Anitra
  d. Dans le halle du Roi de la
    montagne
Beethoven: Septet
Chabrier: España
Massenet: Dernier sommeil de la
Vierge
Bolzoni: Minuetto for strings
Meyerbeer: Marche aux
flambeaux

**GRAND ITALIAN OPERA
SEASON**
Angelo Ferrari, Impresario
Aug 19 to Sept 15

Conductors: Edoardo Mascheroni
and Pietro Nepoti (assistant)
Chorus Master: Achille Clivio
Band Conductor: Guglielmo
Belluci
Director: Rinaldo Rossi
Choreographer: Cesare Conti

Aug 19, Sept 9
LA GIOCONDA (Ponchielli)
Gioconda: Bonaplata-Bau
Enzo Grimaldo: De Lucia
Laura: Guerrini
La cieca: Berlendi
Barnaba: Sammarco
Alvise Badoero: G. Rossi

Aug 21
L'AFRICANA (Meyerbeer) (It)
Selika: Bonaplata-Bau
Vasco da Gama: Mariacher
Nelusko: Scotti
Inez: Torresella

Aug 22, 25, Sept 4
LA BOHEME (Puccini)
Mimì: Ferrani
Rodolfo: De Lucia
Musetta: Torresella

Aug 24, Sept 11
ANDREA CHENIER (Giordano)**
Andrea Chénier: Mariacher
Madeleine de Coigny: Bonaplata-
Bau
Carlo Gerard: Sammarco
Bersi: Guerrini
Incroyable: Zucchi
Contessa de Coigny: Berlendi

Aug 25
Uruguayan National Anthem
LA BOHEME (Puccini)
[The Teatro Solís 1897 box office
register contained the following
entry: "This performance has
been canceled due to the

assassination of the president of Uruguay, Juan Idiarte-Borda, today at 2:50 P.M."]

Aug 28
WERTHER (Massenet) (It)**
Werther: De Lucia
Charlotte: Berlendi
Sofia: Ferrani
Alberto: Sammarco
Alguazil: Rossi

Aug 29
TANNHÄUSER (Wagner) (It)
Tannhäuser: Mariacher
Elisabetta: Bonaplata-Bau
Volframo di Escimbac: Scotti
Venere: Guerrini
Germano: Rossi
Pastore: Berlendi

Aug 31
MANON LESCAUT (Puccini)
Manon: Ferrani
Des Grieux: De Lucia
Lescaut: Sammarco

Sept 1
PAMPA (A. Berutti)**
Sets painted by Ballerini
Giovanni Moreira: Mariacher
Vincenza: Bonaplata-Bau
Francesco il Napoletano: G. Rossi
L'amico Gimenez: Sammarco
Don Gregorio: Monchero
Il payador: Berlendi

Sept 2
MEFISTOFELE (Boito)
Margherita: Ferrani
Faust: De Lucia
Mefistofele: A. Rossi
Marta: Berlendi
Wagner: Zucchi
Elena: Ferrani
Pantalis: Berlendi

Sept 5
IL FIGLIUOL PRODIGO (Ponchielli)**
Jeftele: Bonaplata-Bau
Nefte: Guerrini
Azaele: Mariacher
Amenofi: Scotti
Un vecchio: Rossi

Sept 7
RIGOLETTO (Verdi)
Gilda: Torresella
Il Duca di Mantova: De Lucia
Rigoletto: Sammarco
Maddalena: Berlendi

Sept 12
AIDA (Verdi)
Aida: Bonaplata-Bau
Radamès: Mariacher
Amneris: Guerrini
Amonasro: Scotti
Il Re: Rossi

Sept 15
Operatic Concert
Soloists: Miró <s>, Baños <vc>, Brando <pf>, and Italian Company artists

Sept 23, Oct 9
Sociedad Beethoven Concerts
Soloists: Gallo <pf>, M. de Gaos <pf>
Rossini: Guglielmo Tell Overture
Rubinstein: Feramors, ballet music
   a. Dance of Kasehmir Brides
   b. Bayadere Dance
Gounod: Marche festival
Rubinstein: Piano concerto op. 70 <Gallo>
Chabrier: España
Mendelssohn: Andante from violin concerto (pf transcription) <M. de Gaos>
Saint-Saëns: Introduction and rondo capriccioso <M. de Gaos>

Massenet: Sevillanas from Don Cesar de Bazan

OPERA AND OPERETTA
PERFORMANCES
Sept 25 to 28
Conductor: Riccardo Cendalli

Sept 25
BOCCACCIO (Suppé)
Boccaccio: Gori-Pasquali
Fiametta: Pavan
Lambertuccio: Poggi

Sept 28
Pescatori di Napoli: Acts 2 and 3
CAVALLERIA RUSTICANA (Mascagni)
Santuzza: Pavan
Lola: Gori-Pasquali
Turiddu: Michelotti
Alfio: Poggi

Sept 30
DONNA JUANITA (Suppé)
Donna Juanita: Gori-Pasquali

Oct 1
Sociedad Beethoven Concert
Soloist: A. Gaos <vn>
Nicolai: The Merry Wives of Windsor Overture
Bolzoni: Minuetto for strings
Wieniawski: Polonaise <vn / orch>
Haydn: Symphony no. 3, first movement
Grieg: Mort d'Ase from Peer Gynt
Meyerbeer: Danse aux flambeau

FRENCH OPERETTA AND
DRAMA SEASON
Oct 17 to Nov 3
Artists: Roger, Laurent, Beaucaurt

Oct 17, 23
NINICHE (Boullard)

Oct 19
LE BOSSU (Sardou) [French drama]

Oct 21, 26
LES VINGT-HUIT JOURS DE CLAIRETTE (Roger)

Oct 28
DURAND-DURAND (Valabregue)

Oct 30
MONSIEUR CHOUFLEURI (Offenbach)

Nov 3
LILI (Hervé)

Nov 10 to 15
Spanish Dramatic Company
Mariano Galé

Dec 14
Sociedad Beethoven Concert
Including
Luis Sambucetti's Indiana****

1898

Female artists
Ferrari, Elvira <mez>
Paltrinieri, Antonieta <s>
Rosa, Alina <s>
Tetrazzini, Luisa <s>

Male artists
Athos, Santos <bar>
Ciampi, Giuseppe <buffo-b>
Cesari, Pietro <bar>
Elías, Cándido <t>
Foresti, Luis V.
Maini, Primo <t>
Resplendino, Adolfo <b>
Valenziani, Signor <b>
Zucchi, Dante <t>

Jan 27 to Feb 2
Pantomime and Comedy Company
Hanlon-Less-Ommers

Feb 5 to 28
Carnival Masked Balls

April 28 to May 31
Spanish Dramatic Company

June 5 to 30
Italian Dramatic Company
Teresa Mariani

June 27
Sociedad Beethoven Concert
Conductor: Manuel Pérez-Badía
In program:
Sambucetti: La Garde Passe****

July 1 to 31
[Theaters closed due to political revolution.]

SPANISH ZARZUELA SEASON
Pretel-Pinedo Company
Aug 3 to 22

GRAND ITALIAN OPERA SEASON
Aug 24 to Sept 11
Conductor: Riccardo Bonicioli

Aug 24
LUCIA DI LAMMERMOOR (Donizetti)
Lucia: Tetrazzini
Edgardo: Maini
Enrico: Athos

Aug 25
Uruguayan National Anthem
IL BARBIERE DE SIVIGLIA (Rossini)
Rosina: Tetrazzini
Conte di Almaviva: Elías
Figaro: Athos

Don Bartolo: Cesari
Don Basilio: Ciampi

Aug 27
RIGOLETTO (Verdi)
Gilda: Tetrazzini
Il Duca di Mantova: Elías
Rigoletto: Athos
Sparafucile: Resplendino
Maddalena: Ferrari

Aug 28
FAUST (Gounod) (It)
Margherita: Tetrazzini
Faust: Elías
Mefistofele: Resplendino

Aug 31
FRA DIAVOLO (Auber)
Zerlina: Tetrazzini
Lorenzo: Zucchi
Fra Diavolo: Maini
Lord Rocburg: Cesari
Pamela: Ferrari
Matteo: Resplendino

Sept 1, 10
I PURITANI (Bellini)
Elvira: Tetrazzini
Lord Arturo: Elías
Riccardo Forth: Athos

Sept 3
DINORAH (Meyerbeer) (It)
Dinorah: Tetrazzini
Corentino: Zucchi
Hoel: Cesari
Cacciatore: Resplendino

Sept 8
LA TRAVIATA (Verdi)
Violetta: Tetrazzini
Alfredo Germont: Maini
Giorgio Germont: Athos

Sept 11
Operatic Concert

Sept 22 to Oct 9
Italian Dramatic Company
Teresa Mariani

Oct 12
Sociedad Beethoven Concert
Conductor: Manuel Pérez-Badía
Giribaldi: Sinfonía
Glinka: Scherzo
Marques: Polonesa
Wagner: Rienzi Overture
Saint-Saëns: Tarantelle
Mancinelli: Cleopatra Overture
Chapí: Fantasía morisca

Oct 21 to Nov 9
Spanish Dramatic Company

SPANISH ZARZUELA SEASON
Nov 13 to 22

Dec 7 to 18
Spanish Comedy Company
María Tubau

1899

Female artists
Ankermann, Carolina <s>
Belloni, Signora
Bottari, Adelina <mez>
Cassandro, Lina <s>
Colonnese, Elvira <s>
Ferri, Margherita <s>
Golfieri, Maria <mez>
Iracema, Amalia <mez>
Lerena, Ema <pf>
Longhi, Emma <mez>
Montalcini, Zaira <mez>
Pacini, Regina <s>
Perego, Anita <s>
Sedelmeier, Amelia <s>
Stinco-Palermini, Anunziata <s>

Male artists
Bergonzoni, E. <t>
Caruson, Guglielmo <bar>

Castellano, Edoardo <t>
Ceppi, Antonio <t>
Conti, Giuseppe <b>
De Marco, G. <bar>
De Segurola, Andrea P[erelló]
<b>
Droetto, Antonio <bar>
Federici, Francesco <bar>
Mori, Signor <b>
Quiroli, Giorgio <t>
Rotoli, Donato <b>
Stinco, Enrico <bar>
Ventura, Elvino <t>

Feb 4 to 20
Carnival Masked Balls

**FALL ITALIAN OPERA
SEASON**
March 4 to 24
Conductors: Giorgio Polacco and
Rinaldo Giovanelli (assistant)

March 4, 7
LA GIOCONDA (Ponchielli)
Gioconda: Stinco-Palermini
Enzo Grimaldo: Castellano
Laura: Longhi
Barnaba: Stinco

March 5
La bohème: Acts 1 and 2
La Gioconda: Act 4

March 9, 16
LA BOHEME (Puccini)
Mimì: Stinco-Palermini
Rodolfo: Ventura
Musetta: Cassandro
Marcello: Caruson
Schaunard: Federici
Colline: Rotoli

March 11
LA BOHEME (Leoncavallo)**
Musette: Stinco-Palermini
Mimì: Cassandro
Eufemia: Golfieri

Marcello: Ventura
Rodolfo: Stinco
Schaunard: Rotoli
Barbemuche: Conti
Visconte Paolo: De Marco
Colline: Droetto
Gaudenzio: De Marco
Durand: Bergonzoni

March 14
PAGLIACCI (Leoncavallo)
Nedda: Cassandro
Canio: Castellano
Tonio: Federici
Beppe: De Marco
CAVALLERIA RUSTICANA
(Mascagni)
Turiddu: Ventura
Santuzza: Stinco-Palermini
Lola: Longhi
Alfio: Federici

March 18, 21, 26
MANON (Massenet) (It)
Manon: Colonnese
Des Grieux: Castellano
Lescaut: Stinco

March 23
LA FAVORITA (Donizetti) (It)
Leonora: Longhi
Fernando: Ventura
Alfonso XI: Stinco

March 24
Mefistofele: Prologue
LA RISURREZIONE DI
LAZZARO(Perosi)**

June 3 to 23, Nov 4 to 15
Italian Dramatic Company Clara
Della Guardia

June 28 to July 14
Spanish Dramatic Company
María Guerrero

**GRAND ITALIAN OPERA
SEASON**
Bernabei, Impresario
July 15 to Aug 26
Conductor: Arnaldo Conti
Chorus Master: Achille Clivio
Band Conductor: Guglielmo
Belluci
Director: Rinaldo Rossi

July 15, 22, Aug 1
AIDA (Verdi)
Aida: Stinco-Palermini
Amneris: Montalcini
Radamès: Ceppi
Amonasro: Stinco
Il Re: De Segurola

July 17
LA GIOCONDA (Ponchielli)
Gioconda: Stinco-Palermini
Enzo Grimaldo: Ceppi
Laura: Montalcini
Barnaba: De Segurola

July 18
Uruguayan National Anthem
LUCIA DI LAMMERMOOR
(Donizetti)
Lucia: Pacini
Edgardo: Castellano
Enrico: Federici
Raimondo: De Segurola

July 20
MANON (Massenet) (It)
Manon: Sedelmeier
Des Grieux: Castellano
Lescaut: Federici

July 23, 27
IL TROVATORE (Verdi)
Leonora: Stinco-Palermini
Manrico: Ceppi
Azucena: Montalcini
Conte di Luna: Caruson
Ruiz: Mori

July 25, Aug 17
IL BARBIERE DI SIVIGLIA
(Rossini)
Rosina: Pacini
Conte di Almaviva: Quiroli
Figaro: Caruson
Don Basilio: De Segurola

July 29
GLI UGONOTTI (Meyerbeer) (It)
Margherita de Valois: Pacini
Raul de Nangis: Ceppi
Valentina: Stinco-Palermini
Urbano: Montalcini
Il Conte di Nevers: Federici
Marcello: De Segurola

July 30, Aug 5
LA BOHEME (Puccini)
Mimì: Sedelmeier
Rodolfo: Quiroli(1) /
Castellano(1)
Musetta: Perego
Marcello: Caruson
Schaunard: Federici
Colline: Rotoli

Aug 2, 25
I PURITANI (Bellini)
Elvira: Pacini
Lord Arturo: Quiroli
Riccardo Forth: Caruson
Sir Giorgio: De Segurola

Aug 8
CARMEN (Bizet) (It)
Carmen: Montalcini
Micaela: Perego
Don José: Castellano
Escamillo: Federici

Aug 10
LA FORZA DEL DESTINO (Verdi)
Leonora: Stinco-Palermini
Preziosilla: Montalcini
Don Alvaro: Ceppi
Don Carlo: Federici
Padre Guardiano: Rotoli

Aug 12
RIGOLETTO (Verdi)
Gilda: Pacini
Il Duca di Mantova: Castellano
Rigoletto: Caruson
Maddalena: Montalcini
Sparafucile: De Segurola

Aug 15
LA SONNAMBULA (Bellini)
Amina: Pacini
Elvino: Quiroli
Rodolfo: De Segurola
Lisa: Montalcini
Teresa: Belloni

Aug 19
PARISINA (Giribaldi)
[Revised version]
Parisina: Stinco-Palermini
Imelda: Bottari
Ugo: Castellano
Azzo: Caruson
Ernesto: De Segurola

Aug 22
PAGLIACCI (Leoncavallo)
Nedda: Sedelmeier
Canio: Castellano
Tonio: Caruson
Silvio: Federici
Beppe: De Marco
CAVALLERIA RUSTICANA
(Mascagni)
Turiddu: Ceppi
Santuzza: Stinco-Palermini
Lola: Belloni
Alfio: Federici

Aug 24
FAUST (Gounod) (It)
Margherita: Sedelmeier
Faust: Castellano
Mefistofele: De Segurola
Siebel: Belloni
Valentin: Caruson

Aug 26
L'AFRICANA (Meyerbeer) (It)
Selika: Stinco-Palermini
Inez: Perego
Vasco da Gama: Ceppi
Nelusko: Stinco
Don Pietro: De Segurola
Sacerdote: Rotoli

Sociedad Beethoven Concerts
Conductor: Manuel Pérez-Badía
Sept 29 to Nov 8

Sept 29
Sociedad Beethoven Concert
Works by Beethoven,
Mendelssohn, Wagner, and
Sambucetti: Suite
d'orchestre****
   a. Rêve des bois
   b. Serénade á la lune
   c. Farandole

Oct 18
Sociedad Beethoven Concert
Soloist: Lerena <pf>
Beethoven: Piano Concerto no.
2
Haydn: Symphony in D Major
Brüll: Polacca di concerto
Tchaikovsky: Slavonic March
Grieg: Peer Gynt Suite no. 1
Wagner: Prelude to Lohengrin
Thomas: Variations sur Le
Carnaval de Venice

Nov 8
Sociedad Beethoven Concert
Works by Saint-Saëns, Dumkler,
Gade, Mozart, Chapí, Massenet,
and León Ribeiro.

Dec 21 to 30
Portuguese Dramatic Company
Lucinda Simoes

1900

Female artists
Giuliani, Adela <s>
Golfieri, Maria <mez>
Jacoby, Rosita <s>
Longone, Lina <s>
Marcomini, Elisa <mez>

Male artists
Albaredo, Signor <t>
Arrighetti, Silvio <bar>
Bonini, Francesco Maria <bar>
Cirotto, Sebastiano <b>
Ferrari, Pedro <t>
Ghilardini, Enzo <t>
Resplendino, Adolfo <b>
Russomano, Signor <t>
Villani, Horacio <b>

Feb 24 to March 11
Carnival Masked Balls

June 16 to 27
French Comedy and Vaudeville
Company

July 12 to Aug 5
Italian Dramatic Company Tina
di Lorenzo–Flavio Ando

**GRAND ITALIAN OPERA
SEASON**
Bernabei, Impresario
Aug 9 to Sept 9
Conductors: Alfredo Donizetti
and Rinaldo Giovanelli
(assistant)

Aug 9
L'EBREA (Halévy) (It)
Rachel: Giuliani
Eleazar: Ghilardini
Principessa Eudoxia: Longone
Cardinal Brogni: Cirotto
Alberto: Arrighetti

Aug 11, 24
LA BOHEME (Puccini)
Mimì: Jacoby
Musetta: Longone
Rodolfo: Albaredo
Colline: Cirotto
Marcello: Arrighetti
Alcindoro: Resplendino

Aug 12, 30
AIDA (Verdi)
Aida: Giuliani
Amneris: Marcomini
Radamès: Ghilardini
Amonasro: Bonini
Il Re: Villani

Aug 14
MANON LESCAUT (Puccini)
Conductor: Giovanelli
Manon: Jacoby
Des Grieux: Ferrari
Lescaut: Bonini
Geronte de Revoir: Resplendino

Aug 15
RUY BLAS (Marchetti)
La Regina: Jacoby
Ruy Blas: Ghilardini
Don Salustio de Bazan: Bonini

Aug 18
LA GIOCONDA (Ponchielli)
Gioconda: Giuliani
Laura: Marcomini
Enzo Grimaldo: Albaredo
Barnaba: Bonini
Alvise Badoero: Cirotto

Aug 19
IL TROVATORE (Verdi)
Leonora: Jacoby
Manrico: Ghilardini
Azucena: Marcomini
Conte di Luna: Bonini

Aug 21, 25
OTELLO (Verdi)

Desdemona: Jacoby
Otello: Ghilardini
Iago: Bonini
Ludovico: Cirotto

Aug 23
CARMEN (Bizet) (It)
Carmen: Marcomini
Don José: Ghilardini
Escamillo: Bonini
Micaela: Longone
Zúñiga: Villani

Aug 26
RIGOLETTO (Verdi)
Gilda: Longone
Il Duca di Mantova: Ferrari
Rigoletto: Bonini
Maddalena: Marcomini
Sparafucile: Cirotto

Aug 28
FAUST (Gounod) (It)
Margherita: Jacoby
Faust: Ferrari
Mefistofele: Cirotto

Sept 1, 2, 8
FEDORA (Giordano)**
Fedora: Jacoby
Conte Loris: Ferrari
Contessa Olga: Longone
De Sirieux: Bonini
Cirillo: Arrighetti
Gretch: Villani

Sept 4
L'AFRICANA (Meyerbeer) (It)
Conductor: Giovanelli
Selika: Giuliani
Vasco da Gama: Russomano
Nelusko: Bonini
Don Pietro: Cirotto
Inez: Longone

Sept 6
UN BALLO IN MASCHERA (Verdi)
Amelia: Giuliani

Riccardo: Ghilardini
Renato: Bonini

Sept 9
CAVALLERIA RUSTICANA
(Mascagni)
Santuzza: Jacoby
Lola: Marcomini
Turiddu: Ghilardini
Alfio: Arrighetti
PAGLIACCI (Leoncavallo)
Nedda: Jacoby
Canio: Ghilardini
Tonio: Bonini
Silvio: Arrighetti

Sept 13 to Oct 1
Magic Company Mr. and Mrs.
Watry

Nov 10 to 20
Spanish Dramatic Company
Concepción Ferrer

Nov 30
Sociedad Beethoven Concert
Conductor: Manuel Pérez-Badía
Including
Tomás Giribaldi: Ateneo,
symphonic poem****

SPANISH ZARZUELA SEASON
Vidal-Silva-Campos Company
Dec 27 to 31

1901

Female artists
Barrientos, María <s>
Benzelum, Helena <s>
Borlinetto-Conti, Erina <mez>
Manfredi, Signora <a>
Melsa, Mary <s>
Micucci-Betti, Linda <s>
Routin, Teresa <s>
Santarelli, Amadea <s>

Male artists
Betti, Gino <t>
Bonini, Francesco Maria <bar>
Carazzi, Signor <b>
Cartica, Carlo <t>
Gregoretti, Signor <bar>
Lucenti, Luigi <b>
Paulincini, Signor <bar>
Ventura, Elvino <t>

SPANISH ZARZUELA SEASON
Vidal-Silva-Campos Company
[continuing from 1900] Jan 2 to
12

SPANISH ZARZUELA SEASON
Rogelio Juárez Company
Jan 26 to Feb 14, March 1 to 10

Feb 16 to 28
Carnival Masked Balls

April 15
Sociedad Beethoven Concert
In Memoriam Giuseppe Verdi
Orchestra and chorus
Conductors: Manuel Pérez-Badía
and Luis Logheder
Chorus Master: Adolfo Errante
Soloists: Benzelum <s>, Routin
<s>
Introductory remarks: Arturo
Pozzoli
Giovanna d'Arco: Sinfonia
I lombardi: Chorus
La traviata: Prelude to Act 4
Aroldo in Italia: Sinfonia
La forza del destino: Pace, pace
mio Dio (Benzelum)
Nabucco: Va pensiero
Nabucco: Scena e aria (Routin)
La forza del destino: Sinfonia
Aida: Prelude to Act 1
Aida: Soprano aria, Act 3
(Routin)
Otello: Ave Maria (Benzelum)
I vespri siciliani: Sinfonia

Closing remarks by Samuel
Blixen

May 11 to 31
Spanish Dramatic Company
Leopoldo Buron

June 1 to 30
Italian Dramatic Company Clara
Della Guardia

July 4 to 22
Spanish Dramatic Company
María Guerrero–F. Díaz de
Mendoza

July 29
Sociedad Beethoven Concert
In Memoriam Manuel Pérez-
Badía
Conductor: Luis Sambucetti

**GRAND ITALIAN OPERA
SEASON**
Antonio Bernabei, Impresario
Aug 1 to 25
Conductor: Arnaldo Conti

Aug 1
LA SONNAMBULA (Bellini)
Amina: Barrientos
Elvino: Betti
Rodolfo: Lucenti
Lisa: Borlinetto

Aug 3
AIDA (Verdi)
Aida: Micucci-Betti
Amneris: Borlinetto
Radamès: Cartica
Amonasro: Bonini
Ramfis: Lucenti

Aug 4, 20
IL BARBIERE DI SIVIGLIA
(Rossini)
Rosina: Barrientos
Conte di Almaviva: Betti

Figaro: Gregoretti
Don Basilio: Lucenti

Aug 6, 25
GLI UGONOTTI (Meyerbeer) (It)
Margherita de Valois: Barrientos
Raul de Nangis: Cartica
Valentina: Santarelli
Conte di Saint-Bris: Bonini
Marcello: Lucenti

Aug 8
LUCIA DI LAMMERMOOR
(Donizetti)
Lucia: Barrientos
Edgardo: Cartica
Enrico: Bonini

Aug 10, 14
IRIS (Mascagni)**
Iris: Santarelli
Osaka: Ventura
Kyoto: Gregoretti
Il cieco: Carazzi

Aug 11
RIGOLETTO (Verdi)
Gilda: Barrientos
Il Duca di Mantova: Betti
Rigoletto: Bonini

Aug 15
LAKME (Delibes)
Lakmé: Barrientos
Gerald: Betti
Frederick: Paulincini
Nilakantha: Lucenti

Aug 17
LE MASCHERE (Mascagni)**
Rosaura: Santarelli
Florindo: Ventura
Arlecchino: Betti
Pantaleone: Bonini

Aug 18
I PURITANI (Bellini)
Elvira: Barrientos

Lord Arturo: Betti
Riccardo Forth: Bonini

Aug 22
LA GIOCONDA (Ponchielli)
Gioconda: Micucci-Betti
Enzo Grimaldo: Cartica
Laura: Borlinetto
La cieca: Manfredi
Barnaba: Bonini

Aug 23
DINORAH (Meyerbeer) (It)
Dinorah: Barrientos
Corentino: Ventura
Hoel: Bonini

Aug 24
LA BOHEME (Puccini)
Mimì: Santarelli
Rodolfo: Ventura
Musetta: Melsa
Marcello: Bonini

Aug 31 to Sept 10
Italian Dramatic Company
Jacinta Pezzana

Oct 24
Concert Benefit for Isidoro
Hermann
[Teatro Solís employee]

1902

Female artists
Annini, Anna de <mez>
Bruno, Signora <s>
Cabrini, R. <child actress>
Colombini, Adelina <mez>
Cucini, Alice <mez>
Darclée, Hariclea <s>
De Lerma, Matilde <s>
Galvany, María <s>
Giacomini, Signora <mez>
Lanzi, Sylvia
Many, Juanita <s>

Mazzuchelli, Tina <a>
Paulini, Signora <mez>
Stehle, Adelina <s>
Timroth, Irma <s / mez>

Male artists
Ancona, Mario <bar>
Anselmi, Giuseppe <t>
Arrighetti, Silvio <b>
Biel, Julián <t>
Boudouresque, Marcel <b>
Ciccolini, Ettore <b>
Cubellini, Pietro <t>
Ercolani, Remo <b>
Fari, Edoardo <t>
Ferrari d'Alvaredo, Pietro <t>
Fiegna, Signor <b>
Foglia, Felice <bar>
Franceschi, N. de
Garbin, Edoardo <t>
Giacomello, Pietro <bar>
Marini, Pio <bar>
Mazzanti, Gaetano <t>
Orefice, Francesco
Pasti, Augusto <b>
Ruffo, Titta <bar>
Ruggiero, Teobaldo
Sartori, Signor <t>
Wigley, Michele <b / bar>
Zanzini, Giuseppe <bar>
Zucchi, Dante <t>

Jan 18 to Feb 22
Carnival Masked Balls

April 5 to May 8
Spanish Dramatic Company
Soledad Pestalardo—Andrés
Cordero

May 10 to June 8
Italian Dramatic Company
Teresa Mariani

ITALIAN OPERA SEASON
Ferrari d'Alvaredo Company
June 14 to 23
Conductor: Pedro Duffau

June 14, 22
LA SONNAMBULA (Bellini)
Amina: Galvany
Elvino: Ferrari
Rodolfo: Fiegna
Lisa: Annini
Teresa: Mazzuchelli

June 15, 21
LUCIA DI LAMMERMOOR
(Donizetti)
Lucia: Galvany
Edgardo: Ferrari
Enrico: Marini

June 17
IL BARBIERE DI SIVIGLIA
(Rossini)
Rosina: Galvany
Conte di Almaviva: Ferrari
Figaro: Marini
Don Basilio: Fiegna

June 19
RIGOLETTO (Verdi)
Gilda: Galvany
Il Duca di Mantova: Ferrari
Rigoletto: Marini
Maddalena: Annini
Sparafucile: Fiegna

ITALIAN OPERETTA SEASON
July 2 to 15
Conductor: Ciro Sconamiglio

July 2, 4, 6, 18
SALTIMBACHI (Ganne) (It)
Cast: Many, Paulini, Bruno;
Sartori, Orefice, Fari

July 3, 8, 16
LA GEISHA (Jones) (It)**
O Mimosa San: Many
Roli Poli: Bruno
Captain Katana: Sartori
Juliette: Paulini
Marquis Imari: Fari

July 5
IL VENDITORE DI UCCELI (Zeller)
Cast: Bruno, Paulini, Sartori,
Fari, Orefice

July 9, 13
Uruguayan National Anthem
Argentinean National Anthem
LA CIGALE ET LA FOURMI
(Audran) (It)

July 10, 13
IL GRANADERI (Valenti)
IL DUETTO DELL'AFRICANA
(Fernández-Caballero) (It)

July 11
LA FIGLIA DE MADAMA ANGOT
(Lecocq) (It)
Clairette: Many
Mademoiselle Lange: Paulini

July 12
BOCCACCIO (Suppé)

July 13
LA CIGALE ET LA FOURMI
(Audran)
IL DUETTO DELL'AFRICANA
(Fernández-Caballero) (It)

July 15
LES P'TITES MICHU (Messager)
(It)**
Cast: Lanzi, Paulini, Orefice

Aug 10 to 15
French Dramatic Company
Gabrielle Rèjane

GRAND ITALIAN OPERA SEASON
Nardi and Bonetti, Impresarios
Aug 17 to 31
Conductor: Leopoldo Mugnone

Aug 17, 26
TOSCA (Puccini)**

Tosca: Darclée
Mario Cavaradossi: Garbin
Barone Scarpia: Ancona
Angelotti: Giacomello
Il sagrestano: Ercolani
Spoletta: Zucchi
Sciarrone: Wigley
Carceliere: Foglia

Aug 19
AIDA (Verdi)
Aida: De Lerma
Radamès: Biel
Amneris: Cucini
Amonasro: Ruffo
Sacerdote: Boudouresque

Aug 21
GERMANIA (Franchetti)**
Ricke: De Lerma
Federico Loewe: Garbin
Carlo Worms: Ancona
Giovanni Palm: Ercolani
Shapp: Ercolani

Aug 23, 25
MANON (Massenet) (It)
Manon: Darclée
Des Grieux: Anselmi
Lescaut: Giacomello
Conte des Grieux:
Boudouresque
Bretigny: Wigley

Aug 24
LA BOHEME (Puccini)
Mimì: Stehle
Rodolfo: Garbin
Musetta: Timroth
Marcello: Giacomello
Schaunard: Ercolani
Colline: Boudouresque

Aug 28
DON GIOVANNI (Mozart)**
Donna Anna: De Lerma
Donna Elvira: Timroth
Don Giovanni: Ancona

Zerlina: Darclée
Don Ottavio: Anselmi
Leporello: Ercolani
Masetto: Wigley
Il Commendatore:
Boudouresque

Aug 29
IL TROVATORE (Verdi)
Leonora: Darclée
Manrico: Biel
Azucena: Cucini
Conte di Luna: Ruffo
Ferrando: Ercolani

Aug 30
IRIS (Mascagni)
Iris: Darclée
Osaka: Biel
Kyoto: Giacomello
Il cieco: Ercolani
and Concert
Wagner: Prelude to I maestri
cantori**

Aug 31
ZAZA (Leoncavallo)**
Zazà: Darclée
Milio Dufresne: Garbin
Cascart: Ruffo
Anaide: Giacomini
Malardot: Boudouresque
Bussy: Wigley
Totò: Cabrini
and Concert
Wagner: Prelude to I maestri
cantori

Sept 20 to 21
French Dramatic Company
Gabrielle Rèjane

1903

Female artists
Borghi, Mlle. <d>
Capeletti, Georgina <d>

Clasenti, Esperanza <s>
Darclée, Hariclea <s>
Dussert, Adine <s>
Farneti, Maria <s>
Ferraris, Teresina <mez>
Fusco, Amelia <s>
Garavaglia, Lina <s>
Garavaglia, Rosa <mez>
Guerrini, Virginia <mez>
Mei-Figner, Medea <s>
Ronzio, Ida <d>
Sallaz, Anna <s>
Valery, Odette <d>

Male artists
Arimondi, Vittorio <b>
Articci, Francesco <b>
Bergamaschi, E. <t>
Bonora, G. <t>
Caruso, Enrico <t>
Cerri, Francesco <b>
Constantino, Florencio <t>
Corradi, C. <t>
De Luca, Giuseppe <bar>
Ercolani, Remo <b>
Fabini, Eduardo <vn>
Foglia, Felice <bar>
Giacomello, Pietro <bar>
Giraldoni, Eugenio <bar>
López, Martín <pf>
Pablo, Vicente <pf>
Pini-Corsi, Gaetano <t>
Thomson, César <vn>
Thos, Constantino <b>
Wigley, Michele <b / bar>
Zenatello, Giovanni <t>
Zucchi, Dante <t>

Feb 14 to March 15
Carnival Masked Balls

SPANISH ZARZUELA SEASON
Federico Carrasco Company
April 22 to May 21

May 28 to June 29
Spanish Dramatic Company
Carmen Cobeña

FRENCH BALLET AND OPERETTA SEASON

July 17 to 28
Conductor: Arnaldo Dominici
Dancers: Borghi, Capeletti,
Ronzio, Valery

July 17, 18
POUR LE TROU DE LA SERRURE
(?)
BRAHMA (Dall'Argine)
Cast: Lafone, D'Aurigny,
Dussert, Valery, Ronzio

July 21
LE HOMARD (Gandillot)
IL CAVALIERI DEI FIORI (?,
ballet)

July 22
CAKE WALK, ballet from Down
South (Myddleton)
BRAHMA (Dall'Argine)
with Mlle. Borghi

July 23, 25
Three ballets:
IL CAVALIERI DEI FIORI (?)
CAKE WALK (Myddleton) and
L'HISTOIRE D'UN PIERROT (M.
Costa)
First ballerina: Capeletti

July 26
COPPELIA (Delibes)

July 28
IN ORIENTE (?, ballet)
First ballerina: Ronzio

Aug 7, 12
Symphonic Concerts
Conductor: Gino Puccetti
Soloist: Thomson <vn>
in an all-Paganini program

GRAND ITALIAN OPERA SEASON

Nardi and Bonetti, Impresarios
Aug 15 to 31
Conductors: Arturo Toscanini
and Pietro Sormani, Francesco
Romei (assistants)
Band Conductor: Guglielmo
Belluci
Choreographer: Ludovico
Saracco
Costume Designer: Zamperoni
from Milan
Scenography: Rovescalli from
Milan and Ferri from Milan

Aug 15
LA DANNAZIONE DI FAUST
(Berlioz) (It)**
Faust: Zenatello
Margherita: Sallaz
Mefistofele: Ercolani
Brander: Giraldoni

Aug 16, 29
MANON LESCAUT (Puccini)
Manon: Farneti
Des Grieux: Caruso
Lescaut: Giacomello
Geronte de Revoir: Ercolani
Edmondo: Pini

Aug 18
GRISELDA (Massenet) (It)**
Griselda: Farneti
Alain: Constantino
Marchese de Saluzzo: De Luca
Gondebaut: Giraldoni
Flammina: L. Garavaglia
Lucifer: Ercolani
Priore: Thos

Aug 21
ADRIANA LECOUVREUR (Cilea)**
Adriana: Mei-Figner
Maurizio di Sassonia: Caruso
Principessa Bouillon: Guerrini
Michonnet: De Luca

Mlle. Jouvenot: L. Garavaglia
Mlle. Dangeville: R. Garavaglia

Aug 22
AIDA (Verdi)
Aida: Darclée
Amneris: Guerrini
Radamès: Zenatello
Amonasro: Giraldoni
Ramfis: Arimondi
Il Re: Thos

Aug 23
IRIS (Mascagni)
Iris: Farneti
Osaka: Caruso
Kyoto: Giraldoni
Il cieco: Arimondi

Aug 24
L'ELISIR D'AMORE (Donizetti)
Adina: Clasenti
Nemorino: Caruso
Belcore: De Luca
Dulcamara: Ercolani
Gianetta: L. Garavaglia

Aug 25
Uruguayan National Anthem
MEFISTOFELE (Boito)
Margherita: Farneti
Fausto: Zenatello
Mefistofele: Arimondi

Aug 27
I MAESTRI CANTORI (Wagner)
(It)**
Hans Sachs: Giraldoni
Veit Pogner: Arimondi
Kunz Volgelge: Zucchi
Konrad Nachtigal: Wigley
Sisto Beckmesser: De Luca
Fritz Kothner: Giacomello
Baldassare Zorn: Corradi
Ulrich Eisslinger: Bergamaschi
Agostino Moser: Bonora
Hermann Ortel: Articci
Hans Schwar: Cerri

Hans Foltz: Thos
Walter di Stolzing: Zenatello
David, garzone: Pini
Eva: Darclée
Maddalena: Guerrini
Un guardiano: Ercolani

Aug 31
TOSCA (Puccini)
Tosca: Darclée
Mario Cavaradossi: Caruso
Barone Scarpia: Giraldoni
Spoletta: Ercolani

Sept 3 to 10
Italian Dramatic Company Clara
Della Guardia

Sept 4
Chamber Music Recital
Thomson <vn>, Pablo <pf>,
López <pf>
Grieg: Romanza with variations
<2 pf>
Corelli: Sonata 12, La folia <vn /
pf>
Handel: Largo and
Passacaglia<vn / pf>
Sarasate: Aires bohemios <vn / pf>
Variations after a Beethoven
theme <2 pf>
Tartini: Divertimento L'arte
dell'arco <vn / pf>

Oct 14 to 18
Argentinean Comedy Company
Podestá

SPANISH ZARZUELA SEASON
Oct 22 to 30

Nov 8 to 18
Spanish Dramatic Company
Alejandro Almada

Nov 19, 25
Symphonic Concerts
Conductor: Virgilio Scarabelli

Soloists: Thomson <vn>, Fabini
<vn>, Pablo <pf>
Mendelssohn: Overture for
orchestra
Bach: Concerto for 2 violins
Brahms: Hungarian Dances nos.
5 and 6
Spies:
  a. Romanza <vn / pf>
    (Thomson / Pablo)
  b. Passacaglia <vn / pf> (Fa-
    bini / Pablo)
Sinding: Violin Concerto
(Fabini)
Grieg:
  a. La morte d'Ase
  b. Danse d'Anitra
Vieuxtemps: Concerto No.1 in E
Minor (Thomson)
Tartini: Il trillo del diavolo
(Thomson / Pablo)
Aromati: Gavotta all'antica for
orchestra
Paganini: Fantasia on La
cenerentola (Thomson)

Nov 28 to Dec 31
Italian Dramatic Company
Ferruccio Garavaglia

1904

Female artists
Aranda, Angela <mez>
Didur, Maria <mez>
Farneti, Maria <s>
Fortini, Juana S. de <s>
Frigeri, Rina <s>
Garavaglia, Lina <s>
Garavaglia, Rosa <mez>
Ghibaudo, Euvige <mez>
González, Elisa <s>
Mantegazza, Anunziata B. de <s>
Parsi-Petinella, Armida <a>
Pandolfini, Angelica <s>
Storchio, Rosina <s>
Torretta, Anna <mez>
Tuene, Angelita <s>

Male artists
Amato, Pasquale <bar>
Andolfi, Ernano <pf>
Baldassari, Luigi <bar>
Borgatti, Giuseppe <t>
Cetrullo, S. <mandolin>
Didur, Adamo <b>
Ercolani, Remo <b>
Frigeri, R. <bar>
Garbin, Edoardo <t>
Giacomello, Pietro <bar>
Gonzalez, Juan A. <bar>
Lena, Alfredo <t>
Mafioli, Juan <vn>
Nannetti, Augusto <t>
Sammarco, Mario <bar>
Santucci, José <t>
Schiavazzi, Piero <t>
Thos, Constantino <b>
Venturini, Alfredo <t>

Jan 1 to July 3
[Theaters closed due to political
revolution.]

July 5 to 10
Italian Dramatic Company Clara
Della Guardia

July 27 to Aug 4
Italian Dramatic Company
Ermete Zacconi

**GRAND ITALIAN OPERA
SEASON**
Nardi and Bonetti, Impresarios
Aug 18 to 25
Conductors: Arturo Toscanini
and Pietro Sormani, Francesco
Romei (assistants)
Band Conductor: Guglielmo
Bellucci

Aug 18
LOHENGRIN (Wagner) (It)
Elsa di Brabante: Farneti
Lohengrin: Borgatti
Ortruda: Parsi-Petinella

Federico di Telramondo: Amato
Enrico: Didur

Aug 20
LINDA DI CHAMOUNIX
(Donizetti)
Linda: Storchio
Visconte di Sirval: Schiavazzi
Marquis Boisfleuris: Sammarco
Maddalena: Parsi-Petinella
Prefetto: Ercolani
Intendente: Didur

Aug 21
MANON (Massenet) (It)
Manon: Storchio
Des Grieux: Garbin
Lescaut: Sammarco

Aug 23
FAUST (Gounod) (It)
Margherita: Storchio
Faust: Schiavazzi
Mefistofele: Didur
Valentin: Sammarco
Siebel: Torretta

Aug 24
LA WALLY (Catalani)**
Wally: Farneti
Stromminger: Ercolani
Afra: Torretta
Walter: Frigeri
Hagenbach: Garbin
Gellner: Amato
Il pedone: Baldassari

Aug 25
Uruguayan National Anthem
MADAMA BUTTERFLY (Puccini)**
Cio-Cio-San: Storchio
Pinkerton: Garbin
Bonzo: Ercolani
Sharpless: Amato

Oct 9, 19, 20
Recitals in Celebration of the
Peace Treaty

Mantegazza <s>, González <s>,
Tuene <s>, Fortini <s>, Lena
<t>, González <bar>, Cetrullo
<mandolin>, Santucci <t>,
Mafioli <vn>, Andolfi <pf>

Oct 29 to Nov 6
Italian Dramatic Company
Ermete Novelli

Nov 12 to Dec 7
Spanish Comedy Company
Serrador–Mari

1905

Female artists
Barbiere, Elvira <s>
Barrientos, María <s>
Berti-Cecchini, Anna <mez>
Cerratelli, Polissena <mez>
Burzio, Eugenia <s>
Evangelisti, Signora <mez>
Fálleri, Agar <pf>
Garavaglia, Lina <s>
Garavaglia, Rosa <mez>
Garibaldi, Luisa (Luigia) <mez>
Giachetti, Rina <s>
Gobatto, Ida <s>
Lambiase, Signora <s>
Lavin de Casas, Blanca <mez>
Parisetti, Luisa <a>
Perosio, Giuseppina <mez>
Poggi, Signora <s>
Russ, Giannina <s>
Seinescu, Caliope <s>
Severini, Gina <mez>
Soldemeier, Amelia <s>
Storchio, Rosina <s>
Zani, Bianca <s>
Zeppilli, Alice <mez>

Male artists
Andreini (Andreoni), Remo <t>
Anselmi, Giuseppe <t>
Arcangelli, Alessandro <bar>
Armanini, Giuseppe <t>

Baldassari, Luigi <bar>
Baños, Avelino <vc>
Bonini, Francesco Maria <bar>
Brombara, Vittorio <bar>
Bucalo, Emmanuele <bar>
Butti, Carlo <bar>
Ciccolini, Ettore <b>
Colombo, Natalio <t>
D'Albori (D'Albore), Emilio
<bar>
De Segurola, Andrea P[erelló]
<b>
Didur, Adamo <b>
Di Genaro, Osvaldo <t>
Ercolani, Remo <b>
Etchepare, Esteban <t>
Evangelisti, Signor <bar>
Fálleri, Oseas <ob>
Fornari, A. <bar>
Gabardo, Plinio <t>
Genari, Oreste <t>
Giraldoni, Eugenio <bar>
Gubellini, Pietro <t>
Izquierdo, Manuel <t>
Martinotti, Bruno <b>
Nani, Enrico <bar>
Nannetti, Augusto <t>
Ottonello, Felix <t>
Palet, José <t>
Perico, Atilio <t>
Pulcini, Atilio <b / bar>
Rattaggi, E. <b>
Rossini, Luciano <t>
Roussel, Mario <bar>
Sesona, Emilio <b>
Spangher, Francesco <b>
Tavecchia (Tarecchia), Luigi <b>
Thos, Constantino <b>
Zenatello, Giovanni <t>
Zucchi, Dante <t>
Zucchi, Ettore <t>

Feb 25 to March 19
Carnival Masked Balls

April 19 to 27
Sacred Drama Company José
Fernández

April 28
Symphonic Concert
Soloists: A. Fálleri <pf>, O.
Fálleri <ob>, Baños <vc>
In program:
Rubinstein: Piano Concerto no. 4
Chopin: Polonaise and Berceuse

May 27 to July 30
Italian Dramatic Company
Antonio Bolognesi

**WINTER ITALIAN OPERA
SEASON**
Antonio Bernabei, Impresario
Aug 5 to 16
Conductors: Ettore Perosio and J.
Armani (assistant)
Directors: Giacomo Puccini and
Egidio Scarlatti
Chorus Master: Francesco
Codivilla

Aug 5, 11
TOSCA (Puccini)
Tosca: Burzio
Mario Cavaradossi: Armanini
Barone Scarpia: Arcangelli

Aug 6
LUCIA DI LAMMERMOOR
(Donizetti)
Lucia: Barrientos
Edgardo: Izquierdo
Enrico: Arcangelli
Raimondo: Ciccolini

Aug 8
AIDA (Verdi)
Aida: Burzio
Radamès: Izquierdo
Amneris: Cerratelli
Amonasro: Arcangelli
Ramfis: Pulcini
Il Re: Ciccolini

Aug 10
L'ELISIR D'AMORE (Donizetti)

Adina: Barrientos
Nemorino: Andreini
Dulcamara: Tavecchia
Belcore: D'Albori

Aug 11
TOSCA (Puccini) [same cast as
Aug 5]
Special Gala Performance to
honor Giacomo Puccini
Director: Puccini

Aug 12
LA SONNAMBULA (Bellini)
Amina: Barrientos
Elvino: Andreini
Conte Rodolfo: De Segurola

Aug 13
RIGOLETTO (Verdi)
Gilda: Barrientos
Il Duca di Mantova: Armanini
Rigoletto: Arcangelli
Maddalena: Cerratelli
Sparafucile: Ciccolini

Aug 15
IL BARBIERE DI SIVIGLIA
(Rossini)
Rosina: Barrientos
Conte di Almaviva: Andreini
Figaro: D'Albore
Don Basilio: Ciccolini
Don Bartolo: Tavecchia

Aug 16
MANON LESCAUT (Puccini)
Special Farewell Gala
Performance
Director: Puccini
Manon: Gobatto
Des Grieux: Armanini
Lescaut: D'Albore
Geronte de Revoir: De Segurola

**GRAND ITALIAN OPERA
SEASON**
Nardi and Bonetti, Impresarios

Aug 19 to 31
Conductors: Leopoldo Mugnone,
and Francesco Romei, Fernando
Tanara (assistants)
Band Conductor: Guglielmo
Bellucci
Chorus Master: M. Jurilli
Director: E. Reale
Choreographer: E. Dell'Agostini
Scenography: G. Carmigiani

Aug 19
AIDA (Verdi)
Aida: Russ
Radamès: Zenatello
Amneris: Lavin de Casas
Amonasro: Nani
Ramfis: Didur
Il Re: Thos

Aug 20
MANON LESCAUT (Puccini)
Manon: Giachetti
Des Grieux: Zenatello
Lescaut: Brombara
Geronte de Revoir: Ercolani

Aug 22
MANON (Massenet) (It)
Manon: Storchio
Des Grieux: Anselmi
Lescaut: Brombara
Guillot: Didur

Aug 24
AMICA (Mascagni)**
Amica: Russ
Giorgio: Anselmi
Rinaldo: Giraldoni
Padron Camoine: Ercolani

Aug 25
Uruguayan National Anthem
UN BALLO IN MASCHERA (Verdi)
Amelia: Russ
Riccardo: Zenatello
Renato: Bonini
Ulrica: Lavin de Casas

Oscar: Zeppilli
Sam: Ercolani
Tom: Thos

Aug 26
LA DANNAZIONE DI FAUST
(Berlioz) (It)
Margherita: Russ
Faust: Zenatello
Mefistofele: Bonini

Aug 27
DON PASQUALE (Donizetti)
Don Pasquale: Ercolani
Norina: Storchio
Ernesto: Anselmi

Aug 29
VITA BRETTONE (Mugnone)**
Glaud: Giachetti
Yann: Zenatello
Gaos: Giraldoni
Lania: Lavin de Casas

Aug 30
ROMEO E GIULIETTA (Gounod)
(It)
Giulietta: Storchio
Romeo: Anselmi
Stefano: Garibaldi
Mercurio: Giraldoni
Fra Lorenzo: Didur

Aug 31
LORELEY (Catalani)**
Loreley: Russ
Walter: Anselmi
Herrmann: Bonini
Anna di Rehberg: Lavin de
Casas
Rudolfo: Didur

Sept 12 to Nov 1
Spanish Dramatic Company
Lerena–Díaz

**SPRING ITALIAN OPERA
SEASON**
Rendina and Co., Impresarios

Nov 11 to Dec 2
Conductor: Rinaldo Giovanelli
Chorus Master: Francesco
Codivilla
Choreographer: Rosita
Plantanida

Nov 11, 21
GLI UGONOTTI (Meyerbeer) (It)
Margherita de Valois: Seinescu
Raul de Nangis: Perico
Valentina: Barbieri
Urbano: Berti-Cecchini
Conte di Nevers: Roussel
Conte di Saint-Bris: Spangher

Nov 12, 26
UN BALLO IN MASCHERA (Verdi)
Amelia: Barbieri
Riccardo: Perico
Renato: Roussel
Ulrica: Berti-Cecchini
Oscar: Seinescu
Sam: Spangher
Tom: Sesona

Nov 14
LA BOHEME (Puccini)
Mimì: Gobatto
Rodolfo: Gubellini
Musetta: Severini
Marcello: Roussel

Nov 16
TOSCA (Puccini)
Tosca: Gobatto
Mario Cavaradossi: Gubellini
Barone Scarpia: Bucalo

Nov 17
RIGOLETTO (Verdi)
Gilda: Seinescu
Rigoletto: Bucalo
Il Duca di Mantova: Gubellini
Maddalena: Berti-Cecchini
Sparafucile: Sesona

Nov 18
IL TROVATORE (Verdi)
Leonora: Barbieri
Manrico: Perico
Conte di Luna: Roussel
Azucena: Berti-Cecchini
Ferrando: Spagher

Nov 19
CAVALLERIA RUSTICANA
(Mascagni)
Santuzza: Barbieri
Turiddu: Gubellini
Lola: Severini
Alfio: Bucalo
PAGLIACCI (Leoncavallo) [and
Nov 25]
Nedda: Gobatto
Canio: Perico
Tonio: Roussel
Silvio: Pulcini
Beppe: Rossini

Nov 22
MANON LESCAUT (Puccini)
Manon: Gobatto
Des Grieux: Gubellini
Lescaut: Bucalo
Geronte de Revoir: Spangher

Nov 23
AIDA (Verdi)
Aida: Barbieri
Radamès: Perico
Amneris: Berti-Cecchini
Amonasro: Roussel
Ramfis: Spangher
Il Re: Sesona

Nov 25
Lucia di Lammermoor: Acts 2
and 3
Lucia: Seinescu
and PAGLIACCI (Leoncavallo)

Nov 27
Operatic Concert

OPERA-OPERETTA PERFORMANCES

Nov 28, Dec 3
FRA DIAVOLO (Auber)
Zerlina: Poggi
Fra Diavolo: Gabardo
Lorenzo: Zucchi
Lord Rockburg: Evangelisti
Pamela: Signora Evangelisti
Matteo: Ottonello

Nov 30
LA POUPEE (Audran)
with Signora Lambiase

Dec 2
BOCCACCIO (Suppé)
Boccaccio: Signora Evangelisti
Fiametta: Lambiase
Pietro: Zucchi
Lambertucci: Evangelisti
Beatrice: Poggi

Dec 6
Concert to benefit tenor Esteban
Etchepare

1906 GOLDEN ANNIVERSARY YEAR

Female artists
Alessandrovich, Maria <s>
Barbieri, A. <mez>
Barré, Jeanne <s>
Berti-Marranti, Romilda <s>
Clasenti, Esperanza <s>
Clement, Mlle. <mez>
Courtenay, Vera <s>
Dalila, Signora <s>
Darclée, Hariclea <s>
De Angelis, Signora <s>
De Frate, Ines <s>
De Ter, Marguerite <s / mez>
Depray, Mlle. <s>
Duprez, Mlle. <d>
Favili, Maria <mez>
Franchini, Signora <mez>

Frascani, Nini <mez>
Gagliardi, Cecilia <s>
Garavaglia, Rosa <mez>
Garibaldi, Luigia <mez>
Gautier, Georgine <mez>
Grasse, Signora <mez>
Kruszelnicka [Krusceniski],
Salomea <s>
Leo, Mlle. <s>
Mariani, Signora <mez>
Martini, Signora <s>
Merian, Signora <mez>
Meyer, Mlle. <s>
Nolba, Jeanne <s>
Palatano, Ada <s>
Rodríguez, Señora <s>
Roland, Mlle. <s>
Roli, Signora <mez>
Storchio, Rosina <s>
Talexis, Amelia <s>
Ter, Marguerite de <s>
Vela, Luisa <s>

Male artists
Amato, Pasquale <bar>
Anceschi, Signor <bar>
Anselmi, Giuseppe <t>
Ansorge, Conrad <pf>
Aristide, Monsieur <bar>
Badaracco, Giovanni <t>
Baldassari, Luigi <bar>
Ballin, Monsieur <b>
Barella, Señor <t>
Baroncini, P. <b>
Bertie, Monsieur <bar>
Cappa, Ernesto <b>
Carcan, Monsieur <bar>
Colombo, Natalio <t>
Crams, Monsieur <t>
Cristalli, Italo <t>
Dani, Carlo <t>
De Grazia, Giuseppe <b>
De Luca, Giuseppe <bar>
Didur, Adamo <b>
Dubois, Monsieur <b>
Duffray, Monsieur <bar>
Ercolani, Remo <b>
Falieres, Monsieur <bar>

Garbin, Edoardo <t>
García, Señor <t>
Godard, Monsieur <b>
Godefroy, Monsieur <bar>
Leonard, Monsieur <t>
Longobardi, Luigi <t>
Mansueto, Gaudio <b>
Mardones, José <b>
Martinotti, Bruno <b>
Nadin, Monsieur <bar>
Newstead, Arthur <pf>
Noel, Albert <t>
Poggi, Giovanni <bar>
Polimeni, Franco <bar>
Reguier, Monsieur <bar>
Reuter, Florizel von <vn>
Sagi-Barba, Emilio <bar>
Stracciari, Riccardo <bar>
Thos, Constantino <b>
Valoris, Monsieur <t>
Villiers, Monsieur <t>
Walter, Carlo <b>

Feb 17 to March 16
Carnival Masked Balls

FALL ITALIAN OPERA SEASON
Bonelli and Marranti,
Impresarios
March 17 to April 22
Conductors: Antonio Marranti,
and Luigi Villata (assistant)
Director: Oreste Berti

March 17, 22, April 17
NORMA (Bellini)
Norma: De Frate
Adalgisa: Palatano
Pollione: Badaracco
Oroveso: Cappa

March 18, April 7
TOSCA (Puccini)
Tosca: Del Frate
Mario Cavaradossi: Colombo
Barone Scarpia: Polimeni

March 20, 25
AIDA (Verdi)
Aida: De Frate
Radamès: Badaracco
Amneris: Franchini

March 21
LA BOHEME (Puccini)
Mimì: Palatano
Rodolfo: Colombo
Musetta: De Angelis
Marcello: Poggi
Colline: Cappa

March 24, April 1
IRIS (Mascagni)
Iris: Berti-Marranti
Osaka: Colombo
Kyoto: Poggi
Il cieco: Cappa

March 27
FAUST (Gounod) (It)
Margherita: Palatano
Faust: Colombo
Mefistofele: Cappa
Valentin: Polimeni

March 28
CAVALLERIA RUSTICANA
(Mascagni)
Santuzza: Del Frate
Turiddu: Colombo
PAGLIACCI (Leoncavallo)
Canio: Badaracco
Nedda: Berti-Marranti
Tonio: Polimeni

March 29
IL TROVATORE (Verdi)
Manrico: Badaracco
Leonora: Del Frate
Conte di Luna: Polimeni
Azucena: Franchini

March 31
LA GIOCONDA (Ponchielli)
Gioconda: De Frate

Enzo Grimaldo: Colombo
Laura: Franchini
Barnaba: Polimeni
Alvise Badoero: Cappa

April 3, 15
RUY BLAS (Marchetti)
La Regina: De Frate
Ruy Blas: Badaracco
Casilda: Franchini
Don Salustio de Bazan: Polimeni
Don Guritano: Cappa

April 4
LA TRAVIATA (Verdi)
Violetta: Berti-Marranti
Alfredo Germont: Colombo
Giorgio Germont: Polimeni
Flora: Franchini

April 5
UN BALLO IN MASCHERA (Verdi)
Amelia: De Frate
Riccardo: Badaracco
Renato: Polimeni
Ulrica: Franchini
Oscar: Palatano

April 8
LA FORZA DEL DESTINO (Verdi)
Leonora: De Frate
Don Alvaro: Badaracco
Don Carlo: Polimeni

April 10
RIGOLETTO (Verdi)
Gilda: Palatano
Il Duca di Mantova: Colombo
Rigoletto: Polimeni
Maddalena: Franchini
Sparafucile: Cappa
Giovanna: Frascani

April 11 to 13
Sacred Drama Spanish Company
Arnaldo Gómez

April 14
L'AFRICANA (Meyerbeer) (It)
Selika: De Frate
Vasco da Gama: Badaracco
Nelusko: Polimeni
Don Pietro: Cappa

April 18
LINDA DI CHAMOUNIX
(Donizetti)
Linda: Palatano
Maddalena: Franchini
Visconte di Sirval: Colombo
Antonio: Poggi
Marquis Boisfleuris: Cappa

April 19
Uruguayan National Anthem
LUCIA DI LAMMERMOOR
(Donizetti)
Lucia: Berti-Marranti
Edgardo: Colombo
Enrico: Poggi

April 21, 22
ALDA (Rodríguez-Socas)****
Alda: Berti-Marranti
Enrico: Colombo
Lena: De Angelis
Spauri: Cappa
Dr. Sani: Martinotti
and La bohème, Acts 1, 3, and 4

April 22
ALDA (Rodríguez-Socas)
and Lucia di Lammermoor, Acts
3 and 4

April 28 to May 20
Bióscopo Lírico

June 9 to July 1
Italian Dramatic Company
Antonio Brunorini

**SPANISH ZARZUELA AND
OPERA SEASON**
Emilio Sagi Barba–Luisa Vela
July 11 to 31

July 11
LA TEMPESTAD (Chapí)
Angela: Vela
Roberto: Rodríguez
Beltrán: Barella
Simón: Sagi-Barba

July 14
EL JURAMENTO (Gaztambide)

July 15
LA BOHEME (Puccini) (Sp)
Mimì: Vela
Rodolfo: Barella
Marcello: Sagi-Barba
Musetta: Rodríguez
Colline: Mardones

July 17
MARINA (Arrieta)
EL GRUMETE (Arrieta)
EL GUITARRICO (Pérez-Soriano)

July 18
Uruguayan National Anthem
EL MAESTRO CAMPANONE (Lleó
and Mazza)

July 19
LA TELA DE ARAÑA (Nieto) and
TIERRA (Llanos y Berete)

July 22
LA CONQUISTA DE MADRID
(Gaztambide)

July 24
La bohème, Acts 1 and 3,
CAVALLERIA RUSTICANA
(Mascagni) (Sp)

July 25
TOSCA (Puccini) (Sp)
Tosca: Vela
Mario Cavaradossi: Barella
Barone Scarpia: Sagi-Barba
Angelotti: Mardones

July 27
EL REY QUE RABIO (Chapí)

July 28
LA CANCION DEL NAUFRAGO
(Morera)
with Mardones <b>

July 29
LA MUÑECA [La Poupée]
(Audran) (Sp)

July 30
LA GUERRA SANTA (Arrieta)

July 31
EL ANILLO DE HIERRO
(Marqués)
EL DUO DE LA AFRICANA
(Fernández-Caballero)

**WINTER ITALIAN OPERA
SEASON**
Antonio Bernabei, Impresario
Aug 2 to 12
Conductor: Arnaldo Conti

Aug 2
MANON (Massenet) (It)
Manon: Darclée
Des Grieux: Dani
Lescaut: Anceschi
Conte Des Grieux: Mansueto

Aug 4
LOHENGRIN (Wagner) (It)
Lohengrin: Cristalli
Elsa di Brabante: Gagliardi
Ortruda: Grasse
Federico di Telramondo: Amato

Aug 5
TOSCA (Puccini)
Tosca: Darclée
Mario Cavaradossi: Dani
Barone Scarpia: Amato

Aug 7
IRIS (Mascagni)
Iris: Darclée
Osaka: Cristalli
Kyoto: Anceschi
Il cieco: De Grazia

Aug 9
DON PASQUALE (Donizetti)
Norina: Darclée
Ernesto: Dani

Aug 10
LA GIOCONDA (Ponchielli)
Gioconda: Gagliardi
Enzo Grimaldo: Cristalli
Laura: Franchini
Barnaba: Amato
Alvise Badoero: De Grazia

Aug 11
FAUST (Gounod) (It)
Margherita: Darclée
Faust: Dani
Mefistofele: Mansueto
Valentin: Anceschi

Aug 12
GLI UGONOTTI (Meyerbeer) (It)
Margherita de Valois:
Alessandrovich
Valentina: Darclée
Raul de Nangis: García
Conte di Nevers: Anceschi
Conte di Saint-Bris: Mansueto

**GRAND ITALIAN OPERA
SEASON**
Nardi and Bonetti, Impresarios
Aug 18 to Sept 1
Conductor: Arturo Toscanini

Aug 18
MANON (Massenet) (It)
Manon: Storchio
Des Grieux: Anselmi
Lescaut: Stracciari
Conte Des Grieux: Thos

Aug 19
TRISTANO E ISOTTA (Wagner)
(It)**
Isotta: Kruszelnicka
Tristano: Longobardi
Re Marke: Walter
Brangania: Garibaldi
Kurwenal: Stracciari

Aug 21
LA TRAVIATA (Verdi)
Violetta: Storchio
Alfredo Germont: Anselmi
Giorgio Germont: Stracciari
Flora: Garavaglia

Aug 23, Sept 2
LORELEY (Catalani)
Loreley: Kruszelnicka
Walter: Garbin
Anna di Rehberg: Clasenti
Herrmann: Stracciari
Rudolfo: Thos

Aug 24
DON GIOVANNI (Mozart)
Don Giovanni: De Luca
Donna Anna: Talexis
Donna Elvira: Storchio
Zerlina: Clasenti
Don Ottavio: Anselmi
Leporello: Didur

Aug 25
**SOLIS GOLDEN JUBILEE
GALA**
Uruguayan National Anthem
TOSCA (Puccini)
Tosca: Kruszelnicka
Mario Cavaradossi: Garbin
Barone Scarpia: Stracciari

Aug 26
IL BARBIERE DI SIVIGLIA
(Rossini)
Rosina: Storchio
Conte di Almaviva: Anselmi
Figaro: De Luca

Don Bartolo: Ercolani
Don Basilio: Didur
Berta: Garavaglia

Aug 28
LA WALLY (Catalani)
Wally: Kruszelnicka
Afra: Garibaldi
Hagenbach: Garbin
Stromminger: Ercolani
Gellner: Stracciari
Walter: Baldassari

Aug 29
RIGOLETTO (Verdi)
Gilda: Clasenti
Il Duca di Mantova: Anselmi
Rigoletto: De Luca
Maddalena: Franchini
Sparafucile: Ercolani
Giovanna: Garavaglia

Aug 30
MADAMA BUTTERFLY (Puccini)
Cio-Cio-San: Storchio
Pinkerton: Garbin
Sharpless: De Luca
Suzuki: Garibaldi
Bonzo: Ercolani
Yamadori: Thos

Aug 31
Operatic Concert
Artists: Kruszelnicka, Frascati,
Storchio, Clasenti, Talexis;
Alselmi, Garbin, De Luca,
Didur, Stracciari

Sept 1
DON PASQUALE (Donizetti)
Norina: Storchio
Ernesto: Anselmi
Don Pasquale: Ercolani

Sept 5
Recital: Reuter <vn>, Newstead
<pf>
Mendelssohn: Concerto

Scarlatti: Pastorale
Paganini-Liszt: La campanella
(pf solo)
Chopin: Nocturne
Wieniawsky:
    a. Trois tzigane danses
    b. Polonaise
Tartini: Trillo del diavolo
Bazzini: La Ronde des lutins
Chopin: Berceuse (pf solo)
Liszt: Rhapsodie no. 6 (pf solo)
Paganini: Nel cor piu mi sento

Sept 7
Recital: Reuter <vn>, Newstead
<pf>
Beethoven: Concerto in D Major
Beethoven: Sonata op. 27 no. 2
Tartini: Variations après une
Gavotte de Corelli (cadenza von
Reuter)
Wieniawsky: Airs russes
Sarasate: Aires gitanos
Schubert: Impromptu in B-flat
Rubinstein: Etude in C Major
Paganini: Fantasie après Moïses
(G string)

Sept 20 to 30
Spanish Dramatic Company
Miguel Muñoz

Oct 5
Recital: Ansorge <pf>
Chopin: Sonata in B-flat minor
Beethoven: Sonata Appassionata
op.57
Schubert:
    a. Impromptu in C minor
    b. Serenade
    c. Erlkönig
Liszt:
    a. Soirées de Vienne No. 6
    b. Hungarian Rhapsodie no.
    14

Oct 11
Recital: Ansorge <pf>

Bach: Toccata, Adagio, and
Fugue (Ansorge transcription)
Liszt: Après une lecture du
Dante
Chopin:
    a. Impromptu in F-sharp
       Major
    b. Berceuse
    c. Balade in F Major
Rubinstein:
    a. Barcarole in F Minor
    b. Etude in C Major

Oct 14
Recital: Ansorge <pf>
Liszt: Variations sur un thème
de Bach
Beethoven: Sonata op. 111
Schumann:
    a. L'enfant s'ent dorme
    b. Reverie
    c. L'oiseau prophète
    d. Noveletten no. 2
Liszt:
    a. Gondoliera
    b. Tarantella Venezia e Napoli

Oct 30 to Nov 2
Spanish Dramatic Company José
Vico

**FRENCH OPERA AND
OPERETTA SEASON**
Nov 3 to 29
Conductor: Monsieur Reynaud
Dancer: Mlle. Duprez

Nov 3
LE JOUR ET LA NUIT (Lecocq)
Cast: Barré, Nolba; Aristide,
Leonard

Nov 4, 17
LES SALTIMBANQUES (Ganne)
with Godefroy <bar>

Nov 6
LE GRAND MOGOL (Audran)

Cast: Barré, Nolba, Duprez;
Aristide, Ballin

Nov 7
LAKME (Delibes)
Lakmé: Courtenay
Gerald: Valoris
Nilakantha: Godefroy
Rosa: Nolba

Nov 8
LA MASCOTTE (Audran)

Nov 10
LES CLOCHES DE CORNEVILLE
(Planquette)

Nov 11
LA FILLE DE MADAME ANGOT
(Lecocq)
Clairette: Barré

Nov 13
BOCCACCIO (Suppé)
Boccaccio: De Ter
Fiametta: Nolba

Nov 14
LES MOUSQUETAIRES AU
COUVENT (Varney)

Nov 15, 24
WERTHER (Massenet)
Werther: Valoris
Charlotte: Clement
Sophie: Nolba

Nov 18
CARMEN (Bizet)
Carmen: Clement
Micaela: Courtenay
Mercedes: Mariani
Don José: Valoris
Escamillo: Godefroy

Nov 19
CHILPERIC (Hervé)**

Cast: Nolba, De Ter, Noel,
Leonard

Nov 21
LA PERICHOLE (Offenbach)
La Périchole: Barré
Piquillo: Noel
D. Andrés del Ribeira: Aristide

Nov 22
LES VINGT-HUIT JOURS DE
CLAIRETTE (Roger)
Cast: Barré, Nolba; Noel,
Aristide, Ballin

Nov 25
VERONIQUE (Messager)

Nov 27
L'ENLEVEMENT DE LA TOLEDAD
(Audran)

Nov 29
MANON (Massenet)
Manon: Courtenay
Des Grieux: Valoris
Lescaut: Godefroy

Dec 3 to 18
Spanish Comic Company José
Talavera

1907

Female artists
Claessens, Marie <mez>
D'Albert, A. <mez>
Farneti, Maria <s>
Garavaglia, Lina <s>
Kruszelnicka [Krusceniski],
   Salomea <s>
Longari-Ponsoni, Luigia <s>
Paltrinieri, Antonieta <s>
Parsi-Petinella, Armida <a>
Zanardi, M. <silent actress>

Male artists
Bada, Angelo <t>
Baldassari, Luigi <bar>
Chalmin, Vittorio <bar>
De Luca, Giuseppe <bar>
Didur, Adamo <b>
Garbin, Edoardo <t>
Grassi, Rinaldo <t>
Montanari, A. <t>
Nani, Enrico <bar>
Romboli, A. <bar>
Rousselière, Charles <t>
Scampini, Augusto <t>
Thos, Constantino <b>
Tretti, Alessandro <bar>
Vianna da Motta, José <pf>
Walter, Carlo <b>

Feb 2 to 24
Carnival Masked Balls

GRAND ITALIAN OPERA SEASON
Camillo Bonetti, Impresario
Aug 14 to 27
Conductors: Rodolfo Ferrari, and Fernando Tanara (assistant conductor)

Aug 14
MEFISTOFELE (Boito)
Margherita: Kruszelnicka
Faust: Garbin
Mefistofele: Didur
Elena: Kruszelnicka
Marta: Garavaglia
Pantalis: Claessens
Wagner: Bada
Nereo: Montanari

Aug 15
MANON LESCAUT (Puccini)
Conductor: Tanara
Manon: Farneti
Des Grieux: Grassi
Lescaut: Romboli
Geronte de Revoir: Didur

Aug 17, 25
HERODIADE (Massenet) (It)**
Herodes: Nani
Hérodiade: Parsi-Petinella
Salome: Farneti
S. Giovanni: Scampini
Fanuele: Thos
Vitelio: Baldassari
Gran sacerdote: Tretti
Una giovane: Paltrinieri

Aug 18
DON CARLO (Verdi)
Elisabetta de Valois: Kruszelnicka
La Principessa Eboli: Claessens
Don Carlo: Rousselière
Rodrigo, Marchese di Posa: De Luca
Filippo II: Didur
Il grande inquisitore: Walter
Un frate: Thos
Tebaldo, paggio: Garavaglia
Contesa d'Anenberg: Zanardi
Conte di Lerma: Montanari
Un araldo reale: Montanari

Aug 20
THEODORA (Leroux)** (It)
Andrea: Rousselière
Théodora: Claessens
Justiniano: De Luca
Belisario: Didur
Faber: Walter
Antonina: Garavaglia

Aug 21
LORELEY (Catalani)
Loreley: Kruszelnicka
Walter: Garbin
Herrmann: Nani
Anna di Rehberg: D'Albert
Rudolfo: Thos

Aug 22
LA DANNAZIONE DI FAUST (Berlioz) (It)
Margherita: Longari
Faust: Grassi

Mefistofele: De Luca
Brander: Chalmin

Aug 24
SANSONE E DALILA (Saint-Saëns) (It)
Dalila: Parsi-Petinella
Sansone: Scampini
Sommo Sacerdote: Romboli

Aug 27
LOHENGRIN (Wagner) (It)
Elsa di Brabante: Kruszelnicka
Lohengrin: Garbin
Ortruda: Parsi-Petinella
Enrico: Walter
Federico di Telramondo: Romboli
L'araldo del Re: Thos

Sept 10
Recital: Vianna da Motta <pf>
Bach: Chromatic Fantasia and Fugue
Beethoven: Sonata op. 53
Chopin:
  a. Fantasia op. 49
  b. Six Etudes
Liszt: Deux Legendes
  a. St. François d'Assise, la prédication aux oiseaux
  b. St. François de Paule marchant sur les flots
Liszt-Busoni: Mephisto Waltz

Oct 2 to 21, Dec 31
Italian Dramatic Company
Prodigious Children Lambertini-Campagna

Oct 23 to 30
Italian Comic Company Città di Milano

Oct 31 to Dec 15
Spanish Dramatic Company
Tallavi–Sala

1908

Female artists
Agostinelli, Adelina <s>
Alda, Frances <s>
Berlendi, Livia <s>
Bernard, Gabriela <s>
Bianco, L. <mez>
Bornigia, E. <mez>
Capella, Juanita <s>
Claessens, Marie <mez>
De Lerma, Matilde <s>
Dolcorso, E. <mez>
Ferraresi, Signora <s>
Ferrari, L. <s>
Garavaglia, Lina <s>
Garavaglia, Rosa <mez>
Kruszelnicka [Krusceniski],
Salomea <s>
Maggi, Signora <s>
Mazzi, Emma <a>
Michelini, Saffo <s>
Rakowska, Elena <s>
Redaelli, Sandra <mez>
Salazar de Manjón, Señora <pf>
Stuarda-Savelli, Maria <s>
Vaccari, Eduvige <mez>
Zacconi, Alice <mez>
Zani, Bianca <s>

Male artists
Anselmi, Giuseppe <t>
Bada, Angelo <t>
Badini, Ernesto <bar>
Bendirelli, Angiolo <t>
Benedetti, Ermano <bar>
Biase, Pietro <b>
Biel, Giuliano <t>
Bonini, Francesco Maria <bar>
Corradini, Giuseppe <t>
De Luca, Giuseppe <bar>
De Segurola, Andrea P[erelló]
<b>
Didur, Adamo <b>
Drangosch, Ernesto <pf>
Emilia, E. <t>
Grassi, Rinaldo <t>
Manjón, Antonio <gui>

Mansueto, Gaudio <b>
Mazzuchi, Bassano <vc>
Minolfi, Renzo <bar>
Monti, Luigi <b>
Nannetti, Augusto <t>
Nicola, G. <bar>
Novi, Pietro <t>
Passeti, Signor <b>
Paterna, Concetto <b>
Picchi, Italo <b>
Pico, J. <fl>
Poggi, Giovanni <t>
Pulcini, Atilio <b/bar>
Rodati, Fernando <t>
Rousselière, Charles <t>
Silingardi, Arturo <bar>
Spolverini, Arsenio <t>
Stracciari, Riccardo <bar>
Taccani, Giuseppe <t>
Thos, Constantino <b>
Tortorici, J. <bar>
Valles, José <cl>
Zannoli, Guido <b>
Zonzini, Giuseppe <b>

Jan 5 to 12
Italian Dramatic Company
Prodigious Children Lambertini–
Campagna

March 1 to 20
Carnival Masked Balls

March 22, 25, 29
Recitals: Manjón <gui>, S. de
Manjón <pf>

April 14 to 20
Spanish Sacred Dramatic
Company Enrique Arellano

May 23 to July 13
Spanish Dramatic Company
Esteve–Arellano

WINTER ITALIAN OPERA
SEASON
Antonio Bernabei, Impresario

July 16 to 24
Conductors: Gaetano Bavagnelli,
and Guido Farinelli (assistant)
Chorus Master: Paride Soffriti
Director: Giuseppe Cecchetti
Choreographer: Rosa Piantanida
Prompter: Atilio Cerati

July 16
AIDA (Verdi)
Aida: De Lerma
Radamès: Biel
Amneris: Zacconi
Amonasro: Bonini
Ramfis: Mansueto

July 17
MANON LESCAUT (Puccini)
Manon: Agostinelli
Des Grieux: Taccani
Lescaut: Minolfi
Geronte de Revoir: Paterna

July 18
Uruguayan National Anthem
GLI UGONOTTI (Meyerbeer) (It)
Margherita de Valois: Michelini
Raul de Nangis: Biel
Valentina: De Lerma
Conte di Nevers: Minolfi
Conte di Saint-Bris: Picchi
Marcello: Mansueto

July 19
TOSCA (Puccini)
Tosca: Agostinelli
Mario Cavaradossi: Bendirelli
Barone Scarpia: Bonini
Sagrestano: Paterna
Angelotti: Picchi

July 21
CARMEN (Bizet) (It)
Carmen: Zacconi
Micaela: Michelini
Don José: Biel
Escamillo: Bonini

July 22
LA BOHEME (Puccini)
Mimì: Agostinelli
Rodolfo: Taccani
Musetta: Michelini
Marcello: Minolfi
Schaunard: Tortorici
Colline: Picchi
Alcindoro: Paterna

July 23
FAUST (Gounod) (It)
Margherita: De Lerma
Faust: Bendirelli
Mefistofele: Mansueto
Siebel: Maggi
Valentin: Minolfi

July 24
ANDREA CHENIER (Giordano)
Andrea Chénier: Taccani
Maddalena de Coigny:
Agostinelli
Carlo Gérard: Bonini

Aug 2
Recital: Drangosch <pf>
Chopin:
   a. Sonata op. 35
   b. Etude no. 12, op. 35
   c. Etude no. 11, A Minor
Schumann: Carnaval
Liszt: Fantasia après Mozart's
Don Giovanni**
Halfdan Cleve: Cinq Morceaux
de genre op. 10

**GRAND ITALIAN OPERA
SEASON**
Nardi and Bonetti, Impresarios
Aug 12 to 25
Conductor: Leopoldo Mugnone

Aug 12
ROMEO E GIULIETTA (Gounod)
(It)
Giulietta: Alda
Romeo: Anselmi

Mercutio: Badini
Capuleto: De Segurola
Gertrude: L. Garavaglia
Stefano: R. Garavaglia

Aug 13
LA TRAVIATA (Verdi)
Violetta: Alda
Alfredo Germont: Grassi
Giorgio Germont: Stracciari
Flora: R. Garavaglia
Annina: L. Garavaglia
Dottore Grenvil: Thos

Aug 15
MANON (Massenet) (It)
Manon: Berlendi
Des Grieux: Anselmi
Lescaut: Badini
Conte Des Grieux: De Segurola
Una fante: L. Garavaglia
Bretigny: Nicola
Prima guarda: Rodati
Seconda guarda: Emilia

Aug 16
MEFISTOFELE (Boito)
Margherita: Kruszelnicka
Faust: Grassi
Mefistofele: Didur
Pantalis: Claessens

Aug 18
MIGNON (Thomas) (It)
Mignon: Berlendi
Filea: Alda
Federico: R. Garavaglia
Guglielmo: Anselmi
Lotario: De Segurola
Laerte: Badini
Giarno: Thos

Aug 20
THAIS (Massenet) (It)**
Thaïs: Berlendi
Athanael: Stracciari
Nicias: Bada
Palemone: Thos

Un servo: Nicola
Crobila: L. Garavaglia
Mirtale: R. Garavaglia
Albina: Vaccari

Aug 22
LA WALKIRIA (Wagner) (It)**
Brunhilda: Kruszelnicka
Siglinda: Rakowska
Sigmundo: Rousselière
Wotan: Didur
Hunding: De Segurola
Fricka: Claessens
Helmwige: R. Garavaglia
Ortlinde: Ferrari
Gerhilde: L. Garavaglia
Waltraute: Bornigia
Siegrune: Bianco
Rossweisse: Dolcorso
Grimgerde: Vaccari
Schwertleite: Claessens

Aug 23
LORELEY (Catalani)
Loreley: Kruszelnicka
Walter: Grassi
Anna di Rehberg: Bianco
Herrmann: Stracciari
Rudolfo: Thos

Aug 24
FAUST (Gounod) (It)
Margherita: Alda
Faust: Anselmi
Mefistofele: Didur
Siebel: L. Garavaglia
Valentin: Stracciari

Aug 25
Uruguayan National Anthem
RIGOLETTO (Verdi)
Gilda: Alda
Il Duca di Mantova: Anselmi
Rigoletto: De Luca

Aug 30 to Sept 13
Spanish Dramatic Company
Esteve–Arellano

Sept 16
ORQUESTA NACIONAL
Inaugural Concert
Conductor: Luis Sambucetti
Soloist: Mazzuchi <vc>
Cimarosa: Sinfonia Il
matrimonio segreto
Dubois: Exquise <vc / orch>
Mendelssohn: Spring Song
David: La pluie
Wagner: Prelude to Lohengrin
Bizet: Ouverture patrie
Saint-Saëns: Danse de la tzigane
Liszt: Hungarian Rhapsody

SPANISH ZARZUELA SEASON
Julio Ruiz Zarzuela and Sainete
Company
Sept 18 to 27

**SPRING ITALIAN OPERA
SEASON**
Tuffanelli and Company,
Impresarios
Oct 3 to 26
Conductor: Mr. Alitta

Oct 3, 8
IL TROVATORE (Verdi)
Leonora: Capella
Manrico: Novi

Oct 4
LA FAVORITA (Donizetti) (It)
Fernando: Novi

Oct 6
MANON (Massenet) (It)
Manon: Stuarda-Savelli
Des Grieux: Poggi
Lescaut: Zonzini
Conte Des Grieux: Monti

Oct 7
LA TRAVIATA (Verdi)
Violetta: Stuarda-Savelli
Alfredo Germont: Poggi
Giorgio Germont: Benedetti

Flora: Redaelli
Annina: Ferraresi
Dottore Grenvil: Passeti

Oct 10, 22
AIDA (Verdi)
Aida: Capella
Radamès: Novi
Amneris: Redaelli
Ramfis: Zonzini
Il Re: Passeti

Oct 11, 20
LA BOHEME (Puccini)
Mimì: Stuarda-Savelli
Rodolfo: Poggi
Musetta: Ferraresi
Marcello: Benedetti
Schaunard: Zonzini
Colline: Biase
Alcindoro: Passeti

Oct 13, 24
LA GIOCONDA (Ponchielli)
Gioconda: Capella
Enzo Grimaldo: Novi
Barnaba: Zonzini

Oct 15
FAUST (Gounod) (It)
Margherita: Stuarda-Savelli
Faust: Poggi
Mefistofele: Monti
Siebel: Ferraresi
Valentin: Benedetti

Oct 17
OTELLO (Verdi)
Otello: Spolverini
Desdemona: Capella
Iago: Zonzini

Oct 18
TOSCA (Puccini)
Tosca: Capella
Mario Cavaradossi: Poggi
Barone Scarpia: Zonzini

Sagrestano: Passeti
Angelotti: Biase

Oct 23, 26
RIGOLETTO (Verdi)
Gilda: Bernard
Il Duca di Mantova: Novi
Rigoletto: Zonzini

Oct 24
LA GIOCONDA (Ponchielli)
and *Concert*: Capella <s>

Oct 25
CAVALLERIA RUSTICANA
(Mascagni)
Santuzza: Capella
Turiddu: Novi
PAGLIACCI (Leoncavallo)
Nedda: Stuarda-Savelli
Canio: Spolverini
Tonio: Zonzini

Oct 26
RIGOLETTO (Verdi)
and *Concert* to benefit tenor P.
Novi

Nov 6
Orquesta Nacional Concert and
Coro deI Instituto Verdi
Conductor: Luis Sambucetti
Soloists: Pico <fl>, Valles <cl>
Beethoven: Coriolan Overture
Wagner: Prelude to Lohengrin
Massenet: Phèdre ouverture
Sambucetti: Le chant de pèlerins
<choir / orch>
Wagner: Prelude to Tannhäuser
Giribaldi: Scènes militaires,
symphonic poem
Saint-Saëns: Tarantelle <fl / cl /
orch>
Liszt: Hungarian Rhapsody

1909

Female artists

Belloni, Francesca <d>
Bernard, Gabriela <s>
Bruchi, Maria <d>
Cadelli, Gina <d>
Capella, Juanita <s>
Casani, Corina
Citti-Lippi, Ines
Cumeri, Giselda <s>
Delmare, Irma
Erene, Edelvais <d>
Gianetto, Luisa
Gotardi, Emilia <mez>
Guerra, Elvira <mez>
Imbimbo, Ines <s>
Lecardi, Maria <d>
Lyesia, Ester <d>
Marcomini, Elisa <mez>
Marseli, Emma
Morosoni, Giselda <s>
Palazzi, Nazarena <mez>
Pereyra, Malvina <s>
Poser, Emma <d>
Stellini, Corina <d>
Stellini, Maria <s>
Taselli, Anita <s>
Villefleur, Dina <mez>

Male artists

Albinolo, Signor <bar>
Alessandrini, Umberto <t>
Balboni, Augusto <t>
Barbacci, Carlo <bar>
Bertini, Italo <bar>
Bertucci, Signor <t>
Bizzari, Dante
D'Atino, Biaggio
De Franceschi, Enrico <bar>
D'Ottavi, Filippo <t>
Ferrucci, Domenico <bar>
Giovanni, Alvino
Golardi, Luigi
Landi, Alfredo
Lombardi, Olinto <b>
Martinotti, Bruno <b>
Matiotti, Giuseppe

Monti, Luigi <b>
Novi, Pietro <t>
Petrucci, Signor <bar>
Rossini, Francesco
Silvani, Giuseppe <t>
Vitolo, Eugenio

Feb 20 to March
Carnival Masked Balls

July 13
Orquesta Nacional Concert
Conductor: Luis Sambucetti
Included
Sambucetti: Crepuscule****

ITALIAN OPERETTA SEASON
Ettore Vitale Operetta Company
July 17 to Aug 16
Conductors: Francesco Di Gesú,
and Angelo Caccialupi
(assistant)
Choreographer: Constantino
Romano
Dancers: Francesca Belloni,
Maria Bruchi <Ballet Mistress>,
Gina Cadelli, Edelvais Erene,
Maria Lecardi, Ester Lyesia,
Emma Poser, Anna Sei, Corina
Stelline

July 17, 18, Aug 5, 8 (matinée)
IL TOREADOR (Adam) (It)
with G. Morosoni <s>

July 19
PRIMAVERA SCAPIGLIATA (Josef
Strauss) (It)

July 20, 21, 22, 26, Aug 1
(matinée), 4, 10, 15, 18
LA VEDOVA ALLEGRA (Lehár)
(It)**
Hanna Glawari: Morosoni

July 23, Aug 1, 17
LA GEISHA (Jones) (It)
O Mimosa San: Taselli

Roli Poli: Imbimbo
Captain Katana: Alessandrini
Juliette: Guerra
Marquis Imari: Bertucci

July 24
SALTIMBANCHI (Ganne) (It)
Artists: Morosoni; Alessandrini,
Petrucci

July 27 (matinée), 28, 31
IL VIAGGIO DELLA SPOSA (Diet)

July 27
DIE FLEDERMAUS (Strauss) (It)**

July 30
LA POUPEE (Audran) (It)

Aug 3
LA PRINCIPESSA DELLE CANARIE
(Lecocq) (It)**

Aug 6, 7, 8, 11, 15 (matinée)
IL PAESE DELL'ORO (Vasseur)
(It)**

Aug 9
DONNA JUANITA (Suppé) (It)

Aug 12
LA FIGLIA DI MADAMA ANGOT
(Lecocq) (It)
Clairette: Morosoni
Mademoiselle Lange: Imbimbo
Ange-Pitou: Bertini
Pomponnet: Alessandrini

Aug 13, 16
ORFEO ALL'INFERNO (Offenbach)
(It)
Euridice: Taselli
Cupido: Imbimbo
Jupiter: Petrucci
Orfeo: Alessandrini
Mercurio: Bertini

WINTER ITALIAN OPERA SEASON
Riva, Schiaffino, and Tuffanelli, Impresarios
Aug 21 to Sept 5
Conductors: Napoleone Lisko, and Sisto Colleoni (assistant)

Aug 21, 23
AIDA (Verdi)
Aida: Capella
Radamès: D'Ottavi
Amneris: Marcomini
Amonasro: De Franceschi
Ramfis: Lombardi

Aug 22
LUCIA DI LAMMERMOOR (Donizetti)
Lucia: Pereyra
Edgardo: Novi
Enrico: De Franceschi

Aug 24
RIGOLETTO (Verdi)
Gilda: Pereyra
Il Duca di Mantova: Novi
Rigoletto: De Franceschi
Maddalena: Marcomini
Sparafucile: Lombardi

Aug 25
Uruguayan National Anthem
LA GIOCONDA (Ponchielli)
Gioconda: Capella
Enzo Grimaldo: Novi
Laura: Marcomini
Barnaba: De Franceschi

Aug 26
CARMEN (Bizet) (It)
Carmen: Marcomini
Micaela: Pereyra
Don José: Balboni
Escamillo: De Franceschi

Aug 28
FAUST (Gounod) (It)

Margherita: Pereyra
Faust: Balboni
Mefistofele: Lombardi
Valentin: De Franceschi

Aug 29
IL TROVATORE (Verdi)
Leonora: Capella
Manrico: D'Ottavi
Conte di Luna: De Franceschi
Azucena: Marcomini

Aug 31
GLI UGONOTTI (Meyerbeer) (It)
Margherita de Valois: Bernard
Raul de Nangis: D'Ottavi
Valentina: Capella
Conte di Nevers: De Franceschi
Marcello: Lombardi

Sept 2
LA FORZA DEL DESTINO (Verdi)
Leonora: Capella
Don Alvaro: D'Ottavi
Don Carlo: De Franceschi

Sept 3
IL BARBIERE DI SIVIGLIA (Rossini)
Rosina: Bernard
Conte di Almaviva: Balboni
Figaro: De Franceschi
Don Basilio: Lombardi

Sept 4
TOSCA (Puccini)
Tosca: Capella
Mario Cavaradossi: Novi
Barone Scarpia: Albinolo

Sept 5
OTELLO (Verdi)
Desdemona: Capella
Otello: D'Ottavi
Iago: De Franceschi

Sept 9 to Oct 2
Italian Dramatic Company Clara Della Guardia

Oct 7 to Nov 14
Spanish Dramatic Company Pedro Codina

Dec 5
Benefit Performance
Cuadro Filarmónico Centro Catalán

1910

Female artists
Berlendi, Livia <s>
Brede, Martha
Bussolati, Maria
Carpa, Signora <mez>
Clasenti, Esperanza <s>
Costa-Madrugat, B. <mez>
Dietrich, Kaete <s>
Fisbiger, Erna <s>
Galli-Curci, Amelita <s>
Garavaglia, Lina <s>
Garavaglia, Rosa <mez>
Garibaldi, Luigia <mez>
Goergi, Lucie
Koralek (Kuralek), Paula <s>
Kruszelnicka [Krusceniski], Salomea <s>
Lucci, Elena <mez>
Merviola, Miss
Orduña, Felisa (Elisa) <s>
Russ, Giannina <s>
Schneider, Mazzi
Simzis, Olga <s>
Valdés, Luisa <s>
Werber, Miss <s>

Male artists
Anter, Rudolf
Armanini, Giuseppe <t>
Badini, Ernesto <bar>
Brondi, Alfredo <b>
Carpi, Fernando <t>

De Angelis, Nazzareno <b>
Deutsch-Haupt, Mr. <t>
Dygas, Vladimir <t>
Foglia, Felice <bar>
Grunwald, Carl
Ingar, Gerolamo <t>
Leicht, Emil
Manfrini, Luigi <b>
Mardones, José <b>
Nani, Enrico <bar>
Pacini, Adolfo <bar>
Pagin, Mr.
Pico, J. <fl>
Rebollo, Gregorio <bar>
Rodati, Fernando <t>
Romboli, Arturo <bar>
Saludas, Antonio <t>
Sieder, Alfred <t>
Smirnov, Dmitri <t>
Steiner, Rudolf
Stracciari, Riccardo <bar>

Jan 2 to Feb 4
Dramatic Company Pablo
Podestá

Feb 5 to 15
Carnival Masked Balls

March 5 to April 30
Supparo Dramatic Company

GERMAN OPERETTA SEASON
First season: May 20 to 27
Conductor: Mr. Kappeler
Director: August Papke

May 20
DER GRAF VON LUXEMBURG
(Lehár)**
Cast: Werber, Merviola; Deutsch-
Haupt, Pagin

May 21, 22
EIN HERBSTMANOVER (Kálmán)

May 24
DER FIDELE BAUER (Fall)

May 25
DIE DOLLARPRINZESSIN (Fall)

May 26
DIE GEISHA (Jones) (Gr)

May 27
DIE FLEDERMAUS (Strauss)

June 4 to 10
Spanish Dramatic Company José
Tallaví

June 30
TABARE (Broqua)****
Conductor: Alfonso Broqua
Orchestra and chorus
Soloist: L. Valdés <s>

**WINTER ITALIAN OPERA
SEASON**
Rendina and Company
Impresarios
July 3 to 26
Conductors: Giulio Falconi, and
Signor Colautti (assistant)

July 3, 9
AIDA (Verdi)
Aida: Koralek
Radamès: Saludas
Amneris: Lucci
Ramfis: Brondi
Amonasro: Romboli
Il Re: Manfrini

July 5, 12
LA BOHEME (Puccini)
Mimì: Orduña
Rodolfo: Armanini
Musetta: Simzis
Marcello: Pacini
Schaunard: Rebollo
Colline: Brondi

July 6, 18
MANON (Massenet) (It)
Manon: Orduña

Des Grieux: Ingar
Lescaut: Pacini

July 7
ANDREA CHENIER (Giordano)
Andrea Chénier: Armanini
Maddalena de Coigny: Koralek
Carlo Gérard: Pacini

July 8
Orquesta Nacional Concert and
Coro del Instituto Verdi
Conductor: Luis Sambucetti
Soloist: Pico <fl>
Massenet: Phèdre ouverture
Beethoven: 5th Symphony no. 5
(Andante)
Liszt: Hungarian Rhapsody no.2
Beethoven: Elegy
Sambucetti: Le chant de pèlerins
<choir/orch>
Wagner: Overture to Tannhäuser
Saint-Saëns: Danse macabre
Gluck: Dance of the Blessed
Spirits from Orfeo
Borodin: In Central Asia Plains
Bizet: Farandole

July 10, 20, 23
RIGOLETTO (Verdi)
Gilda: Simzis
Il Duca: Ingar(1) / Armanini (2)
Rigoletto: Romboli
Maddalena: Carpa
Sparafucile: Brondi

July 14, 17
MEFISTOFELE (Boito)
Margherita / Elena: Orduña
Faust: Ingar
Mefistofele: Brondi

July 16
LA GIOCONDA (Ponchielli)
Gioconda: Koralek
Laura: Lucci
La cieca: Carpa
Enzo Grimaldo: Armanini

Barnaba: Romboli
Alvise Badoero: Brondi

July 21, 24
GLI UGONOTTI (Meyerbeer) (It)
Valentina: Koralek
Raul de Nangis: Saludas
Conte di Nevers: Pacini
Marcello: Brondi

July 22
PAGLIACCI (Leoncavallo)
Conductor: Colautti
Nedda: Orduña
Canio: Saludas
SAN FRANCESCO D'ASSISI
(Sambucetti)****
Conductor: Falconi
   I.   La tentazione
   II. Il miracolo delle rose
   III. Morte del Santo
Soloists: Armanini <t>, Pacini
<bar>, Manfrini <b> and
chorus

July 25
TOSCA (Puccini)
Tosca: Koralek
Mario Cavaradossi: Saludas
Barone Scarpia: Romboli
and *Concert*
Overture to Tannhäuser

July 26
CAVALLERIA RUSTICANA
(Mascagni)
Santuzza: Koralek
Turiddu: Saludas
Lola: Carpa
Alfio: Romboli
SAN FRANCESCO D'ASSISI
(Sambucetti)

GERMAN OPERETTA SEASON
Second season: July 27 to Aug 4
Conductor: A. Peisker, and Carl
Dibbern (assistant)
Director: August Papke

July 27, Aug 3
DER ZIGEUNERBARON (J. Strauss)

July 28, Aug 5
MISS DUDELSACK (Nelson)

July 29
DER BETTELSTUDENT (Millöcker)

July 30
DIE SIEBEN SCHWABEN
(Millöcker)***

July 31
DIE LUSTIGE WITWE (Lehár)

Aug 2
MARTHA (Flotow)***

Aug 4
EIN WALTZETRAUM (O. Straus)

**GRAND ITALIAN OPERA
SEASON**
Longinotti, Paradossi, Consigli,
Impresarios
Aug 14 to 30
Conductor: Leopoldo Mugnone,
and Edoardo Vitale (assistant-
cond)
Director: Carlo Ragni
Choreographer: Carolina
Vogliotti

Aug 14
MIGNON (Thomas) (It)
Mignon: Berlendi
Filea: Clasenti
Guglielmo: Carpi
Federico: R. Garavaglia
Lotario: Mardones

Aug 15
MEFISTOFELE (Boito)
Margherita: Kruszelnicka
Faust: Smirnov
Mefistofele: De Angelis

Aug 16
MADAMA BUTTERFLY (Puccini)
Cio-Cio-San: Kruszelnicka
Pinkerton: Carpi
Suzuki: R. Garavaglia
Sharpless: Nani

Aug 18
LOUISE (Charpentier) (It)**
Louise: Kruszelnicka
Julian: Carpi
La Madre: Garibaldi
Il Padre: Nani

Aug 20
IL CREPUSCOLO DEGLI DEI
(Wagner) (It)**
Brunilda: Kruszelnicka
Waltrauta: Garibaldi
Sigfrido: Dygas
Alberico: Nani
Hagen: De Angelis
Gunther: Mardones

Aug 21
RIGOLETTO (Verdi)
Gilda: Galli-Curci
Il Duca di Mantova: Smirnov
Rigoletto: Stracciari
Maddalena: Garibaldi
Sparafucile: Mardones

Aug 23
LOHENGRIN (Wagner) (It)
Elsa di Brabante: Kruszelnicka
Lohengrin: Dygas
Ortruda: Garibaldi
Federico di Telramondo:
Stracciari
Enrico: De Angelis
L'araldo del Re: Badini

Aug 24
LA BOHEME (Puccini)
Mimì: Clasenti
Rodolfo: Smirnov
Musetta: Berlendi
Marcello: Nani

Schaunard: Foglia
Colline: Mardones

Aug 25, 30
Uruguayan National Anthem
UN BALLO IN MASCHERA (Verdi)
Amelia: Kruszelnicka
Riccardo: Dygas
Renato: Stracciari
Ulrica: Garibaldi
Oscar: L. Garavaglia

Aug 27
MANON (Massenet) (It)
Manon: Berlendi
Des Grieux: Carpi
Lescaut: Nani

Aug 28
NORMA (Bellini)
Norma: Russ
Adalgisa: Garibaldi
Pollione: Dygas
Oroveso: De Angelis

SPANISH ZARZUELA AND SAINETE SEASON

Emilio Carreras Company
Sept 8 to Nov 7
Conductor: Amadeo Barbieri

ITALIAN OPERETTA SEASON

Ettore Vitale Operetta Company
Dec 31 to Jan 25, 1911

Dec 31
IL CONTE DI LUSSEMBURGO
(Lehár) (It)

1911

Female artists
Almansi, Margherita <s>
Bernard, Gabriela <s>
Bertolozzi, Paula <mez>
Boninsegna, Celestina <s>
Brosio, Olimpia <s>

Cavalli, Lucia <s>
Cesti, Giulietta <s>
Ciotti, Pina <s>
Colombo, Amalia <mez>
Corsini, Bice <s>
Farneti, Maria <s>
Gaudiero, Lina <s>
Gotardi, Emilia <mez>
Hotkowska, Ladislava <mez>
Luccardi, Ana <s>
Marcomini, Elisa <mez>
Nava, Angelica <mez>
Pozzi, Maria <a>
Rizzola, Olga <s>
Simzis, Olga <s>
Torriani, Signora

Male Artists
Aineto, Marino <bar>
Antimo, Natale <b>
Arrighetti, Silvio <bar>
Bertini, Italo <bar>
Biancafiore, Mr. <bar>
Carnevale, Abele <b>
Centi, Cesare <t>
Cristalli, Italo <t>
Da Ferrara, Pietro <bar>
De Cerser, Carlo <buffo-b>
De Martino, Carlo <b>
De Tura, Gennaro <t>
Dentale, Teofilo <b>
Dezenser, Signor <b>
Etchepare, Esteban <t>
Favi, Gaspare <t>
Ferrario, Arturo <t>
Fiore, Michele <b>
Galazzi, Paolo <bar>
Galeffi, Carlo <bar>
Jedliczka, Carlo <b>
La Puma, Giuseppe <buffo-b>
Mansueto, Gaudio <b>
Meyer-Radon, Walter <pf>
Novi, Pietro <t>
Petrucci, Arturo
Romboli, Arturo <bar>
Saludas, Antonio <t>
Teodoro, Luigi <t>

Vecsey, Ferenc de <vn>
Vitolo, Eugenio

SUMMER ITALIAN OPERETTA SEASON

Ettore Vitale Operetta Company
[continuing from 1910] Jan 2 to 25

Jan 2, 3, 8
IL SOGNO D'UN VALSER (O. Straus)

Jan 4
LA POUPEE (Audran)
Cast: Rizzola; Bertini

Jan 5, 6
SCUOLA D'AMORE (Korolani)**
Cast: Torriani, Gotardi; Centi, Bertini, Petrucci, Vitolo

Jan 7
SALTIMBANCHI (Ganne)

Jan 8 (matinée), 19, 24, 26
IL CONTE DI LUSSEMBURGO
(Lehár) (It)

Jan 9, 10
MANOVRA D'AUTUNNO (Kálmán)
(It)

Jan 11, 16
PRIMAVERA SCAPIGLIATA (J. Strauss) (It)
O. Rizzola <s>

Jan 12, 14, 15, 21
LA VEDOVA ALLEGRA (Lehár) (It)
Hanna Glawari: Cesti
Conte Danilo: Bertini

Jan 17, 18
IL TOREADOR (Adam) (It)

Jan 20
LA GEISHA (Jones) (It)

Jan 23
IL MILLIONARIO ACCATTONE
(Ascher)**

Jan 25
SANTARELLINA (Hervé) (It)
[Mam'zelle Nitouche]
Celestino: Bertini

SPANISH ZARZUELA SEASON
Arsenio Perdiguero Company
Feb 2 to 16

Feb 25 to March 12
Carnival Masked Balls

March 25 to April 9
Spanish Dramatic Company
Francisco A. de Villagómez

**FALL ITALIAN OPERA
COMPANY**
April 15 to 22
Conductors: Alfredo (Arturo)
Padovani, and
Enrico Romeo (assistant)

April 15
AIDA (Verdi)
Aida: Cavalli
Amneris: Bertolozzi
Radamès: Novi
Amonasro: Aineto
Ramfis: Antimo

April 16, 19
IL TROVATORE (Verdi)
Leonora: Cavalli
Manrico: Novi
Conte di Luna: Aineto
Azucena: Bertolozzi

April 18
RIGOLETTO (Verdi)
Gilda: Gaudiero
Il Duca di Mantova: Novi
Rigoletto: Aineto
Maddalena: Bertolozzi

April 20
LA BOHEME (Puccini)
Mimì: Cavalli
Rodolfo: Novi
Marcello: Aineto

April 21, 23
L'EBREO (Apolloni)
Leila: Gaudiero
Adel-Muza: Novi
Issachar: Arrighetti
Ferdinando Re di Aragona:
Antimo

April 22
Rigoletto: Acts 1, 2, and 3
CAVALLERIA RUSTICANA
(Mascagni)

April 24
Symphonic-Choral Concert
Conductor: Alfonso Broqua
In program:
Broqua: La Cruz del Sud****

**FALL ITALIAN OPERETTA
SEASON**
Ettore Vitale Operetta Company
May 6 to 20

May 6, 19
IL CONTE DI LUSSEMBURGO
(Lehár) (It)

May 7
IL TOREADOR (Adam) (It)

May 8
IL SOGNO D'UN VALSER (O.
Straus) (It)
Cast: Ciotti, Almansi

May 9
LA VEDOVA ALLEGRA (Lehár) (It)

May 10, 12
LA DANZATRICE SCALZA
(Cellini)**

May 11
LA GEISHA (Jones) (It)

May 13
MANOVRA D'AUTUNNO (Kálmán)
(It)

May 16, 17 (It)
KUNSTLERBLUT (Eysler)**

May 18, 20
SALTIMBANCHI (Ganne) (It)

May 22
Operatic Recital: Etchepare <t>

SPANISH ZARZUELA SEASON
Rogelio Juárez Company
June 8 to July 9

July 15 to 31
Italian Comedy Company
Giuseppe Sichel

Aug 8
Recital: Vecsey <vn>, Meyer-
Radon <pf>
Vieuxtemps: Concert in E Major
Tartini: Trillo del diavolo
Vieniawski: Souvenir de Moscou
Bazzini: Ridda dei folletti
Paganini: Le streghe

Aug 10
Recital [same as Aug 8]
Mendelssohn: Concerto
Hubay: Fantasie après Carmen
Schubert: Ave Maria
Dvořák: Humoresque
Vieuxtemps: Rêverie
Vieniawski: Scherzo tarantella
Paganini: I palpiti

**GRAND ITALIAN OPERA
SEASON**
Aug 12 to 27
Conductors: Pietro Mascagni and
Guido Farinelli (assistant)

Chorus Master: Dante Zucchi
Director: A. Superti
Choreographer: Giuseppina Mari

Aug 12, 16
AIDA (Verdi)
Aida: Boninsegna
Amneris: Hotkowska
Radamès: De Tura
Amonasro: Romboli
Ramfis: Mansueto
Messagero: Favi

Aug 13, 27 (matinée)
IRIS (Mascagni)
Iris: Farneti
Osaka: Cristalli
Geisha: Colombo

Aug 15
Mascagni: Overture Le Maschere
Wagner: Overture Tannhäuser
AMICA (Mascagni)
Amica: Boninsegna
Giorgio: Saludas
Rinaldo: Galeffi
Padron Camoine: Carnevale
Maddalena: Colombo

Aug 17, 20
ISABEAU (Mascagni)**
Isabeau: Farneti
Ermyntrude: Simzis
Giglietta: Pozzi
Ermyngarde: Colombo
Folco: Saludas
Re Raimondo: Galeffi
Messer Cornelius: La Puma
Cavaliere Faidit: Dentale

Aug 18
MEFISTOFELE (Boito)
Margherita: Boninsegna
Faust: Cristalli
Mefistofele: Mansueto

Aug 19
LA BOHEME (Puccini)

Mimì: Farneti
Rodolfo: Cristalli
Marcello: Romboli

Aug 20 (matinée)
Conductor: Farinelli
PAGLIACCI (Leoncavallo)
Nedda: Corsini
Canio: De Tura
Tonio: Galeffi
Silvio: Biancafiore
CAVALLERIA RUSTICANA
(Mascagni)
Santuzza: Boninsegna
Turiddu: Cristalli
Lola: Colombo

Aug 21, 26
Operatic Concert
CAVALLERIA RUSTICANA
(Mascagni)

Aug 22
GUGLIELMO RATCLIFF
(Mascagni)**
Guglielmo Ratcliff: De Tura
Maria: Boninsegna
Lord Douglas: Galeffi
Margherita: Pozzi
Tom: Mansueto

Aug 24
LA GIOCONDA (Ponchielli)
Gioconda: Boninsegna
Enzo Grimaldo: Cristalli
Barnaba: Galeffi

Aug 25
Uruguayan National Anthem
FATA MORGANA (De Mero)****
Morgana: Farneti
Luciano: De Tura
Marcelin: Galeffi
Doctor: Fiore

Aug 26
Concert
L'Amico Fritz: Intermezzo

Iris: Inno al sole
Tchaikovsky: Symphony no. 6
CAVALLERIA RUSTICANA
(Mascagni)

Aug 27
IL TROVATORE (Verdi)
Leonora: Boninsegna
Manrico: De Tura
Conte di Luna: Romboli
Azucena: Pozzi

Sept 19 to 22
French Dramatic Company
Lucien Guitry–Marie Magnier

Sept 26 to Oct 2
Italian Dramatic Company Mimì
Aguglia

**SPRING ITALIAN OPERETTA
SEASON**
Ettore Vitale Operetta Company
Oct 4 to 29

Oct 4, 20
IL CONTE DI LUSSEMBURGO
(Lehár) (It)

Oct 5
LA DANZATRICE SCALZA (Cellini)

Oct 6, 7, 12, 29
LA CASTA SUSANA (J. Gilbert)**
(It)

Oct 8, 9
IL TOREADOR (Adam) (It)

Oct 10
SCUOLA DI SIGNORINE (J.
Gilbert) (It)

Oct 11, 23 (It)
LA VEDOVA ALLEGRA (Lehár) (It)

Oct 13, 22
L'AMORE DI ZINGARO (Lehár)
(It)

Oct 15, 27
ORFEO ALL'INFERNO (Offenbach)
(It)

Oct 16
SALTIMBANCHI (Ganne) (It)

Oct 17
LA POUPEE (Audran) (It)

Oct 18, 21
IL CONTADINO ALLEGRO (Fall)
(It)

Oct 19
BOCCACCIO (Suppé) (It)

Oct 24, 26
MAM'ZELLE CARABIN (Pessard)
(It)**

Oct 28
SANTARELLINA (Hervé)
[Mam'zelle Nitouche] (It)

Nov 1 to 12
Spanish Dramatic Company
Mariano Díaz de Mendoza

Nov 11
Viento Norte (Thevenin)****
Incidental music by Alfonso
Broqua

SPANISH ZARZUELA SEASON
Emilio Carreras Company
Nov 30 to Dec 31

1912

Female artists
Alvarez, Regina <mez>
Bassi, Giulia <s>
Buño, Isabel <s>

Castaldi, Luisa <s>
Cecarelli, Signora <s>
Cenami, Carlotta <mez>
Cervi-Carolli, Ersilde <s>
De Waldis, Cina <s>
Del Lago, Italia <mez>
Dorini, Signora <s>
Eirín, Berta <narrator>
Galli-Curci, Amelita <s>
Gardini-Marchetti, Eva <s>
Ivanisi, Maria <s>
Marek, M. <mez>
Nicastro, Celika <pf>
Rakowska, Elena <s>
Storchio, Rosina <s>
Vernink de Sambucetti, María
<pf>

Male artists
Argentini, Paolo <b>
Arriola, José (Pepito) <pf>
Baridon, Pedro <vn>
Caramba, Signor
Cirino, Giulio <b>
D'Argento, N. <cl>
Delfino, J. <Enghn>
Dentale, Teofilo <b>
Faticanti, Edoardo <bar>
Fatti-Cunti, Edoardo <b>
Gamba, Adolfo <t>
Geeraert, Mauricio <pf>
Macchi, Plácido <fl>
Manfredi, Signor <t>
Marini, Luigi <t>
Mazzuchi, Bassano <vc>
Minolfi, Renzo <bar>
Mora, Florencio <vn>
Nicastro, M. Miguel <vn>
Nicastro, Oscar <vc>
Polverosi, Manfredo <t>
Rovescalli, Signor
Scampini, Augusto <t>
Stracciari, Riccardo <bar>
Taccani, Giuseppe <t>
Vianna da Motta, José <pf>
Walter, Carlo <b>
Zani, Signor <t>
Zoffoli, Giusto <t>

SPANISH ZARZUELA SEASON
Zarzuela Company Emilio
Carreras
Jan 1 to 29

Feb 18 to March 10
Carnival Masked Balls

ITALIAN OPERETTA SEASON
March 14 to 29

March 14, 24, 28
LA GEISHA (Jones) (It)

March 15
IL CONTE DI LUSSEMBURGO
(Lehár) (It)

March 16
LA VEDOVA ALLEGRA (Lehár) (It)

March 17
IL SOGNO D'UN VALSER (O.
Straus) (It)

March 18, 20, 21, 23, 27
LA CASTA SUSANA (J. Gilbert)
(It)

March 22, 26
AMORE DI PRINCIPE (Eysler) (It)

March 29
PRIMAVERA SCAPIGLIATA (Josef
Strauss) (It)

AMATEUR ITALIAN OPERA
COMPANY
March 25
LA SONNAMBULA (Bellini)
Amina: Castaldi
Conte Rodolfo: Gamba

**ORQUESTA NACIONAL
SEASON** (ON)
April 2 to May 28
Music Director and Conductor:
Luis Sambucetti

April 2, 3, 4 (ON)
Mozart: Overture to Le nozze di
Figaro
Beethoven: Symphony no. 2
Sambucetti: Suite d'orchestre
Haydn: Rondo
Massenet: Sevillanas
Brahms: Hungarian Dance no. 2

April 5, 6, 7 (ON)
Sambucetti: Suite d'orchestre
Haydn: Rondo
Massenet: Sevillanas
Brahms: Hungarian Dance no. 2
Cimarosa: Overture to Il
matrimonio segreto
Beethoven: Symphony no. 5

April 9 (ON)
Soloist: Buño <s>
Saint-Saëns: Ballet Suite from
Henry VIII
Wagner: Prelude and Death of
Isolde
Schumann: Kinderszenen
Massenet: Sevillanas
Bizet: Farandole

April 10, 11, 12 (ON)
Soloist: Baridon <vn>
Cimarosa: Overture to Il
Matrimonio segreto
Saint-Saëns: Ballet Suite from
Henry VIII
Schumann: Kinderszenen
Mendelssohn: Chanson de
printemps
Gluck: Gavota
Saint-Saëns: Déluge (prelude)
Bizet: Farandole

April 13, 14 (ON)
Soloist: Macchi <fl>
[same as April 10]
Mozart: Overture to Le nozze di
Figaro
Gluck: Orfeo's Dance of the
Blessed Souls

April 16, 21, 23 (ON)
Soloists: Baridon <vn>,
D'Angento <cl> Geeraert <pf>,
Mazzuchi <vc>
Massenet: Scènes alsaciennes
Grieg: Piano Concerto op. 16
Wagner: Wedding March from
Lohengrin
Bach: Aria for violin
Mozart: Larghetto for clarinet
Brahms: Hungarian Dance no. 2
Reyer: Paso Guerrero

April 17, 18 (ON)
[same as April 16]
Rossini: Overture to Guglielmo
Tell

April 19, 20 (ON)
Uruguayan National Anthem
Soloists: Eirín <narrator>,
Geeraert <pf>
Zorrilla de San Martin: La
Leyenda Patria (poem)
Saint-Saëns: Ballet Suite from
Henry VIII
Grieg: Piano Concerto op. 16

April 24, 25 (ON)
Soloist: Baridon <vn>
Saint-Saëns: Déluge, for violin
Bizet: L'arlesienne (First Suite)
Saint-Saëns: Overture Etienne
Marcel
Borodin: In the Steppes of
Central Asia
Dramatic School Performances
of two plays: La Grande del
Miércoles and Primavera

April 26, 27 (ON)
Soloists: Mazzuchi <vc>,
D'Argento <cl>
[same as April 24]
Massenet: Scènes alsaciennes
    a. Dimanche matin
    b. Au cabaret

    c. Sous le tilleuls
    d. Dimanche soir

April 30 (ON)
Soloist: Mora <vn>
Saint-Saëns: Ballet Suite from
Henry VIII
Martínez de Ferrari: Overture
op. 18
Rimsky-Korsakoff: Concert
Fantasy <vn / orch>
Broqua: Impresiones
Sinfónicas****
    a. Alba entre los ceibos
    b. Ante una tapera
    c. Pamperada
Wagner: Wedding March from
Lohengrin

May 2 (ON)
Bizet: L'arlésienne (First Suite)
Rossini: Overture to Guglielmo
Tell
and Blixen: "Primavera" (one-
act play)

May 3 (ON)
Bizet: L'arlésienne (First Suite)
Wagner: Wedding March from
Lohengrin
Rossini: Overture to Guglielmo
Tell
Sambucetti: Indiana
Borodin: In the Steppes of
Central Asia
Saint-Saëns: Overture Etienne
Marcel

May 4 (ON)
Soloists: Macchi <fl>, Baridon
<vn>
Martínez de Ferrari: Overture
op. 18
Bizet: L'arlésienne (First Suite)
Borodin: In the Steppes of
Central Asia

Sambucetti: Indiana
Gluck: Orfeo's Dance of the
Blessed Souls
Bach: Aria Suite in D
Massenet: Sous le tilleuls
Rossini: Overture to Guglielmo
Tell

May 7, 8 (ON)
Rossini: Overture to Guglielmo
Tell
Schumann: Kinderszenen
Beethoven: Symphony no. 5
Saint-Saëns: Déluge (prelude)
Mozart: Larghetto
Pierné: Marche aux petits
soldats de plomb
Wagner: Wedding March from
Lohengrin

May 9 (ON)
Rossini: Overture to Guglielmo
Tell
Saint-Saëns: Idylle écossais
Schumann: Kinderszenen
Bizet: L'arlésienne (First Suite)
Chabrier: España (rhapsody)

May 10, 11 (ON)
Weber: Invitation to the Dance
Pierné: Marche aux petits
soldats de plomb
Schubert: Moment musicaux
Chabrier: España (rhapsody)
Beethoven: Symphony no. 5

May 14, 15, 16 (ON)
Massenet: Scènes alsaciennes
Mendelssohn: Italian Symphony
no. 4
Saint-Saëns: Déluge (prelude)
Weber: Invitation to the Dance
Chabrier: España (rhapsody)

May 17 (ON)
Mendelssohn: Italian Symphony
no. 4

Bizet: L'arlésienne (First Suite)
Chabrier: España (rhapsody)

May 18 (ON)
Mendelssohn: Italian Symphony
no. 4
Sambucetti: Indiana
Borodin: In the Steppes of
Central Asia
Weber: Invitation to the Dance
Massenet: Aragonaisse**

May 21, 22 (ON)
Weber: Overture Preciosa
Pierné: Marche aux petits
soldats de plomb
Massenet: Aragonaisse
Sambucetti: Indiana
Saint-Saëns: Tarantella
Bizet: L'arlésienne (First Suite)

May 23, 24 (ON)
Bizet: L'arlésienne (First Suite)
Saint-Saëns: Tarantella
Chabrier: España (rhapsody)
Dramatic School Performance

May 25 (ON)
Uruguayan National Anthem
Bizet: L'arlésienne (Second
Suite)
J. Strauss: Waltzes
Wagner: Wedding March from
Lohengrin
Dramatic School Performance

May 27
Recital: O. Nicastro <vc>, S.
Nicastro <pf>, M. M. Nicastro
<vn>
Schubert: Trio
Lalo: Concert in D for cello
(with pf)
Corelli: Sonata <pf / vc>
Kreisler: Lieberlied <vc / pf>
Becker: Minuetto <vc / pf>
Popper: Tarantella <vc / pf>

May 28 (ON)
All Saint-Saëns program:
Soloists: V. de Sambucetti <pf>,
Baridon <vn>, Macchi <fl>
Ballet Suite from Enrique VIII
Concerto <pf / orch>
Deluge <vn / orch>
Tarantella for flute
Overture to Etienne Marcel

ITALIAN OPERETTA SEASON
Sconamiglio-Caramba Company
Conductor: Signor Marchetti
May 30 to July 3

May 30, June 13, 16 (matinée)
LA PRINCIPESSA DELLE DOLAR
(Fall)

May 31, June 6 (matinée)
IL CONTE DI LUSSEMBURGO
(Lehár) (It)

June 1
LA DUCHESSA DI DANZICA
(Caryll) (It)
[Madame Sans-Gêne]

June 3, 6, 12, 22, July 5
LA CASTA SUSANA (J. Gilbert)
(It)

June 4
VALSE D'AMORE (Grumbaum)
(It)**

June 5
LA DIVORZIATA (Fall) (It)

June 7, 8, 9, 15, 21, July 6, 7
(matinée)
EVA (Lehár) (It)**
Eva: Gardini-Marchetti

June 11
MANOVRA D'AUTUNNO (Kálmán)
(It)
with C. De Waldis <s>

June 14, 16, 19
LA BELLE HELENE (Offenbach)
(It)

June 18
SOGNO D'UN VALSER (O. Straus)
(It)

June 20
LA VEDOVA ALLEGRA (Lehár) (It)

June 24 to 30
Motion Pictures Festival: Italian-
Turkish War

July 1
AMORE DI PRINCIPE (Eysler) (It)

July 2
LA SIRENA (Fall) (It)**

July 3
LE CAMPANNE DI CORNEVILLE
(Planquette) (It)

July 13 to 30
Spanish Dramatic Company
Rosario Pino

Aug 4
Recital: Vianna da Motta <pf>
Beethoven: Sonata op. 57
("Appasionatta")
Bach-Busoni: Prelude Choral
Rachmaninoff: Preludes
Schubert-Liszt: Soirée de Vienne
Chopin: Polonaise op. 53
Paderewsky: Capriccio
Liszt:
  a. Sposalizio
  b. Au bord d'une source
  c. Hungarian Rhapsody no. 9

Aug 7
Recital: Vianna da Motta <pf>
Bach-Busoni: Prelude and Fugue
Beethoven-Liszt: Adelaide
Weber: Polacca in E Minor

Schumann: Etudes
Symphoniques op. 13
Chopin: Four Etudes
Liszt: St. François de Paule
marchant sur les flots
Vianna da Motta: Balada sobre
cantos populares portugueses
Liszt: Scene après Le Prophète

GRAND ITALIAN OPERA SEASON

Walter Mocchi and Company
Impresarios
Aug 10 to 28
Conductor: Gino Marinuzzi

Aug 10, 15 (matinée)
AIDA (Verdi)
Aida: Rakowska
Amneris: Alvarez
Radamès: Taccani
Amonasro: Faticanti
Ramfis: Walter
Il Re: Argentini

Aug 11, 14
LA TRAVIATA (Verdi)
Violetta: Storchio
Alfredo Germont: Polverosi
Giorgio Germont: Stracciari

Aug 13, 18 (matinée)
RIGOLETTO (Verdi)
Gilda: Galli-Curci
Il Duca di Mantova: Polverosi
Rigoletto: Stracciari
Sparafucile: Walter

Aug 15
LA WALLY (Catalani)
Wally: Cervi-Carolli
Stromminger: Cirino
Hagenbach: Marini
Geller: Faticanti
Walter: Galli-Curci

Aug 17
MADAMA BUTTERFLY (Puccini)
Cio-Cio-San: Storchio
Pinkerton: Marini
Sharpless: Minolfi

Aug 18
MEFISTOFELE (Boito)
Margherita: Cervi-Carolli
Faust: Polverosi
Mefistofele: Cirino
Elena: Rakowska
Wagner: Manfredi

Aug 20
CARMEN (Bizet) (It)
Carmen: Alvarez
Micaela: Galli-Curci
Don José: Taccani
Escamillo: Faticanti

Aug 22
MANON LESCAUT (Puccini)
Manon: Cervi-Carolli
Des Grieux: Taccani
Lescaut: Faticanti

Aug 24
IL BARBIERE DI SIVIGLIA
(Rossini)
Rosina: Galli-Curci
Conte di Almaviva: Polverosi
Figaro: Stracciari

Aug 25 (matinée)
LA BOHEME (Puccini)
Musetta: Galli-Curci
Rodolfo: Polverosi

Aug 25
Uruguayan National Anthem
MANON (Massenet) (It)
Manon: Storchio
Des Grieux: Taccani
Lescaut: Faticanti

Aug 27
CONCHITA (Zandonai)**

Conchita: Cervi-Carolli
Don Mateo: Taccani

Aug 28
LIROPEYA (Ribeiro)****
Liropeya: Cervi-Carolli
Guaziola: Marek
Abayubá: Scampini
Zapicán: Cirino
Carvallo: Faticanti
Magaluna: Dentale

Aug 31
Recital: Vianna da Motta <pf>
Bach-Busoni: Prelude, adagio
and fugue
Schumann: Carnaval
Bellini-Liszt: Fantasie après
Norma

Sept 1
Recital: Vianna da Motta <pf>
Beethoven: Sonata op. 53
Brahms: Sixteen Waltzes op. 39
Schubert-Liszt: Poésies
Thomas: Fantasie après Mignon
Beethoven-Rubinstein: Turkish
March
Mozart-Liszt: Fantasie après Don
Giovanni

ITALIAN OPERETTA SEASON
Sept 7 to 27
Conductor: Vincenzo Bellezza,
and Giovanni Gemme (assistant)

Sept 7
DER ZIGEUNERBARON (Strauss)
(It)

Sept 9, 15 (matinée)
LA CASTA SUSANA (J. Gilbert)
(It)

Sept 10, 11, 15, 19
CAPRICCIO ANTICO (Darclée)
(It)**
Cast: Ivanisi, Cenami

Sept 12
EVA (Lehár) (It)

Sept 13, 14, 18
LA REGINETTA DELLE ROSE
(Leoncavallo)**
Lilian: Ivanisi

Sept 16
L'AMORE DI ZINGARO (Lehár)
(It)

Sept 17, 21
LA PRINCIPESSA DELLE DOLAR
(Fall) (It)
Conductor: Gemme
with I. Del Lago

Sept 20, 25
Uruguayan National Anthem
Italian Royal March
Garibaldi Anthem
IL CAPITANO FRACASSA
(Costa)**
Cast: Caramba and Rovescalli

Sept 23, 27
LA BELLA RISETTE (Fall) (It)
Cast: Cenami; Caramba,
Rovescalli

Sept 24, 26
LA VEDOVA ALLEGRA (Lehár) (It)
Hanna Glawari: Ivanisi
Danilo: Zoffoli

Oct 5
Recital: Arriola <pf>
Beethoven: Sonata op. 53
Chopin:
  a. Nocturne
  b. Four Preludes
  c. Polonaise op. 53
Rachmaninoff: Prelude
Schumann: Oiseau prophète
Drangosch: Tema y variaciones
Liszt: Hungarian Rhapsody No.
6

Oct 8, Dec 3
Recitals: Arriola <pf>

Oct 13 to Nov 10
Spanish Zarzuela Company
Antonio Perdiguero

SUMMER ITALIAN OPERETTA
SEASON
Ernesto Lahoz Italian Company
Dec 10 to 12

Dec 10
EVA (Lehár) (It)

Dec 11
LA CASTA SUSANA (J. Gilbert)
(It)

Dec 12
IL CONTADINO ALLEGRO (Fall)
(It)

1913

Female artists
Alemanni, Maria <s>
Alvarez, Regina <mez>
Bassi, Giulia <s>
Benincori, Maria <s>
Bucciarelli, Assunta <mez>
Capazza, Signora <s>
Capella, Juanita <s>
Casazza, Elvira <mez>
Chaplinska, Janka <s>
Csillag (Seillag), Steffi <s>
De Angelis, Maria <a>
De Waldis, Cina <s>
Del Lago, Italia <mez>
Farneti, Maria <s>
Flory, Gilda <mez>
Galeffi, Maria <mez>
Ghirelli, Tina <s>
Giacomucci, Anneta <s>
Guerra, Vittoria <a>
Ivanisi, Maria <s>
Ivner, Emma <s>

Karsavina, Tamara <d>
Maicherska, Mlle. <d>
Mangini, Bianca <s>
Morini, Jeanne <s>
Morini, Martha <s>
Pasquini, Annita <s>
Pouget, Mlle. <s>
Rakowska, Elena <s>
Rosa, Alba <vn>
Ruggero, Maria <s>
Serafino, Signora <s>
Stellina, M. <s>
Tchernicheva, Lubov <d>
Van Loo, Angèle <s>
Vassilievska, Alexandra <d>
Weiss, Clara <s>

Male artists
Alessandrini, Umberto <t>
Barrios, Agustín <gui>
Berardi, Berardo <b>
Bettazoni, Amedeo <bar>
Bolm, Adolphe <d>
Boscachi, Signor
Ciprandi, Carlo <t>
Cirino, Giulio <b>
De Luca, Giuseppe <bar>
De Muro, Bernardo <t>
Dutilloy, Henri <t>
Faticanti, Edoardo <bar>
Geeraert, Mauricio <pf>
Janni, Roberto <bar>
Micheluzzi, Leopoldo <t>
Mussi, Guido <t>
Nijinsky, Vaslav <d>
Palet, José <t>
Pasquini, Giuseppe <t>
Perea, Emilio <t>
Perise, Signor <bar>
Rizzo, Arturo <b>
Stabile, Mariano <bar>
Tessari, Gino <bar>
Vaccari, Guido <t>
Vorontzov, Mr. <d>
Zoffoli, Giusto <t>

Feb 1 to 22
Carnival Masked Balls

March 18 to 27
Italian Dramatic Company Clara
della Guardia

March 29 to April 8
French Cinematographic
Pantomime Troupe André Deed

April 30 to May 25
Dramatic Company Enrique
Arellano

ITALIAN OPERETTA SEASON
Città di Milano Operetta
Company
May 28 to June 27
Conductor: Constantino
Lombardo

May 28, 31
LA BELLA RISETTE (Fall) (It)

May 29, June 5
IL CONTE DI LUSSEMBURGO
(Lehár) (It)

May 30
LA REGINETTA DELLE ROSE
(Leoncavallo)

June 2
SALTIMBANCHI (Ganne) (It)

June 3, 7
DONNA JUANITA (Suppé) (It)

June 6
EVA (Lehár) (It)

June 9, 15
AMORE DI ZINGARO (Lehár) (It)

June 10, 14, 16
IL BIRICHINO DI PARIGI
(Montanari)**

June 11
IL SOGNO D'UN VALSER (O.
Straus) (It)

June 12, 16
Eva: Acts 1 and 2
MOLINOS DE VIENTO (Luna) (It)

June 13
LA SECCHIA RAPITA (Burgmein)
(It)

June 16
MOLINOS DE VIENTO (Luna) (It)
IL BIRICHINO DI PARIGI
(Montanari)

June 17, 18, 20
LA POLVERA DE PIRLIMPIMPIN
(Lombardo)

June 19, 25
LA DIVORZIATA (Fall) (It)

June 21
LA VEDOVA ALLEGRA (Lehár) (It)

June 24
HANS, IL SUONATORE DI FLAUTO
(Ganne) (It)

June 26, 27
LA CREOLA (Berté)**

June 28 to July 1
Italian Dramatic Company
Ermete Zacconi

FRENCH OPERETTA SEASON
Company from L'Opéra-
Comique
July 3 to 14
Conductor: Luigi Dall'Argine

July 3
LA VEUVE JOYEUSE (Lehár) (Fr)
Hanna Glawari: Van Loo
Danilo: Dutilloy

July 4
LA FILLE DE MADAME ANGOT
(Lecocq)

July 5, 11
LE SOLDAT DE CHOCOLAT (O.
Straus) (Fr)

July 7
LE JOUR ET LA NUIT (Lecocq)

July 9
LE REVE D'UN VALS (O. Straus)
(Fr)

July 10, 13
LE GRAND MOGOL (Audran)

July 12
LES MOUSQUETAIRES AU
CONVENT (Varney)

July 13 (matinée)
LA MASCOTTE (Audran)

July 14
Uruguayan National Anthem
La Marseillaise
LE PETIT DUC (Lecocq)

July 23 to Aug 1
French Dramatic Company
Marthe Regnier

Aug 3
Recital: Barrios <gui>

**GRAND ITALIAN OPERA
SEASON**
Walter Mocchi and Company,
Impresarios
Aug 5 to 25
Conductor: Gino Marinuzzi
Chorus Master: Romeo Romei

Aug 5
ISABEAU (Mascagni)
Isabeau: Farneti

Folco: De Muro
Ermyntrude: Benincori
Giglietta: Casazza
Ermyngarde: Giacomucci
Re Raimondo: Janni
Cavaliere Faidit: Rizzo

Aug 7
LA WALKIRIA (Wagner) (It)
Brunhilda: Rakowska
Sigmundo: Vaccari
Siglinda: Ruggero
Fricka: Casazza
Wotan: Faticanti
Hunding: Berardi
Helmwige: Bucciarelli
Ortlinde: Giacomucci
Gerhilde: Benincori
Waltraute: Alemanni
Siegrune: Galeffi
Rossweisse: De Angelis
Grimgerde: Guerra
Schwertleite: Flory

Aug 9
AIDA (Verdi)
Aida: Capella
Amneris: Casazza
Radamès: Palet
Amonasro: Faticanti
Ramfis: Cirino
Il Re: Berardi

Aug 10 (matinée)
CAVALLERIA RUSTICANA
(Mascagni)
Santuzza: Rakowska
Turiddu: De Muro
PAGLIACCI (Leoncavallo)
Nedda: Ruggero
Canio: Palet
Tonio: Faticanti
Silvio: Janni

Aug 10
LOHENGRIN (Wagner) (It)
Lohengrin: Perea
Elsa di Brabante: Farneti

Ortruda: Casazza
Enrico: Cirino
Federico di Telramondo:
Faticanti

Aug 12
IRIS (Mascagni)
Iris: Farneti
Osaka: De Muro
Kyoto: Stabile
Il cieco: Berardi
Geisha: Benincori

Aug 13
LA DANNAZIONE DI FAUST
(Berlioz) (It)
Margherita: Ruggero
Faust: Palet
Mefistofele: De Luca
Brander: Berardi

Aug 14, 24
RIGOLETTO (Verdi)
Gilda: Mangini
Il Duca di Mantova: Palet
Rigoletto: Faticanti
Maddalena: Casazza
Sparafucile: Berardi

Aug 15, 19
PARSIFAL (Wagner) (It)**
Parsifal: Vaccari
Kundry: Rakowska
Amfortas: De Luca
Gurnemanz: Cirino
Klingsor: Stabile
Titurel: Berardi

Aug 16, 20
CARMEN (Bizet) (It)
Carmen: Alvarez
Micaela: Ruggero
Don José: De Muro
Escamillo: Faticanti

Aug 17 (matinée), 25
IL BARBIERE DI SIVIGLIA
(Rossini)

Rosina: Mangini
Conte di Almaviva: Perea
Figaro: De Luca
Don Basilio: Cirino
Don Bartolo: Berardi

Aug 17, 26
MADAMA BUTTERFLY (Puccini)
Cio-Cio-San: Farneti
Pinkerton: Perea
Suzuki: Casazza
Sharpless: Janni

Aug 21
ABUL (Nepomuceno)**
Abul: Palet
Iskah: Farneti
Terak: Stabile
Shinah: Casazza
Amrafel: Berardi

Aug 23
MEFISTOFELE (Boito)
Margherita: Farneti
Faust: Perea
Mefistofele: Cirino
Elena: Rakowska
Pantalis: Capazza
Wagner: Boscachi
Marta: Flory

Aug 25
Uruguayan National Anthem
IL BARBIERE DI SIVIGLIA
(Rossini)
[same cast as Aug 17]

Aug 31
Recital: Rosa <vn>, Geeraert
<pf>
Bach: Chaconne
Beethoven: Romanza in G
Mendelssohn: Concerto op. 64
Tartini: Trillo del diavolo
Paganini: Capriccio on "God
Save the King"

SPANISH ZARZUELA SEASON
José Moncayo Zarzuela
Company
Sept 5 to 19, 21 to 28

Sept 20
Recital: Barrios <gui>

BALLETS RUSSES COMPANY
Cesare Ciacchi, Impresario
Oct 7 and 8
Conductor: René Baton
Principal dancers: Bolm,
Karsavina, Maicherska, Nijinsky,
Tchernicheva, Vassilievska,
Vorontzov

Oct 7
Tcherepnin: Le Pavillon
d'Armide (Karsavina / Bolm)
Schumann: Carnaval
Colombine: Karsavina
Chiarina: Tchernicheva
Estrella: Maicherska
Pierrot: Bolm
Arlequin: Nijinsky
Weber: Le spectre de la rose
(Karsavina / Nijinsky)
Borodin: Marche et Danses
Polovsiennes from Prince Igor

Oct 8
Tchaikovsky: Le Lac des cygnes
(Karsavina / Bolm)
Tchaikovsky: Pas de deux from
L'oiseau et le prince
Borodin: Danses Polovsiennes
(Bolm, Vassilievska. Vorontzov)
Chopin: Les silphides (Karsavina
and Nijinsky)

ITALIAN OPERETTA SEASON
Sconamiglio-Caramba Operetta
Company
Oct 15 to 31
Conductors: Vincenzo Bellezza,
and Edoardo Buccini (assistant)

Oct 15
CAPRICCIO ANTICO (Darclée) (It)

Oct 16, 26
EVA (Lehár) (It)

Oct 17
LA BELLA RISETTE (Fall) (It)

Oct 18, 19, 23, 31
AMORE IN MASCHERA (Darclée)
(It)**

Oct 20
LA REGINETTA DELLE ROSE
(Leoncavallo)

Oct 21
MALBROUCK, "Fantasia Comica
Medioevale" (Leoncavallo)

Oct 22
LA CASTA SUSANA (J. Gilbert)
(It)

Oct 24, 25, 27
13 (medley by several
composers)

Oct 28
LA PRINCIPESSA DELLE DOLLAR
(Fall) (It)

Oct 29
LA FIGLIA DI MADAMA ANGOT
(Lecocq) (It)
Conductor: Buccini
Clairette: Morini
Mademoiselle Lange: Chaplinska

Oct 30
LA VEDOVA ALLEGRA (Lehár) (It)

Nov 1 to 16
Spanish Dramatic Company
Pablo Podestá

Nov 19 to Dec 10
Marco Antonio and Cleopatra
and other motion pictures

1914

Female artists
Aifos, Sofia <s>
Benincori, Maria <s>
Bermiconi, Margherita <s>
Carelli, Emma <s>
Catterini, A. <s>
Catterini, Ida <mez>
Cavalieri, Maria <s>
Cristofeanu, Florica <s>
Dalla-Rizza, Gilda <s>
De Hidalgo, Elvira <s>
De Lerma, Matilde <s>
Dorelli, Signora <s>
Franzi, Bianca <s>
Gari, Nelly <s>
Garibaldi, Luigia <mez>
Giacomucci, Anneta <s>
Gramegna, Anna <mez>
Manarini, Giulia <mez>
Pasini-Vitale, Lina <s>
Ponzano, Signora <mez>
Roselli de Ruiz, Señora <s>
Storchio, Rosina <s>
Theor, Dora <s>
Vallarino, Signora <s>
Verbich, Carmen <s>

Male artists
Berardi, Berardo <b>
Bergamini, Signor <t>
Buscachi, Romeo
Campos, Francisco <bn>
Caronna, Ernesto <bar>
Cirino, Giulio <b>
Danise, Giuseppe <bar>
Dentale, Teofilo <b>
Estela, Enrique <tpt>
García, Francisco <fl>
González, José <cl>
Lázaro, Hipólito <t>
Maestri, Catullo <t>

Martínez, Tomás <hn>
Olivero, Ludovico
Oneto, Signor <t>
Palet, José <t>
Patino, Ciro <bar>
Pesce, Signor <bar>
Pierucetti, Signor <b>
Prudenza, Signor <bar>
Righi, Angelo <t>
Rizzo, Arturo <b>
Sammarco, Mario <bar>
Schipa, Tito <t>
Schottler, Giorgio <b>
Turturiello, Signor <bar>
Venancio, Juan <ob>
Zanasi, Guglielmo <t>
Zoffoli, Giusto <t>

Feb 14 to March 8
Carnival Masked Balls

March 25 to 31
Professor Mapelli <hypnotist>

April 4 to 10
Spanish Dramatic Company José
Berrio

**SPANISH OPERETTA AND
OPERA SEASON**
April 11 to May 3

April 11, May 2
LA PRINCESA DEL DOLLAR (Fall)
(Sp)

April 12, 23, May 3 (matinée)
EVA (Lehár) (Sp)

April 13 (matinée)
LA CASTA SUSANA (J. Gilbert)
(Sp)

April 13, 14
EL ANILLO DE HIERRO (Marqués)

April 15, 17
EL CONDE DE LUXEMBURGO
(Lehár) (Sp)

April 16, 25, May 3
LA VIUDA ALEGRE (Lehár) (Sp)

April 18
MARINA (Arrieta)

April 20
LA REINITA DE LAS ROSAS
(Leoncavallo) (Sp)

April 21
LA TEMPESTAD (Chapí)

April 22
EL LEGO DE SAN PABLO
(Caballero)

April 24
LA DOLORES (Bretón)

April 28
LOS SOLDADITOS DE PLOMO
(Strauss) (Sp)

April 29
LA NIÑA MIMADA (Penella)

April 30
EL JURAMENTO (Gaztambide)

May 4 to 12
Cinematographic ballet
performances with orchestra
Conductor: Signor Viscardini

May 13 to 17
Professor Mapelli <hypnotist>

May 18 to 20
Espartaco (motion picture)

May 21 to June 1
Watry and Maieroni <magicians>

ITALIAN OPERETTA SEASON
Città di Milano Operetta
Company
June 5 to 28
Conductor: Constantino
Lombardo

June 5, 9, 11, 25
EVA (Lehár) (It)
Cast: Franzi; Righi

June 6, 7
LA BELLA RISETTE (Fall) (It)

June 8, 10, 13, 15, 19, 21
(matinée)
FINALMENTE SOLI! (Lehár) (It)**
Cast: Cristofeanu; Zoffoli

June 12, 14
IL CONTE DI LUSSEMBURGO
(Lehár) (It)

June 16, 17
LA DAMA VERDE (Ferraresi)
(It)**
Cast: Gari, Franzi; Zanasi

June 18, 20
IL SOGNO D'UN VALSER (O.
Straus) (It)

June 21, 26
LA VEDOVA ALLEGRA (Lehár) (It)

June 23, 24, 27, 28
IL CAVALIERE DELLA LUNA
(Ziehrer) (It)**
Cast: Cristofeanu, Zanasi

July 10
LA BOHEME (Puccini)
Uruguayan Lyric Association
Conductor: Ernesto Ruiz
Mimì: Roselli de Ruiz
Rodolfo: Bergamini
Musetta: Vallarino
Marcello: Pesce

Schaunard: Turturiello
Colline: Pierucetti

July 11 to 26
Spanish Dramatic Company
Guerrero–Díaz de Mendoza

July 30 to Aug 6
Kinetophono Edison

Aug 8 to 11
Italian Dramatic Company Clara
Zorda

GRAND ITALIAN OPERA
SEASON
Walter Mocchi and Company,
Impresario
Aug 20 to Sept 5
Conductors: Edoardo Vitale and
Teofilo De Angelis (assistant)

Aug 20
MANON (Massenet) (It)
Manon: Storchio
Des Grieux: Schipa
Conte des Grieux: Cirino

Aug 21
RIGOLETTO (Verdi)
Gilda: De Hidalgo
Il Duca di Mantova: Lázaro
Rigoletto: Sammarco
Maddalena: Ponzano
Sparafucile: Berardi

Aug 22
LA FANCIULLA DEL WEST
(Puccini)*
Minnie: Dalla-Rizza
Dick Johnson (Ramerrez):
Lázaro
Jack Rance: Danise

Aug 24, 30
IL BARBIERE DI SIVIGLIA
(Rossini)
Rosina: De Hidalgo

Conte di Almaviva: Schipa
Figaro: Sammarco(1) / Danise(1)
Don Basilio: Cirino

Aug 25
Uruguayan National Anthem
LA TRAVIATA (Verdi)
Violetta: Storchio
Alfredo Germont: Schipa
Giorgio Germont: Sammarco

Aug 26
LA FAVORITA (Donizetti) (It)
Leonora: Garibaldi
Fernando: Lázaro
Alfonso XI: Danise
Baldassare: Berardi

Aug 27
GLI UGONOTTI (Meyerbeer) (It)
Margherita de Valois: De
Hidalgo
Raul de Nangis: Palet
Valentina: De Lerma
Urbano: Garibaldi
Conte di Nevers: Danise
Conte di Saint-Bris: Cirino
Marcello: Berardi

Aug 28, Sept 2
MEFISTOFELE (Boito)
Margherita: Dalla-Rizza
Faust: Palet
Mefistofele: Cirino
Elena: Dalla-Rizza

Aug 29
TOSCA (Puccini)
Tosca: De Lerma
Mario Cavaradossi: Schipa
Barone Scarpia: Sammarco

Aug 30
IL BARBIERE DI SIVIGLIA
(Rossini)
CAVALLERIA RUSTICANA
(Mascagni)
Santuzza: Dalla-Rizza

Turiddu: Lázaro
Lola: Garibaldi
Alfio: Danise

Aug 31
AIDA (Verdi)
Aida: De Lerma
Amneris: Garibaldi
Radamès: Palet
Amonasro: Danise
Il Re: Berardi

Sept 1
DON PASQUALE (Donizetti)
Norina: De Hidalgo
Ernesto: Schipa
Don Pasquale: Schottler
Dottore Malatesta: Danise

Sept 3
CAVALLERIA RUSTICANA
(Mascagni)
[same as Aug 30]
PAGLIACCI (Leoncavallo)
Nedda: Benincori
Canio: Palet
Tonio: Danise

Sept 4
LA BOHEME (Puccini)
Mimì: Dalla-Rizza
Musetta: A. Catterini
Rodolfo: Lázaro
Marcello: Caronna
Schaunard: Dentale
Colline: Cirino
Benoit: Schottler

Sept 5
RIGOLETTO (Verdi)
Gilda: Dorelli
Il Duca di Mantova: Schipa
Rigoletto: Danise
Maddalena: Garibaldi
Sparafucile: Cirino

Sept 12, 13, Oct 2, 4
Recitals: Sexteto Eslava–

Conjunto Valenciano with
García <fl>, Venancio <ob>,
González <cl>, Campos <bn>,
Martínez <hn>, Estela <tpt>
Works by Granados, Estela,
Saint-Saëns, Grieg Veiga, and
Bretón

Sept 19 to 30
Spanish Dramatic Company
Juan Domenech–Carmen Jarque

Oct 10 to Dec 10
Grand Cine-Concert
Conductor: Luigi Dall'Argine
Works by Massenet, Saint-Saëns,
Haydn, Wagner, Verdi,
Ponchielli, Lehár, Strauss,
Schumann, Puccini, and Bizet

1915

Female artists
Alemanni, Maria <s>
Camarano, M. <s>
Dalla-Rizza, Gilda <s>
Escriche, C. <s>
Fornaroli, Cia <d>
Frascani, Nini <mez>
Galeffi, Maria <mez>
Galli-Curci, Amelita <s>
Giachino, Signora <s>
Mannarini, Ida <mez>
Mattinzoli, Signora <s>
Melsa, Mary <s/mez>
Perini, Flora <mez>
Raisa, Rosa <s>
Russ, Giannina <s>
Sabaino, R. <mez>
Saggese, Albina <s>
Torelli, Lucia <s>
Vix, Geneviève <s>
Zoffoli, Giuseppina <mez>

Male artists
Arcelli, Umberto <b>
Bannino, E. <t>

Bassi, Ugo <bar>
Berardi, Berardo <b>
Cairo, Grillo <b>
Capra, Luigi <bar>
Caronna, Ernesto <bar>
Caruso, Enrico <t>
Cesari, Pietro <b>
Cirino, Giulio <b>
Civai, G. <bar>
Danise, Giuseppe <bar>
De Franceschi, Enrico <bar>
De Muro, Bernardo <t>
Dentale, Teofilo <b>
Figueras, Luis <vc>
Freixas, Arturo <bar>
Granforte, Apollo <bar>
Lázaro, Hipólito <t>
Lussardi, Dino <bar>
Nardi, Luigi <t>
Niola, Gugliemo <buffo/b>
Paltrinieri, Giordano <t>
Pietri, N. de <t>
Quatrina, Pietro <t>
Ruffo, Titta <bar>
Sammarco, Mario <bar>
Tabanelli, Pietro <t>
Tedeschi, Alfredo <t>

Jan 9 to 30
Cinematographic performances

Feb 4 to 21
Carnival Masked Balls

Feb 24 to 28
Prof. Mario Mirabello
<hypnotist>

**FALL ITALIAN OPERA
SEASON**
Orchestral Cooperative Society,
Impresario
Conductor: Bruno Mari
April 17 to May 16

April 17, 28
LA GIOCONDA (Ponchielli)
Gioconda: Escriche

Enzo Grimaldo: Bannino
Laura: Zoffoli
La cieca: Sabaino
Barnaba: De Franceschi(1) /
Granforte(1)
Alvise Badoero: Arcelli

April 18 (matinée), May 8
LA BOHEME (Puccini)
Mimì: Saggese
Rodolfo: Quatrina
Musetta: Camarano
Marcello: Freixas
Schaunard: Civai
Colline: Cairo

April 18, 23, May 13 (matinée)
CAVALLERIA RUSTICANA
(Mascagni)
Santuzza: Mattinzoli
Turiddu: Quatrina
PAGLIACCI (Leoncavallo)
Nedda: Giachino
Canio: Bannino
Tonio: De Franceschi

April 19, May 4
RIGOLETTO (Verdi)
Gilda: Saggese
Il Duca di Mantova: Tabanelli
Rigoletto: De Franceschi
Sparafucile: Cairo

April 20, 25, May 10
AIDA (Verdi)
Aida: Escriche
Radamès: Bannino
Amonasro: Granforte
Ramfis: Cairo

April 21, 27
LA TRAVIATA (Verdi)
Violetta: Giachino
Alfredo Germont: Quatrina
Giorgio Germont: Granforte

April 22
FAUST (Gounod) (It)

Margherita: Mattinzoli
Faust: Tabanelli
Mefistofele: Cairo

April 24
IL BARBIERE DI SIVIGLIA
(Rossini)
Rosina: Saggese
Conte di Almaviva: Tabanelli
Figaro: De Franceschi
Don Bartolo: Cairo
Don Basilio: Cesari
Berta: Melsa

April 26, May 2, 15
LA FORZA DEL DESTINO (Verdi)
Leonora: Escriche
Don Alvaro: Bannino
Don Carlo: De Franceschi
Padre guardiano: Cairo

April 29
LUCIA DI LAMMERMOOR
(Donizetti)
Lucia: Saggese
Edgardo: Quatrina
Enrico: Granforte
Raimondo: Cairo

April 30
TOSCA (Puccini)
Tosca: Mattinzoli
Mario Cavaradossi: Tabanelli
Barone Scarpia: De Franceschi

May 1, 7, 16
IL TROVATORE (Verdi)
Leonora: Escriche
Manrico: Bannino
Conte di Luna: Granforte
Azucena: Zoffoli

May 3, 13
LA FAVORITA (Donizetti) (It)
Leonora: Zoffoli
Fernando: Tabanelli
Alfonso XI: Granforte
Baldassare: Cairo

May 5
UN BALLO IN MASCHERA (Verdi)
Amelia: Escriche
Riccardo: Bannino
Renato: Freixas
Ulrica: Zoffoli
Oscar: Saggese
Tom: Cairo
Samuel: Arcelli

May 6, 9
MADAMA BUTTERFLY (Puccini)
Cio-Cio-San: Mattinzoli
Pinkerton: Tabanelli

May 10 (matinée), 12
ERNANI (Verdi)
Elvira: Escriche
Ernani: Bannino
Don Carlo: De Franceschi
D. Ruy Gomez de Silva: Arcelli

May 10
Uruguayan National Anthem
Brazilian National Anthem
AIDA (Verdi)
and Concert
Il Guarany: Sinfonia

May 11
IRIS (Mascagni)
Iris: Mattinzoli
Osaka: Quatrina
Kyoto: Freixas
Il cieco: Arcelli

May 14, 16 (matinée)
Uruguayan National Anthem
La Marseillaise
Russian Anthem
English Anthem
MANON (Massenet) (It)
Manon: Mattinzoli
Des Grieux: Tabanelli
Lescaut: Freixas

May 17 to 23
Prof. Mapelli <hypnotist>

May 29 to June 24
Spanish Ballet and Tonadilla
Company
Aurorita Jauffre ("La Goya")

SPANISH OPERETTA SEASON
Esperanza Iris Operetta
Company
July 3 to Aug 2
Conductor: Mario Sánchez

July 3, 4 (matinée), 28
LA CRIOLLA (Berté)

July 4, 10, 14, 27
EL SOLDADO DE CHOCOLATE (O.
Straus) (Sp)

July 5
LA PRINCESA DEL DOLAR (Fall)
(Sp)

July 6, 11 (matinée), 22
MUJERES VIENESAS (Lehár)
(Sp)**

July 7, 12, 26
LA CASTA SUSANA (J. Gilbert)
(Sp)

July 8
LA POUPEE (Audran) (Sp)

July 9, 19
JUAN II (Eysler) (Sp)

July 11, 15, 18 (matinée)
LA VIUDA ALEGRE (Lehár) (Sp)

July 13
EL CONDE DE LUXEMBURGO
(Lehár) (Sp)

July 16, 18, 25 (matinée), Aug 1
EVA (Lehár) (Sp)

July 17
AIRES DE PRIMAVERA (?) (Sp)

July 20
LA GEISHA (Jones) (Sp)

July 21, 25 (Sp)
PETIT CAFE (I. Caryll)

July 23
SANGRE DE ARTISTA (Eysler)
(Sp)

July 24, 31
LA PRINCESA DE LOS BALCANES
(Eysler) (Sp)**

July 30
LA REINITA DE LAS ROSAS
(Leoncavallo) (Sp)

July 31 (matinée)
EL CUENTO DEL DRAGON
(Giménez [Jiménez])

Aug 2
EL VALS DE AMOR (Ziehrer) (Sp)

Aug 7, 8, 10
Dance Recital: Felyne Verbist
Saint-Saëns: Swan's Death

**GRAND ITALIAN OPERA
SEASON**
Da Rosa, Mocchi, and Company
Impresarios
Aug 14 to 26
Conductors: Gino Marinuzzi, and
Giuseppe Sturani, Attico
Bernabini, Riccardo Dellera,
Alfredo Martino (assistant-
conductors)
Chorus Masters: Enrico Romeo
and Clemente B. Greppi
Director and Choreographer:
Romeo Francioli
Dancer: Cia Fornaroli

Aug 14
MANON (Massenet) (It)
Conductor: Sturani

Manon: Vix
Des Grieux: Caruso
Lescaut: Sammarco

Aug 15
IL BARBIERE DI SIVIGLIA
(Rossini)
Rosina: Galli-Curci
Conte di Almaviva: Tedeschi
Figaro: Ruffo
Don Basilio: Cirino
Don Bartolo: Niola
Berta: Torelli
Fiorello: Paltrinieri

Aug 17, 20
AIDA (Verdi)
Aida: Raisa
Amneris: Frascani
Radamès: De Muro
Amonasro: Danise
Ramfis: Cirino

Aug 18
IL CAVALIERE DELLA ROSE (R.
Strauss) (It)**
Mariscala: Raisa
Octavio: Dalla-Rizza
Sofia: Galli-Curci
Barone Ochs: Cirino
Annina: Perini
Maggiordomo: Nardi

Aug 19
LA FANCIULLA DEL WEST
(Puccini)
Minnie: Dalla-Rizza
Dick Johnson: De Muro
Jack Rance: Sammarco
Jack Wallace: Berardi
Billy Jackrabbit: Niola
Nick: Paltrinieri
Joe: Capra
Larkens: Dentale
Happy: Pietri

Aug 21
AMLETO (Thomas) (It)

Amleto: Ruffo
Ofelia: Galli-Curci

Aug 22
LE JONGLEUR DE NOTRE DAME
(Massenet) (It)**
Giovanni: Vix
Bonifacio: Danise
Il Prior: Berardi
Lucia: Act 3, with Galli-Curci <s>

Aug 24
FRANCESCA DA RIMINI
(Zandonai)**
Francesca: Raisa
Paolo: Lázaro
Malatestino: Paltrinieri
Giovanni Gianciotto: Danise
Altichiara: Mannarini
Donella: Galeffi

Aug 25
Uruguayan National Anthem
CARMEN (Bizet) (It)
Carmen: Vix
Micaela: Russ
Don José: Lázaro
Escamillo: Galeffi
Concert
Prelude to La última gavota
(Cortinas)****

Aug 26
RIGOLETTO (Verdi)
Gilda: Galli-Curci
Il Duca di Mantova: Lázaro
Rigoletto: Ruffo
Sparafucile: Cirino

Sept 21 to 29
French Dramatic Company Felix
Huguenet

Sept 30
Recital: Figueras <vc>

Oct 2 to 10
Monsieur Raymond
<prestidigitator>

Oct 16
Dramatic Art School short-play
performances

Nov 5 to 10
Spanish Ballet Company Pastora
Imperio

Nov 20 to 29
Spanish Ballet and Tonadilla
Company Aurorita Jauffre ("La
Goya")

Dec 21 to 31
Molasso Ballet and Pantomime
Company
Conductor: Luigi Dall'Argine

1916

Female Artists
Barrientos, María <s>
Bertolozzi, Paula <mez>
Capsir, Mercedes <s>
Carton, N.
Clasenti, Esperanza <s>
Dalla-Rizza, Gilda <s>
Giacomucci, Anneta <s>
Leonardi, Signora
Raisa, Rosa <s>
Roessinger, Elvira <mez>
Royer, Jacqueline <mez>
Stora, Juliette <s>
Torelli, Lucia <s>
Vallin (Vallin-Pardo), Ninon <s>

Male artists
Algos, Angelo <t>
Belletti, Alfredo <t>
Bettazoni, Amedeo <bar>
Crabbé, Armand <bar>
Crimi, Giulio <t>

De Giovanni, Edoardo [Edward
Johnson] <t>
Journet, Marcel <b>
Lafitte, Léon <t>
Mansueto, Gaudio <b>
Martinelli, Giovanni <t>
Maury, Sinai <t>
Merli, N. <b>
Mora, Florencio <vn>
Niola, Guglielmo <buffo/b>
Rimini, Giacomo <bar>
Rona, Mr. <child actor>
Ruffo, Titta <bar>
Saint-Saëns, Camille <pf/c>
Schipa, Tito <t>

March 4 to April 2
Carnival Masked Balls

April 22 to 26, June 28 to July 3
Spanish Dance Company
Tórtola Valencia

April 27 to May 9
Fátima Miris <"Transformist
Queen">

May 19
Symphonic Concert
Sociedad Filarmónica de
Montevideo
Conductor: Mauricio Geeraert
Soloist: Mora <vn>
Haydn: Symphony no. 104
Wagner: Overture to Faust
Bach: Violin Concerto in G
Major
Lekew: Fantasia

May 27 to June 13
Spanish Dramatic Company de
Isaura-Arcos

SPANISH OPERETTA SEASON
Esperanza Iris Operetta
Company
June 16 to 25

June 16, 18 (matinée)
AMOR ENMASCARADO (Darclée)
(Sp)

June 17
EL SOLDADO DE CHOCOLATE (O.
Straus) (Sp)

June 18
LA PRINCESA DEL DOLAR (Fall)
(Sp)

June 19
EVA (Lehár) (Sp)

June 20, 22
EL MERCADO DE LAS
MUCHACHAS (Jacobi) (Sp)

June 21
LA CASTA SUSANA (J. Gilbert)
(Sp)

June 23
SANGRE DE ARTISTA (Eysler)
(Sp)

June 24
LA VIUDA ALEGRE (Lehár) (Sp)

June 25 (matinée and evening)
EL CONDE DE LUXEMBURGO
(Lehár) (Sp)

July 8 to 11
My Little Baby (motion picture)

July 13
SAINT-SAËNS SYMPHONIC
CONCERT
Conductors: Camille Saint-Saëns
and Mauricio Geeraert
Soloist: Saint-Saëns <pf>
Weber: Overture to Der
Freischütz
Mozart: Piano Concerto no. 23
Mozart: Divertimento
Saint-Saëns works:

a. Ballet Music from Henry
VIII
b. Piano Concerto no. 5
c. Phaéton (poème sympho-
nique)
d. Rhapsodie d'Auvergne <pf
/ orch>
e. Marche héroïque

ITALIAN OPERETTA SEASON
Sconamiglio-Caramba Operetta
Company
July 15 to 31

July 15
EVA (Lehár) (It)

July 16 (matinée)
LA BELLA RISETTE (Fall) (It)

July 16
AMORE IN MASCHERA (Darclée)
(It)

July 17, 23 (matinée), 26
LA SIGNORA DEL
CINEMATOGRAFO (Lombardo)**

July 18
LA VEDOVA ALEGRA (Lehár) (It)

July 19, 21 to 24, 31, Aug 1
LA DUCHESSA DEL BAL TABARIN
(Bard) (It)

July 20, 25
LA CASTA SUSANA (J. Gilbert)
(It)

July 27
IL CONTE DI LUSSEMBURGO
(Lehár) (It)

July 28
IL DUCA CASIMIRO (Ziehrer)

July 29
FINALMENTE SOLI! (Lehár) (It)

July 30
LA PRINCIPESSA DELLE DOLAR
(Fall) (It)

GRAND ITALIAN OPERA
SEASON
Walter Mocchi and Company,
Impresarios
Aug 14 to 27
Season Conductor: Giuseppe
Barone
Guest Conductors: Xavier Leroux,
André Messager, and Gennaro
Papi

Aug 14
AIDA (Verdi)
Aida: Raisa
Amneris: Bertolozzi
Radamès: Crimi
Amonasro: Rimini
Ramfis: Mansueto

Aug 15
LA SONNAMBULA (Bellini)
Amina: Barrientos
Elvino: Schipa
Alessio: Journet
Lisa: Roessinger
LES CADEAUX DE NOEL
(Leroux)**
Conductor: Leroux
Emma: Roessinger
Claire: Royer
Mère: Vallin
Petit Louis: Rona
Père Jean: Crabbé

Aug 16
AMLETO (Thomas) (It)
Amleto: Ruffo
Ofelia: Clasenti
Polonio: Journet
Gertruda: Royer

Aug 18
FALSTAFF (Verdi)
Falstaff: Ruffo

Mistress Meg Page: Roessinger
Mistress Alice Ford: Raisa
Nannetta: Vallin
Dame Quickly: Bertolozzi
Fenton: Schipa
Bardolfo: Maury
Pistola: Mansueto
Dr. Cajus: Algos

Aug 19, 26
GLI UGONOTTI (Meyerbeer) (It)
Margherita de Valois: Clasenti
Raul de Nangis: Martinelli
Valentina: Raisa
Urbano: Bertolozzi
Conte di Nevers: Crabbé
Conte di Saint-Bris: Journet
Maurevert: Mansueto

Aug 20
ANDREA CHENIER (Giordano)
Andrea Chénier: De Giovanni
Maddalena de Coigny: Dalla-
Rizza
Carlo Gérard: Rimini
LES CADEAUX DE NOEL (Leroux)
[same cast as Aug 15]

Aug 21
IL BARBIERE DI SIVIGLIA
(Rossini)
Rosina: Barrientos
Conte di Almaviva: Schipa
Figaro: Ruffo
Don Basilio: Mansueto
Berta: Roessinger

Aug 22
BEATRICE (Messager)**
Conductor: Messager
Béatrice: Vallin
Musidora: Royer
La Bohemiènne: Carton
La Supérieure: Roessinger
La Vierge: Giacomucci
Florise: Torelli
Lelia: Leonardi
Laurence: Lafitte

L'Evêque: Journet
Tiberio: Bettazoni
Beppo: Niola
Fabio: Maury
HUEMAC (De Rogatis) (It)**
Xiutzal: Dalla-Rizza
Mayabel: Royer
Huemac: Crimi
Ixicohuatl: Merli
Cavaliere dell'Aquila: Belletti
Cavaliere delle Smeraldo:
Bettazoni

Aug 23
LUCIA DI LAMMERMOOR
(Donizetti)
Lucia: Barrientos
Edgardo: Martinelli
Enrico: Rimini

Aug 24
RIGOLETTO (Verdi)
Gilda: Barrientos
Il Duca di Mantova: Schipa
Rigoletto: Ruffo
Maddalena: Bertolozzi
Sparafucile: Mansueto

Aug 25
Uruguayan National Anthem
SAMSON ET DALILA (Saint-Saëns)
Conductor: Messager
Dalila: Royer
Samson: Lafitte
Abimélech: Journet
LA ULTIMA GAVOTA
(Cortinas)****
Conductor: Papi
Duquesa de Bouffers: Dalla-
Rizza
Caballero de Saint Lambert:
Schipa
Duque de Bouffers: Rimini

Aug 27
MANON (Massenet)
Conductor: Leroux
Manon: Vallin

Des Grieux: Schipa
Lescaut: Crabbé
Conde des Grieux: Journet

Sept 16 to Oct 5
Spanish Dramatic Company
Guerrero–Díaz de Mendoza

Oct 6
Lecture: Eduardo Marquina on
"En Flandes se ha puesto el sol"

Oct 7 to Dec 10
Spanish Dramatic Company
Salvat–Olona

Dec 28
Lecture: José Ortega y Gasset on
"Imágenes de España"

1917

Female artists
Anitúa, Fanny <mez>
Barsanti, Emma <mez>
Burchi, Teresina <s>
Canasi, Ida <mez>
Dalla-Rizza, Gilda <s>
Giacomucci, Anneta <s>
Koklova, Olga <d>
Lopokova, Lydia <d>
Marmora, Nera <s>
Melis, Carmen <s>
Moreno, Blanca <s>
Pflanz, Sophia <d>
Pouyanne, Mlle. <pf>
Roselli de Ruiz, Señora <s>
Tchernicheva, Lubov <d>
Torelli, Lucia <s>
Vallin (Vallin-Pardo), Ninon <s>
Vassilievska, Alexandra <d>

Male artists
Azzolini, Gaetano <b>
Caruso, Enrico <t>
Cortis, Antonio <t>
Crabbé, Armand <bar>

De Franceschi, Enrico <bar>
Dentale, Teofilo <b>
Giraldoni, Eugenio <bar>
Gavrilovi, Alexander <d>
Hackett, Charles <t>
Journet, Marcel <b>
Lafuente, Pedro <t>
Maestri, Catullo <t>
Nijinsky, Vaslav <d>
Paltrinieri, Giordano <t>
Rubinstein, Artur <pf>
Stalkiewki, Maximilian <d>
Tabanelli, Pietro <t>
Urízar, Marcelo <bar>
Zverciff, Mr. <d>

Feb 17 to March 3
Carnival Masked Balls

March 10 to June 3
Spanish Dramatic Company
Salvat–Olona

June 12 to 25
Spanish Dramatic Company
Ricardo Simó-Raso

July 21
Recital: Rubinstein <pf>
Bach: Toccata and Fugue in D
Minor
Beethoven: Sonata op. 53
Chopin:
  a. Scherzo in C-sharp Minor
  b. Nocturne in F-sharp
  c. Ballade in A-flat
  d. Waltz in C-sharp Minor
  e. Polonaise in A
Debussy: L'isle joyeuse
Ravel: Ondine
Scriabin: Nocturne pour la main
gauche
Liszt: Rhapsody no. 12

July 22
Recital: Rubinstein <pf>
Schumann: Carnaval
Albéniz:

a. El Albaicín
b. Triana
Chopin: Polonaise op. 44
Liszt: Rhapsody no. 12
Wagner: Death of Isolde

BALLET RUSSES SEASON
July 25 to Aug 5
Conductor: Ernest Ansermet
Director: Mr. Kremenev
Stage Manager: Mr.
Tschaussowsky
Principal dancers: Gavrilovi,
Koklova, Lopokova, Nijinsky,
Pflanz, Stalkiewki, Tchernicheva,
Vassilievska, Zverciff

July 25
Chopin: Les sylphides
Schumann: Carnaval
Borodin: Polovtsian Dances
from Prince Igor
Rimsky-Korsakoff: Scheherazade

July 26
Chopin: Les sylphides
Rimsky-Korsakoff: Le soleil de la
nuit
Borodin: Polovtsian Dances
from Prince Igor
Arensky, Liadov, Glazunov,
Tcherepnin, and Rimsky-
Korsakoff: Cléopâtre

July 28
Schumann: Carnaval
Weber: Le spectre de la rose
(Nijinsky and Lopokova)
Schumann: Papillons
Rimsky-Korsakoff: Scheherazade

July 29
Arensky, Liadov, Glazunov,
Tcherepnin, and Rimsky-
Korsakoff: Cléopâtre
Tchaikovsky: La princesse
enchantée (Nijinsky and
Lopokova)

Borodin: Polovtsian Dances
from Prince Igor
Schumann: Carnaval

July 31
Schumann: Papillons
Rimsky-Korsakoff: Le soleil de la
nuit
Weber: Le spectre de la rose
(Nijinsky and Lopokova)
Scarlatti: Les femmes de bonne
humeur

Aug 2
Schumann: Papillons
Weber: Le spectre de la rose
(Nijinsky and Lopokova)
Rimsky-Korsakoff: Sadko
Arensky, Liadov, Glazunov,
Tcherepnin, and Rimsky-
Korsakoff: Cléopâtre

Aug 4
Chopin: Les sylphides
Balakirev: Thamar
Scarlatti: Les femmes de bonne
humeur
Arensky, Liadov, Glazunov,
Tcherepnin, and Rimsky-
Korsakoff: Cléopâtre

Aug 5
Rimsky-Korsakoff: Les delices du
puissance
Balakiriev: Thamar
Scarlatti: Les femmes de bonne
humeur
Borodin: Polovtsian Dances
from Prince Igor
Fauré: Las Meninas

**URUGUAYAN LYRIC
ASSOCIATION**
Aug 8
LA BOHEME (Puccini)
Conductor: Ernesto Ruiz
Mimì: Roselli de Ruiz

Rodolfo: Tabanelli
and *Concert*

Aug 9
LA SULAMITA (Cortinas)****
Incidental Music after Arturo
Capdevila's Poem
Conductor: César Cortinas
Cast: Eirín <narrator>, singers,
and Asociación Lírica del
Uruguay chorus and orchestra

**GRAND ITALIAN OPERA
SEASON**
Da Rosa, Mocchi and Company,
Impresarios
Aug 14 to 26
Season Conductor: Gino
Marinuzzi
Guest Conductors: Franco
Paolantonio and Vincenzo
Bellezza
Director: Romeo Francioli

Aug 14
MAROUF (Rabaud)**
Saamscheddine: Vallin
Fattoumah: Moreno
Mârouf: Crabbé
Ahmad: De Franceschi
Sultan: Journet
Vizir: Azzolini
Fellah: Paltrinieri
Ali: Dentale

Aug 15
SANSONE E DALILA (Saint-Saëns)
(It)
Conductor: Paolantonio
Dalila: Anitúa
Sansone: Lafuente
Un Vecchio ebreo: Journet

Aug 16
L'ELISIR D'AMORE (Donizetti)
Adina: Vallin
Nemorino: Caruso

Dottore Dulcamara: Azzolini
Belcore: De Franceschi

Aug 18
ARDID DE AMOR (C. Pedrell)
(Fr)**
Laura: Vallin
Don Ramón: Crabbé
Doña Oromasia: Barsanti
Marqués de Carabaña: Azzolini
Don Diego: Paltrinieri
PAGLIACCI (Leoncavallo)
Conductor: Bellezza
Nedda: Vallin
Canio: Caruso
Tonio: Urízar
Silvio: De Franceschi
Beppe: Cortis

Aug 19
LA RONDINE (Puccini)**
Magda de Civry: Dalla-Rizza
Ruggero Lastouc: Hackett
Lisette: Giacomucci
Prunier: Cortis

Aug 20
IL BARBIERE DI SIVIGLIA
(Rossini)
Rosina: Anitúa
Conte di Almaviva: Hackett
Figaro: Crabbé
Don Basilio: Journet
Don Bartolo: Azzolini

Aug 21
TOSCA (Puccini)
Tosca: Dalla-Rizza
Mario Cavaradossi: Caruso
Barone Scarpia: Giraldoni
Angelotti: Azzolini

Aug 22
TRISTANO E ISOTTA (Wagner)
(It)
Isotta: Burchi
Tristano: Maestri

Aug 24
IL CAVALIERE DELLA ROSA (R.
Strauss) (It)
La Mariscala: Melis
Octavio: Dalla-Rizza
Sofia: Marmora
Faninal: De Franceschi
Barone Ochs: Giraldoni

Aug 25
Uruguayan National Anthem
SIBERIA (Giordano)**
Stephana: Dalla-Rizza
Ivan: Cortis
Vassili: Lafuente
Gleby: Urízar
Walitzin: Dentale
Alexis: Paltrinieri
Nikona: Barsanti
Miskinsky: De Franceschi

Aug 26
CARMEN (Bizet) (It)
Carmen: Anitúa
Micaela: Vallin
Don José: Caruso
Escamillo: Journet

Sept 15 to 30
Spanish Dramatic Company
Emilio Thuillier–María Palou

Sept 24
Recital: A. Rubinstein <pf>
Schumann: Etudes
symphoniques
Chopin:
    a. Fantasia Polonaise
    b. Impromptu in F-sharp
    c. Two Etudes
    d. Scherzo in B-flat
Rachmaninoff: 2 Preludes
Granados: La maja y el ruiseñor
Falla: Andaluza
Wagner: Death of Isolde

Oct 1
Recital: Rubinstein <pf>

Beethoven: Sonata op. 31
Schubert: Impromptu
Brahms:
  a. Intermezzo in E-flat
  b. Rhapsody in G Minor
Mendelssohn: La fileuse
Medtner: Ditirambo
Albeniz: Navarra
Debussy: Soirée dans Grenade
Scriabin: Fantasia

Oct 26
CONCERT AND BALLET
PERFORMANCE
Allies' Red Cross Benefit
Rubinstein <pf>, Nijinsky <d>,
Pouyanne <pf>
I: Rubinstein <pf>
Uruguayan National Anthem
English Anthem
Medtner: Ditirambo
Ravel: Ondine
Debussy: Poisson d'or
Debussy: L'isle joyeuse
II: Nijinsky <d> [his last
performance on the stage],
Pouyanne <pf>
La Marseillaise
Poetry reading: Carlos César
Lenzi
Chopin:
  a. Two Mazurkas, op 67 and
    33
  b. Two Waltzes, op. 64 and
    70 <dance / pf>
III: Rubinstein <pf>
The Star-Spangled Banner
Albéniz: Navarra
Rachmaninoff: Prelude
Chopin: Polonaise in A Minor

Nov 3 to 14
Argentinean Dramatic Company
Pagano–Ducasse

Nov 29
Recital: Rubinstein <pf>
Chopin: Sonata in B-flat Minor

Schumann: Carnaval
Mendelssohn: La fileuse
Brahms:
  a. Intermezzo in E-flat Minor
  b. Capriccio in B Minor
Liszt: Rhapsody no. 12

1918

Female artists
Agozzino, Rina <mez>
Aleardi, Egle <s>
Bernard, Gabriela <s>
Bossetti, Elisa <a>
Cesti, Giulietta <s>
Csillag, Steffi <s>
Dolcey, Marta <s>
Franceschi, Elina <s>
Granelli, Annetta <s>
Misselli, Maria <s>
Pangrazi, Rosalia <s>
Signorelli, Olga <a>
Simzis, Olga <s>
Viscardi, Maria <s>
Weiss, Clara <s>

Male artists
Arcelli, Umberto <b>
Baldrich, Rogelio <t>
Bergamaschi, E. <t>
Cairo, Giovanni <b>
Carreras, E. <b>
Cavalotti, Juan <t>
De Angelis, Raimondo <t>
De Franceschi, Enrico <bar>
Federici, Francesco <bar>
Fiore, Michele <b>
Francesconi, Luigi <bar>
Grand, Walter <t>
Marchessiari, Signor <t>
Massé, Raúl <bar>
Mussi, Guido <t>
Novi, Pietro <t>
Pagés-Rosés, Señor <pf>
Pinheiro, Mario <b>
Savorini, Signor <t>
Salvi, Guido de <t>

Signorelli, Signor <t>
Terrones, Señor <bar>

Jan 7 to 13
American Musical Comedy
Company of Baxter and Willard

ITALIAN OPERETTA SEASON
Walter Grant Operetta Company
Jan 15 to 30

Jan 15, 28
MADAME SANS-GENE
(Dall'Argine)

Jan 16
SOGNO D'UN VALSER (O. Straus)
(It)

Jan 17, 20, 30
LA REGINA DEL FONOGRAFO
(Lombardo)

Jan 18, 20 (matinée), 22
LA DUCHESSA DEL BAL TABARIN
(Bard) (It)

Jan 19
ADDIO GIOVINEZZA (Montanari)

Jan 21, 26
BOCCACCIO (Suppé) (It)

Jan 23, 27 (matinée), 29
LA VEDOVA ALLEGRA (Lehár) (It)
Conte Danilo: Cavalotti

Jan 24, 27
EVA (Lehár) (It)

Jan 25
LA CASTA SUSANA (J. Gilbert)
(It)

Feb 2 to 24
Carnival Masked Balls

March 1 to June 18
Spanish Dramatic Company
Salvat–Olona

June 19
Recital: Pagés-Rosés <pf>

June 23
Recital: Pagés-Rosés <pf>
Beethoven: Sonata op. 27, no. 2
Chopin:
   a. Scherzo in C-sharp Minor
   b. Polonaise in A-flat
Albéniz:
   a. Evocación
   b. Triana
Granados: El pelele
Grieg: The Lonely Traveler
Liszt: Hungarian Rhapsodies 11
and 12

ITALIAN OPERA SEASON
Antonio Marranti Company
June 28 to July 20
Conductor: Antonio Marranti

June 28, July 4 (matinée), 18
AIDA (Verdi)

June 29, 30 (matinée), July 7, 10
LA BOHEME (Puccini)
Mimì: Dolcey

June 30, July 4, 7 (matinée)
IL TROVATORE (Verdi)

July 1
RIGOLETTO (Verdi)
Gilda: Bernard
Rigoletto: Terrones

July 2
LA FORZA DEL DESTINO (Verdi)

July 5, 12, 14 (matinée)
FAUST (Gounod) (It)
Faust: Signorelli

July 6
PAGLIACCI (Leoncavallo)
CAVALLERIA RUSTICANA
(Mascagni)

July 8, 17
UN BALLO IN MASCHERA (Verdi)

July 9, 16
LA FAVORITA (Donizetti)

July 11, 14, 21 (matinée)
CARMEN (Bizet) (It)
Carmen: Bossetti

July 13
Il trovatore: Acts 1, 2, and 3
CAVALLERIA RUSTICANA
(Mascagni)

July 15, 18 (matinée), 20
TOSCA (Puccini)

July 19, 21
GLI UGONOTTI (Meyerbeer) (It)

July 20
TOSCA (Puccini)
Cleopatra: Overture
Mefistofele: Prologue

July 27 to 29
Motion Picture Showings

ITALIAN OPERETTA SEASON
Aug 1 to Sept 4
Conductors: Riccardo Cendalli
and Ernesto Lahoz
Director: G. Caracciolo

Aug 1, 6, 11
IL GIORNO E LA NOTTE (Lecocq)
(It)

Aug 3, 7, 9, 29, 31 (matinée)
TOM MIGLER (Jacobi) (It)
Lucy Harrison: Aleardi

Aug 4
EVA (Lehár) (It)
Eva: Aleardi

Aug 8, 10, 18
IL CAVALIERE DELLA LUNA
(Bard) (It)**

Aug 11 (matinée), 13
CINEMA STAR (J. Gilbert) (It)

Aug 18 (matinée), 28
LA GEISHA (Jones) (It)
O Mimosa San: Weiss

Aug 19
LE MASCHERE (Mascagni)
Rosaura: Aleardi
Florindo: De Angelis
Arlecchino: Mussi

Aug 21
LA PRINCIPESSA WANDI (Nelson
and Igrun) (It)
Zezé: Weiss

Aug 27
LA DUCHESSA DEL BAL TABARIN
(Lombardo) (It)

Aug 30
IL CONTE DI LUSSEMBURGO
(Lehár) (It)
Angela Didier: Pangrazi
Giulietta Vermonde: Misselli

Aug 31
LA REGINA DEL CINEMATOGRAFO
(Lombardo?)
Chiffon: Weiss

Sept 4
L'UOMO ELETTRICO (Chylton)

Sept 19 to Oct 7
Spanish Dramatic Company
Guerrero–Díaz de Mendoza

Oct 17 to 27
Motion Picture Showings

Oct 30 to Nov 15
[Theaters closed due to an influenza epidemic.]

SUMMER ITALIAN OPERA SEASON
Loureiro and Company, Impresarios
Dec 7 to 15
Conductor: Arturo De Angelis

Dec 7
AIDA (Verdi)
Aida: Viscardi
Amneris: Agozzino
Radamès: Bergamaschi
Amonasro: De Franceschi
Ramfis: Pinheiro
Il Re: Fiore

Dec 8
L'ELISIR D'AMORE (Donizetti)
Adina: Simzis
Nemorino: Baldrich
Dottore Dulcamara: Fiore
Belcore: De Franceschi

Dec 9
TOSCA (Puccini)
Tosca: Viscardi
Mario Cavaradossi: Bergamaschi
Barone Scarpia: De Franceschi

Dec 10
LUCIA DI LAMMERMOOR (Donizetti)
Lucia: Simzis
Edgardo: Baldrich
Enrico: Federici
Raimondo: Fiore
Normanno: Marchessiari
Arturo: Savorini

Dec 11
MANON LESCAUT (Puccini)

Manon: Viscardi
Des Grieux: Bergamaschi
Lescaut: De Franceschi

Dec 12
IL TROVATORE (Verdi)
Leonora: Viscardi
Manrico: Novi
Conte di Luna: De Franceschi
Azucena: Agozzino
Ferrando: Fiore

Dec 13
LA FAVORITA (Donizetti) (It)
Leonora: Agozzino
Fernando: Baldrich
Alfonso XI: Federici
Gaspare: Pinheiro

Dec 14
LA GIOCONDA (Ponchielli)
Gioconda: Viscardi
Laura: Agozzino
Enzo Grimaldo: Bergamaschi
Barnaba: De Franceschi

Dec 15
PAGLIACCI (Leoncavallo)
Canio: Novi
Tonio: De Franceschi
CAVALLERIA RUSTICANA (Mascagni)
Santuzza: Viscardi
Lola: Agozzino
Turiddu: Bergamaschi

1919

Female artists
Bergé, Laura <s>
Blanco-Sadun, Matilde <mez>
Bonieska, Janina <d>
Butzova, Hilda <d>
Canasi, Ida <mez>
Cattaneo, Giannina (Celestina) <s>
Chabelska, Gala <d>

Chabelska, Maria <d>
Claessens, Marie <mez>
Gianni, Adalgisa <s>
Kroner, Helena <d>
Labia, Maria <s>
Lago, Pura <pf>
Lucci, Gianna <mez>
Mathieu, Maddalena <s>
Mazzoleni, Ester <s>
Merö, Yolanda <pf>
Monti, Rosina <s>
Muró de Lacarte, Julieta <s>
Muzio, Claudia <s>
Pavlova, Anna <d>
Piccone, Giuditta <mez>
Rakowska-[Serafin], Elena <s>
Scarabelli, Catalina D. de <pf>
Spani, Hina <s>
Tesana, Rina
Vecart, Raymonde <s>

Male artists
Bergheens (Behgerens), Alfred <pf>
Bettazoni, Amedeo <bar>
Bettoni, Vincenzo <b>
Bolazzi, Giovanni <t>
Bonfanti, Carlo <t>
Cassia, Vincenzo <b>
Charmat, Claude <bar>
Cigada, Francesco <bar>
Dufranne, Louis <t>
Dumesnil, Maurice <pf>
Gigli, Beniamino <t>
Grassi, Rinaldo <t>
Huberty, Albert <b>
Jacovieff, Alexandre <d>
Kaweski, Jan <d>
Manén, Juan <vn>
Masini-Pieralli, Angelo <b>
Menni, Giuseppe <b>
Muratore, Lucien <t>
Nascimbene, Tommaso <bar>
Nemanoff, Richard <d>
Nessi, Giuseppe <t>
Parmentier, V. <bar>
Pintucci, Angelo <t>
Poggi, Alberto

Risler, Edouard <pf>
Roggio, Emilio <bar>
Tegani, Riccardo <bar>
Tarantoni, G. <t>
Vanni-Marcoux, Jean <bar>
Viglione-Borghese, Domenico
<bar>
Volinine, Alexandre <d>
Vorontzov, Mr. <d>

SPANISH ZARZUELA SEASON
José Viñas Zarzuela Company
Jan 24 to Feb 25

Feb 28 to March 9
Carnival Masked Balls

March 13
Recital: Muró de Lacarte <s>,
Bergheens <pf>
Works by Gounod, Verdi,
Brahms, Chaminade, Wagner,
Granados, Cortinas, and Strauss

March 14 to May 3
Spanish Dramatic Company
Salvat–Olona

PAVLOVA BALLET SEASON
Anna Pavlova Ballet Company
Da Rosa, Mocchi and Company,
Impresarios
May 15 to 21
Principal dancers: Pavlova,
Butzova, Volinine, Vorontzov

May 15
Weber: Invitation to the Dance
Saint-Saëns: Thaïs
Kreisler: La libellule
Lincke: Gavotte Pavlova

May 17
Tchaikovsky: Amarilla <Pavlova,
Volinine, and corps de ballet>
Verdi: Egyptian Ballet from Aida
<Butzova, Vorontzov, and corps
de ballet>

Saint-Saëns: La mort du cygne
<Pavlova>

May 18 (matinée)
Saint-Saëns: La mort du cygne
Lincke: Gavotte Pavlova
Divertissements

May 18
Weber: Invitation to the Dance
Saint-Saëns: Thaïs
Divertissements

May 19
Gluck: Orphée aux les Champs
Elisées
Tchaikovsky: Snow Flakes
Gounod (Faust): Walpurgis
Night
Saint-Saëns: Assyrian Dance

May 21
Tchaikovsky: Amarilla
Glazunov: Chopiniana
Massenet: Slaves Dance
Saint-Saëns: La mort du cygne
Ponchielli: The Dance of the
Hours <Pavlova, Volinine, and
corps de ballet>

May 22
Spanish Dramatic Company
Salvat–Olona

June 9
Recital: Manén <vn>, Lago <pf>
Mozart: Concerto no. 4
Bach: Sonata for violin solo
Paganini-Manén: Il palpiti
Beethoven: Romanza in F
Sarasate: Canto del ruiseñor
Gluck: Ballet
Bazzini: Dance of the Witches

June 13
Recital: Manén <vn>, Lago <pf>
Saint-Saëns: Concerto in B
Minor

Porpora: Sonata in G Major
Paganini-Manén: Le streghe
Bach: Sarabande et double
(violin solo)
Manén: Canción
Sarasate: Capricho vasco

June 20
Recital: Manén <vn>, Lago <pf>
Bruch: Fantasie écossaise
Tartini: Sonata Il trillo del
diavolo
Wieniawski: Airs russes
Schubert: La abeille
Sarasate: Serenata andaluza

KAWESKI BALLET SEASON
Jan Kaweski Ballet Company
Da Rosa, Mocchi and Company,
Impresarios
June 21 to July 20
Conductor: Alfredo Padovani
Principal dancers: Kaweski,
Bonieska, G. and M. Chabelska,
Kroner, Jacovieff, Nemanoff

July 12
Recital: Manén <vn>, Lago <pf>

July 31
Recital: C. D. de Scarabelli <pf>

Aug 15
Recital: Merö <pf>
W. F. Bach: Organ Concerto in
D Minor
Chopin:
    a. Barcarole
    b. Waltz in C-sharp Minor
    c. Etude in C Minor
    d. Scherzo in C-sharp Minor
Debussy:
    a. Clair de lune
    b. Jardins sous la pluie
Merkler: Waltz Intermezzo
Liszt:
    a. Harmonies du soir
    b. Rhapsodie no. 2

Aug 16
Recital: Merö <pf>
Bach: Overture
Beethoven: Sonata no. 111
Chopin: Bolero
Jacoby: Marche miniature
Paul de Slozer: Etude de concert
Rachmaninoff: Serenade
Schubert
   a. Impromptu
   b. Moments musicaux
Liszt: Funerailles

Aug 17
Recital: Dumesnil <pf>

Aug 23
Recital: Merö <pf>

**GRAND ITALIAN OPERA
SEASON**
Camillo Bonetti and Company,
Impresarios
Aug 25 to Sept 22
Season Conductor: Tullio Serafin
Guest Conductors: Arturo Vigna,
Franco Paolantonio, and Aldo
Canepa; Achille Lietti, and
Beniamino Moltrasio (assistant
conductors)
Chorus Masters: Silvio Pierligi
and Giuseppe Pappi (assistant)

Aug 25
Uruguayan National Anthem
LORELEY (Catalani)
Loreley: Muzio
Anna di Rehberg: Spani
Walter: Grassi
Rudolfo: Cassia
Herrmann: Roggio

Aug 26
LA GIOCONDA (Ponchielli)
Gioconda: Mazzoleni
Laura: Claessens
Enzo Grimaldo: Gigli
Barnaba: Viglione-Borghese

Aug 30, 31
Recitals: Merö <piano>
Works by Bach, Beethoven,
Chopin, Debussy, and Liszt

Sept 6, 7
Chopin Recitals
Dumesnil <pf>

Sept 12
LUCREZIA BORGIA (Donizetti)
Conductor: Vigna
Lucrezia: Mazzoleni
Gennaro: Gigli
Duca Alfonso: Masini-Pieralli
Maffio Orsini: Blanco-Sadun

Sept 13
MADAME SANS-GENE
(Giordano)**
Madame Sans-Gêne: Muzio
Toniotta Stiratrice: Gianni
Giulia Stiratrice: Cattaneo
La Rosa Stiratrice: Piccone
Lefèbvre: Grassi
Fouché: Tegani
Conte di Neipperg: Bonfanti
Vinaigre, tamburino: Nessi
Maturino, ragazzo: Bolazzi
Regina Carolina: Claessens
Principessa Elisa: Gianni
Cameriera di Caterina: Monti
Despréaux, maestro di ballo:
Nessi
Gelsomino, valetto: Cassia
Leroy, sarto: Bettazoni
De Brigode: Menni
Napoleone: Viglione-Borghese
Signora di Bulow: Tesana
Roustan: Nascimbene
Constant: Poggi

Sept 14
MANON (Massenet)
Manon: Vecart
Des Grieux: Muratore
Lescaut: Charmat
Comte Des Grieux: Huberty

Sept 16
MONNA VANNA (Février)**
Prinzivalle: Muratore
Monna Vanna: Bergé
Guido: Vanni-Marcoux
Marco: Huberty
Vedio: Dufranne
Borso: Nessi
Torello: Bettazoni
Trivulzio: Charmat

Sept 17
LA BOHEME (Puccini)
Mimì: Muzio
Rodolfo: Gigli
Marcello: Viglione-Borghese
Musetta: Gianni

Sept 19
TOSCA (Puccini)
Conductor: Vigna
Tosca: Muzio
Mario Cavaradossi: Gigli
Barone Scarpia: Viglione-
Borghese

Sept 20
AIDA (Verdi)
Aida: Muzio
Amneris: Blanco-Sadun
Radamès: Grassi
Ramfis: Viglione-Borghese

Sept 21
CARMEN (Bizet)
Carmen: Bergé
Don José: Muratore
Micaela: Vecart
Escamillo: Viglione-Borghese

Sept 22
Wagnerian Concert
Conductor: Serafin
Soloists: Rakowska <s>, Masini-
Pieralli <b>, and the Asociación
Coral de Montevideo chorus
Die Meistersinger: Overture
Siegfried: Forest Murmurs

Die Götterdämmerung: Funeral
March
Tannhäuser: Overture
Siegfried: Idyll
Die Götterdämmerung:
Immolation Scene
Tristan und Isolde: Prelude and
Liebestod
Die Walküre:
   a. Final Duet
   b. Magic Fire Music

Sept 24
Recital: Risler <pf>
Beethoven: Sonatas op. 26 and
57
Schumann: Kinderszenen
Granados: Dos danzas españolas
Debussy: Soirée dans Grenade
Liszt:
   a. Etude "Un soupir"
   b. Polonaise in E Minor

Sept 27, 28, 30
Recitals: Risler <pf>
Works by Beethoven, Schumann,
Liszt, Couperin, Daquin,
Rameau, Saint-Saëns, Chopin

Oct 2 to 14
Spanish Dramatic Company
Guerrero–Díaz de Mendoza

Oct 18 to 29
Spanish Comedy Company
Antonia Plana

Oct 31 to Nov 14
Spanish Dance Company
Antonia Mercé
("La Argentina")

Nov 22
Recital: Risler <pf>
Beethoven: Sonatas op. 13 and
op. 27, no. 2
Chopin: B-flat Minor Nocturne,

A-Minor Mazurka, Impromptu
op. 36, Fantasia op. 49
Liszt: Liszt Légende no. 1, Etude,
"Un sospir," Hungarian
Rhapsody no. 11

Nov 23
Beethoven Recital: Risler <pf>
Sonatas op. 26, 53, 57, and 111

Dec 2
Recital: Risler <pf>
Works by Mozart, Beethoven,
Couperin, Hahn, and Liszt

Dec 4 to 28
Argentinean Dramatic Company
Camila Quiroga

1920

Female artists
Anitúa, Fanny <mez>
Berthon, Mireille <s>
Campiña, Fidela <s>
Caracciolo, Juanita <s>
Claessens, Marie <mez>
Csillag, Steffi <s>
Donbrawska, Asta <pf>
Gallo [de Giucci], Luisa <pf>
Guerrieri, Olga <mez>
Laborde, Ema <pf>
Muró de Lacarte, Julieta <s>
Muzio, Claudia <s>
Nash, Frances <pf>
Rakowska-[Serafin], Elena <s>
Romo, Amparo <tiple>
Sassone, Anna <s>
Scarabelli, Catalina D. de <pf>
Valdés, Luisa <s>
Vallin, Ninon <s>

Male artists
Arriola, José <pf>
Azzolini, Gaetano <b>
Barrios, Agustín <gui>
Cassadó, Gaspar <vc>

Cerdan, Marcel <b>
Cigada, Francesco <bar>
Ciniselli, Francesco
(Ferdinando)<t>
Costa, Francisco <vn>
D'Alessandro, Andrea <bar>
Donarelli, Hugo <bar>
Drangosch, Ernesto <pf>
Dumesnil, Maurice <pf>
Ferrari-Fontana, Edoardo <t>
Fraikin, M. <t>
Franco, José María <pf>
Friedman, Ignaz <pf>
Galeffi, Carlo <bar>
Lazzari, Virgilio <b>
Ludikar, Pavel <b>
Mariani, Hugo <vn>
Medici, Alfredo <t>
Merli, Francesco <t>
Meyer-Radon, Walter <pf>
Muñoz, Luis <bar>
Prihoda, Wasa <vn>
Risler, Edouard <pf>
Rubinstein, Artur <pf>
Segovia, Andrés <gui>
Vecsey, Ferenc de <vn>
Viñes, Ricardo <pf>
Voltolini, Ismaele <t>

SPANISH ZARZUELA SEASON
Romo-Viñas Company
Jan 9 to Feb 8

Feb 14 to 22
Carnival Masked Balls

Feb 26 to March 21
Comedy Company Roberto
Casaux

March 25 to May 9
Spanish Dramatic Company
Antonia Plana–Emilio Díaz

SPANISH OPERETTA SEASON
Valle-Csillag Operetta Company
Director: Enrique Valle
May 13 to 16

May 13
LA DUCHESSA DEL BAL TABARIN
(Lombardo) (Sp)

May 14, 16 (matinée)
LA BELLA RISETTA (Fall) (Sp)

May 15
EL PILLUELO DE PARIS (?) (Sp)

May 16
LA CORSETERIA DE MONTMARTRE
(Nelson) (Sp)

May 17
SOCIEDAD WAGNERIANA DE
MONTEVIDEO (SW)
Inaugural Recital
Drangosch <pf> in Wagner's
piano transcription
Die Meistersinger: Prelude
(Bülow transcription)
Der fliegende Holländer:
Spinning Chorus (Drangosch
transcription)
Tristan und Isolde: Liebestod
(Liszt transcription)
Siegfried: Forest Murmurs
(Drangosch transcription)
Die Walküre:
    a. Siegmund Love Song
    b. Magic Fire Music
    c. Ride of the Walkyries (Bas-
       sini transcription)
Lohengrin: Act 3 duet
Tannhäuser: Overture (Liszt
transcription)

May 18
Recital: Muró de Lacarte <s>

May 22
Recital: Arriola <pf>
J. S Bach:
    a. Italian Concerto
    b. Chromatic Fantasy and
       fugue
Brahms: Rhapsody

Schubert: Impromptu
Chopin:
    a. Ballade op. 38
    b. Two Studies
    c. Nocturne
    d. Impromptu
    e. Scherzo op. 20
Liszt:
    a. Two Legends: St. François
       d'Assise: La prédication
       aux oiseaux and St. Fran-
       çois de Paule marchant sur
       les flots
    b. Consolation
    c. Au bord d'une source
    d. La campanella

May 23, 29
Recitals: J. Arriola <pf>

May 25
ASOCIACION CORAL DE
MONTEVIDEO (ACM)
Symphonic-Choral Concert
Conductor: Wilhelm Kolischer
Soloist: Valdés <s>
Wagner: Pilgrim's Chorus
Franck: Rebecca for soprano
and chorus
Guy de Rogartz: Psalm 136

May 28
Recital: Vecsey <vn>, W. Meyer-
Radon <pf>
Tartini: Sonata Il Trillo del
diavolo
Beethoven: Romanza in A Major
Bach: Prelude and Aria
Vieuxtemps: Concerto in D
Wieniawski: Russian airs
Bazzini: La ridda dei polletti

May 30, June 6
Recitals: de Vecsey <vn>, Meyer-
Radon <pf>

June 5
Recital: Friedman <pf>

Mozart: Larghetto
Chopin:
    a. Polonaise
    b. Waltz
Scriabin: Prelude
Liszt:
    a. Variations on Don Gio-
       vanni
    b. La campanella

June 10
Chopin Recital: Friedman <pf>

June 12, 13, 17, 20, 29, 30
Recitals: Friedman <pf>

June 14
Recital: Drangosch <pf>

June 22
Recital: Costa <vn>
Franck: Sonata
Tartini: Concerto in D Minor
F. Bach: Grave
Couperin: Chanson et Pavane
Francoeur: Siciliana et Rigodon
Kreisler: Love Song
Pugnani: Prelude and Allegro

June 24, July 3, 29
Recitals: Costa <vn>

June 27
Recital: Segovia <gui>
Sors:
    a. Andante and allegro
    b. Estudio
    c. Danza
Tárrega: Capricho árabe
Bach: Bourrée
Beethoven: Andante
Schubert: Minuetto
Mendelssohn: Canzonetta
Granados: Two Dances
Albéniz:
    a. Granada
    b. Cádiz
    c. Sevilla

July 4, 25
Recitals: Segovia <gui>

July 10
Recital: Rubinstein <pf>
Bach-Liszt: Fantasia and Fugue
in G Minor
Gluck: Alceste (ballet music)
Saint-Saëns: Turkish March
Beethoven: Choral from Les
ruines d'Athenes
Chopin:
  a. Berceuse
  b. Scherzo
  c. Ballade op. 49
Albéniz: Corpus Christi en
Sevilla
Debussy:
  a. Minstrels
  b. Cake Walk
Falla: Dance from El amor brujo
Liszt:
  a. Rêve d'amour
  b. Hungarian Rhapsody no.
     10

July 11, 17, 31, Aug 1 (6:30 P.M.)
Recitals: Rubinstein <pf>

July 13
Recital: Nash <pf>
Works by Bach, Chopin, Liszt,
Saint-Saëns, and MacDowell's
Sonata Eroica**

July 14, 21, Aug 4 (matinée)
Recitals: Cassadó <vc>, J. M.
Franco <pf>
Works by Bocherini, Chopin,
Cassadó, Rubinstein, and
Popper

July 15
Recital: Nash <pf>

July 18
SW Symphonic Concert
Conductor: Ernesto Drangosch

July 28
ACM Symphonic Concert
Conductor: Maurice Dumesnil
Soloist: Rubinstein <pf>
Beethoven: Symphony no. 5
Saint-Saëns: Piano Concerto in
G Minor
Debussy: L'Après-midi d'un
faune
Falla: Noches en los jardines de
España
Dukas: L'apprenti sorcier

Aug 4, 6 (matinée)
Recitals: Prihoda <vn>,
Donbrawska <pf>
Works by Dvořák, Chopin,
Paganini

Aug 5 to 7, 10 to 12
French Dramatic Company from
the Thèâtre Odéon de Paris

Aug 7 (matinée)
Lieder Recital: Vallin <s>,
Franco <pf>

Aug 9
Recital: Barrios <gui>

GRAND ITALIAN OPERA SEASON

Camillo Bonetti and Company
Impresario
Aug 15 to 31
Conductors: Tullio Serafin and
Fernand Masson (assistant
conductor)

Aug 15
LA TRAVIATA (Verdi)
Violetta: Muzio
Alfredo Germont: Ciniselli
Giorgio Germont: Galeffi

Aug 17
MADAMA BUTTERFLY (Puccini)
Cio-Cio-San: Caracciolo

Pinkerton: Ciniselli
Suzuki: Guerrieri
Sharpless: Donarelli
Il Bonzo: Azzolini

Aug 18
THAIS (Massenet)
Conductor: Masson
Thaïs: Berthon
Nicias: Fraikin
Athanael: Cerdan
Ballet Performance by Chabelska
and Jakovieff

Aug 19, 28
AIDA (Verdi)
Aida: Muzio
Amneris: Anitúa
Radamès: Voltolini
Amonasro: Galeffi
Ramfis: Lazzari
Il Re: Muñoz

Aug 20
Dance Recital: Alexandre
Jakovieff Ballet Company with
G. and M. Chabelska, Jakovieff
Borodin: Prince Igor's Polovtsian
Dances
Weber: Le spectre de la rose and
Divertissements

Aug 21
FEDRA (Pizzetti)**
Fedra: Rakowska
Teseo: Cigada
Ippolito: Merli
Etra: Anitúa
La schiava tebana: Sassone
La nutrice gorgo: Claessens
L'auriga: Ludikar

Aug 22
RE DI LAHORE (Massenet) (It)**
Nair: Campiña
Alim: Voltolini
Scindia: Galeffi

Timur: Lazzari
Indra: Muñoz

Aug 24
TRISTANO E ISOTTA (Wagner)
(It)
Isotta: Rakowska
Tristano: Ferrari-Fontana
Brangania: Claessens
Re Marke: Ludikar
Kurvenal: Cigada
Melot: D'Alessandro

Aug 25
Uruguayan National Anthem
LORELEY (Catalani)
Loreley: Muzio
Anna di Rehberg: Sassone
Walter: Merli
Herrmann: Cigada
Rudolfo: Muñoz

Aug 26, 29
MEFISTOFELE (Boito)
Margherita: Caracciolo
Faust: Ciniselli(1) / Merli(1)
Mefistofele: Lazzari

Aug 31
LOHENGRIN (Wagner) (It)
Elsa di Brabante: Muzio
Ortruda: Anitúa
Lohengrin: Merli
Federico di Telramondo: Galeffi
Enrico: Lazzari
L'araldo del Re: Muñoz

Sept 4
Two-Piano Recital: Risler and
Rubinstein
Mozart: Sonata in D Major
Saint-Saëns: Variations on a
Beethoven theme
Taillaferre: Jeux de plein air
Saint-Saëns:
  a. La Tirelitentaine
  b. Cache-cache-mitoulá
  c. Scherzo

Chabrier: Trois valses
romantiques
Liszt: Les préludes

Sept 5, 9
Tabare (Motion Picture)

Sept 8
Lieder Recital: Vallin <s>, Risler
<pf>
Schumann: Dichterliebe**
Wagner: Wesendonk lieder
Duparc:
  a. L'invitation au voyage
  b. Phidylé
Deodac de Severac: Chanson
pour mon petit cheval
Fauré:
  a. Clair de lune
  b. Nell

Sept 10 to 26
Spanish Dramatic Company
María Guerrero–Fernando Díaz
de Mendoza

Sept 28
Recital: Medici <t>, Mariani
<vn>

Sept 30
Recital: Risler <pf>
Works by Beethoven, Chopin,
and Liszt

Oct 2
Recital: Vallin <s>, Viñes <pf>
I—Solo piano
Fauré: Impromptu
Debussy:
  a. Prelude
  b. Sarabande
  c. Toccata
II—voice and piano
Franck: Rédemption (Chant du
arcangel)
Ravel:
  a. Sainte

b. Cinq melodies populaires
grecques
Debussy: Proses liriques
  a. De rêve
  b. De soir
Rimsky-Korsakoff: On the Hills
of Georgia
Tchaikovsky: Pendant de bal
Glazunov:
  a. Roman oriental
  b. Les larmes
Grechaninov:
  a. Berceuse
  b. Triste es la steppe
III—Solo piano
Glinka: Berceuse
Borodin: Scherzo
Musorgsky: Tableaux d'une
exhibition (Danse des petit
poulets)
Balakirev: Islamey
Granados: La maja y el ruiseñor
Falla: Seguidillas from El
sombrero de tres picos
Albeniz: El puerto
Chavarri: El viejo castillo moro
Turina: Miramar
IV—voice and piano
Falla: Seis canciones populares
españolas

**WEINGARTNER CONCERTS
SEASON**
Walter Mocchi and Company
Impresario
Oct 7 to 17
ACM orchestra
Conductor: Felix Weingartner
Guest Conductor: Virgilio
Scarabelli

Oct 7
Beethoven: Symphony no. 5
Liszt: Tasso
Wagner:
  a. Siegfried's Idyll
  b. Overture to Tannhäuser

Oct 9
Beethoven: Symphony no. 6
Mozart: Hostias
Berlioz: La damnation de Faust
    a. Ballet follet
    b. Marche hongrois
    c. Danse des sylphes
Wagner: Prelude to Die
Meistersinger

Oct 11
Beethoven: Symphony no. 5
Respighi: Danza antica
Dukas: L'apprenti sorcier
Mendelssohn: Overture to A
Midsummer Night's Dream
Wagner: Prelude and Liebestod
of Isolde

Nov 17
Conductor: Scarabelli
Soloist: Gallo de Giucci <pf>
Raff: In the Forest (Sinfonia)
    a. The Day
    b. Sunset (Réverie)
    c. Scherzo (dance)
    d. The Night—Fantastic Hunt
Beethoven: Fidelio's Overture
Weber: Concertstuck <pf/rch>
Cluzeau-Mortet: Danza****
Weingartner: Serenade**
Wagner:
    a. Liebestod of Isolde
    b. Overture to Tannhäuser

SPANISH BALLET SEASON
Raquel Meller Ballet Company
from Madrid's Teatro Lara
Oct 16 to 31

Nov 6, 7
Cinematographic exhibitions

Nov 23 to Dec 12
Spanish Dramatic Company
Salvat–Olona

**SPANISH ZARZUELA AND
OPERETTA SEASON**
Helena D'Algy Zarzuela and
Operetta Company
Dec 14 to 28

1921

Female artists
Alzáibar, María D. de <s>
Francillo-Kauffman, Hedwig <s>
Galeazzi, Elvira <s>
Lerner, Tina <pf>
Paltrinieri, Velia <s>
Pangrazi, Rosalia <mez>
Sanguinetti, María Elena <a>
Sanz, Pepita <s>
Valdés, Luisa <s>
Zorrilla de San Martín, Elvira <s>

Male artists
Baldrich, Rogelio <t>
Cairo, Giovanni <b>
Cluzeau-Mortet, Luis <pf>
De Franceschi, Enrico <bar>
De Luca, G. <t>
Domínguez, Ricardo <t>
Dumesnil, Maurice <pf>
Franco, José María <pf>
Herrera-McLean, Carlos <t>
Linsen, Kurt <b>
Milli, Attilio <b>
Mora, Florencio <vn>
Vecsey, Ferenc de <vn>

SPANISH BALLET SEASON
Raquel Meller Ballet Company
from Madrid's Teatro Lara
Jan 11 to 23

Jan 24 to 26
Motion Picture Showings

Jan 29 to Feb 13
Carnival Masked Balls

Feb 24 to March 21
Argentinean Comedy Company
Roberto Casaux

March 26 to May 15
Spanish Dramatic Company
Cervantes Antonia Plana

April 23
Recital: Dumesnil <pf>
I—J. S. Bach
    a. Introduction and Coral
       Cantata XV
    b. Aria from Cantata XXXV
    c. Bourée Violin Sonata no. 6
II—Chopin
    a. Polonaise in C-sharp
    b. Impromptu in A-flat
    c. Waltz in F-sharp
    d. Ballade in G-Minor
C. Scott: Asphodel
Rachmaninoff: Prelude in G
Minor
Orstein: Impressions from
Chinatown
R. Strauss: Serenade
A. Williams: Segundo aire de
vals
Wagner-Liszt: Death of Isolde

May 17 to 22
Argentinean Folkloric Dance
Company Andrés A. Chazarreta

May 27 to June 17, 19, to July 11
Spanish Dramatic Company
Antonia Herrero

June 18
Recital: Vecsey <vn>, Franco
<pf>
Tartini: Sonata Trillo del diavolo
Vieuxtemps: Concerto in D
Minor
J. S. Bach: Aria from Suite in D
Paganini-Kreisler: Prelude and
Allegro

Sibelius:
a. Nocturne
b. Vals triste
Sarasate: Zapateado
Paganini: Moto Perpetuo

July 16 (matinée)
Symphonic Concert
Conductor: Wladimir Shavitch
All-Russian music program
Soloists: Lerner <pf>, Mora <vn>
Borodin: Dans les steppes de
l'Asie Centrale
Rimsky-Korsakoff:
a. Russian Fantasy for Violin
and Orchestra
b. Sheherazade
Tchaikovsky: Piano Concerto
no. 2

ITALIAN OPERA SEASON
Antonio Marranti Company

July 12 to 31
Conductor: Antonio Marranti

July 12, 14 (matinée)
LA GIOCONDA (Ponchielli)
Gioconda: Galeazzi
Enzo Grimaldo: Baldrich
Laura: Pangrazi
Barnaba: De Franceschi
Alvise Badoero: Cairo

July 13, 18 (matinée)
IL BARBIERE DI SIVIGLIA
(Rossini)
Rosina: Sanz
Figaro: De Franceschi
Conte di Almaviva: De Luca
Don Basilio: Cairo
Don Bartolo: Milli

July 14
La Marseillaise
FAUST (Gounod)
Margherita: Galeazzi
Faust: Baldrich
Mefistofele: Cairo

July 15, 17, 24
IL TROVATORE (Verdi)
Leonora: Galeazzi
Manrico: Domínguez
Conte di Luna: De Franceschi

July 16, 31 (matinée)
RIGOLETTO (Verdi)
Gilda: Sanz
Il Duca di Mantova: De Luca
Rigoletto: De Franceschi
Sparafucile: Cairo

July 17 (matinée)
LA TRAVIATA (Verdi)
Violetta: Sanz
Alfredo Germont: De Luca
Giorgio Germont: De Franceschi

July 18
Uruguayan National Anthem
AIDA (Verdi)
Aida: Galeazzi
Radamès: Baldrich
Amonasro: De Franceschi
Amneris: Pangrazi
Ramfis: Cairo

July 19, 24 (matinée), 28
(matinée)
I PESCATORI DI PERLE (Bizet)
(It)
Leila: Paltrinieri
Nadir: Baldrich
Zurga: De Franceschi
Nourabad: Cairo

July 20
NORMA (Bellini)
Norma: Galeazzi
Pollione: De Luca

July 21 (matinée), 31 (5:00 P.M.)
CAVALLERIA RUSTICANA
(Mascagni)

July 21
LA BOHEME (Puccini)

Mimì: Paltrinieri
Rodolfo: Baldrich
Marcello: De Franceschi

July 22
LUCIA DI LAMMERMOOR
(Donizetti)
Lucia: Sanz
Edgardo: De Luca
Enrico: De Franceschi

July 23 (matinée)
PAGLIACCI (Leoncavallo)

July 23, 31
MEFISTOFELE (Boito)
Margherita: Galeazzi
Faust: Baldrich
Mefistofele: Cairo

July 21 and 23 (matinée), 26, 31
(6:00 P.M.)
CAVALLERIA RUSTICANA
(Mascagni)
PAGLIACCI (Leoncavallo)

July 27
La bohème: Acts 3 and 4
AMLETO (Thomas) (It)
Amleto: De Franceschi
Ofelia: Sanz

July 28
TOSCA (Puccini)
Tosca: Galeazzi
Mario Cavaradossi: Baldrich
Barone Scarpia: De Franceschi

July 29 (matinée)
La bohème: Acts 3 and 4

July 29
LA FAVORITA (Donizetti) (It)
Leonora: Pangrazi
Fernando: Baldrich
Alfonso XI: De Franceschi

July 30
LA FORZA DEL DESTINO (Verdi)
Leonora: Galeazzi
Don Alvaro: Domínguez
Don Carlo: De Franceschi

July 31 (10:00 P.M.)
MEFISTOFELE (Boito)
Company Farewell *Concert*

Aug 2 to 18
Spanish Dramatic Company
Cervantes Antonia Herrero

Aug 25
Vocal Concert
Chorus Master: Carlos Correa-Luna
Soloists: Valdés <s>, Cluzeau-Mortet <pf>

Sept 2 to 9, 11
Mr. Carter <magician>

Sept 10
Symphonic Concert
Conductor: Wladimir Shavitch
Soloists: Lerner <pf>, Francillo-Kauffman <s>
Tchaikovsky: Symphony no. 6
Mozart: No, non che non sei capace <s/orch>
Schubert: Wandererfantasie
Rimsky-Korsakoff: Scheherazade

Sept 25
Celebration of Dante Alighieri
IV Centennial
ACM chorus and orchestra
Conductor: Domingo Dente

Oct 2, 7
ACM Symphonic-Choral Concerts
Conductor: Carlos Correa-Luna
Soloists: Alzáibar <s>, Zorrilla de San Martín<s>, Sanguinetti

<a>, Herrera-McLean <t>, Linsen <b>
Anonymous: Chansons françaises du XVI siècle
Debussy: Danse chansons avec paroles de Charles d'Orléans
Palestrina: Missa Brevis (Kyrie/Gloria/Credo)
Mendelssohn: Overture to Ruy Blas
Chausson: Chant funèbre
Borodin: Polovtsian Dances from Prince Igor

Oct 27 to Nov 12
Argentinean Dramatic Company
Armando Discépolo

1922

Female artists
Benedetti, Massina <s>
Diez, Matilde <pf>
Lampaggi, Maria Luisa <mez>
Lloret, Dora <s>
Melly, Elena <s>
Mistinguette [Jeanne Marie Bourgeois] <d>
Soler, Adriana <s>

Male artists
Ayala, Alcides <vn>
Bertolini, Signor <bar>
Boraglia, G. <t>
Damiani, Víctor <bar>
De Angelis, Fortunato <t>
De Carlo, Carlo <t>
De Salvi, Guido <bar>
Llobet, Miguel <gui>
Macchi, Plácido <fl>
Mansueto, Gaudio <b>
Moreno, Giacomo <bar>
Vela, José <bar>
Vianna da Motta, José <pf>
Zonzini, Giuseppe <b>

Jan 5 to 22
Chilean Dramatic Company
María Padin–Arturo Mario

Feb 1 to 9
Motion Picture Showings

Feb 18 to March 5
Carnival Masked Balls

March 10 to April 18
Spanish Dramatic Company
Manuel Salvat–Antonia Herrero

April 19 to 24
Spanish Dramatic Company
Flora Drago

SPANISH OPERETTA SEASON
Vela-Guiró Operetta Company
May 5 to June 4
Director: Guido de Salvi

May 5, 6, 7, 12, 19
LA PRINCESA DE LAS CZARDAS (Kálmán) (Sp)

May 8, 14 (matinée)
LA BELLA RISETTA (Fall) (Sp)

May 9, 10, 11, 13, 14, 18 (matinée), June 1
LA CONDESA BAILARINA (Stolz) (Sp)

May 15
LA PRINCESA DEL DOLAR (Fall) (Sp)

May 16, June 4 (9:00 P.M.)
EVA (Lehár) (Sp)

May 17, 18, 20, 21, 30
LA MASCOTITA (J. Gilbert) (Sp)

May 20 (matinée)
Recital: Llobet <gui>
Works by Sors, Tárrega, Mozart,

Mendelssohn, Falla, Granados and Albéniz

May 21 (matinée)
MOLINOS DE VIENTO (Luna)

May 22, 31
LA REINA DEL FONOGRAFO (Lombardo) (Sp)

May 23, 25 (matinée), **27, June 4** (6:00 P.M.)
EL CABALLERO DE LA LUNA (Ziehrer) (Sp)

May 24, 25
LA DUQUESA DEL BAL TABARIN (Bard) (Sp)

May 26, 28 (matinée)
EL MERCADO DE LAS MUCHACHAS (Jacobi) (Sp)

May 28
BOHEMIOS (Vives)

May 29, June 4 (matinée)
EL CONDE DE LUXEMBURGO (Lehár) (Sp)

June 2
LA CASTA SUSANA (J. Gilbert) (Sp)

June 3
CINEMA STAR (J. Gilbert) (Sp)

June 14 to July 16
Spanish Dramatic Company
Manuel Salvat–Antonia Herrero

July 1
Symphonic Concert
Conductors: Luis Sambucetti
Soloist: Ayala <vn>, Macchi <fl>
Beethoven:
  a. Symphony no. 7
  b. Violin concerto

Ayala: La cacería, tone poem**** [conducted by the composer]
Bizet: L'arlésienne, second suite

July 18 to 30
French Music Hall from Paris' Théâtre Ba-Ta-Clan
Director: Madame Rasimi with Mistinguette <d>

Aug 1
ACM chorus and orchestra
Conductor: Carlos Correa-Luna
Soloist: Damiani <bar>
Schubert: Dieu dans la nature
Bach: Incarnatus from B Minor Mass
Cortinas: Elegía a Rodó
Berlioz: Roman Carnival Overture
Dubois: Bergerette
D'Indy: Sainte Marie Madeleine
Franck: Hereuse les misericordieux
Musorgsky: Scene du temple from Oedipe
Borodin:
  a. Aria from Prince Igor
  b. Polovtsian Dances

Aug 3, 9
Recitals: Vianna da Motta <pf>
Works by Busoni, Rameau, Paderewski, Chopin, Vianna da Motta, Chopin-Liszt, and Liszt

VIENNA PHILHARMONIC CONCERTS
Vienna Philharmonic Orchestra
Walter Mocchi, Impresario
Aug 5 to 7
Conductor: Felix Weingartner

Aug 5
Beethoven: Egmont Overture
Wagner: Tannhäuser Bacchanal

Respighi: The Fountains of Rome
Berlioz: Symphonie fantastique

Aug 6
Weingartner: Symphony in G
Vivaldi: Concerto
Smetana: The Moldau
Beethoven: Symphony no. 5

Aug 7
Goldmark: Overture Sakuntala
Weingartner: Dame Kobold Overture
Beethoven: Symphony no. 1
Wagner:
  a. Funeral March from Göt- terdämmerung
  b. Tannhäuser Overture

Aug 10 to Sept 4
Spanish Dramatic Company
Lola Membrives
Director: Jacinto Benavente

Aug 18, 23
Lectures by Jacinto Benavente (winner of the Nobel Prize for Literature in 1922)

Sept 5, 6
French Dramatic Company G. Signoret

Sept 23, 24
Recitals: Diez <pf>
Works by Beethoven, MacDowell, Chopin, Moszkowski, and Liszt

Oct 13 to 15
Motion Picture Showings

Oct 17 to 31
Italian Dramatic Company
Dario Niccodemi

SPRING ITALIAN OPERA SEASON

Nov 4 to 11
Conductor: Bruno Mari
Director: Alfredo Isidoro Landi

Nov 4, 5
MEFISTOFELE (Boito)
Margherita: Benedetti
Faust: Boraglia
Mefistofele: Mansueto

Nov 5 (matinée)
AIDA (Verdi)
Aida: Benedetti
Radamès: Boraglia
Amneris: Lampaggi
Amonasro: Bertolini
Ramfis: Zonzini

Nov 6
CAVALLERIA RUSTICANA
(Mascagni)
PAGLIACCI (Leoncavallo)
Canio: Boraglia
Tonio: Moreno

Nov 7, 11
LA GIOCONDA (Ponchielli)
Gioconda: Benedetti
Laura: Lampaggi
Enzo Grimaldo: Boraglia
Barnaba: Moreno

Nov 9
IL TROVATORE (Verdi)
Leonora: Benedetti
Manrico: Boraglia
Azucena: Lampaggi
Conte di Luna: Bertolini
Ferrando: Zonzini

Nov 10
FAUST (Gounod) (It)
Margherita: Benedetti
Faust: Boraglia
Mefistofele: Mansueto

Dec 7 to 31
Argentinean Comedy Company
Florencio Parravicini

1923

Female artists
Aldabe, María Luisa <pf>
Bertana, Luisa <mez>
Bland, Elsa <s>
Castagneta, Olga <s>
Cattaneo, Gina <mez>
Dahmenn, Charlotte <s>
Dal Monte, Toti <s>
Dragoni, Bruna <s>
Gioana, Pina <s>
Kruszelnicka [Krusceniski],
Salomea <s>
Lilloni, Maria <mez>
Mistinguette [Jeanne Marie
Bourgeois] <d>
Muzio, Claudia <s>
Olczewska, Maria <mez>
Perini, Flora <mez>
Salterain, Margarita de <pf>
Spani, Hina <s>
Vallin, Ninon <s>

Male artists
Blumen, Alfred <pf>
Braun, Carl <b>
Busbaum, Frederick <vc>
Cirino, Giulio <b>
Damiani, Víctor <bar>
De Vecchi, Gino <b>
Fiore, Michele <b>
Fleta, Miguel <t>
Freith, Karl <vla>
Galeffi, Carlo <bar>
Huberman, Bronislaw <vn>
Journet, Marcel <b>
Kirchhoff, Walther <t>
Nardi, Luigi <t>
O'Sullivan, John <t>
Pablo, Vicente <pf>
Palai, Nello <t>
Pertile, Aureliano <t>

Scafa, Ciro <bar>
Schipper, Emil <bar>
Schult, Siegfried <pf>
Segura-Tallien, José <bar>
Thiemer, Heinrich <bar>
Valles, José <cl>

Jan 1 to 7
Argentinean Comedy Company
Florencio Parravicini

Feb 4 to 18
Carnival Masked Balls

Feb 24 to March 18
Comedy Company Roberto
Casaux

March 31 to May 2
Spanish Dramatic Company
Concepción Olona–Rafael
Barden

May 3 to 9
French Dramatic Company
Gabrielle Dorziat

May 25
Sociedad Orquestal del Uruguay
Concert
Conductors: Virgilio Scarabelli
and Vicente Pablo
Soloists: Salterain <pf>, Aldabe
<pf>, Pablo <pf>, Valles <cl>
Uruguayan National Anthem
Argentinean National Anthem
Franck: Symphony in D Minor
Bach: Concerto in C Major for
three pianos
Fabini: Campo
Musorgsky: Intermezzo
Mozart: Larghetto <cl / orch>
Wagner: Solemn March

June 2 to 24
Spanish Zarzuela Company
Manuel Casas

July 17 to 30
French Music Hall from Paris's
Théâtre Ba-Ta-Clan
Director: Madame Rasimi with
Mistinguette <d> and Earl Leslie
<modern jazz dancer>

**VIENNA PHILHARMONIC
CONCERTS**
Vienna Philharmonic Orchestra
Walter Mocchi and Company,
Impresario
August 1 to 5
Conductor: Richard Strauss

Aug 1
All-Strauss program
Ein Heldenleben, tone poem
Till Eulenspiegels
Salome's dances
Tod und Verklärung, tone poem

Aug 2
Mendelssohn: A Midsummer
Night's Dream
Strauss: Also sprach Zarathustra
Wagner:
  a. Overture to Tannhäuser
  b. Siegfried's Idyll
  c. Prelude to Die Meister-
     singer

Aug 3
Weber: Euryanthe Overture
Beethoven: Symphony no. 7
Strauss: Don Juan, tone poem
Strauss: Symphonia domestica

Aug 4
Soloist: Blumen <pf>
Mozart: Symphony no. 41
Beethoven: Piano Concerto no.
3
Strauss: Eine Alpensinfonie**

Aug 5
Soloists: Busbaum <vc>, Freith
<vla>

Beethoven:
  a. Symphony no. 6
  b. Overture to Leonora
Strauss: Don Quixote
Wagner:
  a. Overture to Der fliegende
     Holländer
  b. Funeral March from Göt-
     terdämmerung
  c. Prelude and Liebestod of
     Isolde

Aug 18
Recital: Huberman<vn>,
Schult<pf>
Beethoven: Kreutzer Sonata
Bach: Concerto in D
Chopin-Sarasate: Nocturne
Chopin-Huberman: Waltz
Paganini: La campanella

Aug 19, Sep 2, 22 (matinée)
Recitals: Huberman <vn>,
Schult <pf>
Works by Brahms, Glazunov,
Chopin, Wilhermy, Elgar, Bizet,
and Sarasate

**GRAND ITALIAN OPERA
SEASON**
Walter Mocchi and Company,
Impresario
Aug 21 to 26
Season Conductor: Gino
Marinuzzi
Guest Conductors: Richard
Strauss and Franco
Paolantonio
Director: Mario Sammarco

Aug 21
AIDA (Verdi)
Aida: Muzio
Radamès: Pertile
Amneris: Perini
Ramfis: Journet
Amonasro: Galeffi
Il Re: Cirino

Aug 22
TRISTAN UND ISOLDE (Wagner)
Isolde: Bland
Tristan: Kirchhoff
Brangäne: Olczewska
König Marke: Braun
Kurwenal: Schipper
Melot: Thiemer

Aug 23
RIGOLETTO (Verdi)
Conductor: Paolantonio
Gilda: Dal Monte
Il Duca di Mantova: Fleta
Rigoletto: Damiani
Maddalena: Bertana
Sparafucile: Cirino
Monterone: Fiore
Conte di Ceprano: De Vecchi
Borsa: Palai
Marullo: Scafa
Contessa di Ceprano: Lilloni
Giovanna: Cattaneo

Aug 24
ELEKTRA (Strauss)**
Conductor: Strauss
Elektra: Bland
Klytemnästra: Olczewska
Orestes: Shipper
Chrysotemis: Dahmenn
Aegisthus: Kirchhoff
I COMPAGNACCI (Riccitelli)**
Conductor: Marinuzzi
Anna Maria: Vallin
Baldo: Fleta
Bernardo: Segura-Tallien
Noferi: Nardi

Aug 25
Uruguayan National Anthem
MANON (Massenet)
Manon: Vallin
Des Grieux: Fleta
Lescaut: Segura-Tallien
Comte Des Grieux: Journet
Guillot: De Vecchi

Aug 26 (matinée)
GUGLIELMO TELL (Rossini) (It)
Arnoldo: O'Sullivan
Guglielmo Tell: Galeffi
Matilde: Spani
Hedwige: Perini
Jemmy: Dragoni
Gualtiero: Mansueto

Aug 26
LUCIA DI LAMMERMOOR
(Donizetti)
Conductor: Paolantonio
Lucia: Dal Monte
Edgardo: Pertile
Enrico: Segura-Tallien
Raimondo: Cirino
Alisa: Cattaneo
Arturo: Nardi
Normanno: Palai

Sept 4 to 17
Spanish Dramatic Company
María Guerrero–Fernando Díaz
de Mendoza

ITALIAN OPERETTA SEASON
Bertini-Gioana Operetta
Company
Sept 18 to October 14
Conductor: Vincenzo Bellezza

Sept 18 to 23, 28 (matinée), Oct
1, 8
LA DANZA DELLE LIBELLULE
(Lehár) (It)

Sept 24, 29
ACQUA CHETA (Pietri)

Sept 25 to 27
LA BAYADERA (Kálmán) (It)

Sep 28, 29 (matinée), Oct 2, 11
SALTIMBANCHI (Ganne) (It)

Oct 3, 5, 7 (matinée), 14
SANTARELLINA (Hervé) (It)

Oct 4
ADDIO GIOVINEZZA (Pietri)

Oct 6, 7, 12, 14 (matinée)
DOVE CANTA L'ALLODOLA
(Lehár) (It)

Oct 9
MADAME DE TEBAS (Lombardo)

Oct 10
LA MAZURKA AZZURRA (Lehár)
(It)

Oct 12 (matinée)
LA CASA DELLE TRE RAGAZZE
(Schubert) (It)

Oct 13
LA PRINCIPESSA DELLE CZARDE
(Kálmán) (It)

Oct 14
SANTARELLINA (Hervé) (It)
Farewell Company *Concert*

Oct 23 to 30
Italian Dramatic Company
Maria Melato

Nov 1 to 18, 20 to 25
Italian Dramatic Company
Ermete Zacconi

Nov 19
Recital: Kruszelnicka <s>
Brahms: La domenica
Bassani: Se tu dormi ancora
Chausson: Au temps de lilas
Chaminade: Reste
Pizzetti: I pastori
Santoliquido: Poesia persa
Castelnuovo: Girotondo dei
Golosi
Severac: Ma poupée
López-Buchardo: Las rosas de
Noel

Ugarte: Bajo el parral
Williams: Vidalita

Dec 1 to 14, 16 to 31
Argentinean Comedy Company
Florencio Parravicini

Dec 15
Recital: Kruszelnicka <s>
Brahms: All usignuolo
Wolff: A l'aube
Strauss: Al mio bambino
Bimboni: Melodia
Luizzi: Canto d'amore
Respighi: Nebbie
Roosen-Regalia: La Lune
Cluzeau-Mortet: La noche
blanca de luna
Soria-Gowland: Les griffes d'or
Fabini: Flores del monte
Obradors: Canciones populares
españolas

1924

Female artists
Aldabe, María Luisa <pf>
Besanzoni, Gabriella <mez>
Chabannes, Mlle. <s>
Corucci, Zoraida <s>
Dalla-Rizza, Gilda <s>
Dagmara, Francine <d>
Vera Elisius, Vera <d>
Gabinska, Vera <d>
Galantha, Ekaterine de <d>
Gramegna, Anna <a>
Hols de Schusselin, Josefina <s>
Jabovich, Eugenia <mez>
Koshetz, Nina <s>
Metallo de Maza, Maria Antonia
<s>
Micoulina, Mlle.<d>
Migliacci, Margherita <mez>
Muzio, Claudia <s>
Nemeroff, Maria <d>
Pangrazi, Rosalia <mez>
Rizal, N. <s>

Rosso, Elcira <s>
Scacciati, Bianca <s>
Schouvaloff, Efrosine <mez>
Shereshevkaya, Elise <s>
Simzis, Olga <s>
Syril, Jenny <s>
Wait-Gagliasso, Helen <s>
Zamboni, Maria <s>
Zotti, Clelia <mez>

Male artists
Alsina, Joaquín <b>
Bielina, Stephan <t>
Bonanova, Fortunio <bar>
Cassia, Vincenzo <b>
Chiolo, Oscar <vn>
Corallo, Giovanni <t>
Crimi, Giulio <t>
Damiani, Víctor <bar>
De Vecchi, Gino <bar>
Fleta, Miguel <t>
Fiore, Michele <b>
Frank, Mr. <bar>
Gerardi, Signor <t>
Griff, Alexander <b>
Horszowski, Mieczyslaw <pf>
Lavretzky, Nicolai <t>
Mansueto, Gaudio <b>
Melnikoff, Nicolai <bar>
Michalowski, Pierre <d>
Minghetti, Angelo <t>
Mirassou, Pedro <t>
Nardi, Luigi <t>
Oukranisky, Serge <d>
Pasero, Tancredi <b>
Pastorino, Alfredo I. <t>
Pavley, André <d>
Pilotto, Angelo <bar>
Ponce, Jorge <t>
Ponzio, Leon <bar>
Re, Vittorio <t>
Redondo del Castillo, Señor <b>
Salvatti, Salvatore <t>
Schinca, Luis <bar>
Segura-Tallien, José <bar>
Sgarbi, Luis <t>
Urízar, Marcelo <bar>
Valles, José <cl>

Wesselovsky, Alexander <t>
Zalewsky, Sigismund <b>
Zaporojetz, Kapiton <b>
Zonzini, Giuseppe <b>

March 1 to 10
Carnival Masked Balls

RUSSIAN BALLET SEASON
Russian Ballet Company
March 14 to 30
Conductor: Alexis Abutkoff
First dancer: Michalowski
Dancers: Gabinska, Galantha,
Micoulina

April 3
Poetic recital: Heraclio Sena

**FALL ITALIAN OPERA
SEASON**
April 19 to May 18
Conductor: Arturo De Angelis

April 19, 20 (matinée), May 8
AIDA (Verdi)
Aida: Scacciati
Amneris: Pangrazi
Radamès: Mirassou
Amonasro: Urízar
Ramfis: Alsina
Il Re: Zonzini

April 20, 30
RIGOLETTO (Verdi)
Gilda: Wait-Gagliasso
Il Duca di Mantova: Salvatti
Rigoletto: Urízar

April 21, 29, May 2 (matinée), 11
LA TRAVIATA (Verdi)
Violetta: Corucci
Alfredo Germont: Salvatti
G. Germont: Pilotto(3) /
Urízar(1)

April 22, May 10
MEFISTOFELE (Boito)

Margherita: Scacciati
Elena: Hols
Faust: Salvatti
Mefistofele: Mansueto

April 23, 27 (matinée), May 18
(matinée)
LA BOHEME (Puccini)
Mimì: Simzis
Rodolfo: Re
Marcello: Pilotto
Musetta: Hols

April 24, 27, May 2, 4 (matinée),
12
IL BARBIERE DI SIVIGLIA
(Rossini)
Rosina: Wait-Gagliasso
Figaro: Pilotto
Conte di Almaviva: Salvatti
Don Basilio: Mansueto
Don Bartolo: Alsina
Berta: Pangrazi

April 25, May 17 (matinée)
IL TROVATORE (Verdi)
Leonora: Scacciati
Manrico: Mirassou
Conte di Luna: Pilotto(1) / Urízar
(1)

April 26, May 3, 7
MANON (Massenet)
Manon: Corucci
Des Grieux: Salvatti
Lescaut: Pilotto

April 28
LUCIA DI LAMMERMOOR
(Donizetti)
Lucia: Wait-Gagliasso
Edgardo: Mirassou
Enrico: Pilotto
Raimondo: Alsina

May 1
ANDREA CHENIER (Giordano)
Maddalena de Coigny: Scacciati

Andrea Chénier: Re
Carlo Gérard: Pilotto

May 4, 11 (matinée)
CAVALLERIA RUSTICANA
(Mascagni)
Lola: Scacciati
Turiddu: Re
PAGLIACCI (Leoncavallo)
Nedda: Hols
Canio: Mirassou
Tonio: Pilotto
Silvio: Pilotto

May 5, 6
FAUST (Gounod) (It)
Margherita: Simzis
Faust: Re
Mefistofele: Mansueto
Valentin: Urízar

May 9, 16
LA WALLY (Catalani)
Wally: Scacciati
Hagenbach: Corallo
Gellner: Urízar

May 10 (matinée)
Recital: Horszowski <pf>
Bach: English Suite
Beethoven: Sonata op. 31, no. 1
Musorgsky: Pictures at an
Exhibition
Chopin:
  a. Nocturnes op.27, nos. 1
     and 2
  b. Polonaise op. 22

May 13
LORELEY (Catalani)
Loreley: Corucci
Walter: Salvatti
Herrmann: Urízar
Anna di Rehberg: Pangrazi
Rudolfo: Mansueto

May 14
LA SONNAMBULA (Bellini)

Amina: Wait-Gagliasso
Elvino: Salvatti
Conte Rodolfo: Mansueto

May 15
TOSCA (Puccini)
Tosca: Corucci
Mario Cavaradossi: Mirassou
Barone Scarpia: Urízar

May 18 (6:00 P.M.)
PAGLIACCI (Leoncavallo) [same
cast as May 4]

May 18
THAIS (Massenet) (It)
Thaïs: Corucci
Athanael: Urízar
Nicias: Salvatti

May 23 to June 8
Italian Dramatic Company
Alfredo Sainati

June 17
Symphonic Concert (Homage to
Carmelo Calvo)
Conductor: Vicente Pablo
Soloists: Aldabe <pf>, Chiolo
<vn>, Valles <cl>
Uruguayan National Anthem
Beethoven: Overture Leonora
no. 3
Bach: Violin Concerto
Busoni: Clarinet Concertino
Chopin: Andante and Polonaise
op. 22
Fabini: Campo
Wagner: Overture to Rienzi

RUSSIAN BALLET SEASON
Pavley-Oukranisky Russian
Ballet Company
June 20 to July 3
Conductor: Fively Schmid
Dancers: Dagmara, Elisius,
Nemeroff, Oukranisky, Pavley

July 4 to 15
Italian Comedy Company
Antonio Gandusio

**GRAND ITALIAN OPERA
SEASON**
Walter Mocchi and Company
Impresario
July 18 to 25
Season Conductor: Vincenzo
Bellezza
Guest Conductors: Emil Cooper
and Alceo Toni
Director: Mario Sammarco

July 18
Uruguayan National Anthem
LA TRAVIATA (Verdi)
Conductor: Toni
Violetta: Dalla-Rizza
Alfredo Germont: Minghetti
Giorgio Germont: Damiani

July 19
LA FORZA DEL DESTINO (Verdi)
Leonora: Muzio
Don Alvaro: Crimi
Don Carlo: Damiani
Preziosilla: Besanzoni
Marchese di Calatrava: Pasero

July 20, 23
BORIS GODUNOV (Musorgsky)**
Conductor: Cooper
Boris Godunov: Zalewsky
Xenia: Shereshevkaya
Feodor: Schouvaloff
Nurse of Xenia: Gramegna
Prince Vassili: Wesselovsky
Andrei Shchelkalof: Melnikoff
Pimen: Griff
Grigory: Bielina
Marina: Koshetz
Missail: Lavretzky
Varlaam: Zaporojetz
Hostess of the Inn: Jabovich
The Simpleton: Nardi

July 21
MADAMA BUTTERFLY (Puccini)
Cio-Cio-San: Dalla-Rizza
Pinkerton: Minghetti
Suzuki: Gramegna
Sharpless: Melnikoff
Goro: Nardi
Yamadori: De Vecchi
Bonzo: Fiore

July 22
LORELEY (Catalani)
Loreley: Muzio
Walter: Crimi
Herrmann: Damiani
Anna di Rehberg: Gramegna
Rudolfo: Fiore

July 24
ANDREA CHENIER (Giordano)
Maddalena de Coigny: Dalla-Rizza
Andrea Chénier: Fleta
Carlo Gérard: Damiani

July 25
MEFISTOFELE (Boito)
Margherita: Zamboni
Elena: Koshetz
Faust: Minghetti
Mefistofele: Zalewsky

July 26 (5.30 P.M.)
Symphonic Concert
Conductor: Bellezza
Beethoven: Symphony no. 1
Pick-Mangiagalli: Notturno e
rondo fantastico
Wagner: Prelude and Liebestod
from Tristan und Isolde
Verdi: Overture to La forza del
destino

July 26, 27, 28, 29
Poetry Recitals: Berta Singerman

July 30 to Aug 18
Spanish Dramatic Company
Enrique Borrás

SPANISH ZARZUELA SEASON
Amadeo Vives, Impresario
Aug 19 to Sept 8
Conductors: Francisco Palos and
Amadeo Riera
Director: Amadeo Vives

Aug 19 to Sept 3 (17
performances)
DOÑA FRANCISQUITA (Vives)**

Aug 22 to 28 (5 performances)
BOHEMIOS (Vives)**

Aug 29, 31
BOHEMIOS (Vives)
MARUXA (Vives)**

Aug 30
EL DUQUESITO (Vives)**

Sept 3
Uruguayan National Anthem
Italian Royal March
Gala Performance to honor
Prince Umberto di Savoia
Vives: Prelude to Maruxa
DOÑA FRANCISQUITA (Vives)

Sept 4 to 7
EL BARBERILLO DE LAVAPIES
(Barbieri)
DOÑA FRANCISQUITA (Vives)

Sept 8
DON LUCAS DEL CIGARRAL
(Vives)**

FRENCH OPERETTA SEASON
Marcel Castrix Operetta
Company
Sept 17 to 28

Sept 17, 20 (matinée)
LA MASCOTTE (Audran)

Sept 18, 21 (matinée), 25
LA-HAUT! (Yvain)**

Sept 19
LES MOUSQUETAIRES AU
CONVENT (Varney)

Sept 20
MADAME (Christiné)**

Sept 21, 28 (matinée)
LA FILLE DE MADAME ANGOT
(Lecocq)
Clairette: Syril

Sept 22
LE GRAND MOGOL (Audran)

Sept 23
L'AMOUR MASQUE (Messager)

Sept 24, 27 (matinée)
LAS CLOCHES DE CORNEVILLE
(Planquette)

Sept 26
CIBOULETTE (Hahn)**

Sept 27
LA FILLE DU TAMBOUR MAJOR
(Offenbach)

Sept 28
LE PETIT CHOC (Szule)**

Oct 2 to 12
Troupe Ateniense

Oct 15 to 19
Edmond de Bries <transformist>

Oct 25
Sociedad Orquestal del Uruguay
Concert
Conductor: Felipe Larrimbe
Soloists: Maza <s>, Pastorino
<t>, Sgarbi <t>, Schinca <bar>
All-Wagner program
Lohengrin: Prelude
Parsifal: Good Friday Spell
Meistersinger: Prelude

Tristan und Isolde: Prelude and liebestod
Der fliegende Holländer: Chorus

Nov 13
Children's Comedy Company

Nov 15 to 28
Italian Dramatic Company
Tatiana Pavlowa

Dec 3 to 31
Argentinean Comedy Company
Roberto Casaux

1925

Female artists
Acosta y Lara, Judith <s>
Anido, María Luisa <gui>
Anitúa, Fanny <mez>
Barsanti, Emma <mez>
Corchs, María Delia <s>
Corucci, Zoraida <s>
Dalla-Rizza, Gilda <s>
Fálleri, Agar <pf>
Fantuzzi, Emma <mez>
Francillo-Kauffman, Hedwig <s>
Garinska, Lydia <s>
Gramegna, Anna <a>
Hayes, Louise <s>
Lampaggi, Maria Luisa <mez>
Pangrazi, Rosalia <mez>
Revalles, Flora <s>
Salvi, Margarita de <s>
Scacciati, Bianca <s>
Simzis, Olga <s>
Vitulli, Thea <s>

Male artists
Aguirre, Pedro <bn>
Ansaldi, Pablo <bar>
Arcelli, Umberto <b>
Barbacci, Carlo <bar>
Borgatti, Giuseppe <t>
Brailowsky, Alexander <pf>
Cairo, Giovanni <b>

Cassia, Vincenzo <b>
Cavalotti [Enrique Bosch] <t>
Cirino, Giulio <b>
Corallo, Giovanni <t>
Crabbé, Armand <bar>
Cristalli, Italo <t>
Dente, Domingo <pf>
Fabini, Eduardo <pf/c>
Figueras, Luis <vc>
Freixas, Arturo <bar/b>
Granforte, Apollo <bar>
Guasqui, Augusto <b>
Larralde, Pedro <hn>
Llobet, Miguel <gui>
Marinari, Alejandro <ob>
Martínez, V. <bar>
Minghetti, Angelo <t>
O'Sullivan, John <t>
Pasero, Tancredi <b>
Risler, Edouard <pf>
Rodríguez, Abelardo <gui>
Romay, Luis <t>
Russo, Francisco <fl>
Savorini, Mario <t>
Sous, Roberto <pf>
Tomassini, Gustavo <t>
Urízar, Marcelo <bar>
Valles, José <cl>
Venturino, Francisco <bar>
Viviani, Gaetano <bar>
Zannoli, Guido <b>

Jan 2 to 6
Argentinean Comedy Company
Roberto Casaux

Jan 8 to Feb 3
Argentinean Dramatic Company

Feb 21 to March 1
Carnival Masked Balls

FALL ITALIAN OPERA SEASON

Antonio Chechi, Impresario
April 11 to 26
Conductor: Arturo De Angelis
Director: Renato Salvati

April 11, 12 (matinée), 19
RIGOLETTO (Verdi)
Gilda: Vitulli
Il Duca di Mantova: Cavalotti
Rigoletto: Urízar
Maddalena: Pangrazi
Giovanna: Fantuzzi
Sparafucile: Cairo
Monterone: Arcelli
Mateo Borsa: Savorini
Conte Ceprano: Zannoli

April 12
AIDA (Verdi)
Aida: Corucci
Amneris: Lampaggi
Radamès: Corallo
Amonasro: Urízar
Ramfis: Ansaldi

April 13, 16, 20, 26 (matinée)
LA BOHEME (Puccini)
Mimì: Simzis
Musetta: Acosta y Lara
Rodolfo: Borgatti
Marcello: Ansaldi
Colline: Guasqui

April 14, 18, 25
LOHENGRIN (Wagner) (It)
Lohengrin: Cristalli
Elsa di Brabante: Simzis
Ortruda: Lampaggi
Federico di Telramondo: Ansaldi
Enrico: Guasqui (2) / Cairo(1)
L'araldo del Re: Freixas

April 15, 17, 19 (matinée), 24
LA TRAVIATA (Verdi)
Violetta: Corucci
Alfredo Germont: Borgatti
G. Germont: Urízar(2) /
Ansaldi(2)
Gastone: Savorini
Flora: Fantuzzi
Barone Douphol: Martínez
Marchese D'Obigny: Barbacci
Dottore Grenvil: Arcelli

April 21, 26
THAïS (Massenet) (It)
Thaïs: Corucci
Athanael: Urízar
Nicias: Cristalli

April 22
CARMEN (Bizet) (It)
Carmen: Barsanti
Micaela: Vitulli
Don José: Romay
Escamillo: Urízar

April 23
IRIS (Mascagni)
Iris: Simzis
Osaka: Cristalli

April 25
Gala performance to honor
Albert Einstein
LOHENGRIN (Wagner) [same cast
as April 14]

April 26 (6.30 P.M.)
CAVALLERIA RUSTICANA
(Mascagni)

May 9
Recital: Francillo-Kauffman <s>,
Dente <pf>
Works by Buzzi, Verdi, Rossini,
Cilea, Schubert, Schumann,
Ponchielli, Wagner, and Denza

May 12, 14, 16, 17
Berta Singerman: Poetry Recitals

May 22, 24, 28
Recitals: Llobet <gui>
Works by Rubinstein, Sors, J. S.
Bach, Costa, Albéniz, Granados,
Schubert, and Tárrega

May 23, 25, 30, 31, June 13, 14
Recitals: Risler <pf>
Works by Couperin, Rameau,
Daquin, Schubert,

Mendelssohn, Mozart,
Beethoven, Chopin, Schumann,
Debussy, Saint-Saëns,
Tchaikovsky, and Liszt

May 31
Beethoven Recital: Risler <pf>
Sonatas op. 26, op. 27, no. 2,
op. 53; op. 111

June 9 to 15
Chinese Magic Company Li-Ho-
Chang

June 16 to 21
Fatima Miris <transformist>

June 22 to 25
English Dramatic Company
P. H. Lloyd Davidson

June 24, 27 (6:30 P.M.)
Recitals: Llobet and Anido <gui-
duet>

**EGYPTIAN OPERETTA
PERFORMANCES**
Operetta Company Naguib
Rihani
June 26 to 28

June 26
DER BARBER VON BAGDAD
(Cornelius)

June 27
THE PRINCESS (?)

June 28
THE ADVENTURES OF KICH-KICH-
BEY (?)

July 4
Recital Música Pura Ensemble:
Fálleri <pf>, Valles <cl>,
Aguirre <bn>, Larralde <hn>,
Marinari <ob>, Russo <fl>

Hugues: Quartet in G Minor <fl
/ cl / bn / ob>
Beethoven: Quintet op. 16 <pf /
hn / bn / ob / cl>
Saint-Saëns: Caprice op.79 <pf /
fl / ob / cl>

July 11 to 27
Mexican Comedy Company
Lupe Rivas-Cacho

July 28 to Aug 7 (5.30 P.M.)
Nov 17 to 24
Italian Dramatic Company
Dario Niccodemi

Aug 7
Recital: Figueras <vc>, Fálleri
<pf>

**GRAND ITALIAN OPERA
SEASON**
Walter Mocchi and Company,
Impresario
Aug 11 to 25
Conductors: Edoardo Vitale, and
Alceo Toni (assistant conductor)

Aug 11, 15
AIDA (Verdi)
Aida: Scacciati
Amneris: Anitúa
Radamès: Tomassini
Amonasro: Viviani
Ramfis: Pasero

Aug 12
RIGOLETTO (Verdi)
Il Duca di Mantova: Minghetti
Rigoletto: Granforte
Maddalena: Gramegna
Sparafucile: Pasero

Aug 13
IL BARBIERE DI SIVIGLIA
(Rossini)
Rosina: Salvi
Conte di Almaviva: Minghetti

Figaro: Crabbé
Don Basilio: Cirino

Aug 14
Gala Performance to honor
H.R.H. The Prince of Wales
MADAMA BUTTERFLY (Puccini)
Cio-Cio-San: Dalla-Rizza
Suzuki: Gramegna
Pinkerton: Tomassini
Sharpless: Barbacci

Aug 16, 22
GLI UGONOTTI (Meyerbeer) (It)
Margherita de Valois: Salvi
Raul de Nangis: O'Sullivan
Valentina: Scacciati
Conte di Nevers: Crabbé
Conte di Saint Bris: Cirino
Il paggio: Garinska
Marcello: Pasero

Aug 18
LA TRAVIATA (Verdi)
Violetta: Dalla-Rizza
Alfredo Germont: Minghetti
Giorgio Germont: Granforte

Aug 19
SANSONE E DALILA (Saint-Saëns)
(It-Fr bilingual version)
Dalila: Anitúa
Sansone: O'Sullivan
Il sommo sacerdote: Cirino
Vecchio ebreo: Pasero
Abimélech: Barbacci

Aug 20
IL TROVATORE (Verdi)
Conductor: Toni
Leonora: Scacciati
Manrico: Tomassini
Conte di Luna: Viviani
Azucena: Gramegna
Ferrando: Pasero

Aug 21
ORFEO (Gluck)**

Orfeo: Anitúa
Euridice: Hayes
Amore: Garinska

Aug 23
LA CENA DELLE BEFFE
(Giordano)**
Ginevra: Revalles
Giannetto Malaspini: Tomassini
Neri Chiaramantesi: Granforte
Tornaquinci: Pasero

Aug 24
MONNA VANNA (Février)
Conductor: Toni
Monna Vanna: Revalles
Prinzivalle: O'Sullivan
Guido Colonna: Crabbé
Marco Colonna: Cirino

Aug 25
Uruguayan National Anthem
MANON (Massenet) (It)
Manon: Dalla-Rizza
Des Grieux: Minghetti
Lescaut: Crabbé
Conte des Grieux: Pasero

Aug 27
Recital: Sous <pf>
Works by Mendelssohn,
MacDowell, Chopin, Paderewski,
and Liszt

Aug 29
Recital: Brailowsky <pf>
Bach: Prelude and fugue in C-
sharp Major
Scarlatti: Pastorale e capriccio
Beethoven: Sonata op. 57
Chopin:
    a. Fantasia-Impromptu
    b. Ballade
    c. Three Etudes
    e. Polonaise in A-flat
Rachmaninoff: Prelude in G
Major
Scriabin: Etude

Musorgsky: The Seamstress
Liszt: Hungarian Rhapsody no. 6

Aug 30
Recital: Brailowsky <pf>
Works by Bach, Chopin, Weber,
Palmgren, Leschetitzky, Rimsky-
Korsakov, and Liszt

Sept 5 to 21
Italian Dramatic Company
Melato–Betrone

Sept 26 to Oct 1, 25 to Nov 6
Troupe Ateniense

Oct 3
Recital: Llobet <gui>

Oct 5 to 14
French Dramatic Company
Victor Francen–Germaine
Dermoz

Oct 23, Nov 7
Asociación Coral de Montevideo
Concert
Conductor: Eduardo Fabini
Soloists: Corchs <s>, Fabini
<pf>, Rodríguez <gui>

Dec 12 to 31
Argentinean Comedy Company
Roberto Casaux

1926

Female artists
Algozzino, Nini <mez>
Bianchi, Gina <s>
Braccony, Maria <s>
Carrara, Olga <s>
Corchs, María Delia <s>
Darmia, Gina
Galli, Gabriella <mez>
Gargano, Maria
Kaneline, Martha <mez>

Leman [de Quiroga], Marta <pf>
Leonard, Lotte <s>
Parigi, Margherita <s / mez>
Salvini, L. <mez>
San Marco, Rossana <s>
Saraceni, Adelaida <s>
Sasso, Rosina <s>
Tagliaferro, Magda <pf>
Vidach, Gina <s>
Weiss, Clara <s>

Male artists
Albanese, Mario <bar>
Amoros, Emilio <t>
Bernardi, Dante
Bertelli, Nino <t>
Borracelli, Giovanni <t>
Braccony, Roberto <bar>
Carnevale, Abele <b>
Cremonini, Guido
Damiani, Víctor <bar>
Della Guardia, Luigi
Evans, C. Warwick <vc>
Fabini, Eduardo <pf>
Favi, Gaspare
Ferroni, Luigi <b>
Furlay, Gino
Gargano, Olimpo
Gatti, M. <bar>
Levey, James <vn>
Melandri, Antonio <t>
Miselli, Manfredo
Moiseiwitsch, Benno <pf>
Pavia, A. <t>
Quiroga, Manolo <vn>
Romaniello, Aldo <pf>
Rubinstein, Artur <pf>
Sempere, Vicente <t>
Serpo, A. <bar>
Tagliabue, Carlo <bar>
Turolla, Enrico
Venturino, Francisco A. <bar>
Virgo, Edwin <vn>
Warner, H. Waldo <vla>

Jan 3 to 10
Argentinean Comedy Company
Roberto Casaux

Jan 11 to 22
Li-Ho-Chang <magician>

Jan 23, 30
Orquesta Nacional Concerts
Conductor: Luis Sambucetti [The
last time Sambucetti conducted;
he died on September 7, 1926.]
Beethoven: Symphony no. 6
Galli:
  a. Lontananza
  b. Toccata in D Major
Ascone: Preludio y Marcha de
los Bramines from "Malini"
[conducted by the composer]
Tchaikovsky: 1812 Overture

Jan 26 to Feb 5
Li-Ho-Chang <magician>

Feb 6 to 11
Music Hall Company from
Buenos Aires

Feb 13 to 21
Carnival Masked Balls

March 6 to May 28
Spanish Dramatic Company
Concepción Olona–Pedro
Codina

May 8
Recital: Tagliaferro <pf>
Beethoven: Sonata op. 26
Bach: Organ Concerto
Chopin:
  a. Scherzo no. 1
  b. Two Etudes
  c. Waltz
Poulenc: Trois mouvements
perpétuels
Villalobos: O Polichinelo
Mompou: Muchachas en el
jardín
Granados: Danza
Falla: El amor brujo

May 13, 20, 29, July 14, 17, 28
Recitals: Moiseiwitsch <pf>
Works by Bach, Beethoven,
Brahms, Palmgren, Musorgsky,
Chopin, Falla, Rachmaninoff,
Debussy, and Liszt

May 15
Recital: Tagliaferro <pf>
Works by Bach, Schubert,
Chopin, Debussy, and Albéniz

June 1 to June 25
Spanish Dramatic Company
Plana–Díaz Baena
Director: Manuel Linares-Rivas

June 26, 27, July 6, 11
Recitals: Quiroga <vn>, Leman
<pf>

July 4
Recital: M. Quiroga <vn>,
Leman <pf>
Tartini: Sonata in G Minor
Lalo: Symphonie espagnole
Weber: Larghetto
Dvořák:
  a. Indian Lament
  b. Slave Dance
Rimsky-Korsakov: Himne du
soleil
Paganini: Capricci nos. 20 and
24

July 24, 25, Aug 7, 8 (matinée)
Recitals: Rubinstein <pf>

July 29 to Aug 8
French Dramatic Company
Valentine Tessier–Jacques
Gretillat

July 31
Recital: Rubinstein <pf>
Chopin:
  a. Polonaise
  b. Two Mazurkas

c. Nocturne
d. Scherzo op. 39
Debussy:
a. La Cathédrale engloutie
b. Poissons d'or
c. Hommage à Rameau
d. Ondine
e. L'isle joyeuse
Albéniz: Suite Iberia

Aug 14, 15
Recitals: Quiroga <vn>, Leman
<pf>

**WINTER ITALIAN OPERA
SEASON**
Segreto, Bonacchi, and Pierligi,
Impresarios
Aug 17 to Sept 8
Conductors: Federico Del
Cupolo, and Silvio Pierligi
(assistant conductor)

Aug 17, Sept 3
AIDA (Verdi)
Aida: Carrara
Amneris: Galli
Radamès: Sempere
Amonasro: Tagliabue
Ramfis: Ferroni
Il Re: Carnevale

Aug 18, 24
MANON (Massenet) (It)
Manon: Saraceni
Des Grieux: Bertelli
Lescaut: Albanese
Bretigny: Serpo
Guillot: Pavia
Conte des Grieux: Carnevale

Aug 19, 28
UN BALLO IN MASCHERA (Verdi)
Amelia: Carrara
Riccardo: Melandri
Renato: Tagliabue
Ulrica: Kaneline

Aug 20 (matinée)
Spanish Music Recital:
Rubinstein <pf>
Works by Albéniz, Granados,
Turina, Mompou, and Falla

Aug 20, 22 (matinée)
MEFISTOFELE (Boito)
Margherita: Sasso
Faust: Bertelli
Mefistofele: Ferroni
Elena: Sasso

Aug 21, 29 (matinée), Sept 7
RIGOLETTO (Verdi)
Gilda: Saraceni
Il Duca di Mantova: Sempere
Rigoletto: Tagliabue(2) /
Damiani(1)
Maddalena: Algozzino
Giovanna: Parigi
Sparafucile: Carnevale
Monterone: Serpo
Contessa Ceprano: Salvini
Marullo: Gatti
Borsa: Pavia

Aug 22
IL TROVATORE (Verdi)
Leonora: Carrara
Manrico: Sempere
Conte di Luna: Albanese
Azucena: Galli
Ferrando: Carnevale
Ruiz: Pavia
Ines: Parigi

Aug 23, Sept 5 (matinée)
LA TRAVIATA (Verdi)
Violetta: Saraceni
Alfredo Germont: Melandri
G. Germont: Albanese(1) /
Venturino(1)

Aug 25
Uruguayan National Anthem
LA GIOCONDA (Ponchielli)
Gioconda: Carrara

Laura: Galli
La cieca: Algozzino
Enzo Grimaldo: Melandri
Barnaba: Tagliabue
Alvise Badoero: Ferroni

Aug 26, 29
CARMEN (Bizet) (It)
Carmen: Galli
Don José: Sempere
Escamillo: Tagliabue

Aug 27
MANON LESCAUT (Puccini)
Manon: Carrara
Des Grieux: Melandri
Lescaut: Albanese
Geronte de Revoir: Carnevale

Aug 30, Sept 8
TOSCA (Puccini)
Tosca: Carrara
Mario Cavaradossi: Melandri
Scarpia: Albanese(1) / Damiani(1)

Aug 31
LOHENGRIN (Wagner) (It)
Elsa di Brabante: Sasso
Lohengrin: Sempere
Ortruda: Galli
Federico di Telramondo:
Tagliabue
Enrico: Ferroni
L'araldo del Re: Serpo

Sept 1
FAUST (Gounod) (It)
Margherita: Saraceni
Faust: Bertelli
Mefistofele: Ferroni
Valentin: Albanese
Siebel: Algozzino
Marta: Parigi
Wagner: Serpo

Sept 2
CAVALLERIA RUSTICANA
(Mascagni)

Santuzza: Sasso
Turiddu: Bertelli
Lola: Parigi
Alfio: Albanese
Mamma Lucia: Salvini
PAGLIACCI (Leoncavallo)
Nedda: Sasso
Canio: Sempere
Tonio: Damiani
Silvio: Serpo
Arlecchino: Gatti

Sept 4
IL GUARANY (Gomes)
Cecilia: Saraceni
Pery: Melandri
Gonzalez: Albanese
El cacico: Ferroni
Don Antonio de Mariz:
Carnevale
Don Alvaro: Pavia
Ruy Bento: Gatti
Alonso: Serpo

Sept 5
ANDREA CHENIER (Giordano)
Andrea Chénier: Sempere
Maddalena de Coigny: Carrara
Carlo Gérard: Damiani

Sept 6
LA BOHEME (Puccini)
Mimì: Sasso
Musetta: Parigi
Rodolfo: Bertelli
Marcello: Albanese

LONDON STRING QUARTET
SEASON
Levey <vn>, Virgo <vn>,
Warner <vla>, Evans <vc>
Aug 27 to Sept 12

Aug 27 (matinée)
Haydn: Quartet op. 64, no. 5
Debussy: Quartet op. 10
Beethoven: Quartet op. 50, no. 1

Aug 28 (matinée)
Mozart: Quartet in D Minor
Borodin: Nocturne
Scontrine: Menuetto
Dvořák: Quartet op. 96

Sept 4 (matinée)
Schumann: Quartet op. 41, no. 3
Bridge: Londonderry Air
Kreisler: Scherzo
Beethoven: Quartet op. 18, no. 2

Sept 5 (6:30 P.M.)
Haydn: Quartet op. 76, no. 3
Borodin: Quartet no. 2
Schubert: Quartettsatz
Waldorf: Peter Pan Suite
    a. Peter's Lullaby
    b. Peter's Glad Heart

Sept 11, 12
London String Quartet Last
Recitals

Sept 14
Gala Concert to Homage
Eduardo Fabini
Sociedad Orquestal del Uruguay
and Asociación Coral de
Montevideo
Conductors: Carlos Correa-Luna
and Eduardo Fabini
Soloists: Corchs <s>, Fabini <pf>
All-Fabini program
Campo, symphonic poem
La isla de la ceibos****
Triste, for orchestra
El Rancho, chorus
A mi río, chorus

Sept 15 to Oct 13
Spanish Dramatic Company
Antonia Plana–Emilio Díaz
Director: Federico García-Lorca

Sept 17
Lieder Recital: Leonard <s>,
Romaniello <pf>

Works by Bach, Handel,
Schubert, R. Strauss, and
Pfitzner

Sept 18
Lieder Recital: Leonard <s>,
Romaniello <pf>
Lieder by Gluck and Haydn
Schumann: Frauenliebe und
-leben
Old English Minstrel Songs

Sept 21, 22, 23, 25, Oct 10, 12, 14
Lectures: Federico García-
Sanchiz

Oct 15 to 29
Italian Dramatic Company Italia
Almirante

Oct 30 to Nov 23
Argentinean Comedy Company
Roberto Casaux

ITALIAN OPERETTA SEASON
Clara Weiss Italian Operetta
Company
Dec 11 to 31 (20 performances)
Conductors: Lamberto Baldi and
Ernesto Mogavero
Directors: Guido Agnoletti,
Roberto Braccony
Choreographer: Ginevra
Pratolongo

Dec 11
MEDI (Stoltz) (It)**
and the following works until
Dec 31
[no other information available]
SCUGNIZZA (Costa)**
L'ORLOFF (Granichtaedten) (It)**
LA DANZA DELLA LIBELULLE
(Lehár) (It)
AMORE UNGHERESI (Krausz)
(It)**
MARIETTA (Stoltz) (It)**
DUE PER UNO (J. Gilbert) (It)**

PAGANINI (Lehár) (It)**
SILHOUETTE (Bellini)**
LA PRINCIPESSA OLA-LA! (Fall)
(It)**
KATYA LA BALLERINA (J. Gilbert)
(It)**
BERGERETTE (Ferrarese)**
CANTATRICE DELLA STRADA
(Fall) (It)**
SELVAGGIA (Bellini)**
SOGNO IN RIVIERA (Stoltz) (It)**
THERESINA (J. Gilbert) (It)**

1927

Female Artists
Agostinelli, Adelina <s>
Aldabe, María Luisa <pf>
Bruel [de Elizalde], Andrée <s>
Corchs, María Delia <s>
Iris, Esperanza <s>
Morton, Lily <a>
Tellez de Mendoza, Julieta <s>
Vega, Marta de la <s>
Yéregui-Lerena, Ema <pf>

Male artists
Ansaldi, Pablo <bar>
Arcelli, Umberto <b>
Backhaus, Wilhelm <pf>
Baños, Avelino <vc>
Braga, Ernani <pf>
Chiolo, Oscar <vn>
Cluzeau-Mortet, Luis <vla>
Correa-Luna, Carlos <vn>
Fiammengo, Rómulo <vn>
Fischerman, Jacobo <pf>
Gardel, Carlos <folk / tango
singer>
Hermelin, Arthur <pf>
Iturbi, José <pf>
Milstein, Nathan <vn>
Pablo, Vicente <pf>
Palacios, Armando <pf>
Romaniello, Aldo <pf>
Schinca, Luis <bar>
Schipa, Tito <t>

Segú, José <pf>
Sgarbi, Luis <t>
Spivak, Raúl <pf>
Tabanelli, Pietro <t>
Valles, José <cl>

Feb 26 to March 6
Carnival Masked Balls

SPANISH SAINETE SEASON
[folk farces and comedies]
Rogelio Juárez–San Juan Spanish
Sainete Company
March 11 to May 8, April 1 to 24
Folk songs by Gardel <folk /
tango singer>

**SYMPHONIC CONCERT
SERIES**
Beethoven Centennial
Celebrations
Orquesta Nacional Concerts
Conductor: Vicente Pablo
April 18 to May 14 [see also Sept
6]

April 18
Soloist: Aldabe <pf>
Symphony no. 1, in C Major
Piano Concerto no. 4
Symphony no. 2, in D Major

April 30
Egmont Overture
Symphony no. 4, in B-flat Major
Symphony no. 3, in E-Flat
Major

May 7
Overture Leonora no. 3
Symphony no. 6 ("Pastoral")
Symphony no. 5, in C Minor

May 12
Soloists: Segú <pf>, Chiolo
<vn>, Baños <vc>
Symphony no. 8, in F Major

Triple Concerto in C Major
Symphony no. 7, in A Major

May 14
Soloist: Aldabe <pf>
Symphony no. 3, in E-flat Major
Piano Concert no. 4
Symphony no. 5, in C Minor

May 18, 19, 22
Recitals: Milstein <vn>,
Hermelin <pf>

May 21, 25
Recitals: Backhaus <pf>
Works by Bach, Beethoven,
Schumann, Chopin,
Debussy, Mozart, Smetana, Liszt,
Musorgsky, and Delibes

May 28
Beethoven Recital: Backhaus <pf>
Sonatas op. 53; op. 27, No. 2,
op. 13, op. 57

June 2
Chopin Recital: Backhaus <pf>

June 5, 9, 12, 18, 19
Recitals: Czech String Quartet
Zika

June 24
Beethoven Centennial
Celebrations
Asociación Uruguaya de Música
de Cámara
Chiolo <vn>, Correa-Luna
<vn>, Cluzeau-Mortet <vla>,
Baños <vc>, Pablo <pf>
Trio op. 70, no. 1
Sonata op. 47 ("Kreutzer")
String quartet op. 59, no. 1

June 25 to Sept 8
Spanish Dramatic Company
Pedro Codina

July 26
Symphonic Concert
Conductor: Virgilio Scarabelli
Soloist: Yéregui-Lerena <pf>
Rimsky-Korsakoff: Symphony
no. 3
Tchaikovsky: Piano Concerto
no. 1
Rabaud: Egloga
Wagner: Overture to Tannhäuser

Aug 3
Beethoven Centennial
Celebrations
Asociación Coral de Montevideo
Concert
Conductor: Carlos Correa-Luna
Soloists: Corchs <s>, Correa-
Luna <p>

Aug 6, 13
Recitals: Milstein <vn>,
Hermelin <pf>

Aug 10
Recital: Schipa <t>, Romaniello
<pf>
Pergolesi: Nina
Scarlatti: La violetta
Massenet: Il sogno, from Manon
Schipa: Ave Maria
Franck: Panis Angelicus
Liszt-Schipa: Sogno d'amore
Massenet: Ah! non mi ridestar,
from Werther
Debussy: La mandoline
Paladilhe: Suzanne
Padilla: Princesita
Lacalle: Amapola
Esparza-Oteo: Mi viejo amor
Tagliaferri:
   a. Piscatori e Pasile
   b. Mandulinata a Napoli
Barthelmy: Cui se me acorda
ebia

Aug 12
Lieder Recital: Bruel <s>, Spivak
<pf>

Aug 20
Recital: Iturbi <pf>

Aug 23
Albéniz Recital: Iturbi <pf>

**WINTER OPERA
PERFORMANCE**
Conductor: Bruno Mari
Aug 24
DON PASQUALE (Donizetti)
Norina: Agostinelli
Ernesto: Tabanelli
Don Pasquale: Arcelli
Dottore Malatesta: Ansaldi

Aug 25, Sept 3
Rossini Concerts
Coral Palestrina and orchestra
Conductor: Domingo Dente
Uruguayan National Anthem
Overture to Il barbiere di
Siviglia
Overture to Guglielmo Tell
Stabat Mater

Sept 1
Recital: Palacios <pf>
Works by Bach, Chopin, Falla,
and Debussy

Sept 6, 7
Beethoven Centennial
Celebrations
Asociación Coral de Montevideo
chorus
Conductor: Vicente Pablo
Chorus Master: José Segú
Soloists: Corchs <s>, Morton
<a>, Sgarbi <t>, Schinca <bar>
Beethoven: Symphony no. 9, in
D Minor

Sept 9 to 16
French Dramatic Company Vera
Sergine

Sept 17 to 26
Raymond <magician>

Sept 24
Lecture and Recital on Russian
Music: R. Soriano <lecturer>, J.
Fischerman <pf>

Oct 1 to 4
Motion Picture Showings with
performers:
Esmé Davis <d>, Buddie
<comic>

Oct 6 to 16, 18 to 20 (matinée)
Troupe Ateniense

Oct 20, 21, 22
Beethoven Centennial
Celebrations
Trio in B-flat, op. 11
Sonata op. 24 ("Spring Sonata")
String Quartet op.18, no.9, in G
Major [same artists as June 24]
plus J. Valles <cl>

Oct 23
Brazilian Music Recital
Tellez de Mendoza <s>, E.
Braga <pf>
Vocal works by Nepomuceno,
Francisco Braga, Glauco
Velasquez, Felix Otero, Barrozo
Neto, Paolo Florence, Homero
Barreto, Guy D'Auberval,
Luciano Gallet, I. Octaviano,
Lorenzo Fernandez, and
Villalobos
Piano works by Henrique
Oswald, Nepomuceno, Barrozo
Neto, Villalobos, and Ernani
Braga

Oct 25 to Nov 3
Spanish Dramatic Company
Pedro Codina

MEXICAN VAUDEVILLE AND OPERETTA SEASON
Esperanza Iris Company
Nov 4 to 28

Nov 4, 5, 6
KISS-ONE (Clará) (Sp)

Nov 7
LA PRINCESA DE LAS CZARDAS
(Kálmán) (Sp)

Nov 8
LA MOZA DE CAMPANILLAS
(Luna)

Nov 9, 17, 18, 19 (6
performances)
KISS-ME (Clará) (Sp)

Nov 10 to 20 (9 performances)
LOVE-ME (Clará, Font, and
Olvadora) (Sp)

Nov 14
Uruguayan National Anthem
La Marseillaise
In honor of French pilots Costes
and Le Brix
CHIC REVUE (Potpourri)

Nov 16 to 20 (6 performances)
YES-YES (Clará) (Sp)

Nov 18 to 23
ZIG-ZAG (Potpourri) (Sp)

Nov 19, 26 (both midnight)
LA REVUE DE FOLIES (Potpourri)
(Sp)

Nov 20 (3.45 P.M.)
CHIC-REVUE (Potpourri) (Sp)

Nov 20 (6.50 P.M.)
NOUVELLE REVUE (Potpourri)
(Sp)

Nov 21, 27 (9.30 P.M.)
LA DUQUESA DEL BAL TABARIN
(Bard) (Sp)

Nov 22
LA PRINCESA DEL DOLAR (Fall)
(Sp)

Nov 23, 27 (6.30 P.M.)
ZIG-ZAG (Potpourri) (Sp)
JOY-JOY (Clará) (Sp)

Nov 24
LA CASA DE LAS TRES NIÑAS
(Schubert) (Sp)

Nov 25 (6.30 P.M.)
Lecture on Operetta
Presentation for ladies only

Nov 25 (9.30 P.M.)
EL CONDE DE LUXEMBURGO
(Lehár) (Sp)

Nov 26 (9:00 P.M.) 27 (3.30
P.M.)
LA VIUDA ALEGRE (Lehár) (Sp)

Nov 28
SANGRE DE ARTISTA (Eysler)
(Sp)

Dec 3
Beethoven Centennial
Celebrations
[same artists as June 24]
Serenade op. 8 <vn/vla/vc>
Sonata op. 30, no. 3 <vn/pf>
String quartet op. 18, no. 1

Dec 4
Recital: Vega <s>

Dec 9
Beethoven Centennial
Celebrations
[same artists as June 24]
Trio op. 70 <pf/vn/vc>

Sonata op. 5, no. 2 <pf/vc>
String Quartet op. 18, no. 6

Dec 10
Classical Dance Festival
Dance Mistress: Miss Agnes

Dec 17 and 18
National Comedy Company

1928

Female artists
Corchs, María Delia <s>
Del Campo, Sofía <s>
Fálleri, Agar <pf>
García-Quintana, Amanda <s>
Igarzábal de Chiesa, Blanca <s>
Morton, Lily <a>
Peñagaricano, Celia <pf>

Male artists
Arrau, Claudio <pf>
Beltrán, Señor <pf>
Damiani, Víctor <bar>
Dente, Domingo <pf>
Fabini, Eduardo <pf>
Gandós, Rodolfo <bar>
López-Macía, Raúl <t>
Magnan, Charles <pf>
Manén, Juan <vn>
Orloff, Nikolai <pf>
Ruffo, Titta <bar>
Salmon, Roger <vn>
Segovia, Andrés <gui>
Sykora, Bogumil <vc>
Uninsky, Alexandre <pf>
Zecchi, Carlo <pf>

Feb 18 to 26
Carnival Masked Balls

March 1 to 30, April 18 to May
6, May 30 to June 11
Hortensia Zamora Spanish
Dramatic Company
Director: Francisco Villaespesa

March 31 to April 17
National Dramatic Company
Blanca Podestá

April 14
Recital: Arrau <pf>
Scarlatti: Two Sonatas
Bach: Two Preludes and Fugues
Chopin:
  a. Ballade
  b. Nocturne
  c. Deux études
  d. Scherzo
Sauguet: Françaises
Busoni: Fantasie aprés Carmen
Liszt:
  a. Etude in F
  b. Mephisto Waltz

April 20, 26, 29 (11:00 A.M.)
Recitals: Sykora <vc>, Fálleri
<pf>
Works by Haydn, Piatti, Mulert,
Sykora, Fabini, and Boellmann

April 21
Recital: Arrau <pf>
Brahms: Variations on a
Paganini Theme
Chopin:
  a. Polonaise Fantasie
  b. Tarantelle
  c. Impromptu
  d. Mazurka
  e. Scherzo in B Minor
Debussy:
  a. Minstrels
  b. Mouvement
  c. Au bord d'une source
Balakirev: Islamey

April 28
Recital: Arrau <pf>
Bach: Partita in G
Beethoven: Two rondos
Liszt: Sonata
Ravel: Ondine
Debussy: Feux d'artifice

Stravinsky: Petrushka (three
movements)

May 6 (11:00 A.M.)
Recital: Arrau <pf>
Bach: Fantasia in C Minor
Mozart: Rondo in D Major
Haydn: Fantasia
Scarlatti: Two Sonatas
Chopin: Sonata op. 58
Schubert: Impromptu
Mendelssohn: Scherzo a
capriccio
Liszt:
  a. Les Jeux d'eau à la Villa
     d'Este
  b. Etude in C Minor
  c. Valse mélancolique
Balakirev: Islamey

May 7
Sociedad Coral Uruguaya
Concert
Conductor: Vicente Pablo
All Eduardo Fabini Works
Campo, symphonic poem
Choral works:
  a. El arroyo
  b. A mi río
La isla de los ceibos

May 8 to 20, June 26 to July 11
Italian Dramatic Company
Menichelli–Migliari–Pescatori

May 11, 17, 26, June 30
Recitals: Uninsky <pf>
Works by Bach, Tausing,
Scarlatti, Brahms, Chopin,
Rachmaninoff, Prokofiev,
Debussy, and Liszt

May 18
Chopin Recital: Uninsky <pf>

May 21, 28
Sociedad Filarmónica de

Montevideo Concert
Conductor: Vicente Pablo
Beethoven: Overture to Fidelio
Franck: Le chausseur maudit**
Pick-Mangiagalli: Notturno e
rondo fantastico
Rabaud: Procession nocturnelle
Chabrier: España

May 22 to 27
National Memorial Homage to
playwright Florencio Sánchez
Performances of all his plays

May 28
Asociación Coral de Montevideo
Concert
Conductor: Carlos Correa-Luna
Soloist: Corchs <s>
All Eduardo Fabini Works

June 9, 10, 16, 23
Recitals: Orloff <pf>

June 22
Recital: Manén <vn>

July 5, 10, 12, Aug 10, 15
Recitals: Segovia <gui>
Works by Bach, Sors, Haydn,
Tchaikovsky, Moreno-Torroba,
Tárrega, Turina, Granados, and
Albéniz

July 13 to Aug 8
Spanish Dramatic Company
Ernesto Vilches

Aug 10 to 23 (6.30 P.M.)
Italian Dramatic Company
Dario Niccodemi

Aug 16, 26 (6:30 P.M.), 30, Sept
26, 27, 29
Spanish Dance Company
Tórtola Valencia

**ORQUESTA FILARMONICA
DE BUENOS AIRES**
Conductor: Clemens Krauss
Aug 23, 24, 25

Aug 23
Concert-Gala Performance
Schubert: Symphony no. 8
("Unfinished")
Fabini: La isla de los ceibos
Ravel: Rhapsodie espagnole
Beethoven: Symphony no.7, in A

Aug 24
Concert-Gala Performance
Debussy: Prélude à L'Après-midi
d'un faune
San Martino: Scherzo
Mozart: Serenade
Beethoven: Symphony no. 6
("Pastorale")
Wagner:
a. Good Friday Spell
b. Prelude to Die Meister-
singer

Aug 25
Concert-Gala Performance
Uruguayan National Anthem
Juan J. Castro: La Chellah
Cortinas: Prelude from La
Ultima Gavota
Fabini: Campo
Beethoven: Symphony no. 3
("Eroica")
Wagner:
a. Prelude from Lohengrin
b. Tannhäuser Overture

Aug 26, Oct 13
MESSA DA REQUIEM (Verdi)
Coral Palestrina and orchestra
Conductor: Domingo Dente
Soloists: García-Quintana <s>,
Morton <a>, López-Macía <t>,
Chiesa <s>, Gandós <bar>

Aug 27 to Sept 5
Motion Picture Showings

Sept 6 to 23
André Rotoucheff Music Hall
and Varieté Company

Sept 8
Recital: Corchs <s>, Damiani
<bar>, Fabini <pf>, Beltrán <pf
accompanist>
Works by Giordano, Fabini,
Verdi, and Leoncavallo

Sept 11, 14
Lieder Recitals: Del Campo <s>,
Magnan <pf>
Works by Paisiello, Gluck,
Rimsky-Korsakov, Mozart,
Dardenne, Grieg, Fabini,
Gounod, Subercasseaux,
Valderrama, Gomes, Brahms,
Schubert, Granados, and
Cluzeau-Mortet

Sept 15
Recital: Zecchi <pf>
Scarlatti:
a. Menuetto
b. Giga
c. Sonata in A Major
Bach-Busoni: Toccata in C
Major
Franck: Prelude, aria, and finale
Castelnuovo-Tedesco: Le danze
del Re David op.37 (1) Violento
e impetuoso (2) Ierático (3)
Rapido e salvatico (4) Lento e
sognatore (5) Ritmico (6)
Adagio (7) Allegro barbaro
Paganini-Liszt: Trois etudes

Sept 22, 25, 29
Recitals: Del Campo <s>,
Damiani <bar>, Sept. 22,
Magnan <pf accompanist>;
Sept. 25 and 29 Dente <pf
accompanist>
Works by Fabini, Verdi,
Schumann, Musorgsky, and
Mozart; Denza, Gounod,

Mendelssohn, Verdi, Falla,
Fabini, and Leoncavallo;
Gounod, Mozart, Massenet,
Boito, Thomas Rachmaninoff,
Beethoven, and Leoncavallo

Oct 2 to 23
National Dramatic Company
Matilde Rivera–Enrique de
Rosas–Eva Franco

Oct 23
Recital: Zecchi <pf>
Works by Vivaldi-Bach, Scarlatti,
Chopin, Mozart, and Liszt

Oct 24 to 29
Motion Picture Showing

TITTA RUFFO RECITAL
Héctor Gandós, Impresario
Oct 31
Ruffo <bar>, Salmon <vn>,
Peñagaricano <pf>, Dente <pf
accompanist>
Vitale: Chacona <vn/pf>
Paladilhe: Excerpts from Patrie
Billi: Canta il grillo (canzone
Toscana)
Pagamucci: Gitano Re
Bruch: Adagio
Sarasate: Aires bohemios
Thomas: Excerpts from Amleto
Pérez-Soriano: El guitarrico
Broggi: Vizione veneziana

Nov 3 to 11
Spanish Dramatic Company
Catalina Bárcena
Director: Gregorio Martínez-
Sierra

SPANISH ZARZUELA SEASON
Nov 14 to Dec 15
Conductor: Felipe Torres

1929

Female artists

Aguilar, Elisa <lute>
Aldabe, María Luisa <pf>
Anday, Rosette <mez>
Anido, María Luisa <gui>
Asroff, Raisa <s>
Bonetti, Lucia <mez>
Cattaneo, Giannina <s>
Corchs, María Delia <s>
Davidoff, Maria <mez>
Ehler, Alice <hpd>
Gjebina, Mlle. <d>
Herrera de Rius, María <pf>
Juárez, Nena <mez>
Karnizka, Maria <a>
Kondaky, Maria <s>
Kusnezoff, Maria <s>
Landowska, Wanda <hpd / pf>
Lareu, Ema <s>
Lareu, Teresa <pf>
Leman [de Quiroga], Marta <pf>
Martínez-Law, Marta <s>
Morton, Lily <a>
Novikova, Anna <s>
Olivieri-Sangiacomo [Respighi], Elsa <s>
Poplavskaya, Mlle. <d>
Quincke de Bergengruen, Erna <pf>
Rasa, Lina Bruna <s>
Rolando, Sara B. de <s>
Sayão, Bidú <s>
Scheitler, Celia Margarita <pf>
Stapran, Ana <mez>
Tikanova, Antoinette <mez>
Torres, Carmen <mez>
Varacomini, Nieves <mez>

Male artists

Aguilar, Ezequiel <lute>
Aguilar, Paco <lute>
Aguilar, Pepe <lute>
Alsina, Juan <b>
Amadei, Luis <vc>
Baranda-Reyes, Santiago <pf>
Baridón, J. P. <vn>
Baydaroff, Nicolai <t>

Brancciatto, Vittorio <b>
Bresciani, Mario <vn>
Bustamante de Camargo, José <t>
Castelli, Angel <cl>
Chiolo, Oscar <vn>
Cluzeau-Mortet, Luis <vla>
Crabbé, Armand <bar>
De Franceschi, Enrico <bar>
Dente, Domingo <pf>
Doucet, Clément <pf>
Dubrovsky, Georges <bar>
Fabini, Eduardo <vn>
Feller, Carlos <b>
Friedman, Ignaz <pf>
Gandós, Rodolfo <bar>
Gitovsky, Michel <b>
Granforte, Apollo <bar>
Guaglianone, Víctor <vc>
Iturbi, José <pf>
Janopoulo, Tasso <pf>
Journet, Marcel <b>
Jukovich, Constantin <b>
Kiepura, Jan <t>
Kranz, Naum <vn>
Lavretzky, Nicolai <t>
Llobet, Miguel <gui>
Melnikoff, Nicolai <bar>
Milstein, Nathan <vn>
Mirassou, Pedro <t>
Moiseiwitsch, Benno <pf>
Muzio, Attilio <b>
Nardi, Luigi <t>
Nicastro, Oscar <vc>
Oksansky, Alexander <b>
Pablo, Vicente <pf>
Piotrovsky, Kiprian <t>
Quiroga, Manolo <vn>
Respighi, Ottorino <pf>
Sainz de la Maza, Regino <gui>
Sdanovsky, Eugene <b>
Solari, Christi <t>
Taneeff, Serge <d>
Thill, Georges <t>
Tretiakoff, Mr. <t>
Vecsey, Ferenc de <vn>
Wiener, Jean <pf>

Feb 9 to March 1
Carnival Masked Balls

March 2 to May 15
Mexican Dramatic Company
María Teresa Montoya

March 14, 16, 21
Modern Dance Company
Russell Meriwether–Hugues ("La Meri")

April 6
Recital: Morton <a>, Gandós <bar>, Dente <pf>
Works by Scarlatti, Verdi, Falla, Wolf, Donizetti, and Usiglio

April 11
Recital: E. Lareu <s>, T. Lareu <pf>
Works by Respighi, Ravel, Rimsky-Korsakov, Fabini, Cluzeau-Mortet, Mondino, Chausson, and Turina

April 13, 16, 20, 25
Recitals: Moiseiwitsch <pf>
Works by Bach, Schubert, Beethoven, Brahms, Chopin, Debussy, Wagner-Liszt, Prokofiev, Stravinsky, Rachmaninoff, Moskowski, Palmgrem, Falla, Chopin, and Liszt

April 30
Asociación Uruguaya de Música de Cámara
Chamber Recital in Homage of César Cortinas: Chiolo <vn>, Kranz <vn>, Cluzeau-Mortet <vla>, Amadei <vc>, Pablo <pf>
Cortinas works:
Poema <pf quintet>
Sonata in D Major <vn/pf>
Sonata in B Minor <vc/pf>

May 4, 9, 11, June 1
Recitals: Iturbi <pf>
Works by Bach, Beethoven, Mozart, Schumann, Chopin,

Liszt, Brahms, Ravel, Albéniz, Stravinsky, Poulenc, and Falla

May 16
Recital: Bustamante de Camargo <t>, Torres <mez>, D. Dente <pf>

May 17 to 27
Troupe Ateniense

May 18, 26
Spanish Music Recitals: Iturbi <pf>
Works by Granados, Falla, Albéniz, Navarro, and Infante

May 21
Recital: Milstein <vn>, Janopoulo <pf>
Vivaldi: Concerto in C
Corelli: La follia
Bruch: Concerto in G minor
Debussy:
    a. En bateau
    b. Minstrels
Falla: Nana
Sarasate: Capricho vasco

May 25, 28
Recitals: Sainz de la Maza <gui>
Works by Handel, Bach, Tárrega, Moreno-Torroba, Albéniz, Turina, López-Chavarri, Granados, and Falla

May 30
Recital: Milstein <vn>, Janopoulo <pf>
Handel: Sonata in D Major
Desplanes-Natchez: Intrata
Pugnani-Kreisler: Prelude-Allegro
Tartini: Trillo del diavolo
Schubert: Rondo
Schumann: Nocturnal Song
Sarasate: Concert fantasy on Carmen

June 2 (6.30 P.M.), 5
Recitals: Llobet <gui>

June 2 to 9
Fu-Man-Chu <magician>

June 4, 12
Recitals: Franceschi <bar>, Dente <pf>
Excerpts from Zazà, Pagliacci, Tannhäuser, Re di Lahore, Un ballo in maschera, Nerone, Il barbiere di Siviglia, and Schumann's Lieder

June 6
Recital: Milstein <vn>, Janopoulo <pf>
Friedman-Bach: Grave
Bach:
    a. Presto
    b. Chaconne for solo violin
Franck: Sonata in A
Chopin: Nocturne
Kreisler: Tambourin chinois
Wieniawsky: Polonaise

June 8
Recital: Milstein <vn>, Janopoulo <pf>
Vivaldi: Concerto in C Major
Mozart: Rondo
Mendelssohn: Concerto in E Minor
Brahms: Hungarian Dance no. 17
Gluck: Melody
Paganini: Capriccio no. 24

June 11
Recital: Milstein <vn>, Janopoulo <pf>
Chausson: Poème
Debussy:
    a. En bateau
    b. Minstrels
Fauré: Après un rêve
L. Boulanger: Cortège
Ravel: Berceuse

Falla:
    a. Nana
    b. Jota from La Vida breve
Sarasate: Capricho vasco

June 13, 15
Recitals: Landowska <hpd / pf>
Harpsichord works by Bach, Pachelbel, and Dandrieu
Piano works by Mozart, Couperin, Scarlatti

June 14 to July 7
Argentinean Dramatic Company Luis Arata
Director: Armando Discépolo

June 18
Albéniz Recital: Iturbi <piano>
Suite Iberia

June 20, 22
Recitals: Vecsey <vn>
Works by Handel, Pugnani-Kreisler, Ravel, Mendelssohn, Vecsey, Paganini-Liszt, Tartini, Bach, Tchaikovsky, Debussy, and Paganini

June 25, 27
Recitals: Moiseiwitsch <pf>

June 26
Recital: Landowska <hpd / pf>, Milstein <vn>
Mozart: Sonata in A Major <vn / hpd>
Bach: Concerto Italiano <hpd>
Mozart: Sonata in E Minor <vn / pf>

June 29, July 11
Recitals: Friedman <pf>

July 1, 8 (6:00 P.M.)
Jazz Recitals: The Virtuosi of Jazz (French piano duet Wiener and Doucet)
Works by J. S. Bach, Gershwin,

J. Strauss, and jazz
improvisations

July 2, 5
Chopin Recitals: Friedman <pf>

July 8 to 12
German Dramatic Company
Paul Wegener

July 9
Recital: Landowska <hpd/pf>,
Milstein <vn>

July 13 to 21
French Dramatic Company
Maurice de Féraudy

July 16, 18, 22, 30, Aug 4 (11:00
A.M.), 15
Recitals: Quiroga <vn>, Leman
<pf>

July 23 to Aug 1
Neapolitan Dramatic Company
Raffaele Viviani

July 24, 26, 28
Eva Paci <poetic recitals>

GUARNIERI STRING QUARTET
SERIES
July 25 to Aug 14

July 25
Mozart: Quartet in D Minor
Beethoven: Serenade op. 8 (trio)
Borodin: Quartet in D Minor

July 27
Haydn: Quartet in G Major
Blumenfeld: Sarabande
Ivanoff: Intermezzo
Tchaikovsky: Scherzo
Beethoven: Quartet op. 59, no.
2, in E Minor

Aug 3, 14 (6:30 P.M.)
Last Guarnieri String Quartet
recitals

July 29
Recital: AUMC [same artists as
April 30 except Bresciani <2nd
vn>]
Works by Brahms, Cluzeau-
Mortet, Tchaikovsky

Aug 2 to 6
Amalia de Isaura Spanish Dance
Company

FRENCH OPERETTA SEASON
Georges Milton French Operetta
Company
Aug 7 to 15

Aug 7
COMTE OUBLIE (Moretti)

Aug 8
QUAND ON EST TROIS . . . (Szulc)

Aug 9, 10 (matinée)
UN BON GARÇON (Yvain)

Aug 10, 11 (matinée)
ELLE EST A VOUS (Yvain)

Aug 11
LULU (Parés and Parys)

Aug 12
PASSIONEMENT (Messager)

Aug 13
COSSE DE RICHE (Yvain)

Aug 14, 15 (matinée)
DESHABILLE-VOUS (Mercier)

Aug 16 to 21
Italian Dramatic Company
Ruggero Ruggeri

Aug 22
Sociedad Orquestal del Uruguay
Conductor: Vicente Pablo
Soloists: Quiroga <vn>,
Fabini<vn>
Beethoven: Overture Leonora,
no. 3
Quiroga: Concerto alla antica
(vn / str)
J. S. Bach: Concerto for two
violins
Fabini:
   a. Fantasia**** Soloist: Qui-
      roga
   b. Triste no. 2
   c. La isla de los ceibos

GRAND ITALIAN OPERA
SEASON
Faustino Da Rosa, Impresario
Aug 23 to 26
Conductor: Franco Capuana

Aug 23
RIGOLETTO (Verdi)
Gilda: Sayão
Il Duca di Mantova: Kiepura
Rigoletto: Granforte
Maddalena: Juárez
Sparafucile: Feller

Aug 24
CARMEN (Bizet)
Carmen: Anday
Don José: Thill
Escamillo: Journet

Aug 25 (matinée)
IL BARBIERE DI SIVIGLIA
(Rossini)
Rosina: Sayão
Conte di Almaviva: Solari
Figaro: Crabbé
Don Basilio: Journet
Don Bartolo: Muzio

Aug 25
Uruguayan National Anthem

ANDREA CHENIER (Giordano)
Andrea Chénier: Thill
Maddalena de Coigny: Rasa
Carlo Gérald: Granforte
Bersi: Cattaneo
Contessa de Coigny: Bonetti

Aug 26
TOSCA (Puccini)
Tosca: Rasa
Mario Cavaradossi: Mirassou
Barone Scarpia: Granforte
Angelotti: Alsina
Il sagrestano: Muzio
Spoletta: Nardi
Sciarrone: Brancciatto

Aug 29
Recital: Fabini<vn>,
Quiroga<vn>, Leman<pf>
Works by Handel, Bach, Fabini,
Giucci, Sarasate, Quiroga, and
Wieniawsky

Aug 31
National Dramatic Company
Director: Miguel Víctor
Martínez

RESPIGHI–OLIVIERI CONCERTS
Sept 2 and 4

Sept 2
Recital: Olivieri-Sangiacomo<s>,
Respighi <pf>
Marcello: Il gelsomino
Caccini: Amarilli
Galuppi: Evviva rosa bella
(Respighi transcription)
Respighi songs:
  a. Notte
  b. Noël ancien
  c. Non, non é morto il figlio
     tuo
  d. La mamma
  e. Io sonno la madre
  f. Rispetto toscano
  g. Stornellatrice

h. Van gli efluvi delle rose
i. La najade
j. Sopra un'aria antica
Canti Populari
  a. Quando io vedo il moretto
     (Toscana)
  b. La bella baganai (Emilia)
  c. U'usignolo (Sardegna)
  d. Il maritimo (Piamonte)
  e. Caru cugnatu (Sicilia)
  f. Tarantella (Sicilia)

Sept 4
Conductors: Otorino Respighi
and Vicente Pablo
Soloists: Olivieri-
Sangiacomo<s>, Respighi<pf>
1. Toccata <pf / orch>**
Conductor: Pablo; soloist: the
composer
2. Il Tramonto, Lyric poem for
soprano and strings**
3. Liriche for soprano and piano
  a. Ballata (Boccaccio)
  b. Serenata Indiana (Shelley)
  c. Scherzo (Zangarini)
  d. Nebbie (Ada Aegri)
  e. Nevicatta
4. Antiche dance e aire per
liuto**
Conductor and pf: Respighi

Sept 3 to 11
Italian Dramatic Company
Ruggero Ruggeri

Sept 6, 10, 16
Recitals: Cuarteto de Laúdes
Aguilar <lute quartet> Elisa,
Ezequiel, Paco and Pepe Aguilar

Sept 12 to 23
Spanish Dramatic Company
Irene López Heredia

Sept 16
Spanish Music Recital: Laúdes
Aguilar

Sept 25, 26
Recitals: Llobet and Anido <gui-
duet>

Sept 26 (10 P.M.)
Berta Singerman <poetic recital>

Sept 28
Sociedad Orquestal del Uruguay
Conductor: Vicente Pablo
Soloist: Aldabe <pf>
Liszt: Les Preludes
Beethoven: Piano Concerto in C
Minor, op. 37
Weber: Invitation to the Dance
Wagner: Overture to Der
fliegende Holländer

Sept 30
Recital [same artists as July 29
except Quincke de Bergengruen
<pf>]
Works by Bridge, Pochon,
Schubert, and Beethoven

Oct 1
Recital: Ehler <hpd>
Works by Handel, Pachelbel,
Bach, Rameau, Couperin, and
Daquin

Oct 2
Recital [same artists as July 29
except Alice Ehler <hpd>]

Oct 3 to 9
Mexican Dramatic Company
María Teresa Montoya

Oct 5
Sociedad Orquestal del Uruguay
Conductor: Vicente Pablo
Soloists: Castelli <cl>, Amadei
<vc>, Scheitler <twelve-year-old
pf>, Baridón <vn>
Mozart: Overture to Le nozze di
Figaro
Massenet: Scènes alsaciennes

Mendelssohn: Piano Concerto in
G Minor
Saint-Saëns: Danse macabre
Tchaikovsky: 1812 Overture

Oct 8
Recital: Sainz de la Maza <gui>

**RUSSIAN OPERA AND
BALLET SEASON**
Privée Opera from Paris
Director: Madame Kusnezoff
Héctor Gandós, Impresario
Oct 11 to 23
Conductor: Gregoire Fittelberg
Directors: Michel Benois,
Theodor Komisargevsky, and
Nicolai Tcherny
Scenery: Nicolai Evreinoff
Principal Dancers: Gjebina,
Poplavskaya, Taneeff

Oct 11, 12, 13 (matinée>, 19
KNYAZ'IGOR' [Prince Igor]
(Borodin)
Igor Svyatoslavich: Melnikoff
Prince Galitzky: Sdanovsky
Khan Konchak: Gitovsky
Skula: Oksansky
Yeroschka: Lavretzky
Yaroslavna: Kusnezoff
Vladimir Igorevich: Baydaroff
A Polovtsian Maiden: Karnizka

Oct 13, 17
TSAR SALTAN [Tsare Saltane]
(Rimsky-Korsakov)
Tsar Saltan: Sdanovsky
Tsaritsa Militrisa: Novikova
Prince Guidon: Piotrovsky
Swan-Princess: Kondaky
Spinning Woman: Tikanova
Matchmaker-Crone Babarikha:
Davidoff
Old Grandpa: Lavretzky
Shipmaster: Jukovich
Messenger: Dubrovsky

Oct 15, 17 (matinée), 23
SOROCHINSKAYA YARMARKA
[Sorochintsy Fair] (Musorgsky)
Solopy Cherevik: Sdanovsky
Parasya: Kusnezoff
Khivrya: Davidoff
Grits'ko: Piotrovsky
A Gipsy: Jukovich
Kum: Dubrovsky
Afanasy Ivanovich: Lavretzky

Oct 16
KITEZH [Legend of the Invisible
City of Kitezh and the Maiden
Fevroniya] (Rimsky-Korsakov)
Fevroniya: Kusnezoff
Princeling Vsevolod Yur'yevich:
Baydaroff
Grishka Kuter'ma: Tretiakoff
Fyodor Poyarok: Melnikoff
Prince Yuri Vsevolodovich:
Gitovsky
Sirin: Novikova
Burunday: Dubrovsky
Bedyay: Oksansky

Oct 17 (5:00 P.M.)
SWAN LAKE (Tchaikovsky) and
SOROCHINSKAYA YARMARKA
[Sorochintsy Fair] (Musorgsky)

Oct 18, 20 (9:35 P.M.), 22
SNEGUROCHKA [The Snow
Maiden] (Rimsky-Korsakov)
Debushka-Snegurochka:
Kusnezoff
Vesna-Krasna [The Bonny
Spring]: Karnizka
Kupava: Asroff
Tsar Berendey: Piotrovsky
Bobïl'-Bakula: Lavretzky
Bobïlikha: Stapran
Cherevik: Jukovich
Lel', a Shepherd: Davidoff
Bermyata: Oksansky
Mizgir': Dubrovsky

Oct 20 (matinée)
SWAN LAKE (Tchaikovsky)

Divertissements
Prince Igor: Act 3

Oct 23
Divertissements
SOROCHINSKAYA YARMARKA
[Sorochintsy Fair] (Musorgsky)

Oct 24 to Dec 30
Argentinean Comedy Company
Luis Arata

**SPRING SOCIEDAD
ORQUESTAL SERIES**
with Asociación Coral chorus
Oct 26 to Dec 21

Oct 26
Conductor: Carlos Correa-Luna
Soloists: Guaglianone <vc>,
Corchs <s>
Mozart: Symphony in E-flat
Major
Debussy:
   a. Prélude à L'Après-midi
      d'un faune
   b. La demoiselle élue
Saint-Saëns: Cello Concerto
Chabrier: Bourrée fantastique**

Nov 9, 14
Recitals: Nicastro <vc>, Baranda-
Reyes <pf>
Works by Bruch, Martini,
Beethoven, Schubert, Nicastro,
Couperin-Kreisler, Chopin,
Popper, Musorgsky, Glazunov,
Handel, Corelli, Granados, and
Paganini

Nov 21
Débora Valiente <poetic recital>

Nov 23
Conductor: Virgilio Scarabelli
Haydn: Symphony no. 12, in B-
flat
Weber: Overture to Oberon

Rimsky-Korsakov: Sadko
Cortinas: Elegía fúnebre
Albéniz: Suite Catalonia**
Wagner:
    a. Siegfried Idyll
    b. Imperial March

Nov 28
Recital: [same artists as July 29
and Herrera de Rius <pf>]
Works by Brahms, Bergmann,
Ivanov, and Tchaikovsky

Dec 7
Conductors: Felipe Larrimbe and
Carlos Correa-Luna
Soloists: Martínez-Law <s>,
Rolando <s>, Varacomini <mez>
Calcavecchia: Pastorale, from
Bocetos uruguayos****
Wagner: Isolde's Liebestod
Puccini: Aria from Suor
Angelica
Thomas: Ofelia ballade from
Amleto
Soloist: Martínez-Law
Alfonso X El Sabio: Cantigas de
Santa María
Conductor: Larrimbe
Soloists: Rolando and
Varacomini

Dec 21
1. *Conductor*: Félix Peyrallo
Schubert: Overture to
Rosamunde
Rossini: Overture to Guglielmo
Tell
Gounod: Petite Marche
2. *Conductor*: José Segú
Liszt: Tasso
Grieg: Peer Gynt Suite
Saint-Saëns: Jota aragonaise
3. *Conductor*: Peyrallo
Wagner: Prelude to Lohengrin
Tchaikovsky: 1812 Overture

1930

Female artists
Aguilar, Elisa <lute>
Aldabe, María Luisa <pf>
Bizzozero, Esther <pf>
Corchs, María Delia <s>
Cuervas, Matilde <gui>
Efron, Natalia <s>
Fiesel, Margarita <s>
García, Marta <s>
Gianelli, Elvira <pf>
Giucci, Esther <pf>
Igarzábal de Chiesa, Blanca <s>
Morton, Lily <mez>
Novaes, Guiomar <pf>
Oliveri, Gilda <pf>
Pereira-Montalvo, Dolly <pf>
Quincke de Bergengruen, Erna
<pf>
Ramírez, María Luisa <s>
Reyles, Alma <s>
Rodríguez-Dutra, Marina <s>
Schumann, Elisabeth <s>
Spendiarova, Helena <s>

Male artists
Aguilar, Ezequiel <lute>
Aguilar, Paco <lute>
Aguilar, Pepe <lute>
Albasinoff, Wassily <b>
Alwin, Karl <pf>
Bresciani, Mario <vn>
Britt, Horace <vc>
Bykoff, Nicolai <b>
Casco, Juan <vn>
Chaliapin, Feodor <b>
Chiolo, Oscar <vn>
Cluzeau-Mortet, Luis <pf>
Damiani, Víctor <bar>
De Giuli, Augusto <t>
Denis, Germán <t>
Dente, Domingo <pf>
Echeverry, Venancio <b>
Elinson, Iso <pf>
Ferreira, José Pedro <vn>
Ferreira, Pedro <gui>
Gandós, Rodolfo <bar>

Giucci, Carlos <pf>
Guaglianone, Víctor <vc>
Janopoulo, Tasso <pf>
Kumok, Herman <pf>
Labrocca, Antonio M. <vn>
Luzzatti, Arturo <pf>
Martínez-Oyanguren, Julio <gui>
Mondino, Luis <pf>
Noviliansky, Nicolai <t>
Pujol, Emilio <gui>
Ramis, Cesáreo <vla>
Rebagliatti, Héctor <t>
Rodríguez, Abelardo <gui>
Rummel, Walter <pf>
Rumneff, Alexandre <bar>
Sacharoff, Gregori <b>
Sainz de la Maza, Regino <gui>
Strnad, Josef <harp>
Thibaud, Jacques <vn>
Zecchi, Carlo <pf>

Feb 27 to March 9
Carnival Masked Balls

March 14 to 23
Doctor Javier <Chilean
hypnotist and telepath>

March 27 to May 19
National Dramatic Company
Carmen Casnell–Santiago Arrieta

April 5, 9
Dance Recitals: C. Strnad <d>/
Strnad <harp>

April 10
Sociedad Orquestal Concert
Conductor: Félix Peyrallo
Beethoven: Symphony no. 5
Weber: Overture to Euryanthe
Wagner: Prelude and Isolde's
Liebestod
Liszt: Hungarian Rhapsody no. 2

April 26, May 3, 15, 17
Recitals: Elinson <pf>
Works by Bach, Beethoven,

Chopin, Schubert, Musorgsky, Liszt, Popoff, and Krjukoff

May 7, 23
Lieder Recitals: Reyles<s>, Cluzeau-Mortet<pf>
Works by Handel, Lully, Gretry, Bach, Ravel, Fauré, Roussel, Rimsky-Korsakov, Broqua, Mondino, Cluzeau-Mortet, Fabini, and López-Buchardo

May 19
Recital: Ramírez <s>, Damiani <bar>, Dente <pf>

May 20 to 26
Baron von Reinhalt <magician>

May 22
Recital: Martínez-Oyanguren <gui>

May 25
Gala Recital: Thibaud <vn>, Janopoulo <pf>
Eccles: Sonata
Corelli: La follia
Lalo: Symphonie espagnole
Beethoven: Romanza in F Major
Leclair: Tambourin
Desplanes: Menuet
Mozart: Rondo

DON COSSACK CHORUS CONCERTS
Don Cossack Chorus "Platoff"
May 27 to June 9 (8 performances)
Chorus Master: Nicolai Kostrukoff

June 5 to 11
Film Documentaries on Spain

June 10, 14, 18
Recitals: Thibaud <vn>, Janopoulo <pf>

June 11 to July 16
Argentinean Dramatic Company Blanca Podestá

June 16, 23, 26
Recitals: Cuarteto de Laúdes Aguilar <lute quartet> Elisa, Ezequiel, Paco and Pepe Aguilar

June 21, 24
Recitals: W. Rummel <pf>

June 28
Recital: Novaes <pf>
Works by Scarlatti, Gluck, Rameau, Chopin, Villa-Lobos, and Strauss-Godowsky

July 1
Chopin Recital: Novaes <pf>

July 2
Recital: Cluzeau-Mortet <pf> playing his own piano works

July 8, 10
Recitals: Sainz de la Maza <gui>

July 17 (5.30 P.M.)
Wally Zenner <poetic recital>

GALA CONCERT / RECITALS
[Celebration of Uruguay Constitution Centennial]
July 17 to Aug 3
Music Director and Conductor: Karl Alwin

July 17
Soloists: Schumann <s>, K. Alwin <c / pf>
Mozart:
   a. Aria from Il re Pastore
   b. Alleluia <s / orch>
Beethoven: Symphony no. 5
Schubert:
   a. Die Forelle
   b. Der Neugierige

   c. Wohin?
   d. Morgen
R. Strauss: Serenata <s / pf>
Wagner: Prelude to Die Meistersinger

July 18
Recital: Damiani <bar>

July 19
Recital: Schumann <s>, Alwin <pf>
Lieder by Mozart, Schubert, and Schumann
Puccini: Excerpts from La bohème

July 20
Recital: Schumann <s>, Alwin <pf>, Reyles <s>, Gianelli <pf>, Aguilar Brothers <lute quartet>, Mondino <pf>
I—Works for lute quartet
II—Lieder by Fauré, Cortinas, and Debussy <Schumann / Alwin>
III—Lieder recital of Uruguayan Music <Reyles / Gianelli>
IV—Mondino: Mar, poem for lute quartet and piano****
<composer and Aguilar Brothers>

Aug 3
Lieder Recital: Schumann <s>, Alwin <pf>
Works by Handel, Bach, Schubert, Brahms, and R. Strauss

July 22
Recital: Rodríguez-Dutra <s>, De Giuli <t>, Dente <pf>
Excerpts from Don Pasquale, Il barbiere di Siviglia, Faust, Mefistofele, La favorita, and La bohème

July 23
French Dramatic Company
André Brulé–Madeleine Lély

Aug 12 to 22
Troupe Ateniense

Aug 16, 22
Recitals: Britt <vc>, Luzzatti <pf>

Aug 19
Recital: Bizzozero <pf>

Aug 29
Asociación Coral Concert
Conductor: Carlos Correa-Luna
Soloists: Corchs <s>, Rebagliatti
<t>
Works by Rodríguez-Socas,
Franck, Fauré, Fabini, and
Handel

Sept 1, 19
Coral Palestrina Concert
Conductor: Domingo Dente
Soloists: I. de Chiesa <s>,
García <s>, Morton <mez>,
Denis <t>, Gandós <bar>,
Echeverry <b>

RUSSIAN OPERETTA AND DRAMA SEASON
Alexandre Tairoff Company
from Moscow's Theater
Kamerny
Sept 10 to 17
Cast: Efron, Spendiarova;
Noviliansky, Rumneff,
Albasinoff, Sacharoff, Bykoff

Sept 10
LE JOUR ET LA NUIT (Lecocq)

Sept 11, 15, 17
SALOME [drama] (Wilde)

Sept 13
GIROFLE-GIROFLA (Lecocq)

Sept 14, 16
GIROFLE-GIROFLA (Lecocq)
Russian Popular and Folk Songs

Sept 18
Recital: Bizzozero <pf>
Works by Scarlatti, Chopin,
Debussy, Villa-Lobos, Prokofiev,
Musorgsky, and Liszt

Sept 23, Oct 2
Recitals: Ferreira <gui>, Ferreira
<vn>, Oliveri <pf>

FEODOR CHALIAPIN RECITAL
Sept 24
Chaliapin <b>, Kumok <pf>
Rimsky-Korsakov: The Prophet
I—Voice and piano
Glinka: Midnight Revue
Grieg: The Swan
Dargominsky: Five Songs
Koeneman: When He Went to
War
II—Piano solo
Chopin:
  a. Mazurkas
  b. Ballade
III—Voice and piano
Mozart: Leporello's aria from
Don Giovanni
Musorgsky: Méphisthophélès'
Song of the Flea
Martini: Plaisir d'amour
Flogier: The Hunting Horn
Beethoven: In questa tomba
oscura
Rubinstein: Persian Song
Sakhnovsky: Death and Life
Tchaikovsky: The Night
Schumann: The Two Grenadiers
IV—Piano solo
Chopin:
  a. Etude
  b. Waltz
  c. Polonaise
V—Voice and piano
Karatyguine: Song of the
Prisoner
Koenemann-Chaliapin: Song of
the Volga Boatmen
Popular: Moskowite Song

Massenet: Elegie
Borodin: Khan Kontchak aria
from Prince Igor

Sept 25
Sociedad Orquestal Concert
Conductor: Vicente Pablo
Soloist: Orlandi <pf>
Fauré: Masques et bergamasques
Turina: Orgía, from Danzas
fantásticas
Grieg: Piano Concerto op. 16
Beethoven: Symphony no. 3
("Eroica")

Sept 26 to Dec 6
Argentinean Comedy Company
Luis Arata

Sept 29, Oct 4
Lieder Recitals
Reyles <s>, Cluzeau-Mortet <pf>
Works by Schubert, Brahms,
Pedrell, Falla, Breville, and
Debussy

Sept 30
Recital: Zecchi <pf>

Oct 8
Recital with Carlos Giucci works
Reyles <s>, E. Giucci <pf>,
Bresciani <vn>, Casco <vn>, C.
Giucci <pf>

Oct 11
Sociedad Orquestal Concert
Conductor: Vicente Pablo
Soloist: Q. de Bergengruen <pf>
Beethoven: Symphony no. 7
Schubert-Liszt: Fantasia op. 15
Weber-Berlioz: Invitation to the
Dance
Wagner: Overture to Tannhäuser

Oct 17, 19
Recitals: Pujol <gui>, Cuervas
<gui>

Works by Sanz, Sors, Broqua, Malats, Pujol, Bizet, Granados, and Falla

SACRED MUSIC CONCERTS SERIES
Oct 18, 21, 22, 25
Societá Polifonica Romana from Vatican's Sistine Chapel
Chorus master: C. Raffaele Monsignor Casimiri
Sacred music from the fifteenth and sixteenth centuries

Nov 21
Recital: Rodríguez <gui>

SOCIEDAD ORQUESTAL CONCERTS SERIES
Nov 8 to Dec 20

Nov 8
Asociación Coral de Montevideo
Conductor: Carlos Correa-Luna
Soloists: Fiesel <s>, Labrocca <vn>
Ribeiro: Symphony no. 2
Chabrier: Scènes lyriques <s/chorus>
Rimsky-Korsakov: Scheherazade

Nov 15
Asociación Coral de Montevideo
Conductor: Carlos Correa-Luna
Soloists: Fiesel <s>, Labrocca <vn>
Works by Wagner, Turina, Charpentier, Cluzeau Mortet, Sambucetti, Chabrier, and Borodin

Nov 22
Sponsored by SODRE
Conductor: Vicente Pablo
Soloist: Aldabe <pf>
Wagner: Prelude and Isolde's Liebestod
Mozart: Piano Concerto
Debussy: Petite suite

Rabaud: Procession nocturne
Dukas: L'apprenti sorcier

Dec 6
Sponsored by SODRE
Conductor: Vicente Pablo
Soloist: Pereira-Montalvo <pf>
Rimsky-Korsakov: Russian Easter Festival
Chopin: Andante Spianato and Polonaise op. 22
Dukas: L'apprenti sorcier
Sibelius: Valse triste
Brahms: Hungarian Dance
Wagner: Overture to Rienzi

Dec 20
Eduardo Fabini's orchestral and choral works, with Asociación Coral de Montevideo
Conductors: Virgilio Scarabelli and Eduardo Fabini
Soloists: Corchs <s>, Chiolo <vn>

1931

Female artists
Candini, Lea <s>
Casadesus, Gaby <pf>
Cobelli, Giuseppina <s>
De Bari, Tina <s>
Giani, Nélida (Nini) <mez>
Hols de Schusselin, Josefina <s>
Lareu, Ema <s>
Marengo, Isabel <s>
Morelli, Adelina <s>
Muller, María V. de <s>
Nastri, María <mez>
Vallin, Ninon <s>
Venturino, Elena <s>

Male artists
Ansaldi, Pablo <bar>
Baccaloni, Salvatore <b>
Bacciato, Vittorio (Nicola) <bar>

Brownlee, John <bar>
Calleja, Francisco <gui>
Casadesus, Robert <pf>
Denis, Germán <t>
Fattori, Mario <b>
Fuster, Joaquín <pf>
Galeffi, Carlo <bar>
Gallinal-Heber, Alberto <b>
Gaudin, André <bar>
Herz, Otto <pf>
Kipnis, Alexander <b>
Kubelik, Rafael <vn>
Marsiglia, Oscar <pf>
Masini, Galliano <t>
Orsini, Alfredo <t>
Ortiz de Taranco, Luis <bar>
Paseyro, Pedro <t>
Pauer, Max <pf>
Pina, Giuseppe <b>
Quintas-Moreno, Washington <pf>
Rodríguez, Carlos <t>
Sagi-Barba, Emilio <bar>
Schipa, Tito <t>
Thill, Georges <t>
Uninsky, Alexandre <pf>
Vela, Telmo <vn>

Jan 4
Sociedad Orquestal del Uruguay Concert
Conductor: Félix Peyrallo

Feb 7 to 28
Carnival Masked Balls

March 7 to May 31
National Dramatic Company
Carmen Casnell–Santiago Arrieta

March 26 (6.30 P.M.)
Recital: Uninsky <pf>
Bach: Prelude
Scarlatti: Two Sonatas
Chopin:
  a. Ballade in G Minor
  b. Two Mazurkas

c. Two Etudes
d. Scherzo in E Minor
Stravinsky: Petrushka

April 11
Sociedad Orquestal del Uruguay
Concert
Conductor: José Segú
Mozart: Overture to The Magic
Flute
Schubert: Symphony no. 4
("Tragic")
Beethoven: Septet op. 20
Calcavecchia: Overture
Grieg: Peer Gynt, Second Suite
Liszt: Hungaria, symphonic
poem

April 21
Recital: Uninsky <pf>
Schumann: Novelletten
Chopin:
a. Berceuse
b. Ballade in F Major
Liszt: Sonata in B Minor
Stravinsky: Etude
Debussy: La fille aux cheveux de
lin
Infante: El Vito

April 23, 26 (11:00 A.M.)
Recitals: Uninsky <pf>
Works by Scarlatti, Bach,
Beethoven, Chopin, Brahms,
Scriabin, Prokofiev, Albéniz,
Giucci, and Liszt

April 29
Sociedad Orquestal del Uruguay
Concert
Conductor: Benone Calcavecchia
Respighi: Fontane di Roma**
Fabini: Campo
Calcavecchia: La Leyenda Patria,
symphonic poem****

May 23 (6.30 P.M.)
Recital: Pauer <pf>

Bach: Prelude and Fugue
Beethoven: Sonata op. 81a ("Les
adieux")
Chopin:
a. Impromptu
b. Mazurka
c. Berceuse
d. Scherzo in B Minor
Debussy: Suite bergamasque
a. Prélude
b. Menuet
c. Clair de lune
d. Passepied
Liszt:
a. Funérailles
b. Sonetto del Petrarca
c. Hungarian Rhapsody no. 3

June 4
Beethoven Recital: Pauer <pf>
Sonatas: op. 31, no. 3; op. 27 no.
2 ("Moonlight"); op. 57 ("Appassionata")

June 5
Sociedad Orquestal del Uruguay
Concert
Conductor: Félix Peyrallo
Saint-Saëns: Suite de Henry VIII
Peyrallo: Las niñas de la fábula,
symphonic suite
Schubert: Unfinished Symphony

June 6
Farewell Recital: Pauer <pf>
Mendelssohn: Prelude and fugue
in E Minor
Scarlatti: Three Sonatas
Schumann: Symphonische
Etüden
Schubert:
a. Two Impromptus
b. Moment musical
Liszt: Polonaise in E

June 9
Recital: Calleja <gui>

Andino-Kreisler: Preludio y
mazurka
Tárrega: Danza
Moreno-Torroba: Sonatina
Bach: Allemande, minuet,
gavotte
Rebikoff: Happy Time
Borodin: Serenade
Chopin: Nocturne
Sors: Andantino
Schumann: Lullaby
Turina: Fandanguillo
Albéniz: Leyenda

June 10
Choral Concert with Vicente
Ascone works
Conductor: Vicente Ascone
Soloists: V. de Muller <s>,
Lareu <s>, Marsiglia <pf>, and
female chorus

June 11
Recital: Casadesus <pf>
Bach: Concerto Italiano
Beethoven: Sonata op. 57
("Appassionata")
Schumann: Papillons
Chopin: Fantasia op. 49
Séverac: Le retour des amis
Debussy: La soirée dans Grenade
Ravel: Alborada del gracioso

June 12
Recital: Calleja <gui>
Beethoven: Scherzo
Malats: Serenata
Albéniz:
a. Torre bermeja
b. Cádiz
Bach: Prelude, bourrée, and
courante
Moreno-Torroba: Burgalesa
Calleja: Tres preludios
Granados: Danza
Bacarisse: Pavana
Chopin: Mazurka

Mozart: Menuetto
Sors: Thème variée

June 13
Recital: Casadesus <pf>
Scarlatti: Six Sonatas
Schumann: Symphonische
Etuden
Chopin: Sonata op. 35
Debussy: Images
  a. Reflets dans l'ean
  b. Hommage à Rameau
  c. Mouvement

June 17 to July 16
Dramatic Company Pepita
Serrador–Narciso
Ibañez–Josefina Mari–Esteban
Serrador

June 18, 20, 25
Recitals: Kubelik <vn>, Herz
<pf>

July 8
Two-Piano Recital: R. and G.
Casadesus
Mozart: Sonata in D Major
Schumann: Andante and
Variations
Saint-Saëns: Variations on a
Theme of Beethoven
Chabrier: Trois valses
romantiques
F. Schmitt: Viennese rhapsodie

July 10
Recital: Casadesus <pf>
Rameau:
  a. Les niais de Sologne
  b. Le rappel des oiseaux
  c. Les Cyclopes
Beethoven: Sonata op. 81a ("Les
Adieux")
Chopin: Quatre Ballades
Ravel:
  a. Jeux d'eau

b. Toccata
c. Forlane

**SPANISH OPERA AND
ZARZUELA SEASON**
Emilio Sagi-Barba Company
July 17 to 31

July 17, 19 (6:30 P.M.)
EL JURAMENTO (Gaztambide)

July 18 (6:00 P.M.), 19 (matinée)
LA DEL SOTO DEL PARRAL
(Soutullo and Vert)

July 18 (9:00 P.M.), 20, 26
(matinée)
MARINA (Arrieta)

July 19
EL GUITARRICO (Pérez-Soriano)

July 21 (6:00 P.M.)
MOLINOS DE VIENTO (Luna)

July 21, 25 (9:30 P.M.), 26, 30, 31
LA ROSA DEL AZAFRAN (J.
Guerrero)

July 22
JUGAR CON FUEGO (Barbieri)

July 23
LOS CADETES DE LA REINA
(Luna)

July 23, 27
LA PARRANDA (Alonso)

July 24 (9:00 P.M.)
LA MEIGA (Guridi)

July 25 (6:30 P.M.)
MARUXA (Vives)

July 26 (9:30 P.M.)
LA TEMPESTAD (Chapí)

July 28, 30 (6:30 P.M.)
EL ANILLO DE HIERRO (Marqués)

July 29
LA DOLORES (Bretón)

July 24 (6:30 P.M.)
Recital: Vela <vn>, Fuster <pf>
Grieg: Sonata in C
Vela:
  a. Improvisación
  b. Habanera
Chopin: Nocturne
Mendelssohn: Rondo capriccioso
Chopin: Fantasia impromptu
Halffter:
  a. Danza de la pastora
  b. Danza de la gitana
  c. Sonatina
Esplá: Cuentos de antaño
Liszt: Napoli

July 31
Recital: Fuster <pf>
Works by Chopin, Esplá,
Mompou, Falla, Granados,
Turina, Albéniz, Debussy, and
Liszt

Aug 4 (6:30 P.M.)
Spanish Music Recital: Vela
<vn>, Fuster <pf>

UKRAINIAN CHORUS
PERFORMANCES
Aug 4 to 9 (eight performances)
Chorus master: Maestro Vorloff
Ukrainian Songs and Dances

GRAND OPERA SEASON
Aug 20 to Sept 6
Season Conductor: Arturo De
Angelis
Guest Conductors: Ferruccio
Calusio, Felipe Larrimbe, Aldo
Romaniello

Aug 20
IL BARBIERE DI SIVIGLIA
(Rossini)
Conductor: Larrimbe
Rosina: Venturino
Conte di Almaviva: Paseyro
Figaro: Ansaldi
Don Basilio: Fattori
Bon Bartolo: Gallinal

Aug 24
MANON (Massenet)
Conductor: Calusio
Manon: Vallin
Des Grieux: Thill
Lescaut: Gaudin

Aug 25
Uruguayan National Anthem
L'ELISIR D'AMORE (Donizetti)
Adina: Morelli
Nemorino: Schipa
Dulcamara: Baccaloni

Aug 26
Recital: Schipa <t>, Romaniello
<pf>
Cesti: Il lamento
Caccini: Amarilli
Pergolesi: Nina
Scarlatti: La violetta
Franck: Panis Angelicus
Rimsky-Korsakov: Chanson
Indoue from Sadko
Thomas: Ah, non credevi tu,
from Mignon
Flotow: M'appari, from Martha
Liszt-Schipa: Liebestraum
Benelli: Nina Nana (Berceuse
Veneziana)
Tosti-D'Annunzio: A vuchela
Tagliaferri:
    a. Mandulinata
    b. Napule

Sept 5
LA BOHEME (Puccini)
Mimì: Vallin

Rodolfo: Masini
Musetta: De Bari
Marcello: Brownlee
Colline: Fattori

Sept 6
RIGOLETTO (Verdi)
Gilda: Venturino
Il Duca di Mantova: Masini
Rigoletto: Galeffi
Maddalena: Giani
Sparafucile: Baccaloni

Aug 28
Recital: Vallin <s>, Romaniello
<pf>
Handel: Aria from Judas
Machabée
Mozart: Vedrai, carino, from
Don Giovanni
Blás de la Serna: Jilgerillo de
pico de oro
Bellini: Casta diva, from Norma
Fauré:
    a. Au bord de l'eau
    b. Nell
    c. La rose
Saint-Saëns: La cloche
Debussy:
    a. Green
    b. Fantoches
Nin: Cantos populares españoles
    a. Canción gallega
    b. Jota tortosina
    c. Canto andaluz
    d. Vito
    e. Paño murciano
    f. Polo

Aug 29, 30, Sept 11, 12, 14, 19,
Oct 17, 20, 22, 25
Lectures: Federico García-
Sanchiz

Aug 31
Dramatic Company Aaron
Walfish

Sept 8 to Oct 1
Spanish Dramatic Company
Pedro Codina

Oct 2 to 22
Argentinean Comedy Company
Florencio Parravicini

SPRING ITALIAN OPERETTA
SEASON
Oct 28 to Nov 2

Oct 28
FRASQUITA (Lehár) (It)
Frasquita: Candini

Oct 29
AMAMI ALFREDO (E. Bellini)
Cast: Candini; Orsini

Oct 30, Nov 1 (6:30 P.M.)
LA CASA DELLE TRE RAGAZZE
(Schubert) (It)

Nov 1, 2 (6:30 P.M.)
LUNA PARK (Ranzato)

Nov 2
L'ULTIMO VALSER (Strauss) (It)

Nov 6 to 8
National Dramatic Company
Pedro Becco–Teresa Lacanau

URUGUAYAN LYRIC COMPANY
Nov 9
TOSCA (Puccini)
Conductor: José Tomás Mujica
Tosca: Hols
Cavaradossi: Denis
Barone Scarpia: Ortiz de
Taranco

Nov 9 (6:30 P.M.) to Nov 16
National Dramatic Company
Carmen Casnell–Santiago Arrieta

Nov 16
Recital: Conjunto de Música de

Cámara del SODRE <string quartet> and Quintas-Moreno <pf>

Nov 17 to 29
Dramatic Company Francisco Bolla

Nov 20
Lieder Recital: Vallin <s>, Romaniello <pf>

Dec 8 to 11
Spanish Zarzuela Company Ibarra

Dec 23 to 31
Argentinean Comedy Company Luis Arata

1932

Female artists
Arata, Obdulia S. de <pf>
Cánepa, Noemí <s>
Maris, Margarita <s>
Massardi, Rina <s>
Musso, Wanda <s>
Quiroga, Ercilia <mez>
Siano, María <mez>
Turturiello, Nélida <s>
Vidal, Berta <mez>

Male artists
Alvarez, Aurelio <t>
Arrau, Claudio <pf>
Bianchi, Bartolomé <t>
Cuiñas, Julio <t>
Fattoruso, Luis <b>
Giammarchi, Luis <t>
Ibarra, Ignacio <bar>
Orloff, Nikolai <pf>
Rebagliatti, Héctor <t>

Jan 2 to 6
Dramatic Company Luis Arata

Feb 6 to 20
Carnival Masked Balls

Feb 27 and 28
Dramatic Company Leonidas Sakaloff

March 4 to May 2
Dramatic Company Carmen Casnell–Miguel Faust-Rocha

April 28
Recital: Arrau <pf>
Mozart: Rondo
Beethoven: Sonata op. 10, no. 3
Chopin:
    a. Ballade in A flat major
    b. 2 Studies
    c. Scherzo in B flat
Debussy:
    a. Danseuse de Delphos
    b. Jardins sous la pluie
Bartók: Allegro barbaro
Albéniz:
    a. El puerto
    b. Triana

May 3 to 18
Italian Company "Teatro dei piccoli" <puppet show>

May 12
Recital: Arrau <pf>
Beethoven: Sonata
Musorgsky: Pictures at an Exhibition
Liszt: Two Studies
    a. F minor
    b. Armonies du soir
Balakirev: Islamey

May 21 (6:30 P.M.)
Recital: Orloff <pf>
Scarlatti: Two Sonatas
Schumann: Symphonische Etüden
Chopin:
    a. Scherzo

b. Nocturne
c. Two Studies
d. Andante spianato and Polonaise brillante
Prokofiev: Toccata
Scriabin: Poem and Study
Rimsky-Korsakov: The Flight of the Bumblebee
Strauss-Tausig:
    a. Nocturne
    b. Papillon

May 21 to July 4
Dramatic Company Cooperativa teatral AETU

May 24
Recital: Orloff <pf>
Works by Beethoven, Chopin, Rachmaninoff, Ibert, and Strauss

July 12
Brazilian Music Recital
Musso <s>, S. de Arata <pf>

July 14
Dramatic Israeli Company Clara Friedman

July 15 to 24
Popular Music and Jazz Concerts Carlos Warren

NATIONAL LYRIC COMPANY
Aug 6 to 28
Conductor: César Augusto Metelli

Aug 6, 7, 9, 11, 14
IL TROVATORE (Verdi)
Leonora: Cánepa(2) /
Turturiello(3)
Manrico: Cuiñas(2) /
Giammarchi(3)
Conte di Luna: Ibarra
Azucena: Quiroga

Aug 7 (6:30 P.M.)
Operatic Recital: Maris <s>,
Vidal <s>, Siano <mez>,
Giammarchi <t>, Bianchi <t>,
Alvarez <t>, Rebagliatti <t>

Aug 13
RIGOLETTO (Verdi)
Gilda: Turturiello
Il Duca di Mantova:
Giammarchi
Rigoletto: Ibarra
Maddalena: Quiroga
Sparafucile: Fattoruso

Aug 24 to 28
MADAMA LYNCH (López-
Buchardo)
Argentinean Lyric Comedy
Company

Sept 20, 21
LUCIA DI LAMMERMOOR
(Donizetti)
Lucia: Massardi
Edgardo: Giammarchi
Enrico: Ibarra
Raimondo: Fattoruso

Aug 10 to 17
German Dramatic Company
Georg Urban

Sept 23 to Oct 23
Argentinean Dramatic Company
Paulina Singerman

1933

Female artists
Furettini, Tina <mez>
Maris, Margarita <s>

Male artists
Brailowsky, Alexandre <pf>
Denis, Germán <t>
Fattoruso, Luis <b>

Goldsand, Robert <pf>
Martínez, Ramón <b>
Nicastro, Oscar <vc>
Sgarbi, Luis <t>

SPANISH ZARZUELA SEASON
Bori—Palacios Company
Jan 1 to 22

Feb 3 to 20
Argentinean Music Hall
Company Rosita Contreras–
Mercedes Simone

Feb 25 to March 19
Carnival Masked Balls

NATIONAL LYRIC COMPANY
April 16, 18, May 13
MADAMA BUTTERFLY (Puccini)
Conductor: César Augusto
Metelli
Cio-Cio-San: Maris
Pinkerton: Denis
Suzuki: Furettini
Sharpless: Martínez
Bonzo: Fattoruso
Goro: Sgarbi

April 21 to 31
Brazilian Vaudeville Company

May 9, 11
Recitals: Goldsand <pf>
Vivaldi: Adagio
Scarlatti: Sonata
Mozart: Sonata in A Major
Chopin:
   a. 3 Studies
   b. Variations on a theme
      from Don Giovanni
Ravel: Sonatina
Palmgren: Raindrops
Stravinsky: Etude
Prokofiev: Gavota and toccata
Schoenberg: Piano piece op. 11,
no. 2
Breitenfeld: Study on octaves

SPANISH ZARZUELA SEASON
May 18 to June 21
Conductor: José Serrano

May 18
LA DOLOROSA (Serrano)**

June 30 to July 9
Italian Puppet Show Enrico
Novelli "Yambo"

July 14
Recital: Brailowsky <pf>
Bach: Overture from Cantata
no. 146
Scarlatti: Pastorale e capriccio
Beethoven: Sonata op. 27, no. 2
Chopin: Twelve Etudes from op.
10 and 25
Rachmaninoff: Prelude
Liapunoff: Leghinka
Ravel: Jeux d'eau
Liszt: Hungarian Rhapsody no. 2

July 21
Recital: Brailowsky <pf>

July 25
Recital: Guarnieri String Quartet
Debussy: Quartet
Glière: Variations from Quartet
in A Major
Tchaikovsky: Scherzo in B-flat
Minor
Ivanoff: Intermezzo
Taneiev: Scherzo
Beethoven: Quartet op. 59, no. 2

July 28 to Aug 25
Dramatic Company Concepción
Olona

Aug 26 to 31, Sept 23 to 27
French Dramatic Company
Germaine Dermoz

Sept 1
Recital: Nicastro <vc>

Sept 2 to 19
Dramatic Company Concepción
Olona

Sept 6, 7, 8
Irene de Noirel <Hungarian
Music Hall Company>

Sept 12
Antonia Mercé ("La Argentina")
Spanish Dance Company

Sept 26
Lecture by playwright Luigi
Pirandello

Oct 7 to 16
Music Hall Company

Oct 17 to Nov 20
Argentinean Dramatic Company
SETO

Nov 22 to Dec 11
Argentinean Musical Comedy
Co. from Buenos Aires' Teatro
Sarmiento

Dec 22 to 31
Argentinean Dramatic Company
Arata–Simari–Franco

1934

Female artists
Bértola, Amalia <mez>
Furettini, Tina <s>
Piave, Emilia <s>
Reyles, Alma <s>
Sebillo, Carmen <s>
Turturiello, Nélida <s>
Vitulli, Thea <s>

Male artists
Balli, Emilio <b>
Barbieri, Lorenzo <t>
Bellussi, Oliviero <t>

Fattoruso, Luis <b>
Heifetz, Jascha <vn>
Queralt, Eulogio <gui>
Rigazzi, Edmundo <bar>
Rosenthal, Moriz <pf>
Sgarbi, Luis <t>
Vales, José <t>
Villa, Joaquín <bar>

Feb 10 to March 4
Carnival Masked Balls

March 16 to 18
Lembranzas d'Ultreya Galician
Regional Ensemble with singers,
dancers, and bagpipe players

March 21 to April 16
Argentinean Music Hall
Company Rosita Contreras

April 16 to May 14
Spanish Dramatic Company
Guerrero–Díaz de Mendoza

FALL OPERA SEASON
National Lyric Company
May 17 to June 5
Conductor: César Augusto
Metelli

May 17, 19
AIDA (Verdi)
Aida: Piave
Radamès: Bellussi
Amneris: Bértola
Amonasro: Villa
Il Re: Fattoruso
Ramfis: Balli
Messagero: Sgarbi

May 18, 20 (matinée), 25
LA TRAVIATA (Verdi)
Violetta: Vitulli
Alfredo Germont: Vales
Giorgio Germont: Villa

Mayo 20, 23
IL TROVATORE (Verdi)
Leonora: Piave
Manrico: Bellussi
Conte di Luna: Rigazzi
Azucena: Bértola
Ferrando: Balli
Inez: Furettini
Ruiz: Sgarbi

May 22
TOSCA (Puccini)
Tosca: Piave
Mario Cavaradossi: Vales
Barone Scarpia: Rigazzi
Angelotti: Balli
Il sagrestano: Fattoruso
Spoleta: Sgarbi

May 24, 30
CAVALLERIA RUSTICANA
(Mascagni)
Santuzza: Piave
Lola: Bértola
Turiddu: Vales
Alfio: Rigazzi
PAGLIACCI (Leoncavallo)
Nedda: Vitulli
Canio: Bellussi
Tonio: Villa

May 26
RIGOLETTO (Verdi)
Gilda: Sebillo
Il Duca di Mantova: Barbieri
Rigoletto: Villa
Maddalena: Bértola
Sparafucile: Balli

May 31, June 2, 3 (matinée)
MADAMA BUTTERFLY (Puccini)
Cio-Cio-San: Piave
Pinkerton: Bellussi
Sharpless: Rigazzi

June 4
LA BOHEME (Puccini)
Mimì: Vitulli

Rodolfo: Vales
Musetta: Piave
Marcello: Villa
Schaunard: Rigazzi
Colline: Balli
Benoit: Fattoruso

June 5
IL BARBIERE DI SIVIGLIA
(Rossini)
Rosina: Vitulli
Conte di Almaviva: Vales
Figaro: Villa
Don Basilio: Balli
Don Bartolo: Fattoruso

May 19 (6:30 P.M.)
Recital: Queralt <gui>

June 23 to July 15
Spanish Dramatic Company
Aurora Redondo–Valeriano León

July 3
Recital: Heifetz <vn>
Vitalli: Chaconne
Lalo: Symphonie espagnole
Achron: Hebraic Melody
Schubert: Rondo
Debussy: La fille aux cheveux de
lin
Dinicu: Hora staccato
Falla: Jota
Mendelssohn: On the Wings of
a Song
Paganini: Capriccio no. 24

July 10, 25
Recitals: Heifetz <vn>

July 16, 17
German Dramatic Company
Ingolf Kuntze

Aug 24, 28
Recitals: Rosenthal <pf>
Works by Beethoven, Chopin,

Liszt, Scriabin, Schubert,
Rosenthal, and Strauss

Sept 2
Lieder Recital: Reyles <s>,
Turturiello <s>

Sept 4 to 9
German Dramatic Company
Riesch–Buhne

Sept 8 (6:30 P.M.)
Antonia Mercé ("La Argentina")
Spanish Dance Company

Sept 28 to Oct 7
Puppet Show from the Barnum
Circus

Oct 25 to Nov 11
Spanish Dramatic Company
Carmen Sanz–Juan Bonafé–
Teresa Senén

Nov 13 to Dec 2
Argentinean Dramatic Company
Camila Quiroga

Dec 4 to 25
Brazilian Musical Comedy Jardel
Jercolis

Dec 28 to 31
Spanish Musical Comedy
Company Alegría–Enhart

1935

Female Artists
Asencio, Cándida <s>
Faccioni, Pina <s>
Guerrito, Nina <s>
Sportelli, Victoria <s>

Male artists
Arrau, Claudio <pf>
Barreta, Andrés <bar>

Borowsky, Alexandre <pf>
Caiafa, Vincenzo <t>
Cantoni, Giuseppe
Furlai, Giovanni
Frutos, Luis Pascual <t>
Iturbi, José <pf>
Kreisler, Fritz <vn>
Lamond, Frederic <pf>
Lusso, Alberto
Moiseiwitsch, Benno <pf>
Rupp, Franz <pf>

Jan 2 to Feb 10
Spanish Musical Comedy
Company Alegría–Enhart

Feb 15 to 24
Wu-Li-Chang <magician>

March 2 to 8
Carnival Masked Balls

March 15 to April 1
Dramatic Company Blanca
Podestá

April 2 to May 12
Spanish Dramatic Company
Joaquín García Leon–Socorrito
Martínez–Manuel Perales

May 22
Chopin Recital: Moiseiwitsch
<pf>
Nine Preludes
Impromptu in A-flat Major
Nocturne in C Minor
Sonata op. 35
Seven Etudes op. 10 and 25

May 24
Recital: Moiseiwitsch <pf>
Beethoven: Andante "Favori"
Schumann: Etudes
symphoniques
Chopin:
    a. Ballade in F
    b. Deux Etudes

c. Berceuse
d. Polonaise in A-flat
Mendelssohn-Rachmaninoff:
Fantasy from A Midsummer
Night's Dream
Debussy:
a. La fille aux cheveaux de lin
b. Minstrels
Chassins:
a. Flirting in the garden
b. A Hasty time at Hong
Kong
Strauss-Godowing: Paraphrase of
Die Fledermaus

May 29
Recital: Kreisler <vn>, Rupp <pf>
Handel: Sonata in A
Bach: Chaconne (solo violin)
Mozart: Concerto no.4, in D
Schubert-Kreisler: Music from
Rosamunde
Kreisler: Variations on a Corelli
Theme
Debussy: La fille aux cheveaux
de lin
Albéniz: Malagueña
Kreisler:
a. Caprice Viennoise
b. Tambourin
chinois

June 5 (6:30 P.M.)
Recital: Kreisler <vn>, Rupp <pf>
Beethoven: Sonata Kreutzer
Mendelssohn: Concerto
Gluck-Kreisler: Melody
Mozart-Kreisler: Rondo in G
Major
Kreisler:
a. La chasse, caprice
b. Gypsy
c. Malagueña
d. Gypsy caprice

**SPANISH ZARZUELA AND
OPERA SEASON**
Andrés Barreta Company

June 2 to 16, Sept 25 to Oct 27
Director: Andrés Barreta with
Cándida Asencio and Luis
Pascual Frutos

June 2 (matinée and 9:00 P.M.)
ALMA DE DIOS (Serrano)
MARUXA (Vives)
DONNA JUANITA (Suppé) (Sp)

June 3 (matinée and 9:00 P.M.)
EL PUÑAO DE ROSAS (Chapí)
LOS CLAVELES (Serrano)
DONNA JUANITA (Suppé) (Sp)

June 4 (matinée and 9:00 P.M.)
BOHEMIOS (Vives)
GIGANTES Y CABEZUDOS
(Fernández-Caballero)

June 5 (9:00 P.M.)
LA ALEGRIA DEL BATALLON
(Serrano)
LA CANCION DEL OLVIDO
(Serrano)

June 6 (matinée and 9:00 P.M.)
EL HUESPED DEL SEVILLANO
(Guerrero)
DONNA JUANITA (Suppé) (Sp)

June 7
LA ROSA DEL AZAFRAN
(Guerrero)
LOS DE ARAGON (Serrano)

June 8 (matinée and 9:00 P.M.)
AVENIDA (sainete)
DONNA JUANITA (Suppé) (Sp)
LA DOLORES (Bretón)

June 9 (matinée and 9:00 P.M.),
10
AVENIDA (sainete)
LOS CLAVELES (Serrano)
MOLINOS DE VIENTO (Luna)
LA DOLORES (Bretón)
LAS CASTAÑUELAS (Jimenez)

June 11
AVENIDA (sainete)
LA DEL SOTO DEL PARRAL
(Soutullo and Vert)

June 12
MARUXA (Vives)
Maruxa: Asencio

June 13
AVENIDA (sainete)
LA CALESERA (Alonso)

June 14 (6:30 P.M.)
Spanish Dance Company
Encarnación López ("La
Argentinita")

June 14 (9:00 P.M.)
LOS GAVILANES (Guerrero)
LA VERBENA DE LA PALOMA
(Bretón)

June 15
LA CALESERA (Alonso)
LA LEYENDA DEL BESO (Soutullo
and Vert)

June 16 (matinée and 9:00 P.M.)
DOLORETES (sainete)
GIGANTES Y CABEZUDOS
(Fernández-Caballero)
LA LEYENDA DEL BESO (Soutullo
and Vert)
LA TEMPESTAD (Chapí)

**ITALIAN MUSICAL COMEDY
SEASON**
Canzone di Napoli Company
June 18 to July 8
Conductor: Giovanni Gemme
Director: Salvatore Rubino
O MARE E' MARGELLINA
(Lambiasso)

July 10
Recital: Lamond <pf>

Brahms: Variations on a
Paganini Theme
Beethoven: Sonata op. 53
Chopin: Two Preludes
Liszt:
    a. Campanella
    b. Capriccio in E
Rubinstein: Barcarolle in G
Liszt: Venezia e Napoli

July 13 to 16
Dramatic German Company
Director: Werner Krauss

July 14 (6:30 P.M.)
Beethoven Recital: Lamond <pf>
Fantasia op. 77
Three Sonatas
Rondo op. 51, no. 2
Sonata op. 57

July 17 to 21
Argentinean Dramatic Company
Antonio Podestá

July 23 to 30
French Dramatic Company
Tovarich

July 31
Berta Singerman <poetry recital>

Aug 22
Recital: Arrau <pf>
Bach: Preludes and Fugues from
The Well-Tempered Clavier
Mozart: Sonata in G Mayor
Musorgsky: Pictures at an
Exhibition
Ravel:
    a. Jeux d'eau
    b. Scarbo
Debussy:
    a. Hommage à Rameau
    b. L'isle joyeuse

Aug 23 to Sept 1
Buenos Aires' Teatro Odeon
Music Hall, with Amanda Varela

Aug 29, Sept 5
Berta Singerman <poetry recitals>

Sept 3
Recital: Borowsky <pf>
Bach:
    a. Two Preludes and Figures
       from The Well-Tempered
       Clavier
    b. Fantasia and fugue
Scarlatti:
    a. Pastorale
    b. Sonata in A Major
Brahms: Variations on Handel
Stravinsky: First movement from
Petroushka
Litolff: The Music Box
Prokofiev:
    a. Barcarole
    b. Prelude in C Major
Rachmaninoff: Prelude in G
Minor

Sept 7, 11, 15
Spanish Ballet Company
Antonia Mercé ("La Argentina")

Sept 8
Recital: Borowsky <pf>
Bach-Busoni: Three Chorales
Beethoven: Sonata no.7, in D
Major
Ravel: Toccata
Debussy:
    a. Des pas sur la neige
    b. Jardins sous la pluie
Albéniz:
    a. El Puerto
    b. Málaga
Chopin:
    a. Four Etudes
    b. Nocturne no. 5
    c. Grand polonaise

Sept 17 to 19
French Dramatic Company
Germaine Langier–Jean Marchat

Sept 20 to 22
Lupe Vélez <motion picture
actress>

Sept 21 to 24
Troupe Ateniense

Oct 8
Recital: Iturbi <pf>
Haydn: Sonata in D
Beethoven: Sonata in C
("Waldstein")
Schubert: Impromptu in B-flat
Liszt: Hungarian Rhapsody no.
11
Ravel: Pavane pour une infante
défunte
Granados:
    a. La maja y el ruiseñor
    b. El pelele

Nov 1 to 24
Argentinean Musical Comedy
Olinda Bozán

Nov 26 to Dec 10
Argentinean Comedy Company
Enrique Muiño–Elías Alippi

Dec 11 to 29
Argentinean Comedy Company
Florencio Parravicini

1936

Female artists
Alessandri, Adina <s>
Anitúa, Fanny <mez>
Boni, Franca <s>
Davis, Amata <s>
Díaz, América <tiple>
León, Soledad <tiple>
Luciano, Isabel <s>

Manrique, Carmen <s / mez>
Marini, Angela <s>
Marrone, Elena <s>
Piantanelli, Nené <s>
Rossi, Lidya <s>
Samsó, Nora <tiple>
Vallin, Ninon <s>

Male artists
Barreta, Andrés <bar>
Brailowsky, Alexandre <pf>
Cazenave, Juan de <t>
Cortot, Alfred <pf>
Dark, Pierre <pf>
Di Pietro, Edoardo
Ferrini, Adolfo <t>
Feuermann, Emanuel <vc>
Gallego, Rafael
Heifetz, Bener <vc>
Hoffman, Josef <pf>
Ibarra, Ignacio <bar>
Kolish, Rudolf <vn>
Kuhner, Felix <vn>
Lehner, Jence <vla>
Orsini, Alfredo <t>
Petri, André <pf>
Rabner, Wolfgang <pf>
Reboredo, Luis <t>
Serrano, Manuel
Szigeti, Joseph <vn>
Vicente, Ernesto <bar>
Zuckermann, Virgilio <t>

Jan 3 to 15
Music Hall Company Francisco
Canaro

Jan 18 to Feb 16
Spanish Musical Comedy
Company
Enrique Delfino

Feb 22 to March 1
Carnival Masked Balls

March 6 to June 2
Spanish Dramatic Company
Mari–Serrador

May 21
Recital: Cortot <pf>
Vivaldi: Concerto da camera
Chopin:
    a. Andante spianato and Pol-
       naise op.22
    b. Twenty-four Preludes
Schumann: Carnaval

May 28
Recital: Cortot <pf>
Schumann: Symphonische
Etüden
Chopin: Sonata op. 35
Debussy: Préludes (book 1)

June 3
Recital: Cortot <pf>
Works by Beethoven, Chopin,
Wagner-Liszt, and Liszt

June 4
French Dramatic Company
Roland–Jourdan

June 6 to 14
Vocal Concerts: Vienna Choir
Boys

June 9
Chopin Recital: Cortot <pf>
Sonata op. 59
Four Ballades
Ten Etudes (op. 10 and op. 25)

June 16
Recital: Brailowsky <pf>
Bach: Toccata and fugue
Hummel: Rondo
Beethoven: Sonata op. 57
Chopin:
    a. Impromptu
    b. Ballade in G Minor
    c. Nocturne in D-flat
    d. Waltz in A-flat
    e. Polonaise in A-flat
Debussy: La plus que lente

Rachmaninoff: Prelude in G
Minor
Ravel: Jeux d'eau
Liszt: Hungarian Rhapsody no. 5

June 25 (6:30 P.M.)
Recital: Brailowsky <pf>
Works by Bach, Scarlatti,
Beethoven, Schumann, and
Chopin

July 5 (6:30 P.M.)
Bertha Singerman <poetry
recital>

ITALIAN OPERETTA SEASON
Boni-Orsini Company
June 18 to July 11
Conductor: Filippo Caparros

June 18, 22
VITTORIA E IL SUO USSARO (Paul
Abraham)**

June 19
LA PRINCIPESA DELLE CZARDE
(Kálmán) (It)

June 20, 21 (6:30 P.M.), 26, July
13
LA VEDOVA ALLEGRA (Lehár) (It)
Hanna Glawari: Boni
Count Danilo: Ferrini

June 21, 24, July 11 (6:30 P.M.)
SCUGNIZZA (Costa)

June 23
LUNA PARK (Ranzato)
Charlot: Orsini
Thea d'Orsay: Rossi
Sergio de Bligny: Ferrini
Garçonne: Marini
Tubulo Baluskan: Di Pietro

June 25, 28 (6:30 P.M.)
LA PRINCIPESA DELLE DOLAR
(Fall) (It)

June 27
CIN-CIN-LA (Ranzato)**
BOCCACCIO (Suppé) (It)

June 28, 30
LA DUCHESSA DEL BAL TABARIN
(Lombardo)

June 29, July 4 (6:30 P.M.)
IL PAESE DEL CAMPANILLE
(Ranzato)

July 1, 12
LA CASTA SUSANNA (J. Gilbert)
(It)
Recital by Fanny Anitúa <mez>
Carmen: Habanera
Samson et Dalila: Mon coeur
s'ouvre à ta voix

July 2
LA GATTA NELL SACCO
(Eisemann)**

July 3, July 5 (3:30 P.M.)
SOGNO D'UN VALSER (O. Straus)
(It)

July 4, 12 (6:30 P.M.)
IL CONTE DI LUSSEMBURGO
(Lehár) (It)

July 5, 7
LA DANZA DELLA LIBELLULE
(Lehár) (It)

July 6
BAMBOLA LENCI (Mario
Rosseger)**

July 8
LA CONTESSA MARIZA (Kálmán)
(It)

July 9
LA PRESIDENTESSA (Stolz) (It)

July 10
EVA (Lehár) (It)
Eva: Boni
Gipsi: Davis
Dagoberto: Orsini
Ottavio: Ferrini
Bernardo Larousse: Di Pietro
Elli: Piantanelli
Recital by Fanny Anitúa <mez>

July 11
SFILATA DEL'AMORE
(Caparros)**

July 8 (6:30 P.M.)
Recital: Hoffman <pf>
Bach: Prelude and fugue
Gluck: Melody from Orfeo
Beethoven: Sonata op. 27, no. 2
Chopin:
  a. Waltz
  b. Nocturne in F-sharp Major
  c. Sonata in B Minor, op. 58
Debussy: Clair de lune
Prokofiev: Marche
Liadov: Tabatière à musique
Liszt: Hungarian Rhapsody no.
12

July 10 (6:30 P.M.)
Recital: Szigeti <vn>, Petri <pf>
Corelli: La follia
Bach: Sonata in G Minor for
violin solo
Debussy: Sonata
Schubert: Sonatina in A Major
Bartók-Szigeti: Hungarian Folk
Songs
Ravel: Habanera
Paganini: Capriccio in G Major
Stravinsky: Scherzo from The
Firebird

July 14 to 21
Vocal Concerts: Don Cossacks
Chorus
Chorus Master: Jaroff

July 15
Recital: Hoffman <pf>
Works by Handel, Beethoven,
Brahms, Chopin, Hoffman,
Rubinstein, and J. Strauss

July 17, 21, 23, 30
Recitals: Szigeti <vn>, Petri <pf>
Works by Handel, Mozart,
Pugnani-Kreisler, Beethoven,
Milhaud, Hubay, Falla, and
Stravinsky-Szigeti

Spanish Musical Comedy Season
July 24 to Aug 24, Sept 4 to 20
Conductor: Manolo Casas

July 31
Recital: Anitúa <mez>
Pergolesi: Si tu m'ami
Caldara: Come raggio di sole
Caccini: Amarilli
Gluck:
  a. Lascia ch'io pianga
  b. O del mio dolce ardor
Bizet: Agnus Dei
Franck: Panis Angelicus
Böhm: Still wie die nacht!
Rossini: Aria from Il barbiere di
Siviglia
Del Moral:
  a. Por unos ojos
  b. Déjame que te bese
Cárdenas
  a. Rayito de sol
  b. Nunca
Ponce: Estrellita

Aug 3
Chamber Music Recital
Kolish String Quartet: Kolish/
Kuhner <vns>, Lehner<vla>,
Heifetz<vc>
Beethoven: Quartet op. 18, no. 2
Debussy: Quartet in G Minor
Schubert: Quartet "Der Tod und
das Mädchen"

Aug 5
Kolish String Quartet, second
Recital
Brahms: Quartet in C Minor
Mozart: Quartet in D Minor, K.
421
Dvořák: Quartet in F Major, op.
96

Aug 17
Lieder Recital: Vallin <s>, Dark
<pf>
Lully: L'amour tournera
Gluck: O del dolce mio ardor
Handel: French Song
Schumann: Five Lieder
Schubert:
  a. Lied
  b. Der Tod und das Mädchen
  c. Gretchen am Spinnrade
Fauré:
  a. Poème d'un jour
  b. La rose
Debussy: Air de Lia from
L'enfant prodigue
Falla:
  a. Nana
  b. El Paño moruno
  c. Seguidilla murciana
  d. Jota
Obradors: Coplas de Curro
Dulce
Nin:
  a. Montañesa
  b. El vito

Aug 25 to Sept 1
Germaine Dermoz–Jane Chevrel–
René Rocher Dramatic
Company from Paris's Vieux
Colombier

Sept 2, 21, 22
Israeli Dramatic Company Ben
Ami

Sept 4 (6:30 P.M.)
Lieder Recital: Vallin <s>, Dark
<pf>

Works by Handel, Mozart,
Gluck, Brahms, Duparc,
Chausson, Debussy, Nin, and
Granados

Sept 8
Recital
Feuermann <vc>, Rabner <pf>

Sept 14
Amneris Bosco Garbisso
<poetry recital>

Sept 18
GESTA DE LA EMANCIPACION
(Zarrilli)
Historical Drama with incidental
music by Vicente Ascone
Conductor / Director: Ascone
Scenography: Norberto Berdía
Cast: Children from the
"República Argentina" School

SPANISH LYRIC ZARZUELA
SEASON
Sept 25 to Oct 19
Conductor: Manuel Palacios

Sept 25
LUISA FERNANDA (Moreno-
Torroba)**
Luisa Fernanda: Manrique
Carolina: Samsó
Mariana: Luciano
Rosita: Díaz
Vidal Hernando: Ibarra
Javier: Cazenave
Aníbal: Vicente
Nogales: Barreta
Don Florito: Gallego
Bizco Porras: Serrano

Oct 22 to Nov 8
Magician and Music Hall
Company Chang

Nov 10 to 29
Argentinean Comedy Company
Enrique Muiño–Elías Alippi

Dec 1
Bertha Singerman <poetry
recital>

Dec 4 to 31
Spanish Dramatic Company
Joaquín García Leon–Manuel
Perales

1937

Female artists
Anderson, Marian <a>
Barlett, Ethel <pf>
Bertramo, Franca
Bizzo, Pina
Boni, Franca <s>
Bregis, Danielle <s>
Debret, Lucy <s>
Delaval, Andrée <s>
Francell, Jacqueline <s>
Lambert, Andrée <s>
Lane, Josyane <s>
Marini, Angela <s>
Petschick, Anneliese <d>
Piantanelli, Nené <s>
Regina, Alba <s>
Ribelle, Nella <s>
Vignoli, Olga <s>
Volnay, Jaulette <s>

Male artists
Di Toto, Umberto <t>
Duluart, Jacques <t>
Bertini, Italo <bar>
Ferrini, Adolfo <t>
Foglizzo, Edoardo <t>
Fougères, Jacques <bar>
Fujiwara, Yosie <t>
Grandi, Paride
Kempff, Wilhelm <pf>
Lehamann, Claude
Mareul, Jacques

Milstein, Nathan \<vn\>
Mittman, Leopold \<pf\>
Mojica, José \<t\>
Mujica, José Tomás \<pf\>
Orloff, Nikolai \<pf\>
Orsini, Alfredo \<t\>
Parys, Pierre
Petrone, Emiremo
Riccio, Beniamino \<bar\>
Robertson, Rao \<pf\>
Rupp, Franz \<pf\>
Salvatti, Tomasso
Schmidt, Berthold \<d\>
Segovia, Andrés \<gui\>
Singher, Martial \<bar\>
Sportelli, Italo
Thibaudet, Edouard \<t\>
Zuckermann, Virgilio \<t\>

Jan 1 to 4
Spanish Dramatic Company
Joaquín García Leon–Manuel
Perales

Jan 5 to 26
Music Hall Company Francisco
Canaro

Feb 6 to 14
Carnival Masked Balls

Feb 19 to 28
Musical Comedy Company
Enrique Santos Discépolo-Tania

ITALIAN OPERETTA SEASON
Italo Bertini Italian Operetta
Company
March 5 to 28

March 5, 6 (6:00 P.M.), 11
IL CONTE DI LUSSEMBURGO
(Lehár) (It)
Angela Didier: Vignoli
Conte Rene: Di Toto
Basilio Basilovich: Bertini

March 6, 7 (6:00 P.M.), 16
LA DANZA DELLA LIBELULLE
(Lehár) (It)

March 7, 13 (6:00 P.M.)
LA VEDOVA ALLEGRA (Lehár) (It)
Hanna Glawari: Vignoli

March 8, 9, 13, 14 (6:00 P.M.), 25
SOGNO D'AMORE DE LISZT (Karl
Komjati) (It)**

March 10, 28
ACQUA CHETA (Pietri)

March 12, 21, 27 (6:00 P.M.)
LA PRINCIPESSA DELLE CZARDE
(Kálmán) (It)

March 14, 17, 20 (6:00 P.M.)
LA CASTA SUSANNA (J. Gilbert)
(It)

March 15, 18 (6:00 P.M.)
SANTARELLINA [Mam'zelle
Nitouche](Hervé) (It)
Dionisia: Regina
Organista: Bertini
Teniente de Wancy: Foglizzo

March 18, 22, 25 (6:00 P.M.)
IL TANGO DI MEZZANOTTE
(Komjati)**

March 19
LA PRESIDENTESSA (Stolz) (It)

March 20, 21 (6:00 P.M.), 23
SCUGNIZZA (Costa)

March 24, 26
SOGNO D'UNA NOTTE (Allegra
and Pittaluga)**

March 27, 28 (6:00 P.M.)
LA PRINCIPESSA DEL CIRCO
(Kálmán) (It)

April 1, 29
Amalia Molina Spanish Ballet
Company

SECOND ITALIAN OPERETTA SEASON
Franca Boni Italian Operetta
Company
April 2 to 18

April 2, 3 (6:00 P.M.)
IL PAESE DEL CAMPANILLE
(Ranzato)
Bombon: Boni
Nella: Ribelle
La Gaffe: Orsini
Hans: Ferrini
Pomerania: Marini
Attanasio: Grandi
Ethel: Piantanelli

April 3, 4 (6:00 P.M.)
LA PRINCIPESSA DELLE DOLAR
(Fall) (It)

April 4, 13
LA VEDOVA ALLEGRA (Lehár) (It)
Hanna Glawari: Boni

April 5, 9
SCUGNIZZA (Costa)
Salome: Boni

April 6
LA DANZA DELLA LIBELULLE
(Lehár) (It)

April 7
CIN-CI-LA (Ranzato)

April 8, 10 (6:00 P.M.)
IL CONTE DI LUSSEMBURGO
(Lehár) (It)

April 10, 11 (6:00 P.M.)
LA DUCHESSA DEL BAL TABARIN
(Lombardo)

April 11, 12
BOCCACCIO (Suppé) (It)

April 14, 17 (6:00 P.M.)
LA GEISHA (Jones) (It)

April 15
FRASQUITA (Lehár) (It)
Frasquita: Boni

April 16
LA PRINCIPESSA DELLE CZARDE
(Kálmán) (It)

April 17
SOGNO D'UN VALSER (O. Straus)
(It)

April 18
EVA (Lehár) (It)
Eva: Boni

April 15 (6:30 P.M.)
Recital: Riccio <bar>, Mujica
<pf>
Works by Verdi, Musorgsky,
Brahms, Schubert, and Rossini

April 23 to June 2
Spanish Comedy Company
Casimiro Orta

May 5, 12
Recitals: Segovia <gui>
Works by Scarlatti, Bach,
Moreno-Torroba, Castelnuovo-
Tedesco, Chilesotti, Albéniz, and
Turina

May 14
Recital: Milstein <vn>, Mittman
<pf>
Vivaldi: Sonata in A Major
Lorent: Prelude and Capriccio
Bach: Chaconne
Brahms: Sonata in D Minor
Smetana: From my Land
Chopin: Nocturne

Rimsky-Korsakoff: The Flight of
the Bumblebee
Liszt: Consolation
Paganini: La campanella

May 19
Recital: Kempff <pf>
Bach: Capriccio in B Major
Mozart: Sonata in F, K. 332
Schumann:
    a. Träumerei
    b. Aufschwung
Schubert: Sonata in A Minor

May 21, June 23
Recitals: Milstein <vn>,
Mittman <pf>

May 26
Beethoven Recital: Kempff <pf>
Sonata op. 24, no. 2
Rondo in G Major
Ecossaises
Sonata op. 53 ("Walstein")

June 5, 8
Recitals: José Mojica <t and
motion picture actor>

June 9
Two-piano Recital by Barlett
and Robertson
Handel: Arrivée de la Reine de
Saba
Bach:
    a. Choral
    b. Sonata in E-flat Major
Saint-Saëns: Variations on a
Beethoven Theme
Rachmaninoff: Romance
Arensky: Waltz and Scherzo
Debussy: Lindaraja
Infante: Ritmo

June 11 to 27
Music Hall Company Francisco
Canaro

June 29 to July 1
Israeli Dramatic Company Berta
Gersten

June 30 (6:30 P.M.)
Recital: Anderson <a>, Rupp
<pf>
Handel: Ombra mai fu
Veracini: Pastorale
Mozart: Aleluya
Schubert:
    a. Aufenthalt
    b. Der Tod und das Mädchen
    c. Erlkönig
Verdi: O don fatal, from Don
Carlo
Sibelius: Die liebelle
Tcherepinne: A Kiss
Chaminade: Eté
Negro Spirituals:
    a. Sometimes I Feel Like a
       Motherless Child
    b. Heav'n, heav'n
    c. Trampling
    d. I Know the Lord

**SPANISH MUSICAL COMEDY
SEASON**
July 2 to Aug 8
Conductor: Manolo Casas

July 5
Recital: Orloff <pf>
Scarlatti: Two Sonatinas
Beethoven: Sonata op. 31, no. 3
Franck: Prelude, Fugue and
Variations
Chopin:
    a. Ballade
    b. Impromptu in A-sharp
       Major
    c. Two Mazurkas
    d. Six Studies
Brahms: Variations on a Theme
of Paganini

July 7, 14, 28, Aug 18 (6:30 P.M.)
Recitals: Anderson <a>, Rupp

Works by Gluck, Handel,
Frescobaldi, Beethoven,
Schubert, Schumann, Sadero,
Hummel, Brahms, Bianchini,
Sibelius, Donizetti, Cimara,
Respighi, Obradors, Granados,
and Negro Spirituals

Aug 3, 4
Vocal Concerts: Ratisbone
Cathedral Choir

Aug 9, 13
Delia Iñiguez <poetry recitals>

Aug 10 to 18
Italian Dramatic Company
Director: Giulio Bragaglia

Aug 11, Sept 8
Dance recitals
Berthold Schmidt and Anneliese
Petschick

Aug 20 to Sept 7
Carmen Amaya Spanish Dance
Company

Aug 23
Recital: Singher <bar>
Cinq ancient françaises melodies
Fauré:
    a. La chanson du pêcheur
    b. Poème d'un jour
Hahn:
    a. Paysage
    b. D'une prison
Debussy: Deux ballades de
François Villon
Beethoven:
    a. Prière
    b. La Morte
    c. Dieu loué par la nature
    d. A la bien aimée absente

Sept 9 to 19
Charlo Music Hall Company

FRENCH OPERETTA SEASON
Francell-Bregis French Operetta
Company
Sept 21 to Oct 1
Conductor: René Mercier

Sept 21
OH PAPA! (Yvain)
Nane: Francell
Jule: Delaval
Monique: Lane
Danielle: Debret
Andrée: Lambert
Godin Dinan: Thibaudet
Robert Bossin: Fougères

Sept 22, 23 (6:30 P.M.), 25
(6:30 P.M.)
COUCHETTE no. 3 (Szulc)

Sept 23
SIMONE EST COMME ÇA
(Moretti)

Sept 24
FAITES ÇA POUR MOI
(Gabaroches and Pearly)

Sept 25, 30 (6:30 P.M.)
FLOSSIE (Szulc)

Sept 26 (6:30 P.M.)
QUAND ON EST TROIS (Szulc)

Sept 26, 28 (6:30 P.M.)
PASSIONEMENT (Messager)

Sept 27
LES AVENTURES DU ROI PAUSOLE
(Honegger)**
Blanche Aline: Francell
"Favesti": Bregis
Giglio, un page: Duluart
Jolande: Lehamann

Sept 28
MADAME (Christiné)

Sept 29
LE COEUR Y EST (Van Parys and
Paises)

Sept 30
L'AMOUR MASQUE (Messager)

Oct 1
PHI-PHI (Christiné)

Oct 2 to 17
Argentinean Comedy Company
Enrique Muiño–Elías Alippi

Oct 5
Recital: Fujiwara <t>
Handel: Aria from Semele
Scarlatti:
    a. La violetta
    b. Gia il sole del Ganges
Galuppi: Quando si tristano . . .
Schubert:
    a. Du bist die Ruh
    b. Der Wanderer
Rimsky-Korsakoff: Lewko's
Song, from May's Night
Five Japanese Songs

Oct 15
Recital: Fujiwara <t>
Lotti: Pur dicesti
Pergolesi: Nina
Bonancini: Per la gloria
Mozart: Dalla sua pace, from
Don Giovanni
Schumann: Ich had im Traum
geweinet
Brahms:
    a. Wiegenlied
    b. Sonntag
Debussy: Azoel's recitative and
aria, from L'enfant prodigue
Rimsky-Korsakoff: Oriental
romance
Seven Japanese Songs by
Tauyuki, Yamada, Hasimoto,
and Itow

Oct 20 to Nov 7
Spanish Dramatic Company
Joaquín García-León–Manuel
Perales

Nov 10 to 29
Spanish Dramatic Company
Lola Membrives

Dec 2 to 12
Comedy Company Fanny Brena

Dec 18 to 31
Chang <magician>

1938

Female artists
Anderson, Marian <a>
Feraldy, Germaine <s>
Laudy, Rachel <s>
Maricarmen <tiple>
Matthaeus, Marion <s>
Pardo, Amalia <s>
Pibernat, Maruja <tiple>
Rappol, Anna
Rappol, Esther
Zoriga, Mlle. <d>

Male artists
Dubressy, Monsieur <b>
García Martí, Andrés <bar>
Kaisin, Francy <t>
Moiseiwitsch, Benno <pf>
Niedzielski, Mr. <pf>
Nicastro, Oscar <vc>
Prizant, Heimi <t>
Rupp, Franz <pf>
Sagi-Vela, Luis <bar>
Sauvegeot, Maurice <bar>
Singer, Werner <pf>
Vela, Antonio <t>

Jan 1 to 6
Chang <magician>

Jan 7 to 24
Spanish Comedy Company
Aurora Redondo–Valeriano Leon

Jan 25 to 31
Music Hall Company Francisco
Canaro

Feb 3 to 20
Alcoriza Andalusian Lyric
Comedy Company

Feb 25 to March 13
Carnival Masked Balls

March 16 to 22
Spanish Dance Company Raquel
Meller <tonadillera and dancer>

March 23
Recital: Nicastro <vc>
Vivaldi: Sonata
Corelli: La follia
Bach: Aria
Beethoven: Minuetto
Schubert-Nicastro: Lullaby
Chopin: Nocturne
Sarasate: Malagueña
Debussy: La fille aux cheveux de
lin
Glazunov: Spanish Dance
Popper: Spindle's Song

March 25 to June 19
Comedy Company Pablo Palitos–
Alfredo Carmiña

May 4
Lieder Recital: Matthaeus <s>,
Singer <pf>
Giordano: Caro mio bene
Handel: Largo
Schubert:
  a. Erlkönig
  b. Der Tod und das Mädchen
  c. Lied
  d. Ungeduld
Brahms: Four Lieder

Singer: A Sunny Fall Day
Roger: Lullaby of the Virgin
Marz: Love Is For You
Weingartner: Love Feast
R. Strauss: Four Lieder

May 11
Lieder Recital: Matthaeus <s>,
Singer <pf>
Works by Gluck, Schumann,
Wolff, Singer, Santoliquido, and
R. Strauss

May 25, 26, June 24, 25
Vocal Concerts
The Comedian Harmonists

June 8
Chopin Recital: Niedzielski <pf>
Polonaise op. 40, no. 1
Ballade in A-flat Major
Two Mazurkas, op. 33
Waltz in E-flat Minor
Six Studies: op. 10, nos. 3, 4, 5
and 9; op. 25, nos. 3 and 9

June 21 to July 11
Mexican Musical Comedy
Company Antonieta Lorca–
Ernesto Tanco

July 6
Recital: Moiseiwitsch <pf>
Beethoven: Andante
Schumann: Carnaval
Chopin:
  a. Two Impromptus
  b. Sonata op. 35
Ravel: Jeux d'eau
Prokofiev: Suggestion diabolique
Poulenc: Mouvement perpétuel
Ibert: Le petit âne blanc
Granados: La maja y el ruiseñor
Paganini-Brahms: Variations

July 12
Recital: Moiseiwitsch <pf>

Schubert: Impromptu
Hummel: Rondo in E-flat
Chopin:
a. Ballade in G Minor
b. Nocturne in G Major
c. Three Studies
Debussy:
a. Jardins sous la pluie
b. Minstrels
Poulenc: Pastorale and Presto
Liszt: Hungarian Rhapsody no. 2

July 14 to Aug 4
Musical Comedy Company Fu-
Manchu

FRENCH OPERA / OPERETTA / BALLET SEASON
Aug 6 to 14
Conductors: Henri Gustave
Goublier and Edouard Frigara
Director and ballet mistress:
Zoriga

Aug 6, 7 (6:30 P.M.)
MIREILLE (Gounod)**
Mireille: Feraldy
Vincenette: Laudy
Vincent: Kaisin
Ourrias: Sauvegeot
Maître Ramon: Dubressy
FARANDOLE (ballet)

Aug 7
LA COCARDE DE MIMI PINSON
(Goublier)**
Mimi: Laudy

Aug 8, 13 (6:30 P.M.)
LE PETIT DUC (Lecocq)

Aug 9
LA DEMOISELLE DU PRINTEMPS
(Goublier)**

Aug 10 (6:30 P.M.)
Recital: Anderson <a>, Rupp
<pf>

Schubert:
a. Dem Unendlichen
b. Die Vögel
c. Von Mitleiden Mariä
d. Verherrlichung
Franck:
a. Nocturne
b. Lied
c. S'il est un charmant gazon
Handel: Cantata O numi eterni
(La Lucrezia)
Sibelius:
a. Idle Words
b. Solitude
Respighi: Pioggia
Ravel: Habanera
Five Negro Spirituals

Aug 10, 14 (6:30 P.M.)
LES SALTIMBANQUES (Ganne)

Aug 11 (6:30 P.M.)
VERONIQUE (Messager)

Aug 11
LA FILLE DE MADAME ANGOT
(Lecocq)

Aug 12
LAS CLOCHES DE CORNEVILLE
(Planquette)
Conductor: Frigara

Aug 13
LES MOUSQUETAIRES AU
CONVENT (Varney)

Aug 14
LA FILLE DU TAMBOUR MAJOR
(Offenbach)

GRAND SPANISH ZARZUELA SEASON
Luis Sagi-Vela Zarzuela
Company
Aug 19 to Oct 9
Conductor: Rafael Palacios

Aug 19
LUISA FERNANDA (Moreno-
Torroba)
Luisa Fernanda: Pardo
Carolina: Maricarmen
Javier: Vela
Vidal Hernando: Sagi-Vela

Aug 24
Recital: Anderson <a>, Rupp
<pf>
Works by Handel, Carissimi,
Gluck, Russotto, Cohen, Wolff,
Sadero, Vehanan, and Negro
Spirituals

Oct 11 to 25
Italian Dramatic Company Paola
Borboni–Luigi Cimara

Oct 29, 30 (4 performances)
Argentinean Dramatic Company
Paulina Singerman

Nov 1
BEI MIR BIS DU SCHEIN
(Olschamiezky)
Israeli Operetta Company Heimi
Prizant

Nov 3 to Dec 5
Spanish Dramatic Company
Lola Membrives

Nov 23, Dec 2
Trinidad Soler Spanish Dance
Company

Dec 7 to 25
Musical Comedy Company Fu-
Manchu

Dec 30, 31
Argentinean Comedy Company
Héctor Torres

1939

Female artists
Grey, Madeleine <s>
Ibels, Jacqueline <pf>
Iturbi, Amparo <pf>
Petschick, Anneliese <d>
Raitzin, Florence <pf>

Male artists
Arrau, Claudio <pf>
Brailowsky, Alexandre <pf>
Elman, Misha <vn>
Fritzsche, Gustave <vn>
Gebhardt, Lothar <vn>
Hartman, Imre <vc>
Iturbi, José <pf>
Kohischuetter, Volkmar <vc>
Lener, Jeno <vn>
Longas, Federico <pf>
Oelsner, Johannes <vla>
Padwa, Vladimir <pf>
Roth, Sandor <vla>
Sandor, Gyorgy <pf>
Schipa, Tito <t>
Schmidt, Berthold <d>
Segovia, Andrés <gui>
Smilovitz, Joseph <vn>

Jan 4 to 16
Spanish Comedy Company
Aurora Redondo–Valeriano León

Jan 19 to Feb 12
Spanish Ballet Company
Angelillo–Conchita Martínez

Feb 18 to March 12
Carnival Masked Balls

March 16 to 29
Argentinean Dramatic Company
Mecha Ortiz

March 31 to May 28
Argentinean Comedy Company
Elsa O'Connor–Alfredo Camiña–
María Esther Duckse

April 29, 30 (4 performances)
Music Hall Company Josephine
Baker

May 10
Recital: Grey <s>, Ibels <pf>
Handel: Aria from Joshua
Hüe: Sur l'eau
Pierné: Le petit rentier
Delannoy: Chant du Galérien
Roussel: Coeur en peril
Milhaud: Deux chansons de
négresses
Musorgsky: Chambre des
enfants
   a. Avec Niania
   b. Fi! que esplegie
   c. La Hanneton
   d. Le chat matelot
   e. Un cheval du bâton

May 19
Recital: Segovia <gui>
Visée: Ancient dances
Frescobaldi:
   a. Aria variada
   b. La Frescobalda
   c. Corrente
Rameau: Minuetto
Sor: Variaciones
Bach: Suite
Castelnuovo-Tedesco: Tarantella
Turina: Fandanguillo
Granados: Danza
Albéniz: Torre bermeja

May 22
Recital: Grey <s>, Ibels <pf>
Works by Cimarosa, Debussy,
Nin, Rosenthal, Ravel,
Villalobos, Camargo-Guarnieri,
and Métra

May 24
Two-Piano Recital: A. and J.
Iturbi <pf>
Mozart: Sonata in D Major

Schumann: Theme and
Variations
Chabrier: Two Waltzes
Saint-Saëns: Caprice arabe
Gershwin: Rhapsody in Blue

May 26
Recital: Segovia <gui>
Works by Moreno-Torroba,
Turina, Haydn, Ponce,
Pachelbel, Scarlatti,
Mendelssohn, Villalobos, and
Albéniz

June 1 to July 2
Spanish Dramatic Company
Joaquín García Leon–Manuel
Perales

June 2
Recital: Iturbi <pf>
Soler: Sonata
M. Albéniz: Sonata
Haydn: Sonata in D Major
Schumann: Papillons
Liszt: Hungarian Rhapsody no.
12
Mendelssohn: Rondo capriccioso
Fauré: Impromptu in A
Infante:
   a. Pochades
   b. Andaluzas
Granados:
   a. La maja y el ruiseñor
   b. El pelele

June 6
Recital: Iturbi <pf>
Handel: Harmonious Blacksmith
Bach: Capriccio sopra la
lontananza del suo fratello
dilettissimo
Beethoven: Sonata op. 27, no. 2

June 7, 23, 26
Trinidad Soler Spanish Dance
Company

June 20, 28, July 5
Recitals: Iturbi <pf>
Works by Bach, Schumann,
Liszt, Chopin, Albéniz, and Falla

July 3, 12, 20, Sept 1
Spanish Ballet Company
Encarnación López ("La
Argentinita")

July 4 to 18
Italian Dramatic Company
Maria Melato

July 10
Recital: Arrau <pf>
Bach: Italian Concerto
Beethoven: Sonata op. 18, in E-
flat
Brahms: Variations and Fugue
on a Handel Theme
Ravel: Jeux d'eau
Debussy:
    a. Danse
    b. Voiles
    c. Feux d'artifice

July 19
Chamber Music Recital
Fritzsche Quartet: Fritzsche and
Gebhardt <vns>, Oelsner <vla>,
Kohischuetter <vc>
Haydn: Quartet in F Major, op.
3
Beethoven: Quartet op. 59, no. 2
Schubert: Quartet "Der Tod und
das Mädchen"

July 19, 23 (10:30 A.M.)
Recitals: Isa Kremer <folk
melodist>

July 21 to Aug 27
Musical Comedy Company
Gloria Guzmán–F. Parravicini

Aug 2
Chamber Music Recital

Lener String Quartet: Lener and
Smilovitz <vns>, Roth <vla>,
Hartman <vc>
Schubert: Quartet "Der Tod und
das Mädchen"
Beethoven: Quartet op. 59, no. 3
Haydn: Quartet op. 3, no. 5

Aug 8 (6:30 P.M.)
Recital: Brailowsky <pf>
Bach-Busoni: Toccata and fugue
in D Minor
Scarlatti: Pastoral and Capriccio
Beethoven: Sonata op. 27, no. 2
Chopin: Twelve Studies, op. 10
and 25
Debussy: Reflets dans l'eau
Falla: Danza del fuego
Rachmaninoff: Prelude in G
Major
Balakirev: Islamey

Aug 10 (6:30 P.M.)
Recital: Schipa <t>, Longas <pf>
Pergolesi: Tre giorni son che
Nina
Sadero: Nina Nanna
Scarlatti: La violetta
Flotow: M'apparì, from Martha
Cimarosa: Tenor's aria from Il
matrimonio segreto
Donizetti: Una furtiva lagrima,
from L'elisir d'amore
Tosti: Malia
Padilla: Princesita
Esparza-Otero: Mi viejo amor
Barthelmy: Chi se me scorda
chiu
Piano Recital by Longas with
works by Granados, Albéniz,
and Longas

Aug 14
Recital: Elman <vn>, Padwa <pf>
Handel: Sonata in D Major
Beethoven: "Kreutzer" Sonata
Lalo: Symphonie espagnole
Chopin: Nocturne

Dinicu: Hora staccato
Vieuxtemps: Ballade et polonaise

Aug 16
Dance recital: Anneliese
Petschick and Berthold Schmidt

Aug 21
Recital: Elman <vn>, Padwa <pf>
Valentino: Sonata in B Minor
Franck: Sonata in A Major
Mendelssohn: Concerto in E
Minor
Mozart: Adagio
Brahms: Hungarian Dance in B
Minor
Chopin: Nocturne
Sarasate: Aires bohemios

Sept 1 to 18
Spanish Ballet Company
Angelillo–Conchita Martínez

Sept 11
Recital: Sandor <pf>
Bach:
    a. Prelude and Choral
    b. Fantasia and Fugue
Liszt: Après une lecture de
Dante
Chopin:
    a. Ballade
    b. Waltz
    c. Six Studies
    d. Polonaise in A Major
Schumann: Papillons
Prokofiev: Marche
Debussy:
    a. La Terrasse des audiences
       du clair de lune
    b. Feux d'artifice
Stravinsky: Russian Dance

Sept 21 to Oct 8
Argentinean Comedy Company
Tito Lusiardo

Oct 2
Recital: Raitzin <pf>
Vivaldi: Presto
Bach: Fantasia in C Minor
Mozart: Reveille in C Major
Schumann: Kinderszenen op. 15
Chopin: Ballade op. 38
Debussy:
  a. Jardins sous la pluie
  b. La fille aux cheveux de lin
  c. L'isle joyeuse

Oct 12 to 31
Andalusian Musical Company
"El Niño de Utrera"

Nov 1
Comedy Company Antonio
Gandia

Nov 3 to 5
Musical Comedy Company
Maria Ofelia Cortesina

Nov 8 to 13
Italian Musical Comedy
Company Canzone di Napoli

Nov 14 to 27
Dramatic Company Blanca
Podestá

Nov 30 to Dec 11
Musical Comedy Company
Francisco Canaro

Dec 12 to 21
Comedy Company Pierina
Dealessi

Dec 23 to 27
Gala Chabelska Ballet Company

Dec 28 to 31
Spanish Musical Comedy
Company Juanita Quesada

1940

Female artists
Arce, Merceditas <tiple>
Brizzio, Emma <mez>
Broders, Matilde <s>
Burzio, Dina <s>
Cetera, Amanda <s>
Eggerth, Martha <s>
Espalter, Dora <s>
Gallego, Elcira <s>
Hauser, Blanca <s>
Lange, Herta <pf>
Oyuela, Clara <s>
Pissani, Fina <mez>
Poussin-Despouey, Haydée <s>
Rodríguez, María <s>
Sarria, Lucrecia <s>
Vialade-Vigil, Solange <a>

Male artists
Alsina, Joaquín <b>
Arenas, Joaquín <b>
Arrau, Claudio <pf>
Balli, Emilio <bar>
Bandini, Alvaro <t>
Brocchi, Umberto <t>
Campos, Nemesio <bar>
Delfino, Julio <b>
Dumesnil, Maurice <pf>
Fernandi, Luis <bar>
Hertogs, Pablo <bar>
Ilabarca, Oscar <t>
Kusrow-Corma, Carlos <pf>
Martínez, José <t>
Mastronardi, Domingo <t>
Rigazzi, Edmundo <bar>
Rubinstein, Artur <pf>
Sirvent, Adolfo <t>
Szenkar, Alexandre <pf>
Villa, Joaquín <bar>

Jan 1 to 9
María Antinea Spanish Dance
Company

Jan 13 to 23
Musical Comedy Company
Francisco Canaro

Feb 3 to 18
Carnival Masked Balls
Típica Canaro–Jazz Vinicio
Ascone

March 7 to 18
Trio Moreno Musical Comedy

SPANISH ZARZUELA / OPERA SEASON
Pablo Hertogs–Merceditas Arce
Lyric Company
March 23 to April 21
Conductor: Francisco Gil Saenz

March 23
MARINA (Arrieta)
Marina: Arce
Jorge: Sirvent
Roque: Hertogs
Pascual: Arenas
Teresa: Gallego
Capitán Alberto: Campos
Marinero: Martínez

FALL ITALIAN OPERA SEASON
April 23 to May 4
Conductors: Emilio Cappuzano
and Tino Cremagnani

April 23, 27
IL TROVATORE (Verdi)
Leonora: Hauser
Azucena: Brizzio
Manrico: Mastronardi
Conte di Luna: Villa

April 24, 28 (6:30 P.M.)
LA TRAVIATA (Verdi)
Violetta: Burzio
Alfredo Germont: Bandini
Giorgio Germont: Villa

April 25
CAVALLERIA RUSTICANA
(Mascagni)
Santuzza: Hauser

Turiddu: Brocchi
Lola: Pissani
Alfio: Rigazzi
PAGLIACCI (Leoncavallo)
Nedda: Cetera
Canio: Mastronardi
Tonio: Villa

April 26, 30
LA BOHEME (Puccini)
Mimì: Broders
Musetta: Oyuela
Rodolfo: Bandini
Marcello: Rigazzi
Schaunard: Fernandi
Colline: Balli

April 28
LUCIA DI LAMMERMOOR
(Donizetti)
Lucia: Sarria
Edgardo: Ilabarca
Enrico: Rigazzi

April 29, May 2, 5 (6:30 P.M)
AIDA (Verdi)
Aida: Hauser
Amneris: Brizzio
Radamès: Brocchi
Amonasro: Villa
Il Re: Balli
Ramfis: Alsina

May 1, 5
RIGOLETTO (Verdi)
Gilda: Rodríguez
Il Duca di Mantova: Bandini
Rigoletto: Villa
Maddalena: Brizzio
Sparafucile: Alsina

May 3
IL BARBIERE DI SIVIGLIA
(Rossini)
Rosina: Rodríguez
Conte di Almaviva: Bandini
Figaro: Villa
Don Basilio: Alsina

May 4
CARMEN (Bizet)
Conductor: Cremagnani
Carmen: Pissani
Don Jose: Bandini
Escamillo: Rigazzi

May 9 to 28
Spanish Dramatic Company
Catalina Bárcena–Josefina Díaz–
Manuel Collado

June 4 to 16
Musical Comedy Company
Libertad Lamarque

June 17
Actress Ruth Draper
<soliloquies>

June 18 to 21
Parisian Music Hall Lucienne
Noel Company
Conductor: Jack Hilson

June 26 to Aug 18
Spanish Dramatic Company
Pepita Serrador–Esteban
Serrador–Narciso Ibañez Menta

July 1
Recital: Arrau <pf>
Bach: Concerto Italiano
Beethoven: Sonata op. 81a
Musorgsky: Pictures at an
Exhibition
Ravel: Jeux d'eau
Granados: La maja y el ruiseñor
Liszt:
    a. Au bord d'une source
    b. Mephisto Waltz

July 16
Dance Recital: Sai Shoki
<Korean dancer>

Aug 1
Recital: Eggerth <s>, Szenkar
<pf>
Donizetti: Aria from Don
Pasquale
O. Badero: Fa la nana bambini
Mozart:
    a. Alleluia
    b. Das Veilchen
Donizetti: Aria from Lucia
Dell'Acqua: Villanella
René Rabey: Tes jeux
Schubert:
    a. Ständchen
    b. Ave Maria
Delibes:
    a. Bonjour Suzon
    b. Chanson espagnole from
       Les filles de Cadix

Aug 9
Recital: Kusrow-Corma <pf>
Bach-Busoni: Toccata and Fugue
in D Minor
Bach: Concerto Italiano
Schubert: Impromptu in A-flat
Schumann: Arabesque
Chopin:
    a. Study
    b. Waltz
    c. Ballade in A-flat
Turina: Danza fantástica
Pahissa: Cant de Muntaya
Albéniz: Córdoba
Granados: Allegro de concierto
Albéniz: Evocación
Liszt: Hungarian Rhapsody no.
15

Aug 12
Recital: Rubinstein <pf>
Works by Beethoven, Stravinsky,
Debussy, Ravel, and Albéniz

Aug 20
Bible-Bach Recital: Raul Lange
<narrator>, H. Lange <pf>

Aug 25 (11:00 A.M.)
Spanish Music Recital:
Rubinstein <pf>
Albéniz:
  a. Navarra
  b. Córdoba
  c. Sevilla
  d. Triana
Granados: La maja y el ruiseñor
Mompou: Canción y danza
Falla:
  a. Danza del miedo
  b. Danza de la molinera
  c. Andaluza
Albéniz:
  a. Jerez
  b. Lavapies
Falla: Pantomima and Danza del
fuego

Aug 28 to Sept 22
Angelillo Spanish Musical
Comedy and Dance Company

Sept 2
Asociación Coral de Montevideo
Concert
Conductor: Carlos Correa-Luna
Soloists: Poussin-Despouey <s>,
Espalter <s>, Vialade <a>,
Delfino <b>
Chabrier:
  a. Suite pastorale for orches-
     tra
  b. A la musique, for soprano,
     chorus and orchestra
Fauré: Cantique de Jean Racine,
for chorus
Bach: Cantata "Sehet, welch eine
Liebe," BWV 64
Schubert: Dieu dans la Nature,
psalm

Sept 22 to Oct 3
Galician Regional Art Company
Marujita Villanueva

Oct 8
Bertha Singerman <poetic recital>

Oct 9 to 16
Dramatic Company Pedro López
Lagar–Vilma Vidal

Oct 21
Recital: Dumesnil <pf>
Haydn: Andante and variations
Schumann: Arabesque
Mendelssohn: Scherzo in B
Minor
Chopin: Sonata op. 35
Debussy:
  a. Danseuses de Delphes
  b. Le vent dans la plaine
  c. Brouillards
  d. Les collines d'Anacapri
Ravel: Jeux d'eau
Ibert: Le petit âne blanc
Liszt:
  a. Etude in D-flat
  b. Hungarian Rhapsody no.
     12

Oct 24 to Nov 4
Carmen Amaya Spanish Dance
Company

Oct 25
Recital: Dumesnil <pf>
Mozart: Pastorale variée
Beethoven: Sonata op. 57
Schumann: Etudes
symphoniques op. 13
Granados: Danza española
Albéniz: Sevilla
Lieurance: Indian Flute Call and
Love Song
Lehmann: Southland Frolic
Debussy:
  a. La soirée dans Grenade
  b. Poisson d'or
Chopin: Grande polonaise
brillante op. 22

Nov 8 to 20
Dramatic Spanish Company
Josefina Díaz–Manuel Collado

Nov 21 to Dec 2
Comic Company Paquito Busto

ISRAELI OPERETTA SEASON
Israeli Operetta Company Gita
Galina–Max Perlman

Dec 5 to 29
Conductor: Jeremías Giganeri

Dec 5, 7, 9
DIE DORRISCHE PRINZESSIN
(Maizzels)

Dec 6
UN ROMANCE EN EL DESIERTO
(Marcovich)

Dec 8 (6:30 and 10:00 P.M.)
LA NIETA DEL OTRO MUNDO
(Witmatak)

Dec 28, 29 (6:30 P.M.)
LA MUJER DEL PANADERO
(Maizzels)

Dec 29
EL ALEGRE LOVA (Olschaneski)

Dec 10 to 22
Argentinean Dramatic Company
Mecha Ortiz

1941

Female artists
Arce, Aida <tiple>
Campiña, Fidela <s>
Fleurquin, Clara <s>
Gaveau, Colette <pf>
Maricarmen <tiple>
Odnoposoff, Nélida <pf>
Palazón, Carmen <tiple>
Sakharoff, Clotilde <d>
Vila, Lola <s>
Zug, Elizabeth <pf>

Male artists
Arenas, Joaquín <b>
García-Martí, Andrés <bar>
Guichandut, Carlos <bar>
Hertogs, Pablo <bar>
Malcuzinski, Witold <pf>
Odnoposoff, Ricardo <vn>
Sakharoff, Alexandre <d>
Vela, Antonio <t>

Jan 10 to 19
Spanish Comic Company
(Pochade and Vaudeville)

Jan 24 to Feb 16
Spanish Dramatic Company
Socorrito González–Tino
Rodríguez

Feb 22 to March 23
Carnival Masked Balls

March 27 to April 7
UN GUAPO DEL 900
(Eichelbaum)
Dramatic Argentinean Company
from Teatro Nacional de Buenos
Aires

SPANISH ZARZUELA SEASON
Spanish Zarzuela Company
Pablo Hertogs–Carmen Palazón–
Antonio Vela
April 9 to 28
Conductor: Rafael Palacios

April 9
LUISA FERNANDA (Moreno
Torroba)
Luisa Fernanda: Vila
Carolina: Palazón
Javier Moreno: Vela
Vidal Hernando: Hertogs

May 1 to 31
House dark due to preparation
of the Juan Manuel Blanes
Exhibition

June 19
Official opening, "Complete
Works of Painter Juan Manuel
Blanes (1830–1901)"

Aug 25
Closing ceremonies of Blanes
Exhibition with Uruguayan
President Alfredo Baldomir

SPANISH ZARZUELA SEASON
Spanish Zarzuela Company
Fidela Campiña–Antonio Vela–
Carlos Guichandut
Aug 30 to Sept 22
Conductor: Rafael Palacios

Aug 30
LA VERBENA DE LA PALOMA
(Bretón)
and LA MUSA GITANA (José
Baylac)**

Sept 5
Recital: Odnoposoff <vn>, N.
Odnoposoff <pf>
Joachim: Variations in E Minor
Bach: Sonata no. 1 for violin
solo
Goldmark: Concerto op. 20 in A
Minor
Szymanowski: Nocturne and
Tarantella
Leemans: Croquis chinois
Mignone: Variaciones sobre un
tema brasileiro
Paganini: La campanella

Sept 12, 14, 15
Vocal Concerts with Petit
Chanteurs de la Croix de Boix
from Paris

Sept 19, Oct 2
Dance Recitals

Clotilde and Alexandre
Sakharoff

Sept 24 to 30
Comedie Française Louis Jouvet–
Madeleine Ozeray

Oct 4 to 14
Galician Regional Art Company
Marujita Villanueva

Oct 17 (6:30 P.M.)
Recital: Gaveau <pf>
Schumann:
    a. Novellette in F Major
    b. Novellette in D Major
    c. Symphonische Etüden
Chopin:
    a. Ballade in A Major
    b. Nocturne in B-flat Major
    c. Three Studies: op 10 (F
    Major), op. 25 (F Minor),
    and D-flat Major
Debussy: L'isle joyeuse
Fauré: Nocturne in E-flat Minor
Ravel: Toccata

ITALIAN MUSICAL COMEDY
SEASON
Oct 17 to Nov 4
CANZONI DI NAPOLI

Oct 22
Rosario and Coral Peñalver
Spanish Dance Company

Oct 27
Recital: Zug <pf>
Bach: Largo
Paradial: Toccata
Beethoven: Sonata op. 31, no. 2
Chopin:
    a. Nocturne
    b. Etude in thirds
    c. Etude in sixths
    d. Etude op. 10, no. 6
    e. Polonaise op. 44

Brahms: Variations on a
Paganini Theme
Jonas: Humoresque
Tcherepin: Three Bagatelles op. 5
Sapeinikoff: Song Without
Words
Liszt: Hungarian Rhapsody no.
10

Nov 7 (6:30 P.M.)
Recital:
I—Gaveau <pf> plays French
music
Hahn: Sonatina
Debussy:
   a. Prelude in A
   b. Clair de lune
   c. Jardins sous la pluie
Fauré: Impromptu in F Minor
Ravel: Toccata
II—Malcuzinski <pf> plays
Chopin
   a. Polonaise in F-sharp Mi-
      nor
   b. Nocturne in C Minor
   c. Three Studies op. 10
   d. Mazurka
   e. Scherzo in B-flat Minor

Nov 7 to 9
Spanish Dramatic Company
Josefina Díaz–Manuel Collado

Nov 10
Symphonic Concert
Escuela Experimental de Arte
Musical y Lírico Orchestra
Conductor: Pablo Komlós
Soloist: Fleurquin <s>
Wagner: Prelude and Liebestod
from Tristan und Isolde
Mozart: Aria from Die
Zauberflöte
Beethoven: Symphony no. 5
Fabini: La isla de los ceibos
Rossini: Aria from Il barbiere di
Siviglia

Falla: El sombrero de tres picos'
excerpts
Berlioz: Hungarian March

Nov 12 to 20
Angelillo and the López
Brothers Spanish Dance
Company

Nov 20 to Dec 14
Spanish Dramatic Company
Lola Membrives

Dec 16 to 28
Comic Company Tito Martínez
Delbox

1942

Female artists
Asencio, Cándida <s>
Lange, Herta <pf>
Lerena, Argentina <tiple>
Mariño, Nibya <pf>
Salmon, Celia P. de <pf>
Sanchez-Elía de Quintana,
Carmen <s>
Sportelli, Victoria <s>
Vila, Lola <s>

Male artists
Arenas, Joaquín <b>
Arrau, Claudio <pf>
Brailowsky, Alexandre <pf>
Hertogs, Pablo <bar>
Lange, Raul <actor>
La Vía, Luis <pf>
Reboredo, Luis <t>
Salmon, Roger <vn>
Sirvent, Adolfo <t>
Szeryng, Henryk <vn>
Uninsky, Alexandre <pf>

Jan 1 to 6
NOCHEBUENA GITANA
Juan José Padilla Company

Jan 9 to 12
Teatro Criollo Company Nelly
Omar–Maruja Roig

Feb 14 to March 8
Carnival Masked Balls
Jazz Vinicio Ascone

March 14 to 22
Leon Zárate Comic Company

SPANISH ZARZUELA SEASON
Spanish Zarzuela Company
Pablo Hertogs
March 27 to April 20
Conductor: Rafael Palacios

March 27
LUISA FERNANDA (Moreno-
Torroba)
Luisa Fernanda: Vila
Carolina: Asencio
Javier Moreno: Sirvent
Vidal Hernando: Hertogs

May 6, 15, June 3
Bertha Singerman <poetic
recitals>

BEETHOVEN COMPLETE PIANO-
SONATA CYCLE
Arrau <pf>
April 22: Sonatas nos. 1, 2, 3, 25,
26
April 29: Sonatas nos. 5, 7, 22,
23
May 8: Sonatas nos. 4, 9, 10, 15,
12, 14
May 11: Sonatas nos. 16, 17, 18,
19, 20, 21
May 13: Sonatas nos. 6, 8, 11
May 29: Sonatas nos. 29, 27, 28,
30, 31, 32

April 24 to July 31
Spanish Dramatic Company
Guerrero–Díaz de Mendoza–
Romeu

May 22
Recital: Uninsky <pf>
Bach: Toccata in C Major
Mozart: Variations on Come un
agnello
Chopin: Sonata op. 35
Tchaikovsky: Dumka
Liszt: Sonetto del Petrarca
Debussy: Feux d'artifice
Infante: El vito

May 25
Recital: Uninsky <pf>
Bach: Partita in C Minor
Liszt: Sonata in B Minor
Ravel: Ondine
Albéniz:
   a. Córdoba
   b. Triana
Chopin:
   a. Nocturne
   b. Etude
   c. Polonaise op. 53

June 8
Farewell Recital: Arrau <pf>
Works by Mozart, Schumann,
and Liszt

June 15
Recital: Joaquín Pérez Fernández
Dance Company

June 26
Recital: Uninsky <pf>
Scarlatti: Three Sonatas
Beethoven: Sonata op. 57
Schumann: Novellette in
C-sharp Minor
Brahms: Variations on a
Paganini Theme
Liszt: Funérailles
Chopin: Two Mazurkas
Debussy: Jardins sous la pluie
Ravel: Oiseaux tristes
Dohnányi: Capriccio

June 29
Recital: Salmon <vn>, C. P. de
Salmon <pf>
Corelli: Sonata La follia
Chopin: Concerto in E-flat
Sarasate:
   a. Romanza andaluza
   b. Zapateado

July 3
Russian Music Recital: Uninsky
<pf>

July 15
Recital: Szeryng <vn>, La Vía
<pf>
Vieniawski: Scherzo and
tarantella
Saint-Saëns: Habanera
Paganini: Capriccio no. 20
Brahms: Sonata no. 3 in D
Minor
Szimanowski: Song to Roxana

Musical Comedy Company
Pepita Llaser
July 16 to 31

July 21, 24
EL CID CAMPEADOR
Poetic-Musical Performances
R. Lange <actor>, H. Lange <pf>

July 28
Recital: Szeryng <vn>, Mariño
<pf>
Mozart: Sonata in B-flat Major
Schumann: Sonata in D Minor
Franck: Sonata in A Major

July 31 to Aug 7
Spanish Musical Comedy
Company España y América

Aug 9 to 11, Dec 26 to 31
Spanish Dramatic Company
Josefina Díaz–Manuel Collado

Aug 14 to Sept 6
Musical Comedy Company
Canaro–Pelay

CHOPIN COMPLETE WORKS CYCLE
Brailowsky <pf>

Aug 6 (first recital)
Polonaise op. 26
Eight Mazurkas
Fantasie-Impromptu op. 66
Polonesa op. 44
Sonata op. 58
Three Nocturnes
Three Waltzes

Aug 17 (second recital)
Two Nocturnes
Six Mazurkas
Two Polonaises: op. 40, no. 2
and op. 71, no. 2
Four Studies op. 10
Eight Studies op. 25
Scherzo op. 54
Two Nocturnes
Ballade op. 38
Impromptu op. 29
Waltz op. 34, no. 3
Andante spianato and polonaise
op. 22

Aug 19 (third recital)
Ten Mazurkas
Fantasie op. 49
Two Polonaises: op. 40, no. 1
and op. 71, no. 1
Three Nocturnes
Three Ecossaises
Scherzo op. 20
Impromptu op.51
Four Studies op. 10
Two Studies op. 25
Two Waltzes
Ballade op. 47

Aug 31 (fourth recital)
Ten Mazurkas
Three Nocturnes

Scherzo op. 39
Sonata op. 35
Two Polonaises: op. 71, no. 3
and op. 26 no. 1
Tarantella op. 43
Three Waltzes
Bolero op. 19

Sept 7 (fifth recital)
Prelude op. 45
Eight Mazurkas
Three Studies
Polonaise fantasia op. 61
Impromptu op. 6
Three Waltzes
Ballade op. 52
Three Nocturnes
Scherzo op. 31

Sept 15 (sixth recital)
Three Nocturnes
Nine Mazurkas
Twenty-four Preludes op. 28
Barcarolle op. 60
Two Waltzes
Polonaise op. 52

Sept 7 (10:30 P.M.)
Biblia-Bach Recital
R. Lange <actor>, H. Lange <pf>

Sept 9 to 14
National Dramatic Company
Carmen Casnell—José Franco,
with Guarnero, Otero, Teresa
Puente

SPANISH ZARZUELA SEASON
Lyric Zarzuela Company Pablo
Hertogs–Victoria Sportelli
Sept 18 to Oct 19
Conductor: Rafael Palacios

Sept 18
LA CALESERA (Alonso)

Oct 22 to Nov 15
Dramatic Company Paulina
Singerman

Oct 23
OSSODRE Symphonic-vocal
Concert
Conductor: José María Castro
Soloist: S.E. de Quintana <s>
Esteve: Canciones del siglo XVI
Juransky: Copla y vidala
Granados:
 a. La maja y el ruiseñor
 b. El majo discreto
Guastavino: Se equivocó la
paloma
Vives:
 a. Canciones epigramáticas
 b. El amor y los ojos
 c. El retrato de Isabella
Haydn: Symphony no. 1
J. M. Castro: Obertura para una
ópera cómica
Debussy: Deux nocturnes
Liszt: Les préludes

Nov 18 to Dec 8
Argentinean Dramatic Company
Pepe Arias

Dec 11 to 20
Modern Theatre Company Anita
Jordán–Malisa Zini–Domingo
Marquez–Luis Alberto Negro

1943

Female artists
Amorós, Blanca Luz <s>
Arce, Aida <tiple>
Arce, Merceditas <tiple>
Asencio, Cándida <s>
Campiña, Fidela <s>
Lerena, Argentina <tiple>
Mariño, Nibya <pf>
Paltrinieri, Velia <mez>

Parodi-Invernizzi, Raquel <pf>
Reggiani, Hilde <s>
Regina, Alba <soubrette>
Rosciano, Mafalda <mez>
Siécola, Ema <harp>
Sola, Margherita <s>
Sorella, Grazia <s>
Tagliaferro, Magda <pf>
Valverde, María <s>
Zerite, Princess <d>

Male artists
Arregui, Faustino <t>
Balzo, Hugo <pf>
Bonanni, Oscar <bar>
Casalla, Agustín <b>
Ericourt, Daniel <pf>
Escobal-Vertiz, Venancio <b>
Favila, Sergio <bar>
Firkusny, Rudolf <pf>
Foglizzo, Edoardo <t>
Gaviria, Jesús de <t>
Guichandut, Carlos <bar>
Hertogs, Pablo <bar>
Landi, Bruno <t>
Malcuzinski, Witold <pf>
Mayer, Tomas G. <pf>
Monachesi, Mario <bar>
Pierelli, Franco <t>
Reboredo, Luis <t>
Rolle, Miguel <t>
Villa, Joaquín <bar>

Jan 1 to Feb 21
Spanish Dramatic Company
Díaz–Collado

Feb 25 to March 1
Wu-Li-Chang <magician>

March 6 to 27
Carnival Masked Balls

SPANISH ZARZUELA SEASON
Spanish Zarzuela Company
Merceditas Arce–Arregui–
Guichandut–Campiña

April 2 to May 5
Conductor: Francisco Balaguer

April 2
LUISA FERNANDA (Moreno-
Torroba)
Luisa Fernanda: Campiña
Carolina: M. Arce
Javier Moreno: Arregui
Vidal Hernando: Guichandut

May 5
Recital: Firkusny <pf>
Bach: Toccata in C Minor
Mozart: Variations Minue by
J. P.Duport
Chopin: Sonata op. 58
Debussy:
    a. La puerta del vino
    b. La terrasse des audiences
       du clair de lune
Smetana:
    a. Polka
    b. Czech dance
    c. Furiant

**FALL ITALIAN OPERA
SEASON**
Antonio Marranti Company
May 7 to 23
Conductor: Antonio Marranti

May 7, 9
AIDA (Verdi)
Aida: Campiña
Amneris: Paltrinieri
Radamès: Gaviria
Amonasro: Favila

May 8, 9 (6:30 P.M.), 20
RIGOLETTO (Verdi)
Gilda: Sorella
Il Duca di Mantova: Pierelli
Rigoletto: Villa
Maddalena: Rosciano
Sparafucile: Escobal-Vertiz

May 10, 16 (matinée), 19
LA TRAVIATA (Verdi)
Violetta: Amorós
Alfredo Germont: Pierelli
Giorgio Germont: Monachesi

May 11, 23
LUCIA DI LAMMERMOOR
(Donizetti)
Lucia: Sorella
Edgardo: Rolle
Enrico: Monachesi
Raimondo: Escobal-Vertiz

May 12, 17 (6:30 P.M.)
CAVALLERIA RUSTICANA
(Mascagni)
Santuzza: Campiña
Lola: Rosciano
Turiddu: Rolle
Alfio: Bonanni
PAGLIACCI (Leoncavallo)
Nedda: Amorós
Canio: Gaviria
Tonio: Villa
Silvio: Monachesi

May 13
LA BOHEME (Puccini)
Mimì: Amorós
Rodolfo: Pierelli
Marcello: Monachesi
Colline: Escobal-Vertiz

May 14
TOSCA (Puccini)
Tosca: Campiña
Mario Cavaradossi: Gaviria
Barone Scarpia: Bonanni

May 15
LA FAVORITA (Donizetti)
Leonora: Paltrinieri
Fernando: Pierelli
Alfonso XI: Bonanni
Baldassare: Escobal-Vertiz

May 16
IL TROVATORE (Verdi)
Leonora: Campiña
Manrico: Gaviria
Conte di Luna: Villa
Azucena: Rosciano

May 17, 18, 23 (6:30 P.M.)
IL BARBIERE DI SIVIGLIA
(Rossini)
Rosina: Sorella
Conte di Almaviva: Pierelli
Figaro: Villa
Don Basilio: Escobal-Vertiz
Don Bartolo: Casalla

May 21
MADAMA BUTTERFLY (Puccini)
Cio-Cio-San: Amorós
Pinkerton: Pierelli
Suzuki: Rosciano
Sharpless: Monachesi

May 22
CARMEN (Bizet)
Carmen: Paltrinieri
Don Jose: Gaviria
Escamillo: Villa

May 23
Farewell Operatic Concert

May 13 (6:30 P.M.)
Recital: Firkusny <pf>
Bach: Two Corals
Beethoven: Thirty-two Variations
Chopin:
    a. Mazurka
    b. Deux Etudes
    c. Barcarolle
    d. Ballade
Smetana: Medved (Czech dance)
Ravel: La vallée des cloches
Stravisnky: Petrouchka

May 14 (6:30 P.M.)
Recital: Tagliaferro <pf>
Mozart: Sonata in A Major

Bach: Overture to Cantata no. 23
Chopin: Sonata op. 58
Villa-Lobos: Impresões seresteiras
Poulenc:
  a. Toccata
  b. Pastourelle
Fauré: Deuxième impromptu
Mompou: Muchachas en el jardín
Falla: Danza de La vida breve

May 19 (6:30 P.M.)
Recital: Ericourt <pf>
Bach: Prelude and fugue in D Major
Ravel: Le tombeau de Couperin
Chopin: Sonata op. 35
Debussy:
  a. Serénade interrompue
  b. La terrasse des audiences du clair de lune
  c. Feux d'artifice
Shostakovich: Four Preludes
Balakirev: Islamey

May 26
Recital: Ericourt <pf>
Paradies: Toccata
Bach-Busoni: Two organ preludes
Beethoven: Sonata op. 53
Chopin:
  a. Trois Etudes
  b. Nocturne
  c. Ballade in G Minor
  d. Tarantella
Debussy: Trois images
  a. Cloches à travers les feuilles
  b. Mouvement
  c. Poissons d'or
Roger-Ducasse: Etude
Fauré: Impromptu
Dohnányi: Capriccio

FALL ITALIAN OPERETTA SEASON
Alba Regina Operetta Company
First season: May 28 to June 14
[see second season Nov 18]
Conductor: Giovanni Trave
Principal singers: Sola and Foglizzo

May 28, 29 (6:30 P.M.), June 1, 11
UN BALLO NELLO SAVOY (Abraham)

May 29, 30 (6:30 P.M.), June 4
LA PRINCIPESSA DELLE CZARDE (Kálmán) (It)

May 30, June 2
LA DUCHESSA DEL BAL TABARIN (Lombardo)

May 31, June 3 (6:30 P.M.)
EVA (Lehár) (It)

June 3, 5 (6:30 P.M.)
LA DANZA DELLA LIBELULLE (Lehár) (It)

June 5, 6 (6:30 P.M.), 9
LA VEDOVA ALLEGRA (Lehár) (It)

June 6, 8, 10 (6:30 P.M.)
SCUGNIZZA (Costa)

June 7
IL CONTE DI LUSSEMBURGO (Lehár) (It)

June 10, 12 (6:30 P.M.), 13
LA OSTERIA DELLO CAVALLO BIANCO (Stolz, Gilbert, and Granischataeden) (It)

June 12, 13 (6:30 P.M.)
SOGNO D'UN VALSER (O. Straus) (It)

June 14
LA CASTA SUSANNA (Gilbert) (It)

June 2 (6:30 P.M.)
Recital: Tagliaferro <pf>

June 16 to Aug 8
Spanish Dramatic Company
Guerrero–Díaz de Mendoza–Romeu

BANDA MUNICIPAL 1943 CONCERT SEASON
Banda Municipal de Montevideo
Music Director and Conductor:
Vicente Ascone, and Bernardo Freire-López (assistant conductor)
June 20, Aug 22 (10:45 A.M.)
Conductor: Freire-López
June 27, Aug 1, 8, Sept 26, Oct 3, 10, 24,
Nov 14 (10:45 A.M.)
Conductor: Ascone

July 7
Recital: Firkusny <pf>

July 21
Recital: Malcuzinski <pf>
Beethoven: Thirty-two Variations
Liszt: Sonata in B Minor
Szymanowski: Four Mazurkas op. 50
Chopin:
  a. Nocturne
  b. Etude
  c. Scherzo in B-flat

July 28
Recital: Malcuzinski <pf>
Works by Bach, Chopin, Debussy, Szymanowski, and Paderewski

Aug 4
ABYSSINIAN CHOREOGRAPHIC ART COMPANY

Princess Zerite <Ethiopian dancer>

Aug 6
Farewell Recital: Malcuzinski <pf>
Franck: Prélude, choral et fugue
Chopin:
    a. Scherzo in B Minor
    b. Four Mazurkas
    c. Ballade in G Minor
Scriabin: two Etudes
Szymanowski: Variations on a Polish folk theme

SPANISH ZARZUELA SEASON
(second season)
M. Arce–Arregui–Hertogs
Company
Aug 13 to 30
Conductor: Felipe Torres

Aug 13
LUISA FERNANDA (Moreno-Torroba)
Luisa Fernanda: Asencio
Carolina: M. Arce
Javier Moreno: Arregui
Vidal Hernando: Hertogs

Aug 30
Recital: Parodi-Invernizzi <pf>
Beethoven:
    a. Two Bagatelles
    b. Sonata op. 27, no. 2
Szymanowski: Etude op. 4
Ravel: Pavane pour une infante défunte
Prokofiev: Prelude in C Major
Rachmaninov: Prelude in G Minor
Schumann: Carnaval op. 9

Sept 3 to Oct 12
Musical Comedy Company
Francisco Canaro–Ivo Pelay

Oct 4
Madeleine Ozeray <poetry recital> (from Louis Jouvet Dramatic Company)

Oct 15 to Nov 16
Spanish Dramatic Company
Pepita Meliá–Benito Cibrián

Nov 16
Recital: Reggiani <s>, Landi <t>, Mayer <pf>
Works by Puccini, Tosti, Pergolesi, Verdi, Donizetti, Cilea, Mattei, Pérez-Freire, Serrano, Caccini, Curtis, and Buzzi-Peccia

SPRING ITALIAN OPERETTA SEASON
Alba Regina Operetta Company
Second season: Nov 18 to Dec 5
Conductor: Giovanni Trave

Nov 18, 25 (6:30 P.M.)
VITTORIA E IL SUO USSARO (Abraham)

Nov 19
LA DIVORZIATA (Fall) (It)

Nov 20 (6:30 P.M.)
LA PRINCIPESSA DELLE CZARDE (Kálmán) (It)

Nov 20, 21 (6:30 P.M.)
SALTIMBANCHI (Ganne) (It)

Nov 21
IL PAESE DEL CAMPANILLE (Ranzato)

Nov 22, 28 (6:30 P.M.)
LA PRINCIPESSA DELLE DOLAR (Fall) (It)

Nov 24, 28, Dec 2 (6:30 P.M.)
BOCCACCIO (Suppé) (It)

Nov 25
PAGANINI (Lehár) (It)

Nov 26
LA OSTERIA DELLO CAVALLO BIANCO (Stolz, Gilbert and Granischataeden) (It)

Nov 27 (6:30 P.M.), Dec 5
LA VEDOVA ALLEGRA (Lehár) (It)

Nov 27, 29
SCUGNIZZA (Costa)

Nov 30
LA MASCOTTA (Audran) (It)

Dec 1
PRIMAVERA SCAPIGLIATA (Joseph Strauss) (It)

Dec 2, 4 (6:30 P.M.)
LA DUCHESSA DEL BAL TABARIN (Lombardo)

Dec 3
FRASQUITA (Lehár) (It)

Dec 4
L'AMORE DI ZINGARO (Lehár) (It)

Dec 5 (6:30 P.M.)
IL CONTE DI LUSSEMBURGO (Lehár) (It)

Dec 3 (6:30 P.M.)
Chamber Music Recital:
Valverde <s>, Siécola <harp>, Mariño <pf>, Balzo <pf>
Saint-Saëns: Variations on a Theme of Beethoven <2 pf>
Spanish Songs by Alfonso El Sabio, Milán, Vázquez, and Narvaez <s/harp>
Fauré: Suite Dolly <2 pf>
Infante: Danzas andaluzas <2 pf>

Rachmaninov: Russian Rhapsody
<2 pf>

Dec 7 to 31
[House closed for renovation
and decoration.]

1944

Dec 31, 1943 (at midnight) to
March 31, 1944
GRAND VEGLIONI
(Social and Carnival Masked
Balls)
Orchestras: Típica Juan
D'Arienzo, Jazz Vinicio Ascone,
Alberto Castillo

April 1
Gala Chabelska Ballet
Banda Municipal
Conductor: Vicente Ascone

April 2
EL GATO CON BOTAS (Brusa)
Carlos Brusa Children Theater
Company

April 3 to Dec 31
[House closed for renovation
and decoration.]

1945

Feb 3 to March 11
Carnival Masked Balls
Orchestras: D'Arienzo, Galán,
and Orquesta Casino de
Copacabana

March 12 to Dec 31
[House closed for renovation
and decoration.]

1946

Female artists
Castro, Virginia <s>
Fernández, Aída <s>
Mañé, Adelaida Ramírez de <s>
Soldevila, Blanca Rosa <mez>

Male artists
Algorta, Jorge <b>
Claramunt, Enrique <bar>
Giammarchi, Luis <t>
Luongo, Virgilio <bar>

March 3 to 31
Carnival Masked Balls

April 1st to Aug 24
[House closed for renovation
and decoration.]

Aug 25, 27, Sep 1
NINETIETH ANNIVERSARY
OF THE SOLÍS
REOPENING OF THE HOUSE
Uruguayan National Anthem
"Al Teatro Solís" (poem by
Francisco Acuña de Figueroa)
LA TRAVIATA (Verdi)
Conductor: Domingo Dente
Violetta: Fernández
Alfredo Germont: Giammarchi
Giorgio Germont: Luongo
Flora: Soldevila
Dottore Grenvil: Algorta

Aug 31
LE NOZZE DI FIGARO (Mozart)
Conductor: Carlos Estrada
Susanna: Mañé
Contessa: Soldevila
Cherubino: Castro
Conte Almaviva: Claramunt
Figaro: Algorta

Sept 2 to Dec 31
[House closed for final
decoration.]

1947

Female artists
Correa-Luna, Celia <pf>
Madriguera, Paquita <pf>
Mainor, Dorothy <s>
Mariño, Nibya <pf>
Neveu, Ginette <vn>
Olivera, Mercedes <pf>
Quiroga, Ercilia <mez>
Schenini, Victoria <pf>
Valverde, María <s>
Verbitzky, Sonia <s>
West, María Luisa Fabini de <s>

Male artists
Bergmann, Ludwig <pf>
Carlevaro, Abel <gui>
Damiani, Víctor <bar>
Firkusny, Rudolf <pf>
Jessel, Misha <pf>
Loyonnet, Paul <pf>
Neveu, Jean <pf>
Nicastro, Oscar <vc>
Otnes, Jon <t>
Protasi, Juan <pf>
Rodríguez, Abelardo <gui>
Schenone, Adhemar <pf>
Vertiz, Abel <pf>
Werberg, Otto <d>

Feb 8 to March 23
Carnival Masked Balls

April 17 to 20
THEATRE DU BALLET
Otto Werberg <first dancer of
Vienna's Opera and Ballet Jooss>

April 22
Recital: Mariño <pf>
J. S. Bach: Concerto Italiano
Schumann: Fantasia op.17
Chopin:
  a. Nocturne in E Major
  b. Two Etudes
  c. Scherzo in B-flat Minor

Debussy:
  a. Hommage à Rameau
  b. La plus que lente
  c. Danse
Gershwin: Three Preludes
Scriabin: Sonata no. 4

April 25
Recital: Mariño <pf>
Mozart: Rondo
Franck: Prelude, Choral and
Fugue
Chopin: Sonata op. 58
Schumann: Papillons
Liszt:
  a. Harmonies du soir
  b. Vals oubliée
  c. Saint François de Paule
     marchant sur les flots

May 8
Recital: Mariño <pf>
Bach-Busoni: Toccata,
Intermezzo, and Fugue
Schumann: Kinderszenen
Liszt: Sonata in B Minor
Debussy: Trois préludes
Ravel:
  a. Pavane
  b. Jeux d'eau
Albéniz:
  a. El Albaicín
  b. Córdoba
  c. Triana

May 17
Lecture-Recital
Dr. Emilio Frugoni: Lecture,
"Theater in Russia"
Russian Music Recital: Schenini
<pf>
Musorgsky: Three numbers
from Pictures at an Exhibition
Tchaikovsky: Humoresque
Scriabin: Nocturne pour la main
gauche
Prokofiev: Prelude and Marche

from The Love for Three
Oranges

May 18
Chopin Recital: Mariño <pf>

May 21 to June 9
Dramatic Company Dulcina de
Moraes–Santiago
Arrieta–Fanny Brena

May 30
Recital: Mariño <pf>
Schumann: Papillons
Chopin:
  a. Trois Ecosaises
  b. Barcarole
Liszt:
  a. Funérailles
  b. Harmonies du soir
  c. Saint François de Paule
     marchant sur les flots
Granados: La maja y el ruiseñor
Falla: Andaluza
Albéniz:
  a. Evocación
  b. Navarra
  c. Córdoba
  d. Triana

June 13
Recital: Nicastro <vc>, Protasi
<pf>
Beethoven: Twelve Variations on
Handel's Judas Maccabaeus
Corelli: Sonata
Tartini: Andante cantabile
Lully-Nicastro: Gavotte
Bach: Aria
Beethoven: Minuetto
Cui: Oriental
Beckert: Minuetto
Glazunov: Spanish Serenade
Schubert-Nicastro: Lullaby
Granados-Nicastro: Danza
española no. 5
Popper: Spinnlied

June 14
LA MASQUE BLEU [drama]
Dramatic French Company

June 15
Homage to Eduardo Fabini at
the Twenty-fifth Anniversary
of Campo
Banda Municipal and Coral
Guarda e Passa in a Fabini
Program
Conductor: Vicente Ascone
Chorus Master: Enrique Casal-
Chapí
Soloists: West<s>, Schenone<pf>,
Olivera <pf>
La Patria Vieja (band version)
Songs:
  a. El poncho
  b. Triste
  c. El nido
Piano pieces:
  a. Triste no. 2
  b. Luz mala
String Quintet
Piano pieces:
  a. Triste no. 1
  b. Intermezzo
Choral works:
  a. Las flores del campo
  b. A mi río
Campo, symphonic poem (band
version)

June 18 to July 6
Argentinean Musical Comedy
Company Enrique Santos-
Discépolo

July 8 to 16
Italian Dramatic Company
Emma Gramatica

July 11, 15
Recitals: Mainor <s>, Bergmann
<pf>
Works by Purcell, Handel,
Mozart, Debussy, Massenet, and
Negro Spirituals

BALLET SEASON
Teatro alla Scala Ballet Company
from Milan
July 17 to 30

July 30 (6:30 P.M.)
Recital: Firkusny <pf>
Mozart: Fantasy in C Minor
Beethoven: Sonata op. 27, no. 2
Brahms:
  a. Capriccio op. 76, no. 1
  b. Two Intermezzi, op. 119, nos. 2 and 3
  c. Capriccio, op. 116, no. 1
Mendelssohn: Variations sérieuses
Martinú: Les ritournelles
Smetana:
  a. Furiant
  b. Medved Polka

Aug 5 and 6
French Dramatic Company
Marie Bell–Maurice Escande–
Leo Peltier

Aug 8
Recital: Firkusny <pf>
Bach-Busoni: Two Chorals
Schubert: Three Pieces
Chopin Sonata in B minor op. 58
Martinú:
  a. Study in E Minor
  b. Polka
Debussy: Reflets dans l'eau
Liszt:
  a. Valse oubliée
  b. Mephisto Waltz

Aug 18
"Il Teatro Italiano" (lecture in Italian, presented by Silvio d'Amico [President of the Academy of Dramatic Arts in Rome])

Aug 19
Recital: G. Neveu <vn>, J. Neveu <pf>
Mozart: Concerto in G Minor
Bach: Chaconne for violin solo
Brahms: Sonata no. 2 in A Major
Ravel:
  a. Habanera
  b. Tzigane

Aug 21
Second Lecture in Italian
"Il teatro di Pirandello" by Silvio d'Amico

Aug 22, Oct 10
Recitals: Olivera <pf>

Aug 28
Lecture and Recital
Loyonnet <lecturer / pf>
"Beethoven et son destin"
(Lecture in French)
Beethoven: Sonatas op. 57 and 110

Aug 30
Homage to Florencio Sánchez
Introduction by Roberto Olivencia Marquez and Julio Caporale Scelta
"Mensaje Lírico" by Ovidio Fernández Ríos
Judith Reyes <recitant>
NUESTROS HIJOS (Sánchez) by Agrupación Uruguaya de Teatro Vocacional El Tinglado

Sept 1
Recital: Carlevaro <gui>
R. de Visée: Petite suite
Bach: Sarabande et bourrée
Sor: Tema variado
Moreno-Torroba: Piezas características
Ponce: Vals

Castelnuovo-Tedesco: Vivo e enérgico
Turina: Ráfaga
Albéniz: Asturias

Sept 2
Russian Music Recital: Verbitzky <s>, Jessel <pf>

Sept 5 to 14
Italian Dramatic Company
Emma Gramatica

COMEDIA NACIONAL INAUGURAL SEASON
Oct 2 to Nov 29
EL LEON CIEGO (Herrera)
[also many other plays by Uruguayan playwrights in daily performances]

Oct 15
Recital: Quiroga <mez>, Correa Luna <pf / composer>
1. Correa Luna piano works
  a. Variaciones
  b. Preludio
  c. Hilandera
  d. Vals scherzo
  e. Momentos infantiles (suite)
  f. Baile en la aldea
2. Correa Luna songs:
  a. D'une fontaine
  b. Chant de Mai
  c. El molino quemado
  d. Canción de cuna
  e. El canto del carretero
  f. Dame la mano
  g. Para pasar la ribera
  h. Estilo

Oct 24
Recital: Rodríguez <gui>
Works by Tárrega, Villa-Lobos, Quijano-Llovet, A. Rodríguez, Gómez-Carrillo, Falla, and Albéniz

Oct 26 (10:45 A.M.)
Concert Banda Municipal de
Montevideo
Conductor: Vicente Ascone

Nov 9 (10:45 A.M.)
Banda Municipal / Coral Guarda
e Passa Concert
Conductor: Vicente Ascone

Nov 19
Recital: Otnes <t>, Vertiz <pf>
Works by Handel, Schubert, R.
Strauss, Cilea, Donizetti,
Massenet, and Puccini

Dec 5 to 22
Spanish Dramatic Company
Margarita Xirgu–Esteban
Serrador

Dec 17
Recital:
1. Nicastro <vc> / Protasi <pf>
Tartini: Andante cantabile
Lully-Nicastro: Gavotte
Bach: Aria
Beethoven: Minuetto
Cui: Oriental
Glazunov: Spanish Dance
2. Madriguera <pf>
Mendelssohn: Lieder ohne
Worte
Grabados:
    a. Danza valenciana
    b. La maja y el ruiseñor
Falla: Andaluza
Albéniz: Seguidilla
3. Schenone <pf>
Aguirre: Huella
Villa-Lobos: A lenda do Caboclo
Fabini: Triste no. 2
Cluzeau-Mortet: Junto al fogón
4. Vocal and piano works
J. Vázquez: Duele de mi señora
(sixteenth century)
(Valverde / Schenone)

Respighi: Nebbie (Damiani /
Schenone)
Lohengrin: Duet (Valverde /
Damiani / Schenone)

1948

Female artists
Ayala-Vidal, Ema <pf>
Baigorri, Blanca Rosa <s>
Barbieri, Fedora <mez>
Caniglia, Maria <s>
Di Concilio, Juanita <s>
Estevez, Clara <mez>
Indart, Lyda Mirtha <pf>
Lorusso, María <s>
Mas, Rosa <vn>
Montes, Tila <pf>
Pierri, Olga <gui>
Soldevila, Blanca Rosa <s>
Sportelli, Victoria <s>

Male artists
Abad, Manuel <bar>
Alvarez, Aurelio <t>
Balzo, Hugo <pf>
Colacelli, Donato <pf>
Cortese, Roberto <t>
Cubas, Marcos <t>
Damiani, Víctor <bar>
Escobar-Vertiz, Venancio <b>
Favila, Sergio <bar>
Folgar, Tino <t>
Giammarchi, Luis <t>
Grisoli, Liber <b>
Maggiolo, Roberto <t>
Montes, John <pf>
Morales, Edgardo <t>
Neri, Giulio <b>
Oysher, Moishe <t>
Soler, José <t>
Toso, Vittorio <bar>
Yupanqui, Atahualpa <gui>

Feb 7 to March 14
Carnival Masked Balls

April 1 to 26
Spanish Zarzuela Company
Marcos Cubas–Manuel Abad–
Victoria Sportelli–Clara Estevez

BANDA MUNICIPAL 1948 CONCERT SEASON
April 25, May 2, 10, 17, 23, 30,
June 6, 13, 20, 27, July 4, 11, 18,
25, Aug 15, Oct 3, 10, 17, 24 (10:
45 A.M.)
Banda Municipal de Montevideo
Music Director and Conductor:
Vicente Ascone

April 28 to May 4
Winslow Ballet

May 5, 6
Uruguayan Dramatic Company
La Farándula
Director: Emilio Acevedo Solano

ITALIAN OPERA PERFORMANCES
May 7, 8, 9
Conductors: Ernesto Cogorno,
and Juan Protasi (assistant
conductor)

LUCIA DI LAMMERMOOR
(Donizetti)
Lucia: Baigorri
Edgardo: Maggiolo
Enrico: Favila
Raimondo: Escobar-Vertiz

May 8
LA TRAVIATA (Verdi)
Violetta: Lorusso
Alfredo Germont: Giammarchi
Giorgio Germont: Toso
Dottore Grenvil: Escobar-Vertiz

May 9 (6:00 P.M.)
TOSCA (Puccini)
Conductor: Protasi
Tosca: Lorusso

Mario Cavaradossi: Morales
Barone Scarpia: Toso
Angelotti: Escobar-Vertiz

May 9 (10:30 P.M.)
RIGOLETTO (Verdi)
Gilda: Baigorri
Il Duca di Mantova: Maggiolo
Rigoletto: Favila
Sparafucile: Escobar-Vertiz

May 15 to July 22
EN FAMILIA (Sánchez)
Opening of the Comedia
Nacional 1948 Season

July 2
Paloma de Sandoval Spanish
Ballet Company

July 12
Recital: Mas <vn>, Colacelli <pf>
H. Ecclés: Sonata
Vivaldi: Chaconne
Franck: Sonata in A Major
Pahissa: Nocturno
Fernández-Arbós: Tango
Brahms: Waltz
Novacek: Perpetuum mobile

July 14
Recital: Mas <vn>, Colacelli <pf>
Turina: Sonata española
Paganini: Sonata no. 12
Tartini:
   a. Variations on a Corelli
      Theme
   b. Trillo del diávolo
Dvořák: Slavonic Dance
Saint-Saëns: Habanera
Falla: Pantomima from El amor
brujo
Kreisler: Tambourin chinois

July 23 to Aug 2
Italian Dramatic Company Evi
Maltagliatti–Luigi Cimara

Aug 4
Recital: Oysher <t>

Aug 5
Berta Singerman <poetry recital>

Aug 13
"Límite del progreso" (Lecture
by Juan Ramón
Jiménez [Spanish author, winner
of the 1956 Nobel Prize in
Literature])

Aug 16 (6:30 P.M.)
"Aristocracia inmanente"
(lecture by Juan Ramón
Jiménez)

Aug 16 to 18
French Dramatic Company
Henri Rolland–Julien Bertheau

Aug 25
Gala Performance
Uruguayan National Anthem
IL TROVATORE (Verdi)
Conductor: Ettore Panizza
Leonora: Caniglia
Azucena: Barbieri
Manrico: Soler
Conte di Luna: Damiani
Inez: Soldevila
Ferrando: Neri
Ruiz: Alvarez
Vecchio zingaro: Grisoli
Messagero: Cortese

Sept 1
Two-Piano Recital
T. and J. Montes
Bach: The Art of the Fugue**

Sept 24, 27
Recitals: Yupanqui <gui>

Sept 29, Oct 8
Recitals: Ayala-Vidal <pf>
Works by Mozart, Bach,

Brahms, Beethoven, Liszt, and
Debussy

Oct 22
Recital: Folgar <t>, Indart <pf>
Guerrero: Romanza de la flor
(Los gavilanes)
Guerrero: Mujer de los ojos
negros (El huésped del
sevillano)
Sorozábal: Romanza de Don
Manolito
Padilla: Princesita
Mason: En los jardines de
Granada
Lara: Granada
Chopin: Ah, si j'ossais
Tosti: Ideale
Grieg: I love thee
Folgar: Serenata triste
Bizet: Aria from Les pêcheurs de
perles
Massenet: Il sogno from Manon

Oct 25
PELLEAS Y MELISANDA
(Maeterlinck) (Sp)
(Spanish version by G. Martínez-
Sierra)
Teatro de Cámara de
Montevideo

Nov 4
Choral Concert: Coro
Universitario
Chorus Master: Nilda Muller

Nov 5 to 14
Dramatic Company Emma
Gramatica–Iris Marga–Miguel
Faust Rocha

Nov 17 to December 1
Enrique Serrano Comedy
Company

Dec 2
Drama and Chamber Music
Recital

Casa del Teatro Festival
Di Concilio <s>, Balzo <pf>,
Pierri Guitar Quintet, and
AUDEM Orchestra

Dec 3 to 10
Spanish Dramatic Company
Mario Gabarrón–Asunción
Granados

1949

Female artists
Adler, Hilde <pf>
Ayala-Vidal, Ema <pf>
Danieli de Larrea, Rafaela <pf>
Giacosa-Trujillo, Norma <pf>
Gromova, Irina <s>
Montoya, Fernanda <d>
Pierri, Olga <gui>
Prieto, Margot <gui>
Ricci, Teté <gui>
Rigal, Delia <s>
Rolando, Sarah <a>
Sena, Margarita <gui>
Sena, Matilde <gui>
Soldevila, Blanca Rosa <mez>
Stella Maris <s>
Torraza, Carmen <gui>
Valverde, María <s>
Zunino de Barilari, Ermelinda B.
<harp>

Male artists
Alvarez, Aurelio <t>
Astrinidis, Nicolas <pf/
composer>
Ayestarán, Ramón <gui>
Barletta, Alejandro <bandoneón>
Carbonell, Juan <bar>
Damiani, Víctor <bar>
Kempff, Wilhelm <pf>
Kolischer, Wilhelm <pf>
Michelin, Bernard <vc>
Pacheco, Miguel <d>
Pons, Panchito <bar>
Sgarbi, Luis <t>

Turriziani, Angel <pf/org>
Zamboni, Reynaldo <pf>

Feb 26 to April 3
Carnival Masked Balls
Xavier Cugat's Lecuona Cuban
Boys

April 23 to July 13
EL CENTINELA MUERTO (Bellán)
CANILLITA (Sánchez)
Opening of the Comedia
Nacional Winter Season

BANDA MUNICIPAL 1949 CONCERT SEASON

May 29, July 17, 23, 31, Aug 7,
14, 28, Sept 4, 25, Oct 9, 23, 30
(10:45 A.M.)
Banda Municipal de Montevideo
Music Director and Conductor:
Vicente Ascone, and Bernardo
Freire-López (assistant
conductor)

May 29 (10:45 A.M.)
Banda Municipal Concert
Conductor: Freire-López
Soloist: Pons <bar>
Purcell: The Voluntary Trumpet
Leclerc: Sarabande et Tambourin
Berlioz: Excerpts from La
damnation de Faust
Handel: Largo from Xerxes
Wagner:
  a. Arrival of Lohengrin
  b. Narration of Lohengrin
Siegfried: Forging Song
Verdi: Otello
  a. Esultate!
  b. Ora e per sempre addio
  c. End of Act 3

July 8
Recital: Stella Maris <s>, Danieli
<pf>
Brahms: Lullaby
Schubert: Ungeduld

Mozart:
  a. Voi che sapete
  b. Aria from the Magic Flute
Granados: El majo discreto
Benedit: La Capinera
Verdi: Volta la terrea from Un
ballo in maschera
Delibes: Aria des clochettes
(Lakmé)

July 14 to 25
Dramatic Company Emma
Gramatica

July 26
German Dramatic Company
Viktor de Kowa

July 27 to Aug 7
Italian Dramatic Company
Ruggero Ruggeri
ENRICO IV (Pirandello) [and
other plays]

Aug 9, 10
DIE DREIGROSCHENOPER (Weill)
[The Threepenny Opera]
German Dramatic Ensemble

Aug 10 (6:30 P.M.)
Recital: Ayestarán <gui>
Works by De Viseo, Narvaez,
Ferandiere, Sor, Paganini,
Handel, Musorgsky, Gilardi, and
Granados

Aug 12 to 21, 26 to Sept 4
Dramatic Company Nicolás
Fregues, with Maria Rosa Gallo

Aug 25
Gala Performance
Uruguayan National Anthem
LA TRAVIATA (Verdi)
Conductor: Domingo Dente
Violetta: Rigal
Alfredo Germont: Alvarez

Giorgio Germont: Damiani
Flora: Soldevila
Gastone: Sgarbi
Barone Douphol: Carbonell

Aug 29, Sept 14
Recitals: Barletta <bandoneón>
Scarlatti: Aria and Toccata
Handel: Chaconne in F Major
Haydn: Sonata in E Minor
Beethoven:
    a. Bagatelle op. 119
    b. Four Folk Dances
    c. Sonata in F Major
Musorgsky: Gopak
Prokofiev: Vision Fugitive no. 10
Khachaturian: Dance
García-Caturla: Pastoral
Juan José Castro: Sonata
campestre**

Sept 5
Guitar Recital Olga Pierri Guitar
Ensemble: Pierri, Torraza,
Prieto, Sena sisters, Ricci
Forte: Bailecito
Eisenstein: Cifra
Debali: Media caña y Estilo
from La batalla de Cagancha
Anido: Chacarera
Malats: Serenata
Tárrega: Sueño
Navarro: Pequeña danza
Turina: Fandanguillo
Moreno-Torroba: Sonatina
Cluzeau-Mortet: Vidalita
Aguirre: Huella
Fabini: Two Tristes
Sapere: Gato y Malambo

Sept 9 to 18
Angelita Vélez Argentinean Folk
Dance Company

Sept 10 (10:45 A.M.)
Banda Municipal Special
Concert on Catalonian Music
Conductor: Ascone

Soloists: Valverde <s>, Adler <pf>
Vives: Excerpts from Maruxa
Granados: Tres danzas españolas
Vives: La presumida
Pahissa: La Calcaita
Anónimo: Trois tambors
Albéniz:
    a. Cádiz
    b. Triana
Granados: Intermezzo from
Goyescas
Morera: La santa espina

CENTRO CULTURAL DE MUSICA
(CCM) INAUGURAL YEAR
CONCERT
Sept 12
Orquesta Uruguaya de Cámara
Conductor: Enrique Casal-Chapí
Bassani: Canzone amorosa
Mozart: Eine kleine Nachtmusik
Porter: Music for Strings
Villa-Lobos: Suite for Strings

Sept 18, Oct 16 (10:45 A.M.)
Banda Municipal Concerts
Conductor: Freire-López

Sept 23
CCM Concert: Orquesta
Uruguaya de Cámara
Conductor: Enrique Casal-Chapí
Purcell: King Arthur Suite
Beethoven: Serenade in D Major
Casal-Chapí: Dos piezas
rapsódicas sobre temas
populares de Castilla
    a. Lento
    b. Scherzando
Hindemith: Five Pieces for
String Orchestra

Sept 24 to Dec 29
LA ESPADA DESNUDA
(Bengoa)****
Opening of the Comedia
Nacional Spring Season

Sept 26
Recital: Rolando <a>, A.
Turriziani <pf/ org>
Works by Carisimi, Caccini,
Verdi, Rossini, Ponchielli,
Obradors, and Falla

Sept 28
CCM Symphonic Orchestra
Conductor: Carlos Estrada
Soloist: Kempff <pf>
Rameau: Castor et Polux
Bach: Concerto in A Major
Mozart: Concerto in E-flat
Major

Sept 30
Beethoven Recital: Kempff <pf>
Thirty-two Variations in C
Minor
Sonata op. 111
Rondo op. 51, no. 2
Sonata op. 57 ("Appasionata")

Oct 3
Choreographic Recital: Montoya
and Pacheco <d>, Rolando <a>,
Michelin <vc> and Astrinidis
<composer / pf>

Oct 7
Recital: Giacosa-Trujillo <pf>
Works by Bach, Franck,
Debussy, Ravel, and Albéniz

Oct 16 (10:45 A.M.)
Banda Municipal Concert
Conductor: Freire-López

Oct 17
Chopin Recital: Zunino de
Barilari <harp>
Six Preludes
Eight Studies (op. 10 and op. 25)
Three Nocturnes
Three Mazurkas
Six Waltzes

Oct 24
Recital: Ayala-Vidal <pf>
Debussy:
   a. Feux d'artifice
   b. Etude pour les arpèges
      composés
Ravel: Scarbo
Albéniz: Eritaña
Stravinsky: Study op. 7, no. 4
Gershwin: Three Preludes

Oct 31
Homage to Chopin with
complete piano works
performed by Kolischer
(Sponsored by Uruguayan
Chopin Foundation)
Two Nocturnes
Four Mazurkas
Four Impromptus
Four Balades

Nov 7
Second Chopin Recital
Two Nocturnes: op. 15, no. 2;
op. 27, no. 2
Polonaise op. 71, no. 2
Barcarolle
Fantasie in F Minor
Twelve Mazurkas
Polonaise in A-flat Major

Nov 11
Third Chopin Recital
Four Scherzi
Twelve études (op. 10 and op.
25)

Nov 14 (6:30 P.M.)
Fourth Chopin Recital
Sonatas op. 35 and op. 58

Nov 14 (10:00 P.M.)
Inauguration of the Escuela
Municipal de Arte Dramático
General Director: Margarita
Xirgu

Nov 16
Recital: Gromova <s>, Zamboni
<pf>
Duparc: L'invitation au voyage
Fauré:
   a. Nell
   b. Les berceaux
   c. Rencontre
Chausson:
   a. Le temps de lilas
   b. Le colibri
Debussy: Mandoline
Rubinstein:
   a. The night
   b. The Devil (Romance de
      Thamar)
Gretchaninoff:
   a. Desire
   b. Sad is the steppe (Lullaby)
Rimsky-Korsakov: Enslaved by
the rose, the nightingale
Rachmaninov: Spring waters

1950

Female artists
Ayala-Vidal, Ema <pf>
Bellini, Mariella <s>
Bilbao, Berta <s>
Bonasso, Anita <s>
Di Concilio, Juanita <s>
Golino [de Paternó], Celia <s>
González, Adelita <s>
Iglesias, Sarah <s>
Lanz, Ariel <actress>
Indart, Lyda Mirtha <pf>
Linne, Olga <s>
Kusrow-Korma [de Iniesta],
Yocasta <pf>
Orlandi, Sarah <pf>
Ossona, Paulina <d>
Pantano [de Giucci], Nahyr <pf>
Parodi, Gioconda <pf>
Parodi, Yolanda <s>
Pedragosa, Lita <s>
Preve, Julieta <pf>
Preve, María Esther <pf>

Quincke, Erna <pf>
Quiroga, Ercilia <mez>
Richepin, Eliane <pf>
Roca [de Musetti], Celia <pf>
Rodríguez Dutra, Marina <s>
Ruy, Juliette <s>
Sadowsky, Reah <pf>
Sánchez, Renée <s>
Satre, (Ana) Raquel <s>
Schenini, Victoria <pf>
Susena, Gloria <s>
Traverso, Diana <pf>

Male artists
Algorta, Jorge <b>
Alvarez, Aurelio <t>
Balzo, Hugo <pf>
Campos, Omar <b>
Carrasco, Alberto <vn>
Chelle, Ruben <pf>
Damiani, Víctor <bar>
D'Arnot, Paul <d>
Dobal, Darwin <t>
Fabbri, Juan <vn>
Firkusny, Rudolf <pf>
García de Zúñiga, Eduardo <b>
Gieseking, Walter <pf>
Giovanini, Alejandro <t>
Gittli, Ernesto <pf>
Giuli, Augusto de <t>
Heltai, Francisco <vla>
Hermida, Guillermo <t>
Iniesta, Enrique <vn>
Kreuder, Peter <pf>
Marsiglia, Oscar <org>
Michelin, Bernard <vc>
Morpurgo, Adolfo <vla da
gamba-c>
Musetti, Francisco J. <vn>
Navatta, Vicente <vc>
Protasi, Juan <pf>
Russo, Francisco <fl>
Schoeder, Carlos <bar>
Sosa, Edgardo <b>
Szeryng, Henryk <vn>
Turriziani, Angel <pf/org>
Vernazza, Juan A. <bar>

Feb 18 to March 25
Carnival Masked Balls
Xavier Cugat Orchestra and the
Lecuona Cuban Boys

April 8 to June 22
CANTOS RODADOS (Imhoff)
Opening of the Comedia
Nacional Winter Season

April 12
CCM Symphonic Orchestra
Bach Bicentennial Concert
Season Conductor: Carlos Estrada
Soloists: Balzo and Chelle <pf>,
Iglesias <s>, Alvarez <t>, García
de Zúñiga <b>, Fabbri <vn>,
Russo <fl>
Suite no. 2 in B Minor
Concerto for two pianos in C
Major
Coffee Cantata
Brandenburg Concert no. 5

April 19, 26, 30
Recital: Kreuder <Brazilian
composer and pf>
in popular medleys

April 21
CCM Concert
Morpurgo Ancient-Instrument
Ensemble
Conductor: Adolfo Morpurgo

April 24
CCM Symphonic Orchestra
Soloist: Szeryng <vn>
Rameau: Castor et Pollux
Overture
Bach: Violin Concerto in E
Major
Mozart: Violin Concerto no. 5
Beethoven: Violin Concerto

April 28
Recital: Szeryng <vn>

Tartini: Fugue and Variations on
a Corelli Theme
Beethoven: Sonata in G Major
Lalo: Symphonie espagnole
Prokofiev: Sonata op. 94
Ravel: Tzigane

May 3
CCM Two-piano Recital
Balzo and Chelle
Works by Frescobaldi,
Schumann, Debussy, Stravinsky,
Bartók, and Poulenc

May 10
CCM Symphonic Orchestra
Second Bach Bicentennial
Concert
Soloists: Orlandi <pf>, Ruy <s>
Suite no. 1
Piano Concerto in F Minor
Cantata no. 209, "Non sa che
sia dolore"
Brandenburg Concerto no. 1

May 16
Symphonic Concert
Conductor: Pierino Gamba
<thirteen-year-old>
Mozart: Overture to The Magic
Flute
Beethoven: Symphonies nos. 2
and 5

May 17
CCM Symphonic Orchestra
Soloist: Traverso <pf>
Handel: Concerto Grosso
Mozart: Ave Verum Sancta
Maria
Debussy: Fantaisie for piano and
orchestra
Estrada: Tema y variaciones 1938
Retier: Symphonie no. 3

May 19
Symphonic Concert
Conductor: Pierino Gamba

Schubert: Unfinished Symphony
Wagner: Overture to Tannhäuser
Dvořák: New World Symphony

May 23, 25
Beethoven Festival Concerts
Conductor: Pierino Gamba
Overture to Egmont
Symphonies nos. 2 and 3

May 24
Recital: Firkusny <pf>
Bach: Chromatic fantasia and
fugue
Chopin: Sonata op. 58
Smetana: Two Czech dances
Debussy: La soirée dans Grenade
Ravel: Alborada del gracioso
Prokofiev: Toccata

May 26
Dance Recital: Ossona and
D'Arnot

**BANDA MUNICIPAL 1950
CONCERT SEASON**
May 28, July 2, 16, 30, Oct 22
(all 10:45 A.M.)
Banda Municipal de Montevideo
Music Director and Conductor:
Vicente Ascone, Bernardo Freire-
López (assistant conductor), and
Carlos Estrada (guest conductor)

May 31
CCM Symphonic Orchestra
Soloist: Firkusny <pf>
Mozart:
    a. Overture to Le Nozze di
       Figaro
    b. Piano Concerto op. 20
Beethoven: Piano Concerto no.
3
Mendelssohn: Piano Concerto
no. 1

June 5
Recital: Firkusny <pf>

Beethoven: Sonata op. 10, no. 3
Schumann: Phantasie op. 17
Fabini: Triste no. 1
Martinú: Polka
Debussy: Prelude
Liszt: Mephisto Waltz

June 6
Italian Operatic Overtures
Concert
Conductor: Pierino Gamba
Verdi: La forza del destino
Bellini: Norma
Mascagni: Intermezzo from
Cavalleria
Verdi: Preludes from La traviata
Mancinelli: Cleopatra
Rossini: Overtures
 a. Il barbiere di Siviglia
 b. L'italiana in Algeri
 c. La gazza ladra

June 7
CCM Recital: Gabriel Fauré
Festival
 a. La Bonne Chanson: Parodi
  <s>, Parodi <pf>
 b. Theme and Variations:
  Schenini <pf>
 c. Fauré Religious Music:
  CCM Chorus and Dobal
  <t>, Vernazza <bar>, Turriziani <org>

June 9
Recital: Hermida <t>, Protasi
<pf>
Works by Schumann, Massenet,
Donaudy, Grieg, Williams,
Leoncavallo, Boero, Puccini,
Bellini, and Giordano

June 11, 18 (10:45 A.M.)
Banda Municipal Concerts
Conductor: Estrada

June 14
CCM Symphonic Orchestra and
Chorus

Soloists: Pantano and Balzo
<piano-duet>, Fabbri and
Carrasco <vns>, Navatta <vc>
Couperin: Four Short Pieces
Corelli: Concerto grosso op. 6,
no. 9
Beethoven: Elegischer Gesang
op. 118
Rodríguez-Socas: Preludio y
Madrigal
Bartók: Sonata for Two Pianos
and Percussion **

June 16
Asociación Coral Orchestra
Conductor: Enrique Casal-Chapí
Soloist: Musetti <vn>
Respighi: Antiche arie e danze
per liuto
Anónimo: Italian Suite
Bach:
 a. Brandenburg Concerto no.
  3
 b. Aria from the D Suite, no.
  3
 c. Two Cantatas
Simó: Preludio y fuga
Hindemith: Five Orchestral
Pieces

June 21
CCM Recital: Linne <s>, García
de Zúñiga <b>, Quincke <pf>
Arias / duettos from Handel,
Bach, and Haydn

June 24 to 29 (8 performances)
Madeleine Renaud and Jean
Louis Barrault
(Directors of Paris' Théâtre
Marigny)

June 30 to July 20
Pilar López Spanish Ballet
Company

July 5
Recital: Ayala-Vidal <pf>

Works by Haydn, Bach,
Schumann, and Ravel

July 12
CCM Symphonic Orchestra and
Chorus
Soloists: Iglesias <s>, Quiroga
<mez>, Indart <pf>, Marsiglia
<org>, Sánchez <s>, Dobal<t>,
Vernazza <bar>
Fabini: Piano and voice works
Fauré:
 a. Messe basse
 b. Tu es Petrus
 c. Tantum ergo
 d. Ave verum corpus

July 19
CCM Recital: Michelin <vc>
Handel: Sonata in G
Bocherini: Andante and Allegro
Franck: Sonata
Falla: Suite española

July 28 to Dec 20
ROMEO Y JULIETA (Shakespeare)
(Sp)
Opening of the Comedia
Nacional Spring Season
Director: Margarita Xirgu

Aug 2
CCM Recital: Schenini <pf>
Haydn: Variations in B-flat
Major
Bach: Sarabande and Partita in
C Major
Chopin: Sonata op. 35
Poulenc: Suite Napoli
Stravinsky: Three movements
from Petrouchka

Aug 7
CCM Symphonic Orchestra
Soloist: Gieseking <pf>
Couperin-Estrada: Scene
pastorale
Mozart: Piano Concerto, K. 331

Beethoven: Piano Concerto no. 4

Aug 9
CCM Recital: Gieseking <pf>
Works by Mozart, Beethoven, Schumann, Debussy

Aug 11
CCM Recital: Gieseking <pf>
Debussy: Complete Preludes (Books 1 and 2)
Ravel: Miroirs

Aug 14
Two-Piano Recital: Preve sisters

Aug 16
CCM Recital: Satre <s>, Indart <pf>, Iglesias <s>, Quincke <pf>, Musetti <vn>, Roca <pf>
Bassani: L'amante placata (cantata)
Roussel: Piano Sonata
Musorgsky: Songs and dances of death
Stravinsky: Duet Concertante <pf / vn>

Aug 20 (10:45 A.M.)
Banda Municipal Concert
Conductor: Freire-López

Aug 30
CCM Recital: Golino <s>, Quincke <pf>
Rameau: Aria from Castor et Pollux
Lully: Four arias from Thésée
Mozart:
  a. Cherubino's aria from Le nozze di Figaro
  b. L'amaro from Il rè pastore
Debussy:
  a. Romance
  b. Fantoches
Ravel: Cinq mélodies populaires grecques

Cluzeau-Mortet:
  a. Llueve
  b. Mar de luna
Storm: Dos muchachas
Vázquez:
  a. De los álamos vengo madre
  b. ¿Con qué la lavaré?

Sept 4
CCM Recital: Iniesta <vn>, Kusrow-Korma <pf>
Bach: Sonata in E
Fauré: Sonata op. 13
Stravinsky: Duo Concertante
Dinicu-Heifetz: Hora Staccato
Ravel: Valses nobles et sentimentales
Albéniz: Malagueña
Bassini: Witches Dance

Sept 11
Operatic Recital
Di Concilio <s>, Protasi <pf>
Mozart: Four arias from Le nozze di Figaro
Godard: Aria from Jocelyn
Bizet: Aria from Carmen
Massenet: Aria from Hérodiade
Puccini: Aria from Turandot
Gomes: Aria from Lo schiavo
Puccini: Aria from Gianni Schicchi
Meyerbeer: Aria from L'africana
Verdi: Aria from Il trovatore
Wagner: Death of Isolde

Sept 13
CCM Recital: Algorta <b>, Indart <pf>
Handel: Aria from Berenice
Lotti: Pur diceste, o bocca bella
Scarlatti: Gia il solo dal Gange
Schubert:
  a. Der Wanderer
  b. Du bist die Ruh
  c. Gruppe aus dem Tartarus

Mozart:
  a. Two arias from Die Zauberflöte
  b. Two arias from Don Giovanni
  c. Aria from Le nozze di Figaro
Fauré: Trois mélodies
Fabini:
  a. Triste
  b. El poncho
  c. Luz mala

Sept 15, 18
Berta Singerman <poetic recitals>

Sept 25
Recital: Sadowsky <pf>
Works by Bach, Brahms, Chopin, Gianner, and Prokofiev

Oct 2
CCM Recital: Musetti <vn>, Roca <pf>, Navatta <vc>
Trios by Leclair, Fauré, and Ravel

Oct 12
CCM Symphonic Orchestra
Soloist: Richepin <pf>
Brahms: Concerto in D
Estrada: Concertino for piano
Bartók: Concerto no. 3

Oct 20
Asociación Coral Chamber Music Ensemble
Conductor: Enrique Casal-Chapí
Gittli <pf>, Musetti <vn>, Heltai <vla>, Navatta <vc>
Handel: Concerto grosso
Esteban Eitler: Policromia 1950
Bach: Piano Concerto in D
Grieg: Aus Holbergs Zeit Suite

Nov 16
LA CONTESSA MARIZA (Kálmán) (Sp)

Conductor: Juan Protasi
Contessa Mariza: Susena
Contessa Lisa: Bonasso
Conte Tassilo: Giovanini
Baron Koloman: Schoeder

Nov 17
Orquesta Uruguaya de Cámara
and Asociación Coral Chorus
Conductor: Enrique Casal-Chapí
Golino <s>, Dobal <t>, Campos
<b>
Works by Estrada, Guarino,
Bach, Kellner, and Chapí

Nov 22
Lecture-Recital
Lauro Ayestarán <musicologist>,
"The Opera in Italy and
Germany"
Linne <s>, Damiani <bar>,
Algorta <b>
Works by Handel, Gluck,
Monteverdi, Mozart, Rossini,
Verdi, Bellini, Weber, and
Leoncavallo

Nov 23
PARANA GUAZU (Ascone)
Conductor: Rogelio Mastrangelo
Doña Sol: Rodríguez-Dutra
José Luis: Giuli
Lola: Bellini
Rosario: González
Don Fernando: Sosa
Don Rodrigo: Lanz
Carmen: Pedragosa
Consuelo: Bilbao

Dec 4
Cristóbal Martínez Spanish
Ballet Company

1951

Female artists
Ayala-Vidal, Ema <pf>
Bourdillon [de Santórsola],
Sarah <pf>

Brizzio, Emma <mez>
Lorenzi, Hebe <pf>
Navarro, Silvia de <pf>
Olivera, Mercedes <pf>
Parodi, Yolanda <s>
Piras, Ada <pf>
Santamarina, María Luisa <pf>
Tuccari, Angelica <s>
Valverde, María <s>
Villegas, Socorrito <s>

Male artists
Bacciato, Vittorio <bar>
Backhaus, Wilhelm <pf>
Cáceres, Oscar <gui>
Cases, Guillermo <pf>
Chelle, Ruben <pf>
Demus, Jorg <pf>
De Raco, Antonio <pf>
Fournier, Pierre <vc>
García de Zúñiga, Eduardo <b>
Gobbi, Tito <bar>
Hajmassy, Imre <pf>
Hermida, Guillermo <t>
Janzer, Georges <vla>
Kempff, Wilhelm <pf>
Neri, Giulio <b>
Nicastro, Oscar <vc>
Olaverri, Lorenzo <pf>
Pons, Panchito <bar>
Redondo, Marcos <bar>
Rosito, Lorenzo <bar>
Rossi, Alfredo <pf>
Rubinstein, Artur <pf>
Santórsola, Guido <vla / vla
d'amore>
Speranza, Alfredo <pf>
Szabó, Paul <vc>
Turriziani, Angel <org>
Valetti, Cesare <t>
Vecino, Walter <t>
Végh, Sándor <vn>
Zóldy, Sándor <vn>

Feb 3 to March 11
Carnival Masked Balls

March 16 to 28
Dramatic Company Aida Luz–
Roberto Airaldi
Direction: Antonio Cunil-
Cabanellas

March 30 to April 22
Dramatic Company Pedro López
Lagar

April 11
CCM Recital: De Raco <pf>
Works by Rafael Anglés, Felipe
Rodríguez, Mateo Albéniz,
Antonio Soler, José Galles, Bach-
Busoni, Beethoven, Ravel,
Chopin, and Liszt

April 18
CCM Concert: Don Cossacks
Chorus

April 26 to May 7
José Greco Spanish Ballet
Company

April 27
Vocal / Piano Recital: Redondo
<bar> Cases <pf>
Falla: Suite from El amor brujo
Millán: Tarantela from La
dogaresa
Mozart: Serenata from Don
Giovanni
Soutullo y Vert: Romanza de
Germán from La del Soto del
Parral
Pérez-Soriano: Jota from El
guitarrico
Albéniz: Two Piano Works
Falla: Jota
Moreno-Torroba: Los vareadores
from Luisa Fernanda
Alonso: Romanza from La linda
tapada
Rossini: Largo al factotum from
Il barbiere di Siviglia

May 2
CCM Recital: Bourdillon <pf>,
Santórsola
<vla / vla d'amore>
Works by Ariosi, Vivaldi,
Rameau, Gluck, Couperin,
Hindemith, Cluzeau-Mortet,
Fabini, Ravel, and Falla

May 11 to July 19
LA RONDALLA (Pérez-Petit)
Opening of the Comedia
Nacional Fifth Season

May 25
Vocal Recital: Hermida <t>,
Olaverri <pf>
Works by Gluck, Thomé, Fauré,
Godard, Donaudy, Jimenez,
Cortinas, Boito, Cilea, Mascagni,
and Meyerbeer

June 6
Recital: Speranza <pf> [winner
of the first prize for piano in
the Salzburg Competition]
Haydn: Sonata no. 7
Beethoven: Sonata op. 27, no. 1
Schumann: Novelette no. 4
Tajčević: Six Barbarian Dances
Weineger: Fantasia

June 8
Recital: Olivera <pf>
Bach: Partita in B-flat
Scarlatti: Three Sonatas
Chopin: Sonata op. 58
Kabalewsky: Sonata op. 3, no. 6
Tajčević: Seven Balkan Dances**
Granados: El pelele

June 15
Beethoven Recital: Backhaus <pf>
Sonatas no. 12, op. 26; no. 18,
op. 31; no. 21
("Waldstein"); and no. 32, op.
111

June 18
Recital: Backhaus <pf>
Bach:
  a. Fantasia in C Minor
  b. Chromatic Fantasy and
     Fugue
  c. French Suite no. 5
Brahms:
  a. Rhapsody in G Minor
  b. Waltzes
  c. Capriccio
Schubert: 6 Momens musicals
  [sic]
Schubert-Liszt: Soirée de Vienne

June 20
Dzigan and Szumacher Yiddish
Musical Comedy Company

June 24 (10:45 A.M.)
Recital: Demus <pf>
Works by Haydn, Beethoven,
Schubert, Schumann, and
Franck

June 29
CCM Recital: Végh String
Quartet
Végh and Zóldy <vn>, Janzer
<vla>, Szabó <vc>
Beethoven Program: Quartets
op. 18, no. 2 in D Minor; op.
95, no. 11 in F Minor; and op.
59, no. 2 in E Minor

July 2
Recital: Kempff <pf>
Schumann: Fantasia op. 17
Schubert: Sonata in B Minor
Liszt: Deux légendes
  a. Saint François d'Assise, la
     prédication aux oiseaux
  b. Saint François de Paule
     marchant sur les flots

July 4
Recital: Kempff <pf>

Handel: Chaconne
Rameau: Four Pieces
Mozart: Sonata K. 532
Chopin: Two Impromptus
Brahms: Sonata in F Minor

July 11
CCM Recital: Nicastro <vc>,
Chelle <pf>
Simpson: Thirteen Variations
Tartini: Sonata in C Minor
Lecillet: Suite in G Minor
Vivaldi: Sonata in C Minor
Corelli: Sonata in D Minor

July 21 to 29
Italian Dramatic Company
Diana Torrieri–Vittorio Gassman

July 23
Recital: Rubinstein <pf>
Bach-Busoni: Chaconne
Schumann: Phantasiestucke
Chopin:
  a. Ballade no. 1
  b. Impromptu no. 1
  c. Scherzo no. 2
Debussy: L'isle joyeuse
Ravel: Ondine
Albéniz: Navarra
Villa-Lobos: Impresoes Seres-
  teiras
Stravinsky: Petrouschka

July 30 to Sept 1 (6
performances)
French Dramatic Company Jean-
Pierre Grenier–Olivier Hussenot

Aug 6
Choral Concert
Coral Amigos de la Música de
Paysandú
Chorus master: Eric Simon
Works by Ingenieri, Bach,
Duffay, Banchieri, Handel,
Fabini, Cluzeau-Mortet, Foster,

Tchaikovsky, Belfritz, and Villa-
Lobos

Aug 8, 9
CCM Choral Concerts
Coral de Pamplona (Spain)
Works by Lasso, Palestrina,
Victoria, Marenzio, Banchieri,
Crocoe-Falla, Reboud, Moreno-
Torroba, and Iparraguirre

Aug 13 to 16
Mariquita Flores–Antonio
Córdoba Spanish Dance
Company

Aug 25
Uruguayan National Anthem
IL BARBIERE DI SIVIGLIA
(Rossini)
Conductor: Nino Stinco
Chorus master: Domingo Dente
Rosina: Tuccari
Conte di Almaviva: Valetti
Figaro: Gobbi
Don Bartolo: Bacciato
Don Basilio: Neri
Fiorello: Pons
Berta: Brizzio
Ufficiale: Rosito

Sept 5
Recital: Lorenzi <pf>
Bach:
  a. Two Choral Preludes
  b. Fantasia and Fugue in G
     Minor
Schumann: Carnaval
Ravel:
  a. Jeux d'eau
  b. Valses nobles et sentimen-
     tales
  c. Sonatina

Sept 7
CCM Recital: Fournier <vc>,
Rossi <pf>
Francoeur: Sonata

Bach: Suite no. 6 in D Major
for violin solo
Beethoven: Sonata op. 69 in A
Major
Stravinsky: Italian Suite
Dvořák:
  a. Romantic Piece
  b. Rondo
Falla:
  a. Pantomima
  b. Danza del fuego

Sept 13 to 19
Italian Dramatic Company
Diana Torrieri–Vittorio Gasman

Sept 22 to Dec 2
Opening of the Comedia
Nacional Spring Season

Sept 26
CCM Recital: Santamarina <pf>
Spanish Music by: Mateo
Albéniz, Soler, Falla, Casal-
Chapí, R. Halffter, Mompou,
and E. Halffter

Oct 3
CCM Recital: Hajmassy <pf>
Bach: Chromatic Fantasia and
Fugue
Schumann: Sonata op. 11
Liszt: Variations on a Bach
Theme

Oct 10
Chamber Music Recital:
Valverde <s>, Cáceres <gui>,
Navarro <pf>
Works by Scarlatti, Rodrigo,
Narvaez, Vives, and Falla

Oct 12, 21 (10:45 A.M.)
Banda Municipal Concerts
Music Director and Conductor:
Vicente Ascone

Oct 16
Choral Concert: Bach Chorus
Chorus master: Ruben
Carámbula
Works by Palestrina, Di Lasso,
Schütz, Bach, Gevaert, Pretorius,
Leontovich, Musorgsky, Donato,
Fabini, and Negro Spirituals

Oct 17
Choral Concert: Bach Chorus
Chorus master: Ruben
Carámbula
Soloists: Parodi <s>, Vecino
<t>, García de Zúñiga <b>,
Turriziani <org>, Piras <pf>
Works by J. S. Bach
Cantatas nos. 78 and 155
Selection from the St. Matthew
Passion

Oct 31
CCM Recital: Closing of 1951
Season
Villegas <s>
Gluck: Aria from Orfeo
Mozart: Batti, batti from Don
Giovanni
Debussy:
  a. Nuit d'étoiles
  b. Recitative and air de Lia
     from L'enfant prodigue
  c. Nöel des enfants qui n'ont
     plus de maison
Milhaud: Trois chansons de
Ronsard
Bach: Two arias
  a. "Vergiss mein nicht," lied
     BWV 504
  b. "Sich Üben im Lieben,"
     no. 7 from Cantata BWV
     202

Nov 4 (10:45 A.M.)
Banda Municipal Concert
Conductor: Bernardo Freire-
López

Nov 7
Recital: Ayala-Vidal <pf>
Works by Handel, Bach, Mozart,
Beethoven, and Liszt

Dec 2
Choral Concert
Alpargatas Coral, Coro
Municipal Infantil,
with AUDEM Orchestra
Chorus master: Kurt Pahlen

Dec 26 to Jan 31, 1952
Historical Exhibition "Artigas en
la Historia y en el Arte."
Bicentennial Commemorative
Exhibition on General José G.
Artigas (1764–1850). [Display of
documents, paintings, and
memorabilia related to the
Uruguayan national hero.]

1952

Female artists
Airaldi, Ernestina L. de <pf>
Amorós, Tere <d>
Bernhardt, Carlota <a>
De los Reyes, Paloma <pf>
Di Concilio, Juanita <s>
Golino [de Paternó], Celia <s>
Heinitz, Eva <vc>
Helguera, Haydée <pf>
Hoyer, Dore <d>
Indart, Lyda Mirtha <pf>
Linne, Olga <s>
Mariño, Nibya <pf>
Markova, Alicia <d>
Olivera, Mercedes <pf/hpd>
Orlandi, Sarah <pf>
Pierri, Olga <gui>
Prieto, Margot <gui>
Quincke Erna <pf>
Quiroga, Ercilia <mez>
Ramírez [de Mañé], María
Adelaida <s>

Reiner, Catherine <s>
Ricci, Teté <gui>
Richepin, Eliane <pf>
Rodríguez-Dutra, Marina <s>
Santamarina, María Luisa <pf>
Satre, (Ana) Raquel <s>
Sena, Margarita <gui>
Sena, Matilde <gui>
Siano, Matilde <a>
Tagliaferro, Magda <pf>
Traverso, Diana <pf>
Urquizú, Marta <s>
Varsi, Dinorah <pf>
Vischnia, María <vn>

Male artists
Algorta, Jorge <b>
Alonso, Julio <gui>
Alvarez, Aurelio <t>
Amadei, Luis <vc>
Arzarello, Juan <pf>
Balzo, Hugo <pf>
Batlle, Luis <pf>
Beck, Melchor <pf>
Berges, Michel <hn>
Boutard, André <cl>
Canessa, José <pf>
Carbonell, Juan <b>
Cassier, Robert <ob>
Castagner, Jacques <fl>
Chorberg, Israel <vn>
Coirolo, Armando <vn>
Cortot, Alfred <pf>
Demicheri, Carlos <vn>
Di Carlo, Ruben <t>
Faisandier, Gerard <bn>
Fabbri, Juan <vn>
Fernández de Guevara, Luis
<bar>
García de Zúñiga, Eduardo
<b>
Gieseking, Walter <pf>
Giovanini, Alejandro <t>
Gittli, Ernesto <pf>
Gulda, Friedrich <pf>
Heltai, Francisco <vla>
Iraola, Horacio <pf>
Jasinski, Roman <d>

Johannesen, Grant <pf>
Kaufman, Louis <vn>
Kreutzberg, Harald <d>
Otonello, Adhemar <t>
Prissing, Guillermo <b>
Rosito, Lorenzo <b>
Sancan, Pierre <pf>
Schenone, Adhemar <pf>
Schnabel, Karl Ulrich <pf>
Schwartz, Leo <pf>
Spagnolo, Paolo <pf>
Szeryng, Henryk <vn>
Tosar, Héctor <pf and c>
Weissenberg, Sigi [Alexis] <pf>

Jan 31
Closing of Historical Exhibition
"Artigas en la Historia y en el
Arte"

Feb 16 to March 23
Carnival Masked Balls

April 17 to July 6
SANTOS VEGA (Silva Valdés)
Opening of the Comedia
Nacional Sixth Season

April 30
CCM Recital: Schnabel <pf>
Brahms: Sonata in F Minor
Schubert: Trois Moments
Musicaux
Debussy: Three Preludes
    a. La sérénade interrompue
    b. La cathédrale engloutie
    c. La danse de Puck
Chopin:
    a. Nocturne op. 32, no. 1
    b. Polonaise op. 40, no. 1

May 6
Recital: Spagnolo <pf>
Works by Scarlatti, Brahms,
Beethoven, Debussy, and
Prokofiev

**SODRE SYMPHONIC
ORCHESTRA (OSSODRE)
SEASON**
May 10 to Oct 25 [40 concerts]
Season Conductor: Paul Paray
Guest Conductors: Carlos
Estrada, Héctor Tosar, Nino
Stinco

May 10, 12
OSSODRE Concerts
Soloists: Urquizú <s>, Carbonell
<b>
Beethoven:
    a. Overture to Egmont
    b. Symphony No. 7
Fauré: Requiem

May 14
CCM Recital: Tosar <pf>
Bach: Chromatic Fantasia and
Fugue
Mozart: Variations from Duport
Minuet
Brahms: Variations and Fugue
on a Handel Theme
Honegger: Prelude, Arioso, and
Fuguetta on B.A.C.H.
Tosar:
    a. Toccata
    b. Vals (Homenaje a Ravel)
Prokofiev: Sonata op. 83, no. 7

May 17
OSSODRE Concert
Soloist: Balzo <pf>
Haydn: The "Surprise"
Symphony
Fabini: Campo
Liszt: Piano Concerto in E-Flat
Major
Ravel: La valse

May 19
OSSODRE Concert
Conductor: Estrada
Rameau: Second Suite from
Dardamus

Beethoven: Symphony no. 8
Debussy: Prélude à l'après-midi
d'un faune
Rimsky-Korsakoff: Capriccio
espagnol

May 21
CCM Choral Concert: Coro
Oriana
Chorus Master: Nilda Muller
Works by Claude Le Jeune, Jean
Mouton, Jacuppus Gallus,
Hindemith, and XVI Century
Polyphonists

May 24
OSSODRE Concert
Schumann: Symphony no. 3
Dukas: La Péri
Liszt: Les préludes

May 26
OSSODRE Concert
Soloist: Balzo <pf>
Franck: Symphony in D Major
Liszt: Piano Concerto no. 1
Fabini: Campo

May 28
CCM Concert: Orquesta
AUDEM
Conductor: Guido Santórsola
Soloist: Varsi <twelve-year-old
pf>
Beethoven: Overture to Corolian
Mozart: Piano Concerto in D
Minor
Oswald: Bebé s'endort
Fabini: Triste
Rimsky-Korsakoff: Capriccio
espagnol

May 30
CCM Recital: Weissenberg <pf>
Bach: Chromatic Fantasia and
Fugue
Mozart: Sonata in G Major
Schumann: Fantasia in D Minor

Musorgsky: Pictures at an
Exhibition

May 31
OSSODRE Concert
Soloist: Vischnia <vn>
Brahms: Symphony no. 2
Tchaikovsky: Violin Concerto
Wagner: Overture to Tannhäuser

June 2
OSSODRE Concert
Conductor: Estrada
Soloists: Fabbri / Coirolo <vns>,
Amadei <vc>
Corelli: Concerto grosso no. 2
Schubert: Unfinished Symphony
Roussel: Concert pour une
petite orchestre

June 3
Dance Recital: Kreutzberg <d>

June 4
Recital: Olivera <hpd>
Italian, French and Spanish
composers of the seventeenth
and eighteenth centuries

June 7
OSSODRE Concert
Soloist: Weissenberg <pf>
Mozart:
    a. Overture to Don Giovanni
    b. Symphony in G Minor
Tchaikovsky: Piano Concerto
op. 23
Dukas: L'apprenti sorcier

June 9
OSSODRE Concert
Conductor: Estrada
Corelli: Concerto grosso no. 2
Schubert: Unfinished Symphony
Roussel: Concert pour une
petite orchestre
Ascone: Sobre el río Uruguay
Borodin: Polovtsian Dances

June 11
CCM Recital: Weissenberg <pf>
Franck: Prelude, Fugue and
Variations
Scarlatti: Six Sonatas
Chopin: Sonata op. 58
Debussy: Suite bergamasque
Kabalewski: Sonata

June 13
Recital: Szeryng <vn>
Tartini: Trillo del diavolo
Bach: Chaconne for violin solo
Glazunov: Concerto op. 82
Chausson: Poème
Saint-Saëns: Rondo capriccioso
López-Buchardo: Campera
Rolón: Danza mejicana
Suk: Burlesque

June 14
OSSODRE Concert
Soloist: Weissenberg <pf>
Franck: Symphony in D Minor
Milhaud: La création du monde
Chopin: Piano Concerto no.1

June 15
OSSODRE Concert
Soloist: Vischnia <vn>
Haydn: The "Surprise"
Symphony
Tchaikovsky: Violin Concerto
Ravel: La valse

June 18
CCM Recital: Indart <pf>
Beethoven:
    a. Sonata op. 90
    b. Rondo a Capriccio
Debussy:
    a. Preludes:
    1. La puerta del vino
    2. Des pas sur la neige
    3. Bruyères
    4. Général Lavine-excentric
    5. La danse de Puck

6. Hommage a Pickwick Esq.,
    P.P.M.P.C.
    b. L'isle joyeuse
Poulenc: Trois mouvements
perpetuelles
Bartók:
    a. Rondo no. 1
    b. Allegro barbaro

June 21
OSSODRE Concert
Beethoven: Symphony no. 3
Debussy: La mer

June 23
OSSODRE Concert
Schumann: Symphony no. 3
Milhaud: La création du monde
Dukas: L'apprenti sorcier

June 24
Recital: Spagnolo <pf>
Mozart: Fantasia K. 475
Beethoven: Waldstein Sonata
Brahms: Variations on a
Paganini Theme
Toch: Burlesque op. 31
Chopin:
    a. Two Polonaises
    b. Ballade op. 52

June 25
CCM Two-Piano Recital: Balzo
and Tosar
Bach: Sonata in G Major
Debussy: En blanc et noir
Hindemith: Sonata
Britten: Introduction and Rondo
alla Burlesca

June 27
CCM Recital: Kaufman <vn>
Telemann: Sonata
Bach: Concerto in E Major
Franck: Sonata
Dvořák: Two Romantic Pieces
Camargo-Guarnieri: Canti 1
Grant-Kaufman: Blues
Copland: Ukelele Serenade

June 28
OSSODRE Concert
Soloist: Richepin <pf>
Weber: Overture to Der
Freischütz
Schumann: Symphony no. 4
Honegger: Pastorale d'été
Rachmaninoff: Second Piano
Concerto

BANDA MUNICIPAL 1952
CONCERT SEASON
June 29, July 6, 20, Aug 3, 10, 17,
24, 31, Sept 28, Oct 5, 26 (10:45
A.M.)
Banda Municipal de Montevideo
Music Director and Conductor:
Vicente Ascone, and Bernardo
Freire-López (assistant
conductor)

June 30
OSSODRE Concert
Conductor: Estrada
Beethoven: Symphony no. 5
Ravel: Ma mère l'oye
Rodrigo: Zarabanda lejana y
villancico
Estrada: Symphony no. 1

July 2
Recital: Kaufman <vn>
Tartini: Adagio
Schumann: Sonata op. 105
Saint-Saëns: Concerto in B, op.
61
Kodaly: Adagio
Milhaud: Ipanema
Prokofiev: Gavotte op. 132
Copland: Hoedown from Rodeo

July 3
Recital: Gulda <pf>
Galuppi: Sonata in D Major
Mozart: Sonata K. 310
Beethoven: Sonata op. 109
Chopin:
    a. Ballade in F Minor

b. Nocturne in F
c. Polonaise in F-sharp
d. Nocturne in B
e. Scherzo C-sharp Minor

July 5
OSSODRE Concert
Tchaikovsky: Symphony no. 6
Debussy: Trois nocturnes
Wagner: Overture to Die
Meistersinger

July 7
CCM Recital: Helguera <pf>
Mozart: Sonata K. 576
Brahms:
    a. Two Intermezzi op. 117 no.
       2, and op. 118 no. 6
    b. Rhapsody op. 79
Schumann: Sonata op. 22
Debussy: Hommage à Rameau
Shostakovich: Two Preludes, op
34, nos. 16 and 24
Falla: Andaluza
Turina: Orgía

July 9 to 15 (10 performances)
LE BOURGEOIS GENTILHOMME
(Molière)
Comedie Française opening
performance

July 17, 18
Orquesta AUDEM Concerts
Conductor: Guido Santórsola
Uruguayan National Anthem
Handel: Three Dances
Bach-Santórsola: Prelude and
Fugue
Mozart: Eine kleine Nachtmusik

July 19
Chopin Recital: Cortot <pf>
Twenty-four Preludes
Twelve Etudes op. 10, and
twelve Etudes op. 25

July 20
Vocal Recital: Reiner <s>, Tosar
<pf>

Haydn: Del mio core from
Orfeo e Euridice
Pergolesi: Nina
Mozart: Louise
Schubert:
    a. Die Post
    b. Der Wanderer
Schumann:
    a. Frühlingsnacht
    b. Der Leuchtkäfer
Brahms: Two Lieder
Fabini:
    a. Las flores del campo
    b. El poncho
Two Negro Spirituals
Berg: Two Songs
Bartók: Two Hungarian
Folksongs

July 24 (6:30 P.M.)
Recital: Cortot <pf>
Chopin:
    a. Fantasia op. 49
    b. Waltz op. 64, no. 2
    c. Berceuse op. 57
    d. Scherzo op. 31
    e. Sonata op. 35
Schumann: Kinderszenen

July 24 to Nov 23
Comedia Nacional Spring
Season

July 25
Vocal Recital: Fernández de
Guevara <bar>, Di Carlo <t>,
Prissing <bar>, Airaldi <pf>
Works by Wagner, Giordano,
Verdi, Soriano, Guerrero,
Milans, Lecuona, and Morales

July 26
OSSODRE Concert
Beethoven: Overture to Leonora,
no. 3
Schubert: Unfinished Symphony
R. Strauss: Tod und Verklärung

Berlioz: Excerpts from La
damnation de Faust

July 28
OSSODRE Concert
Conductor: Stinco
Soloist: Schenone <pf>
Mendelssohn: Overture to A
Midsummer Night's Dream
Franck: Psyché
Casella: Scarlatianna for piano
and orchestra
Dvořák: From the New World
Symphony

July 29
Recital: Cortot <pf>
Mendelssohn: Variations
sérieuses op. 54
Schubert: Moments musicals
Weber: Invitation to the Dance
Chopin:
    a. Ballade in G Minor
    b. Nocturne in E Minor
    c. Taratella
    d. Waltz
    e. Polonaise héroïque
Schumann: Symphonische
Etüden
Liszt: Hungarian Rhapsody no. 2

Aug 1
Chamber Music Recital:
Quintette á vent de Paris
Castagner <fl>, Cassier <ob>
Boutard <cl>, Berges <hn>,
Faisandier <bn>
Works by Mozart, D'Anches,
Ibert, Milhaud and Hindemith

Aug 2
OSSODRE Concert
Soloist: Olivera <hpd>
Beethoven: Symphony no. 6
Haydn: Concerto op. 21 for
harpsichord
Falla: El amor brujo

Aug 4
OSSODRE Concert
Conductor: Estrada
Brahms: Symphony no. 2
Tosar: Momento sinfónico
Bartók: Romanian folkdances
Ravel: Alborada del gracioso

Aug 6
CCM Recital: Vischnia <vn>,
Olivera <pf>
Vivaldi-Kreisler: Concerto
Bach: Chaconne for violin solo
Franck: Sonata
Ravel: Tzigane
Stravinsky: Two Excerpts from
Petrouschka

Aug 7
Istituto Italiano di Cultura
Symphonic Concert: Orquesta
AUDEM
Conductor: Carmen De Campori
Mozart: Overture to Le nozze di
Figaro
Beethoven: Symphony no. 2
Wagner: Siegfried Idyll
Rossini: Sonata per cordi**
Enzo Masetti: Gioco di nascosto

Aug 9
OSSODRE Concert
Soloist: Tagliaferro <pf>
Bach-Respighi: Passacaglia
Mendelssohn: Nocturne and
Scherzo from A Midsummer
Night's Dream
R. Strauss: Don Juan
Brahms: Piano Concerto in D

Aug 11
OSSODRE Concert
Tchaikovsky: Symphony no. 6
Wagner: Overture to Tannhäuser
Falla: El amor brujo

Aug 13
CCM Recital: Olivera <hpd>

Lully: Allemande, sarabande, et
fugue
Couperin:
  a. La bandoline
  b. Les petit moulins à vent
Rameau:
  a. La poule
  b. Rigodon
Scarlatti: Three sonatas
Soler: Three sonatas
Bach:
  a. Prelude and Fugue in C
    Minor
  b. French Suite in G Major

Aug 15
Recital: Tagliaferro <pf>
Bach: Coral
Bach-Busoni: Toccata in C
Schumann: Sonata op. 11
Debussy: Pour le piano
Albéniz:
  a. Evocación
  b. Triana

Aug 16
OSSODRE Concert
Soloist: Sancan <pf>
Bach: Suite no. 3
Mozart: Piano Concerto in C
Cluzeau-Mortet: Preludio y
Danza****
Fauré: Pelléas et Mélisande
Liszt: Piano Concerto no. 2

Aug 18
OSSODRE Concert
Conductor: Stinco
Rimsky-Korsakoff: Scheherazade
Respighi: Antiche arie e danze
per liuto (set 1)
Zandonai: Excerpts from Romeo
e Giulietta

Aug 20
Recital: Heinitz <vc>, Schwartz
<pf>
Vivaldi: Sonata in B-flat Major

Bach: Suite in C Major for cello
solo
Martinú: Arabesques
Schubert: Sonata in A Minor
Nin: Suite española

Aug 23
OSSODRE Concert
Beethoven: Symphony no.1
Wagner:
  a. Overture to Der fliegende
    Holländer
  b. Bacchanal from Tannhäu-
    ser
  c. Prelude to Lohengrin
  d. Prelude and Liebestod
    from Tristan und Isolde

Aug 25
OSSODRE Concert with SODRE
Chorus
Soloist: Satre <s>
Uruguayan National Anthem
Saint-Saëns: Marche héroïque
Broqua: Excerpts from Tabaré
Beethoven: Symphony no.5

Aug 27
CCM Recital: Gieseking <pf>
Bach: Partita no. 1
Beethoven: Sonata op. 111
Schubert: Two Impromptus
Brahms: Two Intermezzi
Mendelssohn: Rondo capriccioso
Debussy:
  a. Hommage à Haydn
  b. Mouvement
  c. Cloches à travers les feuil-
    les
  d. Poissons d'or
Ravel: Ondine

Aug 29
CCM Recital: Gieseking <pf>
Paradisi: Sonata in G Major
Mozart: Sonata in D Major
Schumann: Davidsbündlertänze

Debussy: Children's Corner
Ravel: Jeux d'eau

Aug 30
OSSODRE Concert with SODRE
Chorus
Soloists: Urquizú <s>, Siano
<a>, Alvarez <t>, García de
Zúñiga <b>
Beethoven: Symphony no. 9

Sept 1, 3
Dance Recitals: Markova and
Jasinski <d> with the OSSODRE
Conductor: Robert Zeller

Sept 6
OSSODRE Concert
Soloist: Orlandi <pf>
Mozart: Jupiter Symphony
Ravel: Piano Concerto in G
Borodin: On the Steppes of
Central Asia
Rimsky-Korsakoff: Capriccio
espagnol

Sept 8
OSSODRE Concert
Soloist: Batlle <pf>
Beethoven:
    a. Overture to Coroliano
    b. Piano Concerto no. 4
Wagner: Prelude and Liebestod
from Tristan und Isolde
Liszt: Les préludes

Sept 10
CCM Recital: Johannesen <pf>
Bach: Prelude and Fugue in A
Minor
Schumann: Phantasie op. 17
Fauré: Impromptu op. 34
Debussy:
    a. Cloches à travers les feuil-
    les
    b. L'isle joyeuse
Chopin:

a. Mazurka op. 17 no. 4
b. Polonaise op. 44

Sept 12
CCM Recital: Johannesen <pf>
Mozart: Fantasia in C Minor, K.
396
Mendelssohn: Scherzo
capriccioso
Grieg: Five lyric pieces
Chopin: Sonata op. 58
Bartók: Suite op. 14
Chabrier: Impromptu
Fauré: Nocturne
Roussel: Bourrée op. 14

Sept 13
OSSODRE Concert
Soloists: Heltai <vla>, Mariño
<pf>
Berlioz: Harold en Italie
Schumann: Piano Concerto in A
Musorgsky: St. John's Night on
the Bare Mountain
Wagner: Excerpts from Die
Meistersinger

Sept 14, Oct 19 (10:45 A.M.)
Banda Municipal Concert
Conductor: Freire-López

Sept 20
OSSODRE Concert
Conductor: Estrada
Handel: Concerto grosso no.7
Boyce: Symphony no. 2
Beethoven: Symphony no. 5
Roussel: Bacchus et Arianne

Sept 22
OSSODRE Concert
Conductor: Stinco
Soloist: Algorta <b>
Mendelssohn: Italian Symphony
Wagner:
    a. Wotan's Farewell
    b. Magic Fire Music

c. Murmurs of the Forest
d. Siegfried Idyll

Sept 24
CCM Recital: Gittli <pf>
Works by Beethoven, Chopin,
Smetana, Falla, Cluzeau-Mortet,
Ravel, and Poulenc

Sept 27, Oct 4
OSSODRE Concerts with
SODRE Chorus
Soloists: Ramirez <s>, Quiroga
<mez>, Giovanini <t>, García
de Zúñiga <b>
Mozart: Requiem

Oct 1
CCM Recital: Chorberg <vn>
De los Reyes <pf> Iraola <pf>
Works by Vitale-Auer, Bach,
Beethoven, Prokofiev, Novacek,
Scarlatti, Chopin, Debussy,
Poulenc, and Gershwin

Oct 6, 13
IL MATRIMONIO SEGRETO
(Cimarosa)
Sponsored by CCM
Conductor: Juan Protasi
Director: Antonio Larreta
Don Geronimo: Rosito
Carolina: Golino
Elisetta: Satre
Fidalma: Bernhardt
Paolino: Otonello
Conte Robinson: García de
Zúñiga

Oct 8
CCM Recital: De los Reyes <pf>
Mozart: Sonata K. 311 in D
Major
Beethoven: Fifteen Variations
and a Fugue on an
Original Theme (Eroica
variations)

Schumann: Novelette op. 21, no. 8
Brahms:
  a. Intermezzi
  b. Rhapsody op. 119
Tosar: Danza criolla
Prokofiev:
  a. March from The Love for Three Oranges
  b. Toccata op. 11

Oct 11
OSSODRE Concert
Conductor: Estrada
Soloist: Santamarina <pf>
Bach: Suite no. 2
Falla: Noches en los jardines de España
Milhaud: Saudades do Brazil
Honegger: Symphony no. 5

Oct 15
CCM Recital: Traverso <pf>
Works by Scarlatti, Beethoven, Chopin, Schumann, Debussy, and Juan J. Castro

Oct 16
Chamber Music Recital: Pierri Guitar Quintet
Works by Debali, Sapere, Aguirre, Gianneo, Fabini, Cluzeau-Mortet, Escobar, and Soriano

Oct 18
OSSODRE Concert
Conductor: Stinco
Soloist: Indart <pf>
Weber: Overture to Oberon
Grieg: Piano Concerto op.16
Giacobbe: Suite Música muchacha
Martucci: Noveletta
Respighi: Pini di Roma

Oct 20
OSSODRE Concert

Conductor: Estrada
Soloist: Vischnia <vn>
Mozart: Overture to Le nozze di Figaro
Bruch: Violin Concerto op. 26
Berlioz: Symphonie fantastique

Oct 25
OSSODRE Concert
Conductor: Tosar
Haydn: Symphony no. 104
Schumann: Overture Genoveva
Debussy: Berceuse héroïque
Tosar: Oda a Artigas****

Oct 27
Recital-Benefit for the Chopin Piano Competition
Batlle <pf>
Bach-Busoni: Chaconne in D
Beethoven: Sonata op. 101
Schumann: Fantasia op. 17

Oct 29
Dance Recital: Hoyer <German expressionist d>

Nov 3
Recital: Demicheri <vn>, Beck <pf>
Works by Vivaldi, Vieuxtemps, Arzarello, Ponce-Heifetz, Sarasate, Juon, and Falla-Kochanski

Nov 4
Vocal Recital: Di Concilio <s>
Works by Pergolesi, Cesti, Gluck, Verdi, Halevy, Giordano, Ponchielli, and Puccini

Nov 5
CCM Concert Coro Universitario
Homage to Carlos Vaz-Ferreira
Soloists: Tosar <pf>, Linne <s>
Quincke <pf>
Chorus Master: Nilda Muller

Schubert: Piano Sonata in C Minor
Schubert: Lieder
Bach: Cantata no. 12

Nov 10 to 25, Dec 20, 21
Spanish Dance Recitals
Amorós <d>, Alonso <gui>
Canessa <pf>

Nov 19
Vocal Recital: Rodríguez-Dutra <s>, Arzarello <pf>
Songs of America and Spain

Nov 25
Choral Concert: Coro Oriana
Chorus Master: Nilda Muller
Works by Victoria, Monteverdi, Debussy, Ravel, Costeley, and Claude Le Jeune

Nov 27
Escuela Municipal de Arte Dramático (final examination/performance)
Director: Margarita Xirgu

Nov 29, 30
"Taller de Teatro"
Dramatic performances
Director: Antonio Larreta

Dec 2
Victoria Tomina Ballet Company

Dec 27
Children Chorus Concert
Coro Municipal Infantil
Chorus Master: Kurt Pahlen
Christmas Program

1953

Female artists
Adonaÿlo, Raquel <s>
Bonifacino, María G. de <s>

Castro, Virginia <s>
Cruz-López, María de Lourdes <s>
Golino [de Paternó], Celia <s>
Gómez-Carrillo, Carmen Rosa <s>
Flórez, Lyda <pf>
Handel, Ida <vn>
Hautbourg, Simone de <mez>
Hoyer, Dore <d>
Laffrá, Annie <vn>
Linne, Olga <s>
Olivera, Mercedes <pf>
Pedemonte, Rosalía O. de <pf>
Pérez-Barranguet, Mirtha <pf>
Pierri, Olga <gui>
Prieto, Margot <gui>
Quincke, Erna <pf>
Ricci, Teté <gui>
Rodríguez-Dutra, Marina <s>
Satre, (Ana) Raquel <s>
Schenini, Victoria <pf>
Schiaffarino, Raquel <pf>
Sena, Margarita <gui>
Sena, Matilde <gui>
Tipo, Maria <pf>
Wagner, Anna <s>

Male artists
Arzarello, Juan <pf>
Baldwin, Dalton <pf>
Balzo, Hugo <pf>
Barani, Felipe <t>
Barletta, Alejandro <bandoneón>
Basseux, Pierre <vc>
Benda, Sebastian <pf>
Bizzozero, Hugo <pf>
Carrasco, Alberto <vn>
Diehl, Heriberto <pf>
García de Zúñiga, Eduardo <b>
Giuli, Augusto de <t>
Gómez-Carrillo, Jr., Manuel <t>
Gómez-Carrillo, Julio <bar>
Gómez-Carrillo, Jorge <b>
Heltai, Francisco <vla>
Hermida, Guillermo <t>
Kaemper, Gerd <pf>
Kolischer, Wilhelm <pf>

Loewenguth, Alfred <vn>
Malcuzinski, Witold <pf>
Murgier, Jacques <vn>
Musetti, Francisco J. <vn>
Navatta, Vicente <vc>
Olaverri, Lorenzo <pf>
Otero, Ramón <actor>
Otonello, Adhemar <t>
Quintas-Moreno, Washington <pf>
Roche, Roger <vla>
Rosito, Lorenzo <b>
Sancan, Pierre <pf>
Schaia, Wolff <bar>
Schenone, Adhemar <pf>
Segovia, Andrés <gui>
Sorín, Darío <pf>
Sosa, Edgardo <b>
Souzay, Gerard <bar>
Taschner, Gerard <vn>
Tosar, Héctor <pf>
Varga, Ruben <vn>
Viatovich, Dimitri <pf>

Jan 11, June 16
Cristóbal Martínez Ballet Company

Jan 17, Aug 7, Dec 5
Paula Jarmalovich Ballet Company

Feb 14 to 22
Carnival Masked Balls

April 10 to Nov 15
BARRANCA ABAJO (Sánchez)
Opening of the Comedia Nacional Seventh Season

April 22
CCM Recital: Benda <pf>
Bach: Fugue in A Minor
Beethoven
   a. Thirty-two Variations
   b. Sonata op. 31
Schumann: Carnaval
Chopin: Sonata op. 35

April 28
Recital: Segovia <gui>
Works by Milán, Galileo, De Visée, Bach, Villalobos, Castelnuovo-Tedesco, Cassadó, Torroba, Tansman, Granados, and Albéniz

April 29
CCM Recital: Kaemper <pf>
Schumann: Humoresque op. 2
Brahms:
   a. Ballade in G Minor
   b. Intermezzo in A Major
   c. Rhapsody in G Minor
Berg: Sonata no. 1
Schoenberg: Six pieces op. 19
Bartók: Six Romanian Dances
Beethoven: Sonata op. 110

BANDA MUNICIPAL 1953 CONCERT SEASON
May 3, 10, 31, June 7, July 12, Aug 23, 30, Sept 6, 22, Oct 4, 18, 25 (10:45 A.M.)
Banda Municipal de Montevideo
Music Director and Conductor:
Vicente Ascone, and Luis D'Andrea, Bernardo Freire-López (assistant conductors)

May 6
CCM Recital: Cruz-López, <s>, Olivera <pf>
Works by Handel, Schubert, Chausson, Debussy, Musorgsky, Fabini, Nin, and Villalobos

May 11, June 1
COSI FAN TUTTE (Mozart)
Sponsored by CCM
Conductor: Juan Protasi
Director: Antonio Larreta
Fiordiligi: Satre
Dorabella: Linne
Despina: Golino
Guglielmo: García de Zúñiga

Fernando: Otonello
Don Alfonso: Rosito

May 13
CCM Concert: Stuttgart
Orchestra
Conductor: Karl Munchinger
J. S. Bach:
  a. Two Fugues
  b. Brandenburg Concerto no.
  3
J. C. Bach: Concerto for viola
and strings in C Minor
Pergolesi: Concertino in F
Mozart: Eine kleine Nachtmusik

May 19, Aug 2
Choral Festival Homage to
Eduardo Fabini
"Coros Unidos de Montevideo"
Chorus Master: Kurt Pahlen
Flórez and Diehl <pf>, Ramón
Otero <speaker>, Bonifacino
<s>, Bizzozero <pf>
All Fabini works: piano pieces,
choral songs, and La Patria Vieja
<speaker, chorus, pf>

May 24, Aug 2, 9, Sept 13, 20 (10:
45 A.M.)
Banda Municipal Concerts
Conductor: Freire-López

May 27
CCM Recital: Olivera <pf>
Ravel: Le tombeau de Couperin
Poulenc:
  a. Deux novelettes
  b. Suite in C Major
Brahms: Variations and Fugue
on a Handel Theme
Soler: Three Sonatas
Scarlatti: Three Sonatas

June 1 (6:30 P.M.)
Operatic Recital: Wagner <s>,
Hermida <t>, Olaverri <pf>,
Pedemonte <pf>

Works by Massenet, Ponchielli,
Halevy, Puccini, Verdi, and
Giordano

June 3
CCM Choral Concert: Coro
"Oriana"
Chorus Master: Nilda Muller
Works by Di Lasso, Monteverdi,
Costeley, Pasereau, Debussy,
Jannequin, Valenti-Costa,
Camargo-Guarnieri, and
Villalobos

June 9
CCM Recital: Taschner <vn>,
Olivera <pf>
Handel: Sonata in D Major
Bach: Chaconne for violin solo
(fourth partita)
Brahms: Sonata in G Major
Bartók: Sonata for violin solo**
Falla: Danzas de La vida breve
Sarasate: Zapateado

June 10
CCM Recital: Castro <s>, Sorín
<pf>
Poulenc: Cinq poèmes
Ravel:
  a. Deux mélodies hébraïques
  b. Don Quichotte à Dulcinée
Musorgsky: La chambre des
enfants

June 12, July 14
Expressionist Dance Recital
Hoyer <d> and Viatovich <pf>

June 15
Dramatic Company "Teatro
Alvarez Quintero"

June 17
CCM Recital: Taschner <vn>,
Olivera <pf>
Bach: Chaconne for violin solo
(Fourth partita)

Franck: Sonata
Bartók: Sonata for violin solo

June 22, Dec 1
Tamara Grigorieva Ballet
Company

June 24
CCM Lieder Recital: Linne <s>,
García de Zúñiga <b>, Olivera
<pf>
Wolff: Five Lieder for bass
Schumann: Liederkreis op. 24
Haydn: Duet from The Creation
Bach: Excerpts from Cantata no.
212

June 26
Recital: Sancan <pf>
Bach: Three Chorales
Mozart: Sonata in G Major
Schumann: Carnaval
Schubert: Impromptu
Debussy: Trois préludes
Ravel: Sonatina

July 1
CCM Recital: Hautbourg
<mez>, Sorín <pf>
Works by Handel, Lully,
Rameau, Fauré, Ravel, and
Messiaen

July 7
Recital: Kolischer <pf>
Beethoven: Sonata Waldstein
Liszt:
  a. Arbre de Noël, four pieces
  b. Annés de pélerinage, three
  pieces
Brahms:
  a. Rhapsody in G Minor
  b. Fantasy and Fugue on a
  Handel Theme

July 8, 10
Choral Concerts: Les petites
chanteurs de la Provence
Chorus Master: Abbot Geoffroy

July 9
CCM Recital: Handel <vn>,
Olivera <pf>
Beethoven:
   a. Sonata no. 10
   b. Adagio and Fugue from
     Sonata no. 1
Brahms:
   a. Sonata op. 108
   b. Hungarian Dance

July 15
Lieder Recital: Souzay <bar>,
Baldwin <pf>
Strozzi: Four Italian arias
Schubert: Five Lieder
Debussy:
   a. Deux ballades de Villon
   b. Mandoline
Fauré: Two Songs
Ravel: Don Quichotte à
Dulcinée

BEETHOVEN STRING QUARTETS
CYCLE
Sponsored by CCM
Loewenguth String Quartet from
Paris
Loewenguth and Murgier
<vns>, Roche <vla>, Basseux
<vc>
July 20 (first recital)
Op. 18, no. 1; op. 74, no. 10; op.
59, no. 3

July 21 (second recital)
Op. 18, no. 2; op. 59, no. 1; and
op. 127

July 24 (third recital)
Op. 18, no. 3; op. 58, no. 2; and
op. 135

July 27 (fourth recital)
Op. 18, no. 2; op. 95; and op.
132

July 29 (fifth recital)
Op. 18, no. 4, and op. 132

July 27
LA FIACCOLA SOTTO IL MOGGIO
(D'Annunzio)
Italian Dramatic Company

July 31
CCM Recital: Loewenguth String
Quartet
Schubert: Der Tod und das
Mädchen
Debussy: Quartet op. 10
Ravel: Quartet no. 1 in F

Aug 5
CCM Recital: Laffrá <vn>,
Quintas-Moreno <pf>
Francoeur: Sonata no. 2
Boelman: Symphonic Variations
Beethoven: Sonata no. 2
Tchaikovsky: Variations on a
Rococo Theme

Aug 10
Lieder Recital: Souzay <bar>,
Baldwin <pf>
Lully:
   a. Aria de Caron (Alceste)
   b. Aria de Cadmus (Cadmus
     et Ermione)
Mozart: Die betrogene Welt
Beethoven: In questa tomba
oscura
Mozart: Dans un bois solitaire
Brahms: Vergebliches Ständchen
Duparc:
   a. Soupir
   b. Le manoir de Rosemonde
Musorgsky:
   a. The Garden by the Don
   b. Lullaby from Songs and
     Dances of Death
   c. Savishna
Poulenc:
   a. Priez pour paix
   b. Le Bestiaire

Legnerai: A son page
Falla:
   a. Seguidilla murciana
   b. Asturiana
   c. Jota

Aug 14, 28, Sept 1
CCM Choral Concerts: Jubilee
Singers
Chorus Master: Mrs. Myers

Aug 16, Sept 27 (10:45 A.M.)
Banda Municipal Concert
Conductor: D'Andrea

Aug 18
Lieder Recital: Souzay <bar>,
Baldwin <pf>
Works by Monteverdi, Bach,
Berlioz, and Schumann's
Dichterliebe

Aug 19
CCM Lieder Recital: Satre <s>,
Olivera <p>
Fauré: Five Songs
Schumann: Frauenliebe und
-leben
Nin: Cinco villancicos

Aug 26
Two-Piano Recital: Tosar and
Balzo
Bach: Three Chorales
Brahms: Variations on a Handel
Theme
Hindemith: Sonata
Tosar:
   a. Preludio fugado
   b. Toccata alla Burlesca****
Casadesus: Four pieces
Bartók: Microcosmos, six pieces

Sept 2
Recital: Varga <vn>, Tosar <pf>
Beethoven: Kreutzer Sonata
Bach: Sonata in G for solo
violin

Debussy: Sonata in G Minor
Varga: Oriental Fantasy
Paganini: Capricci Nos. 17, 13, 9, 24

Sept 7, 12 (matinée)
THE MIKADO (Sullivan)
Conductor: Juan Protasi
Orquesta AUDEM
The Montevideo Musical Society
Players and Singers

Sept 9
CCM Recital: Barletta
<bandoneón>
Bach:
   a. Seven Variations
   b. Toccata and Fugue in D
      Minor
Haydn: Sonata in D Major
Grieg: Six Nordic Folk Melodies
and Dances
Koc:
   a. Dos invenciones para ban-
      doneón
   b. Coral para bandoneón
Orrego-Salas: Pequeña suite para
bandoneón
Bartók: Five Romanian Dances

Sept 16
CCM Recital: Golino <s>,
Quincke <pf>
Works by Varlderrábano, Milán,
Vázquez, Marín, Schubert,
Schumann, Brahms, Grétry, and
Vivaldi

Sept 23
CCM Recital: Pérez-Barranguet
<pf>
Handel: Chaconne
Mozart: Sonata in C
Chopin: Sonata op. 35
Bartók: Suite op. 14
Roussel: Bourrée op. 14
Martinon: Introduction et
toccata

Sept 28
CCM Recital: Tipo <pf>
Scarlatti: Two Sonatas
Beethoven: Sonata op. 53
Bloch: Poems of the Sea
Chopin:
   a. Nocturne no. 4
   b. Ballade in G Minor
   c. Andante spianato et polo-
      naise op. 22

Sept 29
Recital: Malcuzinski <pf>
Bach: Chromatic Fantasia and
Fugue
Brahms: Variations / Fugue on a
Handel Theme
Chopin:
   a. Nocturne
   b. Etude
   c. Mazurka
   d. Waltz
Liszt: Spanish Rhapsody

Sept 30
CCM Recital: Tipo <pf>
Mozart: Sonata in E-flat Major
Schumann: Davidsbündlertänze
Ravel: Jeux d'eau
Bartók: Romanian Dances

Oct 2
Recital: Malcuzinski <pf>
Works by Franck, Liszt,
Szymanowski, Prokofiev, and
Chopin

Oct 5
Chopin Recital: Malcuzinski <pf>
Polonaise in E-flat minor
Nocturne
Sonata op. 58
Four Mazurkas
Etude
Waltz
Scherzo no. 2

Oct 7
CCM Two-Piano Recital:
Schenini and Schenone
J. C. Bach: Sonata
Mozart: Sonata
Poulenc: Concerto in D-minor
Ravel: Ma mère l'oye
Stravinsky: Russian Dance

Oct 14
CCM Closing of 1953 Season
Concert
Adonaylo <s>, Tosar <pf>,
Musetti <vn>, Carrasco <vn>,
Heltai <vla>, V. Navatta <vc>
Works by Héctor Tosar:
   a. Suite for piano
   b. Two Songs: Mundo and
      Solitude
   c. Sonata for violin and pi-
      ano
   d. String Quartet no. 1

Oct 16
Recital: Schiaffarino <fourteen-
year-old pf>
Bach: Partita in B-flat Major
Beethoven: Thirty-two variations
in C Minor
Chopin:
   a. Deux Etudes op. 10
   b. Polonaise op. 26, no. 2
   c. Scherzo op. 20, no. 1
Esplá: Chants d'Antán
Falla: Aragonesa
Infante: Gitanerías

Oct 19
Chamber Music Recital:
Schenini <pf>, Pierri
Guitar Quintet: Ricci, M. & M.
Sena, Prieto <gui>, Coro Oriana
Conductor: Nilda Muller
Latin American Composers:
works by Mignone, Villalobos,
Guastavino, Cluzeau-Mortet,
Fabini, J. Aguirre, Sapere,

Escobar, Debali, and Gutiérrez del Barrio

Oct 21, 23, 27
Vocal Concerts: Carmen, Manuel Jr., Julio, and Jorge Gómez-Carrillo Vocal Quartet
Works by French composers from the sixteenth century, Di Lasso, Bach, Debussy, Guastavino, García-Caturla, André, Henrique, Manuel Gómez-Carrillo, and Negro spirituals

Nov 4
Lecture-Recital
Sponsored by Instituto Uruguay-Brazil: "La evolución de la música en el tiempo y en la psicología de los pueblos" by Dr. L. Romanowski, with Barani <t>, Schaia <bar>, and Roberval <chansonnier>

Nov 8, 22 (10:45 A.M.)
Choral Concerts: Coro Municipal Infantil
Chorus Master: Kurt Pahlen
Works by Palestrina, Schubert, Fabini, and folksongs from around the world

Nov 9
Vocal Recital: Rodríguez-Dutra <s>, Giuli <t>, Sosa <b>, Arzarello <pf>

Nov 17
Wilfredo Toamarán Ballet

Nov 23
Gala Chabelska Ballet

Dec 15, 22
Choral Concerts: Coro Municipal Infantil
Chorus master: Kurt Pahlen

Works by Pahlen, Mozart, Brahms, Fabini, Villalobos, and folksongs

---

1954

Female artists
Berger, Erna <s>
Bernhardt, Carlota <a>
Castro, Virginia <s>
Freeden, Mlle. <d>
Gil-Janeiro, Noemí <s>
Golino [de Paternó], Celia <s>
Handel, Ida <vn>
Indart, Lyda Mirtha <pf>
López-Lomba, Violeta <d>
Linne, Olga <s>
Mariño, Nibya <pf>
Olivera, Mercedes <pf>
Orlandi, Sarah <pf>
Satre, (Ana) Raquel <s>
Schenini, Victoria <pf>
Toumanova, Tamara <d>

Male artists
Batlle, Luis <pf>
Beck, Melchor <pf>
Borstein, Adolfo <vn>
Botto, Jorge <bar>
Bresciani, Mario <vn>
Cuevas, Germán <fl>
García de Zúñiga, Eduardo <b>
Demicheri, Carlos <vn>
Demus, Jorg <pf>
Fiorentino, Sergio <pf>
Forino, Gerardo <cl>
Gamba, Rubén <bn>
Giammarchi, Luis <t>
Haase, Gerhard <bn>
Heltai, Francisco <vla>
Jasinsky, Roman <d>
Izzi, Italo A. <pf>
Le Roux, Jean-Louis <ob>
Navatta, Vicente <vc>
Nicastro, Oscar <vc>
Otonello, Adhemar <t>
Pellejero, Emilio <vn>

Pons, Panchito <bar>
Puchelt, Gerhard <pf>
Romaniz, Miguel <vla>
Rosito, Lorenzo <b>
Schenone, Adhemar <pf>
Schwartz, Leo <pf>
Tagliavini, Ferruccio <t>
Tosar, Héctor <pf>
Turriziani, Angel <org>
Vernazza, Juan A. <bar>
Virtuoso, Antonio <hn>

Feb 27 to March 20
Carnival Masked Balls

April 2
CCM Lieder Recital: Berger <s>, Schwartz <pf>
Mozart: Seven Lieder
Schubert:
   a. Lachen und Weinen
   b. Nacht und Träume
   c. Ave Maria
   d. Rosa, denkst du an mich?
   e. Delphine
Brahms: Six Lieder
Wolff:
   a. Frühling
   b. Schmetterling
   c. Mädchen mit dem roten
   d. Lied
   e. Stolz
Debussy:
   a. Pantomime
   b. Clair de lune
   c. Pierrot
   d. Apparition

April 23 to June 6
OFICIO DE TINIEBLAS (Larreta)
Opening of the Comedia Nacional Eighth Season
Director: Orestes Caviglia

April 28
Recital: Drolc String Quartet from Berlin
Mozart: "Jagd" Quartet

Beethoven: Quartet op. 59 in F Minor
Schubert: Der Tod und das Mädchen

April 30
Recital: Drolc String Quartet from Berlin
Debussy: Quartet in G Minor
Hindemith: Quartet op. 16
Beethoven: Quartet op. 59 in C Major

May 3
CCM Lieder Recital: Berger <s>, Schwartz <pf>
Pergolesi: Arietta
Schubert:
    a. Du bist die Ruh
    b. Ave Maria
Brahms: Two Lieder
Mozart: Exsultate jubilate
Wolff: Three Lieder
Debussy:
    a. Pantomime
    b. Clair de lune
    c. Pierrot
    d. Apparition

May 10, Nov 27
LA NOVIA VENDIDA [The Bartered Bride]
(Smetana) (Sp)
Sponsored by CCM
Conductor: Juan Protasi
Director: Fritz Kalmar
Chorus Master: Dante Magnone
Dancer: Freeden
Mařenka: Castro
Jenik: Giammarchi
Vašek: Pons
Krušina: Vernazza
Ludmila: Bernhardt
Micha: Botto
Háta: Gil-Janeiro
Esmeralda: Freeden

May 19
CCM Recital: Demus <pf>

Bach: French Suite no. 5
Brahms: Two Intermezzi
Beethoven: Sonata op. 110
Debussy: Images
Franck: Prelude, Chorale, and Fugue

May 21
CCM Bach Recital: Demus <pf>
The Well-Tempered Clavier
1. Seven Preludes and Fugues
2. Five Preludes and Fugues
Chromatic Fantasia and Fugue
Italian Concerto

BANDA MUNICIPAL 1954 CONCERT SEASON
May 23, July 11 (10:45 A.M.)
Banda Municipal de Montevideo
Music Director and Conductor:
Vicente Ascone Bernardo Freire-López, Luis D'Andrea (assistant conductors)

May 26
Recital: Fabini String Quartet
Borstein and Pellejero <vns>, Romaniz <vla>, Navatta <vc>
Works by Haydn, Stravinsky, and Brahms

May 31, June 3
Dance Recitals: Toumanova and Jasinsky <d>, Izzi <pf>

June 2
Schumann Memorial Recital:
Mariño <pf>
Kinderszenen
Papillons
Fantasia op. 17
Etudes Symphoniques op. 13

June 4, 7, 11
Vocal Recitals: Tagliavini <t>, Schenone <pf>
Works by Cilea, Gluck, Paisiello, Sibella, Donizetti, Puccini, Lalo,

Massenet, Sadero, Gastalton, De Curtis

June 6, 20, 27, July 18, Aug 1, 8, 15, 29, Sept 5, 12, 19, 26, Oct 10, 17, 24, 31 (10:45 A.M.)
Banda Municipal Concerts
Conductor: Freire-López

June 10 to 22
French Dramatic Company
Madeleine Renaud–Jean Louis Barrault

June 25 to July 2
Italian Dramatic Company
Piccolo Teatro della Città di Milano

July 5 to 30
Folies Bergère from Paris

July 7
CCM Recital: Trio Le Roux: Le Roux <ob>, Haase <bn>, Indart <pf>
Works by Marcelo, Telemann, Poulenc, Hindemith, and Wolff-Ferrari

July 9
CCM Recital: Handel <vn>, Olivera <pf>
Schumann: Sonata op. 121
Bach: Chaconne (second partita)
Franck: Sonata in A Major

July 12, Aug 1
CCM Two-Piano Recitals:
Mariño and Batlle
Mozart:
    a. Sonata in C Major
    b. Adagio in C Minor
Saint-Saëns: Variations on a Beethoven Theme
Fauré: Suite Dolly

Debussy: Petite suite
Chabrier: España (rhapsody)

July 14, 16
CCM Recitals: Fiorentino <pf>
Works by Vivaldi, Scarlatti,
Bach, Mozart, Beethoven,
Schumann, Casella, and Chopin

July 23
Recital: Berlin Philharmonic
Octet
Mozart: Serenade in G
Schubert: "Die Forelle" Quintet
Beethoven: Septet op. 20

July 25, Oct 3 (10:45 A.M.)
Banda Municipal Concerts
Conductor: D'Andrea

July 26
Recital: Berlin Philharmonic
Octet
Brahms: Trio op. 40
Bartók: Contrasts
Schubert: Octet op. 116

July 28
CCM Recital: Puchelt <pf>
Works by Schubert, Blaher,
Bartók, and Brahms

Aug 6 to Nov 21
MACBETH (Shakespeare) [Sp
version]
Opening of the Comedia
Nacional Winter Season

Aug 11
CCM Recital: Trio Uruguayo:
Bresciani <vn>, Heltai <vla>,
Nicastro <vc>
Beethoven program: Trios op. 9,
op. 9, no. 2, and Serenade op. 8

Aug 16
Anfion Chamber Orchestra
Concert

Conductor: Beatriz Tuset
Dall'Abaco: Allegro
Corelli:
    a. Sonata in A Major
    b. Concerto grosso no. 8
Handel: Concerto grosso no. 7

Aug 22
Homage to Vicente Ascone (his
farewell concert as Banda
Municipal music director and
conductor)
Conductor: Vicente Ascone
Dancer: López-Lomba
Verdi: Overture to La forza del
destino
Wagner: Death of Isolde
Tchaikovsky: 1812 Overture
Works by Vicente Ascone:
    a. Danza del gaucho errante
    b. Overture to Santos Vega
    c. Pericón <López-Lomba>

Aug 24
CCM Recital: Tosar <pf>
Bach: French Suite in D
Beethoven: Sonata op. 27, no. 2
Schubert: Fantasia op. 15
Ravel: Sonatina
Prokofiev: Sonata no. 7, op. 83

Aug 25
Choral Concert: Coro Municipal
Infantil
Chorus Master: Kurt Pahlen

Aug 31
Berta Singerman <poetic recital>

Sept 1
CCM Recital: Conjunto
Instrumental Montevideo
Cuevas <fl>, Le Roux <ob>,
Forino <cl>, Haase and Gamba
<bn>, Virtuoso <hn>, Indart
<pf>
Beethoven: Quintet op. 18

Mozart: Two-bassoon Sonata
Thuillet: Sextet op. 6

Sept 8
Recital: Chigiano String Quintet
Mozart: Piano quartet in G
Shostakovich: Quintet
Dvořák: Quintet op. 81

Sept 10
Recital: Chigiano String Quintet
Bocherini: Quintet
Mozart: Piano quartet K. 493
Franck: Quintet in F Major

Sept 15
Choral Concert: Coro Oriana
Chorus Master: Nilda Muller
Works by Monteverdi,
Palestrina, Mudarra, Hidalgo,
Hindemith, Poulenc, Costeley-
Mignone, Mauduit, and
Jannequin

Sept 20
Two-Piano Recital: Schenini and
Schenone

Sept 29
Choral Concert: Coro Juventus
Chorus Master: Dante Magnone
Turriziani <org>
Works by Aichinger, Ingegneri,
Victoria, Vázquez, and J. S. Bach

Oct 1
Recital: Demicheri <vn>, Beck
<pf>
Works by Bruch, Vivaldi,
Tartini, Debussy, Arzarello, and
Falla

Oct 6
Asociación Coral de Montevideo
Concert
Chorus Master: Enrique Casal-
Chapí
Works from the thirteenth,

fourteenth and fifteenth
centuries

Oct 11
Federación Uruguaya de
Puericantores Concert
Chorus Master: Alberto González
Sacred works by Gounod,
Palestrina, Victoria, Van
Berchem, Viadana, Rota, and
González

Oct 13 (6:30 P.M.)
CCM Recital: Orlandi <pf>
Works by Lully, Rameau,
Daquin, Couperin, Scarlatti,
Bach, and Debussy

Oct 13 (9:30 pm)
THE GONDOLIERS (Sullivan)
The Montevideo Musical Society
Conductor: Juan Protasi
Director: Eduardo Malet
Sung by a British cast

Oct 19, Dec 3
Paula Jarmalovich Ballet

Oct 22
CCM Recital: Batlle <pf> and
Conjunto Instrumental
Montevideo [same as Sept 1]
Mozart: Quintet K. 452
Frank Bridge: Two Divertimenti
for 2 flutes, oboe, clarinet, and
bassoon
Villa-Lobos: Quinteto en forma
de choro
Hindemith: Septet

Oct 27
CCM Recital: Olivera <pf>
Works by Bach, Beethoven,
Schumann, Granados

Nov 15, 24
Choral Concert: Coro Municipal

and Coro Municipal Infantil [on
Nov 24]
Chorus Master: Kurt Pahlen

Nov 25
Recital: Homage to the VIII
UNESCO Conference
Batlle <pf>
Mozart: Fantasia in C Minor
Schumann: Phantasie op. 17
Brahms: Two Rhapsodies op. 79
Chopin:
  a. Ballade no. 4
  b. Etude op. 25, no. 7
Debussy: Pour le piano

Nov 27
Homage to the VIII UNESCO
Conference
LA NOVIA VENDIDA [The
Bartered Bride]
(Smetana) (Sp) [same cast as
May 10]

Nov 29
Homage to the VIII UNESCO
Conference
COSI FAN TUTTE (Mozart)
[Sponsored by CCM]
Conductor: Juan Protasi
Director: Antonio Larreta
Fiordiligi: Satre
Dorabella: Linne
Despina: Golino
Guglielmo: García de Zúñiga
Fernando: Otonello
Don Alfonso: Rosito

Nov 30
Escuela Municipal de Arte
Dramático
Final examination / performance
Director: Margarita Xirgu

Dec 1
Homage to the VIII UNESCO
Conference Choral Festival

1. Coro Bach: High polyphony
works
Chorus Master: Eduardo
Carámbula
2. Coro Juventus: Madrigals
Chorus Master: Dante Magnone
3. Coro Municipal: Romantic
period
Chorus Master: Kurt Pahlen
4. Coro Universitario: Poulenc's
Mass in
G Major
Chorus Master: Nilda Muller
5. Coral Guarda e Passa: Latin-
American music
Chorus Master: Jaime Airaldi

Dec 7 to 12
José Limon and Pauline Koney
Modern Dance Company

Dec 15
Coral de Montijo Spanish Ballet
Company

Dec 17
Olga de Hintz Ballet Company

Dec 22
Dance Festival: "Danza y
Cultura"
Sponsored by Musical Teachers
Association

Dec 23
Municipal Ensembles Festival
1. Escuela M. de Arte Dramático:
excerpts from dramatic plays
Director: Margarita Xirgu
2. Coro Municipal sings Mozart,
Schubert, Schumann, Christmas
carols
Chorus Master: Kurt Pahlen
3. Escuela Municipal de Música
Director and Conductor: Vicente
Ascone
Beethoven: Adagio
Ascone: Minué y cielito

1955

Female artists

Alyer, Ethel <s>
Burke, Georgia <a>
Castro, Virginia <s>
Colbert, Helen <s>
Del Castillo, Zulma <a>
Davy, Gloria <s>
De los Angeles, Victoria <s>
Flórez, Lyda <pf>
Flowers, Martha <s>
François, Jacqueline
<chansonnière>
Heinitz, Eva <vc / vla da gamba>
Hopper, Joyce <s>
Kallay, Maria <s>
Kamendrowska, Ina <s>
Linne, Olga <s>
Malnou, Marie Louise <s>
Mattauch, Hilde <s>
Mariño, Nibya <pf>
Olivera, Delmira <s>
Olivera, Mercedes <pf>
Parodi, Yolanda <s>
Quincke, Erna <pf>
Rolando, Sarah <mez>
Sabatés, Elsa <pf>
Sánchez-Raña, Polonia <pf>
Souza, Noemí <a>
Thigpen, Helen <s>
Tipo, Maria <pf>

Male artists

Baldwin, Dalton <pf>
Ballestero, Omar <b>
Batlle, Luis <pf>
Beck, Melchor <pf>
Borstein, Adolfo <vn>
Bresciani, Mario <vn>
Carbonell, Juan <b>
Carsi, Héctor <pf>
Cuevas, Germán <fl>
Delfino, Roberto <t>
Demicheri, Carlos <vn>
Dorsey, Pierre <pf>
Dobrache, Wladimir <vc>
Fariña, Gianfranco <vn>

Fasoli, Adolfo <pf>
Fuller, Lawrence <t>
García de Zúñiga, Eduardo <b>
Giammarchi, Luis <t>
Giannazza, Luis <t>
Giovanini, Alejandro <bar>
Haase, Gerhard <bn>
Heltai, Francisco <vla>
Hermida, Guillermo <t>
Istomin, Eugene <pf>
James, Joseph <bar>
Laws, Jerry <t>
Lisy, Alberto <vn>
Martínez-Buelta, Fernando <t>
McCurry, John <bar>
Mendeguía, Walter <bar>
Navatta, Vicente <vc>
Nicastro, Oscar <vc>
Ortiz, Juan Carlos <b>
Pellejero, Emilio <vn>
Ramírez, Ariel <pf>
Ricci, Ruggero <vn>
Romaniz, Miguel <vla>
Roselen, Santo <t>
Schwartz, Leo <pf>
Scott, Leslie <b/bar>
Serrato, Víctor <pf>
Simon, Abbey <pf>
Souzay, Gerard <bar>
Tilche, Jean-Jacques <gui>
Tauriello, Antonio <pf>
Tosar, Héctor <pf>
Vercelli-Maffei, Eduardo <pf>
Vernazza, Juan A. <bar>
Vinitzky, Carlos <vn>
Wright, Ned <t>

Feb 19 to March 13
Carnival Masked Balls

March 26, 27
CCM presents Teatro Colón
Ballet
Choreographer: César Purekoff
Fasoli and Carsi <pf>
Works by Tchaikovsky, Minkus,
Rimsky-Korsakov, Egk, J. Strauss

AUDAL ITALIAN OPERA
PERFORMANCES
April 9, 16, 17
IL BARBIERE DI SIVIGLIA
(Rossini)
Conductor: Carlos Estrada
Rosina: Hopper
Figaro: Giovanini
Conte di Almaviva: Martínez
Don Bartolo: Vernazza
Don Basilio: Carbonell
Berta: Rolando
Fiorello: Delfino

April 18, 23
DON PASQUALE (Donizetti)
Conductor: Jaime Airaldi
Norina: Parodi
Don Pasquale: Ballestero
Ernesto: Giannazza
Dottore Malatesta: Mendeguía

April 29
CCM Concert: Euterpe
Chamber Orchestra
Conductor: Jean-Louis Le Roux
Soloists: Batlle <pf>, Cuevas
<fl>, Vinitzky <vn>
Bach: Concerto for piano,
violin, and flute
Corelli: Concerto grosso no. 8
Tchaikovsky: Serenade op. 48

May 6 to July 10
LA GRINGA (Sánchez)
Opening of the Comedia
Nacional Ninth Season

**BANDA MUNICIPAL 1955
CONCERT SEASON**
May 8, 15, 22, June 12, 19, 26,
July 10, 17, 24, Aug 7, 14, 21,
Sept 4, 11, Oct 2, 9, 23, 30 (10:45
A.M.)
Banda Municipal de Montevideo
Music Director and Conductor:

Bernardo Freire-López, Luis
D'Andrea (assistant conductor)

May 11
CCM Recital: Batlle <pf> and
Trío Uruguayo de Cuerdas with
Bresciani<vn>, Heltai <vla>,
Nicastro <vc>
Weber: Piano quartet op. 8
Schumann: Piano quartet op. 47
Fauré: Piano quartet op. 15

May 20
CCM Recital: Fabini String
Quartet
Borstein and Pellejero <vns>,
Romaniz <vla>, Navatta <vc>
Haydn: Quartet in D Minor op.
70, no. 2
Casal-Chapí: Dos piezas
rapsódicas
  a. Lento
  b. Scherzando
Guarnieri: Cinco piezas
infantiles
Borodin: Quartet in A Minor

May 25
CCM Concert: Munich
Orchestra
Conductor: Christoph Stepp
Purcell: Suite for Strings
Vivaldi: Concerto grosso no. 3
Bach:
  a. Brandenburg Concerto no.
    3
  b. Concerto for two violins in
    D Minor
Mozart: Divertimento K. 136
Bartók: Divertimento for strings

May 27
CCM Concert: Munich
Orchestra
Conductor: Christoph Stepp
Bach: Ricercare
Karl Heller: Fugue for strings
Beethoven: Grosse Fuge op. 133

Mozart: Eine kleine Nachtmusik
Bartók: Divertimento for strings

June 1
CCM Recital: Istomin <pf>
Bach: Toccata and Fugue in E
Minor
Mozart: Rondo in A Minor
Schumann: Abegg Variations
Beethoven: Waldstein Sonata
Ravel: Gaspar de la nuit

June 5, July 3, Sept 18, 25, Oct 16
Banda Municipal Concert
Conductor: D'Andrea

June 10
CCM Recital: Mattauch <s>
Works by Handel, Mozart,
Schubert, Brahms, and Wolf

June 15
CCM Concert: Euterpe
Chamber Orchestra
Conductor: Jean-Louis Le Roux
Soloists: Malnou <s>, Dobrache
<vc>
Handel: Concerto grosso no.6
Vivaldi: Concerto for cello in E
Minor
Britten: Les illuminations
Tassman: Varíations on a
Frescobaldi Theme

June 20
Concert: Anfión Chamber
Orchestra
Conductor: Beatriz Tuset

June 29
CCM Recital: Simon <pf>
Beethoven: Sonata op. 110
Liszt: Sonata in B Minor
Chopin:
  a. Nocturne op. 27, no. 2
  b. Scherzo op. 31

  c. Posthumous Waltz
  d. Andante spianato and Pol-
    onaise op. 22

July 6
CCM Concert: Conjunto
Instrumental Montevideo
Conductor: Jean-Louis Le Roux
Works by Roussel and Poulenc

July 8
Vocal Recital: Olivera <s>, Del
Castillo <a>, Hermida <t>
Works by Scarlatti, Puccini,
Verdi, Giordano, and Bizet

July 11
CCM Recital: Ricci <vn>, Tosar
<pf>
Locatelli: Sonata
Beethoven: Sonata in A Minor,
op. 25
Bach: Partita for solo violin
Bartók: Sonatina
Webern: Four Pieces

July 13 to 24
Théâtre National de Belgique
Director: Jacques Huisman

July 26 to 31 (7 performances)
PORGY AND BESS (Gershwin)**
Lumbroso and Jean Clairjois,
Impresarios
AUDEM Orchestra
Conductor: Alexander Smallens
Director: Robert Breen
Clara: Colbert
Mingo: Laws
Sportin' Life: Fuller
Serena: Thigpen
Jake: James
Robbins: Wright
Maria: Burke
Porgy: Scott
Bess: Flowers / Alyer
Crown: McCurry

July 27
CCM Schumann Lieder Recital:
Souzay <bar>, Baldwin<pf>
  a. Lieder
  b. Dichterliebe

Aug 1, 3
CCM Choral Concerts
Saint Thomas of Leipzig Choral
Chorus Master: Gunther Ramin
Works by anonymous fifteenth-
century composers, Gabrielli,
Gallus, Brahms, Weismann, and
J. S. Bach

Aug 4, 8, 12
Vocal Recitals: François
<chansonnière>, Dorsey <pf>,
Tilche <gui>

Aug 6 to 16
Compagnia dell Teatro Italiano
Renzo Ricci–Eva Magni

Aug 10
CCM Recital: Heinitz <vla da
gamba, vc>
Valentine: Sonata in E Major
Bach: Suite no. 1 for solo cello
Marcello: Sonata for viola da
gamba
Abel: Prelude and Allegro for
solo viola da gamba
Haydn: Divertimento for viola
da gamba
Marais: Suite for viola da gamba
and piano
Schumann: Adagio and Allegro
op. 70 for violoncello and piano
Dvořák: Waldesruh for cello
Bartók: Romanian Dances

Aug 20
CCM Recital: Tipo <pf>
Bach: French Suite
Schumann:
  a. Noveletten
  b. Arabesque

  c. Toccata
Ravel: Alborada del gracioso
Stravinsky: Pulcinella

Aug 21
CCM Recital: M. Tipo <pf>
Schumann: Kinderszenen
Chopin:
  a. Trois Etudes op. 10
  b. Trois Etudes op. 25
  c. Polonaise

Aug 24
CCM Lieder Recital: Linne <s>,
García de Zúñiga <b>, Quincke
<pf>
Brahms Lieder Program

Aug 24 to Dec 3
Comedia Nacional Spring
Season

Aug 25 (10:30 A.M.)
Choral Concert: Coro Municipal
Chorus Master: Kurt Pahlen
Flórez <pf>
Uruguayan National Anthem
I—Songs by Uruguayan
composers
II—Folksongs from around the
world

Aug 31
CCM Recital: De los Angeles <s>
Sacratti: Proserpina
Scarlatti: La violetta
Handel: Aria from Radamisto
Schubert:
  a. Der Tod und das Mädchen
  b. Wohin?
  c. An die Musik
Brahms:
  a. Das Mädchen spricht
  b. Die Mainacht
  c. Vergebliches Ständchen
Fauré:
  a. En prière
  b. Chanson d'amour

  c. Fleur jetée
Granados:
  a. Tres tonadillas
  b. El majo tímido
  c. Amor y odio
  d. El tra la lá y el punteado
Nin:
  a. Canto andaluz
  b. El vito
Falla: Soneto a Córdoba

Sept 7
CCM Latin-American Recital:
Sabatés <pf>
Cortinas: Balada
García-Morillo:
  a. Canción triste
  b. Danza alegre
Bisquertt: Misceláneas
  a. Aires chilenos
  b. Marcha grotesca
  c. Claro de luna
  d. Arlequín
  e. Bodas de Pierrot
Guarnieri: Cavalhino da perna
quebrada
González:
  a. Fiesta en el solar
  b. Danza de la negra triste
Soriano: Sonatina
González-Gamarra: Noche de
luna en el Cuzco
Gnatalli: Rapsodia brasileira

Sept 13
CCM Recital: Mariño <pf>
Mozart: Sonata in D Minor
Beethoven: Sonata op. 53
Liszt: Sonata in B Minor
Cluzeau-Mortet: Pericón
Ravel:
  a. Pavane pour une infante
    défunte
  b. Jeux d'eau
  c. Toccata

Sept 16
CCM Recital: Tipo <pf>

Schumann: Noveletten
Bach: Sonata op. 2
Debussy:
  a. Reflet dans l'eau
  b. Général Lavine-excentric
  c. Ondine
  d. La cathédrale engloutie
  e. Feux d'artifice
Prokofiev:
  a. Prelude
  b. Suggestion diabolique

Sept 28
CCM Recital: Vercelli-Maffei <pf>
Scarlatti: Five Sonatas
Schubert: Two Impromptus
Schumann: Arabesque
Liszt: Funérailles
Chopin: Sonata op. 58

Oct 5
CCM Recital: Pasquier Trio
Beethoven: Trio op. 9, no. 1
Roussel: Trio op. 52
Mozart: Divertimento K. 563

Oct 6
CCM Recital: Tipo <pf>
Bach: Sonata in G Major
Chopin:
  a. Scherzo in B Minor
  b. Nocturne no. 24
  c. Ballade op. 23 in G Minor
Cassella: Sei pezzi infantile op. 35
Debussy:
  a. Clair de lune
  b. Général Lavine-excentric
  c. Feux d'artifice
Ravel:
  a. Jeux d'eau
  b. Toccata

Oct 10
CCM Concert: Sodca Vocal Ensemble
Kallay <s>, Souza <a>, Roselen <t>, Ortiz <b>

Works by Schumann, Gratzer, Jurafsky, and Brahms

Oct 12, 17
Coro Municipal Choral Concerts
Chorus Master: Kurt Pahlen

Oct 14
CCM Recital: Trío Uruguayo de Cuerdas Bresciani <vn>, Heltai <vla>, Nicastro <vc>, with Batlle <pf>
Brahms: Quartets
  a. Op. 60 in C Minor
  b. Op. 26 in A Major

Oct 18
Concert: Anfión Chamber Orchestra
Conductor: Beatriz Tuset
Soloists: Olivera <pf>, Haase <bn>
Albinoni: Sonata in A Major
Vivaldi: Concerto grosso no. 11
Geminiani: Concerto grosso no. 2
Soriano: Divertimento for bassoon and strings
Bach: Piano concerto in F

Oct 19
CCM Recital: Lisy <vn>, Tauriello <pf>
Piatti: Sonata in G Major
Bach: Sonata in A Major
Milhaud: Deuxième sonata
Falla-Kochansky: Suite popular española
Gianneo: Chacarera
Stravinsky: Russian Dance
Szimanowsky: Roxana's Song
Smetana: My Fatherland

Oct 24
CCM Recital: Kamendrowska <s>, Serrato <pf>
Works by Tchaikovsky, Musorgsky, Tcherepin, Cui,

Debussy, Strauss, López-Torres, and Guarnieri

Oct 28
Recital: Demicheri <vn>, Beck <pf>
Works by Beethoven, Loeillet, Vitalli, Bruch, Francoeur, Ponce, Kreisler, Falla, Sarasate

Oct 30
CCM Concert: OSSODRE and Coro Juventus
Conductor: Juan Protasi
Chorus Master: Dante Magnone
Soloists: Castro <s>
Giammarchi <t>, Carbonell <b>
Haydn: The Creation

Nov 6, 10, 13, 20, 27
Choral Concerts: Coro Municipal
Chorus Master: Kurt Pahlen

Nov 8, Dec 13
Escuela Municipal de Arte Dramático
Final examination/performances
Director: Margarita Xirgu

Nov 9
Recital: Batlle <pf>
Mozart: Sonata K. 310
Beethoven: Sonata op. 111
Chopin: Sonata op. 35
Liszt: Dante Sonata

Dec 10
Folk Recital: Ramírez <pf>
Folk music from the River Plate and Northern Argentina

Dec 14, 16
Gala Chabelska Ballet Company

Dec 21 (9:30 P.M.)
Concert: Escuela Municipal de Música Student Orchestra

Conductor: Vicente Ascone
Soloists: Fariña <vn>, Sánchez-Raña <pf>
Haydn: Quartet in G Major
Serebrier: Preludio y danza
Bruch: Concerto in G Minor <vn pf>
Bach: Sarabande and dance
Anonymous: Italiana [Respighi orch]
Ascone: Pericón no. 4

1956—CENTENNIAL YEAR

Female artists
Ayala-Vidal, Ema <pf>
Bandín, Sofía <s>
Faig, Leticia <s>
Flórez, Lyda <pf>
Giucci, Esther <pf>
Golino [de Paternó], Celia <s>
Ingold, Fanny <pf>
Linne, Olga <s>
Maresca de Marsiglia, Amalia <harp>
Mariño, Nibya <pf>
Olivera, Mercedes <pf>
Perdomo, Marita <s>
Quincke, Erna <pf>
Romay, Elena <fl>
Schenini, Victoria <pf>
Schwartz, Fanny <vn>
Staricco, Delia <a>
Steuber, Lilian <pf>
Toumanova, Tamara <d>

Male artists
Altieri, Juan B. <vc>
Balzo, Hugo <pf>
Batlle, Luis <pf>
Battesini, Rodolfo <db>
Botto, Jorge <bar>
Bresciani, Mario <vn>
Cáceres, Oscar <gui>
Camponi, Alfredo <vn>
Carbonell, Juan <b>
Casadesus, Jean <pf>

Cavallaro, Carmen <pf>
Colacelli, Donato <pf>
Cuevas, Germán <fl>
Damiani, Víctor <bar>
Dumont, Pierre <hn>
Fabbri, Juan <vn>
Graffman, Gary <pf>
Gulda, Friedrich <pf>
Heltai, Francisco <vla>
Hermida, Guillermo <t>
Honegger, Henri <vc>
Kafka, Karel <vc>
Kayan, Alexander <pf>
Kratochvil, Jiri <vla>
Kraus, Detlef <pf>
Kroyt, Boris <vla>
Mesa, Sadhi <pf>
Oukhtomsky, Wladimir <d>
Paolillo, Jorge <t>
Pasquet, Luis <pf>
Pinto, Walter <tpt>
Quartino, Rafael <t>
Roisman, Josef <vn>
Rossi, Alfredo <pf>
Rossi, Wilser <pf>
Salaberry, Walter <bar>
Schenone, Adhemar <pf>
Schneider, Mischa <vc>
Schneider, Alexander <vn>
Scholz, Alexander <vn>
Schwartz, Leo <pf>
Soler, José <t>
Stenzel, Gerhard <vc>
Sykora, Adolf <vn>
Terrasa, Miguel <b>
Tomasow, Jan <vn>
Travnicek, Jiri <vn>
Virtuoso, Antonio <hn>

Jan 31 to Feb 8, March 6 to 14
LAS MANOS DE EURIDICE (Bloch)
Spanish Dramatic Company
Enrique Guitart

Feb 16 to March 1
Carnival Troupes Parade

March 15 to April 15
Spanish Dramatic Company
María Guerrero–Pepe Romeu

April 6, 8, 9, 16
Los Chalchaleros <folk ensemble>

April 17 to 25
SPIEL IM SHOLLS (Molnar)
German Dramatic Company
from Frankfurt

April 27 (6:40 and 9:40 P.M.)
DIE ZAUBERFLOTE (Mozart)
CCM: Salzburg Marionetten Company

April 28 (6:40 and 9:40 P.M.)
DON GIOVANNI (Mozart)
CCM: Salzburg Marionetten Company

April 29 (6:40 and 9:40 P.M.)
BASTIEN UND BASTIENNE (Mozart)
SWAN'S DEATH (Saint-Saëns)
EINE KLEINE NACHTMUSIK (Mozart)
CCM: Salzburg Marionetten Company

April 30 (6:40 and 9:40 P.M.)
DIE FLEDERMAUS (Strauss)
CCM: Salzburg Marionetten Company

May 5, 6, 10
Ricardo Solé Spanish Ballet Company

BANDA MUNICIPAL 1956 CONCERT SEASON
May 6, 13, 20, June 3, 10, 17, July 1, 8, 15, 19, 29, Aug 5, 12, 19, 26, Sept 9 (10:45 A.M.)
Banda Municipal de Montevideo
Music Director and Conductor:

Bernardo Freire-López, Luis D'Andrea (assistant conductor)

May 9
CCM Recital: Casadesus <pf>
Works by Rameau, Schumann, Chopin, Ravel, and Chabrier

May 12 to 27
THE TEAHOUSE OF THE AUGUST MOON (Vern Sneider [John Patrick]) American Dramatic Company Rosita Díaz-Gimeno
Director: Romney Brent

May 16
Euterpe Orchestra Concert
Conductor: Jean-Louis Le Roux
Soloists: Dumont and Virtuoso <hns>, Schenini<pf>
Mozart: Divertimento no.7
Bach: Three Concerti for piano

May 17
Beethoven Recital: Gulda <pf>
Sonatas op. 31, no. 2, no. 23, no. 32; op. 111

May 23
Budapest String Quartet Recital
Roisman and A. Schneider <vns>, Kroyt <vla>, M. Schneider <vc>
Mozart: Quartet K. 465
Bartók: Quartet no. 1
Beethoven: Quartet op. 59, no. 2

May 28
CCM Recital: Steuber <pf>
Works by Scarlatti, Mozart, Reger, William Schuman, and Brahms

May 30
CCM Recital: Tomasow <vn>, Schwartz <pf>
Leclair: Sonata no. 3 in D Major
Debussy: Sonata in G Minor

Prokofiev: March from The Love for Three Oranges
Aguirre: Aires criollos
Wieniawsky: Polonaise brillant in D Major

June 6
CCM Recital: Kayan <pf>
Handel: Chaconne in G Major
Bach: Grand Fantasia and Fugue
Schumann: Kreisleriana
Chopin: Sonata op. 58
Bartók: Sonatina
Prokofiev: Sonata op. 3, no. 2

June 8 to Sept 30
BARRANCA ABAJO (Sánchez) Opening of the Comedia Nacional Tenth Season

June 11, 18
Folk Indo-American Music Recital
Yupanki <voice/gui>

June 13
Recital: Trío Uruguayo de Cuerdas
Bresciani <vn>, Heltai <vla>, Altieri <vc>
Beethoven: Trio op. 9
Mozart: Divertimento K. 563

June 22
CCM Recital: Scholz <vn>, Colacelli <pf>
Vitali: Chaconna
Bach: Grave
Pugnani: Preludio and Allegro
Grieg: Sonata in G Minor
Debussy: Sonata
Scholz: Capricho criollo
Ravel: Tzigane

June 24
Banda Municipal Concert
Conductor: D'Andrea

June 27
CCM Recital: Kraus <pf>
Scarlatti: Three Sonatas
Brahms: Variations and Fugue on a Handel Theme
Prokofiev: Sonata no. 3
Liszt:
  a. Les cloches de Genève
  b. Les jeux d'eau à la Villa d'Este
  c. Danse des gnomes
Albéniz: El puerto
Chopin: Scherzo in E Major

July 4
Renate Schottelius and her Contemporary Dance Ensemble

July 8 (3:15 P.M.)
Hot Club Jazz Ensemble Concert

July 9
CCM Recital: Camponi <vn>, A. Rossi <pf>
Handel: Sonata in A Major
Bach: Partita No. 3 for solo violin
Franck: Sonata in A Major
Poulenc: Sonata 1944
Dohnanyi: Ruralia hungarica op. 32

July 10
Vocal Recital: Faig <s>, Hermida <t>, Mesa <pf>
Works by Scarlatti, Brahms, Schumann, Fauré, Massenet, Donizetti, Halévy, Albéniz, Verdi, and Puccini

July 11
Recital: Janáček String Quartet from Prague
Travnicek and Sykora <vns>, Kratochvil <vla>, Kafka <vc>, and Battesini <db>
Mozart: Quartet K. 387

Janáček: Quartet no. 2
("Intimate letters")
Debussy: Quartet op. 10

July 13
Recital: Janáček String Quartet
from Prague and Schenini <pf>
Beethoven: Quartet op. 59, no. 2
Smetana: Quartet From my Life
Schubert: Piano Quintet ("Die
Forelle")

July 16, 23, 31
Ludnica Ensemble Czech Folk
Ballet

July 20
Pop Concert: Cavallaro <pf>
Melodic music arrangements
and fantasies

**ORQUESTA SINFONICA
MUNICIPAL SEASON** (OSM)
Season Conductor: Bernardo
Freire-López

July 24
OSM Mozart Concert
Soloist: Ingold <pf>
Symphony no. 31
Piano Concerto K. 488
Symphony no. 40 in G Minor

July 25
CCM Schumann Memorial
Recital: Kraus <pf>, Linne <s>,
Quincke <pf accompanist>
Two Romanzen op. 28
Eight Phantasiestücke op. 12
Eleven Lieder voice and piano
Phantasie op. 17

July 27
Berlin Chamber Orchestra
Concert
Conductor: Hans von Benda
Soloist: Stenzel <vc>
Handel: Concerto grosso

Mozart: Symphony no. 40
Haydn: Concerto in D for cello
Schubert: Symphony no. 5

July 30
OSM Mozart Concert
Soloists: Maresca <harp>,
Romay <fl>
Concerto for flute, harp, and
orchestra, K. 299
Symphony no. 41 ("Jupiter")

Aug 1, 3
Dance Recitals: Toumanova and
Oukhtomsky <d>

Aug 6 (6:30 P.M.)
Wilfredo Toamarán and Ballet
Experimental Uruguayo

Aug 6
Coro Municipal Concert
Chorus Master: Kurt Pahlen

Aug 10
CCM Recital: Graffman <pf>
Haydn: Sonata in D Major
Beethoven: Sonata op. 109
Schumann: Sonata op. 22
Musorgsky: Pictures at an
Exhibition

Aug 14
Anfión Chamber Orchestra
Concert
Conductor: Beatriz Tuset
Soloists: Schwartz <vn>, Cuevas
<fl>, Giucci <pf>
Handel: Concerto grosso op. 6,
no.1
Corelli: Concerto fatto per la
notte di Natale
Bach: Brandenburg Concert no.
5
Holst: Saint Paul Suite

Aug 15
CCM Recital: M. Olivera <pf>

Mozart:
  a. Variations on a minuet de
     Duport
  b. Sonata K. 333
Schumann:
  a. Zwei Nachtstücke op. 23
  b. Sonata op. 11

**TEATRO SOLÍS CENTENNIAL
CELEBRATIONS**
Aug 21 to Sept 4

Aug 21 (6:30 P.M.)
Opening of the Theatrical
Exhibition and Centennial
Lecture Series (held in foyer)
First Lecture: "The Artistic
Development of the Teatro
Solís" by Professor Juan Carlos
Sabat-Pebet

August 23 (6:30 P.M.)
Teatro Solís Centennial Lecture
Series
Second Lecture: "The Musical
History of the Teatro Solís" by
Professor Lauro Ayestarán

August 25 (11:00 A.M.)
**CENTENNIAL CELEBRATION
DAY**
Dedication of the bust of the
Uruguayan playwright Florencio
Sánchez in the Teatro Solís foyer
Choral Concert by the Coro
Municipal
Chorus Master: Kurt Pahlen

Aug 25 (9:30 P.M.), 26, 28
TEATRO SOLIS CENTENNIAL
CELEBRATION GALA
Uruguayan National Anthem
Opening address by a
representative of the
Municipality of Montevideo
ERNANI (Verdi)
Conductor: Domingo Dente

Director: Fritz Kalmar
Elvira: Bandín
Ernani: Soler
Don Carlo: Damiani
D. Ruy Gomez de Silva:
Carbonell
Giovanna: Perdomo
Don Riccardo: Paolillo
Jago: Terrasa

Aug 26 (10:45 A.M.)
Teatro Solís Centennial
Celebrations
Banda Municipal Concert
Conductor: Freire-López

Aug 26, Sept 1, 2 (2:00 to 4:30
P.M.)
Teatro Solís Centennial
Celebrations
Open House (house and
backstage tours)

Aug 27 (6:30 P.M.)
Teatro Solís Centennial Lecture
Series
Third Lecture: "The
Architectural History of the
Teatro Solís" by architect Carlos
Pérez-Montero

Aug 29 (6:30 P.M.)
Teatro Solís Centennial Lecture
Series
Fourth Lecture: The
Development of the Comedia
Nacional by Angel Irisarri

Aug 31 (6:30 P.M.)
Teatro Solís Centennial Lecture
Series
Fifth Lecture: "Portrayal of an
Epoch: Uruguay at the Middle
of the Nineteenth Century" by
Professor Juan Pivel-Devoto

Aug 31 (9:30 P.M.)
Teatro Solís Centennial
Celebrations

OH! QUE APUROS (Xavier de
Acha)
EL PELO DE LA DEHESA (Bretón)
Comedia Nacional
Director: Margarita Xirgu

Sept 2 (10:45 A.M.)
Teatro Solís Centennial
Celebrations
Coro Municipal Concert
Chorus Master: Kurt Pahlen
Works by Beethoven, Schubert,
and Mozart

Sept 4 (6:30 P.M.) (held in
house)
Teatro Solís Centennial Lecture
Series
Sixth Lecture: "The History of
the Teatro Solís" by Professor
Juan Carlos Sabat-Pebet [For
high school students]

Aug 22
CCM Spanish Composers
Recital: Golino <s>, Olivera <pf>
Music from the Thirteenth and
Twentieth centuries

Sept 3, 5
CCM Choral Concert: The
Jubilee Singers
Chorus Master: Mrs. Myers

Sept 12
CCM Mozart Celebration
OSSODRE and Juventus Choral
Conductor: Juan Protasi
Chorus Master: Dante Magnone
Soloists: Ayala-Vidal <pf>,
Golino <s>, Staricco <a>,
Quartino <t>, Botto <bar>
German Dances
Piano Concerto K. 488
"Coronation" Mass

Sept 16, 23 (10:45 A.M.)
Coro Municipal Concert
Chorus Master: Kurt Pahlen

Sept 17, 19
CCM Recital: Honegger <vc>
J. S. Bach: Suites for Cello

Sept 24
American Saxophone Quartet
and Vocal Concert
Soloists: Salaberry <bar>,
Pasquet <pf>
Works by Scarlatti, Mozart,
Cluzeau-Mortet, Brodi, Verdi,
Debussy, Pérez-Soriano, Soutullo
y Vert, and Wagner

Sept 25 (6:30 P.M.), 28
Berta Singerman <poetic recitals>

Sept 25
OSM Concert
Soloists: Schenini and Schenone
<pf>
Weber: Der Freischütz Overture
Mozart: Two-piano Concerto K.
365
Beethoven: Symphony no. 7

Oct 1 (6:45 P.M.)
CCM Recital: Mariño <pf>
Mozart: Fantasia in C Minor
Bach-Busoni: Chaconne in D
Minor
Mendelssohn: Variation sérieuses
Poulenc: Suite Napoli

Oct 1 (10:00 P.M.)
OSM Concert
Soloist: Fabbri <vn>
Tartini: Violin Concerto in D
Minor
Haydn: Symphony no. 10
Wagner: Siegfried Idyll
Rimsky-Korsakov: Russian
Easter Festival

Oct 2 to 8
Italian Dramatic Company
Peppino de Filippo

Oct 10
Schumann Memorial Centennial
Recital:
Batlle <pf>, Quartino <t>
Phantasiestücke op. 12
Dichterliebe op. 48 <t / pf>
Symphonische Etüden op.13

Oct 13
OSM Concert
Soloists: Heltai <vla>, W. Rossi
<pf>
Cluzeau-Mortet: Llanuras
W. Castro: Concierto elegíaco
<vla / orch>****
Gershwin:
  a. Rhapsody in Blue
  b. An American in Paris

Oct 14
Coro Municipal Concert
Chorus Master: Kurt Pahlen

Oct 16
Choral Concert
1. Johann Sebastian Bach
Chorus
Chorus Master: Eduardo
Carámbula
Works by Bach, Di Lasso,
Palestrina, Jannequin, Cavalieri,
Orff
2. SODRE Chamber Chorus
Chorus Master: Nilda Muller
Works by Jannequin,
Guastavino, Gutiérrez del
Barrio, Schiar, and Negro
spirituals

Oct 19 to Nov 18
Comedia Nacional Spring
Season

Oct 22
OSM Concert
Soloist: Balzo <pf>
Bach: Aria Suite in D, no. 3
Mozart: Eine kleine Nachtmusik
Turina: Rapsodia sinfónica
Tchaikovsky: Serenade op. 48

Oct 24
Homage to the United Nations
OSM and Coro Municipal
Chorus Master: Kurt Pahlen
Soloist: W. Rossi <pf>
Debussy: Preludes
Wagner: Siegfried Idyll
Gershwin: Rhapsody in Blue
Rimsky-Korsakov: Russian
Easter Festival

Nov 5
OSM Schumann Memorial
Concert
Soloist: Ingold <pf>
Kinderszenen op. 15
Symphony no. 3 ("Rhenish")
Piano Concerto in A Minor,
Op. 54

Nov 13
OSM Concert
Soloists: Cáceres <gui>, Pinto
<tpt>
Rossini: Overture to La scala di
seta

Haydn: Concerto for Trumpet
Rodrigo: Concierto de Aranjuez
Grofé: Grand Canyon Suite

Nov 23 to Dec 3
DIALOGUES DES CARMELITES
(Bernanos) (Sp)
Dramatic Company Teatro
Astral (Buenos Aires)
Josefina Díaz–Antonia Herrero–
Susana Campos
Director: José Tamayo

Dec 5, 11
Escuela Municipal de Arte
Dramático
Final examination/performances
Director: Margarita Xirgu

Dec 6 to 17
CAT ON A HOT TIN ROOF
(Williams) (Sp)
Francisco Petrone Dramatic
Company

Dec 19
Olga de Hintz Ballet Company

Dec 22
Paula Jarmalovich Ballet
Company

Dec 29
Coro Municipal Holiday
Concert
Chorus Master: Kurt Pahlen
Flórez <pf>

B: *Artists Who Performed at the Teatro Solís (1856–1956)*

(Singers, instrumentalists, dancers, conductors, chorus masters, opera directors)

Abad, Manuel \<bar\> 1948

Abutkoff, Alexis \<c\> 1924

Acosta y Lara, Judith \<s\> 1925

Adler, Hilde \<pf\> 1949

Adonaylo, Raquel \<s\> 1953

Ageno, Enrico \<t\> 1887

Agnoletti, Guido \<dir\> 1926

Agostinelli, Adelina \<s\> 1908, 1927

Agostinelli, Signor \<b\> 1873

Agostini, Angelo \<c\> 1869

Agozzino, Rina \<mez\> 1918

Aguilar, Elisa \<lute\> 1929, 1930

Aguilar, Ezequiel \<lute\> 1929, 1930

Aguilar, Paco \<lute\> 1929, 1930

Aguilar, Pepe \<lute\> 1929, 1930

Aguirre, Avelino \<c\> 1880, 1885

Aguirre, Pedro \<bn\> 1925

Aifos, Sofia \<s\> 1914

Aineto, Marino \<bar\> 1911

Airaldi, Ernestina L. de \<pf\> 1952

Airaldi, Jaime \<chor / c\> 1954, 1955

Albanese, Mario \<bar\> 1926

Albaredo, Signor \<t\> 1900

Albasinoff, Wassily \<b\> 1930

Albinolo, Signor \<bar\> 1909

Alda, Frances \<s\> 1908

Aldabe, María Luisa \<pf\> 1923, 1924, 1927, 1929, 1930

Aleardi, Egle \<s\> 1918

Alemanni, Maria \<s\> 1913, 1914

Alessandri, Adina \<s\> 1936

Alessandrini, Umberto \<t\> 1909, 1913

Alessandrovich, Maria \<s\> 1906

Algorta, Jorge \<b\> 1946, 1950, 1952

Algos, Angelo \<t\> 1916

Algozzino, Nini \<mez\> 1926

Alhaiza, Aline \<s\> 1876, 1877

Alitta, Signor \<c\> 1908

Allú, Ricardo S. \<c\> 1874

Almansi, Margherita \<s\> 1911

Alonso, Julio \<gui\> 1952

Alsina, Joaquín \<b\> 1924, 1940

Alsina, Juan \<b\> 1929

Altieri, Giuditta \<s\> 1862

Altieri, Juan B. \<vc\> 1956

Alvarez, Aurelio \<t\> 1932, 1948 to 1950, 1952

Alvarez, Regina \<mez\> 1912, 1913

Alwin, Karl \<c / pf\> 1930

Alyer, Ethel \<s\> 1955

Alzáibar, María D. de \<s\> 1921

Amadei, Luis \<vc\> 1929, 1952

Amat, José \<t\> 1856

Amato, Pasquale \<bar\> 1904, 1906

Amaya, Carmen \<d\> 1937, 1940

Ambrosi, Fernando \<t\> 1874

Amey, Giuseppina \<s\> 1864

Amigó de Lara, Señor \<pf\> 1856, 1857

Amoros, Emilio \<t\> 1926

Amorós, Blanca Luz \<s\> 1943

Amorós, Tere \<d\> 1952

Anceschi, Signor \<bar\> 1906

Ancona, Mario \<bar\> 1902

Anday, Rosette \<mez\> 1929

Anderson, Marian \<a\> 1937, 1938

Andolfi, Ernano \<pf\> 1904

Andreff, Maria Solowieff \<s\> 1876

Andreini (Andreoni), Remo \<t\> 1905

Andreoli, C. \<b\> 1887, 1896

Angelillo \<d\> 1939, 1940, 1941

Angelini, Emma \<s\> 1895

Angelini, Mario \<bar\> 1883

Angioletti, Signora \<mez\> 1878

Anido, María Luisa \<gui\> 1925, 1929

Anitúa, Fanny \<mez\> 1917, 1920, 1925, 1936

Ankermann, Carolina \<s\> 1895, 1899

Annini, Anna de \<mez\> 1902

Annovazzi, Antonio \<t\> 1884, 1892

Ansaldi, Pablo \<bar\> 1925, 1927, 1931

Anselmi, Giuseppe \<t\> 1902, 1905, 1906, 1908

Ansermet, Ernest \<c\> 1917

Ansorge, Conrad \<pf\> 1906

Anter, Rudolf 1910

Antimo, Natale \<b\> 1911

Antinea, María \<d\> 1940

Antinori, Vicente <t> 1870

Antoni, Giulietta (Giuditta) <mez> 1860, 1861

Antoni, Pietro de <b> 1860, 1861, 1863

Antonietti, Ida <mez> 1879

Appiani, Antonio <b> 1895

Aramburo, Antonio <t> 1877, 1883, 1886, 1894, 1896

Aranda, Angela <mez> 1904

Arata, Obdulia S. de <pf> 1932

Arcangelli, Alessandro <bar> 1905

Arce, Aida <tiple> 1941, 1943

Arce, Merceditas <tiple> 1940, 1943

Arcelli, Umberto <b> 1915, 1918, 1925, 1927

Arditi, Giulietta <s> 1861

Ardizzoni, Ernestina <d> 1869

Arenas, Joaquín <b> 1940, 1941, 1942

Argentini, Paolo <b> 1912

Arimondi, Vittorio <b> 1890, 1903

Aristide, Monsieur <bar> 1906

Arkel, Teresa <s> 1894

Armani, J. <c> 1905

Armanini, Giuseppe <t> 1905, 1910

Arnaldi, Francesco <b> 1864, 1865

Arnaud, Giacomo <bar> 1859, 1860

Arpisella-Romano, C. <mez> 1887

Arrau, Claudio <pf> 1928, 1932, 1935, 1939, 1940, 1942

Arreglia, Signora <a> 1892

Arregui, Faustino <t> 1943

Arrighetti, Silvio <b / bar> 1900, 1902, 1911

Arrigone, Cesare <t> 1881

Arriola, José (Pepito) <pf> 1912, 1920

Articci, Francesco <b> 1903

Arzarello, Juan <pf> 1952, 1953

Ascone, Vicente <c> 1931, 1943, 1944, 1947 to 1955

Asencio, Cándida <s> 1935, 1942, 1943

Asroff, Raisa <s> 1929

Astengo, Carlos <pf> 1859

Astrinidis, Nicolas <pf> 1949

Athos, Santos <bar> 1898

Aubriot, Enrique <t> 1875, 1876, 1878

Augier, Achille <b> 1876 to 1878

Augier, Signora <mez> 1876

Aulés, Antonio <pf> 1856

Avalli, Lucia <mez> 1878 to 1880

Ayala, Alcides <v / c> 1922

Ayala-Vidal, Ema <pf> 1948, 1949, 1950, 1951, 1956

Ayestarán, Ramón <gui> 1949

Azzolini, Gaetano <b> 1917, 1920

Baccaloni, Salvatore <b> 1931

Bacciato, Vittorio (Nicola) <bar> 1931, 1951

Backhaus, Wilhelm <pf> 1927, 1951

Bada, Angelo <t> 1907, 1908

Badaracco, Giovanni <t> 1906

Badini, Ernesto <bar> 1908, 1910

Baigorri, Blanca Rosa <s> 1948

Bajetti, Teresa <s> 1858, 1859, 1866

Baker, Josephine <d> 1939

Balaguer, Francisco <c> 1943

Balbiani, Felice <t> 1892

Balboni, Augusto 1909

Baldassari, Luigi <bar> 1887, 1904 to 1907

Baldassari, Signora <mez> 1887

Baldelli, Antonio <t> 1884

Baldi, Carolina <s> 1873

Baldi, Lamberto <c> 1926

Baldrich, Rogelio <t> 1918, 1921

Baldwin, Dalton <pf> 1953, 1955

Ballerini, Emidio (Emilio) <t> 1860 to 1863, 1870

Ballestero, Omar <b> 1955

Balli, Emilio <bar / b> 1934, 1940

Ballin, Monsieur <b> 1906

Bálsamo, Virginia <d> 1876

Balsinelli, Paolo <c> 1884, 1885, 1889

Balzo, Hugo <pf> 1943, 1948, 1950, 1952, 1953, 1956

Bandín, Sofía <s> 1956

Bandini, Alvaro <t> 1940

Bannino, E. <t> 1915

Baños, Avelino <vc> 1897, 1905, 1927

Baracchi, Cesare <bar> 1887

Baranda-Reyes, Santiago <pf> 1929

Barani, Felipe <t> 1953

Barbacci, Carlo <bar> 1909, 1925

Barbé, Henri <bar> 1881

Barbiere, Elvira <s> 1905

Barbieri, A. <t> 1894

Barbieri, A. <mez> 1906

Barbieri, Amadeo <c> 1910

Barbieri, Emilio <bar> 1890

Barbieri, Fedora <mez> 1948

Barbieri, Lorenzo <t> 1934

Barella, Señor <t> 1906

Baridon, J. P. <vn> 1929

Baridon, Pedro <vn> 1912

Barlett, Ethel <pf> 1937

Barletta, Alejandro <bandoneón> 1949, 1953

Baroncini, P. <b> 1906

Barone, Giuseppe <c> 1916

Barré, Jeanne <s> 1906

Barreta, Andrés <bar / dir> 1935, 1936

Barrientos, María <s> 1901, 1905, 1916

Barrios, Agustín <gui> 1913, 1920

Barry, Emily <s / pf> 1867

Barsanti, Emma <mez> 1917, 1925

Basetti, Signor <bar> 1868

Basseux, Pierre <vc> 1953

Bassi, Giulia <s> 1912, 1913

Bassi, Niccola <c> 1884, 1886

Bassi, Ugo <bar> 1915

Bassori, Pietro <t> 1860, 1861

Bastoggi, Gaetano <bar> 1858

Bastoggi, Signora <mez> 1858

Batlle, Luis <pf> 1952, 1954, 1955, 1956

Baton, René <c> 1913

Battesini, Rodolfo <db> 1956

Battistini, Mattia <bar> 1889

Bavagnelli, Gaetano <c> 1908

Bay, Enriqueta <d> 1869

Baydaroff, Nicolai <t> 1929

Bayo, Gioacchino <t> 1892

Bazelli, Lorenzo <b> 1879 to 1882

Bazin, Monsieur <b> 1876, 1877

Beaucaurt, Henri de <t> 1897

Beccario, Giuseppe <bar> 1887

Beck, Melchor <pf> 1952, 1954, 1955

Bedey, Maria (Marietta) <s> 1857, 1859 to 1862

Belia, Signora <s> 1875

Bellazi, Vittorio <bar> 1894

Belletti, Alfredo <t> 1916

Bellezza, Vincenzo <c> 1912, 1913, 1917, 1923, 1924

Belli, Signor 1862

Bellincioni, Gemma <s> 1886

Bellini, Mariella <s> 1950

Bello, Luigi <t> 1892

Belloni, Francesca <d> 1909

Belloni, Signora <mez> 1879, 1899

Bellucci, Guglielmo <band c> 1892, 1894, 1895, 1897, 1903 to 1905

Belluci, H. <vn> 1879

Bellussi, Oliviero <t> 1934

Belmondo, Signora <s> 1883

Beloff, Erminia <s / mez> 1884, 1885

Beltrán, Señor <pf> 1928

Benda, Sebastian <pf> 1953

Bendazzi-Ruiz, Gertrude <s> 1872

Bendirelli, Angiolo <t> 1908

Benedetti, Ermano <bar> 1908

Benedetti, Massina <s> 1922

Benedetti, Oreste <bar> 1887, 1888

Bengochea, Pedro D. <vn> 1859

Bengoechea, Pedro <pf> 1867

Benincori, Maria <s> 1913, 1914

Benois, Michel <dir> 1929

Bensaude, Mauricio <bar> 1896

Bensberg, Kate <s> 1894

Benucci, Signor 1885

Benzelum, Helena <s> 1901

Beracoechea, Sebastián <t> 1880

Berardi, Berardo <b> 1913 to 1915

Bergamaschi, Adolfo <b / bar> 1868

Bergamaschi, E. <t> 1903, 1918

Bergamaschi, Giovanni <bar> 1858

Bergamini, Signor <t> 1914

Bergé, Laura <s> 1919

Berger, Erna <s> 1954

Berges, Michel <hn> 1952

Bergheens (Behgerens), Alfred <pf> 1919

Bergmann, Ludwig <pf> 1947

Bergonzoni, E. 1899

Bergonzoni, Filippo <dir> 1884

Berlendi, Livia <s / mez> 1897, 1908, 1910

Bermiconi, Margherita <s> 1914

Bernabini, Attico <c> 1915

Bernard, Gabriela <s> 1908, 1909, 1911, 1918

Bernardi, Dante 1926

Bernardi, Signora <s> 1883

Bernhardt, Carlota <a> 1952, 1954

Bertana, Luisa <mez> 1923

Bertelli, Nino <t> 1926

Berthon, Mireille <s> 1920

Berti, Ernesto <t> 1875, 1876

Berti-Cecchini, Anna <mez> 1905

Berti-Marranti, Romilda <s> 1906

Bertie, Monsieur <bar> 1906

Bertini, Italo <bar> 1909, 1911, 1937

Bertini, Tobias <t> 1882

Bértola, Amalia <mez> 1934

Bertolini, Giuseppe <bar> 1860, 1861, 1863

Bertolini, Signor <bar> 1922

Bertolozzi, Paula <mez> 1911, 1916

Bertramo, Franca 1937

Bertucci, Signor <t> 1909

Besanzoni, Gabriella <mez> 1924

Bettazoni, Amedeo <bar> 1913, 1916, 1919

Betti, Gino <t> 1901

Bettini, Signor <t> 1891

Bettoni, Vincenzo <b> 1919

Betz, Signor 1896

Bevilacqua, Concetta <s> 1887

Bezzi, Jaime de <dir> 1874, 1878

Bezzoni, Pietro <bar> 1860

Biancafiore, Signor <bar> 1911

Bianchi, Bartolomé <t> 1932

Bianchi, Gina <s> 1926

Bianchi Mancini, Carolina <mez> 1883

Bianco, L. <mez> 1908

Biancolini, Marietta <s> 1873, 1875

Biase, Pietro <b> 1908

Biel, Julián <t> 1902, 1908

Bielina, Stephan <t> 1924

Bignami, César <vc> 1871, 1883

Bignami, Pompeo (Pompeyo) <vn> 1871, 1883, 1889

Bilbao, Berta <s> 1950

Bimboni, Oreste <c> 1877, 1879

Bishop, Anna <s> 1858

Bizzari, Dante 1909

Bizzo, Pina 1937

Bizzozero, Esther <pf> 1930

Bizzozero, Hugo <pf> 1953

Blanc, Hubert de <pf> 1880

Blanche, Mlle. <s> 1881

Blanco-Sadun, Matilde <mez> 1919

Bland, Elsa <s> 1923

Blechschmidt, Julia <vn> 1878

Blume, Bianca <s> 1880

Blumen, Alfred <pf> 1923

Boccalari, Edoardo 1895

Bolazzi, Giovanni <t> 1919

Bolesio, Signor <vc> 1896

Bolm, Adolphe <d> 1913

Bomon, E. <vc> 1879

Bonanni, Oscar <bar> 1943

Bonanova, Fortunio <bar> 1924

Bonaplata-Bau, Carmen <s> 1895, 1897

Bonasso, Anita <s> 1950

Bonetti, Edoardo <bar> 1867 to 1872, 1875

Bonetti, Lucia <mez> 1929

Bonfanti, Carlo <t> 1919

Bonfanti, Enrico <bar> 1887

Boni, Franca <s> 1936, 1937

Bonicioli, Riccardo <c> 1898

Bonieska, Janina <d> 1919

Bonifacino, María G. de <s> 1953

Bonini, Francesco Maria <bar> 1900, 1901, 1905, 1908

Boninsegna, Celestina <s> 1911

Bonora, G. <t> 1903

Bonora, Pietro <b> 1881

Boraglia, G. <t> 1922

Bordalba, Concetta <s> 1892

Borelli, Ettore <t> 1884

Borgatti, Giuseppe <t> 1904, 1925

Borghi, Mlle. <d> 1903

Borlinetto-Conti, Erina <mez> 1887, 1888, 1892, 1901

Bornigia, E. <mez> 1908

Borowsky, Alexandre <pf> 1935

Borra, Rosa <vn> 1856

Borracelli, Giovanni <t> 1926

Borrucchia, Ettore <b> 1892

Borsi, Signora <s> 1873

Borstein, Adolfo <vn> 1954, 1955

Boscachi, Signor 1913

Bosch, Enrique <t> 1925 (*see* Cavalotti)

Boschini, Leonida <bar / b> 1877

Bossetti, Elisa <a> 1918

Bossi, Carlotta <s> 1873

Bottari, Adelina <mez> 1899

Bottero, Alessandro <b> 1873, 1889

Bottesini, Giovanni <db> 1879

Botto, Jorge <bar> 1954, 1956

Bouchet, Monsieur 1862

Boudouresque, Marcel <b> 1902

Bourdillon de Santórsola, Sarah <pf> 1951

Bourman, Amalia <s> 1896

Boutard, André <cl> 1952

Bouzzoni, Isauro <vla> 1889

Bovi, Enrico <c> 1886

Braccony, Maria <s> 1926

Braccony, Roberto <bar / dir> 1926

Braga, Ernani <pf> 1927

Braham, Leonora <s> 1890, 1891

Brailowsky, Alexandre <pf> 1925, 1933, 1936, 1939, 1942

Brambilla, Elvira V. <s / mez> 1874, 1887, 1888

Brancciatto, Vittorio <b> 1929

Brando, A. <pf> 1897

Braun, Carl <b> 1923

Brede, Martha 1910

Breen, Robert <dir> 1955

Bregis, Danielle <s> 1937

Bresciani, Mario <vn> 1929, 1930, 1954 to 1956

Briol, Carolina <s> 1865 to 1868

Britt, Horace <vc> 1930

Brizzio, Emma <mez> 1940, 1951

Brocchi, Umberto <t> 1940

Broders, Matilde <s> 1940

Brogini, Amalia <s> 1883

Broglio, Luigi <b> 1894

Brombara, Vittorio <bar> 1890, 1905

Brondi, Alfredo <b> 1910

Broqua, Alfonso <c> 1910, 1911

Brosio, Olimpia <s> 1911

Browne, Walter <bar> 1890

Brownlee, John <bar> 1931

Bruce, May <mez> 1890

Bruchi, Maria <d> 1909

Bruel de Elizalde, Andrée <s> 1927

Bruni, Signora <s> 1883

Bruni, Rinaldi <t> 1883

Bruno, Elisa <a> 1896

Bruno, Signora <s> 1902

Bruzzone, Elvira <s> 1868

Bruzzone, Signor <t> 1868

Bruzzone, Rosita <s / mez> 1862, 1868, 1869

Bucalo, Emmanuele <bar> 1905

Bucciarelli, Assunta <mez> 1913

Buccini, Edoardo <c> 1913

Buil, Eloisa <s / mez> 1861, 1863, 1865, 1866, 1868, 1870

Bulterini, Carlo <t> 1873, 1878

Buño, Isabel <s> 1912

Buonaguida, Concetta <s> 1883

Burchi, Teresina <s> 1917

Burke, Georgia <a> 1955

Burzio, Dina <s> 1940

Burzio, Eugenia <s> 1905

Busacchi, Signor 1896, 1914

Busbaum, Frederick <vc> 1923

Busi, Adriana <s> 1887, 1888

Bussolati, Maria 1910

Bussoni, Pietro <b> 1861

Bustamante de Camargo, José <t> 1929

Buti, Ludovico <bar> 1874

Butti, Carlo <bar> 1905

Butzova, Hilda <d> 1919

Buzzi, Attilio <b> 1872, 1873, 1882

Bykoff, Nicolai <b> 1930

Cabrini, R. <child-actress> 1902

Caccialupi, Angelo <c> 1909

Cáceres, Oscar <gui> 1951, 1956

Cadelli, Gina <d> 1909

Cadwalar, L. <bar> 1890

Caiafa, Vincenzo <t> 1935

Cailly, Clarisse <s> 1858 to 1860

Caire, T. <s> 1887

Cairo, Giovanni <b> 1918, 1921, 1925

Cairo, Grillo <b> 1915

Calcavecchia, Benone <c> 1929, 1931

Caldi, Angelo <t> 1895

Calisto-Piccioli, María <s> 1872, 1873, 1875

Calleja, Francisco <gui> 1931

Calusio, Ferruccio <c> 1931

Calvera, S. <fl> 1894

Calvo, Carmelo <c / pf / org> 1870, 1871, 1895

Camarano, M. <s> 1915

Camboggi, Signora <mez> 1886

Cambroni, Vicente <bar> 1859

Camera, Edoardo <bar> 1895, 1896

Campiña, Fidela <s> 1920, 1941, 1943

Camponi, Alfredo <vn> 1956

Campos, Francisco <bn> 1914

Campos, Nemesio <bar> 1940

Campos, Omar <b> 1950

Camps, Antonio <armonium> 1870

Canasi, Ida <mez> 1917, 1919

Candini, Lea <s> 1931

Canepa, Aldo <c> 1919

Cánepa, Noemí <s> 1932

Caneschi, Alceo <vn> 1874

Canessa, José <pf> 1952

Caniglia, Maria <s> 1948

Cannonero, Carlotta <mez> 1856, 1857

Cantieri, Luigi <b> 1883

Cantoni, Giuseppe 1935

Caparros, Filippo <c> 1936

Capazza, Signora <s> 1913

Capeletti, Georgina <d> 1903

Capella, Juanita <s> 1908, 1909, 1913

Capelli, Clelia <mez> 1884, 1886

Capelli, F. <bar / b> 1886, 1889

Cappa, Ernesto <b> 1906

Cappuzano, Emilio <c> 1940

Capra, Luigi <bar> 1915

Capri, Signor <b> 1882

Capsir, Mercedes <s> 1916

Capuana, Franco <c> 1929

Caracciolo, Juanita <s> 1920

Caracciolo-Strozzi, Laura <mez / a> 1878, 1887, 1888

Caramba, Signor 1912

Carámbula, Eduardo <chor> 1954, 1956

Carámbula, Ruben <chor> 1951

Carazzi, Signor <b> 1901

Carbonell, Juan <b / bar> 1949, 1952, 1955, 1956

Carbonetti, Federico <b-buffo> 1886

Carcan, Monsieur <bar> 1906

Cardinali, Franco <t> 1888

Carelli, Emma <s> 1914

Cariano, Vicente <bar> 1856

Carlany, Eva <mez> 1877

Carlevaro, Abel <gui> 1947

Carmona, Eduardo <t-comico> 1874

Carnevale, Abele <b> 1911, 1926

Carobbi, Silla <bar> 1887, 1888

Caronna, Ernesto <bar> 1914, 1915

Caroselli, Signor <t> 1882

Carotini, Tilde <a> 1895

Carozzi-Zucchi, Carlotta <s> 1868, 1869, 1875

Carpa, Signora <mez> 1910

Carpi, Fernando <t> 1910

Carrara, Olga <s> 1926

Carrasco, Alberto <vn> 1950, 1953

Carreras, E. <b> 1918

Carsi, Héctor <pf> 1955

Cartica, Carlo <t> 1901

Carton, N. 1916

Caruso, Enrico <t> 1903, 1915, 1917

Caruson, Guglielmo <bar> 1894, 1899

Casadesus, Gaby <pf> 1931

Casadesus, Jean <pf> 1956

Casadesus, Robert <pf> 1931

Casal-Chapí, Enrique <c / chor> 1947, 1949, 1954

Casali, Julio <c> 1885

Casalla, Agustín <b> 1943

Casaloni, Annetta <mez> 1857, 1859, 1860

Casals, Señora <s> 1896

Casani, Corina 1909

Casanova, Carlo <b> 1858

Casanova de Cepeda, Carolina <s> 1872

Casas, Manolo <c> 1936, 1937

Casazza, Elvira <mez> 1913

Casco, Juan <vn> 1930

Cases, Guillermo <pf> 1951

Casimiri, [Monsignor] C. Raffaele <chor> 1930

Cassadó, Gaspar <vc> 1920

Cassaglia, Giuditta <mez> 1882

Cassandro, Lina <s> 1892, 1899

Cassia, Vincenzo <b> 1919, 1924, 1925

Cassier, Robert <ob> 1952

Castagner, Jacques <fl> 1952

Castagneri, Clemente <c> 1857, 1859, 1860

Castagneta, Olga <s> 1923

Castaldi, Luisa <s> 1912

Castellano, Edoardo <t> 1899

Castelli, Angel <cl> 1929

Castelmary, Armand <b> 1874

Castro, José María <c> 1942

Castro, Virginia <s> 1946, 1953, 1954, 1955

Cataneo, Aurelia <s> 1886

Cattaneo, Giannina (Celestina) <s> 1919, 1929

Cattaneo, Gina <mez> 1923

Catterini, A. <s> 1914

Catterini, Ida <mez> 1914

Cavalieri, Maria <s> 1914

Cavallaro, Carmen <pf> 1956

Cavalli, Lucia <s> 1911

Cavalotti, Juan <t> 1918

Cavalotti (*see* Enrique Bosch) <t> 1925

Cavedagni, Luigi <b / bar / dir> 1858, 1859, 1866, 1873

Cavedagni, Signora <s> 1858

Cazenave, Juan de <t> 1936

Cazmill, Adela 1897

Cecarelli, Signora <s> 1912

Cecchetti, Giuseppe <dir> 1908

Celada, Augusto <t> 1874

Celestino, Antonio Ma. <bar> 1865 to 1868

Celestino, A. Jr. <pf> 1867

Cellai, Giuseppe <t> 1883

Celsetti, Signor <harmonium> 1871

Cenami, Carlotta <mez> 1912
Cendalli, Riccardo <c> 1897, 1918
Centi, Cesare <t> 1911
Ceppi, Antonio <t> 1899
Cerdan, Marcel <b> 1920
Ceresa, Luigi <t> 1881
Cerezo, Cruz <c> 1895
Cerioli, F. <bar / chor> 1871, 1895
Cerratelli, Polissena <mez> 1905
Cerri, Francesco <b> 1903
Cervi-Carolli, Ersilde <s> 1912
Cesari, Giulia <s / mez> 1883, 1887
Cesari, Inocente <bar> 1864
Cesari, P. A. de <c> 1884
Cesari, Pietro <bar / b> 1882, 1883, 1887 to 1889, 1898, 1915
Cesarotto, Vittorio <bar> 1895, 1896
Cesti, Giulietta <s> 1911, 1918
Cetera, Amanda <s> 1940
Cetrullo, S. <mandolin> 1904
Chabannes, Mlle. <s> 1924
Chabelska, Gala <d> 1919, 1920, 1939, 1944, 1953, 1955
Chabelska, Maria <d> 1919, 1920
Chaliapin, Feodor <b> 1930
Chalmin, Vittorio <b> 1907
Chaplinska, Janka <s> 1913
Charmat, Claude <bar> 1919
Charnod, Monsieur <b-buffo> 1879
Chateauford, León <bar> 1856, 1857
Chazarreta, Andrés <d> 1921
Chelle, Ruben <pf> 1950, 1951
Chinelli, Angelo <t> 1886
Chiodini, Angelo <b> 1856, 1861 to 1863, 1868, 1870, 1872
Chiolo, Oscar <vn> 1924, 1927, 1929
Chizzoni, Antonio <t> 1860 to 1862
Chorberg, Israel <vn> 1952
Ciampi, Giuseppe <buffo-b> 1898
Ciapini, Signor <bar> 1873

Ciccolini, Ettore <b> 1902, 1905
Cigada, Francesco <bar> 1919, 1920
Cima, Giuseppe <bar> 1856, 1857, 1859, 1860
Cimini, Gaetano <c> 1892
Ciniselli, Francesco (Ferdinando) <t> 1920
Cioci, Amos <t> 1883
Cioni, Cesare <bar> 1895
Ciotti, Pina <s> 1911
Ciprandi, Carlo <t> 1913
Cirino, Giulio <b> 1912 to 1915, 1923, 1925
Cirotto, Sebastiano <b> 1900
Citti-Lippi, Ines 1909
Civai, G. <bar> 1915
Claessens, Marie <mez> 1907, 1908, 1919, 1920
Claramunt, Enrique <bar> 1946
Clasenti, Esperanza <s> 1903, 1906, 1910, 1916
Clement, Mlle. <mez> 1906
Clergeaud, Monsieur <bar> 1876, 1877
Clivio, Oreste <chor> 1892, 1894, 1895, 1897, 1899
Clotilde, Signora <s / mez> 1875
Cluzeau-Mortet, Luis <pf / vla> 1921, 1927, 1929, 1930
Cobelli, Giuseppina <s> 1931
Cobianchi, Angelina <mez> 1883
Cochelin, L. <c> 1878, 1879
Cockburn, George <b / bar> 1890
Codivilla, Francesco <chor> 1905
Cogorno, Ernesto <c> 1948
Coirolo, Armando <vn> 1952
Colacelli, Donato <pf> 1948, 1956
Colautti, Signor <c> 1910
Colbert, Helen <s> 1955
Colleoni, Sisto <c> 1909
Colli, Ernesto <t> 1895
Colombini, Adelina <mez> 1902
Colombo, Amalia <mez> 1911

Colombo, Natalio <t> 1905, 1906
Colonnese, Elvira <s> 1899
Comolli, Giovanni <t> 1856, 1859
Conde, Lola <mez> 1895
Consolani-Piazza, Signora <a> 1876
Constantino, Florencio <t> 1896, 1903
Contarini, Signor 1896
Conti, Arnaldo <c> 1888, 1892, 1899, 1901, 1906
Conti, Giuseppe <b> 1899
Conti Marroni, Luigi <b> 1869
Conti-Foroni, Amalia <s> 1879
Contini, Achille <b> 1886
Contini, Luis <t> 1859
Cook, Aynsley <a> 1891
Coop, Colin <bar> 1891
Cooper, Emil <c> 1924
Copca, Fanny <s> 1886
Copetti, Juanita <pf / musical glasses> 1883, 1887
Corallo, Giovanni <t> 1924, 1925
Corchs, María Delia <s> 1925 to 1930
Córdoba, Antonio <d> 1951
Core, Lucia <mez> 1873
Core, Maria <a> 1873
Corradi, C. <t> 1903
Corradini, Giuseppe <t> 1908
Correa-Luna, Carlos <c / vn / chor> 1921, 1922, 1926 to 1930, 1940
Correa-Luna, Celia <pf> 1947
Corsi, Emilia <s> 1895
Corsi-Toressi, Linda <s> 1875, 1876
Corsini, Baldassare <b-buffo> 1886
Corsini, Bice <s> 1911
Cortese, Roberto <t> 1948
Cortesi, Ersilia <s> 1878
Cortinas, César <c> 1917
Cortini, Zaira <mez> 1886
Cortis, Antonio <t> 1917
Cortot, Alfred <pf> 1936, 1952

Corucci, Zoraida <s> 1924, 1925

Costa, Dalmiro <pf> 1867, 1871

Costa, Enrico <chor> 1886

Costa, Francisco <vn> 1920

Costa, Pablo <b> 1858, 1862

Costa-Madrugat, B. <mez> 1910

Cottone, Vincenzo <bar> 1878, 1879

Courtenay, Vera <s> 1906

Crabbé, Armand <bar> 1916, 1917, 1925, 1929

Crams, Monsieur <t> 1906

Cremagnani, Tino <c> 1940

Cremonesi, Luis <vn> 1883

Cremonini, Giuseppe <t> 1894

Cremonini, Guido 1926

Crimi, Giulio <t> 1916, 1924

Crippa, Emma <a> 1892, 1896

Cristalli, Italo <t> 1906, 1911, 1925

Cristino, Ida <s> 1884

Cristofeanu, Florica <s> 1914

Crocci, Clotilde <mez> 1872

Croce, Luisa <mez> 1873

Croner, Rafael <cl> 1867

Cruz-López, María de Lourdes <s> 1953

Csillag, Steffi <s> 1913, 1918, 1920

Cubas, Marcos <t> 1948

Cubellini, Pietro <t> 1902

Cucini, Alice <mez> 1902

Cuervas, Matilde <gui> 1930

Cuevas, Germán <fl> 1954, 1955, 1956

Cuiñas, Julio <t> 1932

Cumeri, Giselda 1909

Cusano, Antonio <bar> 1858, 1862

D'Adini, Ada <s> 1877

D'Albert, A. <mez> 1907

D'Albori (D'Albore), Emilio <bar> 1905

D'Alessandro, Andrea <bar> 1920

D'Amico, Giuseppina <s> 1874

D'Andrea, Luis <c> 1953 to 1956

D'Argento, N. <cl> 1912

D'Arnot, Paul <d> 1950

D'Astragna, Eduvige <mez> 1889

D'Atino, Biaggio 1909

D'Hervil, Eloisa <pf> 1872

D'Orcanti, Signora <s> 1878

D'Ottavi, Filippo 1909

Da Ferrara, Pietro <bar> 1911

Dagle, Mariana <s> 1863

Dagmara, Francine <d> 1924

Dahmenn, Charlotte <s> 1923

Dal Monte, Toti <s> 1923

Dal Negro, Domenico <b> 1882, 1883

Dal Negro, Giulio <b> 1883

Dalceo, Clementina <s> 1887

Dalila, Signora <s> 1906

Dall'Argine, Luigi <c> 1913 to 1915

Dalla-Rizza, Gilda <s> 1914 to 1917, 1924, 1925

Dalnegro, Julio <dir> 1891

Damiani, Víctor <bar> 1922 to 1924, 1926, 1928, 1930, 1947 to 1950, 1956

Dangón, Victor <c> 1881

Dangón, Monsieur <b> 1881

Dani, Carlo <t> 1906

Danieli de Larrea, Rafaela <pf> 1949

Danise, Giuseppe <bar> 1914, 1915

Darclée, Hariclea <s> 1896, 1902, 1903, 1906

Dark, Pierre <pf> 1936

Darmia, Gina 1926

Davidoff, Maria <mez> 1929

Davis, Amata <s> 1936

Davis, Esmé <d> 1927

Davy, Gloria <s> 1955

De Angelis, Arturo <c> 1918, 1924, 1925, 1931

De Angelis, Fortunato <t> 1922

De Angelis, Maria <a> 1913

De Angelis, Nazzareno <b> 1910

De Angelis, Raimondo <t> 1918

De Angelis, Signora <s> 1906

De Angelis, Teofilo <c> 1914

De Armas, Signor <t> 1883

De Bari, Tina <s> 1931

De Bezzi, Signor <t> 1873, 1875 to 1877, 1878

De Camilli, Antonio <bar> 1859

De Camilli, Matilde <s> 1859

De Campori, Carmen <c> 1952

De Carlo, Carlo <t> 1922

De Cerser, Carlo <b-buffo> 1911

De Cré, Pomponet <t> 1876, 1877

De Ferrari, Serafino <c> 1863, 1870

De Franceschi, Enrico <bar> 1909, 1915, 1917, 1918, 1921, 1929

De Frate, Ines <s> 1906

De Giovanni, Edoardo [Edward Johnson] <t> 1916

De Giuli, Augusto <t> 1930

De Grazia, Giuseppe <b> 1895, 1896, 1906

De Hidalgo, Elvira <s> 1914

De la Costa, Joaquín <t> 1874

De la Grange, Anna <s> 1859, 1860

De Lerma, Matilde <s> 1902, 1908

De los Angeles, Victoria <s> 1955

De los Reyes, Paloma <pf> 1952

De Luca, Giuseppe <bar> 1903, 1906 to 1908, 1913

De Luca, G. <t> 1921

De Lucia, Fernando <t> 1897

De Marchi (Demarchi), Emilio <t> 1895, 1896

De Marco, G. <bar> 1899

De Martino, Carlo <b> 1911

De Muro, Bernardo <t> 1913, 1915

De Negri, Giambattista <t> 1889

De Raco, Antonio <pf> 1951

De Salvi, Guido <bar> 1922

De Santis, Angelo <t> 1882

De Segurola, Andrés [Andrea] Perelló <b> 1899, 1905, 1908

De Ter, Marguerite <s/mez> 1906

De Tura, Gennaro <t> 1911

De Vecchi, Gino <b/bar> 1923, 1924

De Vere, Clementina <s> 1884

De Waldis, Cina <s> 1912, 1913

Debret, Lucy <s> 1937

Del Campo, Sofía <s> 1928

Del Castillo, Zulma <a> 1955

Del Cupolo, Federico <c> 1926

Del Lago, Italia <mez> 1912, 1913

Del Re, Enrico <b> 1887

Delaval, Andrée <s> 1937

Delfino, J. <enghn> 1912

Delfino, Julio <b> 1940

Delfino, Roberto <t> 1955

Deliliers, Vittorio <t> 1883, 1884, 1887

Della Guardia, Luigi 1926

Dellera, Riccardo <c> 1915

Delmare, Irma 1909

Delorme, Mlle. <mez> 1881

Demicheri, Carlos <vn> 1952, 1954, 1955

Demus, Jorg <pf> 1951, 1954

Dengremont, Maurice <vn> 1874, 1880

Denis, Germán <t> 1930, 1931, 1933

Dentale, Teofilo <b> 1911, 1912, 1914, 1915, 1917

Dente, Domingo <pf/c/chor> 1921, 1925, 1927 to 1930, 1946, 1949, 1951, 1956

Depray, Mlle. <s> 1906

Derezzi, Giacomo <t> 1872

Derubeis, Signor <t> 1896

Desiré, Monsieur <t> 1878, 1879

Deutsch-Haupt, Mr. <t> 1910

Devotti, Ugo <t> 1858, 1859

Dezenser, Signor <b> 1911

Di Carlo, Ruben <t> 1952

Di Concilio, Juanita <s> 1948, 1950, 1952

Di Genaro, Osvaldo <t> 1905

Di Gesú, Francesco <c> 1909

Di Pietro, Edoardo 1936

Di Toto, Umberto <t> 1937

Díaz, América <tiple> 1936

Dibbern, Carl <c> 1910

Didot, Alfred <b/bar> 1859, 1860

Didur, Adamo <b> 1904 to 1908

Didur, Maria <mez> 1904

Diehl, Heriberto <pf> 1953

Dietrich, Kaete <s> 1910

Diez, Matilde <pf> 1922

Dimier, Mlle. <s> 1876, 1877

Dionesi, Romeo <t> 1871

Dobal, Darwin <t> 1950

Dobrache, Wladimir <vc> 1955

Dodero, Signor 1859

Dodero, Rosa <s/mez> 1859, 1861, 1862

Dolcey, Marta <s> 1918

Dolcorso, E. <mez> 1908

Domínguez, Ricardo <t> 1921

Dominici, Arnaldo <c> 1903

Dominici, Giuseppe <bar/t> 1879, 1880

Donarelli, Hugo <bar> 1920

Donati, Vittorio <b> 1885

Donbrawska, Asta <pf> 1920

Dondi, Enrico <b> 1864, 1876, 1882

Donizetti, Alfredo <c> 1900

Dorelli, Signora <s> 1914

Dorina, Rosita <mez> 1859

Dorini, Signora <s> 1912

Dorini, Signor <t> 1886

Dorsey, Pierre <pf> 1955

Doucet, Clément <pf> 1929

Dragoni, Bruna <s> 1923

Drangosch, Ernesto <pf/c> 1908, 1920

Droetto, Antonio 1899

Drog, Livia <s> 1888

Dubois, Monsieur <b> 1906

Dubressy, Monsieur <b> 1938

Dubrovsky, Georges <bar> 1929

Duchamont, Mlle. <s> 1862

Duchamont, Monsieur <t> 1862

Duclós, Carolina <s> 1858, 1859

Duclós, Matilde <s> 1857 to 1859

Duffau, Pedro <c> 1902

Duffray, Monsieur <bar> 1906

Dufranne, Louis <t> 1919

Duluart, Jacques <t> 1937

Dumesnil, Maurice <pf/c> 1919, 1920, 1921, 1940

Dumont, Pierre <hn> 1956

Duprez, Mlle. <d> 1906

Dussert, Adine <s> 1903

Dutilloy, Henri <t> 1913

Dygas, Vladimir <t> 1910

Ebendinger, Monsieur <b> 1862

Echeverry, Venancio <b> 1930

Efron, Natalia <s> 1930

Eggerth, Martha <s> 1940

Ehler, Alice <hpd> 1929

Elías, Cándido 1898

Elinson, Iso <pf> 1930

Elisins (Elisius), Vera <d> 1924

Elman, Misha <vn> 1939

Emilia, E. <t> 1908

Emiliani, Orestes <t> 1886

Emon, Monsieur <bar> 1862

Enamorado, José <t> 1857 to 1859, 1862

Engelbrecht, Enrique <pf> 1886

Ercolani, Remo <b> 1892, 1894 to 1896, 1902 to 1906

Erene, Edelvais <d> 1909

Ericourt, Daniel <pf> 1943

Errante, Adolfo <chor> 1901

Escalante, Isabella M. <s> 1869, 1870, 1873, 1875

Escobal-Vertiz, Venancio <b> 1943, 1948

Escriche, C. <s> 1915

Espalter, Dora <s> 1940

Estagel, Signora <mez> 1870, 1872

Estela, Enrique <tpt> 1914

Estevenet, Señor <fl> 1894

Estevez, Estela <mez> 1948

Estrada, Carlos <c> 1946, 1949, 1950, 1952, 1955

Etchepare, Esteban <t> 1905, 1911

Etienne, Monsieur <b> 1879, 1881

Evangelisti, Signora <mez> 1905
Evangelisti, Signor <bar> 1905
Evans, C. Warwick <vc> 1926
Evreinoff, Nicolai <dir> 1929

Fabbri, Guerrina <mez> 1888
Fabbri, Juan <vn> 1950, 1952, 1956
Fabini, Eduardo <vn / pf / c> 1903, 1925, 1926, 1928, 1929
Facci, Pio <t> 1887
Faccioni, Pina <s> 1935
Faff, Enrique <b> 1896
Faget, Eduardo <pf> 1867, 1868
Faget, Paul <pf> 1867, 1868, 1875
Faig, Leticia <s> 1956
Faisandier, Gerard <bn> 1952
Falconet, Mlle. <mez> 1876, 1877
Falconi, Giulio <c> 1910
Falconis, Vittoria <mez> 1885
Falieres, Monsieur <bar> 1906
Fálleri, Agar <pf> 1905, 1925, 1928
Fálleri, Oseas <ob> 1905
Falleti, Ernesto 1892
Fancioli, Romeo <c> 1917
Fantuzzi, Emma <mez> 1925
Fari, Edoardo 1902
Farinelli, Guido <c> 1908, 1911
Fariña, Gianfranco <vn> 1955
Farneti, Maria <s> 1903, 1904, 1907, 1911, 1913
Fasoli, Adolfo <pf> 1955
Faticanti, Edoardo <bar> 1912, 1913
Fatti-Cunti, Edoardo <b> 1912
Fattori, Mario <b> 1931
Fattoruso, Luis <b> 1932, 1933, 1934
Favi, Gaspare <t> 1911, 1926
Favila, Sergio <bar> 1943, 1948
Favili, Maria <mez> 1906
Federici, Francesco <bar> 1899, 1918
Felice, Carlotta <mez> 1877
Felicio, Mlle. <mez> 1879
Felicio, Monsieur 1879
Felix, Signora <mez> 1877

Feller, Carlos <b> 1929
Feraldy, Germaine <s> 1938
Feratoni, Signor <bar> 1878
Ferdinando, Signor <t> 1875
Fernández, Aída <s> 1946
Fernández de Guevara, Luis <bar> 1952
Fernández-Caballero, Manuel <c> 1885
Fernandi, Luis <bar> 1940
Fernando, Señor 1862
Feroldi, Ippolita <s> 1895
Ferrani, Cesira <s> 1897
Ferranti, Pedro 1856
Ferraresi, Signora <s> 1908
Ferrari, Angelo <pf> 1858
Ferrari d'Alvaredo, Pietro <t> 1902
Ferrari, Elvira <mez> 1898
Ferrari, L. <s> 1908
Ferrari, Signor 1887
Ferrari, P. <b> 1870
Ferrari, Pedro <t> 1900
Ferrari, Rodolfo <c> 1907
Ferrari, Virginia <d> 1861
Ferrari-Fontana, Edoardo <t> 1920
Ferrario, Arturo <t> 1911
Ferraris, Teresina <mez> 1903
Ferreira, José Pedro <vn> 1930
Ferreira, Pedro <gui> 1930
Ferreti, Adelina (Adele) <s> 1885, 1886
Ferreti, Signor <b> 1883
Ferri, G. <c> 1881, 1882
Ferri, Margherita Alda <mez> 1881, 1899
Ferri, Signora <mez> 1881
Ferrini, Adolfo <t> 1936, 1937
Ferroni, Luigi <b> 1926
Ferroni, Miguel <vla> 1874, 1883, 1890
Ferroni, Vicente <fl> 1874
Ferrucci, Domenico 1909
Feuermann, Emanuel <vc> 1936
Fiammengo, Rómulo <vn> 1927
Fiegna, Signor <b> 1902
Fiesel, Margarita <s> 1930

Figari, Pietro <b> 1856, 1857, 1859, 1860, 1862
Figari, Roberto <t> 1856
Figner, Nikolay <t> 1884
Figueras, Luis <vc> 1915, 1925
Fiore, Michele <b> 1911, 1918, 1923, 1924
Fiorentino, Sergio <pf> 1954
Fiorini, Signor <b> 1888
Fiorio, L. <mez> 1873
Firkusny, Rudolf <pf> 1943, 1947, 1950
Firpo, Signora 1892
Fisbiger, Erna <s> 1910
Fischerman, Jacobo <pf> 1927
Fisher, Mr. <bar> 1891
Fitelberg, Gregoire <c> 1929
Fleta, Miguel <t> 1923, 1924
Fleurquin, Clara <s> 1941
Flores, Mariquita <d> 1951
Flórez, Lyda <pf> 1953, 1955, 1956
Flory, Gilda <mez> 1913
Florit, Jaime <bar> 1893
Flowers, Martha <s> 1955
Foglia, Felice <bar> 1902, 1903, 1910
Foglizzo, Edoardo <t> 1937, 1943
Folgar, Tino <t> 1948
Fons, Luisa <s> 1894
Forest, Monsieur <t> 1870
Foresti, Luis V. 1898
Foresti, Oreste <bar> 1883
Forino, Gerardo <cl> 1954
Forlivesi, Felicita <mez> 1868
Formentini, Camilo <c / bn / db> 1874, 1883, 1886, 1887, 1889, 1891, 1894, 1896
Formilli, Signor <bar> 1876
Fornari, A. <bar> 1905
Fornaroli, Cia <d> 1915
Forsten (Foster), Signor <bar> 1878
Forti, Gaetano <bar> 1874, 1881, 1882
Fortini, Juana S. de <s> 1904
Fougères, Jacques <bar> 1937
Fournier, Pierre <vc> 1951

Fradelloni, Achille <b> 1879,
　1880
Fraikin, M. <t> 1920
Francell, Jacqueline <s> 1937
Franceschi, Elina <s> 1918
Franceschi, N. de 1902
Francesconi, Luigi <bar> 1918
Franchi, Paolo <b-buffo> 1860
Franchini, Signora <mez> 1906
Francillo-Kauffman, Hedwig <s>
　1921, 1925
Francioli, Romeo <dir> 1917
Francisco, Julián <t> 1856
Franciscolo, Luigi <c / chor>
　1883, 1887
Franco, Antonio <t> 1879
Franco, José María <pf> 1920,
　1921
Franco, Matilde <s> 1880, 1885
Franco, Señor <harp> 1869
　[member of Franco duet]
Franco, Señor <vn> 1869
　[member of Franco duet]
François, Jacqueline
　<chansonnière> 1955
Frank, Antonio <fl> 1883
Frank, Mr. <bar> 1924
Franzi, Bianca <s> 1914
Franzini, Rocco <b> 1894, 1895,
　1897
Frascani, Nini <mez> 1906, 1915
Freeden, Miss <d> 1954
Freire-López, Bernardo <c>
　1943, 1949 to 1956
Freith, Karl <vla> 1923
Freixas, Arturo <bar / b> 1915,
　1925
Frery, Señora <vn> 1856
Friedman, Ignaz <pf> 1920, 1929
Frigara, Edouard <c> 1938
Frigeri, Rina <s> 1904
Frigerio, Maria <s> 1883
Fritzsche, Gustave <vn> 1939
Frutos, Luis Pascual <t> 1935
Fujiwara, Yosie <t> 1937
Fuller, Lawrence <t> 1955
Furettini, Tina <mez / s> 1933,
　1934

Furlay, Gino 1926
Furlay, Giovanni 1935
Furlotti, Signor <c> 1886
Fusco, Amelia <s> 1903
Fusoni, Angelina <mez> 1858,
　1859
Fuster, Joaquín <pf> 1931

Gabardo, Plinio <t> 1905
Gabinska, Vera <d> 1924
Gabrielesco, Gabriel <t> 1890
Gaddi, Luigi <b> 1862, 1868 to
　1870
Gadilhe, M. <t> 1876, 1877
Gagliardi, Cecilia <s> 1906
Gaito, G. <vn> 1879
Galantha, Ekaterine de <d>
　1924
Galassi, Egisto <b> 1887
Galazzi, Paolo <bar> 1911
Galeazzi, Elvira <s> 1921
Galeffi, Carlo <bar> 1911, 1920,
　1923, 1931
Galeffi, Maria <mez> 1913, 1915
Galleani, Armando <c> 1915
Gallego, Elcira <s> 1940
Gallego, Rafael 1936
Galli, Balestra <t> 1859
Galli, Ferdinando <t> 1883
Galli, Gabriella <mez> 1926
Galli, Signora 1883
Galli-Curci, Amelita <s> 1910,
　1912, 1915
Gallinal-Heber, Alberto <b> 1931
Gallo [de Giucci], Luisa <pf>
　1874, 1878, 1897, 1920
Gallori, Sebastiano <t> 1883
Galván, Cristóbal <t> 1880
Galván, Tomás <t-comico> 1874
Galvany, Maria <s> 1902
Gamba, Adolfo <t> 1912
Gamba, Pierino <c> 1950
Gamba, Rubén <bn> 1954
Gandós, Rodolfo <bar> 1928 to
　1930
Ganthong, Nellis <a> 1890
Gaos, Andrés <vn> 1897
Garagnani, Signora <mez> 1889

Garavaglia, Lina <s> 1903 to
　1905, 1907, 1908, 1910
Garavaglia, Rosa <mez> 1903 to
　1906, 1908, 1910
Garbin, Edoardo <t> 1902, 1904,
　1906, 1907
Garbini, Adela <s> 1879
García de Zúñiga, Eduardo <b>
　1950 to 1955
García, Francisco <fl> 1914
García, Josefa <tiple> 1874
García, Marta <s> 1930
García Martí, Andrés <bar>
　1938, 1941
García, Señor <t> 1906
García-Quintana, Amanda <s>
　1928
Gardel, Carlos <folk and tango
　singer> 1927
Gardini-Marchetti, Eva <s> 1912
Gargano, Maria 1926
Gargano, Olimpo 1926
Gari, Nelly <s> 1914
Garibaldi, Luigia (Luisa) <mez>
　1905, 1906, 1910, 1914
Garinska, Lydia <s> 1925
Gatti, M. <bar> 1926
Gaudiero, Lina <s> 1911
Gaudin, André <bar> 1931
Gautier, Georgine <mez> 1893,
　1906
Gaveau, Colette <pf> 1941
Gaviria, Jesús de <t> 1943
Gazull, Adele <mez> 1894, 1895
Gazzo, Luis <b> 1859
Gear, Pauline <mez> 1890
Gebhardt, Lothar <vn> 1939
Geeraert, Mauricio <pf / c> 1912,
　1913
Gemme, Giovanni <c> 1912,
　1935
Genari, Oreste <t> 1905
Geoffroy, Abbot Bernard <chor>
　1953
Gerardi, Signor <t> 1924
Gerome, Emma <s> 1876
Gery, Agzema <s> 1870
Ghezzi, Signor <cl> 1890

Ghibaudo, Euvige <mez> 1904

Ghignatti, G. <vla> 1879

Ghilardini, Enzo <t> 1900

Ghinon, Signor <t> 1859

Ghirelli, Tina <s> 1913

Ghizone, N. <t> 1881

Ghizzoni, Signor <b> 1875

Giachetti, Rina <s> 1905

Giachino, Signora <s> 1915

Giacomello, Pietro <bar> 1902
to 1904

Giacomini, Signora <mez> 1902

Giacomucci, Anneta <s> 1913,
1914, 1916, 1917

Giacosa-Trujillo, Norma <pf>
1949

Giamari, Signor 1883

Giammarchi, Luis <t> 1932,
1946, 1948, 1954, 1955

Gianelli, Elvira <pf> 1930

Gianetto, Luisa 1909

Giani, Nélida (Nini) <mez> 1931

Giannazza, Luis <t> 1955

Gianni, Adalgisa <s> 1919

Gianni, Francesco <bar> 1857,
1858

Gianni, Giovanni B. <bar> 1858,
1859

Giannini, Clotilde <mez> 1874

Giannini, Francesco <t> 1879

Giannini, Filippo <b> 1883

Gibboni, Elisa <s> 1896

Gieseking, Walter <pf> 1950,
1952

Giganeri, Jeremías <c> 1940

Gigli, Beniamino <t> 1919

Giglioni, Ida <s> 1883, 1889

Gil Saenz, Francisco <c> 1940

Gil (Gilboni), Lucia Boni de <s>
1890

Gil-Janeiro, Noemí <s> 1954

Gilioni, Ida <s> 1883

Gini-Pizzorni, Adele <s> 1892,
1896

Gioana, Pina <s> 1923

Giordani, Signor <b> 1876

Giottanti (Giottanli), Signor <t>
1878

Giovanelli, Matilda <mez> 1862,
1863

Giovanelli, Rinaldo <c> 1899,
1900, 1905

Giovanini, Alejandro <t / bar>
1950, 1952, 1955

Giovanini, Signor 1881

Giovanni, Alvino 1909

Giraldoni, Eugenio <bar> 1903,
1905, 1917

Girardi, Vittorio <b> 1889

Gitovky, Michel <b> 1929

Gittli, Ernesto <pf> 1950, 1952

Giucci, Camillo <pf> 1887

Giucci, Carlos <pf> 1930

Giucci, Esther <pf> 1930, 1956

Giucci, Luisa Gallo de (*see* Gallo
[de Giucci], Luisa)

Giudice, Maria <mez / a> 1894,
1897

Giuffra, Señor <pf> 1864

Giuli, Augusto de <t> 1950, 1953

Giuliani, Adela <s> 1900

Giutti, Emilia <s> 1879

Gjebina, Mlle. <d> 1929

Gobatto, Ida <s> 1905

Gobbi, Tito <bar> 1951

Godard, Monsieur <b> 1906

Godefroy, Monsieur <bar> 1893,
1906

Goergi, Lucie 1910

Golardi, Luigi 1909

Goldsand, Robert <pf> 1933

Golfieri, Maria <mez> 1899,
1900

Golino [de Paternó], Celia <s>
1950, 1952 to 1954, 1956

Gómez-Carrillo, Carmen Rosa
<s> 1953

Gómez-Carrillo, Jorge <b> 1953

Gómez-Carrillo, Julio <bar>
1953

Gómez-Carrillo, (Junior),
Manuel <t> 1953

González, Adelita <s> 1950

González, Alberto <chor> 1954

González, Elisa <s> 1904

González, José <cl> 1914

González, Juan A. <bar> 1904

González, Señor <b> 1879

Gori, Ferruccio <b> 1883

Gori-Pasquali, Cesira <s / mez>
1885, 1887, 1896, 1897

Gotardi, Emilia <mez> 1909,
1911

Gottardi, Signor <t> 1878

Gottschalk, Louis Moreau <pf / c>
1867, 1868

Goublier, Henri Gustave <c>
1938

Graffman, Gary <pf> 1956

Gramegna, Anna <mez / a> 1914,
1924, 1925

Grand, Walter <t> 1918

Grandi, Paride 1937

Granelli, Annetta <s> 1918

Granforte, Apollo <bar> 1915,
1925, 1929

Grasse, Signora <mez> 1906

Grassi, Signor <fl> 1883

Grassi, Rinaldo <t> 1907, 1908,
1919

Grasso, Gerardo <c> 1885, 1886

Grau, Maurice <dir> 1881

Gravenstein, Mr. <c> 1881

Gravilovi, Alexander <d> 1917

Greco, José <d> 1951

Gregoire, Mlle. <mez> 1881

Gregoretti, Signor <bar> 1901

Greppi, Clemente B. <chor>
1915

Grey, Madeleine <s> 1939

Griff, Alexander <b> 1924

Griffon, Celestino <c> 1858

Grigorieva, Tamara <d> 1953

Grisoli, Liber <b> 1948

Gromova, Irina <s> 1949

Grondona, Emilio <b> 1895

Grondone, M. <bar> 1887

Grunwald, Carl 1910

Guaglianone, Victor <vc> 1929,
1930

Guasqui, Augusto <b> 1925

Gubellini, Pietro <t> 1905

Guerin, Victor <c> 1861

Guerra, Elvira 1909

Guerra, Vittoria <a> 1913
Guerrici, Signora <mez> 1874
Guerrieri, Olga <mez> 1920
Guerrini, Virginia <mez> 1895
   to 1897, 1903
Guerrito, Nina <s> 1935
Guichandut, Carlos <bar> 1941,
   1943
Guille, Mlle. <s> 1862
Guille, Monsieur <c> 1862
Guinei, Augusta <mez> 1874
Gulda, Friedrich <pf> 1952, 1956
Gurtubay, Saturnino de <vn>
   1874

Haase, Gerhard <bn> 1954, 1955
Hackett, Charles <t> 1917
Hajmassy, Imre <pf> 1951
Handel, Ida <vn> 1953, 1954
Hartman, Imre <vc> 1939
Hauser, Blanca <s> 1940
Hautbourg, Simone de <mez>
   1953
Hayes, Louise <s> 1925
Heifetz, Bener <vc> 1936
Heifetz, Jascha <vn> 1934
Heine, Ada <pf> 1870
Heine, José <vn> 1870
Heinitz, Eva <vc / vla da gamba>
   1952, 1955
Helguera, Haydée <pf> 1952
Hellstrom, Luisa <s> 1880
Heltai, Francisco <vla> 1950,
   1952 to 1956
Henri, Mlle. <s> 1877, 1878
Hericourt, Luis <t> 1860, 1864
   to 1866, 1872 to 1874
Hermelin, Arthur <pf> 1927
Hermida, Guillermo <t> 1950,
   1951, 1953, 1955, 1956
Hernández, Félix <sax> 1871,
   1872
Herrera de Rius, María <pf>
   1929
Herrera-McLean, Carlos <t>
   1921
Hertogs, Pablo <bar> 1940 to
   1943

Herz, Otto <pf> 1931
Hilson, Jack <c> 1940
Hines, Miguel <pf> 1861
Hintz, Olga de <d> 1954, 1956
Hipolito, Señor <t> 1858
Hoffman, Josef <pf> 1936
Hols de Schusselin, Josefina <s>
   1924, 1931
Honegger, Henri <vc> 1956
Hopper, Joyce <s> 1955
Horszowski, Mieczyslaw <pf>
   1924
Hotkowska, Ladislava <mez>
   1911
Hoyer, Dore <d> 1952, 1953
Huberman, Bronislaw <vn> 1923
Huberty, Albert <b> 1919

Ibarguren, Clemente <vn> 1889
Ibarra, Ignacio <bar> 1932, 1936
Ibels, Jacqueline <pf> 1939
Igarzábal de Chiesa, Blanca <s>
   1928, 1930
Iglesias, Sara <s> 1950
Ilabarca, Oscar <t> 1940
Imbimbo, Inés 1909
Indart, Lyda Mirtha <pf> 1948,
   1950, 1952, 1954
Ingar, Gerolamo <t> 1910
Ingold, Fanny <pf> 1956
Iniesta, Enrique <vn> 1950
Innocenti, Cesare <bar> 1865,
   1866
Iracema, Amalia <mez> 1899
Iraola, Horacio <pf> 1952
Irfré, Héctor <t> 1868, 1869
Irigoyen, Juan <pf> 1890, 1891,
   1896
Iris, Esperanza <s> 1927
Isaura, Amalia de <d> 1929
Istomin, Eugene <pf> 1955
Iturbi, Amparo <pf> 1939
Iturbi, José <pf> 1927, 1929,
   1935, 1939
Ivanisi, Maria <s> 1912, 1913
Ivner, Emma <s> 1913
Izquierdo, Manuel <t> 1905
Izzi, Italo A. <pf> 1954

Jabovich, Eugenia <mez> 1924
Jacobson, Amalia <s> 1856,
   1857
Jacoby, Rosita <s> 1900
Jacovieff, Alexandre <d> 1919,
   1920
James, Joseph <bar> 1955
Jancsi, Kiss <c> 1890
Janni, Roberto <bar> 1913
Janopoulo, Tasso <pf> 1929,
   1930
Janzer, Georges <vla> 1951
Jarmalovich, Paula <d> 1953,
   1954, 1956
Jaroff, Serge <chor> 1936, 1951
Jasinsky, Roman <d> 1952, 1954
Jedliczka, Carlo <b> 1911
Jessel, Misha <pf> 1947
Jiske, N. <bar> 1891
Johannesen, Grant <pf> 1952
Jones, Barter <c> 1890, 1891
Jouffre, Monsieur <pf> 1867,
   1868
Journet, Marcel <b> 1916, 1917,
   1923, 1929
Juárez, Nena <mez> 1929
Juárez, Rogelio <b / bar> 1894
Jukovich, Constantin <b> 1929
Julien, Elodie <pf> 1865, 1866
Julien, George <fl> 1894
Julien, Paul <vn> 1863, 1865,
   1866
Jurilli, M. <chor> 1905
Jurkowski, José <pf> 1874, 1875

Kaemper, Gerd <pf> 1953
Kafka, Karel <vc> 1956
Kaisin, Francy <t> 1938
Kallay, Maria <s> 1955
Kalmar, Fritz <dir> 1954, 1956
Kamendrowska, Ina <s> 1955
Kaneline, Martha <mez> 1926
Kapeller, Mr. <c> 1910
Karnizka, Maria <a> 1929
Karsavina, Tamara <d> 1913
Kaweski, Jan <d> 1919
Kaufman, Louis <vn> 1952
Kayan, Alexander <pf> 1956

Kempff, Wilhelm <pf> 1937,
   1949, 1951
Kiepura, Jan <t> 1929
Kipnis, Alexander <b> 1931
Kirchhoff, Walther <t> 1923
Kitzú, Aurelia <s> 1890
Kohischuetter, Volkmar <vc>
   1939
Koklova, Olga <d> 1917
Kolisher, Wilhelm <pf / c> 1920,
   1949, 1953
Kolish, Rudolf <vn> 1936
Komisargevsky, Theodor <dir>
   1929
Komlós, Pablo <c> 1941
Kondaky, Maria <s> 1929
Koney, Pauline <d> 1954
Koralek (Kuralek), Paula <s>
   1910
Koshetz, Nina <s> 1924
Kostrukoff, Nicolai <chor>
   1930
Kranz, Naum <vn> 1929
Kratochvil, Jiri <vla> 1956
Kraus, Detlef <pf> 1956
Krauss, Clemens <c> 1928
Kreisler, Fritz <vn> 1935
Kremenev, Mr. <dir> 1917
Kreuder, Peter <pf> 1950
Kreutzberg, Harald <d> 1952
Kroner, Helena <d> 1919
Kroyt, Boris <vla> 1956
Kruszelnicka [Krusceniski],
   Salomea <s> 1906 to 1908,
   1910, 1923
Kubelik, Rafael <vn> 1931
Kuhner, Felix <vn> 1936
Kumok, Herman <pf> 1930
Kusnezoff, Maria <s> 1929
Kusrow de Iniesta, Yocasta <pf>
   1950
Kusrow-Corma, Carlos <pf>
   1940

La Puma, Giuseppe <b-buffo>
   1911
Labia, Maria <s> 1919
Laborde, Ema <pf> 1920

Labrocca, Antonio M. <vn>
   1930
Laffrá, Annie <vn> 1953
Lafitte, León <t> 1916
Lafon, Signora 1896
Lafont, Monsieur <b> 1876, 1877
Lafuente, Pedro <t> 1917
Lago, Pura <pf> 1919
Lahoz, Ernesto <c> 1918
Lalloni, Lorenzo <bar> 1877
Lambert, Andrée <s> 1937
Lambiase, Elvira <s / mez> 1887,
   1889
Lambiase, Gaetano <t / bar>
   1884, 1887
Lambiase, Signora <s> 1905
Lambiase, Oreste 1896
Lambra, Carlos <pf> 1856
Lamond, Frederic <pf> 1935
Lampaggi, Maria Luisa <mez>
   1922, 1925
Landi, Alfredo Isidoro <dir>
   1909, 1922
Landi, Bruno <t> 1943
Landowska, Wanda <hpd / pf>
   1929
Lane, Josyane <s> 1937
Lanfredi, Carlo <t> 1889
Lange, Herta <pf> 1940, 1942
Lanz, Ariel <actor> 1950
Lanzi, Sylvia 1902
Lareu, Ema <s> 1929, 1931
Lareu, Teresa <pf> 1929
Lari-Valero, Raya <s> 1882
Larralde, Pedro <hn> 1925
Larraya, Camilo <b> 1874
Larreta, Antonio <dir> 1952,
   1953, 1954
Larrimbe, Felipe <c> 1924, 1929,
   1931
Larrumbe, Adelaida <s> 1862,
   1863
Laserre Brisson, Luis <fl> 1859
Laudy, Rachel <s> 1938
Laura, Mlle. 1862
Laurent, Mlle. 1897
Lauria, J. 1892
La Vía, Luis <pf> 1942

Lavin de Casas, Blanca <mez>
   1905
Lavretzky, Nicolai <t> 1924,
   1929
Laws, Jerry <t> 1955
Lázaro, Hipólito <t> 1914, 1915
Lazzari, Virgilio <b> 1920
Le Roux, Jean-Louis <c / ob>
   1954, 1955, 1956
Lebano, Felice <harp> 1887
Lecardi, Maria <d> 1909
Lecoutex, Mlle. 1862
Lecoutex, Monsieur <dir> 1862
Lehamann, Claude 1937
Lehner, Jence <vla> 1936
Leicht, Emil 1910
Lelmi, Luis <t> 1858 to 1863,
   1865 to 1869, 1875
Leman de Quiroga, Marta <pf>
   1926, 1929
Lena, Alfredo <t> 1904
Lener, Jeno <vn> 1939
Lentz, Julie 1881
Leo, Mlle. <s> 1906
Leon, Monsieur <bar> 1876
León, Soledad <tiple> 1936
Leonard, Lotte <s> 1926
Leonard, Monsieur <t> 1906
Leonardi, Signora 1916
Leone (Leoni), Eugenia <s>
   1883, 1887
Lerena, Argentina <tiple> 1942,
   1943
Lerena, Ema <pf> 1899
Lerner, Tina <pf> 1921
Leroux, Hélène <s> 1881
Leroux, Xavier <c> 1916
Leslie, Earl <d> 1923
Lespagne, Mlle. 1878
Lestellier, Signor <t> 1877
Leuters, Mlle. <s> 1879
Levey, James <vn> 1926
Liard, Vittorina <s> 1858
Lietti, Achille <c> 1919
Liguori, Ermenegildo <pf> 1863
Lilloni, Maria <mez> 1923
Limberti, Giuseppe <t> 1872
Limón, José <d> 1954

Limonta, Napoleone \<b\> 1884, 1889, 1892, 1894 to 1896

Linne, Olga \<s\> 1950, 1952 to 1956

Linsen, Kurt \<b\> 1921

Lippi, Signor 1883

Lisko, Napoleone \<c\> 1909

Lisy, Alberto \<vn\> 1955

Livian, Miss 1890, 1891

Llobet, Miguel \<gui\> 1922, 1925, 1929

Lloret, Dora \<s\> 1922

Llovet y Castellet, Juan \<pf\> 1867

Loewenguth, Alfred \<vn\> 1953

Logheder, Luis \<c / pf\> 1890 to 1892, 1896, 1901

Lombardi, Olinto \<b\> 1909

Lombardo, Constantino \<c\> 1913, 1914

Longari-Ponsoni, Luigia \<s\> 1907

Longas, Federico \<pf\> 1939

Longhi, Emma 1899

Longobardi, Luigi \<t\> 1906

Longone, Lina \<s\> 1900

López Brothers \<d\> 1941

López, Encarnación ("La Argentinita") \<d\> 1935, 1939

López, Isabel \<tiple\> 1894

López, Martín \<pf\> 1903

López, Señor \<c\> 1895

López, Pilar \<d\> 1950

López-Lomba, Violeta \<d\> 1954

López-Macía, Raúl \<t\> 1928

Lopokova, Lydia \<d\> 1917

Loreau, Arthur \<pf\> 1858, 1859

Loredano, Signor \<bar\> 1858

Lorenzi, Hebe \<pf\> 1951

Lorusso, María \<s\> 1948

Loyonnet, Paul \<pf\> 1947

Luccardi, Ana \<s\> 1911

Lucci, Elena \<mez\> 1910

Lucci, Gianna \<mez\> 1919

Lucenti, Luigi \<b\> 1901

Luciano, Isabel \<s\> 1936

Lucignani, Benedetto \<t\> 1887, 1894

Ludikar, Pavel \<b\> 1920

Luongo, Virgilio \<bar\> 1946

Lupino, Miss 1890, 1891

Luppi, Achille \<dir\> 1884

Lussardi, Dino \<bar\> 1915

Lusso, Alberto 1935

Luttichau, Julia de \<s / mez\> 1886, 1892

Luzzardi (Lusiardo), Clementina \<s\> 1895

Luzzatti, Arturo \<pf\> 1930

Luzzetti, Emilia \<mez\> 1872

Lyesia, Ester \<d\> 1909

Lyon, Pauline \<s\> 1862, 1866

Macchi, Plácido \<fl\> 1912, 1922

Madriguera, Paquita \<pf\> 1947

Maestri, Catullo \<t\> 1914, 1917

Maffei, Giovanni \<bar / b\> 1873, 1878

Mafioli, Juan \<vn\> 1904

Maggi, Signora \<s\> 1908

Maggiolo, Roberto \<t\> 1948

Magnan, Charles \<pf\> 1928

Magnone, Dante \<chor\> 1954, 1955, 1956

Maicherska, Miss \<d\> 1913

Máiquez, Francisco L. \<c\> 1896

Maini, Primo \<t\> 1898

Mainor, Dorothy \<s\> 1947

Malbleid, Monsieur 1862

Malcuzynski, Witold \<pf\> 1941, 1943, 1953

Maleroni, Signor 1896

Malet, Eduardo \<dir\> 1954

Malnou, Marie Louise \<s\> 1955

Malvezzi, Stella \<s\> 1887

Malvina, Mlle. \<mez\> 1881

Manaresi, Clarise \<s\> 1864

Manaresi, Giobbe \<t\> 1864, 1865

Manarini, Giulia \<mez\> 1914

Mancinelli, Marino \<c\> 1889

Mancini, Signora \<s\> 1886

Mancini, Roberto \<b\> 1883

Manén, Juan (Juanito) \<vn\> 1893, 1919, 1928

Manfredi, Eugenio \<b\> 1875

Manfredi, Signora \<a\> 1901

Manfredi, Signor \<t\> 1912

Manfredini, Signora \<s\> 1890

Manfrini, Luigi \<b\> 1910

Mangini, Bianca \<s\> 1913

Manjón, Antonio \<gui\> 1908

Mannarini, Ida \<mez\> 1915

Manrique, Carmen \<s / mez\> 1936

Mansueto, Gaudio \<b\> 1906, 1908, 1911, 1916, 1922, 1924

Mantegazza, Anunziata B. de \<s\> 1904

Mantelli, Eugenia \<mez\> 1889

Mantinenghi, Antonio \<t\> 1873

Many, Juanita \<s\> 1902

Manzini, Constanza \<s\> 1860 to 1863

Manzini (Mancini), Signora \<s\> 1892

Mañé, Adelaida Ramírez de \<s\> 1946

Marangoni, Signor 1896

Marasini, Mario \<t\> 1880

Marchapp, Monsieur 1862

Marchessiari, Signor \<t\> 1918

Marchetti, A. \<t\> 1870

Marchetti, Signor \<c\> 1912

Marchesi, Adela \<s\> 1896

Marcomini, Elisa \<mez\> 1900, 1909, 1911

Marconi, Raffaele \<b / dir\> 1874 to 1877, 1887

Mardones, José \<b\> 1906, 1910

Marek, M. \<mez\> 1912

Marengo, Isabel \<s\> 1931

Maresca de Marsiglia, Amalia \<harp\> 1956

Mareul, Jacques 1937

Mari, Bruno \<c\> 1915, 1922, 1927

Mariacher, Michele \<t\> 1892, 1897

Mariani, Hugo \<vn\> 1920

Mariani, Signora \<mez\> 1906

Maricarmen \<tiple\> 1938, 1941

Marié, Paola \<mez\> 1881

Marinari, Alejandro \<ob\> 1925

Marini, Angela \<s\> 1936, 1937

Marini, Luigi \<t\> 1912

Marini, Pio <bar> 1895, 1902

Marino (Marini), C. <bar/b> 1876

Marinuzzi, Gino <c> 1912, 1913, 1915, 1917, 1923

Mariño, Nibya <pf> 1942, 1943, 1947, 1952, 1954 to 1956

Mario, Señor <fl> 1894

Mariotti, Rosina <mez> 1865, 1866

Maris, Margarita <s> 1932, 1933

Maristany, Signor <t> 1896

Markova, Alicia <d> 1952

Marmora, Nera <s> 1917

Marneck, G. Walter <bar> 1890

Marotta, Alessandro <c> 1861

Marranti, Antonio <c> 1906, 1918, 1921, 1943

Marrone, Elena <s> 1936

Marseli, Emma 1909

Marsiglia, Oscar <pf/org> 1931, 1950

Marti, Anita <s> 1862

Martinelli, Giovanni <t> 1916

Martinenghi, Antonio <t> 1873

Martínez, Conchita <d> 1939

Martínez, Cristóbal <d> 1950, 1953

Martínez, José <t> 1940

Martínez, L. <mez> 1870

Martínez, Ramón <b> 1933

Martínez, Tomás <hn> 1914

Martínez, V. <bar> 1925

Martínez-Buelta, Fernando <t> 1955

Martínez-Law, Marta <s> 1929

Martinez-Oyanguren, Julio <gui> 1930

Martini, Gaetano <bar> 1883

Martini, Signora <s> 1906

Martino, Alfredo <c> 1915

Martinotti, Bruno <b> 1905, 1906, 1909

Marucco, Pedro <bar> 1873

Marziali, Cristiano <bar> 1872, 1873, 1875

Marziali-Passerini, Julia <s> 1872, 1873

Mas, Rosa <vn> 1948

Mascagni, Pietro <c> 1911

Mascheroni, Edoardo <c> 1894 to 1897

Maserole, Napoleon <c> 1886

Masi, Romeo <vn> 1883, 1886

Masini, Angelo <t> 1889

Masini, Galliano <t> 1931

Masini-Pieralli, Angelo <b> 1919

Massardi, Rina <s> 1932

Massé, Raúl <bar> 1918

Massi, R. <bar> 1889

Massimi, Massimo <t> 1887

Masson, Fernand <c> 1920

Mastrangelo, Rogelio <c> 1950

Mastronardi, Domingo <t> 1940

Matarelli, Signora 1892

Mathieu, Maddalena <s> 1919

Matiotti, Giuseppe 1909

Matray, Mlle. <a> 1876

Matray, Monsieur <b> 1876, 1877

Mattauch, Hilde <s> 1955

Matthaeus, Marion <s> 1938

Mattinzoli, Signora <s> 1915

Maugé, F. <b/bar> 1881

Maugé, Mlle. <mez> 1881

Mauras, Paul M. <t> 1881

Maury, Sinai <t> 1916

Mayer, Tomas G. <pf> 1943

Mazzanti, Gaetano <t> 1902

Mazzi, Emma <a> 1908

Mazzi, Giuseppe <t> 1862

Mazzini, Signora <s> 1862

Mazzoleni, Ester <s> 1919

Mazzoli, Agustin <bar> 1876, 1879

Mazzolo, Signor <b> 1883

Mazzoni-Osti, Ludovico <bar> 1872, 1873

Mazzuchelli, Tina <a> 1902

Mazzuchi, Bassano <vc> 1908, 1912

Mazzuco, Antonieta <mez/a> 1872

McCurry, John <bar> 1955

Medici, Alfredo <t> 1920

Medori, Giuseppina <s> 1859, 1860

Mei-Figner, Medea <s> 1884, 1903

Melandri, Antonio <t> 1926

Melis, Carmen <s> 1917

Meller, Raquel <d/tonadillera> 1920, 1921, 1938

Melly, Elena <s> 1922

Melnikoff, Nicolai <bar> 1924, 1929

Melsa, Mary <s/mez> 1901, 1915

Mendeguía, Walter <bar> 1955

Menghini, Signora 1883

Menici, Signor <b> 1872

Menni, Giuseppe <b> 1919

Menotti, Delfino <bar> 1882, 1885, 1887 to 1889

Mercé, Antonia ("La Argentina") <d> 1919, 1933, 1934, 1935

Mercier, René <c> 1937

Merea, Carolina <s> 1856

Merian, Signora <mez> 1906

Meriwether-Hugues, Russell ("La Meri") <d> 1929

Merle, Mlle. <mez> 1881

Merle, Monsieur <t> 1881

Merli, Francesco <t> 1920

Merli, N. <b> 1916

Merö, Yolanda <pf> 1919, 1920

Meroles, Pablo <b/bar> 1890

Merviola, Miss 1910

Mesa, Sadhi <pf> 1956

Messager, Monsieur <pf> 1868

Messager, André <c> 1916

Metallo de Maza, Maria Antonia <s> 1924

Metelli, César Augusto <c> 1932, 1933, 1934

Meyer, Mlle. <s> 1906

Meyer-Radon, Walter <pf> 1911, 1920

Michalowski, Pierre <d> 1924

Michelin, Bernard <vc> 1949, 1950

Michelini, Saffo <s> 1908

Michelotti, Signor <t> 1895, 1897

Micheluzzi, Leopoldo <t> 1913

Micoulina, Mlle. <d> 1924

Micucci-Betti, Linda <s> 1901

Migliacci, Margherita <mez> 1924

Migliazzi, Signor 1896

Milani, Signor <t> 1878, 1883

Millanes, Carlota <s> 1893

Milli, Attilio <b> 1921

Milstein, Nathan <vn> 1927, 1929, 1937

Minghetti, Angelo <t> 1924, 1925

Minolfi, Renzo <bar> 1908, 1912

Mirabella, Giovanni <b> 1879

Mirassou, Pedro <t> 1924, 1929

Mirate, Raffaele <t> 1859, 1860

Miró, María <s> 1897

Miselli, Manfredo 1926

Misselli, Maria <s> 1918

Missorta, Palmira <s> 1876

Mistinguette [Jeanne Marie Bourgeois] <d> 1922, 1923

Mittman, Leopold <pf> 1937

Mogavero, Ernesto <c> 1926

Moiseiwitsch, Benno <pf> 1926, 1929, 1935, 1938

Mojica, José <t> 1937

Molina, Amalia <d> 1937

Molinari, Signora 1896

Molla, Signor <b> 1873

Moller, Martha <mez> 1883

Mollo, Marietta <s> 1863, 1865, 1867, 1872

Moltrasio, Beniamino <c> 1919

Monachesi, Mario <bar> 1943

Monchero, Amilcare <b> 1887, 1888, 1897

Mondino, Luis <pf> 1930

Montalicini, Zaira 1899

Montanari, A. <t> 1907

Monteano (Monteoni), Signora <s> 1891

Montenegro de Gaos, America <pf> 1897

Montenegro, Leopoldo <c> 1878

Montes, John <pf> 1948

Montes, Tila <pf> 1948

Monteverde, A. <t> 1858, 1859, 1862, 1863

Monti, Francisco de Paula <b> 1880

Monti, Gaetano <b> 1877

Monti, Luigi <b> 1908, 1909

Monti, Rosina <s> 1919

Montijo, Coral de <d> 1954

Montoya, Fernanda <d> 1949

Mora, Florencio <vn> 1912, 1916, 1921

Morales, Edgardo <t> 1948

Morbini, Luigia <mez> 1885

Moreira de Sá, Bernardo <vn> 1897

Morelli, Adela <s> 1886

Morelli, Adelina <s> 1931

Moreno, Blanca <s> 1917

Moreno, Giacomo <bar> 1922

Moreschi, Enrique <vc> 1889, 1890

Moretti, Giuseppe <t> 1887, 1888

Mori, Signor <b> 1899

Moriami, Gustavo <bar> 1882

Morini, Jeanne <s> 1913

Morini, Luigia <mez> 1864, 1865, 1866

Morini, Martha <s> 1913

Moroni, Signor <b> 1876

Morosoni, Giselda 1909

Morpurgo, Adolfo <vla da gamba / c> 1950

Morton, Lily <a / mez> 1927, 1928, 1929, 1930

Motelli, Signora <mez> 1876, 1877

Mozzi, Eugenio <t> 1882

Mugnone, Leopoldo <c> 1902, 1905, 1908, 1910

Mujica, José Tomás <c / pf> 1931, 1937

Muller, María V. de <s> 1931

Muller, Nilda <chor> 1948, 1952, 1953, 1954, 1956

Munchinger, Karl <c> 1953

Muñoz, Luis <bar> 1920

Muratore, Lucien <t> 1919

Murgier, Jacques <vn> 1953

Muró de Lacarte, Julieta <s> 1919, 1920

Musetti, Francisco J. <vn> 1950, 1953

Mussi, Guido <t> 1913, 1918

Musso, Wanda <s> 1932

Mussy, Monsieur <b> 1881

Muzio, Attilio <b> 1929

Muzio, Claudia <s> 1919, 1920, 1923, 1924

Myers, Mrs. James A. <chor> 1953, 1956

Nadin, Monsieur <bar> 1906

Nani, Enrico <bar> 1905, 1907, 1910

Nannetti, Augusto <t> 1904, 1905, 1908

Napoleão, Arthur <pf> 1857, 1863

Narberti, Antonio <b> 1878

Nardi, Luigi <t> 1915, 1923, 1924, 1929

Nascimbene, Tommaso <bar> 1919

Nash, Frances <pf> 1920

Nastri, María <mez> 1931

Nava, Angelica <mez> 1911

Navarro, Silvia de <pf> 1951

Navatta, Vicente <vc> 1950, 1953, 1954, 1955

Negrini, Signora <s> 1886

Nemanoff, Richard <d> 1919

Nemeroff, Maria <d> 1924

Nepoti, Pietro <c / chor> 1896, 1897

Neri, Giulio <b> 1948, 1951

Nerini, Gian-Carlo <b> 1865 to 1870

Nessi, Giuseppe <t> 1919

Neveu, Ginette <vn> 1947

Neveu, Jean <pf> 1947

Newstead, Arthur <pf> 1906

Nicastro, Celika <pf> 1912

Nicastro, M. Miguel <vn> 1912

Nicastro, Oscar <vc> 1912, 1929, 1933, 1938, 1947, 1951, 1954, 1955

Nicola, G. <bar> 1908
Niedzielski, Mr. <pf> 1938
Nigri, Monsieur <b> 1881
Nijinsky, Vaslav <d> 1913, 1917
Niola, Guglielmo <b-buffo>
1915, 1916
Noel, Albert <t> 1906
Nolba, Jeanne <s> 1906
Noli, Severino <c> 1887
Notargiacomo, Gaetano <b>
1887
Noury, Monsieur <t> 1862, 1866
Novaes, Guiomar <pf> 1930
Novelli, Giulia <mez> 1882
Novi, Pietro <t> 1908, 1909,
1911, 1918
Novikova, Anna <s> 1929
Noviliansky, Nicolai <t> 1930

Odnoposoff, Nélida <pf> 1941
Odnoposoff, Ricardo <vn> 1941
Oelsner, Johannes <vla> 1939
Oksansky, Alexander <b> 1929
Olaverri, Lorenzo <pf> 1951,
1953
Olczewska, Maria <mez> 1923
Oliveira, Claudino J. <ophicleide>
1858
Olivera, Delmira <s> 1955
Olivera, Mercedes <pf / hpd>
1947, 1951 to 1956
Oliveri, Gilda <pf> 1930
Olivero, Ludovico 1914
Olivieri-Sangiacomo [Respighi],
Elsa <s> 1929
Ollandini, Signora <s> 1875
Oneto de Bruzzone, Signora <s>
1875
Oneto, Signor <t> 1914
Ordinas, Juan <b> 1868, 1869
Orduña, Felisa (Elisa) <s> 1910
Orefice, Francesco 1902
Orejón, Isabel <pf> 1889
Orlandi, Sarah <pf> 1950, 1952,
1954
Orlandi, Sofía 1896
Orloff, Nikolai <pf> 1928, 1932,
1937

Orsini, Alfredo <t> 1931, 1936,
1937
Ortisi, Gaetano <t> 1877
Ortiz de Taranco, Luis <bar>
1931
Ortiz, Juan Carlos <b> 1955
Ossona, Paulina <d> 1950
O'Sullivan, John <t> 1923, 1925
Otero, Ramón <actor> 1953
Othon, Salud <s> 1894
Otnes, Jon <t> 1947
Otonello, Adhemar <t> 1952,
1953, 1954
Ottonello, Felix <t> 1885, 1905
Oukhtomsky, Wladimir <d>
1956
Oukranisky, Serge <d> 1924
Oxilia, José <t> 1890, 1891,
1892
Oysher, Moishe <t> 1948
Oyuela, Clara <s> 1940

Pablo, Vicente <pf / c> 1903,
1923, 1924, 1927 to 1930
Pacheco, Miguel <d> 1949
Pacini, Adolfo <bar> 1910
Pacini, Regina <s> 1899
Padovani, Adelina <s> 1896
Padovani, Alfredo (Arturo) <c>
1911, 1919
Padwa, Vladimir <pf> 1939
Pagés-Rosés, Señor <pf> 1918
Pagin, Mr. 1910
Pagliero, Maria <mez> 1877,
1882
Pahlen, Kurt <chor> 1951 to
1956
Palacios, Armando <pf> 1927
Palacios, Manuel <c> 1936
Palacios, Signora <s> 1882
Palacios, Rafael <c> 1938, 1941,
1942
Palai, Nello <t> 1923
Palatano, Ada <s> 1906
Palazón, Carmen <tiple> 1941
Palazzi, Nazarena 1909
Palet, José <t> 1905, 1913, 1914
Palos, Francisco <c> 1924

Paltrinieri, Antonieta <s> 1898,
1907
Paltrinieri, Giordano <t> 1915,
1917
Paltrinieri, Velia <s / mez> 1921,
1943
Pandolfini, Angelica <s> 1904
Pangrazi (Pancrazzi), Rosalia <s
/ mez> 1918, 1921, 1924, 1925
Panizza, Ettore <c> 1948
Pantaleoni, Romilda <s> 1882,
1888
Pantano de Giucci, Nahyr <pf>
1950
Paolantonio, Franco <c> 1917,
1919, 1923
Paoli, Signora <s> 1896
Paolicchi, Domenico <b> 1883
Paolillo, Jorge <t> 1956
Papi, Gennaro <c> 1916
Papke, August <dir> 1910
Pappi, Giuseppe <chor> 1919
Parasini, Signor <t> 1876
Paray, Paul <c> 1952
Pardo, Amalia <s> 1938
Parigi, Margherita <s / mez>
1926
Parisetti, Luisa <a> 1905
Parmentier, V. <bar> 1919
Parmesini, Giovanni <t> 1877
Parodi, Catalina <mez> 1862
Parodi, Gioconda <pf> 1950
Parodi, Luigi <t> 1886
Parodi, Teresa <s> 1862
Parodi, Yolanda <s> 1950, 1951,
1955
Parodi-Invernizzi, Raquel <pf>
1943
Paroli, Paride <t-leggiero> 1886
Parsi-Petinella, Armida <a>
1904, 1907
Parys, Pierre 1937
Pascal-Damiani, Signora <s>
1876
Pasero, Tancredi <b> 1924, 1925
Paseyro, Pedro <t> 1931
Pasi, Amelia <s> 1870
Pasini-Vitale, Lina <s> 1914

Pasquet, Luis <pf> 1956

Pasquini, Annita <s> 1913

Pasquini, Giuseppe <t> 1913

Passeti, Signor <b> 1908

Passeto, Luigi <b> 1892

Passett, Alessandro <t> 1889

Passini, Timoteo <c> 1874

Passini, Tomás <b> 1874

Pasti, Augusto <b> 1902

Pastorino, Alfredo I. <t> 1924

Paterna, Concetto <b> 1908

Patino, Ciro <bar> 1914

Patti, Adelina <s> 1888

Patti, Carlotta <s> 1870

Pattini, Raffaela <s> 1885

Pauer, Max <pf> 1931

Paulincini, Signor <bar> 1901

Paulini, Signora <mez> 1902

Pavan-Moretti (Pavan-Bernini),
    Annetta <s> 1884, 1885, 1897

Pavia, A. <t> 1926

Pavley, André <d> 1924

Pavlova, Anna <d> 1919

Pedemonte, Rosalía O. de <pf>
    1953

Pedotti, T. <b> 1876

Pedragosa, Lita <s> 1950

Peisker, A. <c> 1910

Pellegrini, Signor <t> 1896

Pellejero, Emilio <vn> 1954, 1955

Peñagaricano, Celia <pf> 1928

Peñalver, Coral <d> 1941

Peñalver, Rosario <d> 1941

Perales, Clotilde <s> 1894

Perdomo, Marita <s> 1956

Perea, Emilio <t> 1913

Perego, Anita <s> 1899

Pereira-Montalvo, Dolly <pf>
    1930

Pereyra, Malvina 1909

Pérez-Badía, Manuel <c> 1896
    to 1898, 1900, 1901

Pérez-Barranguet, Mirtha <pf>
    1953

Pérez-Fernández, Joaquín <d>
    1942

Perico, Atilio <t> 1905

Perini, Flora <mez> 1915, 1923

Perini-Verdini, Margherita <a>
    1861

Perise, Signor <bar> 1913

Perosio, Ettore <c> 1905

Perosio, Giuseppina <mez> 1905

Perotti, Julio <t> 1872, 1873

Perret, Monsieur <t> 1881

Pertile, Aureliano <t> 1923

Pesce, Signor <bar> 1914

Pessina, Arturo <bar> 1885

Petri, André <pf> 1936

Petri, Elisa <s> 1894

Petrini, Clotilde <s> 1868

Petrone, Emiremo 1937

Petrucci, Arturo <c> 1911

Petrucci, Signor <bar> 1909

Petschick, Anneliese <d> 1937,
    1939

Pettigiani, Anna <s> 1892

Peydró, Lola <s> 1892

Peyrallo, Félix <c> 1929, 1930,
    1931

Pfeiffer, Oscar <pf> 1858, 1880

Pflanz, Sophia <d> 1917

Piantanelli, Nené <s> 1936, 1937

Piave, Emilia <s> 1934

Piazzini, Signora <s> 1862

Pibernat, Maruja <tiple> 1938

Picchi, Italo <b> 1908

Piccioli, Gerónimo <t> 1872,
    1873, 1875

Piccoletti, Giuseppina <s> 1895

Piccone, Giuditta <mez> 1919

Pico, J. <fl> 1908, 1910

Pierelli, Franco <t> 1943

Pierligi, Silvio <chor/c> 1919,
    1926

Pierri, Olga <gui>, 1948, 1949,
    1952, 1953

Pierucetti, Signor <b> 1914

Pietri, N. de <t> 1915

Pilotto, Angelo <bar> 1924

Pina, Giuseppe <b> 1931

Pinheiro, Mario <b> 1918

Pini-Corsi, Gaetano <t> 1903

Pinkert, Regina <s> 1895

Pinto, Walter <tpt> 1956

Pintucci, Angelo <t> 1919

Piotrovsky, Kiprian <t> 1929

Piras, Ada <pf> 1951

Piroia, Horace <t> 1881

Pirola, Maddalena <s> 1881

Pissani, Fina <mez> 1940

Pizzoloti, Signor <b> 1885

Poggi, Alberto 1919

Poggi, Giovanni <bar/t> 1906,
    1908

Poggi, Signor <b> 1896

Poggi, Signora <s> 1905

Poggi, Tito <bar> 1897

Poggiolesi, Ettore <d> 1869

Pogliami, Enrico <bar> 1883

Polacco, Giorgio <c> 1899

Polimeni, Franco <bar> 1906

Pollero, Emilio <bar> 1892

Pollieri, Signora <s> 1882

Polonini, Alessandro <bar> 1883,
    1884, 1889

Polverosi, Manfredo <t> 1912

Pomè-Penna, Giuseppe <c>
    1880, 1890

Ponce, Jorge <t> 1924

Pons, Panchito <bar> 1949, 1951,
    1954

Pons, Rafael <pf> 1868

Ponte, Carmen del <pf> 1879

Ponzano, Signora <mez> 1914

Ponzio, Leon <bar> 1924

Poplavskaya, Mlle. <d> 1929

Poppe, Monsieur <c> 1866

Porzi, Luigi <t> 1895

Poser, Emma <d> 1909

Potentini, Vittoria <s> 1877

Pother, Monsieur <b> 1876, 1877

Pouget, Mlle. <s> 1913

Poussin-Despouey, Haydée <s>
    1940

Pouyanne, Mlle. <pf> 1917

Poyard, Monsieur <bar> 1881

Pozzi, Francesco <bar> 1886

Pozzi, Maria <a> 1911

Pozzi, Natale <bar/b> 1875,
    1886, 1896

Pozzoli, Emilia <s> 1872

Pozzolini, Atanasio <t> 1865,
    1866, 1868

Pratto-Lalloni, Emma <mez> 1877

Preti, Luigi <c/vn> 1856 to 1868, 1872, 1874 to 1876

Preve, Julieta <pf> 1950

Preve, María Esther <pf> 1950

Prevost, Francesco <t> 1886

Preziosi, Margherita <s/mez> 1883, 1884, 1887, 1889

Prieto, Margot <gui> 1949, 1952, 1953

Prihoda, Wasa <vn> 1920

Prissing, Guillermo <b> 1952

Privat, Anais <mez> 1881

Prizant, Heimi <t> 1938

Protasi, Juan <c/pf> 1947, 1948, 1950, 1952 to 1956

Prudenza, Signor <bar> 1914

Puccetti, Gino <c> 1903

Puccini, Giacomo <dir> 1905

Puchelt, Gerhard <pf> 1954

Pujol, Emilio <gui> 1930

Pulcini, Atilio <b/bar> 1905, 1908

Quartino, Rafael <t> 1956

Quatrina, Pietro <t> 1915

Queralt, Eulogio <gui> 1934

Quesada, Dolores <tiple> 1874

Quincke [de Bergengruen], Erna <pf> 1929, 1930, 1950, 1952, 1953, 1955, 1956

Quintas-Moreno, Washington <pf> 1931, 1953

Quiroga, Ercilia <mez> 1932, 1947, 1950, 1952

Quiroga, Manolo <vn> 1926, 1929

Quiroli, Giorgio <t> 1889, 1899

Rabner, Wolfgang <pf> 1936

Raggi, Carlo 1892

Ragni, Carlo <bar/dir> 1895, 1910

Raisa, Rosa <s> 1915, 1916

Raitzin, Florence <pf> 1939

Rajneri, Emilio <c> 1882 to 1885

Rakowska, Elena <s> 1908, 1912, 1913, 1919, 1920

Rambelli, Signora <mez> 1882

Ramin, Gunther <chor> 1955

Ramini, Roberto <b> 1894

Ramírez, Ariel <pf> 1955

Ramírez de Mañé, María Adelaida <s> 1952

Ramírez, María Luisa <s> 1930

Ramis, Cesáreo <vla> 1930

Ranzati, Ernesto <t> 1874

Rappini, Ida <a> 1892

Rappol, Anna 1938

Rappol, Esther 1938

Rasa, Lina Bruna <s> 1929

Rattaggi, E. <b> 1905

Ratti, Celestina <d> 1869

Ravogli, Julia <mez> 1884

Re, Vittorio <t> 1924

Reali, E. <dir> 1905

Rebagliatti, Héctor <t> 1930, 1932

Rebelly, Monsieur <bar> 1881

Rebollo, Gregorio <bar> 1910

Reboredo, Luis <t> 1936, 1942, 1943

Redaelli, Sandra <mez> 1908

Redondo del Castillo, Señor <b> 1924

Redondo, Marcos <bar> 1951

Reggiani, Hilde <s> 1943

Reggiani, Samuel <b> 1883, 1887

Regina, Alba <s> 1937, 1943

Reguier, Monsieur <bar> 1906

Reina, Giovanni B. <bar> 1859

Reinaldi, José <bar> 1886

Reiner, Catherine <s> 1952

Remondini, Amilcare <b> 1886

Repetto, Signora <s> 1878

Respighi, Ottorino <pf/c> 1929

Resplendino, Adolfo <b> 1898, 1900

Reuter, Florizel von <vn> 1906

Revalles, Flora <s> 1925

Reyles, Alma <s> 1930, 1934

Reynaud, Monsieur <c> 1906

Ribeiro, León <pf> 1888

Ribelle, Nella <s> 1937

Ricci, Matilde <s> 1882

Ricci, Ruggero <vn> 1955

Ricci, Teté <gui> 1949, 1952, 1953

Riccio, Beniamino <bar> 1937

Ricetti, Ida <s> 1889

Richard, Monsieur <t> 1879

Richepin, Eliane <pf> 1950, 1952

Riera, Amadeo <c> 1924

Riera, Miguel <b> 1896

Rigal, Delia <s> 1949

Rigazzi, Edmundo <bar> 1934, 1940

Righi, Angelo <t> 1914

Rigotti, Signora <mez> 1862

Rimini, A. <t> 1890

Rimini, Giacomo <bar> 1916

Risler, Edouard <pf> 1919, 1920, 1925

Ritter, Teodoro <pf> 1870

Rizal, N. <s> 1924

Rizzo, Arturo <b> 1913, 1914

Rizzola, Olga <s> 1911

Robertson, Rao <pf> 1937

Roca de Musetti, Celia <pf> 1950

Roca, Gabriela <s> 1880

Rocca, Clorinda <d> 1876

Roche, Roger <vla> 1953

Rodati, Fernando <t> 1908, 1910

Rodríguez, Abelardo <gui> 1925, 1930, 1947

Rodríguez, Carlos <t> 1931

Rodríguez, María <s> 1940

Rodríguez, Señora <s> 1906

Rodríguez-Dutra, Marina <s> 1930, 1950, 1952, 1953

Roessinger, Elvira <mez> 1916

Roger, Marie <s> 1893, 1897

Roggio, Emilio <bar> 1919

Roisman, Josef <vn> 1956

Roland, Mlle. <s> 1906

Rolando, Sara B. de <s> 1929

Rolando, Sarah <a/mez> 1949, 1955

Roli, Signora <mez> 1906

Rolle, Miguel <t> 1943

Romaniello, Aldo <pf/c> 1926, 1927, 1931

Romaniz, Miguel <vla> 1954, 1955

Romay, Elena <fl> 1956

Romay, Luis <t> 1925

Romboli, Arturo <bar> 1907, 1910, 1911

Romei, Francesco <c> 1903, 1904, 1905

Romei, Romeo <chor> 1913

Romeo, Enrico <c / chor> 1911, 1915

Romo, Amparo <tiple> 1920

Rona, Señor <child actor> 1916

Ronzio, Ida <d> 1903

Rosa, Alba <vn> 1913

Rosa, Alina <s> 1898

Rosa, Elvira <tiple> 1874

Rosciano, Mafalda <mez> 1943

Rosea, Luis <b> 1856, 1859

Roselen, Santo <t> 1955

Roselli de Ruiz, Señora <s> 1914, 1917

Rosensteel, Frank <c> 1887

Rosenthal, Moriz <pf> 1934

Rosito, Lorenzo <bar / b> 1951, 1952, 1953, 1954

Rossi, Alfredo <pf> 1951, 1956

Rossi, Arcangelo <b> 1895 to 1897

Rossi, Giulio <b> 1889, 1891, 1897

Rossi, Lidya <s> 1936

Rossi, Rinaldo <dir> 1886, 1894, 1897

Rossi, Wilser <pf> 1956

Rossi-Ghelli, Achille <bar / b> 1862, 1870, 1873, 1882

Rossi-Trauner, Carolina <s> 1889

Rossini, Francesco 1909

Rossini, Luciano <t> 1905

Rosso, Elcira <s> 1924

Roth, Sandor <vla> 1939

Rotoli, Donato <b> 1899

Round, Señor <org / pf> 1867, 1868

Roussel, Mario <bar> 1905

Rousselière, Charles <t> 1907, 1908

Rousset, Adelaide <d> 1857

Rousset, Carolina <d> 1857

Rousset, Clementine <d> 1857

Rousset, Louis <d> 1857

Rousset, Theresina <d> 1857

Routin, Teresa <s> 1890, 1901

Rovescalli, Signor 1912

Royer, Jacqueline <mez> 1916

Roza, Petronila <mez> 1881

Rubino, Salvatore <dir> 1935

Rubinstein, Artur <pf> 1917, 1920, 1926, 1940, 1951

Ruffo, Titta <bar> 1902, 1915, 1916, 1928

Ruggero, Maria <s> 1913

Ruggiero, Teobaldo 1902

Ruis, Señor <b> 1888, 1890

Ruiz, Ernesto <c> 1914, 1917

Ruiz, Luigi <b> 1872

Rummel, Walter <pf> 1930

Rumneff, Alexandre <bar> 1930

Ruotolo, Signor <b> 1883

Rupp, Franz <pf> 1935, 1937, 1938

Russ, Giannina <s> 1905, 1910, 1915

Russo, Francisco <fl> 1925, 1950

Russomano, Signor <t> 1900

Ruy, Juliette <s> 1950

Sabaino, R. <mez> 1915

Sabatés, Elsa <pf> 1955

Sacharoff, Gregori <b> 1930

Sachetti, Pietro <pf> 1861

Sadowsky, Reah <pf> 1950

Saggese, Albina <s> 1915

Sagi-Barba, Emilio <bar> 1906, 1931

Sagi-Vela, Luis <bar> 1938

Saint-Saëns, Camille <c / pf> 1916

Sainz de la Maza, Regino <gui> 1929, 1930

Sakharoff, Alexandre <d> 1941

Sakharoff, Clotilde <d> 1941

Salaberry, Walter <bar> 1956

Salassa, Signor <bar> 1889

Salazar de Manjón, Señora <pf> 1908

Sallaz, Anna <s> 1903

Salmon, Celia P. de <pf> 1942

Salmon, Roger <vn> 1928, 1942

Salterain, Margarita de <pf> 1923

Saludas, Antonio <t> 1910, 1911

Salvati, Francesco <bar> 1882, 1886

Salvatti, Salvatore <t> 1924

Salvatti, Tomasso 1937

Salvi, Guido de <t> 1918

Salvi, Margherita de <s> 1925

Salvini, Gioachino <c> 1873, 1880, 1882, 1883

Salvini, L. <mez> 1926

Samaniego, Carmen <d> 1934

Sambucetti, Juan José <vn> 1890

Sambucetti, Luis <vn / c> 1875, 1876, 1888 to 1891, 1901, 1908, 1910, 1912, 1926

Sammarco, Mario (Mariano) <bar / dir> 1897, 1904, 1914, 1915, 1923

Sampaio, Juvenal <pf> 1866, 1869

Sampieri, Signor <b> 1885

Samsó, Nora <tiple> 1936

San Marco, Rossana <s> 1926

Sancan, Pierre <pf> 1952, 1953

Sanchez-Elía de Quintana, Carmen <s> 1942

Sánchez, Mario <c> 1915

Sánchez, Ramona <s> 1866, 1867

Sánchez, Renée <s> 1950

Sánchez-Raña, Polonia <pf> 1955

Sandor, Gyorgy <pf> 1939

Sandoval, Paloma de <d> 1948

Sanguinetti, María Elena <a> 1921

Sanjuán, Eliseo <t> 1894

Santamarina, María Luisa <pf> 1951, 1952

Santarelli, Amadea <s> 1901

Santinelli, Giuseppe <t> 1883

Santórsola, Guido <c / vla / vla d'amore> 1951, 1952

Santucci, José <t> 1904

Sanz, Elena <mez / a> 1874

Sanz, Pepita <s> 1921

Saraceni, Adelaida <s> 1926

Sarasate, Pablo de <vn> 1870

Sardou, Paul <t> 1856, 1857, 1859, 1860

Sarria, Lucrecia <s> 1940

Sartori, Elvira <d> 1870

Sartori, G. <b> 1882

Sartori, Ma. Clotilde <mez> 1886

Sartori, R. <t> 1887

Sartori, Signor <t> 1902

Sasso, Rosina <s> 1926

Sassone, Anna <s> 1920

Satre, (Ana) Raquel <s> 1950, 1952, 1953, 1954

Sauvegeot, Maurice <bar> 1938

Savorini, Signor <t> 1918

Sayão, Bidú <s> 1929

Scacciati, Bianca <s> 1924, 1925

Scafa, Ciro <bar> 1923

Scampini, Augusto <t> 1907, 1912

Scarabelli, Catalina D. de <pf> 1920

Scarabelli, L. <b> 1859

Scarabelli, Vincenzo <b> 1860 to 1863, 1868

Scarabelli, Virgilio <c> 1903, 1920, 1923, 1927, 1929, 1930

Scarlatti, Egidio <dir> 1905

Schaia, Wolff <bar> 1953

Scheitler, Celia Margarita <pf> 1929

Schenini, Victoria <pf> 1947, 1950, 1953, 1954, 1956

Schenone, Adhemar <pf> 1947, 1952, 1953, 1954, 1956

Schiaffarino, Raquel <pf> 1953

Schiavazzi, Piero <t> 1904

Schinca, Luis <bar> 1924, 1927

Schipa, Tito <t> 1914, 1916, 1927, 1931, 1939

Schipper, Emil <bar> 1923

Schmid, Fively <c> 1924

Schmidt, Berthold <d> 1937, 1939

Schnabel, Karl Ulrich <pf> 1952

Schneider, Alexander <vn> 1956

Schneider, Mazzi 1910

Schneider, Mischa <vc> 1956

Schoeder, Carlos <bar> 1950

Scholz, Alexander <vn> 1956

Schottelius, Renate <d> 1956

Schottler, Giorgio <b> 1914

Schramm, Carlos <pf> 1865

Schult, Siegfried <pf> 1923

Schumann, Elisabeth <s> 1930

Schuvaloff, Efrosine <mez> 1924

Schwartz, Fanny <vn> 1956

Schwartz, Leo <pf> 1952, 1954, 1955, 1956

Scolara, Francesco <b-buffo> 1886

Scolari, Giovanni <b> 1883

Sconamiglio, Ciro <c> 1902

Scott, Leslie <b / bar> 1955

Scotti, Antonio <bar> 1892, 1894, 1897

Sdanovky, Eugene <b> 1929

Sebillo, Carmen <s> 1934

Sedelmeier, Amelia <s> 1899

Segovia, Andrés <gui> 1920, 1928, 1937, 1939, 1953

Segú, José <pf / c> 1927, 1929, 1931

Seguí, Francisco <pf / c / chor> 1873 to 1876, 1883, 1886, 1888, 1889

Segura-Tallien, José <bar> 1923, 1924

Sei, Anna <d> 1909

Seillag, Steffi <s> 1913

Seinescu, Caliope <s> 1905

Sempere, Vicente <t> 1926

Sena, Margarita <gui> 1949, 1952, 1953

Sena, Matilde <gui> 1949, 1952, 1953

Serafin, Tullio <c> 1919, 1920

Serafino, Signora <s> 1913

Serini, Ermenegildo de <b> 1892

Serpo, A. <bar> 1926

Serra, Giuseppina <s> 1890

Serrano, José <c> 1933

Serrano, Manuel 1936

Serrano (Sereno), Teresa <s> 1864, 1865, 1867

Serrato, Víctor <pf> 1955

Sesona, Emilio <b> 1905

Setragni, Pietro <t> 1872

Severini, Gina <mez> 1905

Sgarbi, Luis <t> 1924, 1927, 1933, 1934, 1949

Shavitch, Wladimir <c> 1921

Shereshevkaya, Elise <s> 1924

Shoki, Sai <d> 1940

Siano, María <mez / a> 1932, 1952

Siécola, Ema <harp> 1943

Sieder, Alfred <t> 1910

Signorelli, Olga <a> 1918

Signorelli, Signor <t> 1918

Signoretti, Leopoldo <t> 1875, 1885, 1895, 1896

Signori, Signora <mez> 1883

Signorini, Francesco <t> 1885, 1895

Sillich, Aristodemo <b> 1884

Silingardi, Arturo <bar> 1908

Silvani, Giuseppe 1909

Simon, Abbey <pf> 1955

Simon, Eric <chor> 1951

Simonsen, Fanny de <s> 1859

Simonsen, Martin <vn> 1859

Simzis, Olga <s> 1910, 1911, 1918, 1924, 1925

Singer, Teresa (Teresina) <s> 1878, 1887, 1888

Singer, Werner <pf> 1938

Singher, Martial <bar> 1937

Sirvent, Adolfo <t> 1940, 1942

Sismondi, Miss 1890

Sivori, Ernesto <bar> 1895

Smallens, Alexander <c> 1955

Smilovitz, Joseph <vn> 1939

Smirnov, Dmitri <t> 1910

Soffleti, Serafino <bar> 1883

Sola, Margherita <s> 1943

Solano, Atilano <bar> 1874

Solari, Christi <t> 1929
Soldemeier, Amelia <s> 1905
Soldevila, Blanca Rosa <mez / s> 1946, 1948, 1949
Solé, Ricardo <d> 1956
Soler, Adriana <s> 1922
Soler, José <t> 1948, 1956
Soler, Trinidad <d> 1938, 1939
Solffriti, Paride <chor> 1908
Sommelius, Giorgina <mez> 1889
Sorella, Grazia <s> 1943
Sorín, Darío <pf> 1953
Sormani, Pietro <c> 1903, 1904
Sormani, Signora <mez> 1891
Sortini, R. <b> 1878
Sosa, Edgardo <b> 1950, 1953
Sous, Roberto <pf> 1925
Souza, Noemí <a> 1955
Souzay, Gerard <bar> 1953, 1955
Spagnolo, Paolo <pf> 1952
Spangher, Francesco <b> 1905
Spani, Hina <s> 1919, 1923
Spendiarova, Helena <s> 1930
Speranza, Alfredo <pf> 1951
Spinelli, Francisco <c> 1885
Spivak, Raúl <pf> 1927
Spolverini, Arsenio <t> 1908
Sportelli, Italo 1937
Sportelli, Victoria <s> 1935, 1942, 1948
Springer-Dominici, Sidonia <mez / s> 1879
Stabile, Mariano <bar> 1913
Stagi, Carlo <t> 1885
Stagno, Roberto <t> 1886, 1888
Stalkiewki, Maximilian <d> 1917
Stampanoni, A. <s> 1878, 1880
Stampanoni, Americo <t> 1897
Stanfield, Silvestre <t> 1856
Stapran, Ana <mez> 1929
Staricco, Delia <a> 1956
Steel, Hart <chor> 1871
Stehle, Adelina <s> 1902
Steinbach, Emma <mez> 1890
Steiner, Rudolf 1910
Stella Maris <s> 1949
Stellina, M. <s> 1913

Stelline, Corina <d> 1909
Stellini, Maria 1909
Stenzel, Gerhard <vc> 1956
Stepp, Christoph <c> 1955
Steuber, Lilian <pf> 1956
Stinco, Enrico <bar> 1899
Stinco, Nino <c> 1951, 1952
Stinco-Palermini, Anunziata <s> 1899
Stoika, Ernestina <mez> 1874
Stolzmann, Maria <s> 1883
Stora, Juliette <s> 1916
Storchio, Rosina <s> 1904 to 1906, 1912, 1914
Stracciari, Riccardo <bar> 1906, 1908, 1910, 1912
Strauss, Richard <c> 1923
Strigelli, Giuseppe <c> 1882, 1885
Strnad, Camille <d> 1930
Strnad, Josef <harp> 1930
Stuarda-Savelli, Maria <s> 1908
Sturani, Giuseppe <c> 1915
Subirá, José <b> 1880
Subirana, José <bar> 1876
Superti, A. <dir> 1911
Susena, Gloria <s> 1950
Susini, Signor <bar / b> 1857
Sykora, Adolf <vn> 1956
Sykora, Bogumil <vc> 1928
Syril, Jenny <s> 1924
Szabó, Paul <vc> 1951
Szenkar, Alexandre <c / pf> 1940
Szeryng, Henryk <vn> 1942, 1950, 1952
Szigeti, Joseph <vn> 1936
Szollozy, Monsieur <d> 1857

Tabanelli, Pietro <t> 1915, 1917, 1927
Tabellini, Gaetano <t> 1885
Taccani, Giuseppe <t> 1908, 1912
Taffurelli, Dario <cl> 1866
Tagliabue, Carlo <bar> 1926
Tagliaferro, Magda <pf> 1926, 1943, 1952
Tagliapietra, Giovanni <bar> 1872, 1873

Tagliavini, Ferruccio <t> 1954
Talexis, Amelia <s> 1906
Tamagno, Francesco <t> 1884, 1896
Tamberlick, Enrico <t> 1857
Tamburlini, Angelo <b> 1884, 1885, 1886
Tanara, Fernando <c> 1905, 1907
Tanci, Camilo 1897
Tancioni, Annetta <a / mez / s> 1876, 1895
Taneeff, Serge <d> 1929
Tansini, Giovanni <b> 1876
Tappa, P. <tpt> 1871
Tarantoni, G. <t> 1919
Taschner, Gerard <vn> 1953
Taselli, Anita 1909
Tati, Federico <b> 1856
Tati, Felicio <t> 1856
Tati, Giuseppina <mez> 1856, 1857
Tauriello, Antonio <pf> 1955
Tavecchia (Tarecchia), Luigi <b> 1905
Tchernicheva, Lubov <d> 1913, 1917
Tcherny, Nicolai <dir> 1929
Tedeschi, Alfredo <t> 1915
Tegani, Riccardo <bar> 1919
Teggiani, Samuel <b> 1886
Tellez de Mendoza, Julieta <s> 1927
Teodorini, Elena <s> 1884, 1889
Teodoro, Luigi <t> 1911
Ter, Marguerite de <s> 1906
Teresina, Mlle. <s> 1881
Teressi, Giuseppe 1876
Terrasa, Miguel <b> 1956
Terrones, Señor <bar> 1918
Terzi, Titto <bar> 1880, 1892
Tesana, Rina 1919
Tescher, Signora <s> 1886
Tessari, Gino <bar> 1913
Tetrazzini, Eva <s> 1885
Tetrazzini, Luisa <s> 1898
Theor, Dora <s> 1914
Thibaud, Jacques <vn> 1930
Thibaudet, Edouard <t> 1937

Thiemer, Heinrich <bar> 1923

Thigpen, Helen <s> 1955

Thill, Georges <t> 1929, 1931

Thomson, César <vn> 1903

Thos, Constantino <b> 1903 to
1908

Tikanova, Antoinette <mez>
1929

Tilche, Jean-Jacques <gui> 1955

Timroth, Irma <s / mez> 1902

Tipo, Maria <pf> 1953, 1955

Tisci-Rubino, Giuseppe <bar>
1897

Toamarán, Wilfredo <d> 1953,
1956

Tomasow, Jan <vn> 1956

Tomassini, Gustavo <t> 1925

Tomina, Victoria <d> 1952

Toni, Alceo <c> 1924, 1925

Toninelli, Signor <t> 1887

Torelli, Lucia <s> 1915 to 1917

Toressi, Giuseppe <t> 1875, 1876

Torraza, Carmen <gui> 1949

Torrens, Eduardo <c> 1876

Torres, Carmen <mez> 1929

Torres, Felipe <c> 1943

Torresella, Fanny <s> 1889, 1896,
1897

Torretta, Anna <mez> 1904

Torriani, Signora 1911

Tortorici, J. <bar> 1908

Tosar, Héctor <pf / c> 1952, 1953,
1954, 1955

Toscanini, Arturo <c> 1903,
1904, 1906

Toso, Vittorio <bar> 1948

Toumanova, Tamara <d> 1954,
1956

Trabucchi, Ceferino <vn> 1888

Trave, Giovanni <c> 1943

Traverso, Diana <pf> 1950, 1952

Travi, Francesco <b> 1895

Travnicek, Jiri <vn> 1956

Trebbi, Olimpia <s> 1882, 1891

Tretti, Alessandro <bar> 1907

Tronconi, Giovanni <harp>
1857, 1858

Tuccari, Angelica <s> 1951

Tuene, Angelita <s> 1904

Turconi-Bruni, Angelina <s>
1890

Turolla, Enrico 1926

Turriziani, Angel <pf / org>
1949, 1950, 1951, 1954

Turturiello, Nélida <s> 1932,
1934

Turturiello, Signor <bar> 1914

Tuset, Beatriz <c> 1954, 1955,
1956

Ubaldi, M. <mez> 1876

Ughetti, Pietro <bar> 1886

Uguccioni, Alejandro <vn / c>
1865, 1866, 1882, 1886

Uninsky, Alexandre <pf> 1928,
1931, 1942

Urban, Alice <s> 1874

Urízar, Marcelo <bar> 1917,
1924, 1925

Urquizú, Marta <s> 1952

Vaccari, Eduvige <mez> 1908

Vaccari, Guido <t> 1913

Val, Maurice <t> 1876

Val, Signora <s / vn> 1876

Valdés, Luisa <s> 1910, 1920,
1921

Valencia, Tórtola <d> 1916, 1928

Valenziani, Signor <b> 1892,
1898

Valero, Fernando <t> 1882

Valery, Odette <d> 1903

Vales, José <t> 1934

Valetti, Cesare <t> 1951

Vallarino, Signora <s> 1914

Valle, Antonio del <c> 1890

Valle, Enrique <actor> 1920

Valles, José <cl> 1923 to 1925,
1927

Vallin (Vallin-Pardo), Ninon <s>
1916, 1917, 1920, 1923, 1931,
1936

Vallo, A. 1892

Valoris, Monsieur <t> 1906

Valverde, María <s> 1943, 1947,
1949, 1951

Van Loo, Angèle <s> 1913

Van Marke, Gustave <vn / pf>
1857

Vanni, Roberto <t> 1891

Vanni-Marcoux, Jean <bar>
1919

Varacomini, Nieves <mez> 1929

Varga, Ruben <vn> 1953

Varsi, Dinorah <pf> 1952

Vassilievska, Alexandra <d> 1913,
1917

Vassoni (Vassori), Signora <mez>
1867

Vecart, Raymonde <s> 1919

Vecchioni, Francesco <b> 1882,
1885, 1887 to 1889, 1895

Vecino, Walter <t> 1951

Vecsey, Ferenc de <vn> 1911,
1920, 1921, 1929

Vega, Marta de la <s> 1927

Végh, Sándor <vn> 1951

Vela, Antonio <t> 1938, 1941

Vela, José <bar> 1922

Vela, Luisa <s> 1906

Vela, Telmo <vn> 1931

Vélez, Angelita <d> 1949

Vells, Gioachino 1895

Venancio, Juan <ob> 1914

Ventura, Elvino <t> 1899, 1901

Venturini, Alfredo <t> 1904

Venturino, Elena <s> 1931

Venturino, Francisco A. <bar>
1925, 1926

Vera-Lorini, Sofia <s> 1856,
1857

Verbich, Carmen <s> 1914

Verbist, Felyne <d> 1915

Verbitzky, Sonia <s> 1947

Vercelli-Maffei, Eduardo <pf>
1955

Vercolini-Tay, Signora <mez / a>
1873, 1879

Verdini, Albino <bar> 1884

Vernazza, Juan A. <bar> 1950,
1954, 1955

Vernink de Sambucetti, María
<pf> 1912

Vertiz, Abel <pf> 1947

Vialade-Vigil, Solange <a> 1940

Vianna da Motta, José <pf> 1897, 1907, 1912, 1922

Viatovich, Dimitri <pf> 1953

Vicente, Ernesto <bar> 1936

Vidach, Gina <s> 1926

Vidal, Berta <mez> 1932

Vidal, M. <t> 1876

Viglione-Borghese, Domenico <bar> 1919

Vigna, Arturo <c> 1919

Vignoli, Giuseppe <vn> 1861

Vignoli, Olga <s> 1937

Vila, Lola <s> 1941, 1942

Villa, Joaquín <bar> 1934, 1940, 1943

Villani, Horacio <b> 1900

Villanova, Francesco <b> 1878, 1879

Villefleur, Dina 1909

Villegas, Socorrito <s> 1951

Villiers, Monsieur <t> 1906

Vinitzky, Carlos <vn> 1955

Viñes, Ricardo <pf> 1920

Virgo, Edwin <vn> 1926

Virtuoso, Antonio <hn> 1954, 1956

Viscardi, Maria <s> 1918

Viscardini, Signor <c> 1914

Vischnia, María <vn> 1952

Vitale, Edoardo <c> 1910, 1914, 1925

Vitali, Ida <a> 1863

Vitolo, Eugenio 1909, 1911

Vitulli, Thea <s> 1925, 1934

Vives, Amadeo <dir> 1924

Viviani, Gaetano <bar> 1925

Vix, Geneviève <s> 1915

Volinine, Alexandre <d> 1919

Volir (Voliz), Vincenzo <c> 1883, 1889

Volnay, Jaulette <s> 1937

Voltolini, Ismaele <t> 1920

Von Benda, Hans <c> 1956

Vorloff, Mr. <chor> 1931

Vorontzov, Mr. <d> 1913, 1919

Voyer, Capitan <pf> 1885

Wagner, Anna <s> 1953

Wagner, Giuseppe <b> 1875, 1876

Wait-Gagliasso, Helen <s> 1924

Waldteufel, Mlle. <s> 1881

Walter, Carlo <b> 1863, 1906, 1907, 1912

Walter, Luigi <bar / b> 1862, 1867

Warner, Ermelinda <mez / a> 1875

Warner, H. Waldo <vla> 1926

Weingartner, Felix <c> 1920, 1922

Weiss, Clara <s> 1913, 1918, 1926

Weissenberg, Sigi (Alexis) <pf> 1952

Werber, Miss <s> 1910

Werberg, Otto <d> 1947

Werner, Carlos <vn> 1865

Werner, Krauss <dir> 1935

Wesselovsky, Alexander <t> 1924

West, María Luisa Fabini de <s> 1947

White, Mr. <vn> 1879

Widmar, E. <s / mez> 1882, 1895

Wiener, Jean <pf> 1929

Wigley, Michele <b / bar> 1902, 1903

Wilkinson, John <t> 1890, 1891

Wiziack, Emma <s> 1883

Wright, Ned <t> 1955

Wulmann, Paolo <b> 1889

Yéregui-Lerena, Ema <pf> 1927

Yupanqui, Atahualpa <gui> 1948

Zabo, Enrique <d> 1876

Zaccaria, Achille <b> 1894

Zacconi, Alice <mez> 1908

Zacconi Musella, Letizia <s / mez> 1868, 1869

Zalewsky, Sigismund <b> 1924

Zamboni, Maria <s> 1924

Zamboni, Reynaldo <pf> 1949

Zanardi, Clotilde <s> 1881

Zanardi, M. <actress> 1907

Zanasi, Guglielmo <t> 1914

Zani, Bianca <s> 1905, 1908

Zani, Diomira <mez> 1883, 1887, 1892

Zani, Signor <t> 1912

Zannoli, Guido <b> 1908, 1925

Zanzini, Giuseppe <bar> 1902

Zaporojetz, Kapiton <b> 1924

Zawner, Carolina <a> 1894

Zecchi, Carlo <pf> 1928, 1930

Zeller, Robert <c> 1952

Zenatello, Giovanni <t> 1903, 1905

Zennari, Angelo <t> 1868, 1869

Zeppilli, Alice <mez> 1905

Zerite, Princess <d> 1943

Ziglioli, A. <dir> 1895

Zoffoli, Giuseppina <mez> 1915

Zoffoli, Giusto <t> 1912, 1913, 1914

Zóldy, Sándor <vn> 1951

Zonzini, Giuseppe <bar / b> 1908, 1922, 1924

Zoriga, Mlle. <d / ballet mistress> 1938

Zorrilla de San Martín, Elvira <s> 1921

Zotti, Clelia <mez> 1924

Zucchi, A. <bar> 1887

Zucchi, Dante <t / chor> 1895, 1897, 1898, 1902, 1903, 1905, 1911

Zucchi, Ettore <t> 1905

Zucchi, Francisco <t> 1873

Zucchi, Signor <b> 1883

Zuckermann, Virgilio <t> 1936, 1937

Zug, Elizabeth <pf> 1941

Zunino de Barilari, Ermelinda B. <harp> 1949

C: *Musical Works Performed at the Teatro Solís (1856–1956)*

(Operas, operettas, ballets, zarzuelas)

Note: The numbers beside each year indicate how many times the work was performed during that given year.

Note: Titles of works are listed according to the language in which the work was sung.

Abul (Nepomuceno) 1913 <1>
Acqua Cheta (Pietri) 1923 <2>, 1937 <2>
Addio giovinezza (Montanari) 1918 <1>
Addio giovinezza (Pietri) 1923 <1>
Adriana Lecouvreur (Cilea) 1903 <1>
Adventures of Kich-Kich-Bey, The (?) 1925 <1>
Africana, L'(Meyerbeer) 1869 <13>, 1873 <4>, 1882 <8>, 1883 <5>, 1885 <9>, 1886 <4>, 1887 <3>, 1888 <3>, 1892 <1>, 1894 <1>, 1899 <1>, 1900 <1>, 1906 <1>
Aida (Verdi) 1877 <9>, 1878 <7>, 1879 <6>, 1882 <8>, 1883 <1>, 1885 <8>, 1888 <4>, 1890 <3>, 1892 <1>, 1894 <1>, 1895 <3>, 1900 <2>, 1896 <3>, 1899 <3>, 1901 <1>, 1902 <1>, 1903 <1>, 1905 <3>, 1906 <2>, 1908 <3>, 1909 <2>, 1910 <2>, 1911 <3>, 1912 <2>, 1913 <1>, 1914 <1>, 1915 <4>, 1916 <1>, 1918 <4>, 1919 <1>, 1920 <2>, 1921 <1>, 1922 <1>, 1923 <1>, 1924 <3>, 1925 <3>, 1926 <2>, 1934 <1>, 1940 <3>, 1943 <2>

Aires de primavera (?) 1915 <1>
Alda (Rodríguez-Socas) 1906 <2>
Alegre Lova, El (Olschaneski) 1940 <1>
Alegría del batallón, La (Serrano) 1935 <1>
Ali-Pot-d-Rhum (F. Bernicat) 1894 <1>
Alma de Dios (Serrano) 1935 <1>
Amami Alfredo! (Ettore Bellini) 1931 <1>
Amica (Mascagni) 1905 <1>, 1911 <1>
Amico di casa, L' (Cortesi) 1884 <2>
Amico Fritz, L' (Mascagni) 1892 <1>
Amleto (Thomas) 1889 <1>, 1915 <1>, 1916 <1>, 1921 <1>
Amor enmascarado (Darclée) 1916 <2>
Amore di principe (Eysler) 1912 <3>
Amore di zingaro, L' (Lehár) 1911 <2>, 1912 <1>, 1913 <2>, 1943 <1>
Amore in maschera (Darclée) 1913 <3>, 1916 <1>

Amore ungheresi (Krausz) 1926 <2>
Amour masqué, L' (Messager) 1924 <1>, 1937 <1>
Amour au moulin, L' (Lanciani) 1894 <1>
Amours du diable, Les (Grisar) 1876 <2>, 1877 <1>
Andrea Chénier (Giordano) 1897 <2>, 1908 <1>, 1910 <1>, 1916 <1>, 1923 <2>, 1924 <2>, 1926 <1>, 1929 <1>
Anillo de hierro, El (M. Marqués) 1879 <3>, 1906 <1>, 1914 <2>, 1931 <1>
Ardid de amor (C. Pedrell) 1917 <1>
Armi ed amore (Varney) 1885 <2>
Aroldo (Verdi) 1861 <3>, 1863 <1>
Astas del toro, Las (Gaztambide) 1874 <2>
Atar-Gull (Mason) 1866 <1>
Attila (Verdi) 1858 <3>, 1861 <1>, 1881 <2>
Aventures du roi Pausole, Les (Honegger) 1937 <1>

Babolin (Varney) 1887 <1>
Ballo in maschera, Un (Verdi) 1862 <3>, 1863 <5>, 1865 <1>, 1866 <5>, 1867 <2>, 1868 <2>, 1869 <5>, 1870 <4>, 1872 <9>, 1873 <10>, 1874 <3>, 1875 <3>, 1876

<4>, 1877 <1>, 1878 <4>,
1879 <2>, 1882 <3>, 1885
<5>, 1895 <1>, 1900 <1>,
1903 <3>, 1905 <3>, 1906
<1>, 1910 <2>, 1915 <1>, 1918
<2>, 1926 <2>

Ballo nello Savoy, Un
(Abraham) 1943 <4>

Bambola lenci (M. Rosseger)
1936 <1>

Barbe-Bleue (Offenbach) 1881 <1>

Barbier von Bagdad, Der
(Cornelius) 1925 <1>

Barberillo de Lavapiés, El (F. A.
Barbieri) 1879 <4>, 1924 <1>

Barbier de Seville, Le (Rossini)
1862 <1>

Barbiere di Siviglia, Il (Rossini)
1856 <3>, 1859 <2>, 1860
<1>, 1862 <1>, 1863 <2>,
1866 <1>, 1870 <3>, 1872
<5>, 1873 <6>, 1874 <3>,
1875 <1>, 1876 <2>, 1878 <1>,
1882 <3>, 1883 <4>, 1884
<2>, 1886 <2>, 1888 <1>,
1889 <1>, 1895 <1>, 1898 <1>,
1899 <2>, 1901 <2>, 1902
<1>, 1905 <1>, 1906 <1>,
1909 <1>, 1912 <1>, 1913 <2>,
1914 <2>, 1915 <1>, 1916 <1>,
1917 <1>, 1921 <2>, 1924 <5>,
1925 <1>, 1929 <1>, 1931 <1>,
1934 <1>, 1940 <1>, 1943
<3>, 1951 <1>, 1955 <3>

Battaglia di Legnano, La (Verdi)
1861 <1>

Bayadera, La (Kálmán) 1923 <3>

Béatrice (Messager) 1916 <1>

Bebé (Hennequin) 1879 <1>

Bei mir bist du schein
(Olschamiezky) 1938 <1>

Belisario (Donizetti) 1858 <3>

Bella Risetta, La (Fall) 1920 <2>,
1922 <2>

Bella Risette, La (Fall) 1912 <2>,
1913 <3>, 1914 <1>, 1916 <1>

Belle Hélène, La (Offenbach)
1912 <3>

Belle meunière, La (?) 1894 <1>

Bergerette (Ferrarese) 1926 <2>

Bettelstudent, Der (Millöcker)
1910 <1>

Birichino di Parigi, Il
(Montanari) 1913 <3>

Black Crook, The (various
composers) 1874 <14>

Boccaccio (Suppé) 1883 <7>,
1884 <3>, 1885 <3>, 1887 <1>,
1889 <1>, 1896 <1>, 1897 <1>,
1902 <1>, 1905 <1>, 1906
<1>, 1911 <1>, 1918 <2>, 1937
<2>, 1943 <3>

Bohème, La (Leoncavallo) 1899
<1>

Bohème, La (Puccini) 1896 <3>,
1897 <2>, 1899 <5>, 1900
<1>, 1901 <1>, 1902 <1>, 1905
<1>, 1906 <2>, 1908 <3>,
1910 <3>, 1911 <2>, 1912 <1>,
1914 <2>, 1915 <2>, 1917 <1>,
1918 <4>, 1919 <1>, 1921 <1>,
1924 <3>, 1925 <4>, 1926
<1>, 1931 <1>, 1934 <1>, 1940
<2>, 1943 <1>

Bohemios (Vives) 1922 <1>, 1924
<6>, 1935 <1>

Bon garçon, Un (Yvain) 1929 <2>

Bondelmonte (Pacini) 1861 <4>,
1862 <2>, 1863 <1>, 1867 <3>

Boris Godunov (Musorgsky)
1924 <2>

Brahma (Dall'Argine) 1886 <2>,
1903 <2>

Braconniers, Les (Offenbach)
1894 <1>

Brigands, Les (Offenbach) 1876
<3>, 1877 <4>, 1878 <1>, 1885
<1>

Briganti, I (Offenbach) 1883 <1>

Caballero de la luna, El
(Ziehrer) 1922 <4>

Cadeaux de Nöel, Les (Leroux)
1916 <2>

Cadetes de la reina, Los (Luna)
1931 <1>

Cake Walk (W. H. Myddleton)
1903 <2>

Calesera, La (Alonso) 1935 <2>,
1942 <4>

Cantatrice della strada (Fall)
1926 <2>

Campani di Corneville, Gli
(Planquette) 1883 <2>

Campanne de Corneville, Le
(Planquette) 1896 <1>

Campanone [El maestro
Campanone] (Mazza) 1874
<4>, 1881 <3>, 1906 <1>

Canción del náufrago, La
(Mazza & Lleó) 1906 <1>

Canción del olvido, La (Serrano)
1935 <1>

Canotiers de la Seine, Les (A. M.
Orey) 1868 <1>

Capitano fracassa, Il (Costa) 1912
<2>

Capriccio antico (Darclée) 1912
<3>, 1913 <1>

Capuleti e i Montecchi, I
(Bellini) 1862 <2>, 1873 <7>,
1875 <2>

Carmen (Bizet) 1881 <1>, 1883
<3>, 1884 <2>, 1887 <3>,
1889 <1>, 1894 <1>, 1896
<1>, 1899 <1>, 1900 <1>,
1906 <1>, 1908 <1>, 1909
<1>, 1912 <1>, 1913 <2>, 1915
<1>, 1917 <1>, 1918 <3>, 1919
<1>, 1925 <1>, 1926 <2>,
1929 <1>, 1940 <1>, 1943 <1>

Carnaval (Schumann)
[performed as a ballet] 1913
<1>, 1917 <2>

Casa delle tre ragazze, La
(Schubert) 1923 <1>, 1931
<2>

Casa de las tres niñas, La
(Schubert) 1927 <1>

Casta Susana, La (J. Gilbert) 1911
<4>, 1912 <13>, 1913 <1>,
1914 <1>, 1915 <3>, 1916 <1>,
1918 <1>, 1922 <1>, 1936 <2>,
1937 <3>, 1943 <1>

Castañuelas, Las (Giménez
   [Jiménez], Jerónimo) 1935 <2>
Cavaliere della luna, Il (Ziehrer)
   1914 <2>, 1918 <3>
Cavaliere della rosa, Il (Richard
   Strauss) 1915 <1>, 1917 <1>
Cavalieri dei fiori, Il (?, ballet)
   1903 <2>
Cavalleria rusticana (Mascagni)
   1892 <4>, 1894 <1>, 1896
   <1>, 1897 <1>, 1899 <2>,
   1905 <1>, 1906 <2>, 1908
   <1>, 1910 <1>, 1911 <3>, 1913
   <1>, 1914 <2>, 1915 <3>, 1918
   <3>, 1921 <3>, 1922 <1>, 1924
   <2>, 1925 <1>, 1926 <1>,
   1934 <2>, 1940 <1>, 1943 <2>
Cena delle beffe, La (Giordano)
   1925 <1>
Cenerentola, La (Rossini) 1859
   <1>
Ce que femme veut!!!
   (Lauzanne) 1886 <1>
Chanteuse d'Anesse (?) 1862 <1>
Chatte metamorphosée en
   femme, La (Offenbach) 1868
   <2>
Charles VI (Halévy) 1881 <2>
Chic revue (Potpourri) 1927 <2>
Chilpéric (Hervé) 1906 <1>
Ciboulette (Hahn) 1924 <1>
Cigale et la fourmi, La (Audran)
   1902 <2>
Cin-Cin-La (Ranzato) 1936 <1>,
   1937 <1>
Cinema star (J. Gilbert) 1918
   <2>, 1922 <1>
Claudia (Cagnoni) 1873 <5>
Claveles, Los (Serrano) 1935 <2>
Cleopatra (Arensky and others)
   1917 <3>
Cloches de Corneville, Las
   (Planquette) 1878 <5>, 1879
   <4>, 1880 <1>, 1881 <2>,
   1906 <1>, 1924 <2>, 1938 <1>
Cocarde de Mimi Pinson, La
   (Goublier) 1938 <1>

Coeur y est, Le (Van Parys and
   Paises) 1937 <1>
Comediantes de antaño, Los
   (Barbieri) 1879 <2>
Compagnacci, I (Riccitelli) 1923
   <1>
Comte oublié (Moretti) 1929 <1>
Conchita (Zandonai) 1912 <1>
Conde de Luxemburgo, El
   (Lehár) 1914 <2>, 1915 <1>,
   1916 <1>, 1922 <2>, 1927 <1>
Condesa bailarina, La (Stoltz)
   1922 <5>
Conquista de Madrid, La
   (Gaztambide) 1906 <1>
Contadino allegro, Il (Fall) 1911
   <2>, 1912 <1>
Conte di Lussemburgo, Il
   (Lehár) 1910 <1>, 1911 <8>,
   1912 <3>, 1913 <2>, 1914 <2>,
   1916 <1>, 1918 <1>, 1936 <2>,
   1937 <5>, 1943 <2>
Contessa d'Amalfi, La (Petrella)
   1872 <4>
Contessa Mariza, La (Kálmán)
   1936 <1>, 1950 <1>
Contributions indirectes, Les (?)
   1868 <1>
Coppelia (Delibes) 1903 <1>
Corsetería de Montmartre, La
   (Nelson) 1920 <1>
Così fan tutte (Mozart) 1953
   <2>, 1954 <1>
Cosse de riche (Yvain) 1929 <1>
Couchette no. 3 (Szulc) 1937 <3>
Creola, La (Berté) 1913 <2>
Crepuscolo degli dei, Il
   (Wagner) 1910 <1>
Criolla, La (Berté) 1915 <3>
Crispino e la comare (Ricci,
   Federico, and Luigi) 1867
   <2>, 1872 <4>, 1873 <3>,
   1884 <4>, 1885 <1>, 1886 <1>
Croix d'or (?) 1862 <1>
Croquefer (Offenbach) 1866 <1>
Cuento del dragón, El (Giménez
   [Jiménez], Jerónimo) 1915 <1>

Cuore e la mano, Il (Lecocq)
   1884 <5>

Dama verde, La (Ferraresi) 1914
   <1>
Dame blanche, La (Boieldieu)
   1877 <1>
Dannazione di Fausto, La
   (Berlioz) 1903 <1>, 1905 <1>,
   1907 <1>, 1913 <1>
Danza della libelulle, La (Lehár)
   1923 <9>, 1926 <3>, 1936
   <2>, 1937 <4>, 1943 <2>
Danzatrice scalza, La (Cellini)
   1911 <3>
Delicias del poder, Las (Rimsky-
   Korsakov) 1917 <1>
Demoiselle du printemps, La
   (Goublier) 1938 <1>
Deshabillé-vous (Mercier) 1929
   <2>
Deux pecheurs, Les (Offenbach)
   1866 <3>
Diablo en el poder, El (Barbieri)
   1880 <1>
Diamants de la couronne, Les
   (Auber) 1862 <1>, 1879 <2>
Dinorah (Meyerbeer) 1898 <1>,
   1901 <1>
Divorziata, La (Fall) 1912 <1>,
   1913 <2>, 1943 <1>
Dollarprinzessin, Die (Fall) 1910
   <1>
Dolores, La (Bretón) 1896 <8>,
   1914 <1>, 1931 <1>, 1935 <1>
Dolorosa, La (Serrano) 1933
   <8>
Domino noir, Le (Aubert) 1862
   <1>
Domino rose, Le (Hennequin)
   1879 <1>
Doña Francisquita (Vives) 1924
   <19>
Don Bucefalo (Cagnoni) 1873
   <6>, 1889 <1>
Don Carlo (Verdi) 1892 <1>,
   1907 <1>

Fille de Madame Angot, La
(Lecocq) 1875 <5>, 1877 <5>,
1878 <2>, 1879 <2>, 1881
<1>, 1913 <1>, 1924 <2>, 1938
<1>

Fille du regiment, La (Donizetti)
1862 <1>, 1877 <2>, 1879
<2>, 1881 <1>

Fille du tambour major, La
(Offenbach) 1881 <1>, 1882
<1>, 1924 <1>, 1938 <1>

Finalmente soli! (Lehár) 1914
<6>, 1916 <1>

Fledermaus, Die (Johann
Strauss) 1909 <1>, 1910 <1>

Flossie (Szulc) 1937 <2>

Fornaretto, Il (Sanelli) 1858 <3>

Forza del destino, La (Verdi)
1867 <8>, 1869 <5>, 1873
<3>, 1876 <6>, 1879 <4>,
1880 <3>, 1882 <3>, 1883
<4>, 1885 <6>, 1886 <2>,
1887 <1>, 1888 <2>, 1895
<2>, 1896 <1>, 1906 <1>,
1909 <1>, 1915 <3>, 1918 <1>,
1921 <1>, 1924 <1>

Fra diavolo (Auber) 1886 <1>,
1887 <1>, 1889 <1>, 1892 <1>,
1898 <1>, 1899 <1>, 1905 <2>

Francesca da Rimini (Zandonai)
1915 <1>

Frasquita (Lehár) 1931 <1>, 1937
<1>, 1943 <1>

Gallina ciega, La (Fernández-
Caballero) 1879 <2>

Gato con botas, El (Brusa) 1944
<1>

Gatta nell sacco, La (Eisemann)
1936 <1>

Gavilanes, Los (Guerrero) 1935
<1>

Geisha, La (Jones) 1902 <3>,
1909 <3>, 1910 <1>, 1911 <2>,
1915 <1>, 1918 <2>, 1937 <2>

Gemma di Vergy (Donizetti)
1861 <2>, 1865 <1>, 1879 <1>

Germania (Franchetti) 1902 <1>

Gigantes y cabezudos
(Fernández-Caballero) 1935
<2>

Gioconda, La (Ponchielli) 1884
<3>, 1886 <4>, 1887 <4>,
1888 <6>, 1889 <2>, 1890
<1>, 1892 <3>, 1894 <3>,
1895 <4>, 1896 <2>, 1899
<1>, 1900 <1>, 1901 <1>,
1906 <1>, 1908 <2>, 1909
<1>, 1910 <1>, 1911 <1>, 1915
<2>, 1918 <1>, 1919 <1>, 1921
<2>, 1922 <2>, 1926 <1>

Giorno e la notte, Il (Lecocq)
1918 <3>

Giroflé-Giroflá (Lecocq) 1881
<1>, 1930 <3>

Giselle (Adam) 1857 <1>, 1869
<3>

Giulietta e Romeo (Vaccai) 1875
<2>

Giuramento, Il (Mercadante)
1883 <4>

Gondoliers, The (Sullivan) 1954
<1>

Graf von Luxemburg, Der
(Lehár) 1910 <1>

Granaderi, Il (Valenti) 1896 <3>,
1902 <1>

Grand Casimir, Le (Lecocq) 1879
<1>

Grand Mogol, Le (Audran)
1906 <1>, 1913 <2>, 1924
<1>

Grande Duchesse de Gerolstein,
La (Offenbach) 1868 <1>,
1879 <1>, 1881 <2>

Griselda (Massenet) 1903 <1>

Grumete, El (Arrieta) 1906 <1>

Guarany, Il (Gomes) 1876 <10>,
1877 <8>, 1879 <3>, 1882
<2>, 1926 <1>

Guerra santa, La (Arrieta) 1906
<1>

Guglielmo Ratcliff (Mascagni)
1911 <1>

Guglielmo Tell (Rossini) 1870
<3>, 1896 <2>, 1923 <1>

Guitarrico, El (Pérez-Soriano)
1906 <1>, 1931 <1>

Hamlet (Thomas) 1876 <3>

Hans, Il suonatore di flauto
(Ganne) 1913 <1>

Haydée (Aubert) 1876 <1>, 1877
<1>

Herbstmanover, Ein (Kálmán)
1910 <1>

Hijas de Eva, Las (Gaztambide)
1874 <4>

Histoire d'un pierrot, L' (M.
Costa) 1903 <1>

Hérodiade (Massenet) 1907 <2>

Homard, Le (Gandillot) 1903 <1>

Homme n'est pas parfait, L'
(Thiboush) 1866 <1>

Huemac (De Rogatis) 1916 <1>

Huésped del sevillano, El
(Guerrero) 1935 <2>

Huguenots, Les (Meyerbeer)
1877 <3>

Indígena, La (Fumi) 1862 <1>

In Oriente (?, ballet) 1903 <1>

Iris (Mascagni) 1901 <2>, 1902
<1>, 1903 <1>, 1906 <3>, 1911
<2>, 1913 <1>, 1915 <1>, 1925
<1>

Isabeau (Mascagni) 1911<2>,
1913<1>

Jauja (Errante) 1896 <1>

Jone (Petrella) 1866 <3>, 1867
<5>, 1870 <4>, 1875 <4>,
1879 <3>

Jongleur de Notre Dame, Le
(Massenet) 1915 <1>

Jour et la nuit, Le (Lecocq) 1906
<1>, 1913 <1>, 1930 <1>

Joy-Joy (Clará) 1927 <2>

Juan II (Eysler) 1915 <2>

Juan de Urbina (Barbieri) 1879
<2>

Jugar con fuego (Barbieri) 1931
<1>

Juramento, El (Gaztambide)
1906 <1>, 1914 <1>, 1931 <2>

Katya la ballerina (J. Gilbert)
1926 <2>
Kiss-Me (Clará) 1927 <4>
Kiss-One (Clará) 1927 <3>
Kitezh [Legend of the Invisible
City of Kitezh and the
Maiden Fevroniya] (Rimsky-
Korsakov) 1929 <1>
Knyaz' Igor' [Prince Igor]
(Borodin) 1929 <4>
Kunstlerblut (Eysler) 1911 <1>

La del soto del parral (Soutullo
and Vert) 1931 <2>, 1935 <2>
Lac des cygnes, Le
(Tchaikovsky) 1913 <1>
Là-Haut! (Yvain) 1924 <3>
Lakmé (Delibes) 1888 <1>, 1901
<1>, 1906 <1>
Lego de San Pablo, El
(Caballero) 1914 <1>
Leyenda del beso, La (Soutullo
and Vert) 1935 <2>
Lili (Hervé) 1897 <1>
Linda di Chamounix (Donizetti)
1856 <2>, 1858 <1>, 1872
<4>, 1874 <3>, 1878 <1>,
1886 <1>, 1888 <1>, 1904
<1>, 1906 <1>
Liropeya (Ribeiro) 1912 <1>
Lituani, I (Ponchielli) 1888 <3>
Lohengrin (Wagner) 1892 <1>,
1894 <1>, 1895 <1>, 1896 <1>,
1904 <1>, 1906 <1>, 1907
<1>, 1910 <1>, 1913 <1>, 1920
<1>, 1925 <3>, 1926 <1>
Lombardi alla prima crociata, I
(Verdi) 1858 <2>, 1862 <1>
Loreley (Catalani) 1905 <1>,
1906 <2>, 1907 <1>, 1908
<1>, 1919 <1>, 1920 <1>, 1924
<2>
L'Orloff (Granichtaedten) 1929
<2>

Louise (Charpentier) 1910 <1>
Los de Aragón (Serrano) 1935 <1>
Love-Me (Clará, Font and
Olvadora) 1927 <9>
Lucia di Lammermoor
(Donizetti) 1856 <3>, 1859
<3>, 1860 <4>, 1861 <2>,
1862 <4>, 1863 <2>, 1865
<1>, 1866 <1>, 1867 <1>,
1869 <3>, 1870 <1>, 1872
<9>, 1873 <3>, 1874 <2>,
1876 <1>, 1877 <3>, 1878 <1>,
1879 <2>, 1881 <1>, 1882
<4>, 1888 <1>, 1891 <1>, 1892
<1>, 1895 <1>, 1896 <1>, 1898
<1>, 1899 <1>, 1901 <1>,
1902 <2>, 1905 <1>, 1906
<1>, 1909 <1>, 1915 <1>, 1916
<1>, 1918 <1>, 1921 <1>, 1923
<1>, 1924 <1>, 1932 <2>,
1940 <1>, 1943 <2>, 1948 <1>
Lucie de Lammermoor
(Donizetti) 1876 <2>, 1877 <1>
Lucrezia Borgia (Donizetti) 1859
<5>, 1860 <3>, 1861 <1>,
1862 <1>, 1867 <1>, 1868
<2>, 1869 <2>, 1872 <3>,
1873 <2>, 1874 <3>, 1875
<2>, 1876 <2>, 1878 <5>,
1881 <1>, 1884 <1>, 1887 <2>,
1888 <1>, 1889 <1>, 1890
<2>, 1919 <1>
Luisa Fernanda (Moreno-
Torroba) 1936 <8>, 1938
<10>, 1942 <4>, 1943 <3>
Luisa Miller (Verdi) 1856 <3>,
1857 <1>, 1859 <1>, 1860 <1>,
1861 <3>, 1863 <2>, 1870
<2>, 1887 <2>
Luisa Strozzi (Sanelli) 1856 <6>
Lulú (Parés and Parys) 1929 <1>
Luna Park (Ranzato) 1931 <2>,
1936 <1>
Lustige Witwe, Die (Lehár) 1910
<1>

Macbeth (Verdi) 1860 <1>, 1877
<5>

Madama Butterfly (Puccini)
1904 <1>, 1906 <1>, 1910
<1>, 1912 <1>, 1913 <2>, 1915
<2>, 1920 <1>, 1924 <1>,
1925 <1>, 1933 <3>, 1934 <3>,
1943 <1>
Madame (Christiné) 1924 <1>,
1937 <1>
Madame de Tebas (Lombardo)
1923 <1>
Madame Favart (Offenbach) 1881
<2>
Madame Sans-Gêne
(Dall'Argine) 1918 <2>
Madame Sans-Gêne (Giordano)
1919 <1>
Maestri cantori, I (Wagner) 1903
<1>
Magyares, Los (Gaztambide)
1874 <4>
Maître Baton (Dufresne) 1861
<1>
Maître de chapelle, Le (Paer)
1862 <1>
Malbrouck (Leoncavallo) 1913 <1>
Mam'zelle Carabin (Pessard)
1911 <2>
Mam'zelle Nitouche (Hervé)
1893 <1>
Manfredi di Svevia (Giribaldi)
1882 <3>
Manon (Massenet) 1899 <3>,
1902 <2>, 1904 <1>, 1905
<1>, 1906 <3>, 1908 <2>,
1910 <3>, 1912 <1>, 1914 <1>,
1915 <3>, 1916 <1>, 1919 <1>,
1923 <1>, 1924 <3>, 1925 <1>,
1926 <2>, 1931 <1>
Manon Lescaut (Puccini) 1894
<3>, 1895 <1>, 1896 <2>,
1900 <1>, 1903 <1>, 1905
<3>, 1907 <1>, 1908 <1>,
1912 <1>, 1918 <1>, 1926 <1>
Manovra d'autunno (Kálmán)
1911 <2>, 1912 <1>
Marceau (?) 1878 <1>
Marco Visconti (Petrella) 1859
<3>, 1894 <3>, 1895 <1>

Maria di Rohan (Donizetti) 1859
<3>, 1870 <3>

Mari à la porte, Le (Offenbach)
1868 <1>

Marie Jeanne (Mallian) 1866 <1>

Mariée du Mardi Gras, Le
(Thiboush) 1866 <1>

Marietta (Stoltz) 1926 <2>

Marina (Arrieta) 1874 <3>, 1879
<4>, 1906 <1>, 1914 <1>, 1931
<3>, 1940 <3>

Marjolaine, La (Lecocq) 1881 <1>

Mârouf (Rabaud) 1917 <1>

Maruxa (Vives) 1924 <2>, 1931
<1>, 1935 <1>

Martha (Flotow) 1866 <8>, 1867
<7>, 1870 <1>, 1872 <7>,
1884 <2>, 1910 <1>

Marthe (Flotow) 1877 <1>

Martiri, I (Donizetti) 1860 <3>,
1875 <1>

Maschere, Le (Mascagni) 1901
<1>, 1918 <1>

Mascotita, La (J. Gilbert) 1922
<4>

Mascotta, La (Audran) 1889
<2>, 1896 <1>, 1943 <1>

Mascotte, La (Audran) 1881 <1>,
1887<1>, 1906 <1>, 1913 <1>,
1924 <2>

Masnadieri, I (Verdi) 1859 <1>,
1866 <3>

Matrimonio segreto, Il
(Cimarosa) 1952 <2>

Mazurca azzura, La (Lehár) 1923
<1>

Medea (Pacini) 1866 <1>

Mefistofele (Boito) 1884 <1>,
1886 <2>, 1890 <1>, 1892
<2>, 1894 <1>, 1896 <1>,
1903 <1>, 1907 <1>, 1908
<1>, 1910 <3>, 1911 <1>, 1912
<1>, 1913 <1>, 1914 <2>, 1920
<2>, 1921 <2>, 1922 <1>,
1924 <3>, 1926 <2>

Meiga, La (Guridi) 1931 <1>

Meninas, Las (Fauré) 1917 <1>

Mercado de las muchachas, El
(Jacobi) 1916 <2>, 1922 <2>

Messa da Requiem (Verdi) 1888
<2>, 1928 <2>

Michele Perrin (Cagnoni) 1873
<5>

Mignon (Thomas) 1876 <2>,
1881 <1>, 1889 <1>, 1908 <1>,
1910 <1>

Mikado, The (Sullivan) 1890
<2>, 1891 <2>, 1953 <2>

Millionario Accatone (Asher)
1911 <1>

Mireille (Gounod) 1938 <2>

Miss Dudelsack (Nelson) 1910
<2>

Misteres de l'eté, Les (?) 1866 <1>

Mosè in Egitto (Rossini) 1870
<2>, 1883 <3>

Molinero de Subiza, El (Oudrid)
1874 <3>

Molinos de viento (Luna) 1913
<2>, 1922 <1>, 1931 <1>, 1935
<1>

Monna Vanna (Février) 1919
<1>, 1925 <1>

Monsieur Choufleuri
(Offenbach) 1897 <1>

Mosqueteros grises, Los (?) 1889
<1>

Mousquetaires au convent, Les
(Varney) 1906 <1>, 1913 <1>,
1924 <1>, 1938 <1>

Mousquetaires de la reine, Les
(Halévy) 1862 <1>, 1877 <1>

Moza de campanillas, La (Luna)
1927 <1>

Mujer del panadero, La
(Maizzels) 1940 <2>

Mujeres vienesas (Lehár) 1915 <3>

Muñeca, La (Audran) 1906 <1>

Musa gitana, La (Baylac) 1941 <5>

Nabucco (Verdi) 1859 <1>, 1865
<1>, 1870 <5>, 1881 <3>

Napoli in Carnevale (De Giosa)
1884 <2>

Nieta del otro mundo, La
(Witmatak) 1940 <2>

Niniche (Boullard) 1897 <2>

Niña mimada, La (Penella) 1914
<1>

Noces d'Olivette, Les (Audran)
1881 <1>

Norma (Bellini) 1858 <1>, 1859
<4>, 1860 <4>, 1861 <5>,
1862 <2>, 1863 <3>, 1864
<3>, 1866 <2>, 1867 <3>,
1868 <5>, 1869 <8>, 1870
<2>, 1872 <4>, 1873 <4>,
1874 <4>, 1875 <6>, 1876
<6>, 1877 <1>, 1878 <4>, 1881
<2>, 1885 <2>, 1906 <3>,
1910 <1>, 1921 <1>

Nouvelle revue (Potpourri) 1927
<1>

Novia vendida, La [The
Bartered Bride] (Smetana)
1954 <2>

Nozze di Figaro, Le (Mozart)
1946 <1>

Nozze di Juanita, Le (Massé)
1857 <1>

Nuit blanche, Une (Offenbach)
1894 <1>

Ofelia (Calvo) 1880 <1>

Oh Papa! (Yvain) 1937 <1>

Oiseau et le prince, L'
(Tchaikovsky) 1913 <1>

Orfeo (Gluck) 1925 <1>

Orfeo all'inferno (Offenbach)
1885 <3>, 1896 <2>, 1909
<2>, 1911 <2>

Orloff, L' (Granichstaedten) 1926
<2>

Orphée aux enfers (Offenbach)
1868 <1>, 1879 <2>

Osteria dello cavallo bianco, La
(Stolz, Gilbert, and
Granischataeden) 1943 <4>

Otello (Rossini) 1862 <1>

Otello (Verdi) 1888 <4>, 1889
<2>, 1890 <1>, 1892 <1>,

1896 <1>, 1900 <2>, 1908
<1>, 1909 <1>

Papillons, Les (Schumann) 1917
<2>

P'tites michu, Les (Messager)
1902 <1>

Paese del campanille, Il
(Ranzato) 1936 <2>, 1937
<2>, 1943 <1>

Paese dell'oro, Il (Vasseur) 1909
<4>

Paganini (Lehár) 1926 <2>, 1943
<1>

Pagliacci (Leoncavallo) 1896
<4>, 1899 <2>, 1905 <2>,
1906 <1>, 1908 <1>, 1910
<1>, 1911 <1>, 1913 <1>, 1914
<1>, 1915 <3>, 1917 <1>, 1918
<2>, 1921 <2>, 1922 <1>,
1924 <3>, 1926 <1>, 1934
<2>, 1940 <1>, 1943 <2>

Pampa (Berutti) 1897 <1>

Papa Martin (Cagnoni) 1873
<7>, 1883 <3>, 1884 <1>,
1887 <2>, 1889 <2>

Paraná Guazú (Ascone) 1950 <1>

Parisina (Giribaldi) 1878 <4>,
1899 <1>

Parranda, La (Alonso) 1931 <2>

Parsifal (Wagner) 1913 <2>

Passionement (Messager) 1929
<1>, 1937 <2>

Patience (Sullivan) 1891 <1>

Paul et Virginie (Massé) 1881 <1>

Pavillon d'Armide, Le
(Tcherepiene) 1913 <1>

Pepita (Solomon) 1890 <1>

Perichole, La (Offenbach) 1881
<1>, 1906 <1>

Pescatori di Napoli (Sarria) 1889
<2>

Pescatori di perle, I (Bizet) 1889
<1>, 1921 <3>

Petit cafe (I. Caryll) 1915 <2>

Petit choc, Le (Szule) 1924 <1>

Petit duc, Le (Lecocq) 1878 <1>,

1879 <1>, 1881 <1>, 1882 <1>,
1913 <1>, 1938 <2>

Petit Faust, Le (Hervé) 1878 <3>

Petite mariée, La (Lecocq) 1878
<2>

Petite Pologne, La (Poppe) 1866
<1>

Phi-Phi (Christiné) 1937 <1>

Pilluelo de París, El (?) 1920 <1>

Pipelet (A. S. De Ferrari) 1870
<4>

Pirates of Penzance, The
(Sullivan) 1890 <1>, 1891
<1>

Pleito, Un (Gaztambide) 1880 <1>

Poliuto (Donizetti) 1868 <1>,
1869 <7>, 1872 <3>, 1873
<2>, 1877 <4>, 1879 <2>,
1883 <4>, 1885 <3>, 1896 <1>

Polvera de Pirlimpimpin, La
(Lombardo) 1913 <2>

Porgy and Bess (Gershwin) 1955
<7>

Postillón de la Rioja, El
(Oudrid) 1879 <2>

Poupée, La (Audran) 1905 <1>,
1909 <1>, 1911 <2>, 1915 <1>

Pour le trou de la serrure (?)
1903 <1>

Pré aux clers, Le (Hérold) 1881
<2>

Precauzione, La (Petrella) 1887
<2>

Prés de Saint Gervais, Les
(Lecocq) 1883 <2>

Presidentessa, La (Stolz) 1936
<1>, 1937 <1>

Primavera scapigliata (Josef
Strauss?) 1909 <1>, 1911 <2>,
1912 <1>, 1943 <1>

Princesa de las czardas, La
(Kálmán) 1922 <3>, 1927 <1>

Princesa de los balcanes, La
(Eysler) 1915 <2>

Princesa del dólar, La (Fall) 1914
<2>, 1915 <1>, 1916 <1>, 1922
<1>, 1927 <1>

Princesse enchantée, La
(Tchaikovsky) 1917 <1>

Princess, The (?) 1925 <1>

Principessa del circo, La
(Kálmán) 1937 <2>

Principessa delle Canarie, La
(Lecocq) 1909 <1>

Principessa delle czarde, La
(Kálmán) 1923 <1>, 1936 <1>,
1937 <4>, 1943 <4>

Principessa delle dolar, La (Fall)
1913 <1>, 1912 <5>, 1916 <1>,
1936 <2>, 1937 <2>, 1943 <2>

Principessa Ola-Lá, La (Fall)
1926 <2>

Principessa Wandi, La (Nelson
and Igrun) 1918 <1>

Profeta, Il (Meyerbeer) 1873 <5>,
1896 <3>

Puchino, Il (Lecocq) 1884 <1>

Puñao de rosas, El (Chapí) 1935
<1>

Puritani, I (Bellini) 1859 <1>,
1860 <2>, 1888 <2>, 1898
<2>, 1899 <2>, 1901 <1>

Quand on est trois . . . (Szulc)
1929 <1>, 1937 <1>

Raffaelo e la Fornarina (Maggi)
1896 <1>

Re coscritto, Il [El rey que
rabió] (Chapí) 1896 <3>

Re di Lahore (Massenet) 1920
<1>

Regina del cinematografo, La
(Lombardo?) 1918 <1>

Regina del fonografo, La
(Lombardo) 1918 <3>

Reginetta delle rose, La
(Leoncavallo) 1912 <3>, 1913
<2>

Reina del fonógrafo, La
(Lombardo) 1922 <2>

Reine Indigo, La (Johann
Strauss) 1879 <1>

Reinita de las rosas, La
(Leoncavallo) 1914 <1>, 1915
<1>

Relámpago, El (Barbieri) 1874
<4>

Rendevouz bourgeois, Les (N.
Isouard "Nicolo") 1862 <1>

Retour du saltimbanque, Le (?)
1894 <1>

Rêve d'un vals, Le (O. Straus)
1913 <1>

Revue de folies, La (Potpourri)
1927 <2>

Rey que rabió, El (Chapí) 1906
<1>

Rigoletto (Verdi) 1856 <3>, 1857
<1>, 1859 <1>, 1861 <2>, 1863
<1>, 1865 <1>, 1866 <2>,
1867 <2>, 1868 <3>, 1869
<4>, 1870 <2>, 1872 <6>,
1873 <5>, 1874 <4>, 1876
<2>, 1877 <7>, 1879 <1>, 1881
<3>, 1882 <5>, 1884 <3>,
1885 <6>, 1886 <1>, 1887
<3>, 1888 <2>, 1889 <1>,
1890 <1>, 1891 <1>, 1895 <1>,
1896 <1>, 1898 <1>, 1899
<1>, 1900 <1>, 1901 <1>,
1902 <1>, 1905 <2>, 1906
<2>, 1908 <3>, 1909 <1>,
1910 <4>, 1911 <2>, 1912 <2>,
1913 <2>, 1914 <2>, 1915 <3>,
1916 <1>, 1918 <1>, 1921 <2>,
1923 <1>, 1924 <2>, 1925
<4>, 1926 <3>, 1929 <1>,
1931 <1>, 1932 <1>, 1934 <1>,
1940 <2>, 1943 <3>, 1948 <1>

Risurrezione di Lazzaro, La
(Perosi) 1899 <1>

Roberto Devereux (Donizetti)
1860 <1>

Roberto il diavolo (Meyerbeer)
1869 <7>, 1874 <4>, 1886 <2>

Romance en el desierto, Un
(Marcovich) 1940 <1>

Romeo e Giulietta (Gounod)
1905 <1>, 1908 <1>

Rondine, La (Puccini) 1917 <2>

Ronsette, La (Millaud) 1893 <2>

Rosa del azafrán, La (J.
Guerrero) 1931 <5>, 1935 <1>

Ruy Blas (Marchetti) 1872 <7>,
1873 <5>, 1875 <5>, 1876 <2>,
1878 <3>, 1879 <4>, 1882
<3>, 1883 <1>, 1885 <2>, 1887
<1>, 1888 <1>, 1892 <1>,
1900 <1>, 1906 <2>

Sadko (Rimsky-Korsakov) 1917
<1>

Saffo (Pacini) 1861 <2>, 1862
<1>, 1869 <5>, 1874 <6>,
1879 <1>

Saltimbanchi (Ganne) 1902 <4>,
1909 <1>, 1911 <4>, 1913 <1>,
1923 <4>, 1943 <2>

Saltimbanques, Les (Ganne)
1866 <3>, 1906 <2>, 1938
<2>

Salvator Rosa (Gomes) 1876 <3>

Samson et Dalila (Saint-Saëns)
1916 <1>

Sansone e Dalila (Saint-Saëns)
1896 <2>, 1907 <1>, 1917
<1>, 1925 <1>

San Francesco d'Assisi
(Sambucetti) 1910 <2>

Sangre de artista (Eysler) 1915
<1>, 1916 <1>, 1927 <1>

Santarellina [Mam'zelle
Nitouche] (Hervé) 1911 <2>,
1923 <4>, 1937 <2>

Savetier et le financier, Le
(Offenbach) 1861 <1>

Schahabaham III (Poppe) 1866
<2>

Scheherazade (Rimsky-
Korsakov) 1917 <2>

Scugnizza (Costa) 1926 <2>,
1936 <3>, 1937 <5>, 1943 <5>

Scuola d'amore (Korolani) 1911
<1>

Scuola di signorine (J. Gilbert)
1911 <1>

Secchia rapita, La (Burgmein)
1913 <1>

Selvaggia (Bellini) 1926 <2>

Semiramide (Rossini) 1885 <1>,
1888 <1>

Serafín el grumete (Arrieta) 1883
<1>

Sfilata del'amore (Caparros) 1936
<1>

Si j'etais roi (Adam) 1881 <2>

Siberia (Giordano) 1917 <1>

Sieben Schwaben, Die
(Millöcker) 1910 <1>

Signorina del cinematografo, La
(Lombardo) 1916 <3>

Silhouette (Bellini) 1926 <2>

Simon Boccanegra (Verdi) 1862
<2>, 1889 <1>

Simone est comme ça (Moretti)
1937 <1>

Sirena, La (Fall) 1912 <1>

Snegurochka [Snow Maiden]
(Rimky-Korsakov) 1929
<3>

Sobrinos del capitán Grant, Los
(Fernández-Caballero) 1885
<7>

Sogno d'amore de Liszt (K.
Komjati) 1937 <5>

Sogno d'una notte (Allegra &
Pittaluga) 1937 <2>

Sogno d'un valser (O. Straus)
1911 <3>, 1912 <2>, 1913 <1>,
1914 <2>, 1918 <1>, 1936 <2>,
1937 <1>, 1943 <2>

Sogno in Riviera (Stoltz) 1926
<2>

Soldaditos de plomo, Los
(Johann Strauss) 1914 <1>

Soldado de chocolate, El (O.
Straus) 1915 <4>, 1916 <1>

Soldat de chocolat, Le (O.
Straus) 1913 <2>

Soleil de la nuit, Le (Rimsky-
Korsakov) 1917 <2>

Sonnambula, La (Bellini) 1856
<1>, 1859 <1>, 1862 <1>, 1872

<6>, 1873 <3>, 1874 <1>,
1876 <1>, 1878 <1>, 1884 <3>,
1896 <1>, 1899 <1>, 1901 <1>,
1902 <2>, 1905 <1>, 1912
<1>, 1916 <1>, 1924 <1>

Sorochinskaya Yamarka [The
Fair at Sorochintsï]
(Musorgsky) 1929 <3>

Spectre de la rose, Le (Weber)
1913 <1>, 1917 <3>

Stabat Mater (Rossini) 1857 <1>,
1862 <1>, 1866 <1>, 1869
<1>, 1927 <1>

Still Waters run Deep (Ryssens)
1864 <1>

Sulamita, La (Cortinas) 1917 <1>

Sylphides, Les (Chopin) 1913
<1>, 1917 <3>

Tabaré (Broqua) 1910 <1>

Tango di mezzanotte, Il
(Komjati) 1937 <3>

Tannhäuser (Wagner) 1894 <1>,
1895 <1>

Taras Bulba (Berutti) 1895 <1>

Thamar (Balakirev) 1917 <2>

Tela de araña, La (M. Nieto)
1906 <1>

Tempestad, La (Chapí) 1906
<1>, 1914 <1>, 1931 <1>, 1935
<2>

Thaïs (Massenet) 1908 <1>, 1920
<1>, 1924 <1>, 1925 <2>,

Theodora (Leroux) 1907 <1>

Theresina (J. Gilbert) 1926 <2>

Thirteen (Various composers)
1913 <2>

Tierra (A. Llanos y Berete) 1906
<1>

Tom Migler (Jacobi) 1918 <5>

Toreador, Il (Adam) 1909 <4>,
1911 <3>

Tosca (Puccini) 1902 <2>, 1903
<1>, 1905 <3>, 1906 <5>,
1908 <2>, 1909 <1>, 1910
<1>, 1914 <1>, 1915 <1>, 1917
<1>, 1918 <4>, 1919 <1>, 1921

<1>, 1924 <1>, 1926 <2>,
1929 <1>, 1931 <1>, 1934 <1>,
1943 <1>, 1948 <1>

Traviata, La (Verdi) 1856 <6>,
1859 <2>, 1860 <3>, 1861
<3>, 1862 <2>, 1863 <4>,
1864 <1>, 1865 <3>, 1866
<2>, 1867 <6>, 1868 <1>,
1869 <2>, 1870 <2>, 1872
<7>, 1873 <1>, 1874 <1>, 1876
<6>, 1877 <1>, 1878 <1>, 1879
<4>, 1881 <4>, 1882 <3>,
1884 <1>, 1885 <4>, 1887
<3>, 1888 <2>, 1892 <1>,
1891 <2>, 1896 <2>, 1898
<1>, 1906 <2>, 1908 <2>,
1912 <2>, 1914 <1>, 1915 <2>,
1920 <1>, 1921 <1>, 1924 <5>,
1925 <5>, 1926 <2>, 1934
<3>, 1940 <2>, 1943 <3>,
1946 <3>, 1948 <1>, 1949 <1>

Trial by Jury (Sullivan) 1890 <1>

Tristan und Isolde (Wagner)
1923 <1>

Tristano e Isotta (Wagner) 1906
<1>, 1917 <1>, 1920 <1>

Tromb-al-ca-zar (Offenbach)
1866 <1>

Trouvère, Le (Verdi) 1881 <2>

Trovatore, Il (Verdi) 1856 <3>,
1857 <2>, 1858 <5>, 1859 <3>,
1860 <2>, 1861 <4>, 1862
<4>, 1863 <4>, 1864 <4>,
1865 <1>, 1866 <3>, 1867
<3>, 1868 <5>, 1869 <13>,
1870 <2>, 1872 <7>, 1873
<6>, 1874 <6>, 1875 <4>,
1876 <1>, 1877 <9>, 1878
<2>, 1879 <5>, 1881 <2>,
1882 <6>, 1883 <3>, 1884
<1>, 1885 <3>, 1887 <1>, 1888
<2>, 1891 <1>, 1899 <1>,
1902 <1>, 1905 <1>, 1906
<1>, 1908 <2>, 1909 <1>,
1911 <3>, 1915 <3>, 1918 <4>,
1921 <3>, 1922 <1>, 1924
<2>, 1925 <1>, 1926 <1>, 1932

<5>, 1934 <2>, 1940 <2>,
1943 <1>, 1948 <1>

Tsar Saltan [Tsare Saltane]
(Rimsky-Korsakov) 1929 <2>

Tutti in maschera (Pedrotti)
1884 <1>, 1889 <1>

Ugonotti, Gli (Meyerbeer) 1876
<5>, 1882 <3>, 1884 <2>,
1885 <8>, 1887 <3>, 1888
<1>, 1889 <1>, 1890 <1>,
1892 <2>, 1894 <1>, 1895
<2>, 1896 <2>, 1901 <2>,
1905 <2>, 1906 <1>, 1908
<1>, 1909 <1>, 1910 <2>,
1914 <1>, 1916 <1>, 1918 <2>,
1925 <2>

Última gavota, La (Cortinas)
1916 <1>

Ultimo valser, L' (Strauss) 1931
<1>

Uomo elettrico, L' (Chylton)
1918 <1>

Vals del amor (Ziehrer) 1915 <1>

Valse d'amore (Grumbaum) 1912
<1>

Vedova allegra, La (Lehár) 1909
<7>, 1911 <7>, 1912 <4>, 1913
<2>, 1914 <2>, 1916 <1>, 1918
<3>, 1936 <4>, 1937 <4>,
1943 <5>

Vendetta, Una (Agostini) 1869
<6>

Venditore di ucceli, Il (Zeller)
1896 <1>, 1902 <1>

Verbena de la Paloma, La
(Bretón) 1894 <6>, 1935 <1>,
1941 <3>

Véronique (Messager) 1906 <1>,
1938 <1>

Vespri siciliani, I (Verdi) 1862
<2>, 1877 <3>, 1892 <2>

Veuve joyeuse, La (Lehár) 1913
<1>

Viaggio della sposa, Il (Diet)
1909 <3>

Viejo de la montaña, El (Conti)
1896 <1>

Vingt-huit jours de Clairette, Les
(Roger) 1893 <1>, 1897 <2>,
1906 <1>

Vita brettone (Mugnone) 1905
<1>

Vittore Pisani (Achille Peri) 1867
<5>

Vittoria e il suo ussaro (P.
Abraham) 1936 <2>, 1943 <2>

Viuda alegre, La (Lehár) 1914
<3>, 1915 <3>, 1916 <1>, 1927
<2>

Voyage en Chine, Le (Bazin)
1877 <2>, 1881 <1>

Walkiria, La (Wagner) 1908 <1>,
1913 <1>

Wally, La (Catalani) 1904
<1>, 1906 <1>, 1912 <1>, 1924
<2>

Waltzetraum, Ein (O. Straus)
1910 <1>

Werther (Massenet) 1897 <1>,
1906 <2>

Yes-Yes (Clará) 1927 <5>

Zazà (Leoncavallo) 1902 <1>

Zigeunerbaron, Der (Johann
Strauss) 1910 <2>, 1912 <1>

Zig-Zag (Potpourri) 1927 <4>

D: *Instrumental Ensembles that Performed at the Teatro Solís (1856–1956)*

(Orchestras, chamber groups, bands)

Adolfo Morpurgo Ancient-Instrument Ensemble 1950

Asociación Coral de Montevideo orchestra 1920 to 1922, 1925, 1927, 1950, 1954

Asociación Lírica del Uruguay 1917

Asociación Uruguaya de Música de Cámara 1927, 1929

Banda Escuela de Artes y Oficios (Montevideo) 1885

Bandas Militares de Montevideo 1885

Banda Municipal de Montevideo 1943, 1944, 1947 to 1956

Berlin Chamber Orchestra 1956

Berlin Philharmonic Octet 1954

Budapest String Quartet 1956

Centro Cultural de Música Orchestra 1949, 1950

Cuarteto Americano de Saxofones 1956

Cuarteto de Cuerdas Fabini 1954, 1955

Cuarteto de Laúdes Aguilar (lute quartet) 1929, 1930

Conjunto Instrumental Montevideo 1954

Drolc String Quartet from Berlin 1954

Escuela Municipal de Música Student Orchestra 1954, 1955

Ghigiano String Quintet 1954

Guarnieri String Quartet 1929, 1933

Hot Club Jazz Ensemble 1956

Hungarian National Orchestra 1890

Italian Band 1889

Janáček String Quartet 1956

Kolish String Quartet 1936

Lembranzas d'Ultreya bagpipe players 1934 (*see also* Appendixes E and F)

Loewenguth String Quartet from Paris 1953

London String Quartet 1926

Munich Orchestra 1955

Música Pura Ensemble (chamber group) 1925

Orquesta Anfión 1954, 1955, 1956

Orquesta AUDEM 1952, 1955

Orquesta del Teatro Solís 1856 to 1876

Orquesta de la Sociedad Filarmónica 1866, 1875

Orquesta Euterpe 1955, 1956

Orquesta Filarmónica de Buenos Aires 1928

Orquesta Nacional 1908 to 1910, 1912, 1926, 1927

Orquesta Sinfónica Municipal 1956

Orquesta Sociedad Beethoven 1897 to 1901

Orquesta Sociedad Musical "La Lira" 1877

Orquesta Sociedad Wagneriana de Montevideo 1920

Orquesta Uruguaya de Cámara 1949, 1950

OSSODRE (Orquesta Sinfónica del Servicio Oficial de Difusión Radio Eléctrica) 1952, 1955, 1956

Pasquier Trio 1955

Pierri [Olga Pierri] Guitar Ensemble 1948, 1949, 1952

Quintette à vent de Paris (wind quintet) 1952

Scottish Campanologists (bell's orchestra) 1865

Sexteto Eslava—Conjunto
valenciano (wind sextet) 1914
Sociedad Filarmónica de
Montevideo 1928
Sociedad Coral Uruguaya
Orchestra 1928
Sociedad Orquestal 1896

Sociedad Orquestal del Uruguay
1923, 1924, 1926, 1929 to
1931
Stuttgart Orchestra 1953

Teatro alla Scala Orchestra
members 1903

Trío Jean-Louis Le Roux 1954
Trío Uruguayo de Cuerdas 1954,
1955, 1956

Vegh String Quartet 1951
Vienna Philharmonic Orchestra
1922, 1923

E: *Vocal Ensembles that Performed at the Teatro Solís (1856–1956)*

Asociación Coral de Montevideo chorus 1919 to 1930, 1950, 1954

Asociación Lírica del Uruguay choral 1917

Centro Cultural de Música chorus 1950

Christy's Minstrels 1871

Coral Alpargatas 1951

Coral Amigos de la Música de Paysandú 1951

Coral de Pamplona (Spain) 1951

Coral Guarda e Passa 1947, 1954

Coral Palestrina 1927, 1928, 1930

Coro Bach 1951, 1954, 1956

Coro de Cámara del SODRE 1956

Coro del Teatro Solís 1856 to 1891

Coro Juventus 1954 to 1956

Coro Municipal 1954 to 1956

Coro Municipal Infantil 1951 to 1955

Coro Oriana 1952 to 1954

Coro Sociedad Lega Lombarda 1880

Coro Sociedad Musical La Lira 1880

Coros Unidos de Montevideo 1953

Coro Universitario 1948, 1954

Cuarteto Vocal Gómez-Carrillo 1953

Don Cossack Chorus "Platoff" 1930

Don Cossack Chorus 1936, 1951

Federación Uruguaya de Puericantores 1954

German Vocal Societies of Montevideo and Buenos Aires 1865

Jubilee Singers 1953, 1956

Lembranzas d'Ultreya (vocal part) 1934 (*see also* appendixes D and F)

Officers Choir of H.R.H. Forte 1864

Petit Chanteurs de la Croix de Bois de Paris (boys choir) 1941

Petit Chanteurs de la Provence, Les 1953

Ratisbone Cathedral Choir 1937

Saint Thomas of Leipzig Choral 1955

Sociedad Coral Uruguaya chorus 1928

Sociedad Orquestal del Uruguay chorus 1924

Società Polifonica Romana (Sistine Chapel Chorus) 1930

Sodca Vocal Ensemble 1955

SODRE chorus 1952, 1956

Ukrainian Chorus 1931

Vienna Choir Boys 1936

F: *Ballet Companies that Performed at the Teatro Solís (1856–1956)*

Abyssinian Choreographic Art
Company 1943
Amaya, Carmen, Spanish Dance
Company 1937, 1940
Angelillo Spanish Company
1939, 1940, 1941
Antinea, María, Spanish Dance
Company 1940

Ballet Experimental Uruguayo
1956
Ballets Russes 1913, 1917

Chabelska, Gala, Ballet
Company 1939, 1944, 1953,
1955
Chazarreta, Andrés, Argentinean
Folk Company 1921

Florez, Mariquita and Antonio
Córdoba Spanish Dance
Company 1951

Greco, José, Spanish Dance
Company 1951
Grigorieva, Tamara, Ballet
Company 1953

Hintz, Olga de, Ballet Company
1954, 1956

Imperio, Pastora, Company 1915
Isaura, Amalia de, Spanish
Dance Company 1929

Jakovieff, Alexandre, Ballet
Company 1920
Jarmalovich, Paula, Ballet
Company 1953, 1954, 1956
Jauffre, Aurorita ("La Goya"),
Company 1915

Kaweski, Jan, Ballet Company
1919

Lembranzas d'Ultreya Dancers
1934 (part of ensemble) (*see
also* appendixes D and E)
Limón, José, and Pauline Koney
Modern Dance Company
1954
López, Encarnación ("La
Argentinita"), Spanish Dance
Company 1935, 1939
López, Pilar, Spanish Ballet
Company 1950
Ludnica Czech Folkloric Ballet
1956

Martínez, Cristóbal, Spanish
Ballet Company 1950, 1953
Meller, Raquel, Company 1920,
1921, 1938
Mercé, Antonia ("La
Argentina"), Company 1919,
1933, 1934, 1935
Meriweather-Hugues, Russell

("La Meri"), Modern Dance
Company 1929
Molasso Ballet and Pantomime
Company 1915
Molina, Amalia, Spanish Dance
Company 1937
Montijo, Coral de, Spanish
Ballet Company 1954

Pavley, André and Serge
Oukranisky Russian Ballet
Company 1924
Pavlova, Anna, Ballet Company
1919
Peñalver, Rosario y Coral,
Spanish Dance Company
1941
Pérez-Fernández, Joaquín, Dance
Company 1942

Rousset Ballet Company 1857
Russian Ballet Company
Michalowski 1924
Russian Ballet and Opera
Company Privée (Paris) 1929

Sandoval, Paloma de, Spanish
Ballet Company 1948
Schottelius, Renate,
Contemporary Dance
Ensemble 1956
Solé, Ricardo, Spanish Ballet
Company 1956

Soler, Trinidad, Spanish Dance
  Company 1938, 1939

Teatro Alla Scala Ballet 1947
Teatro Colón de Buenos Aires
  Ballet 1955

Théâtre du Ballet 1947
Thierry Choreographic
  Company 1861, 1862
Toamarán, Wilfredo, Ballet
  Company 1953
Tomina, Victoria, Ballet 1952

Valencia, Tórtola, Company
  1916, 1928
Vélez, Angelita, Argentinean
  Folk Company 1949

Winslow Ballet 1948

NOTES

Chapter 1. 1516–1829

1. Born in Chioggia, Venice (c. 1476?), Sebastian Caboto was the second son of Mattea and Giovanni Caboto. In 1512 he moved to Spain in the service of the Spanish king Fernando de Aragón; he continued his service until 1548. See *The Christopher Columbus Encyclopedia*, Silvio A. Bedini, ed. (New York: Simon & Schuster, 1992) 1:86–87. During his time at the service of the Spanish Crown he was known as Sebastián Gaboto. One of Montevideo's streets bears his name.

2. The most recent studies give December 1726 as the time when the settlement was almost completed and the city established. See María Luisa Coolighan y Juan José Arteaga, *Historia del Uruguay* (A. Barreiro y Ramos, S.A. editores, 1992).

3. Last will and testament of Manuel Cipriano de Melo, 1806 (file no. 45). Mention is made of Cipriano de Melo in Isidoro de María's *Montevideo Antiguo*: "Cipriano de Mello [*sic*] was a good and prosperous neighbor of Montevideo, originally from Portugal." De María goes on to call Melo "Impresario" because of Melo's duty to find artists to perform at the Casa de Comedias; *Montevideo Antiguo*, 4th ed. (Montevideo: 1957), 1:215ff. (Part of the series Montevideo: Ministerio de Instrucción Pública y Previsión Social, Colección de Clásicos Uruguayos, 24:2).

4. Ibid., 23:1.

5. See José Subirá, *La tonadilla escénica*, 3 vols. (Madrid, 1928–30).

6. Ibid., 1:13–32, 2:87–100.

7. Lauro Ayestarán, *La Música en el Uruguay* (Montevideo: SODRE, 1953), 176.

8. The word *zarzuela* comes from *zarza*, which translates as a bramble bush. Zarzuela is a dramatic Spanish form that alternates singing and dancing with spoken language. Its origin comes from the Palacio de la Zarzuela, the hunting lodge surrounded by bramble bushes and built by the Infante Don Fernando about 1634 on El Pardo, near Madrid.

9. Ayestarán, *La Música*, 250.

Chapter 2. 1830–1856

1. *El Universal*, May 9, 1832.

2. *El Comercio del Plata*, January 7–8, 1852.

3. Antoine Sallès, *L'Opéra Italien et Allemand à Lyon aux XIXe siècle (1805–1882)* (Paris: E. Fromont, 1906), 69–92.

4. *El Comercio del Plata*, July 11, 1855.

5. Ibid., June 6, 1855.

6. *Cronología Comparada de la Historia del Uruguay, 1830–1945* (Montevideo: Universidad de la República, 1966) 2d ed. 1969.

Chapter 3. 1839–1856

1. "Actas de la Comisión Censora y Directiva del Teatro, de 1840," *Revista Histórica* 13 (1941–42): 446–48 no. 2.

2. *El Nacional*, July 1, 1840.

3. Many will recognize these names immediately: not only were they prominent citizens; these men were some of the members of the first

Asamblea Legislativa of 1828, the first Congress to be created in Uruguay, just three years after its Declaration of Independence. In addition, all the streets of one of Montevideo's best residential neighborhoods are named in memory of these men.

4. This society is also referred to as the Empresa del Nuevo Teatro; that is, it has been called both the Society of the New Theater or the New Theater Corporation.

5. Arq. [Architect] Eugenio P. Baroffio, "El Teatro Solís," *Revista Histórica* 38 (July 1958). Alfredo R. Castellanos, *La Historia del Teatro Solís* (Montevideo, 1987). It is possible that other circumstances could explain the committee's reaction, for Zucchi was sympathetic to Juan Manuel Rosas, the Argentinean dictator against whom the Uruguayan president Fructuoso Rivera declared war in March 1839.

6. Lauro Ayestarán, *El Centenario del Teatro Solís* (Montevideo, 1956).

7. Baroffio, "El Teatro Solís."

8. The Guerra Grande lasted from 1839 to 1851, but until February 16, 1843—the date marking the beginning of the siege of Montevideo—the battles were fought in the countryside. In spite of the war, materials did begin arriving at the theater's construction site in 1841, and construction continued, on and off, until the middle of 1843, at which time it was totally discontinued.

9. *La Constitución*, November 27, 1852.

10. In doing my research, I was struck by the ethical question of who truly deserves credit for the design of the Teatro Solís. No one has found yet the original plans, and I have only a blueprint of the house floor that I discovered in the archives of the University of Montevideo's School of Architecture during a 1987 trip. (It should be noted that this floor plan was made in 1946, at the time of the existing building's remodeling.) It is not known if Zucchi and Garmendia ever spoke about this project, or even if they knew each other personally. To say that Zucchi was the only architect is untrue, as Garmendia's work was instrumental in the completion of the Teatro Solís; still it cannot be denied that Zucchi's ideas were the mainstay of the theater's ultimate design. I have referred to it as a joint project; nonetheless, there remains a question as to the ethics of Garmendia's use of Zucchi's original plans.

11. *El Comercio del Plata*, November 28, 1852.

12. Ibid., August 2, 1854.

13. Ibid., May 18–19, 1855.

14. Ibid., November 25, 1856.

15. Baroffio, "El Teatro Solís."

16. Alfredo R. Castellanos, *La Historia del Teatro Solís* (Montevideo: Intendencia Municipal de Montevideo, 1987).

17. Ayestarán, *El Centenario*.

18. As of the last remodeling of the house, the Teatro Solís has approximately 2,800 seats.

19. Baroffio, "El Teatro Solís."

20. Castellanos, *Historia*.

21. "The earliest permanent theatre may have been one in Ferrara, Italy, which supposedly burned down in 1532." "Theatre Architecture," *The New Grove Dictionary of Opera*, ed. Stanley Sadie (London: Macmillan, 1992), 4: 709.

22. Early on September 30, 1940, there was a downpour, which continued throughout the afternoon, with near-cyclone winds reaching ninety kilometers per hour. The intensity of the heavy rain and wind were such that in the evening the roof collapsed, crushing the movie patrons below. What is especially tragic is that earlier in the day Faustino García, who rented this space from the municipality, called the municipal authorities to report great patches of humidity and a crack in the ceiling. An inspector arrived and saw that this crack extended to the exterior of the domed roof, yet he proclaimed no immediate danger. Thus assured, García went on to sell more than 200 seats; three hours later, this portion of the building was a mass of flame and rubble. The east wing was practically destroyed yet, miraculously, the main house of the Solís survived. Following this scare it was meticulously surveyed, so any further structural damage was found before it was too late. (See *El Día*, October 2, 1940.)

23. *El Comercio del Plata*, September 20, 1856.

24. Ibid., October 27, 1856.

25. After eighty-one years (1856–1937) of private ownership, the Teatro Solís was bought by the Municipality of Montevideo in the amount of 640,000 pesos according to a contract signed on June 24, 1937. Although the building was sound, there were many items that did not comply with security and building rules and regulations. The house was necessarily closed on December 7, 1943, and with the exception of some annual carnival masked balls, the Solís

remained closed for performances until August 1946 (see 1943–46 chronology). (This three-year closure was completely related to remodeling, painting, and so forth, and was not a reflection of the war years.) The electrical system and plumbing were completely overhauled; backstage new dressing rooms, bathrooms, and showers were all installed; and the theater benefitted from a better and updated heating system. In addition to cosmetic improvements (such as painting, upholstering, and carpeting), the most important change related to safety. A fire-retardant metal curtain was installed, as was a "stage rain," a pipe of water all along the ceiling of the stage (i.e., the space behind the proscenium arch), able to provide 1,200 liters of water per minute to inundate stage and pit. Several huge water tanks were also installed and connected with a special network of pipes and fire hydrants. The biggest decorative challenge came in trying to match the red velvet of the original ninety-year-old upholstering of boxes, curtains, and handrails. After a fruitless search in Montevideo, Buenos Aires, and Río de Janeiro, a similar fabric was found in London. With the assistance of the British Embassy in Montevideo, it was possible to expedite buying and shipping in order to complete the upholstery on time for the August 25 gala. (See *El Día*, February 3, 1945.)

This restoration was done by a team from the Department of Architecture of the Municipality of Montevideo under the general direction of architect Raúl E. Cohe, assisted by engineer Alberto Tournier, director of repair shops and transportation; engineer Romeo Otieri, director of electrical and mechanical engineering; engineer Julio César Arigón of the same division, plus dozens of expert technicians and hundreds of workers of the municipality. (See *El Día*, August 25, 1946.) The Teatro Solís, completely renewed and in all its splendor, celebrated its ninetieth anniversary with a gala performance of Verdi's *La traviata* on August 25, 1946.

Chapter 4. August 25, 1856

1. *El Comercio del Plata*, August 27, 1856.
2. Ibid.
3. Ibid.

Chapter 5. 1857–1858

1. *The Musical World*, vol. 25, no. 14, London, Saturday, April 6, 1850.
2. *El Comercio del Plata*, January 12–13, 1857.
3. Ibid., December 7–8, 1857.
4. See *The New Grove Dictionary of Music and Musicians* (London: Macmillan 1980), 13: p. 32.
5. The Batalla de Quinteros (Battle of Quinteros) took place February 1–6, 1858. The preceding political unrest began on December 16, 1857, when General César Díaz (head of the conservative party), and other citizens, were banished by the government near elections; the government in power was afraid that Díaz and his followers were capable of beginning a revolution. Indeed, Díaz and these supporters went to Buenos Aires to enlist help and returned with a group of seventy revolutionaries on January 6. They were joined by eight hundred men in Montevideo, with the idea of taking over the capital. A confrontation with government forces on January 16 resulted in three hundred deaths. Díaz and his revolutionaries resolved to draw back to the north as far as the Quinteros pass, where they arrived on January 27. Unequal to the task of being soldiers, they capitulated to General Anacleto Medina on January 28. The treaty allowed them to withdraw peacefully to Brazil, but on February 2 the official army killed 152 of these men. In 1865 all victims were declared martyrs to the freedom of Uruguay.
6. *La Nación* (Montevideo), June 17, 1858.
7. *New York Daily Tribune*, Monday, November 1, 1852.
8. Ibid., Tuesday, November 2, 1852.

Chapter 6. 1859–1866

1. *La Nación* (Montevideo), January 19, 1859. The name of this soprano has been spelled in different ways in books and publications. It has been written as Anna De Lagrange, Anna de Lagrange, Anna De La Grange, Anna De la Grange, and Anna de la Grange. However, the most bizarre example is a 1906 book by Antoine Sallès, *L'Opéra Italien et Allemand à Lyon au XIXe. Siècle (1805–1882)*, published in Paris by E. Fromont, where the name of this French singer was written, successively, as Anna de La

Grange (p. 87), Anna de Lagrange (p. 88), and Anna de la Grange (pp. 89, 90, 91, 92) To avoid confusion, I decided on Anna de la Grange.

2. *New York Daily Tribune*, Wednesday, March 25, 1856.

3. *La Nación* (Montevideo), January 20, 1859.

4. Ibid., December 17, 1859.

5. Julian Budden, *The Operas of Verdi*, 3 vols. (New York: Oxford University Press, 1978), 481. (Letter from Piave—in Verdi's *Copialettere*—January 26, 1851.)

6. *El Comercio del Plata*, June 1, 1862.

Chapter 7. 1867–1869

1. Almost seventy years later, on January 25, 1920, Artur Rubinstein would give a recital at the New York Metropolitan Opera House with a similar program, where solo piano works alternated with operatic arias. The concert opened with "Il lacerato spirito" from *Simon Boccanegra* sung by Giovanni Martino, followed by an aria from Gustave Charpentier's *Louise* sung by soprano Marie Sundelius. Rubinstein then played Camille Saint-Saëns' Concerto in G minor. The program's second part began with the "Invocation" from Giacomo Meyerbeer's *Robert le diable*, a song group, and ended with Rubinstein playing two Chopin pieces and Liszt's Hungarian Rhapsody no. 10. For years to come, approximately until the early 1930s, such eminent artists as Pablo Casals, Fritz Kreisler, Mischa Elman, and many others, performed at the Metropolitan Opera concerts in similar programs. They continued to the end of the 1945–46 season.

2. Louis Moreau Gottschalk, *Notes of a Pianist*, ed. Jeanne Behrend (New York: 1964), entry February 11, 1868, p. 391.

3. Ibid., entry December 15, 1868, p. 397.

4. *Palestra* is a Greek word referring to a place of literary competitions, and is often used in Romance languages to refer to the artistic arena.

5. *El Siglo*, September 13, 1867.

6. Gottschalk, *Notes*, entry January 13, 1868, p. 390.

7. *El Siglo*, October 30, 1868.

8. S. Frederick Starr, *Bamboula! The Life and Times of Louis Moreau Gottschalk* (New York: Oxford University Press, 1995).

9. *El Siglo*, November 12, 1868.

10. The Ayestarán Collection of scores is now at the Library of Congress.

Chapter 8. 1870–1876

1. *El Siglo*, October 9, 1870.

2. Around 1824 Rossini settled in Paris, where he became director of the Théâtre des Italiens; his principal interest, however, remained the composition of new works based on French libretti for this house and for the Académie Royale de Musique (the Paris Opéra). Among other new compositions, he adapted two of his early Neapolitan operas to a new French version. *Mosè in Egitto*, was first performed in Naples' San Carlo in 1818, and later became *Moïse* when presented in its new version at the Paris Opéra on March 26, 1827.

3. *El Siglo*, September 1, 1870.

4. Ibid., June 19, 1873.

5. Ibid., August 8, 1873.

6. This information was given to the author by her children, Camillo, Jr., Luisa, and Esther Giucci.

7. Although he lived well into the twentieth century, Luis Sambucetti Jr. composed most of his work in the late nineteenth century (including his greatest work in 1899); later on, his musical career consisted mostly of conducting and teaching.

Chapter 9. 1878–1887

1. *El Siglo*, September 17, 1878.

2. When she was a teenager, my mother Amelia Gómez-Eirín de Salgado, was a cousin and also a bosom friend of Lía Giribaldi (later Mrs. Cyro Giambruno), the only niece of Tomás Giribaldi. Being single all his life, Maestro Giribaldi visited his brother's family every morning after coming from the cemetery. Always arriving punctually at six-thirty in the morning, he required his niece to wake up to brush his top hat (which the young and perky Lía always complained about). Many years later my mother told me that she never could forget Giribaldi's permanent melancholy, which she attributed at that time not only to his solitude and sad story, but to the failure of his operatic career.

3. A select but illustrious group of names would have to include the following: 1882: Romilda Pantaleoni; 1883: Emma Wizziack and Antonio Aramburo; 1884: Medea Mei, Elena Teodorini, Francesco Tamagno, Nikolay Figner, and Angelo Tamburlini; 1885: Eva Tetrazzini, Leopoldo Signoretti, and Francesco Signorini; 1886: Gemma Bellincioni, Fanny Copca, and Roberto Stagno; 1887: Elvira Brambilla; and the culmination, in 1888, with Adelina Patti, as well as Pantaleoni, and Stagno once again.

4. *El Siglo*, July 20, 1882.

5. *La Razón*, July 22, 1882.

6. *El Siglo*, July 20, 1882.

7. *La Razón*, July 21, 1882.

8. Tamagno's 1896 season will be further discussed in chapter 12. It was then that he first sang the Moor, his most renowned role, in Montevideo.

9. See chapter 16 for further discussion.

10. Personal communication with Andrew Farkas.

Chapter 10. 1888–1889

1. Eduard Hanslick, *Montevideo Musical*, nos. 26, 27, 28, July 8, 16, 24, 1888.

2. *La Tribuna Popular*, July 9, 1888.

3. Herman Klein, *The Reign of Patti* (New York: Century, 1920), 244.

4. To appreciate the quality of her singing, it helps to know that four months after she left Montevideo she had one of the most brilliant successes of her life when she sang Gounod's *Roméo et Juliette* under the composer's baton in her Paris Opéra debut. In New York, during the 1891–92 Metropolitan Opera season, she entranced the audiences with her Rosina—when she was forty-nine years old.

5. *El Siglo*, July 13, 1888.

6. *La Tribuna Popular*, July 23, 1888.

7. *The Times*, July 5, 1861.

8. *La Tribuna Popular*, July 30, 1888.

9. Klein, *Reign of Patti*, 328.

10. *Montevideo Musical*, no. 29, August 1, 1888. At that time the exchange rate for 12,000 golden pesos was equivalent to about 2,600 pounds sterling. It is no doubt that Patti was not only a great singer and a woman of good taste, but someone who knew how to invest her earnings.

11. John Frederick Cone, *Adelina Patti: Queen of Hearts* (Portland, Ore.: Amadeus, 1993), 113.

12. *Montevideo Musical*, no. 28, review by Luis D. Desteffanis, July 24, 1888.

13. *El Siglo*, August 10, 1888.

14. Ibid., August 14, 1888.

15. Ibid., August 15, 1888.

16. Ibid., August 17, 1888.

17. *Montevideo Musical*, no. 31, August 16, 1888.

18. My father-in-law, Juan Morassi-Guardia, (an acquaintance of Caruso) was present during the performance when he was booed and then hailed.

19. Roberto Caamaño, *La historia del Teatro Colón, 1908–1968* (Buenos Aires: Editorial Cinetea, 1969), 1:58, 60, 66.

20. Francesco Palmegiani, *Mattia Battistini, il re dei baritoni* New York: Arno, 1977), 73.

Chapter 11. 1890–1894

1. Verdi, *Copialettere*, letter 250; English translation by Charles Osborne (New York: Holt, Rinehart and Winston, 1972), 231–32.

2. *Diario de Barcelona*, February 14, 1884. This information about Oxilia's performances at the Teatro Liceo, as well as the newspaper review, was supplied by Maestro Jaume Tribó, prompter of the Liceo, who has been preparing, for many years, that opera house's chronology.

3. Carlo Gatti, *Il Teatro alla Scala Nella Storia e Nell'Arte* (Milan: Ricordi, 1964), 1: 160; in vol. 2, Annals compiled by Giampiero Tinturi, see 1888–89 season.

4. *El Siglo*, June 30, 1890.

5. Oxilia sang five operas at the Teatro Nuevo Politeama: *Lucia di Lammermoor, La favorita, La Gioconda, Fausto*, and *Carmen*, some of them more than once. (See *El Día*, August and September 1890)

6. Oxilia obituary in *El Día*, May 18, 1919.

7. In Hungarian the names are reversed; i.e., his last name was Kiss.

8. *El Día*, August 19, 1892.

9. Ibid., August 20, 1894.

10. George Bernard Shaw review quoted in *The New Grove Dictionary of Music and Musicians*, 15: 432. See Puccini entry written by Mosco Carner.

11. Only six months after Rosina Storchio gave *Madama Butterfly*'s world premiere at La Scala in February 1904, she sang Cio-Cio-San at the

Solís. This first performance of Puccini's opera would be under Toscanini's baton, an extraordinary event in Solís history. Also it should be pointed out that Storchio sang the revised version in Buenos Aires and Montevideo after creating the role in Milan. See chapter 17 for further discussion.

12. *El Siglo*, August 22, 1894.
13. *El Día*, August 22, 1894.
14. Solís performances of Wagner sung in German would not be heard until the first German conductors arrived after World War I.
15. *El Día*, August 13, 1894.
16. *El Siglo*, August 24, 1894.
17. One of Bretón's operas is based on the poem *Tabaré*, written by the Uruguayan Juan Zorrilla de San Martín (1855–1931). The poet, then regarded as the Bard of Uruguay, was also a lawyer, and founder and director of one of Montevideo's leading newspapers. During the last years of the nineteenth century Dr. Zorrilla was the Uruguayan ambassador to Spain; as a result, he became well known in the Madrid artistic and literary circles frequented by Bretón. In 1910 Bretón visited Montevideo for the first time in order to become acquainted with the country's aboriginal landscape, the setting of *Tabaré*. Three years later Bretón's three-act opera *Tabaré* was created and premiered at Madrid's Teatro Real, on February 26, 1913.

Chapter 12. 1895–1897

1. W. J. Henderson, review of *La bohème*, *New York Times*, December 27, 1900, 6.
2. *El Siglo*, August 2, 1896.
3. *El Día*, August 3, 1896.
4. Ibid., August 7, 1896.
5. Ibid., August 3, 1896.
6. Caruso was not a "tenore di forza" like Tamagno, but is usually considered to be the greatest tenor in the first half of the twentieth century. He started out as a lyrico, but eventually became a lyrico-spinto or even a spinto.
7. *El Siglo*, August 20, 1896.
8. On March 9, 1885, at Naples' San Carlo under conductor Nicola Bassi with Virginia Ferni-Germano as Margherita and Francesco Vecchioni as Mefistofele. See *Teatro San Carlo*, vol. 2, *La cronologia*, by Carlo Marineli Roscioni (Naples, Guida Editori, 1987), 408.

9. *El Día*, September 2, 1897.
10. The establishment of a nationalistic style, which was to use the forms, themes, instruments, and dance types of South American folklore for the first time in art music, was on the horizon. New works, among them opera, with native plots and a new harmony and style derived from autochthonous scales and melodies would soon develop, with the peak of this new nationalism in music taking place between 1910 and 1930.
11. *El Día*, February 7, 1896.
12. This is the correct date and not the year 1892 as is listed under Constantino's entry in *The New Grove Dictionary of Opera* (1:921). See also 1896 chronology.
13. *El Día*, February 11, 1896.
14. Julio Goyén Aguado, *Florencio Constantino—1868–1919. El hombre y el tenor: milagro de una voz* (Diputación Foral de Bizkaia, Departamento de Cultura, 1994), 255
15. *El Día*, February 12, 1896.
16. Goyén Aguado, *Florencio Constantino*, 137, 175, 275, 281

Chapter 13. 1898–1899

1. *El Día*, August 25, 1898.
2. Mario Moreau, *Cantores de ópera portugueses* (Lisbon: Bertrand, 1987), 2: 372–79.
3. *El Día*, July 26, 1899.
4. Howard Greenfeld, *Caruso* (New York: Putnam, 1983), 74.
5. Segurola debuted under the baton of Armando Seppilli in the 1901–1902 Metropolitan season. See William H. Seltsam, *Metropolitan Opera Annals* (New York: Wilson, 1947).
6. *La Razón*, September 30, 1899.
7. Luis Sambucetti, holograph's photocopy score, *Suite d'orchestre*, The Edwin A. Fleisher Music Collection of Orchestral Music, Free Library of Philadelphia, Temporary number RS 1331. (In 1981 I brought the holograph photocopies of Sambucetti's music from Montevideo, at which time they were added to the Free Library of Philadelphia's collection.)

Chapter 14. 1900

1. There were two other very important impresarios in Latin America in those times: Renato

Salvati, who went primarily to Santiago de Chile, Valparaíso, and Lima; and Adolfo Bracale, who regularly visited Havana, San Juan, Caracas, Bogotá, Lima, and San José, frequently stopped in many other cities in the northwestern corner of the continent, and even got as far south as Santiago.

2. A "grillé" box was most often one of the "avant-scène" boxes. It was a regular box, but was screened off with a type of lattice (grillé) that allows anyone in the box to see out without being seen from outside.

3. *El Día*, February 1907.

Chapter 15. 1901–1902

1. At this time, a strong currency and the stability of the Uruguayan peso allowed impresarios to choose and engage star performers, paying them whatever they asked. It was because of this that Solís fans were able to hear the great Adelina Patti. The highest-paid singer in Montevideo at the time, in the 1888 season she earned 14,000 francs per night, with a total of 20,000 pounds sterling for her eight Solís performances, (see Herman Klein, *The Reign of Patti* [New York: Century, 1920], 247). In 1901, Hariclea Darclée was paid 42,000 francs per month. A commentary on the successful Nardi and Bonetti Lyric Company during its 1908 Solís season appears in one Uruguayan music critic's review: "Maestro Leopoldo Mugnone received 24,000 francs monthly, which is the highest salary ever paid to any conductor in South America, if we bear in mind that Toscanini's fee is 20,000 francs. Salomea Krusceniski [*sic*] and Giuseppe Anselmi—the two stars of the season—each have a salary of 45,000 francs per month" (see *El Día*, August 26, 1908).

Such figures demonstrate that at the beginning of the century conductors, regardless of their responsibilities, were still underpaid in comparison to the top-name singers. It is also clear that the Solís audiences had the privilege of hearing the best of the internationally known divas. To understand what these figures mean, it is instructive to compare contemporary prices. If we look at a 1909 Sears, Roebuck and Co. catalogue, we find that the most exclusive imported pair of shoes cost $2.23, and a silk tie could be had for 28 cents. Musical instruments were advertised as going from the most expensive of the upright pianos at $138.00 to a good Chadwick violin from London (with a Turtle bow and leather case with velvet interior) for $23.45. A more common violin could be purchased for as little as $2.95.

2. *El Día*, March 16, 1901.

3. Ibid., August 2, 1901.

4. Ibid., August 5, 1901.

5. *La Vanguardia*, Barcelona, December 28, 1984.

6. In addition *Le maschere* was performed at Naples' San Carlo two days after, on January 19, 1901.

7. *El Día*, August 18, 1902.

8. Henry Krehbiel, review of *Tosca*, *New York Tribune*, February 5, 1901, 6.

9. *El Día*, August 24, 1902.

10. Ibid., August 22, 1902.

11. Ibid., September 1, 1902.

12. Ibid., June 19, 1902.

Chapter 16. 1903

1. Enrico Caruso, Jr., and Andrew Farkas, *Enrico Caruso, My Father and My Family* (Portland, Ore.: Amadeus, 1990), 661

2. Harvey Sachs, *Toscanini* (London: Weidenfeld and Nicolson, 1978), 85.

3. *La Razón*, August 14, 1903.

4. Ibid.

5. Linda B. Fairtile, "The Violin Director in *Trovatore* and *Trouvère*," *Verdi Newsletter* (American Institute for Verdi Studies), no. 21 (1993): 16–23.

6. *La Razón*, July 9, 1903. Three months after this Solís season, New York's Metropolitan manager, Heinrich Conried, also exhibited the house's modern stage machinery, including trapdoors and an elaborate switchboard for lights, in a preview tour for the press (see the *New York Times*, November 21, 1903).

7. On this night Toscanini conducted a performance of Verdi's *Un ballo in maschera*, with Giovanni Zenatello as Riccardo. During the first-act aria, the audience persisted in asking for an encore from Zenatello; Toscanini, however, sensing that the tenor did not wish to give one, proceeded with the performance. Half of the audience yelled more loudly for an encore, the other half just as loudly to proceed. Finally,

after prolonged shouting, the act continued, sans encore. But as soon as the curtain fell, a stagehand walked onstage to announce that an injured Toscanini would be unable to conduct the remainder of the performance. The backstage account reports an angry Toscanini cutting his hand as he furiously pushed through a glass door or window; then and there he left La Scala, vowing never to return. Of course he did return, but only many years later.

8. *El Día*, August 16, 1903.
9. Ibid., August 23, 1903.
10. In this Eugenio Giraldoni echoed the career of his father, Leone Giraldoni, the baritone chosen by Verdi almost half a century earlier for the creation of the title role in *Simon Boccanegra* and Renato in *Un ballo in maschera*.
11. Howard Greenfeld, *Caruso* (New York: Putnam, 1983), 65.
12. *El Día*, August 17, 1903. The reviewer was mistaken about Farneti's age: she was actually twenty-six.
13. Samuel Blixen ["Suplente"], *La Razón*, August 21, 1903. Because these comments were published the same day as the *Adriana Lecouvreur* Solís premiere, it can be pretty certain that these are Blixen's impressions after attending the dress rehearsal.
14. *El Día*, August 24, 1903.
15. Ibid., August 25, 1903.
16. Ibid., September 1, 1903.
17. Samuel Blixen ["Suplente"], *La Razón*, August 19, 1903.
18. Julio Goyén Aguado, *Florencio Constantino—1868–1919. El hombre y el tenor: milagro de una voz* (Diputación Foral de Biskaia, Departamento de Cultura, 1994), 243.

Chapter 17. 1904–1906

1. *El Día*, August 19, 1904.
2. It must be mentioned that Storchio, then pregnant with Toscanini's baby, was the first Cio-Cio-San in the disastrous world premiere of *Madama Butterfly* at La Scala in 1904.
3. *El Día*, August 22, 1904.
4. Ibid., August 24, 1904.
5. Ibid., August 26, 1904.
6. Ibid.
7. Bernabei and Puccini visited both Buenos Aires and Montevideo. Bernabei was the major

competitor of the Nardi and Bonetti Company in both cities. (In Buenos Aires Nardi and Bonetti were at the Teatro de la Opera, while Bernabei was at the Teatro Politeama.)
8. *La Razón*, August 3, 1905. There are no known documents to indicate how the legal dispute was settled.
9. *El Día*, August 6, 1905. See also *Eugenia Burzio, Un secolo dopo l'esordio (1899–1999),* (Comune di Poirino, Citta' di Chieri: Grafica Chierese, Arignano (TO), 1999), 10, 26.
10. *El Día*, August 7, 1905.
11. Ibid., August 17, 1905.
12. Ibid., August 20, 1905.
13. Ibid.
14. Enrico Caruso Jr. and Andrew Farkas, *Enrico Caruso, My Father and My Family* (Portland, Ore.: Amadeus, 1990). See chronology by Thomas G. Kaufman, 706
15. *El Día*, August 21, 1905.
16. Ibid., August 23, 1905.
17. *La Razón*, August 23, 1905.
18. Ibid., August 30, 1905.
19. *El Día*, September 1, 1905.
20. Uruguayan-born Dr. Justo G. Urquiza was a descendant (presumably a son) of General Justo José de Urquiza (1800–1870), statesman, former governor of the Entre Ríos province, and chief of the Argentine Confederation.
21. *El Día*, February 28, 1905.
22. Ibid., September 2, 3, 4, 5 and 6, 1905.
23. Unidentified Uruguayan newspaper clipping, Montevideo, August 1906.
24. *El Día*, August 22, 1906.
25. Ibid., April 22, 1906.
26. The first *Manon* was sung (by Darclée) on August 2, the second (by Storchio) on August 18, and the third (by Courtenay) on November 29, all in 1906.

Chapter 18. 1861–1918

1. Perhaps it would be useful to point out that operetta companies also gave opéra-comiques like the two Auber works cited.
2. *La Razón*, October 21, 1874.
3. Richard Traubner, *Operetta: A Theatrical History* (Garden City, N.Y.: Doubleday, 1983), p. 358.
4. Martin Mayer, *The Met: One Hundred Years of*

Grand Opera (New York: Simon and Schuster, 1983), 68.

5. William H. Seltsam, Metropolitan Opera Annals (New York: Wilson, 1947), 1931–32 season.

Chapter 19. 1907–1914

1. One critic singled out Rousselière as "an excellent tenor," going on to say that he would very much like to hear the singer perform in the original French. El Día, August 22, 1907.
2. El Día, August 10, 1907.
3. Ibid., August 21, 1908.
4. Unidentified newspaper clipping, Montevideo, August 1908.
5. El Día, August 23, 1908.
6. Frances Alda, Men, Women and Tenors (1937; reprint, New York: AMS Press, 1971), 101. See 1859 chronology. Lauro Ayestarán, La Música en el Uruguay (Montevideo: SODRE, 1953).
7. El Día, August 22, 1910.
8. Rivista Teatrale Melodrammatica, Milan, August 29, 1910.
9. El Día, September 8, 1910.
10. La Razón, August 12, 1911.
11. El Día, August 14, 1911.
12. La Razón, August 16, 1911.
13. El Día, August 16, 1911.
14. La Razón, August 18, 1911.
15. Ibid., August 19, 1911.
16. El Día, August 23, 1911.
17. Ibid., August 11, 1912.
18. Ibid., August 18, 1912.
19. Ibid., August 16, 1913.
20. La Razón, August 16, 1913.
21. Ibid., August 22, 1913.
22. Luigi Inzaghi, Il tenore Alessandro Bonci (1870–1940) (Rimini: Raffaelli, 2001), 184ff.
23. El Día, October 8, 1913.
24. Romola Nijinsky, Nijinsky (1934; reprint, New York: Simon and Schuster, 1980), 263–64.

Chapter 20. 1914–1916

1. El Día, August 21, 1914.
2. Ibid., September 2, 1914.
3. Ibid., August 15, 1915.
4. La Razón, August 16, 1915.

5. Enrico Caruso Jr. and Andrew Farkas, Enrico Caruso, My Father and My Family (Portland, Ore.: Amadeus, 1990) 233.
6. La Razón, August 23, 1915.
7. Ibid., August 18, 1915.
8. Antonio Defraia, Bernardo De Muro, Ossia l'utile cronologia (Bologna: Bongiovanni 1982), 19.
9. El Día, August 23, 1915.
10. Bruno Cagnoli, Zandonai Imagini (Rovereto: Longo Editore, 1983). 2d ed., 1994. (Cronologia della vita e delle opere di Riccardo Zandonai.)
11. El Día, August 26, 1915.
12. This information was supplied by the writer Laura Cortinas, the composer's sister, whom I met in 1954. At the time of our meeting she was in her seventies, and I was able to visit her at her home, where she talked extensively about her brother's life, musical education, and works. She also presented me with photographs and musical scores of Cortinas' compositions. I used this background and materials to write an article on the composer; it appeared in El Día's Sunday literary magazine on October 31, 1954. I also participated in a "Cortinas Week" (October 23–29, 1955) sponsored by the Department of Musicology at the School of Humanities. During this week Cortinas was honored by concerts, recitals, and lectures, including my lecture on Cortinas' life and works. My further work on this composer has taken the form of lectures about him in a series on public broadcasting stations on Uruguayan composers, and writing about him in several music dictionaries.
13. La Razón, August 26, 1915. The complete version of La última gavota was finally performed exactly one year later, during the 1916 opera season (as is discussed in its chronological place in this chapter).
14. La Razón, August 26, 1916.
15. El Día, August 26, 1916.
16. Ibid., March 13, 1916.
17. Ibid., July 14, 1916.
18. Ibid., August 20, 1916.
19. Ibid., August 16, 1916.
20. Tenor Léon Lafitte was connected to the Paris Opéra Company, and baritone Armand Crabbé sang several seasons at the Théâtre de la Monnaie Company, in Brussels.
21. El Día, August 23, 1916.
22. Ibid., August 28, 1916.

Chapter 21. 1917

1. Artur Rubinstein, *My Many Years* (New York: Knopf, 1980), 10.
2. *La Razón*, July 21, 1917.
3. Rubinstein, *My Many Years*, 10.
4. *El Día*, July 22, 1917.
5. *La Razón*, July 23, 1917.
6. *El Día*, July 27, 1917.
7. Ibid., August 16, 1917.
8. Ibid., August 19, 1917.
9. Ibid., August 17, 1917.
10. Ibid., August 10, 1917.
11. Ibid., August 15, 1917.
12. Ibid., August 20, 1917.
13. William H. Seltsam, *Metropolitan Opera Annals* (New York: Wilson, 1947); see 1927–28 and 1935–36 seasons.
14. Romola Nijinsky, *Nijinsky* (New York: Simon and Schuster, 1934; reprint, Simon and Schuster, 1980), 395.
15. Rubinstein, *My Many Years*, 13–14.
16. According to the program, the Uruguayan national anthem and the English anthem were played at the beginning of part one, "La Marseillaise" at the beginning of part two, and "The Star-Spangled Banner" at the beginning of part three.
17. Rubinstein, *My Many Years*, 15.
18. Ibid., 16.

Chapter 22. 1918–1922

1. Roberto Caamaño, ed., *La historia del Teatro Colón, 1908–1968* (Buenos Aires: Editorial Cinetea, 1969); see 1918 season.
2. Rodolfo Arizaga, *Enciclopedia de la música argentina* (Buenos Aires: Fondo Nacional de las Artes, 1971), 284.
3. Mario Morini, ed., *Umberto Giordano* (Milan: Casa Musicale Sonzogno di Piero Ostali, 1968).
4. *El Día*, September 14, 1919.
5. Ibid., August 27, 1919.
6. Ibid., September 18, 1919.
7. Ibid., September 20, 1919.
8. Ibid., October 1920.
9. Giuseppe Pugliese, ed., *Gigli* (Treviso, Matteo Editore, 1990), 80; see also *Cronologia*, by Carlo Marinelli Roscioni, 139, 140, 165, 166, and 168.
10. *El Día*, September 15, 1919.
11. Ibid., September 17, 1919.

12. Guglielmo Berutto, *I cantanti Piemontesi, Dagli albori del Melodramma ai nostri giorni* (Italgrafica, Torino), 1972; see Marcoux, Vanni, Basso-Baritone, 169.
13. *El Día*, August 25, 1920.
14. Ibid., August 24, 1920.
15. Ibid., August 22, 1920.
16. K. H. Stottner, special correspondent, New York, *Musical Courier*, (October 14, 1920): 5, 12.
17. *El Día*, May 18, 1919.
18. Ibid., September 5, 1920.
19. Ibid., August 17, 1919.
20. Ibid., October 8, 1920.
21. Ibid., August 6, 1922.

Chapter 23. 1923–1928

1. *El Día*, August 2, 1923.
2. *La Razón*, August 4, 1923.
3. *El Día*, August 22, 1923.
4. Ibid., August 27, 1923.
5. *La Razón*, August 1922.
6. *El Día*, August 23, 1923.
7. Ibid.
8. Ibid., August 24, 1923 (late edition).
9. Carlo Gatti, *Il Teatro alla Scala nella Storia e Nell'Arte*, 2 vols., (Milan: Ricordi, 1964), 329, 335; annals 84 to 87.
10. "The Baritone DAMIANI at La Scala," *Il Corriere della Sera* (Milan, June 1928); review supplied by Juan Pedro Damiani, grandson of the baritone.
11. *Il Corriere della Sera* (Milan, December 12, 1928).
12. See Ronald Davis, *Opera in Chicago, A Social and Cultural History, 1850–1965* (New York: Appleton-Century, 1966). Damiani sang six operas during the 1931–32 season. Guido Leone, *L'Opera a Palermo*, vol. 2, *L'Opera al Teatro Massimo dalle origini (1897) al 1987* (Palermo: Publisicula Editrice, 1988), 1948–49 season, 116 to 119. Jole Tognelli, ed., *Cinquant'anni del Teatro dell'Opera* (Roma: Bestetti, 1979). See *Cronologia* by Carlo Marinelli Roscioni, 1930–31 season; *Il Teatro di San Carlo—La Cronologia, 1737–1987* by Carlo Marinelli Roscioni (Naples: Guida Editori, 1987); see 1923–24, and 1948–49 seasons.
13. *El Plata*, January 29, 1962.
14. *El Día*, August 27, 1923.
15. In spite of what Fleta said, *L'amico Fritz* had

already been given in New York, both at Carnegie Hall and at the Metropolitan.

16. *El Día*, May 20, 1923.

17. These singers had been performing at the Solís for many years. An account of how many seasons each singer had been appearing at the Solís is as follows: Dalla Rizza, fifth year; Muzio, fourth year; Anitúa, third year; Crimi, second year; Borgatti, second year; Cristalli, third year; Urízar, third year; Damiani, third year; Fleta, second year.

18. *El Día*, August 17, 1925.

19. Ibid., August 20, 1925.

20. Ibid., August 24, 1925.

21. Schipa's performance was not reviewed, overshadowed by the opening gala (at the Teatro Urquiza) of Luigi Pirandello's *Six Characters in Search of an Author*. Schipa had the bad luck to precede this performance (directed by the playwright himself) by only one and a half hours. Thus, the newspapers from that entire week are filled with reviews, news, and photographs of Pirandello's play and company—but nothing on Schipa.

22. *El Día*, November 1, 1928.

23. Ibid., April 22, 1928.

24. Ibid., April 29, 1928.

25. Ibid., September 16, 1928.

Chapter 24. 1929–1930

1. *EL Día*, October 12 and 13, 1929.

2. Ibid., October 14, 1929.

3. Ibid., October 16, 1929.

4. "The Opera Public: VIENNA," *Opera News* (January 2, 1988); 14–15.

5. *El Día*, August 24, 1929.

6. Ibid., August 25, 1929.

7. Ibid., September 3, 1929.

8. Ibid., September 4, 1929.

9. Ibid., June 7, 1929.

10. Ibid., May 18, 1930.

11. Ibid., July 19, 1930.

12. Ibid., August 26, 1930.

13. Ibid., September 26, 1930.

Chapter 25. 1931–1955

1. *El Día*, August 21, 1932.

2. James A. Drake and Kristin Beall Ludecke, eds.,

Lily Pons—A Centennial Portrait (Portland, Ore.: Amadeus, 1999), 64.

3. For more information about this 1934 SODRE season see *El Día*, July 14–18, 1934.

4. See *El Día*, September 27 and 28, 1937. Honegger's operetta, was considered a success musically (it ran for almost five hundred performances) and premiered at the Bouffes-Parisiens in Paris, on December 12, 1930. It is still regarded as a "distinctly erotic work." Geoffrey K. Spratt, "Arthur Honegger," *The New Grove Dictionary of Opera* (London: Macmillan, 1992), 2:746.

5. *La Prensa*, May 26, 1946.

6. Alfredo Romea, *El Noticiero Universal*, December 31, 1947, 7.

7. *El Día*, February 22, 1981.

8. *El País*, February 22, 1994, 13.

Chapter 26. 1956–1984

1. From March 1, 1952 to March 1, 1967, a nine-member National Council was Uruguay's new executive authority in place of a president. In 1956 Dr. Alberto F. Zubiría was the council chairman. In 1967 the executive authority was returned to the presidency.

Epilogue

1. Philadelphia, American Academy of Music. Act of incorporation of the American Academy of Music and the supplements thereto; with the by-laws of the Corporation (Philadelphia, Crissy and Markley, 1857).

2. By this time many of the older generation of singers had retired from the stage. The youngest performers were just starting out, and those singers who fell into the middle generation (those between twenty-five and forty-five years of age) began to leave the country either during the time of the Tupamaros (the 1960s) or at the beginning of the military dictatorship (1973). This twenty-five-year-long cultural exodus included my husband, Roberto Morassi, and myself, who have made the United States our home since 1971.

3. Adelaida Negri's appearance in *Ernani* was part of the Metropolitan Opera House centennial celebrations; her illustrious costars were Luci-

ano Pavarotti, Sherrill Milnes, and Ruggero Raimondi.

Appendix A

1. As an example the program of Artur Rubinstein and Vaslav Nijinsky performance, on October 26, 1917—the last appearance of the legendary dancer on the stage, one of the collection's most valuable items, and undoubtedly a collector's item—disappeared after October 1971. (This was the time when the Municipality of Montevideo authorities terminated my research at the Solís Archives.) Fortunately, the central (and most important) page of this program had been photographed before its disappearance and is one of this book's illustrations.

2. Montevideo newspapers usually listed and advertised the major zarzuela companies and the best-known works of that genre. Performances by second- or third-rate companies were seldom listed individually by name of work. Something similar happens with zarzuela singers. Now and then very well known zarzuela companies with seasons that cover two or three consecutive months gave the first few performances at the Solís, continuing their seasons in other houses.

BIBLIOGRAPHY

Books and Articles

Abbiati, Franco. *Storia della Musica*. 4 vols. Milan: Garzanti, 1967–68.

Aguirre, Mirta. *La lírica castellana hasta los siglos de oro*. Havana: Editorial Arte y Literatura, 1977.

Alborghetti, F., and M. Galli. *Gaetano Donizetti e G. Simone Mayr*. Bergamo: Gaffuri e Gatti, 1875.

Alda, Frances. *Men, Women and Tenors*. Boston: AMS Press, N.Y. 1971 (originally published 1937).

Alier I Aixalà, Roger, and Francesc X. Mata. *El Gran Teatro del Liceo (Historia Artística)*. Barcelona: Ediciones Francesc X. Mata, S. L., 1991.

Anglés, H., and J. Pena. *Diccionario de la Música Labor*. 2 vols. Barcelona: Editorial Labor, S.A., 1954.

Arizaga, Rodolfo. *Enciclopedia de la Música Argentina*. Buenos Aires: Fondo Nacional de las Artes, 1971.

Artucio, Leopoldo C. *Montevideo y la Arquitectura Moderna*. Montevideo: Editorial Nuestra Tierra, 1971.

Ashbrook, William. *Donizetti and his Operas*. Cambridge: Cambridge University Press, 1982.

Ayestarán, Lauro. *El Centenario del Teatro Solís, 1856–25 de Agosto 1956*. Montevideo: Comisión de Teatros Municipales, 1956.

———. *Crónica de una Temporada Musical en el Montevideo de 1830*. Montevideo: Impresora L.I.G.U., 1943.

———. *Luis Sambucetti, Vida y Obra*. Montevideo: Museo Histórico Nacional, 1956.

———. *La Música en el Uruguay*. Vol. 1. Montevideo: Servicio Oficial de Difusión Radio Eléctrica. 1953.

Balzo, Hugo. "La Vida Musical (Variaciones sobre el mismo tema)." Montevideo: *Enciclopedia Uruguaya*, no. 35, 1969.

Barigazzi, Giuseppe. *La Scala racconta*. Biblioteca Universale Rizzoli, 1984.

Baroffio, Eugenio P. "El Teatro Solís." *Revista Histórica* 38 (July 1958).

Barrán, José Pedro. *Historia de la sensibilidad en el Uruguay*. 2 vols. Montevideo: Ed. Banda Oriental, 1991.

Barret Puig. *Víctor Damiani, un señor en la escena*. Montevideo: Barreiro y Ramos Editores, 1991.

Bellincioni, Gemma. *Io e il Palcoscenico*. Milan: R. Quintieri, 1920. Reprint, 1977.

Berutto, Guglielmo. *I Cantanti Piemontesi: Dagli albori del Melodramma ai nostri giorni*. Turin: Italgrafica, 1972.

Bing, Sir Rudolf. *5000 Nights at the Opera*. New York: Doubleday, 1972.

Blixen, Josefina L. A. de. *Contraluz*. Montevideo: Talleres Gráficos Gaceta Comercial, 1948.

———. *Novecientos*. Montevideo: Ediciones Río de la Plata, 1967.

Bloomfield, Arthur. *50 Years of the San Francisco Opera*. San Francisco: San Francisco Book Company, 1972. 2d ed., 1978.

Bollo, Sarah. *Literatura uruguaya, 1807–1965*. 2 vols. Montevideo: Ediciones Orfeo, 1965.

Bonaventura, Arnaldo. *L'Opera Italiana*. Florence, 1928.

Bosch, Mariano G. *Historia de la Opera en Buenos Aires*. Buenos Aires: El Comercio, 1905.

Brenet, Michel [pseud. Marie Bobillier]. *Dictionaire Practique et Historique de la Musique*. Paris: Colin, 1926.

[British Broadcasting Corporation]. *BBC Music Library, Choral and Opera Catalogue (Titles)*. British Broadcasting Corporation, 1967.

Brower, Harriete. *Vocal Mastery, Talks with Master Singers and Teachers*. New York: Frederick A. Stokes, 1920.

Bruyr, José. *L'Opérette*. Paris: Presses Universitaires de France, 1962.

Buckle, Richard. *Nijinsky*. London: Weidenfeld and Nicolson, 1971.

Budden, Julian. *The Operas of Verdi*. 3 vols. New York: Oxford University Press, 1978.

———. *Verdi*. London: J. M. Dent and Sons, 1985.

Bushnell, Howard. *Maria Malibran: A Biography of the Singer*. Foreword by Elaine Brody. University Park: The Pennsylvania State University Press, 1979.

Caamaño, Roberto, ed. *La historia del Teatro Colón, 1908–1968*. Buenos Aires: Editorial Cinetea, 1969.

Cagnoli, Bruno. *Pasquale di Costanzo, una vita per il San Carlo*. Naples: Casa Editrice Fausto Fiorentino, 1992.

———. *Riccardo Zandonai a Carpegna*. Rimini: Bruno Ghigi Editore [1981].

———. *Il soprano Nera Marmora*. Comune di Terni, 1989.

———. *Zandonai Imagini*. Rovereto: Longo Editore, 1983. 2d ed., 1994.

———. *Zandonai in America*. Rovereto, 1994.

Cánepa Guzmán, Mario. *La ópera en Chile (1839–1930)*. Santiago: Editorial del Pacífico, 1976.

Caruso, Enrico, Jr., and Andrew Farkas. *Enrico Caruso, My Father and My Family*. Portland, Ore.: Amadeus Press, 1990.

Casals, Pablo. *Joys and Sorrows: His Own Story as Told to Albert E. Kahn*. New York: Simon and Schuster, 1970.

Castellanos, Alfredo R. *La Historia del Teatro Solís*. Montevideo:, Intendencia Municipal de Montevideo, 1987.

Catálogo de Discos Victor. Camden, N.J.: Victor Talking Machine Co., c. 1920.

Celletti, Rodolfo. *Il canto*. Milan: Garzanti Editore 1989.

Cervantes Saavedra, Miguel de. *Comedias y Entremeses*. Madrid: Imprenta de Antonio Marín, 1749.

Cesari, G., e A. Luzio. *I Copialettere di Giuseppe Verdi*. Milano: Forni Editori, 1913.

Chaliapin, Feodor I. *Ma vie*. French translation by André Pierre. Paris: A. Michel, 1932.

Chase, Gilbert. *The Music of Spain*. New York: Dover Publications, 1959.

Chatfield-Taylor, Joan. *San Francisco Opera: The First Seventy-Five Years*. San Francisco: Chronicle Books, 1997.

Clément, Félix, & Pierre Larousse. *Dictionnaire des Opéras (Dictionnaire Lyrique)*. Paris: Librairie Larousse, [1905/1969].

Cohen-Stratyner, Barbara Naomi. *Biographical Dictionary of Dance*. New York: Schirmer Books, 1982.

Colomer Pujol, Josep Maria. *María Barrientos*. Barcelona, Edicions de Nou Art Thor, n.d.

Combarieu, Jules. *Histoire de la musique*. 3 vols. Paris: Librairie Armand Colin, 1920.

———. *La musique, ses lois, son évolution*. Paris: Ernest Flammarion Editeur, 1917.

The Concise Oxford Dictionary of Opera. London: Oxford University Press, 1964.

Cone, John Frederick. *Adelina Patti: Queen of Hearts*. Portland, Ore.: Amadeus Press, 1993.

Coolighan, María Luisa, & Juan José de Arteaga. *Historia del Uruguay*. Montevideo: A. Barreiro y Ramos, S.A., editores, 1992.

Corredor, José María. *Conversaciones con Pablo Casals*. Buenos Aires: Editorial Sudamericana, 1955.

Cowden, Robert H., ed. *Concert and Opera Singers: A Bibliography of Biographical Materials*. Westport, Conn.: Greenwood, 1985.

Cronología Comparada de la Historia del Uruguay, 1830–1945. Montevideo: Universidad de la República, 1966.

Cross, Milton. *Complete Stories of the Great Operas*. New York: Doubleday, 1955.

———, and Karl Kohrs. *More Stories of the Great Operas*. New York: Doubleday, 1971.

Curotto, Angel. "La Vida Teatral Montevideana," *Cuadernos de Marcha*, no. 22 (February 1969): 45.

Dassori, Carlo. *Opere e Operisti-Dizionario Lirico Universale*. Università degli Studi di Bologna, Arnaldo Forni, Editore, 1979.

Davis, Ronald. *Opera in Chicago: A Social and Cultural History, 1850–1965*. New York: Appleton-Century, 1966.

Defraia, Antonio. *Bernardo De Muro: ossia l'utile cronologia*. Bologna: Bongiovanni Editore, 1982.

De María, Isidoro. *Compendio de la Historia de la República O. del Uruguay*. 4 vols. Montevideo: Imprenta El Siglo Ilustrado, 1895.

———. *Montevideo Antiguo*. 2 vols. Colección de Clásicos Uruguayos. Montevideo: Colombino Hnos., 1957.

Dent, Edward J. *The Rise of Romantic Opera*. Cambridge: Cambridge University Press, 1976.

De Oliveira Castro Cerquera, Paulo. *Um Século de Opera em São Paulo.* São Paulo, 1954.

Diccionario Biográfico Anual: Quién es quién en el Uruguay. Montevideo, 1941.

Diccionario de la Zarzuela. Madrid and Barcelona: Ediciones Daimon, Manuel Tamayo, 1986.

Dillón, César A., and Juan A. Sala. *El Teatro Musical en Buenos Aires.* Vol. 1, *Teatro Doria–Teatro Marconi.* Buenos Aires: Ediciones de Arte Gaglianone, 1997. Vol. 2, *Teatro Coliseo, 1907–1937 / 1961–1998.* Buenos Aires: Ediciones de Arte Gaglianone, 1998.

Di Nóbile Terré, Roberto. *Gabriella Besanzoni.* Burgos: Aldecoa, S. L., 1996.

Di Segni, Rosanna, and Angela Pelegrini. *Bosquejos e Impresiones de Montevideo.* Montevideo: Universidad de la República, 1969.

Drake, James A., and Kristin Beall Ludecke, eds. *Lily Pons—A Centennial Portrait.* Portland, Ore.: Amadeus Press, 1999.

D'Urbano, Jorge. *La Música en Buenos Aires.* Buenos Aires: Editorial Sudamericana, 1966.

Ellis, Roberto J. G., *¿Conoce usted Montevideo?* Montevideo: Talleres Gráficos Emecé, 1979.

———. *Crónicas y viejas quintas de Montevideo.* Montevideo: Imprenta Mercur, 1978.

———. *Del Montevideo de ayer y de hoy.* Montevideo: Editorial VYP, 1971.

———. *Evocaciones montevideanas.* Montevideo: Barreiro y Ramos, 1969.

Enciclopedia Salvat de la Música. 4 vols. Barcelona: Salvat, 1967.

Farkas, Andrew. *Opera and Concert Singers: An Annotated International Bibliography of Books and Pamphlets.* New York: Garland, 1985.

———. ed. *Titta Ruffo; An Anthology.* Westport, Conn.: Greenwood, 1984.

Fernández Saldaña, José M. *Diccionario uruguayo de biografías (1810–1940).* Montevideo, n.d.

Fitzgerald, Gerald, ed. *Annals of the Metropolitan Opera.* New York: The Metropolitan Opera Guild, G. K. Hall, 1989.

Furtwängler, Wilhelm. *Problemas de la vida musical.* Spanish translation by Johannes Franze. Buenos Aires: Amigos del Libro, 1950.

García Esteban, Fernando. *Panorama de la pintura uruguaya contemporánea.* Montevideo: Editorial Alfa, 1965.

———. "La Plástica Nacional." *Cuadernos de Marcha,* no. 22 (February 1969): 17.

García Morillo, Roberto. *Estudios sobre música argentina.* Ediciones Culturales Argentinas, Secre-

taría de Cultura, Ministerio de Educación y Justicia, Buenos Aires, 1984.

Gatti, Carlo. *Il Teatro alla Scala nella Storia e Nell'Arte.* 2 vols. Milan: Ricordi, 1964.

Gatti-Casazza, Giulio. *Memories of the Opera.* Edited by John Caldes. London, 1977.

Gesualdo, Vicente. *Historia de la Música Argentina.* 3 vols. Buenos Aires: Editorial Beta, 1961.

Girardi, Michele. *Giacomo Puccini: l'arte internazionale di un musicista italiano.* Venice: Marzilio, 1995.

———. *Puccini, la vita e l'opera.* Rome: Newton Compton, 1989.

Gómez Haedo, Juan Carlos. "Crónica de Fin de Siglo." *Cuadernos de Marcha,* no. 22 (February 1969): 3.

Goss, Madeleine. *Bolero.* Buenos Aires: Ediciones Peuser, 1945.

Gottschalk, Louis Moreau. *Notes of a Pianist.* Edited by Jeanne Behrend. New York: Knopf, 1964.

Goyen Aguado, Julio. *Florencio Constantino, 1868–1919. El hombre y el tenor: milagro de una voz.* Departamento de Cultura, Diputación Floral de Bizkaia, 1994.

Greenfeld, Howard. *Caruso.* New York: Putnam, 1983.

Grun, Bernard. *The Timetables of History* (based on Werner Stein's *Kulturfahrplan*). New York: Simon and Schuster, 1982.

H. D. (Hermano Damasceno) [Eduardo Gilberto Perret]. *Ensayo de Historia Patria.* 2 vols. 10th ed. Barreiro y Ramos, 1955.

Hanslick, Eduard. *De lo bello en la música (Von Musikalisch-schönen;* Spanish translation by Alfredo Cahn). Buenos Aires: Ricordi Americana, 1947.

Henstock, Michael E. *Fernando De Lucia, Son of Naples.* Portland, Ore.: Amadeus Press, 1990.

Hernández-González, Gabriel. *Bretón.* Salamanca: Talleres Gráficos Núñez, 1952.

Historia de la Musica Española. 7 vols. Madrid: Alianza Editorial, 1983.

History's Timeline. London: Grisewood and Dempsey, 1981.

Ignacios, Antonio de. *Historial Rafael Barradas.* Montevideo: Imprenta Letras, 1953.

The International Cyclopedia of Music and Musicians. London: J. M. Dent and Sons, 1975.

Inzaghi, Luigi. *Il tenore Alessandro Bonci (1870–1940).* Rimini: Raffaelli, 2001.

Iovino, Roberto. *Mascagni, l'avventuroso dell'opera.* Milan: Ed. Camunia, 1987.

Janson, H. W. *History of Art*. New York: Abrams, 1969.

Jean-Aubry, Georges. *La musique française d'aujourd'hui*. 2d. ed. Paris, 1916.

Kaufman, Thomas G., Edoardo Ferrati, Giorgio Gualerzi, Giorgio Rampone, Valeria Pregliasco, and Fernando Battaglia. "La carriera (di Eugenia Burzio)." In *Eugenia Burzio, Un secolo dopo l'esordio (1899–1999)*, Comune di Poirino, Citta' di Chieri: Grafica Chierese, Arignano (TO), 1999.

———. "A Chronology of Francesco Tamagno's Appearances." In *Il titanico oricalco-Francesco Tamagno*. Turin: Teatro Regio, 1997.

———. "A Chronology of Mattia Battistini's Appearances." In *Battistini-Le Dernier Divo* by Jacques Chuilon. Paris, 1996.

———. "Cronologia delle rappresentazioni e delle esecuzioni." In *Iris, 1898–1998: Il Centenario*. Leghorn, Italy: A cura di Fulvio Venturi, 1998.

———. *Verdi and his Contemporaries: A Selected Chronology of Performances with Casts*. New York: Garland, 1990.

Klein, Herman. *The Golden Age of Opera*. London: Routledge, 1933.

———. *The Reign of Patti*. New York: Century, 1920.

Kolodin, Irvin. *The Metropolitan Opera*. New York: Knopf, 1967.

———. *New Guide to Recorded Music*. New York: Doubleday, 1947.

Lagarmilla, Roberto E. *Eduardo Fabini*. Montevideo: Organización Medina, 1953.

Lang, Paul Henry. *La música en la civilización occidental*. Buenos Aires: EUDEBA, 1963. [*Music in Western Civilización*; Spanish translation by José Clementi.]

Larionoff, P., and F. Pestellini. *María Malibrán y su época*. Barcelona: Editorial Juventud, 1953.

Lavignac, Albert. *La musique et les musiciens*. Paris: Librairie Ch. Delagrave, 1895.

———. *Le voyage artistique à Bayreuth*. Paris: Librairie Ch. Delagrave, 1900.

Leone, Guido. *L'Opera a Palermo, 1653–1987*. Vol. 2, *L'Opera al Teatro Massimo dalle origini (1897) al 1987*. Palermo: Publisicula Editrice, 1988.

El Libro de la Zarzuela. Madrid, 1982.

El Libro Victrola de la Opera. R.C.A. Victor Co., N.J., 1930.

Lieven, Prince Peter. *The Birth of Ballets-Russes*. New York: Dover Publications, 1973.

Maciel López, Ema. *Aspectos del Montevideo de 1811*. Montevideo, 1963.

Mackinlay, Malcolm Sterling. *Garcia the Centenarian and His Times; Being a Memoir of Manuel Garcia's Life and Labours for the Advancement of Music and Science*. New York: Appleton, 1908.

Marek, George R. *Toscanini*. New York: Atheneum, 1975.

Mariani, Antonio. *Luigi Mancinelli: La Vita*. Orvieto: Akademos, 1998.

Marinelli Roscioni, Carlo, ed. *Il Teatro di San Carlo: La Cronologia, 1737–1987*. Naples: Guida Editori, 1987.

Mascagni, Pietro. *Epistolario*. Libreria Musicale Italiana. Vol 1, 1996. Vol. 2, 1997.

Mauclair, Camille. *Historia de la música moderna, 1850–1914*. Barcelona: Sociedad General de Publicaciones, 1920.

Mayer, Martin. *The MET: One Hundred Years of Grand Opera*. New York: Simon and Schuster, 1983.

Mayer-Serra, Otto. *Música y Músicos de Latinoamérica*. Mexico, D. F.: Editorial Atlante, 1947.

The Mellen Opera Reference Index. Lewiston, N.Y.: Edwin Meller Press, 1986.

Moor, Edward C. *Forty Years of Opera in Chicago*. New York: Horace Liveright, 1930. Reprint, New York: Arno, 1977.

Morassi, Roberto. *Reseña de la pintura uruguaya*. Montevideo: Ministerio de Relaciones Exteriores, 1970.

Morden, Ethan, *Opera anecdotes*. New York: Oxford University Press, 1985.

Moreau, Mario. *Cantores de ópera portugueses*. Lisbon: Bertrand Editora, 1987.

Morini, Mario, ed. *Umberto Giordano*. Milan: Casa Musicale Sonzogno di Piero Ostali, 1968.

Muñoz, Matilde. *Historia del Teatro Real*. Madrid: Editorial Tesoro, 1946.

The New Grove Dictionary of Music and Musicians. 20 vols. London: Macmillan, 1980.

The New Grove Dictionary of Opera. 4 vols. London: Macmillan, 1992.

Nijinska, Bronislava. *Early Memoirs*. New York: Holt, Rinehart and Winston, 1981.

Nijinsky, Romola. *The Last Years of Nijinsky*. New York: Simon and Schuster, 1952.

———. *Nijinsky*. New York: Simon and Schuster, 1980. (Originally published 1934.)

Olavarría y Ferrari, Enrique de. *Reseña histórica del teatro en Mexico, 1538–1911*. 5 vols. Mexico D.F.: Editorial Porrúa, 1895. 3d ed., 1961.

Osborne, Charles, ed. *Letters of Giuseppe Verdi.* New York: Holt, Rinehart and Winston, 1972.

Palmegiani, Francesco. *Mattia Battistini, il re dei baritoni.* New York: Arno, 1977.

Pedrell, Felipe. *Músicos contemporáneos y de otros tiempos.* Paris: Librería Paul Ollendorff, 1910.

Pellicer, A. C. *El Renacimiento en Italia.* Barcelona: Editorial Amaltea, 1956.

Philadelphia, City of *American Academy of Music. Act of incorporation.* Crissy and Markley, printers, 1857.

Pipers Enzyklopädie des Musiktheaters. Vol. 7. Munich: Piper, 1997.

Pugliese, Giuseppe, ed. *Gigli.* Treviso: Matteo Editore, 1990.

Pulido Granata, Francisco Ramón. *La tradición operística en la ciudad de Mexico (Siglo XIX).* Mexico D.F.: Cuadernos de Cultura Popular, 1970.

Rela, Walter. *Poesía Uruguaya, el siglo 20.* Montevideo: Alfar Editores, n.d.

Reparaz, Carmen de. *Maria Malibran.* Madrid: Servicio de Publicaciones del Ministerio de Educación y Ciencia, 1976.

Robinson, Harlow. *The Last Impresario: The Life, Times and Legacy of Sol Hurok.* New York: Viking Penguin, 1994.

Roland-Manuel. *Manuel de Falla.* Buenos Aires: Editorial Losada, 1945.

Rosen, David, and Andrew Porter, eds. *Verdi's Macbeth, A Sourcebook.* New York: Norton, 1984.

Rosenthal, Harold. *Two Centuries of Opera at Covent Garden.* London: Putnam, 1958.

Rostirolla, Giancarlo, ed. *Ottorino Respighi.* Turin: ERI Edizioni RAI Radiotelevisione Italiana, 1985.

Rubinstein, Artur. *My Many Years.* New York: Knopf, 1980.

———. *My Young Years.* New York: Knopf, 1973.

Rudorff, Raymond. *The Belle Epoque: Paris in the Nineties.* New York: Saturday Review Press, 1973.

Ruffo, Titta. *La mia parabola: memorie.* Milan: Fratelli Treves Editori, 1937.

———. *My parabola (La Mia Parabola): The Autobiography of Titta Ruffo.* Translated by Connie Mandracchia DeCaro. Baskerville Publishers, 1995.

Sachs, Harvey. *Toscanini.* London: Weidenfeld and Nicolson, 1978.

Saiz Valdivieso, Alfonso Carlos. *Miguel Fleta: memoria de una voz.* Madrid: Espasa-Calpe, 1986.

Salgado, Susana, *Breve Historia de la Música Culta en el Uruguay.* Montevideo: A. Monteverde & Cía, 1971. 2d ed., 1980.

———. *Cluzeau-Mortet.* Montevideo: A. Monteverde & Cía, 1983.

———. *Compositores Musicales Uruguayos.* Montevideo: Biblioteca del Poder Legislativo, 1969.

———. *Cronología Comparada de la Historia del Uruguay* (Musical section, with professor Lauro Ayestarán). Montevideo: University of Montevideo, 1966.

———. "De la ópera a la música sinfónica." *Cuadernos de Marcha,* no. 22 (February 1969): 39.

———. "Doña Francisquita." *Washington Opera Magazine,* no. 77 (December 1997).

———. *Historia de la Música de Cámara en el Uruguay.* Montevideo, 1967–68.

———. *Los Músicos Uruguayos desde 1830 al Nacionalismo.* Montevideo: Instituto de Estudios Superiores, 1960.

———. "The Spanish Singing Tradition." *Opera America* 2, no. 2 (1998).

———. "Una Sinfonía Inconclusa de Cluzeau-Mortet." *Sodre Magazine,* no. 1 (1967).

Sallès, Antoine. *L'Opéra Italien et Allemand à Lyon au XIXe. Siècle (1805–1882).* Paris: E. Fromont, 1906.

Sánchez Torres, Enrique. *Stagno, Gayarre, Massini, las tres grandes escuelas del canto moderno.* Madrid: Imprenta de los hijos de M. G. Hernández, 1911.

Scarone, Arturo. *Uruguayos contemporáneos: Nuevo diccionario de datos biográficos y bibliográficos.* Montevideo, 1937.

Schickel, Richard. *El mundo de Carnegie Hall.* Mexico, D. F.: Editorial Letras, 1967.

Schwartz, Charles. *Gershwin: His Life and Music.* Indianapolis, Ind.: Bobbs-Merrill, 1973.

Scott, Michael. *The Record of Singing to 1914.* New York: Scribner 1977.

Seltsam, William H., ed., *Metropolitan Opera Annals.* New York: H. W. Wilson, 1947.

Seventy Years of Issues: Historical Vocal 78rpm Pressings from Original Masters, 1931–2001. Compiled with notes by Tom Peel and John Stratton. Toronto: Dundurn Press, n.d.

Shakespeare, William. *The Complete Works of William Shakespeare.* New York: Avenel Books, 1975.

Simpson, Harold. *Singers to Remember.* Lingfield, Surrey, Eng.: Oakwood Press, 1972?

Sokol, Martin L. *The New York City Opera.* New York: Macmillan, 1981.

Stagno Bellincioni, Bianca. *Roberto Stagno e Gemma Bellincioni.* New York: Arno, 1977.

Starr, S. Frederick. *Bamboula! The Life and Times of Louis Moreau Gottschalk.* New York: Oxford University Press, 1994.

Stieger, Franz. *Opernlexicon: Titelkatalog.* Tutzing: Hans Schneider, 1975.

Storti, Amedeo. *Firenze.* Venice: Edizioni Storti, 1977.

———. *Venezia.* Venice: Edizioni Storti, 1977.

Subirá, José. *Historia y anecdotario del Teatro Real.* Madrid: Editorial Plus Ultra, 1949.

———. *La musique espagnole.* Paris: Presses Universitaires de France, 1959.

———. *La tonadilla escénica española.* 4 vols. Madrid, 1928–32.

———. *La tonadilla escénica: sus obras y sus autores.* Barcelona: Ed. Labor, 1933.

Tenenbaum, Barbara A., ed. *Encyclopedia of Latin American History and Culture.* 5 vols. New York: Scribner, 1996.

Thiel, Rudolf. *Firmamento musical.* Madrid: Espasa-Calpe, 1953.

Tognelli, J., ed. *Cinquant'anni del Teatro dell'Opera.* Rome, 1979.

Towers, John. *Dictionary-Catalogue of Opera and Operettas.* Vol. 1, *Dictionary of Operas and Operettas.* Vol. 2, *Composers and Their Operas. Libretti.* New York: Da Capo, 1967.

Traubner, Richard. *Operetta: A Theatrical History.* Garden City, N.Y.: Doubleday, 1983.

Tuggle, Robert. *The Golden Age of Opera.* New York: Holt, Rinehart and Winston, n.d.

Turina Gómez, Joaquín. *Historia del Teatro Real.* Madrid: Alianza Editorial 1997.

Uruguayos Contemporáneos, noticias biográficas. 4 vols. Montevideo: Biblioteca del Poder Legislativo, 1965.

Valenti-Ferro, Enzo. *Teatros Líricos del Mundo.* Buenos Aires: Emecé Editores, 1980.

———. *Las Voces: Teatro Colón, 1908–1982.* Buenos Aires: Ediciones de Arte Gaglianone, 1983.

Vasconcellos, Amilcar. *Febrero amargo.* Talleres Gráficos Vanguardia, 1973.

Visca, Arturo S. "Vida literaria, una visión del novecientos." *Cuadernos de Marcha,* no. 22 (February 1969): 27.

Wagner, Cosima. *Cosima Wagner's Diaries.* Vol 1, *1869–1877.* New York: Harcourt Brace Jovanovich, 1976.

Walter Rubboli, Daniele E. *Rosina Storchio.* Museo R. Storchio, 1994.

Newspapers

The Chicago Daily News, Chicago.
El Comercio del Plata, Montevideo (1861–1886).
La Constitución, Montevideo.
Il Corriere della Sera, Milano.
El Día, Montevideo (1895–1972).
El Diario, Montevideo.
Diario de Barcelona, Barcelona.
Diario Oficial de la República Oriental del Uruguay, Montevideo.
La Mañana, Montevideo.
El Mercurio, Santiago de Chile.
La Nación, Buenos Aires.
La Nación, Montevideo.
New York Daily Tribune, New York.
New York Times, New York.
New York Tribune, New York.
El Noticiero Universal, Barcelona.
El País, Montevideo.
El Plata, Montevideo.
La Prensa, Buenos Aires.
La Razón, Montevideo.
El Siglo, Montevideo.
The Times, London.
La Tribuna Popular, Montevideo.
El Universal, Montevideo.
La Vanguardia, Barcelona.

Periodicals and Musical Magazines

Caras y Caretas, Montevideo (1892).
Clave, Montevideo.
Comentario, Montevideo (1959).
Gazzetta Musicale di Milano, Milano.
The Journal of Musicology, Louisville, Ky.
Montevideo Musical, Montevideo (1906–37).
Mundo Uruguayo, Montevideo.
Musical Courier, New York.
The Musical Leader, Chicago.
The Musical World, London.
Opera America, Washington, D.C.
Opera News, New York.
Opera Quarterly, Durham, N.C.
Orfeo: revista musical uruguaya, Montevideo.
Revista del SODRE, Montevideo.
Rojo y Blanco, Montevideo.
Verdi Newsletter, New York.
The Washington Opera Magazine, Washington, D.C.
The author's personal papers and collection of opera programs and libretti.

ABOUT THE AUTHOR

Susana Salgado is an American musicologist born in Montevideo who settled in the Washington, D.C., area in 1971, and is a consultant to the Library of Congress Music Division. Prior to leaving Uruguay, she was Research Professor and chair of Uruguayan Music in the Department of Musicology at the University of Uruguay in Montevideo. She also organized and directed the preservation and cataloguing of the scores held at the Musical Archives of the Teatro Solís. Author of several books, she has contributed to many scholarly publications, including five Grove dictionaries: *Opera, Music and Musicians* (1980 and 2001 editions), *American Composers*, and *Women Composers*.